The Ideas and Careers of Simon-Nicolas-Henri Linguet

Portrait of Linguet by Saint-Aubin, 1773.
Bibliothèque nationale, Paris.

The Ideas and Careers of
Simon-Nicolas-Henri Linguet

A Study in Eighteenth-Century French Politics

Darline Gay Levy

UNIVERSITY OF ILLINOIS PRESS

Urbana Chicago London

For my parents

Library of Congress Cataloging in Publication Data

Levy, Darline Gay, 1939–
The ideas and careers of Simon-Nicolas-Henri Linguet.

Bibliography: p.
Includes index.
1. Linguet, Simon Nicolas Henri, 1736–1794—Political
science.   I. Title.
JC179.L52L48   320.5 ′3 [B]   79-24109
ISBN 0-252-00311-X

Contents

Illustrations following page 224

Acknowledgments

In researching, writing, and revising this work, I have received essential support and advice from many sources. I am grateful for pre-doctoral support from the Dissertation Committee of the Woodrow Wilson Fellowship Foundation, the American Association of University Women, and the Radcliffe College Special Projects Fund, and for the opportunity to expand my inquiry into Linguet's career as a political journalist during a period as a post-doctoral fellow at the Radcliffe Institute.

I am particularly thankful for the extraordinary privileges extended to me on several occasions by Roger Laslier, librarian of the Bibliothèque municipale in Reims; for the zeal with which he and his staff searched with me for uncatalogued manuscripts; and for the time sacrificed to arrange for photographic and microfilm reproduction of materials. Thanks are also due to the staffs of the institutions cited in my bibliography, but especially to librarians and archivists at the Bibliothèque nationale, the Archives nationales, the Archives of the Ministère des affaires étrangères, the Bibliothèque de l'Arsenal, and the Bibliothèque et Archives de la Préfecture de Police, in Paris; at the Osterreichisches Haus-, Hof, und Staatsarchivs, in Vienna; at the Archives générales du Royaume de Belgique and the Bibliothèque Royale, Albert 1er, in Brussels; and at the Bibliothèque publique et universitaire in Geneva and the Bibliothèque publique de la ville de Neuchâtel. Henri and Monique Lelarge provided encouragement and hospitality during each of my many research trips to Reims. My special thanks also are due to Henri and France Druart of Reims, who opened their home to me and graciously allowed me to consult their splendid collection of Linguet's works.

In Paris, professors René Rémond and Albert Soboul helped me orient my research in its initial stages. I wish to express my appreciation to them for their aid and their interest.

From the beginning of this study, Professor Donald H. Fleming of Harvard University has provided encouragement, along with relentless critical readings, the kind that stimulated my most agonizing reappraisals and a necessary rethinking of all my ideas. In this undertaking, as in so many of my academic projects, I am also thankful for the support of Professor Emeritus Richard B. Morris of Columbia University, mentor and friend. Several friends and colleagues consented to read and criticize portions of this manuscript. I wish to thank Thomas Adams, Gail Lee Bernstein, Robert Darnton, Elizabeth Eisenstein, and Svetlana Kluge Harris. I owe a special debt of gratitude to Eugene McCreary, Alan Spitzer, Steven Kaplan, and Harriet Applewhite for undertaking a full critical reading and evaluation of my entire manuscript at a critical juncture in its preparation, and to Linda K. Kerber, Ann Fagan, and Françoise McCreary for invaluable counsel and unflagging support. Of course I assume full responsibility for all errors and misinterpretations in this study.

The officers of the Voltaire Foundation at the Taylor Institution, Oxford, kindly granted me permission to use portions of my article, "Simon Linguet's Sociological System: An Exhoration to Patience and Invitation to Revolution." which appeared in *Studies on Voltaire and the Eighteenth Century*, LXX (1970), 219-93. The late Dr. Theodore Besterman allowed me to microfilm a copy of an anonymous, spurious Linguet "autobiography" formerly housed at the Institut et Musée Voltaire, in Geneva, and now located at the Voltaire Foundation in Oxford.

Carole Appel, my editor at the University of Illinois Press, gave this manuscript her closest attention. I have benefitted immensely from her continuous support and editorial advice. Virginia Arnett performed the heroic feat of typing the manuscript, and Sophia Thompson offered expert editorial advice.

Virginia Arnett performed the heroic feat of typing the manuscript, and Sophia Thompson offered expert editorial advice.

I cannot begin to express my gratitude to my husband, Peter Levy, for his critical readings of this work in every one of its versions, for his absolutely essential support, and for his tolerance of Simon Linguet's spectre in our midst, for so long.

Abbreviations

Archives

AG	Archives générales du Royaume de Belgique (Brussels)
AM	Archives, Ministère des affaires étrangères (Paris), correspondance politique
AN	Archives nationales de France (Paris)
BM	Bibliothèque municipale (Reims), MSS
BN	Bibliothèque nationale de France (Paris)
OS	Osterreichisches Haus-, Hof, und Staatsarchivs (Vienna)

Works by Linguet

A	*Histoire du siècle d'Alexandre, avec quelques réflexions sur ceux qui l'ont précédé*
A-1769	*Histoire du siècle d'Alexandre,* 2d ed.
Aveu	*L'Aveu sincère, ou Lettre à une mère sur les dangers que court la jeunesse en se livrant à un goût trop vif pour la littérature*
Avis	*Avis aux Parisiens*
CN	*Canaux navigables*
FP	*Le Fanatisme des philosophes*
HR	*Histoire des révolutions de l'Empire romain*
L	*Théorie des lois civiles, ou Principes fondamentaux de la société*
L-1774	*La Théorie des lois civiles,* new ed.
LL	*Lettres sur la "Théorie des lois civiles," & c.*
MB	*Mémoires sur la Bastille*
MOI	*Mémoire sur un objet intéressant pour la province de Picardie*
NR	*Necessité d'une réforme dans l'administration de la justice et dans les lois civiles en France, avec la réfutation de quelques passages de "L'Esprit des lois"*
P	*Point de banqueroute*
PB	*Du pain et du bled*

PHG	*Du plus heureux gouvernement*
Plan	*Plan d'établissemens tendans a l'extinction de la mendicité*
RDM	*Réponse aux docteurs modernes*
RP	"Réflexions préliminaires," *Annales,* vol. 1

Works by Rousseau

R	*Discours sur l'origine de l'inégalité*

ONE

Under the Auspices of
a *Lettre de Cachet*

The Rebel and the Administrator

High noon was hardly the ideal moment for an abduction. The entrance to the Bastille was not the *locus classicus* for an ambush. But if Jean-Charles-Pierre LeNoir, lieutenant general of the Paris police, was oblivious to the picturesque absurdity of the *mise en scène*, he was very much alive to its value as a backdrop for the police exercise he had in mind. His directions in the form of a *lettre de cachet* dated April 18, 1780, and signed Louis and Amelot,[1] called for the arrest and *embastillement* of the notorious Simon-Nicolas-Henri-Linguet, journalist-in-exile, political theorist, sociologist, historian, economist, playwright, self-appointed consultant to European governments, and disbarred lawyer. On Wednesday, September 27, twenty-three weeks after it had been authorized, the scene was about to be played in the most densely populated sector of the *quartier* Saint-Antoine.

A carriage came into view, heading down the jammed thoroughfare of the Rue Saint-Antoine. The hired coachman should have proceeded directly past the Bastille, straight through the Porte Saint-Antoine, and into the Bois de Vincennes via the Rue du Faubourg Saint-Antoine, to a country house at Fontenay-sous-bois where a silk merchant named Memin was preparing a dinner for Simon Linguet and his companions. The coachman, as it turned out, was also a police spy. Executing a sharp turn just before the Porte Saint-Antoine, he brought his vehicle to rest directly in front of the Bastille. Two police officers sprang into action, hustling the occupants of the coach out and into a pressing crowd.[2]

First to descend was Pierre Lequesne, prosperous Parisian cloth merchant, and literary agent and distributor in France for Simon Linguet's *Annales politiques, civiles, et littéraires du dix-huitième siècle*. By accident or design, Lequesne had hired a marked coach and a spy coachman for the day's excursion.[3]

The man the police were really after emerged from the coach struggling, ready for battle or flight[4] —small, rail-thin, giving the appearance of an enraged marionette in full animation: the wild, menacing gestures, the high-tension pitch of a fifelike voice, the dart of a maddened eye. It was reported that one of the police inspectors, fearing an escape, secured the cornered prey in irons and summoned twenty *mouchards* to surround him. Then, a friend of the prisoner, Police commissary Chesnon, led him off into the Bastille.[5]

The journalists were unanimous in their evaluation of the happening at the Bastille. They applauded secretaries of state, the police, anyone who might plausibly be credited with the *coup;* they displayed condescending disdain or gleeful contempt for the victim.

Linguet had once been described in the *Correspondance littéraire*, the philosophes' news and gossip sheet, as "[t]his man so strangely famous, this zealous panegyrist of Asiatic despotism, this raging detractor of all free governments...."[6] Now, in October, 1780, the reporter for the *Correspondance littéraire* commended the good judgment of authorities practiced enough to have removed this deviant from circulation: "The craft of Aretino has always had its perils and its inconveniences. Sieur Linguet, who was very seriously persuaded that he would escape them forever, thanks to his strength of character and a half-dozen pistols which he took great care to display on his desk or to carry around in his pockets, has just been tossed into the Bastille."[7] Searching out motives for Linguet's arrest, the columnist came up with outbursts against the king of Prussia, critiques of the Estates-General, unflattering appraisals of the treaties of the Department of Foreign Affairs with the Americans. Most damning in his repertory of Simon Linguet's crimes was the journalist's letter to a maréchal de France and member of the Académie française, Emmanuel-Félicité de Durfort, duc de Duras. It was a letter unpublished but not undisplayed, in which, the columnist discloses, Linguet refers to Duras, a peer of the realm, as "a son of a...fully written out, signed Linguet."[8]

From the tone of the article, the reader might conclude that the Bastille was an entirely suitable asylum for an unpolished, vulgarly independent journalist.

Joseph de Lanjuinais, masquerading as the correspondent and gossip-columnist Milord All'Ear, wrote a letter to Milord All'Eye describing the protagonist in the events of September 27. He felt compelled to attribute to him every departure from sane thinking known to an enlightened mind.

> ...this attorney for the Neros and Caligulas...this hero of French literature, this implacable enemy of philosophy and the philosophes, this famous detractor of distinguished talents, this modern Aristarchus whose sublime function was to calumniate the most universally recognized merit....this presumptuous writer, hardened against merit, sold to the priests, and devoured by the frenetic ambition to make a name for himself at any cost....this man of bad faith who, armed with the basest jealousy, took pleasure in declaring war upon great talents, and tearing the most distinguished erudites to shreds....among the enemies of the sciences, letters, progress, even the human mind.[9]

Simon Linguet insisted that the only crime that would merit the punishment of an indefinite entombment in the Bastille was *lèse-majesté*.[10] In July, 1780, two months before his arrest, Jean-Jacques Duval d'Eprémesnil, counsellor in the Parlement of Paris, attempted to try Linguet before the parlement's *Chambres des enquêtes* for what sounded like the crime of high treason. The accused was never summoned to testify, and the parlement never took formal action on the charges.[11] D'Eprémesnil published his accusations in full only in 1781. Linguet, however, ran summaries of the sessions in his *Annales* for July, 1780.[12]

D'Eprémesnil was an outspoken defender of the parlement's prerogatives, and a renowned and practiced debater. During each of three hour-and-a-half sessions of the parlement that July, d'Eprémesnil presented his case. His stated purpose: to denounce this "man who has expatriated himself," this author of "a periodic, defamatory, and calumnious libel...whose destiny has become, in a way, an affair of state."[13]

Linguet, d'Eprémesnil charged, had directed a three-year verbal attack against private persons, the Académie française, the Paris Bar, and the French constitution; he had inflamed the nation against its laws and judges. His *Annales* was an intolerable semimonthly barrage of calumny, "and we put up with it!" Most horrible of all was Linguet's political theory: "The Neros in their conduct, the Hobbeses in their writings, offer nothing comparable....This author has been working methodically for thirteen years to overthrow the most salutary ideas on the nature of man and the principles of society."[14] He wanted slavery restored by revolution, d'Eprémesnil continued; he "carries frenzy to the point of provoking all the lower classes of society against the upper."[15] He grants "to the flock, against the shepherd's abuses of property, that is to say, to peoples with respect to kings, no recourse other than open force and revolt....Nothing is sacred for him: the peace and quiet of individuals, the peace of families, public tranquillity, the dignity of courts, the rights of truth, the interest of the laws, the liberty of peoples, the safety of sovereigns, nothing has an effect on him."[16] D'Eprémesnil goes on to say, "Just read his *Annales*, his aim is to foment a revolution in the state; his procedure is to attack successively principles, tribunals, their members."[17]

A brief, shocking list of Linguet's principles follows in the *Dénonciation*.[18] Then comes the ultimate accusation:

> And all that...not in one passage, in one article, in one sheet, but in all the volumes of his *Annales,* which form a body of doctrine meditated, coherent, thought out, developed, with the view to preaching despotism to sovereigns, revolt to peoples, servitude to the human race, [and] to Frenchmen hatred of their laws and judges—which tends to destroy the fundamental principles of society, the general rules of all good government, the constitutive maxims of French monarchy, the rights and influence of bodies that are trustees and guardians of these maxims—in a word, to

compromise the very persons of all sovereigns and the tranquility of all peoples.[19]

D'Eprémesnil rested his case. The parlement took no action on this indictment; key magistrates perhaps already were aware that Linguet had been tried elsewhere, and condemned by order of a *lettre de cachet* dated April 18, 1780.[20]

The paradoxical accusation stood. It might be legitimate to conclude from d'Eprémesnil's indictment of him that Linguet was the parlement's mortal foe— but then whose ally could the man have been? By d'Eprémesnil's concession, Linguet was the most formidable enemy of the *parlementaires'* enemies and a saboteur of the absolute monarchy d'Eprémesnil accused him of supporting. In an age of enlightenment, Nero was acting like Spartacus preparing to lead an uprising of slaves against their monarchical master. An apologist for absolute despotism was fomenting popular revolution. France had produced a maverick Hobbes, a theorist who raised brute force to the power of right, only to oppose as a salutary check upon it the armed force of outraged, expropriated subjects: "...entre les Rois et les sujets, le Ciel s'explique par des Victoires."[21]

The age of reason's posterity might be tempted to expose a colossally trumped-up case against Simon Linguet. But assuming the charges could be substantiated, still, the man's enemies stacked the cards in an arresting manner. What could Linguet's system of thought and style of existence have been for d'Eprémesnil's depiction of it to read like a book of paradoxes? Whatever the man's character, no caricature of it quite held him together in a coherent, readily assimilable attitude. Linguet's enemies and detractors in all camps branded his ideas paradoxical and his professional comportment absurd; but they really were begging some questions. Who was the man behind the paradoxes, and why did his contemporaries find his thought and his behavior so palpably threatening?

Simon Linguet left the Bastille in May, 1782, proclaiming his innocence: "My conduct and my pen have always been pure, as my heart";[22] he defended his blackened *Annales*: "I dare say that literature has produced no work in which king, religion, and state were more scrupulously respected."[23] Linguet had to prove his innocence and have his revenge. Voltaire used his leisure time behind bars to complete his *Oedipus*.[24] The abbé Morellet, the Physiocrat, celebrated his sojourn in the Bastille in paeans of gratitude to his jailors:

> I awoke with the sun and I went to bed with the coming of night; and apart from my mealtime, I read or wrote, without any distraction other than the urge to sing and dance all alone, which came upon me several times a day. Every day, I received a bottle of pretty good wine, a very good one-pound bread;...for lunch, a soup, beef, an entrée, and dessert; at night, a roast and salad....

I saw some measure of literary glory lighting up the walls of my prison; persecuted, I was going to be better known. The men of letters whom I avenged, and philosophy, whose martyr I was, would launch my reputation. Men of the world, who love satire, were going to extend a better welcome than ever before....These six months of Bastille would be an excellent recommendation and would make my fortune without fail.

Such were the hopes in which I cradled myself, and if I must say so, they have not been deceived....[25]

Linguet, confined in the same fortress, was gripped by other compulsions. He was in no mood for song and dance. Convinced that he was being poisoned, he refused to eat at first; then he would ingest only minuscule portions.[26] He experienced imprisonment not as *travaux pratiques* in suffering, a sabbatical for composing poetry and drama, but as a personal and political annihilation. It was not an urge to literary creation, but rather the impulse to physical destruction that his interlude in the Bastille generated. Confinement and isolation within tower walls twelve feet thick, by his own measure,[27] gave Linguet's prophetic hallucinations a form, that of falling fortifications, walls crumbling away, "the walls of this modern Jericho, a thousand times more worthy than were those of the ancient city of the lightning of heaven and the anathema of men."[28] The frontispiece of Linguet's sensational *Mémoires sur la Bastille*, published in January, 1783, is an engraving showing a statue of Louis XVI wielding the royal sceptre; the statue stands in front of a Bastille struck on all sides by bolts of lightning, and toppling into ruin. In the foreground, grateful citizens bow before the statue; on its pedestal is the inscription: *A Louis XVI, sur l'emplacement de la Bastille.*[29]

It is true that in his *Mémoires sur la Bastille* Linguet called upon the monarch to demolish the fortress; he literally placed the emancipating proclamation in Louis' mouth: "soyez libres: vivez."[30] Still, in the engraving, the destructive bolts of lightning issue not from the royal sceptre, but from the heavens themselves, signifying a merciless and inexorable revolution of nature.

D'Eprémesnil might almost have been predicting the form Linguet's incendiary radicalism would take when he branded him an *agent provocateur* of revolution—except that it was he also who had exposed Linguet as a reactionary apologist of Asiatic despotism.

Simon Linguet opened the year 1783 by demolishing the Bastille with his pen. Whatever else he was, this Linguet was a difficult character to contain, or even to deal with rationally. He burst through the categories that ordinarily served to depict the life and thoughts of a man in an age of reason. He was continually breaking the bonds of the usual institutions available for taming or silencing thinkers who publicized explosive doctrines. The principles of his social theories were appalling and unsettling. While his contemporaries expounded laws of social statics, order, harmony, salutary balance, or progress measured in graded phases, Linguet achieved intellectual equanimity in the practice of social sciences where deliberately paradoxical categories called up images of violent social-class antagonisms, hatreds that were unappeasable, exploitations that were socially necessary and existentially intolerable, alienations of self as agonizing as they were irremediable, revolution—inexorable and all-annihilating.

Linguet formulated his social critiques and analyses as paradoxes; perhaps that is another way of saying that he was a dialectic thinker. He was able to develop to its limit the double potential for revolutionary and reactionary resolutions latent in the social contradictions and conflicts he depicted in his paradoxical structuring of social reality.

This thinker willed an engagement of his ideas; and the thinker-in-action can be understood as an eighteenth-century prototype of two types of modern man, the administrator and the rebel. Early in his career, Linguet published a theory in which he accounted for the origins of civil society and the propertied order in acts of violence—usurpation and subjugation—that separated men forever from the condition of independence and equality they enjoyed in a state of nature. He traced the structuring of society into classes and the organization of all its institutions, laws, and norms around a common center of properties; and he developed the dynamics of societal transformation through class struggles. He constructed a model political regime, a paternalistic monarchy, where an all-powerful ruler regulated and attenuated antagonisms built into the class structure of society, denying claims to liberty grounded in appeals to pre-societal and extra-societal norms, but providing protection for the properties and lives of subjects who enjoyed a single countervailing and corrective power, the power of revolution against robber kings and robber barons—despots, in Linguet's reading.

These social sciences embodied knowledge that cut two ways; it could be invoked to undergird or undermine societal order. Notwithstanding his supersensitivity to radical inequalities which all regimes institutionalized and perpetuated and his inability to repress in himself drives for independence and equality that he depicted as absolutely contrary to the dictates of societal order, Linguet committed himself to using his theories to instruct influential contemporaries in the art of saving crisis-ridden monarchies from the disaster of irreversible corruption and dissolution.

Linguet's determination to carve out for himself a career in which his ideas could have an impact multiplied the occasions for confrontations with interlocking networks of public and private institutions and personalities that comprised the liberal establishment in France in the pre-revolutionary decades. When Linguet began making his bids for a place in his culture, even before he fully stated the principles of his social and political philosophies, luminaries among the previous generation of intellectuals and functionaries were already beginning to block off access to positions of power and prestige. Philosophes and their friends and sympathizers in the world of letters, the arts, and administration were able to exert a fairly effective control over entry into positions guaranteeing public recognition for intellectual and professional accomplishment. *Encyclopédistes, économistes,* and others in the party of humanity held and disposed of membership in the Académie française, in the academies of arts and sciences, and in professional bodies and the salons. Entrenched elites defending partisan interests made and unmade careers, opened and closed doors to advancement, and promoted pensions and privileges for selected protégés.[31] They did not accept Linguet, in part because his perspectives on social reality and political necessity were radically contradictory to their own visions and principles, although repeated experiences of exclusion may have provoked Linguet into sharpening these contradictions.

While well-placed contemporaries worked to limit the power of authority in a bid to enlarge the sphere of liberties, Linguet was publicizing convictions that flew in the face of these efforts: in modern societies where economic, social, and cultural transformations only aggravated class tensions and deepened class cleavages, the power of monarchical sovereignty must be concentrated and augmented and the universe of liberties drastically contracted so that governors might continue to fulfill their fundamental political obligations, satisfying their subjects' overriding need and demand for security—protection for threatened holdings in property and life.

Linguet struggled for more than a decade to engage his principles in careers conferring renown and fortune, that is, an honorable place, what passed for an identity in French society. He attempted to practice law. The Order of Lawyers in Paris, threatened by his law-breaking and law-making courtroom deportment, his theories of monarchy, and his attacks on the political pretensions of the *noblesse de robe,* disbarred him. He solicited a place for himself in the Académie française on the strength of his writings in history, sociology, and political science. Members of the Académie, like Charles Duclos—the perpetual secretary to whom Linguet once had sent or mentioned his diatribe against the philosophes, his apologies for autocratic Roman emperors, and his early critiques of Montesquieu—refused to lend his support; and the Académie never seriously considered Linguet's candidacy. He tried editing a government-licensed journal. His heated defense of policies of economic regulation, where priority was assigned not to legislating liberty but to safeguarding life, provoked censors under Turgot's administration into suppressing his articles; more critical, his irreverent tone, but especially his assaults on *littérateurs* in favor, offended the literary estate, and the journal's publisher, pressured by two secretaries of state, fired him. In the end, the king failed to reverse decisions terminating the double career in journalism and law where Linguet had expressed his dedication to the principles of a reformed and strengthened monarchy.

In his most spectacular and successful career, political journalism in exile, Linguet institutionalized his rebellion. He broadcast his intention to use his journal as an independent base for his work of protecting and educating peoples. In fact, he did something else. He generated a role for himself as a political persuader, an intermediary between the authorities and a public whose weight as a political force and pressure group he actively exploited. In journal articles, in polemic pamphlet literature, and in reprints of his early treatises, Linguet advertised his skills as master of the metapolitics of administration; he publicized ideas for reforms to calm classes he believed were at the brink of social revolution and to satisfy their conflicting needs for security and protection. Inherent in this kind of activity was the double potential for preserving and subverting authority. In effect, Linguet provided his public with a clear measure for the viability of modern monarchical regimes—their success in legislating reforms to protect subjects' properties and lives. His unending series of widely circulated revelations of the French authorities' crimes against him and against "the people"—their attacks on properties he was defining in progressively broader terms—tended to undermine the system he claimed he was working to save from disaster.

Linguet's polarization of his public activities looked like a kind of political schizophrenia, a simultaneous and successive self-identification with apparently contradictory and incompatible roles: as administrator, an instructor to kings, their advisers, and supporters—a publicist for programs to regenerate monarchy; as rebel against despots, a spokesman for the interests of threatened and underprotected proprietors (like himself and "the people")—a polemicist whose dramatic case studies in the corruption, abuse, and abdication of power could be read as challenges to the legitimacy of the monarchy.

This kind of extremist politics may have been Linguet's malady. He perhaps was not the only member of his generation exposed to the conditions that favored the ailment; certainly succumbing was one way of being *homo politicus*, given the live options in the political culture of prerevolutionary France.

Under the Auspices of a *Lettre de Cachet*

Simon Linguet's father, Jean Linguet, professor of the second class and subprincipal of the Collège de Navarre at the University of Paris in 1731, was the son and grandson of farmers from the tiny village of Senuc. Jean Linguet's journey from the fields and gently sloping wooded hills of Champagne to the Montagne Sainte-Geneviève in Paris is a success story whose details have not been confided to posterity. As a *roturier*, a commoner, born in 1692, educated in Paris, and established as an academic by 1719, he probably had spent most of his twenty-seven years competing against schoolmates and colleagues, and eluding the pitfalls of the system. As a candidate soliciting the position of professor or regent at a *collège* within the University of Paris, his education would have included, beyond the ordinary *collège* program, a complete two-year course in philosophy. The successful candidate was a *maître ès arts* who had weathered two three-hour oral examinations in philosophy, more precisely, in scholastic logic, conducted in Latin.[32] He never could consider himself an academic with a safe position; the concept of untouchable tenure was incompatible with the parlement's prerogatives, with the power of one's superiors, and certainly with the king's pleasure.[33]

On September 4, 1731, a *lettre de cachet* was addressed to Jean Linguet; he was ordered to retire from his post at once, leave Paris, and establish himself somewhere else no closer than twenty leagues from the capital.[34] Linguet's extracurricular, pro-Jansenist activities had come to the attention of the king's First Minister, André-Hercule, cardinal de Fleury, who was determined to dampen every ember from the recent conflagration of religious enthusiasm and resistence to the Constitution *Unigenitus.*

The University of Paris was ready to fight for Linguet. In a letter to Fleury, University authorities professed obedience to the monarch's will while proclaiming their decision to protest the arbitrary removal of a colleague from his academic position: "We presume that had Sieur Linguet been heard, he would have cleared himself of complaints that may have been lodged against him....we cannot believe that his Majesty's design is to render removable at pleasure positions that are fixed by established custom, and declared so by several decrees. The public good is in question...."[35]

Fleury had heard that argument before.[36] In his official capacity, he was both the source of the accusation against the professor and his only board of appeal. Therefore, in his response of September 18, 1731, the minister could safely deny that judicial formalities invoked by the university existed; he refused to explore His Majesty's *"raisons particulières"* for stamping out Jean Linguet's academic career.[37]

In 1733 Jean Linguet bought the sinecure of *greffe d'élection de Reims,* a registrar's post, for the price of 13,720 *livres.*[38] On March 2, 1734, he married Marie Louis, daughter of Jean-Baptiste Louis, procurator of the presidial court in Reims. On January 23, 1735, a daughter, Marie-Louise Linguet, was born. "Le 14 juillet 1736, à huit heures et demie du matin," Jean Linguet noted in his *livre journal,* "est né Simon Nicolas Henri Linguet....Baptisé le lendemain à cinq heures et demie du soir."[39]

Simon Linguet's understanding of the event was that he had entered the world suffocating beneath the burden of an ominous paternal heritage.

> I was born without fortune, and without shame for [my condition in life]. The son of an esteemed, persecuted man whom I had the misfortune to lose in my earliest youth, I was left with hardly

more than his name and his destiny. In his last moments, he might have instructed me, as Aeneas would: *Disce puer virtutem ex me verumque laborum,/Fortunam ex aliis.* Engaged, I don't know how, in the follies of *Jansenism,* witness, I no longer see how, to a miracle of the blessed *Deacon,* he was the martyr of the despotism of the *exilers* as his son has been of the despotism of the *disbarrers.* Consequently he lost his post as Professor at the University of *Paris,* established himself in *Reims,* married there: and so I was born under the auspices of a *lettre de cachet.*[40]

In January, 1738, a third child was born. She died on March 4, 1738, two days after the death of Linguet's mother. Simon Linguet was not yet two years old. Jean Linguet married again in August, 1738, to Marie Barbe Lalemans, daughter of a merchant in Reims. She bore him seven children in eight years; four survived.[41]

Reflecting on her childhood, Marie-Louise confided to a friend that the Linguet household was totally lacking in maternal warmth. "I was never aware of having touched the maternal breast."[42] This sister, whose relationship with her brother is a study in the jealousy, hatred, possessiveness, and love of a spirited sibling rival, penned from memory the earliest preserved character sketch of Linguet. It is also the one piece of evidence we have of a smoldering civil war between father and son in the Linguet household. Linguet was only five and a half when "...he began to show promise of great intelligence, and we can say that in this respect he surpassed our hopes. At this age, my dearest friend, he already showed astonishing steadfastness." Enraged because a servant had refused him something, Linguet bit her. Jean Linguet stepped into the dispute and demanded an immediate apology, but even with the forceful aid of nine lashings, he failed to elicit it.[43] It is unclear from the available evidence whether Linguet succeeded in assuming attitudes of subservient obedience toward his father; but even if he did, deference under compulsion and subservience against the will might be expected to intensify rage, defiant impulses, and aggressiveness, and in short, to deepen the ambivalence of a son toward his "esteemed" father.

Jean Linguet suffered a partial paralysis and loss of memory in 1744. following a stroke. He died of a second attack in 1747, leaving Simon Linguet with a burdensome legacy: proceeds from the sale of the registrar's post and a responsibility for his four surviving brothers and sisters; some unresolved and possibly radical ambivalence towards paternal authority; and the memory of injustice committed in the king's name by order of a *lettre de cachet.*[44]

Linguet, who had received his early education at the Collège de Bons Enfants in Reims,[45] was enrolled at the University of Paris in the Collège de Dormans-Beauvais. The son of a commoner flung himself into the same milieu that already had molded a commoner's son into a professor of the second class at the Collége de Navarre. The leap out of obscurity was perilous; it might land a man back at the spot where his father had found himself following his own disastrous fall. Linguet was too young, or too naturally contrary, perhaps, to be consciously affected. He had not yet identified himself as a marked man, born under the auspices of a *lettre de cachet*.

What did these auspices augur? What imprint was left by childhood socialization in this Jansenist household? Specifically, how might it have contributed, along with other influences, to shaping Linguet's attitudes and behavior toward authorities in the larger society?

It may be the case, although analysis and interpretation here must be qualified as tentative and speculative, that Linguet speaks to these questions obliquely in his sociology of law, the *Théorie des lois civiles,* published in 1767, when he was thirty years old.[46] In this work, which I analyze in other contexts in the following chapter, Linguet paints a picture of the suffocating oppressiveness of his culture in all its dimensions; but he makes his uneasy, unconvincing peace with it also, embracing the necessity of intolerable societal constraints.

In Book Four of the *Théorie des lois civiles* (the first half of his second volume) Linguet simultaneously accepts and condemns societal oppressiveness in one of its principal expressions when he states the fundamental laws governing relationships between parents and children in society and in nature.

In the earliest societies, also the ideal societies in Linguet's readings, fathers were absolute despots, enjoying unlimited powers over children, wives, slaves, and fields. (*L,* II, 5, 8, 88). These paternal despots themselves were slaves to a totalitarian regime of property, the fundamental institution in the civil laws of all societies. A fear of attacks on their property motivated them to reduce their sons to abject servility; The father "was authorized to punish the slightest deviation as a revolt and to react severely, pitilessly, against the shadow of a disobedience" (*L,* II, 53).

Habit and laziness initially kept children from fleeing to elude the "net that property was readying to spread over them" (*L,* II, 57). Later, the expectation that they would succeed to everything their fathers owned kept these sons from revolting, expropriating their fathers, or committing even worse crimes (*L,* II, 95, 102).

The paternal despots' most refined and effective instrument was the will and testament. When fathers institutionalized the power to disinherit, their children's dependency and bondage was complete, "reestablished in all its rigor" (*L,* II, 154). It extended beyond the grave. "A father was within his rights in disposing of his goods as if he were immortal" (*L,* II, 153).

Linguet concludes this book with effusive panegyrics of paternal and political despotism in the administrations of the Middle East, his models for all societal perfection. There, "Paternal power has suffered almost no alteration...." There, "Filial dependency still subsists in its full scope." There, fathers are the property of rulers as children are the property of fathers (*L*, II, 206-7; 218-22). He laments the dissolution of paternal authority in modern Western societies (*L*, II, 176-85), and insists that once the principle of salutary all-embracing paternal despotism is challenged, the power of political authority is necessarily called into question as well (*L*, II, 228). Submission must be whole, or rebellion will be all-shattering.

Linguet's reconstructions of the character and motivations of paternal despots are striking; so are his analyses of the mechanisms by which a son's impulse to flee or revolt gives way to his freely willed, self-interested capitulation to the justice of authoritarian fathers and the spirit of property. His juxtapositions of nature against society in this context are more remarkable still. Nature is before society, but also coeval with it. It is a place on the map of the mind where the sociologist engineers a total reversal in the tyrannical power relationship he had depicted between parents and children in perfected societies.

"I allege that it is upon parents exclusively that nature imposes obligations, not upon children. Following [nature's] laws, the first are made for giving everything, the others [children] for receiving everything. Following these same laws, the former cannot reclaim anything, and the latter are not obliged to give anything in return. It is to society alone that we owe the change that has taken place in these [nature's] principles" (*L*, II, 14). In nature, the enslaving obligations of parents begin with the birth of their children. "It is he [the child] who can be regarded as exercising a veritable empire over them, and it is they who are condemned to render him arduous services" (*L*, II, 19). Mothers are physiologically bound to nourish their children; otherwise their milk will turn to poison and kill them (*L*, II, 22-24).

The tyranny of infants over their mothers is absolute; but fathers also are bound, less by their bodies than by the invisible chain of commiseration that is forged as they witness the act of childbirth. Nothing about natural paternal compassion, Linguet insists, sanctions a father's despotism over his son. There is no authorization in nature for a son to "divest himself of his own will," to "submit himself to all the caprices one might like to subject him to" (*L*, II, 24-30, 32). As soon as a child no longer requires nourishment and nurture, he "enters with full rights into possession of his liberty" (*L*, II, 18). No one can "claim to direct his movements against his will...." (*L*, II, 45). It is only in society "that the head of the son is caught under a yoke the lines of which lead to the father's hand, and that the will of the latter becomes an imperious spur against which the former cannot revolt" (*L*, II, 36).

Linguet might have imbedded autobiographical material at both poles of his juxtaposition of society against nature, documenting a son's perceptions of and responses to paternal authority and maternal deprivation. If that is the case, then his identifications with the propertied interests of fathers, combined with his extravagant idealizations of absolute authority wielded by parents and kings, were undercut and threatened by his irrepressible, absolute claims upon all authority for goods and rights of nature he may have been most acutely aware of lacking—physical security, parental nurture, and a guiltless and free-wheeling independence.

What is suggested here is that Linguet's ties with parents, living and dead, may have been a complicated and conflict-ridden affair; and that radical ambivalence toward "esteemed" parental authority may have found social and political expression in the revolts, reclamations, identifications, idealizations and collaborations that characterized the man's entangled unstable relations with the powers in his society. If the auspices Simon Linguet was born under augured anything, it was conflict.

Simon Nicolas Henricus Linguet, Remus, was something of an academic prodigy. The records of the *concours général de la Sorbonne* for August 12, 1750, indicate that for the class of the third year, Linguet won second prize for the delivery of a Latin composition, second prize for translation from Latin into French, and fourth honorable mention for his translation from Greek into French. Linguet's showing in the *concours* of the following year was even more impressive. For the class of the second year Linguet was first prize winner for delivery of a Latin composition, for translation of a Greek discourse into French, and for translation of a Latin discourse into French. The records of the *concours* of August 3, 1752, indicate that for the class in rhetoric, Linguet won second prize in French amplification.[47]

It was an imposing record, but what could a sixteen-year-old youth do with it? What was he now equippped to make of himself in the world? Linguet's scholastic record already distinguished him from others in a class of commoners with ignoble family trees and noble aspirations; and it fed his ambition to aim still higher. The one universally recognized elite in the French monarchy was the aristocracy.[48] A man whose genealogical obscurity barred him from admission still might arrive. In rare instances, the aristocracy recognized merit and talent with an award of nobility. The founder of the *Ecole des ponts et chaussées,* Jean-Rodolphe Perronet, forged a path for himself into the ranks of the nobility with feats of engineering. Linguet might have weighed these considerations as he began his formal preparations for study in Perronet's school.

Suddenly, however, he abandoned this training for an interlude of adventure and travel through Germany and Poland as secretary to the duc de Deux-Ponts, future ruler of the Palatinate and Bavaria.[49] Following a path to renown in the footsteps of a patron could prove a waste of time and a dissipation of youth, though the tactic was certainly not uncommon and instances of success were encouraging.

By 1754, Linguet was back in Paris, hounded by rumors that he had been dismissed for stealing a horse from his patron.[50] It was more likely that the employee had repudiated a career as subservient, eternally aspiring *attaché*. Later he confessed: "As for me…I despise stratagems of all kinds. After having wasted a part of my life in a fruitless servitude, I want to spent the rest of it in an independent liberty."[51]

Impoverished and far from independent, Linguet established himself in the cul de sac de Rouen in Les Halles with the future minor master of light verse, Claude-Joseph Dorat. The republic of letters was among the most prestigious elite groups in France. It seemed to be a natural aristocracy of talents, drawing its members from the ranks of genius and deriving its standing from the consensus of all men with a pretension to cultivated taste. In fact, the *sine qua non* conditions for success—in the republic of letters as everywhere else—were good connections. In this domain, Linguet and Dorat could boast frequent invitations to the dinners of Voltaire's arch-enemy and the *bête noire* of the party of humanity, Elie-Catherine Fréron, editor of *L'Année littéraire* and an indefatigable talent scout continually on the lookout for new recruits for the fraternity of anti-philosophes. The cultural pessimism and antipathy toward the liberal establishment which colored the attitudes of Fréron and his circle probably reinforced and gave focus to Linguet's beliefs; and it is also possible that Linguet took some pratical lessons from Fréron in how to organize, operate, and sustain support for a periodical that regularly provoked the wrath of the *philosophaille*.[52]

Using their academic laurels as credentials and their favor with Fréron as a *passe-partout*, Linguet and Dorat set out to become men of letters. Instead they produced a whim in poetry and prose called *Voyage au labyrinthe du jardin du Roi*. Fréron printed a kind review in *L'Année littéraire*.[53] The best lines in the piece could stand as an autocritique.

> Mais plus froide que la saison
> Passant l'univers en revue
> Notre sagesse morfondus
> Traitait comme de pauvres fous
> Tous les humains, excepté nous.[54]

Linguet turned out a parody on Lemierre's *Hypermnestre, Les Femmes-filles*. It was performed twice in 1758.[55] He filled a manuscript notebook with various poetic efforts. "A Mademoiselle…qui avait perdu un petit lièvre qu'elle paraissait regretter beaucoup" is a rimed suggestion that the young lady in mourning roast her beloved deceased, a fitting preparation for entombment in the stomach of a fellow mourner and gourmet, the poet.[56] Linguet refused a request from "Madame" for some verses with this couplet:

> Pour quoy vouloir être ma muse
> Quand vous pouvez être Vénus[57]

and offered still another variation on the same thought:

> Ah quand on s'aime et que l'on n'est que deux
> Il faut des actions et non pas des paroles.
> Après tout quand j'auray chanté
> Le bonheur secret que je goutte
> En aura-t-il plus de réalité?[58]

This was not quite the kind of probing most likely to bring a man to the edge of total understanding. Ambition momentarily reached a dead end in the cul de sac de Rouen, and Linguet and Dorat terminated their short literary liaison. One play performed two times, a jointly written and unsigned frivolity in poetry and prose, a notebook filled with verses, and some "scribbling" for Fréron and dinner talk with him and his friends were Linguet's contributions to date to the world of letters. It was hardly the dossier to pin on a man of diabolic notoriety, an apologist of Neros, a panegyrist of Asiatic despots, fomenter of popular revolution. The beginning was deceptively innocuous for a man claiming birth under auspices as singular and portentous as those of a *lettre de cachet*.

The Rousseauan Perspective on Ancients and Moderns

After his break with Dorat, the poet and playwright turned entrepreneur. According to a chronicle kept by his brother-in-law Jean-Nicolas Dérodé.[59] Linguet returned to Reims in 1760, broke and sick. Received with open arms by his impoverished but loving family, restored to health and outfitted with a new suit, Linguet considered himself sufficiently established to turn down an offer by the baron de Breteuil to employ him as secretary on a diplomatic mission to Russia. Instead, he bounded off into Germany where, Dérodé reported, he had a deal worked out with his former employer, the duc de Deux-Ponts. He had plans for setting up a manufacturing establishment to employ laborers in the duke's territories. At the same time, he mapped out a project for a commerce in wines between Champagne and the duke's estates.

Having embroiled the Dérodé family in his schemes, he then embroiled himself in violent dispute with the duke. The deal for the manufactory was off, but Linguet had another enterprise lined up outside Lyons. Using Dérodé's assets as credit, he acquired a huge house on the outskirts of the city. He had some plans for establishing an industry in cold-water soap. The venture fell through. Leaving the Dérodé family to add up the cost of his industrial exploits and free-wheeling entrepreneurship,[60] Linguet returned to Paris without a career.

He signaled his reappearance in the capital in 1762 by circulating brochures supporting the recently suppressed Company of the Jesuits, a gesture which he may have hoped would bring him some attention from the père Berthier, editor of the Jesuit *Journal de Trévoux*; what is more likely is that he alerted triumphant Jansenists and philosophes to the presence of a foolhardy deviant.[61]

Early in 1762, Linguet published his *Histoire du siècle d'Alexandre, avec Quelques réflexions sur ceux qui l'ont précédé.* He dedicated the work to Stanislas, King of Poland, Duke of Lorraine and of Bar, and Elie Fréron's protector.[62] While he awaited the verdict of public opinion with an anxious impatience (*A*, vii-ix), the real arbiters of taste, the critics, delivered the judgment that consigned the work to oblivion: the history of Alexander's century should not have been published.[63]

The opening pages of Linguet's history were written to please Voltaire. Linguet seemed to be making an overt bid for a place in Voltaire's school for historians. He announced that he was writing the history of Alexander's century for Voltaire; he presumed the philosopher was too occupied with other affairs to do the job himself (A, 9). In fact, the historian of the century of Louis XIV had clearly outlined the task that Linguet was assuming:

> But whoever thinks, and, what is even rarer, whoever has taste, will count only four centuries in the history of the world. These four happy ages are those in which the arts have been perfected and those which, serving as periods of the grandeur of the human mind, are an example for posterity.
>
> The first of these centuries to which true glory is attached is that of Philip and Alexander, of men like Pericles, Demosthenes, Aristotle, Plato, Apollo, Phidias, Praxiteles; and this honor has been confined within the limits of Greece....[64]

Linguet agreed. The study of antiquity is "the fixed point from which one can begin to measure the progress of the human mind" (*A*, 6). "The century of Alexander is therefore the first interesting period in the history of the human mind (*A*, 9).[65]

Would a true Voltairean have found the first interesting period also the most interesting one? Voltaire left no doubt where he stood on the question. In his scheme, the fourth century of the mind's grandeur, not the first, was to have occupied the central position: "The fourth century is that which we name the century of Louis XIV, and it is perhaps that of the four which most nearly approaches perfection.[66]

Linguet saw things another way. For him, the pre-Alexandrian Greeks had realized perfection. Their perfection became his measure of the progress of modern civilizations into decadence. Voltaire's self-appointed apprentice-historian committed a greater sin than that. He depicted perfection in ancient society following the models and ideal types of a very suspect modern, Jean-Jacques Rousseau.

Linguet describes the working of Athenian democracy. Magistrates are elected annually, popular controls are exercised over the administration of justice, taxes are assessed on a proportional basis, the authority of the laws commands universal respect, and citizens participate directly in the affairs of the polis "exercising a portion of the sovereignty": "Only in Rome and in Greece does one see these inconceivable assemblies of the entire nation, where a single man harangues twenty thousand men at once, and this astonishing fact is nonetheless one of the best authenticated of all ancient history" (*A*, 174-80, 181). Men were themselves in this age, open and direct with one another. The words they articulated, undeflected into empty formulae, were intended to strike the listener immediately. Justice was handed down without appeal and to all citizens. Multiple jurisdictions and judicial appeal, both innovations of the moderns, are "far more useful to proud and audacious wealth than to timid and trembling indigence" (*A*, 198-99). A citizen in the polis was considered competent to plead his own case: "It was not supposed that a paid lawyer must have even more knowledge of a case than the litigant who pays him". The laws were clear, simple, and uniform. When a man won his case, at least he won something. "The contested objects were not engulfed in a bottomless pit of chicanery" (*A*, 197, 198).

A lawyer in the polis was an orator, a privileged medium through whom unobstructed truth flowed as eloquence and impressed itself upon the hearer as justice. Lawyers "studied the springs of the human heart, and made themselves masters of the mind by pleasing the ear" (*A*, 200). In modern states the lawyer as orator is barred from the chambers where judicial decisions are made: "Suppleness is more effective there than the power of language, and intrigue is often more useful there than genius."[67] The orator has been barred also from the modern criminal proceeding, an operation now shrouded in secrecy. In the ancient world, it was precisely when life or honor hung in the balance that the lawyer could "bring great passions into play without falling into turgidity, and use the most vehement expressions without fearing that they would appear ridiculous." Eloquence once had been the vehicle of an immediate communication of truth, a stimulus impressing the tone of truth directly upon men's hearts. But the springs of eloquence had dried up; the occasions for employing it had vanished. The modern lawyer was limited to "dry dissertations on obscure laws" (*A*-1769, 262-63).

The ancient democracies were slave societies. There could be no question of strict economic equality and universal liberty there; but at least it was believed that everyone, citizens and slaves, had an equal right to life: "One doesn't remark that there was poverty there. I mean this horrible indigence that removes from a man the right nature gives him over a portion of the fruits of the earth, and that often forces him, for lack of work, either to forfeit his life in the horrors of hunger, or to buy it back through crimes" (*A*, 228).

In the ancient world men were either free or they were slaves. All free men were capable of providing for their basic needs. The slave had been forced to relinquish his liberty, but not his claim to life, not his right to enough food to exist (A, 229).

> What was unknown [there] is this cursed breed of men we call manual laborers [manouvriers] who do not enjoy even the advantages of slavery. Compelled to tear from the earth products that are not for them; weighed down by all the expenses of state; exposed to all the losses caused by the harshness of the seasons; rejected, despised; like animals, knowing hardly any pleasures other than digesting food and perpetuating their species. I do not know whether they feel very forcefully the price of their alleged liberty. But I believe that basically the slavery we consider barbarity is not nearly as barbarous as the degradation in which perhaps two-thirds of the human race languishes today. [A, 229-30]

Armies of day laborers and menials, men in a modern world, had been given their liberty by their masters, and liberty was a fatal sign of their perfect dehumanization. Linguet's description (or invention) of social and cultural bonds uniting masters and their slaves in the ancient world was his measure for the progress of inequality and inhumanity in the moderns' high civilization.[68] He did not propose slavery as a humanitarian model for the moderns to imitate; his striking comparison and scandalous paradox suggested that modern reformers had not yet found even a functional equivalent for the security of slavery.

Slavery notwithstanding, Linguet insisted that culture in ancient society was egalitarian. For example, the music of the ancients worked almost magically to evoke an immediate and involuntary response in all listeners, regardless of education. Sound passed from the sensory receptor directly to the heart, undeflected by the obstacle of a cultivated, critical reason: "It is certain that nature has attached to certain inflections of the voice the power to excite movements of joy or pity in all hearts. The cry that pain pulls out of every one who suffers is a powerful blow which affects us in spite of ourselves; it forces us to share the suffering of our fellow men. Another, and lighter, less anguished cry, dilates our heart agreeably. It announces to us the satisfaction, the happiness of the man who formed it. It makes us feel an agreeable sentiment whose cause and object we know nothing of" (A, 282-83). On these occasions, all men became transparent mediums through whom nature flowed as compassion raised to the power of musical sound. Jean-Jacques Rousseau had offered the same interpretation in his *Julie, ou La Nouvelle Héloïse*,[69] and in his *Dictionnaire de musique*.[70]

Rousseau insisted, and Linguet agreed, that although professional musicians catering to audiences with civilized tastes had constructed an elaborate art of music, it was only artifice, the denaturing of melody, the total perversion of music's essential characteristic, its power to affect everyone, immediately and involuntarily.

Linguet delineates in other ancient customs and institutions expressions of community and humanity denoting an all-embracing unity of men with men, and of men with their world, which the subsequent refinements and contrived complexities of the moderns have smothered. The ancient pagan orgy has its parallel in *mardi gras,* this wild indulgence that civilized French Catholics permit themselves (*A,* 300-301). Still, Linguet forgives these debaucheries in the ancients, while condemning them in the moderns; he even deplores the disappearance of ancient orgies: "What can even make us wish we had them back is that a kind of respect was maintained there for the rights of humanity, too much neglected the rest of the time. This all-precious equality was reborn then, for which no possessions can indemnify mankind. Masters and slaves, seated at the same table, and basking in the bosom of the joy of pure and tangible pleasures, recalled an image of the golden age..." (*A,* 301).

Linguet's sentiment again reflects that of Rousseau's Saint-Preux at the festival of the *vendages.* During these celebrations, Saint-Preux observes, "all live in the greatest familiarity," masters, servants, all: "Everyone is equal. We eat with the peasants at their mealtime, and we work with them as well. We eat with appetite their somewhat crude but good, healthful soup, filled with excellent vegetables....these saturnalias are much more agreeable and wise than those of the Romans. The reversal that the Romans affected was too vain to instruct either the master or the slave; but the gentle equality that reigns here restores the order of nature, forms an instruction for some, consoles others, and creates a bond of friendship for all.[71] Linguet continues his comparison: "With us, the pleasures of the carnival serve only to tire the rich, and often to drive the poor to despair. Their inability to imitate these costly excesses humiliates them and makes them feel much more acutely the degree of vileness to which they are reduced. However you look at them, you will almost always find the maxims, customs, pleasures, and even weaknesses of the ancients more humane than ours" (*A,* 301-2).

The naked, unadorned melody evoked in all listeners immediate joy, involuntary sadness. The communal gathering, whether pagan orgy or festival of the *vendanges,* made it possible, even necessary, for all men to reveal themselves to all, and tearing away the marks of their separateness, become accessible to one another, a community of equals in revelry, seated at the same table, sharing the same food, partaking all alike of the "tender pleasures." The *fête* is a magic happening; it lasts only a night. Equality is epiphenomenal and extra-institutional. Yet men on these extraordinary occasions tore through artificial restraints and broke the chains of subservience to become men to one another again, receptive to one another's persons in a relationship that was immediate, unreflected, reflexive rather, and natural: "the image of the golden age," Linguet wrote; "the tender equality that...restores the order of nature," in Rousseau's phrase.

Linguet was aware that a man might embrace a politics of equality, an economics of equality; he was not advocating that in this context. One of Rousseau's alternatives was enticing. Rousseau taught that there was a psychology of equality, the art of evoking immediately and reflexively the oneness of men in communion with men and with the world. Not all men could be politically free and equal citizens, only the privileged few could be. Rousseau's and Linguet's psychology of equality is a magic substitute for the drastic reform that would realize a universal democratic politics. It does not break the bonds of servitude. It reinforces them. The *Nouvelle Héloïse,* published the year before the *Contract social,* supplies an alternative to universal political autonomy and institutionalized equality in the concept of episodic, universal effusions of fraternity. Far from destroying a social structure grounded in inequalities, the bond of fraternity reinforces inequalities, offering realizable equivalents for an impossible all-embracing democratization of civil society. Apologists for an egalitarianism so deliberately lacking in political dimension hardly qualified as political radicals. They were magicians who invented equality out of the stuff of compassion, mutual devotion, and fraternal solicitude. At least in this early work, Linguet appeared to be captivated by Rousseau's idea. In ritual, through the magic medium of the fraternal embrace, men might overcome alienation, bridging the abyss separating them from their common humanity.

Athenian democracy, comprehending the political and social institutions of the polis, was rigidly exclusive; but that democracy was also a collective state of mind, an illusion of universal equality evoked as spectacle in which all were actors, in dance and song where all joined hands and mingled voices, in shared work and play that broke through convention to recall the reign of an extra-institutional natural equality. The most certain measures of modern man's progress were, first, his estrangement from other selves, and then, his self-alienation.

Printing, an invention of the moderns, is hailed as man's mechanical liberator and the vehicle for propagating enlightenment. Linguet argues that it is the "reef of the happiness of men of letters in general and even more, of philosophers" (*A-1796,* 448). In the ancient world, a man *was* his spoken word:

> He is exposed to the view of a crowd of auditors, persuaded that the truth is in his mouth and learning in his head....His gestures are his demonstrations. The fire in his eyes seems to throw light on everything he says....
>
> But these mute masters that you pick up casually, that you take leave of unceremoniously, these inanimate instructors thrown onto a desk or banished into libraries, can inspire neither respect nor confidence....The latter [books] excite only a reflected and icy admiration....The person [of the author] is separated from the work. [*A-1769,* 445]

The public devours the author's works while the censors and police punish him for the power and genius of his thoughts. Society has divided him against himself, separating his body from his ideas, dissociating the only too fragile man from his immortal genius: "This will never happen to an orator. His glory is attached in its essence to his person. A cruel subtlety does not come to teach his disciples the secret of separating orations from the being who pronounces them. Everything in him is indivisible, and whoever has heard him with pleasure is drawn to defend him with fervor" (*A-1769,* 457).

The orator speaks his whole truth, communicating urgency, outrage, tenderness through intonation, modulation, and inflection. He is as good as his word. The orator speaks his truth as gesture also: defiance in an attitude, compassion in a glance. The orator is an indivisible self. The listener appropriates oratorical truth involuntarily, or rather, the truth appropriates him in the same unmediated way that the purity of the ancient melody strikes the chords of human emotion and provokes an unwilled instantaneous response that is almost reflexive: "…and whoever has heard him with pleasure is drawn to defend him with fervor." Truth is not formal and passive, but lived, a happening among persons.

Athens in the century of Alexander was not only the first interesting period in the history of the human mind; it was, Linguet insisted, the most interesting, and the best. Athens was a high point from which the historian depicted and analyzed society's procession into civilization and decay. In Athens, technical innovation and social pressures had not yet made it possible for men to banish themselves from the earth they tilled, and to condemn themselves to serve the vices of luxury and empty ease. Progress in the science of law had not reached the stage where cunning manipulators flung only legal texts and administrative orders in the path of those seeking immediate satisfaction of grievances. The progress of morals had not advanced to the point where exploiters of human labor used men's liberty as a whip to beat them into economic enslavement. Men were still open, accessible to one another, and receptive to the voice of nature in themselves. They had not yet thrown up walls of empty form and title, elaborate masks, formulae of politeness and gentility, barriers behind which they hurried to carry out their little deceptions. Entertainment and pleasures were accessible to all; progress in the arts had not yet yielded the fatal fruits of artifice, delicacy, luxury. The highest art was artlessness, men's perfect, unconscious imitation of the purity and simplicity of nature.

A culturally sophisticated civilization, Linguet was arguing, could not be a happy one. What Linguet had been portraying all along in his history was anything but artistic and scientific perfection. He had described not the grandeur of the human mind, but its simplicity. He was lauding not the perfection of art but the innocence of artless nations in their infancy.

What corrupted the moderns was their civilization. In the 1762 edition of the *Histoire du siècle d'Alexandre*, Linguet described the arts and sciences as curing balms applied to civilizations ravaged and bled by conquerors (*A*, 4, 5). In the introduction to his second edition, Linguet wrote that he would refrain from asking "whether...progress in the cultivation of the mind might not be for a state the infallible sign of its decadence and imminent fall. It is with the arts as with conquests. Everyone lets himself be seduced by their brilliance" (*A-1769*, 10-11).

Linguet repudiated Voltaire's "four happy ages" of the arts and sciences. He exposed modern civilization's perfections in these areas as a fragile gloss over substructural faults, divisions, and class exploitations. As an apprentice in Voltaire's school of history, Simon Linguet was a failure. Voltaire's *Histoire du siècle de Louis XIV* had not functioned as his historical model, after all. He had patterned his first critical evaluation of modernity and the moderns after the *Nouvelle Héloïse*, the *Discours sur les sciences et les arts*, and the *Discours sur l'origine de l'inégalité*.

In his youthful cult of letters during the 1750s, Linguet had met with frustration, failure, or at best, fruitless, tepid support. It was no wonder. He said little or nothing, although he said it with a tolerable grace. In 1762, he abruptly abandoned a brand of exercise typified by his ridiculous depiction of the charms of the royal labyrinth. Now, he was courting acclaim or notoriety and probably employment with apologies for the vanquished Jesuits, critiques of a flourishing culture of the high Enlightenment, and a Rousseauan profession of faith in the lost perfection of unsophisticated cultures—a combination of allegiances and antipathies which did not turn out to be particularly attractive in the marketplace of ideas.

Law and Disorder

The historian exchanged his pen for a sword in the summer of 1762 and left Paris with the duc de Beauvau's troops bound for campaign duty in Spain and Portugal. As *aide de camp* in the engineering division of the duke's corps, Linguet saw little action except on the stages of Madrid where the works of Lope de Vega and Calderón were being presented.[72] He was released from his military service when peace was arranged in 1763.[73]

He was unpressured by the duties a profession entails; he had avoided committing himself to anything but literature. He had none of the obligations that accompany literary renown, as he had failed to elicit any significant response, positive or negative, to his comprehensive indictment of the civilization of the moderns. He became an adventurer. That was a relatively painless way for a literary failure to postpone a long overdue career decision.

Linguet worked his way back into France from Spain, then traveled to Holland.[74] From Holland, Linguet wandered through the Low Countries into Flanders and Picardy.

In September, 1763, a stranger appeared in the city of Abbeville, in Picardy. People of Abbeville who had interests to protect, secrets to guard, and reports to turn in to superiors, were immediately on guard. The man called himself Monsieur de Beaumont. He was short, and thin; his features were regular, but he had an insolent chin, a darting, questioning glance, and a ferret's nose, marks of a dangerous curiosity. The townsmen watched him pacing along the banks of the sluggish Somme, which flowed through Abbeville. Stopping a sailor, he made an inquiry. How high up the Somme did tides from the sea penetrate? Somehow, Monsieur de Beaumont's question reached the attention of the mayor of Abbeville, Nicolas-Pierre Duval de Soicourt. The mayor demanded an explanation for this stranger's fascination with tides in the city's waters. Monsieur de Beaumont was open and obliging. He explained that he was a wandering philosopher, traveling about, often on foot, following in the paths of Thales and Plato, studying nature and men, stopping wherever he found subjects to scrutinize, quenching his thirst at the first stream. To prove his good faith he offered to give a course in mathematics to military officers stationed in Abbeville, free of charge.

Duval de Soicourt agreed, but remained on his guard against Thales in Abbeville. Another town notable, Jean-Nicolas Douville—a former mayor, a counsellor in Abbeville's presidial court, and Duval de Soicourt's political rival—offered his home as a schoolroom.[75] The itinerant philosopher and self-styled professor of mathematics eventually revealed to the public that he was Simon-Nicolas-Henri Linguet.

While teaching applied mathematics without compensation, Linguet prepared several brochures for publication. One of these works, *Le Fanatisme des philosophes,* was dedicated to Douville.[76] The author confessed in print to his friend in Abbeville that he had fallen victim to the "chimeras of ambition," the "love of pleasure," and the "smoke of glory." At the age of twenty-eight, he already was destined to pass in "cruel regrets and long repentences" the remainder of a life "early poisoned by cruellest afflictions." His consolation in obscurity would be his protector's friendship, and his work, "the study of man's true duties, effaced in my heart for too long by frivolous studies or by even more frivolous occupations and hopes" (*FP*, dedication).

Linguet's *Le Fanatisme des philosophes* was a diatribe against the cultural aristocracy he held responsible for his troubles and failures in the world of letters.[77] It was also a sketch for a general theory of the development and decay of cultures, a study in the cycles of history—an essay in historical pessimism. The frustrated man of letters who dedicated himself to studying man's true duties in obscurity must have studied Jean-Jacques Rousseau's *Discours sur les sciences et les arts* as well (*FP*, 27).[78] He argued in this work that in the first stages of their development, men in society were ignorant, poor, and hard-working; and they were obedient—not from reflection, but out of "love for the laws" and "respect for legitimate authority." A "deplorable curiosity" sparked progress out of this state of happy obscurity; and curiosity found its fullest expression in economic transformations, the development of "the arts, and their whole dangerous train." The arts and sciences, "carried into their final stage, degenerate into philosophy" (*FP*, 19-20, 21). The philosophers advertised their love of humanity and their dedication to principles of public utility and good of country; but the sociologist of their philosophy depicted them as self-interested publicists for civilized society's profiteers, dominators, and exploiters, the leisured elites. Their apologies for luxuries on utilitarian grounds were really justifications of exploitative enterprises that aggravated the masses's degradation. They were particularly dangerous because they succeeded so frequently in seducing authority and because eventually the universally appropriable lessons they offered in the calculus of interest would work to dissolve bonds of obedience, preparing the way for despots whose brute force would replace the salutary social cohesive of instinctive obedience (*FP*, 9, 18, 33, 42).

> The spirit of calculation infects all minds.... Virtues are analyzed, thoughts are measured: there are algebrists, geometricians, physicists—but there are no longer any orators, no longer any poets, and above all, no longer any citizens.

> Having surrendered themselves for some time to this mathematical frigidity which numbs all members of a state, they reason their way into barbarism. And barbarism, like a new deluge, inundates the ill-starred fields where philosophy and the vices once germinated. It disposes them to blossom forth one day, but in a later generation, into ignorance and the virtues. [*FP*, 21-22.]

Rousseauan images of virtuous primitive societies gave Linguet leverage for his critiques of contemporary culture, including his striking correlation of the philosophes' utilitarian philosophy with exploitative and socially corrosive doctrines. However, his primitivist model did not suggest any programs of reform to ward off decay in fully developed societies. The rational moralism that Rousseau structures into his *Du Contract social*, a utopian instrument for transforming the social and political behavior of persons fated to reach the age of reason—and an alternative to the utilitarian philosophies with which the liberals proposed to reform society—finds no place in *Le Fanatisme des philosophes*. "The citizen obeys without reasoning," Linguet insisted. "His heart and his limbs are always in harmony" (*FP*, 19-20). A fixation on the superiority of primitive cultures in the context of a cyclical theory of historical development and decay boxed Linguet into an attitude of fatalistic resignation and detachment. Every society was doomed to run its cyclical course to the end. The inevitable death of a fully developed, perfectly corrupted society only heralded the renaissance of a primitive culture. Criticism was socially useless.

In other essays completed in 1764, Linguet broke the paralyzing mood that marked *Le Fanatisme des philosophes,* although he did not renounce historical pessimism, repudiate his critiques of modern culture, or drop his charges against the philosophes. In his *Nécessité d'une réforme dans l'administration de la justice et dans les lois civiles en France,*[79] Linguet drafted a project for forestalling decadence with reforms calculated to satisfy the material interests and elicit the allegiance of France's propertied Third Estate. Linguet's working assumption in the *Nécessité d'une réforme* was that rulers could command obedience, even in societies where the instinctive will to obey had been destroyed—only now, they had to appeal to their subjects' interests, decreeing and enforcing laws that guaranteed their properties. Where social change created new categories of owners—precisely the case in France, Linguet believed—the laws would have to be reformed to provide protection for their holdings (*NR,* 8, 10-11, 62-63).

In a brief sketch of the development of French legal and social institutions, Linguet documented the thesis that following the collapse of the Roman Empire, the earliest legal establishments in France reflected and protected the interests of the Frankish conquerors exclusively. The rest of the urban and rural population was already enslaved or rapidly became enserfed; its interests were altogether unsatisfied under existing legal conventions. Medieval monarchs first conceived the idea of "unchaining the enslaved multitude" to use it as a "support against the insolence of the small number of free persons," a refractory nobility. They encouraged the serfs to purchase their liberty. "And so was inaugurated the order, unknown in France until that time, to which the name of Third Estate has been given" (*NR,* 25-30, 31, 32). As quickly as members of this estate acquired properties, they began fighting with one another over their respective rights. However, the legal institutions that ought to have regulated their economic activities and facilitated the mediation of disputes remained unaltered, a chaotic heritage from the middle ages. Parlements, presidial courts, seigneurial courts, and bailiwick courts bickered interminably over the assignment of cases (*NR,* 70-81). Institutional reform to pro-

Linguet noted that the presidial courts, administering justice in some cases without appeal, and on the spot, where sums not exceeding 250 *livres* were at stake, had been established by the French monarchs specifically to remedy abuses of seigneurial justice and the inconvenience of appeals through an interminable succession of intermediary jurisdictions. Inflations in monetary values made them virtually powerless (*NR,* 70-81). Institutional reform to protect the property of artisans, merchants, shopkeepers, and other relatively new categories of owners in the Third Estate was a crying necessity; yet the situation remained unchanged. Either new institutions must be created to protect new economic interest groups, or existing institutions, like the presidial courts, must be revived (NR, 98).

The multiplicity of civil laws posed another threat to the operation of the judicial system. France was governed by canon law, Roman law, and French law, "a kind of bizarre patchwork, a ridiculous assortment of provisions, all contradictory...." (NR, 96). Justice as Linguet defined it was precisely the equitable administration of civil laws governing relationships among holders of all kinds of properties, the hard core of the monarch's supporters; but there could be no justice, no equity, where institutions and laws were in such confusion (NR, 96-97).

Again, reform was necessary; it was also unlikely. The monarch feared antagonizing an entrenched aristocratic elite by promulgating new legislation. He refused to bid for the allegiance of a propertied Third Estate. There was no hope then. The judicial structure would crumble altogether, signaling the death of the state: "He [the legislator] is a gardener who, in trimming his trees, spares the parasitic branches because they seem hardy. He does not see that [those] are draining the sap from all the others. The trunk, weakened by them, dries up. The entire tree soon perishes, dragging down with it those fatal branches which caused its ruin. That is what has happened to us, or what will happen to us sooner or later..." (NR, 103).

Unreformed, the state would die. Like the badly pruned tree, it was doomed. There were, of course, a few key differences between trees in gardens and men in society. Trees ruined by ignorant gradeners were docile victims; new proprietors in the Third Estate who feared expropriation by reactionary aristocratic magistrates enforcing archaic laws in the king's name might not be.

Linguet was demanding the kind of institutional reform the king's ministers would invoke in 1788 in their open struggle against the aristocratic party. In 1764, however, he was only an anti-Montesquieuan seer without an audience, a theorist of administrative reform and a publicist for the thèse royale without prestige, portfolio, or backing at even the lowest levels of national administration. He was also the grandson of a procurator in the presidial court at Reims, the protégé of a former counsellor in Abbeville's presidial court, and a commoner himself. He had the makings of a forceful advocate for underprotected proprietors in his estate—like the petite bourgeoisie, the peasantry, and the bourgeoisie de robe—beginning with the officers in Abbeville's presidial court who took the initiative of sending a copy of the Nécessité d'une réforme to the lieutenant general of police in Paris and requesting his permission to have it published.[80] Nonetheless, Linguet's allegiances were mixed. His thesis on the necessity for reform was bound up with an antithesis: a reformed legal system would function all the more efficiently as a safeguard for all those who owned something, and as their protection against the class in society which owned nothing. Civil law was the possessor's permanent defense against the claims of propertyless persons:

> In the position society puts men in, they would not know how to get along without laws. If they lived isolated, they would not need any. If they were all poor, they would need few. If they were all rich, they would require more but far fewer than they do in that singular position where [the inequality of] passions and talents, wealth and poverty, respectively, places them. In general, they are instituted to repress violence, although they often favor it. They are destined above all to guarantee properties. Now, since you can steal much more from someone who has [possessions] than from someone who doesn't, they are evidently a safeguard accorded to the rich against the indigent.
>
> Justice is the art of rendering to each one what belongs to him. *Suum cuique tribuere.* But the poor man has for himself only his poverty. The laws, therefore, cannot maintain anything else for him. They tend to safeguard whoever has superfluities against the attacks of whoever lacks what is necessary; that is their true spirit, and if it is a drawback, it is inseparable from their existence. [*NR*, 6-7]

In putting one issue to rest, the necessity for immediate judicial reform to protect owners in the Third Estate, and by implication, to strengthen political bonds between governors and governed, to reduce disorder in modern society and forestall its collapse, Linguet conspicuously, boldly raised another. How just and how effective could the judicial system be when its spirit was property and its purpose was to perpetuate inequality and deepen class divisions? He attempted to handle this explosive issue by invoking precisely the principles of utility he had cited and condemned the philosophes for embracing: laws that consecrated extremes of possessions and deprivation were not unjust; those who produced everything and were condemned to own nothing nonetheless got something in return, enough to keep alive. "In this way, they [the laws] impose silence upon critics in condemning the multitude to painfully dragging fruits from the bosom of the earth without allowing it to keep for itself anything but the smallest portion" (*NR*, 7-8). The rationalization was unconvincing. In his *Histoire du siècle d'Alexandre* and in *Le Fanatisme des philosophes,* Linguet already had exposed the grim realities it camouflaged: the propertyless class in fully developed societies was no longer getting even the "smallest portion" of what it produced. Among "those same peoples famous for arts and opulence, the sole hope for three-quarters of the nation is death on a dung heap from the first illness brought on by an excess of work and misery. The indigent man's nourishment is a bread moistened only by his tears; and the opulent man to whom he has sacrificed his life will fight with him over the bed of straw where he is about to die" (*FP*, 62; see also *A*, 229-30).

In his *Nécessité d'une réforme*, Linguet championed programs to strengthen the political bond between the French king and the propertied Third Estate. Nonetheless, his observations on the material conditions of the propertyless masses in modern societies as well as his trenchant analyses of how liberal philosophies functioned as apologies and spurs for class exploitation pointed to the dangers and contradictions in an overly facile identification of monarchical principles and reform policies with the needs and interests of proprietors. In the context of these observations and analyses, Linguet's *Nécessité d'une réforme* advertised his real but qualified commitment to the common cause of king and propertied commoners against an economically, politically, and socially resurgent aristocracy.

"Monsieur de Beaumont," the author of the *Nécessité d'une réforme*, was heavily indebted to his friend and protector, Jean-Nicolas Douville, the counsellor in Abbeville's presidial court to whom he had dedicated the work. Douville paid for printing costs and provided the author with source materials.[81] That was not enough.

From his outpost in Abbeville, Beaumont-Linguet was trying to engineer a nationwide exposure for his ideas. He wanted to distribute his *Nécessité d'une réforme* to all the presidial courts in France "on behalf of whom," he announced, "it is written."[82]

Convinced that the literary establishment's approval and connections were essential if he wanted a wide circulation for his work, Linguet persuaded his brother, a lawyer in Paris, to contact the perpetual secretary of the Académie française, Charles Duclos—but without revealing his true identity. Linguet-frère presented Duclos with a copy of his brother's work; when the perpetual secretary objected to some notes in the text, the author obligingly deleted them, returned an expurgated copy of his brochure to Duclos and asked Duclos to find out whether the director of the postal service would be willing to arrange for a national distribution.[83]

Meanwhile, Linguet-frère continued asking for the favor of Duclos's approval.[84] If the perpetual secretary ever intervened, it didn't help. The *Nécessité d'une réforme* was not acclaimed by the literary reviewers; what was even more ruinous, the government proscribed it.[85]

Beaumont-Linguet was experiencing similar difficulties with other works, especially with his *Histoire des révolutions de l'Empire romain*, written, he confessed to Duclos, "to stave off the boredom into which inaction throws me." He dispatched it to Paris to test its acceptance by the censors "although I have for this ceremony all the distaste that it must inspire in a man able and eager to tell the truth." His lack of connections and his "way of thinking," he feared, might cause customs agents to conclude that he was circulating the work illicitly.[86] Linguet's "way of thinking" in this work was to extrapolate from a study of imperial policies some fundamental guidelines for reforms to ward off the collapse of large states. He argued that the most effective emperors—like Tiberius, Caligula, Nero, Trajan—ruthlessly and systematically quashed a dangerously independent, insurrectionary Roman nobility and forged bonds of political allegiance between themselves and the population whose liberty they had recently annihilated. They elicited obedience not by applying force despotically, as their detractors charged, but by satisfying the material interests of their unfree subjects. They legislated protection for properties; they guaranteed subsistence for the masses (*HR*, I, 26-27, 157-73, 184-86, 233-73; II, 127-30). The truly censurable emperors, Linguet observed, were those who supported and practiced philosophy, "the art that weighs all things, discusses everything, substituting words for things," the science that "thinks about the prerogatives of man." Allegiances to philosophy paralyzed them for action on principles of sound imperial administration (*HR*, II, 237-38).

In 1766, when Linguet finally succeeded in publishing the *Histoire des ré-volutions de l'Empire romain,* his critics would draw their own lessons from his characterization of imperial rulers as brilliant administrators, protectors of properties and lives. They would charge that Linguet was an "attorney for the Neros and Caligulas,"[87] an apologist for despots, ancient and modern, when in fact, what he was championing was the unpopular model of an all-powerful ruler who repressed the liberties of aristocrats and guaranteed security to commoners.

In 1764, however, Linguet was not encountering much open opposition; he still had not made the contacts needed to assure circulation and publicity for his works. What depressed him most was the notable failure of authority at any level to recognize a literature he had filled with diagnoses of the maladies of modern culture and with blueprints for reforming its institutions to forestall corruption and dissolution. Although fiercely partisan elites operating out of interconnected bases in social and literary circles and government had not posed fatal obstacles to the upward mobility of this provincial *arriviste,* they also had not chosen to extend the solid support that might have assured his success.

By September, 1764, having produced a library of proscribed, suspect, or unsalable works, Beaumont-Linguet seemed to have reached the depths of despair and the point of real resignation to a fate in obscurity—without the consolation of literature this time, and bereft of the *littérateur*'s eternal hope that successful publications would rescue him from oblivion. He confessed to Charles Duclos that from his earliest youth, he wanted to associate with men of letters. "... I found only unbearable protectors, unfaithful guides, or perfidious friends." They exploited his talents, and claimed his works as their own. Disenchanted, he tried to launch an independent career in literature, and "I saw immediately that I would have done better not to have entered it." He wrote that he tried other employment (probably an allusion to his work for the prince de Beauvau and the duc de Deux-Ponts); even there, he was pursued by "a misfortune which has followed me in a striking way from my birth...." At the age of twenty-four, he made up his mind to retire into obscurity, "and to owe my life, if necessary, to the work of my hands." His friend Douville "revived in me a taste [for literature] I believed extinguished," but what was the good of it all? It was clear that he had wasted his time on the *Nécessité d'une réforme,* and Douville his money; it had been suppressed. Even if he succeeded in finding a publisher and an approving censor for his *Histoire des révolutions de l'Empire romain,* his latest effort, and he insisted, his last, he planned to abandon his career in letters to flee to "another hemisphere." He would go to the American islands, seeking not fortune, but calm. "Finding it impossible to play a brilliant role of any kind whatever, I long only to spend my life untroubled and unknown, and I will doubtless lose nothing by it in any way."[88]

In October, 1764, a month after Beaumont-Linguet promised to seek obscurity and threatened to find it in an American wilderness, Simon Linguet was inscribed as a *stagiaire,* a probationer on the rolls of the Order of Lawyers practicing before the Parlement of Paris.[89] He chose a career in law at a point in his life when multiple experiences of rejection, failure, and frustration, the prospects of oblivion in America, and the necessity of making some kind of living left him confused, depressed, and possibly desperate. "I have never respected the profession of lawyer," Linguet is alleged to have admitted, "and I am going to enter it. That is because one must be something in life; one must make money, and it's better to be a rich cook than a poor and unknown savant."[90]

The decision was not that clean-cut. The lawyer remained a man of letters, *malgré lui.* He never really liquidated Beaumont-Linguet. In *L'Aveu sincère, ou Lettre à une mère sur les dangers que court la jeunesse en se livrant à un goût trop vif pour la littérature,* a work published in 1768 and addressed to his sister, her children, and a generation of young "commoners of no importance,"[91] Linguet cites and condemns teachers who breed intellectual *arrivistes* and turn them loose in a savage environment where only those skilled in intrigue, hypocrisy, and pandery can survive (*Aveu,* v, 35-36). He thought he might save the next generation. He confessed that he was powerless to reform himself (*Aveu,* xvii). Philosophy, as Linguet defined it in *L'Aveu sincère,* the kind of thinking which "accredits egoism, flatters pride, and destroys subordination....lead[ing] one to aspire after equality by sensitizing him to its justice," already had left its imprint on Linguet's character. And literature, unremitting analysis and critique, was his existential necessity (*Aveu*, 79, 63-75). This man of letters would claim for himself—against the grain of all his proclamations about the virtue and necessity of an existence in mediocrity, ignorance, and unreflecting obedience, the absolute freedom of thought he condemned the liberal establishment for encouraging and monopolizing (*FP*, 11), and an equal opportunity to mold the opinions of his contemporaries. In the context of immediate needs, however, Linguet's literary output, and in particular his *Nécessité d'une réforme* and the *Histoire des révolutions de l'Empire romain*, served him as a defense against professional overcommitment to the Paris Order of Lawyers and to the *thèse nobiliaire* espoused by the members of this legal fraternity.[92]

"...as priests and oracles," Linguet wrote in his *Nécessité d'une réforme*, advocates have "the exclusive right to speak to their Goddess, and, as these priests, [advocates also] take great care to collect their fee for opening their mouth....These are what are called lawyers. It is alleged that they can be found as far back as ancient Rome" (*NR, 93*). The celebrated Roman lawyer, as Linguet idealized him, had mastered the arts of pleading and persuasion. He used words to evoke justice by provoking the judges' undeliberated response to the sound of truth. With beautiful voice and seductive gesture, he impressed his convictions upon his hearers; he touched their hearts. "He had to move his judges: he did not think of convincing them by shreds of arid citations, often as unintelligible as they were uncalled for." The modern lawyer poses as mediator between his client and the law, and his mediation takes the form of compilations and citations in mute, depersonalized words (*NR*, 94). Only in the ancient world had a man's true self been his social self, his professional self. As Linguet described it in his *Histoire du siècle d'Alexandre*, the polis was the space in which citizens fulfilled themselves in their professions without corrupting themselves. "Everything in him is indivisible." There, the professional was not the instrument of his calling. He was master of it. His public being, that is, all dimensions of his activity in the polis, constituted his politics. A man's profession in the polis was a political self-expression.

The modern professional was a traitor to himself. He practiced his profession successfully by repressing whole dimensions of himself. To choose a profession was to will a permanent self-division. What was a man, knowing all this, to do in the world? Linguet described this dilemma in 1762. The Jesuit Order had just been suppressed. A young Jesuit, finding himself in a society riddled with corruption, governed exclusively by the law of self-interest, needed somehow to resolve a major identity crisis; he must become someone, choose a profession, be something:

> Viens donc vil intérêt, viens gouverner ma vie,
> Viens tendre dans mon cœur tes ressorts tout puissans;
>
> ...
>
> Irai-je, de mon être oubliant la noblesse,
> D'un Riche dédaigneux courtiser la bassesse?
>
> ...
>
> Et la paix sur le front, la rage au fond du cœur,
> Parasite avili, sans vertu, sans honneur,
> Perdre pour un repas, toute ma renommée?

If loss of autonomy was the price of literary renown, how was a man to embrace a career in letters?

> Faudra-ti-il, apprenant au sein des Facultés
>   A rediger une ordonnance,
>   Vendre chèrement l'espérance
>   Aux malades épouvantés?
> Ministre de la mort, tyran de la nature
> Assassiner par art, guérir par conjecture.

The false promise of health was a commodity sold exclusively to patients who could meet the going market price, and only by physicians who had memorized useless prescriptions in the course of a worthless academic preparation. How could a man of sensitivity and uncalculating sympathy betray himself in a life of professional hypocrisy?

> Faudra-t-il à Thémis consacrant mes talens,
> Du Dédale des Lois, sans en trouver l'issue,
>   Parcourir la route inconnue
>   Et, Novice après quarante ans,
>   Avec une éloquence aisée
>   Débiter quelque phrase usée
>   Devant des Sénateurs dormants?

How could a man become a lawyer: The practice of law was not a self-expression but a self-betrayal. Law had become a fortuitous conjunction of formulas and the lawyer the passive mechanical agent of their transmission through the proper channels.

Did the self's salvation lie in retreat? Was seclusion the only way out for any man revolted by the rottenness in society?

> Et sous l'humilité d'un habit méprisable
> Déguiser du manteau de la Religion,
> La fière austérité d'un Dévot redoutable,
> Et d'un Moine mécontent la sourde ambition?[93]

No. Retreat was the greatest corrupter of all; it only further stimulated the demon of ambition which impelled men to scale the walls of all the self's refuges, physical and intellectual.

Simon Linguet became a lawyer. This lawyer chose to protect his principles and defend his independence in permanent opposition to the values, interests, and conventions of the legal establishment.

The white Christ, a wooden crucifix, had hung for years at the high point on the Pont-Neuf of Abbeville, an object of veneration among the pious of the town. During the night of August 8-9, 1765, the crucified Christ was massacred, its legs lacerated with a sword or a hunting knife, its right arm deeply gashed, a gaping wound pierced through the painted wood at a point just below the heart. Christ had been crucified and resurrected, and now he had been murdered in Abbeville. The cry echoed through the city. The king's procurator, Jean-Clément Hecquet, moved at once to bring action against the perpetrators of this criminal impiety and instructed the assessor of the *lieutenant criminel* of Abbeville to conduct a preliminary investigation. The assessor was Duval de Soicourt, the town's former mayor, a political enemy of Linguet's protector Douville, and a suspicious observer of the activities of Plato in Abbeville.[94]

At the same time the assessor began taking testimony on the incident, the Church issued three *monitoires,* calls to witnesses to depose their testimony with church officials. At this point witnesses began associating the crime against the crucifix with other impieties—singing blasphemous songs, reading forbidden books, desecrating crosses in cemeteries. The names of several young men, including that of the chevalier Francois-Jean de La Barre, began to circulate in connection with these separate misdemeanors. Guillaume-François-Louis Joly de Fleury, procurator-général of the Parlement of Paris, ordered a new investigation to deal with these separate charges, and two of the youths were arrested.

In the course of questioning, the youths implicated others, including Pierre-Jean-François Douville de Maillefeu, the son of Linguet's friend Douville, and Pierre-François Dumaisniel de Saveuse, both of whom escaped before they could be apprehended. The recently inscribed probationary lawyer, summoned by Douville, rushed to the scene, prepared to fight on behalf of the accused. There could be no question of an oral defense. The Criminal Ordinance of 1670 prohibited it. The accused gave their testimony behind closed doors. Their statements were kept strictly secret. The youths were uncounseled; they were even kept ignorant of the charges against them.[95] *Mémoires,* supplications, personal appeals to great men in positions of power—these were the lawyer's only recourse: "suppleness is of more effect there than the power of language, and intrigue more useful than genius" (*A-1769,* 262).

One of the youths, the chevalier de La Barre, was judged and found guilty on charges of singing blasphemous songs, profaning the sign of the cross, and showing a lack of respect for the Holy Sacrament. On February 28, 1766, the presidial court of Abbeville sentenced La Barre to do "honorable penance," to undergo various degrees of torture, to have his tongue cut out, his head cut off, and his body and his head burned in a public ceremony.[96]

Until almost the moment of the execution, Linguet fought to bring the case into the open and to stop the spread of damaging hearsay. Because La Barre was a nobleman and because corporal punishment was involved, he was permitted by the terms of the Criminal Ordinance of 1670 to appeal his case before the Grand'Chambre of the Paris parlement.[97] Linguet was planning to present an appeal himself. He was determined to force his truth, that is, La Barre's innocence, not only upon the magistrates but upon a hostile, ignorant public, seducing them with words and gestures, "bring[ing] the noble passions into play...employ[ing] the most vehement expressions without fear of appearing ridiculous" (A-1769, 262-63). Linguet drew up a *mémoire* for La Barre and submitted it to a *président à mortier* of the Paris parlement, Louis-François Le Fèvre d'Ormesson, La Barre's influential relative. D'Ormesson, seeking desperately to avoid scandal and tragically miscalculating the greatness of La Barre's peril, refused Linguet's offer.[98] "I have endured in this affair every rebuff, every frustration imaginable," Linguet complained; "they have tied my hands; they have closed my mouth; they have not allowed me to publish the least thing for their [the accused boys'] vindication. It was necessary to substitute for printed writings, which would have instructed and disabused the public immediately, procedures, solicitations, manuscript remonstrances that have caused me a hundred times more trouble and which have had no effect."[99]

On June 4, the Grand'Chambre of the Parlement of Paris summoned and questioned La Barre and then confirmed the sentence of the Abbeville court.[100] La Barre was to die on July 1, 1766. Linguet was working against time to complete and circulate a *mémoire* for La Barre when, on June 26, he was advised to calm himself, to keep quiet, and abandon his brief.[101] Trapped, Linguet could only hope for direct clemency from the king for La Barre. He eliminated the chevalier's name from the title of his *mémoire* which appeared on June 27: *Mémoire pour les Sieurs Moynel, Dumesniel de Saveuse et Douville de Maillefeu, impliqués dan l'affaire de la mutilation d'un crucifix arrivée à Abbeville, le 9 août 1765.* Linguet painstakingly had collected the signatures of celebrated lawyers pleading before the Paris parlement; he appended them to the "Consultation" following his brief. This tactic prevented the immediate suppression of the *Mémoire* by judicial act, although Joly de Fleury secretly ordered that distribution be stopped.[102] Nonetheless, as it appeared, and where it appeared, the *Mémoire* communicated an outrage against injustice that nothing could extinguish.

Linguet accused the assessor, Duval de Soicourt, of grave judicial error; he had joined the charge of mutilating the crucifix to charges of impieties and other minor transgressions, and had deliberately confused the gravity of the two groups of accusations.[103] Linguet described the circumstances in which witnesses' testimony had been elicited and recorded. All testimony had been given equal weight and had been accepted indiscriminately—hearsay, bare suspicions, rumors, irrelevant facts.[104] Linguet exposed the reasons for Duval de Soicourt's partiality in the case.[105] He ruthlessly challenged the competence of another of the presiding judges on the presidial court, a pork merchant named de Broutelle.[106] He discounted all confessions drawn from one of the accused, Charles-François-Marcel Moisnel, during the course of strictly secret questioning. His psychological portrait of this young man was brilliant. He had deliberately drawn it to move his readers to tears. Moisnel confronts his judge, but he has no crime to confess. He did not mutilate the crucifix, yet he has been made to suffer. He searches his conscience for some justification for this anguish he has been forced to endure. He is confused, terrified. He begs pardon of his judges as of father-confessors. Yes, he has committed great crimes. He has not removed his hat in public procession; he has sung bawdy songs, although not publicly. "Can you imagine a more moving spectacle than that of this unfortunate child, prostrate at the feet of his judge, baring his conscience, recapitulating his past conduct...."[107]

Imaginative reconstruction in a *Mémoire* calculated to move the reader from rage into action was the limit of Linguet's defense. Linguet reached the limit but failed to capture the public conscience and public sympathies in time.

La Barre was executed on July 1, 1766. Linguet was still combating the machinations of Duval de Soicourt, who was in Paris to demand that Joly de Fleury do something about the *Mémoire*.[108] Duval de Soicourt had not judged the case of the other accused youths. As soon as Linguet got wind of these intrigues, he wrote to Joly de Fleury. Duval de Soicourt, Linguet charged, had promised the parents of the remaining accused youths that he would hear and judge their cases quickly and leniently, on one condition: the government must suppress Linguet's *Mémoire*. Linguet informed Joly de Fleury that he was ready to call witnesses to support his allegations. He also revealed that Duval de Soicourt had terrified Moisnel into disavowing his lawyers' arguments in his defense. While Duval de Soicourt apparently abandoned his functions with impunity to "occupy himself exclusively with his self-interest and his vengeance," the parents of the jailed youths and those who were implicated but had fled to escape imprisonment were still vainly demanding a trial and judgment.[109]

Writing to Joly de Fleury on August 27, 1766, Linguet called Duval de Soicourt's bluff. If the assessor considered himself maligned by the *Mémoire*, if he wanted to challenge Linguet's facts, let him bring his case into the courts. If he dares, "he can run the risks of a judicial discussion.... We await him, our feet firmly planted...." Linguet advised Joly de Fleury that he had "a thousand things, each one more interesting than the next" to relate concerning "this horrible affair." He announced that he would appear the following day to recount them personally. He warned the procurator general that if he solicited a parlementary *arrêt* suppressing the *Mémoire* he would live to regret it because "it could be shown to you that what has been suppressed is the truth."[110] The tactic worked. Duval de Soicourt was forced to step down. On September 10, 1766, Douville de Maillefeu, Dumaisniel de Saveuse, and Moisnel were absolved of the charges against them.[111]

"...all sensitive souls," the journalist Grimm wrote, "have been dismayed by this judgment [against La Barre]....humanity awaits a public avenger, an eloquent and courageous man to transmit this purposeless and unexampled cruelty to the tribunal of the public and for the branding of posterity."[112] Grimm was prepared to nominate Voltaire, avenger of Calas's memory. Then, as though remembering that Voltaire's *Dictionnaire philosophique* (which had been found in La Barre's room, and was alleged to be his favorite reading) had been tossed into the flames at Abbeville along with the parts of La Barre's corpse, Grimm retracted. The avenging philosopher's friends "had to beseech him to prefer his safety and repose to the interest of humanity, and not to risk printing the mark of opprobrium upon bloodthirsty men resolved to pursue him at the slightest move on his part."[113]

Voltaire did not wait upon ceremonies of entreaty. He was frankly frightened. He fled to the safety of Clèves; he begged all the philosophes to join him; he scattered a trail of abuse behind him, against La Barre, this "young fool," against "two scatterbrains whom madness and debauchery have driven to the point of public profanations...."[114]

Once all spectre of danger had vanished and indignant men everywhere could be found to deplore this crime against humanity, Voltaire emerged as defender of the chevalier de La Barre's memory and avenger of one more victim of *l'infâme*.

Linguet was not as politic as the celebrated Voltaire, whose courage in the Calas affair he was conspicuously trying to equal. He had tried to save La Barre's life and failed; he succeeded, however, in rescuing three more lives from the clutches of the law and from the solicitous attentions of a philosophic posterity.

His intrepidity had no bounds. There has been some talk, Linguet remarked in a letter to his brother-in-law, of pursuing the author of the *Mémoire*: "Mais c'est un reste d'écume qui tombât de la gueule du tigre expirant. Je ne crains guère ses menaces...."[115] Linguet was wrong. The tiger was long in expiring. In the preliminary discourse to his magnum opus, his *Théorie des lois civiles*, which he dedicated to Douville, Linguet was still trying to kick it to death. The La Barre case, he wrote, would be the best supplement to the *Théorie des lois civiles*. "If only all the details of that case were well enough known, no other proofs would be required of the necessity of reforming our jurisprudence in almost all its parts" (*L*, I, 4).

Duval de Soicourt was on guard. This time he obtained from the parlement an *arrêt* dated July 14, 1767, directing that offensive passages in Linguet's "Discours préliminaire" be suppressed. The parlement was now on general alert. Suspicions had been aroused by the irreverent boldness of the *stagiaire au Parlement de Paris*. At the end of the *arrêt* it was noted that Linguet's *Théorie des lois civiles* was to be deposited with the court clerk and the remainder of its contents inspected by the procurator general, if necessary.[116]

The probationary lawyer was undaunted by the threats of these magistrates. He seemed to thrive on their machinations. By March, 1767, he was deeply immersed in a new case. He wrote to a friend: "...I hope to emerge with a more complete success than in [the case of] the unfortunate La Barre. The subject of this one is not as tragic, but I am dealing with judges who are hardly lesser rogues than those of Abbeville. I have drawn up a fine big *Mémoire* and nothing has impeded me; I have told all, and it will be clear that these Messieurs, the honest gentlemen, as you can well sense, will not find anything to laugh about."[117]

This lawyer, who published brochures showing how magistrates turned scandalous inequities and procedural irregularities to their own advantage, who called judges "rogues," and boasted and threatened in his *Théorie des lois civiles* that if he ever told the full story of the La Barre affair he would clinch his case for "reforming our jurisprudence in almost all its parts," was inviting future confrontations with the magistrature. The contents of the "Discours préliminaire" and the remainder of the *Théorie* exposed the position of a young man ready to risk his professional security to uncover injustices and to publicize programs for radical judicial reform as prejudicial to entrenched and self-serving *robins* as they were salutary for proprietors in the Third Estate and vital, he believed, for the survival of the monarchy.

At a more basic level, the *Théorie des lois civiles*—in which Linguet refocused earlier reflections on history, retrospective cultural anthropology, law, political economy, and public administration, and integrated them into a theory of the origins of society, the organization of its institutions and cultural superstructures, and the dynamics and directions of its development—can be read as a preface to all his projects for administrative reform: an understanding of the fundamental principles of civil society would dictate the necessity of reform, specify its objectives, and map its limitations.

The lessons Linguet was offering were also a manifesto, the signal and warning of a partially disaffected subject to authorities in a royal administration he burned to serve but into which he could not gain *entrée*: unless government officials adopted the reforms he had constructed on the foundation of his fundamental principles; unless they integrated into their doctrines and policies his understanding of the humanity and social justice that could be attained "in this valley of tears which you embellish with the name of society" (L, II, 448), they would be facing not the consequences of one isolated subject's alienation but the disaster of a nation's estrangement in social revolution.

Perspective

In the 1750s and 1760s, when his renowned contemporaries were capturing the allegiance of some of the brightest young minds in France with their lessons in the art and science of liberating mankind from the shackles of traditional beliefs and institutions, Simon-Nicolas-Henri Linguet, an immigrant from the French provinces, and the son of a Jansenist who was a disgraced ex-professor and officer in the *petite bourgeoisie de robe* in Reims, was acquiring his academic credentials in Paris and working his way through a remarkable series of unsuccessful apprenticeships.

Although he won attention or favors from highly placed influentials in the intersecting byways of *le monde*—the duc de Deux-Ponts, the prince de Beauvau, Charles Duclos—he never mastered the art of advancing himself on the basis of these connections. Instead, like some prototypical protean man, he snatched at opportunities opened up to him by the support of great men, exploited them briefly, and abandoned them noisily, frequently leaving trails of scandal behind him. In a few short years, he considered and rejected study in engineering, an apprenticeship as a secretary, a technical post in the military, several kinds of entrepreneurial activity, playwriting, poetry, and the writing of history. Through all these *engagements* he failed conspicuously to identify himself with the doctrines and activities of the party of humanity—*encyclopédistes, académiciens, économistes*—perhaps in part because the philosophes' liberal ideologies contradicted conceptualizations of authority and liberty that Linguet may have appropriated initially from an education in a Jansenist household and a childhood in a provincial city permeated with the symbols, images, and rituals of paternalistic monarchy. Linguet's passage through the circle of Fréron and the anti-philosophes and his close friendship with the Abbeville notable Jean-Nicholas Douville, who encouraged and supported some of his early publications, may have contributed to crystallizing and strengthening some of his early convictions—like the commitment to autocracy he expressed in the *Histoire des révolutions de l'Empire romain.* An approval of autocrats who, like good Christian kings, guaranteed their subjects security and protection, was combined in Linguet's early writing with a radical pessimism about the fate of the moderns and strong sympathies for simple men in primitive societies—characters modelled after those portrayed by Jean-Jacques Rousseau in his two *Discourses*.

Linguet was bitter about his failures in the world of letters; following Fréron's example he blamed the philosophes for exercising a stultifying monopoly over ideas. He never renounced the convictions that set him apart from them. On the contrary, he seemed to be trying to force the republic of letters to become the open society it advertised itself as being...by letting him in and tolerating his deviant doctrines.

By the time he settled on a career in law, Linguet had done everything to guarantee that he would be practicing the profession under fire from magistrates and advocates: he never repudiated apologies for the Jesuit party which were certain to arouse suspicion among *parlementaires* who had worked to destroy the Company; he did not abjure his defense of Roman autocrats or abandon his demands for reforms in the content and administration of French civil laws—position papers that *parlementaires* and *avocats* found professionally threatening, and therefore doctrinally unacceptable.

In short, Linguet brought with him into the practice of law, and kept on generating in his second career in letters, beliefs which many of his contemporaries in power would have liked to dismiss or stifle as reactionary because they went against prevailing and confluent currents of liberal convictions—like faith in liberty and in liberties, in philosophy and in the philosophes' task of enlightening, and in progress—convictions which had swept up potentates in the world of letters, officers in the royal administration, *parlementaires*, and other notable influentials.

In fact, as I will show in the following chapters, there was at least as much subversiveness in Simon Linguet's anti-liberal ideas as there was in the liberal philosophies of the luminaries of the high enlightenment, and an even greater revolutionary potential.

NOTES

1. Charpentier, *La Bastille dévoilée, ou Recueil des pièces authentiques pour servir à son histoire*, 3 vols. (Paris, 1789-90), III, 114.

2. Louis Petit de Bachaumont, *Mémoires secrets, pour servir à l'histoire de la république des lettres en France, depuis MDCCLXII jusqu'à nos jours; ou Journal d'un observateur*, 36 vols. (London, 1780-89), XVI (Oct. 6, 8, 10, 1780), 17, 18-19, 22-23.

3. *Ibid.* (Oct. 10, 1780), 23; Simon Linguet, *Mémoires sur la Bastille, et la détention de l'auteur dans ce château royal, depuis le 27 septembre 1780 jusqu'au 19 mai 1782* (London, 1783), pp. 36-37.

4. Bachaumont, *Mémoires secrets*, XVI (Oct. 6, 1780), 17.

5. Jakob Friedrich Melchior Grimm, Denis Diderot, Guillaume-Thomas-François Raynal, Heinrich Meister, *Correspondance littéraire, philosophique, et critique*, ed. Maurice Tourneux, 16 vols. (Paris, 1877-82), XII (Oct., 1780), 441, Bachaumont, *Mémoires secrets*, XVI (Oct. 6, 1780), 17.

6. Grimm et al., *Correspondance littéraire*, XI (Feb., 1777), 414.

7. *Ibid.*, XII (Oct., 1780), 441. Pietro Aretino, notorious Renaissance adventurer, had constituted himself diplomatic adviser and confidant to princes, monarchs, and emper-

ors. He presented himself alternately as the panegyrist and calumniator of popes, aristocrats, and artists. At all times, he was his age's most brilliant and acerbic satirist. He disposed of a large fortune, titles, and honors, spoils of intrigues and manipulations. He bore scars of whippings, slashes inflicted by sword, and the marks of numerous tramplings. He had been banished from courts, summoned before kings, exiled by popes.

8. Grimm et al., *Correspondance littéraire,* XII (Oct., 1780), 441. The phrasing in French is "un Jean...en toutes lettres, signé par Linguet."

9. Joseph de Lanjionais, *Supplément à "l'Espion anglois" ou Lettres intéressantes sur la retraite de M. Necker; sur le sort de la France et de l'Angleterre; et sur la détention de M. Linguet à la Bastille. Adressées à Mylord All'Eye. Par l'auteur de "l'Espion anglois"* (London, 1781), pp. 205-7.

10. Linguet, *Mémoires sur la Bastille,* p. 19. See also Linguet to police commissary Chesnon, the Bastille, Sept. 19, 1781, as cited in Charpentier, *La Bastille dévoilée,* III, 123-24.

11. Minutes of the Conseil secret, Parlement de Paris, Tuesday, July 18, 1780, in AN, X1A 3582, fol. 81.

12. D'Eprémesnil's accusations were published in 1781 in the form of a pamphlet signed "M" and entitled *Dénonciation des feuilles du Sr Linguet, faite en Parlement, les chambres assemblées, les mardi 11, vendredi 14, et mardi 18 juillet 1780* (n.p. [1781]). Linguet's comments appear in his *Annales politiques, civiles, et littéraires du dix-huitième siècle,* 19 vols. (London, Brussels, Paris, 1777-92), IX (1780), 201-45.

13. D'Eprémesnil, *Dénonciation,* pp. 4, 9.

14. *Ibid.,* pp. 17, 20-21.

15. *Ibid.,* p. 25, quoting from Linguet's "Réflexions préliminaires" in his *Annales,* I (1777), 102-3; see also Minutes, Conseil secret, July 18, 1780, in AN, X1A 3582, fol. 103.

16. D'Eprémesnil, *Dénonciation,* pp. 34-35, 42; see also Minutes, Conseil secret, in AN, X1A 3582, fols. 103-10, 116v.

17. D'Eprémesnil, *Dénonciation,* p. 44; Minutes, Conseil secret, in AN, X1A 3582, fol. 119.

18. D'Eprémesnil, *Dénonciation,* p. 54; Minutes, Conseil secret, in AN, X1A3582, fols. 119-20.

19. D'Eprémesnil, *Dénonciation,* pp. 54-55; Minutes, Conseil secret, in AN, X1A 3582, fols. 128, 128v.

20. Bachaumont, *Mémoires secrets,* XV (July 21, 1780), 235-36; see also Minutes, Conseil secret, in AN, X1A3582, fols. 81-82. Progress reports on the trial of Linguet and his *Annales* before the Paris parlement were being sent out from the offices of the procurator general to Keeper of the Seals Miromesnil as well as to ministers Maurepas and Amelot. See BN, MSS fr., Fonds Joly de Fleury, doss. 1682, fols. 243, 246ff. The reports are dated July 11, 14, and 18, 1780.

21. D'Eprémesnil, *Dénonciation,* p. 54, paraphrasing from Linguet's article, "Explication du principe avancé dans le Numéro 26 de ces *Annales,* sur les effets de la force, en politique," *Annales,* IV (1778), 227.

22. Linguet, *MB,* p. 27.

23. *Ibid.,* p. 12.

24. Peter Gay, *Voltaire's Politics: The Poet as Realist* (New York, 1965), p. 78.

25. Abbé André Morellet, *Mémoires (inédits) de l'Abbé Morellet, suivis de sa correspondance avec M. le Comte Rxxx, Ministre des finances à Naples,* ed. Saint-Albin Berville and Jean-François Barrière, 2 vols., Collection des mémoires relatifs à la Révolution française, vols. VI-VII (Paris, 1823), I, 97, 99; cited without reference in Léonce de Lavergne, *Les Economistes français du XVIIIe siècle* (Paris, 1870), pp. 342-43.

26. Bachaumont, *Mémoires secrets,* XVI (Oct. 8, 1780), 18; Linguet, *MB,* pp. 71-75.

27. Linguet, *MB,* p. 63.

28. *Ibid.,* p. 110.

29. *Ibid.,* frontispiece and iii-iv. Linguet attributes the idea for the engraving to the editor of the *Courrier du Bas-Rhin,* who had announced the forthcoming publication of

the *Mémoires* in his first number for 1783. Inspired by Linguet's prospectus, he urged that the doors of these "abhorred places" be opened, that the prisoners be released and tried before the law, "that the walls be razed to elevate in their place a statue to the reigning king with this inscription: 'A Louis XVI, sur l'emplacement de la Bastille.' " See *Courrier du Bas-Rhin,* vol. for 1783, no. 1 (Jan. 1), 3-4.

30. Linguet, *MB,* frontispiece.

31. This reading of Linguet's troubled relationship with the literary establishment owes much to Robert Darnton's pioneering work, and in particular to Darnton's "The High Enlightenment and the Low-Life of Literature in Pre-Revolutionary France," *Past and Present,* no. 51 (May, 1971), 81-115.

32. Maxime Targe, *Professeurs et régents de collège dans l'ancienne Université de Paris (XVIIe et XVIIIe siècles)* (Paris, 1902), pp. 71-77, 85.

33. *Ibid.,* pp. 86-124.

34. Lettre de cachet, Sept., 1731, addressed to Jean Linguet, *BM,* no. 1918.

35. Piat, rector in the University of Paris and Ingout, deputy registrar to the Cardinal de Fleury, Sept. 10, 1731, in Charles Jourdain, *Histoire de l'Université de Paris au XVIIe et XVIIIe siècle* (Paris, 1862-66), "Pièces justificatives," p. 186.

36. Charles Jourdain, *Histoire de l'Université de Paris au XVIIe et XVIIIe siècle,* 2d ed., 2 vols. (Paris, 1888), II, 213-15.

37. The Cardinal de Fleury to Piat and Ingout, Sept. 18, 1731, in Jourdain, *Histoire de l'Université de Paris,* "Pièces justificatives," p. 186.

38. Livre Journal de Jean Linguet, in BM, no. 1918. At least a portion of the funds for his investment might have come from the sale of Jean Linguet's last real stake in the venture on the Montagne Sainte-Geneviève, a library left behind in Paris, containing well over three thousand titles, "the only possession remaining to me." Linguet to unnamed correspondent, Feb. 14, 1732, in Bibliothèque de l'Arsenal, Paris, MSS, doss. 11,107. In 1733, Jean Linguet published a catalogue of books in his library, *Catalogue des livres du cabinet de M.L.D.G.* [Monsieur Linguet, Docteur gradué] (Paris, 1733). The only copy found was in the Bibliothèque municipale, Reims. There are 2,604 titles entered.

39. Livre Journal de Jean Linguet, in BM, no. 1918.

40. Linguet, *Annales,* VII (1779), 459. Linguet's phrasing in the French is "*despotisme exileur*" and "*despotisme rayeur.*" Linguet is alluding here to his disbarment in 1775 from the Order of Lawyers practicing before the Parlement of Paris. The Order's custom was to strike the ousted lawyer's name from its professional register, "*rayer.*"

41. Marie-Louise [Linguet] Dérodé to "Thérèse" [Reims], n.d., in BM, uncat. MSS, Coll. Gosset, no. 96. The complete collection of Marie-Louise Dérodé's correspondence with Linguet is contained in the Collection Gosset. (I consulted two genealogies of the Linguet family, one in the Gosset Collection, the other in MS no. 1918 at the Bibliothèque municipale, Reims.)

42. Marie-Louise [Linguet] Dérodé to "Thérèse" [Reims] n.d., in BM, uncat. MSS, Coll. Gosset, no. 96.

43. *Ibid.*

44. *Ibid.*; Jean Cruppi, *Un Avocat journaliste au XVIIIe siècle, Linguet* (Paris, 1895), p. 14.

45. Eugène Ernest Cauly, *Histoire du Collège des Bons-Enfants de l'Université de Reims depuis son origine jusqu'à ses récentes transformations* (Reims, 1885), p. 546.

46. *Théorie des lois civiles, ou Principes fondamentaux de la société,* 2 vols. (London [Paris], 1767), cited hereafter as *L.*

47. *L'Intermédiaire des chercheurs et curieux, correspondance littéraire, historique et artistique, questions et réponses, lettres et documents inédits, communications divers à l'usage de tous,* 103 vols. (1864-1940), XIX (1886), 477-80.

48. Marcel Reinhard, "Elite et noblesse dans la seconde moitié du XVIIIe siècle," *Revue d'histoire moderne et contemporaine,* III (1956), 23-24.

49. Henri Martin, "Etude sur Linguet," in *Travaux de l'Académie nationale de Reims,* vols. XXX (1858-59), 341-425; and XXXI (1859-60), 81-149; see XXX, 346.

50. Cruppi, *Avocat journaliste,* pp. 11-14.

51. Linguet, *Lettres sur les avantages et les inconvéniens de la navigation des ports d'Abbeville, Amiens, Saint-Valery et Le Crotoy,* ed. H. Devérité (Abbeville, 1818), p. 43.

52. For discussion of Fréron's recruitment of talented young men, see Jean Balcou, *Fréron contre les philosophes* (Geneva, 1975), Histoire des idées et critique littéraire, no. 151, p. 78. For reference to Dorat's youthful association with Fréron, see *ibid.,* pp. 93-94. For spare but intriguing mention of Linguet as Fréron's "scribbler" see Turgot to Du Dupont de Nemours, Limoges, Dec. 21, 1770, in Anne-Robert-Jacques Turgot, *Oeuvres de Turgot et documents le concernant,* ed. Gustave Schelle, 5 vols. (Paris, 1913-23), III, 399. I acknowledge Ronald I. Boss's valuable observations on the development of new expressions of pessimism among men in Fréron's circle, including Linguet. Private communication, May 5, 1976.

53. [Linguet, with Claude-Joseph Dorat], *Voyage au labyrinthe du jardin du Roi* (The Hague, 1755); Elie Fréron, *L'Année littéraire,* 292 vols. (Paris and Amsterdam, 1754-90), II (March 15, 1755), 333-34.

54. *Voyage au labyrinthe,* p. 5.

55. Linguet, *Les Femmes filles, ou Les Maris battus, Parodie d'Hipermnestre* [by A.-M. Lemierre] (Paris, 1759).

56. BM, no. 1921, fols. 4, 4v.

57. *Ibid.,* fols. 5, 5v.

58. *Ibid.,* fols. 6, 6v.

59. Jean-Nicolas Dérodé to Linguet, n.p., n.d., BM, uncat. MSS, Coll. Gosset, no. 99 (probably circa 1774-75, at a time when Linguet was combating the Order of Lawyers in Paris; Dérodé makes several references to Linguet's entanglements with his colleagues and threatens litigation if Linguet doesn't settle long-standing accounts with the Dérodé family).

60. *Ibid.* See also Mme. Dérodé to Linguet, March 12, 1774, in BM, uncat. MSS, Coll. Gosset; draft of a letter from Jean Dérodé to a "chef d'un corps respectable" [probably to the *Bâtonnier* of the Order of Lawyers of Paris], n.d. [1774 or 1775], in *ibid.,* no. 73. See also "Journal pour servir à Jean-Nicolas Dérodé, notaire roial à Reims," in BM, no. 1920.

61. [Linguet], *Epitre d'un J* [ésuite] .....*de D....à un de ses amis* (n.p., n.d.); [Linguet], *Lettre du mandarin Oei-Tching à son ami Hoei-Tchang sur les affaires des RR. PP. Jésuites,* 2d ed. (n.p., 1762). For discussion of Linguet's possible motives in risking circulation of these works, see Cruppi, *Avocat journaliste,* pp. 20-22. In a letter to Charles Duclos in 1764, Linguet referred indirectly to the danger he believed he had run in circulating the pro-Jesuit tracts: "I have the misfortune to belong by birth to a sect which today is victorious. I saw myself crushed by it for having refused to prepare and then to share its triumph." Beaumont-Linguet to Charles Duclos, Estreuval, Sept. 1, 1764, in Jacques Brengues, "Duclos dupé par Linguet, ou Quatre lettres inédites de Simon-Nicolas-Henri Linguet à Charles Duclos," *Revue des sciences humaines,* XXXV, no. 137 (1970), 71.

62. *Histoire du siècle d'Alexandre, avec Quelques réflexions sur ceux qui l'ont précédé* (Amsterdam, 1762), iii-vi, cited hereafter as *A.*

63. Bachaumont, *Mémoires secrets,* I (June 12, 1762), 93; Grimm et al., *Correspondance littéraire,* V (July, 1762), 131.

64. Voltaire, *Le Siècle de Louis XIV,* in *Voltaire: Oeuvres historiques,* ed. René Pomeau (Paris, 1957), p. 616.

65. For other evidence of Linguet's conspicuous attempt to link his philosophy of history to Voltaire's, compare *A,* 1-2 with Voltaire, *Nouvelles considérations sur l'histoire,* in *Voltaire: Oeuvres historiques,* ed. Pomeau, p. 49; and see also J. H. Brumfitt, *Voltaire, Historian* (London, 1958), p. 92. Compare *A,* 18-19, with poem by Voltaire in letter of May 26, 1742, in *Voltaire, Oeuvres,* ed. Lequien, L1, 119, as rendered in prose in Ernst Cassirer, *The Philosophy of the Enlightenment,* trans. Fritz C. A. Koelln and James P. Pettegrove (Princeton, 1951), p. 217.

66. Voltaire, *Le Siècle de Louis XIV,* in *Voltaire: Oeuvres historiques,* ed. Pomeau, p. 617.

67. Linguet, *Histoire du siècle d'Alexandre*, 2d ed. (Amsterdam and Paris, 1769), p. 262, cited hereafter as *A-1769*.

68. For comparison, See Jean-François Melon, "Esclavage," *Essai politique sur le commerce* (1734) in *Economistes-financiers du XVIIIᵉ siècle/ Vauban, Boisquillebert, Jean Law, Melon, Dutot*, ed. Eugène Daire, 2d ed. (Paris, 1851), p. 724.

69. Jean-Jacques Rousseau, *Julie, ou La Nouvelle Héloïse*, ed. René Pomeau (Paris, 1960), pp. 596-97.

70. Rousseau, "Romance," *Dictionnaire de musique*, in *Oeuvres complètes*, ed. Louis-Germain Petitain and Victor-Donatien Musset-Pathay, 4 vols. (Paris, 1835-36), III, 795, as cited by Jean Starobinski, *Jean-Jacques Rousseau, la transparence et l'obstacle* (Paris, 1957), p. 109.

71. Rousseau, *La Nouvelle Héloïse*, pp. 593-95.

72. See Simon-Nicolas-Henri Linguet, trans., *Théâtre espagnol*, 4 vols. (Paris, 1770).

73. Cruppi, *Avocat journaliste*, p. 27.

74. For a discussion of Linguet's reform projects, which he partly based on observations he made in Holland, see Chapter Three.

75. Louis-Alexandre Devérité, *Notice pour servir à l'histoire de la vie et des écrits de S.-N.-H. Linguet*, new ed. (Liège, 1782), pp. 18-19.

76. Simon-Nicolas-Henri Linguet, *Le Fanatisme des philosophes*, (London and Abbeville, 1764); cited hereafter in the text as *FP*.

77. Linguet charged that the philosophers, the governors of the literary universe, were fanatics; they excluded and maligned writers who refused to toe the party line (*FP*, 11, 36, 41-42)—writers like the author of the *Histoire du siècle d'Alexandre*. For Linguet's reflections on the failure of this work, see Linguet, *Histoire des révolutions de l'Empire romain, pour servir de suite à celle des révolutions de la République*, 2 vols. (Paris, 1766), I, iv, v, vii; cited hereafter in the text as *HR*. Linguet's accusation that the philosophes were fanatics was remarkable, but not original. Elie Fréron regularly used the label "fanatic" to depict the philosophes' behavior. And yet even he found Linguet's diatribe too extreme for his tastes. Fréron reviewed Linguet's *Le Fanatisme des philosophes* in *L'année littéraire;* while he supported Linguet's condemnation of the philosophes' excesses, he refused to underwrite Linguet's impassioned repudiation of the arts and sciences—just as he had refused to endorse the primitivism that colors Rousseau's *First Discourse*. See *L'Année littéraire*, VII (Nov. 20, 1764), as discussed in Jean Balcou, *Fréron contre les philosophes*, pp. 67-69, 270-71.

78. The historical pessimism that marks this work and the body of Linguet's *œuvre* reflects his reading of Rousseau, but it also reflects an evaluation of the fruits of endeavor based on personal experience and the example of history; and it may have deeper roots in Linguet's Jansenist upbringing. For a brief discussion, see Hans-Ulrich Thamer, *Revolution und Reaktion in der französischen Sozialkritik des 18 Jahrhunderts. Linguet, Mably, Babeuf* (Frankfurt am Main, 1973), p. 56.

79. The full title was: *Nécessité d'une réforme dans l'administration de la justice et dans les lois civiles en France, avec la réfutation de quelques passages de "L'Esprit des lois"* (Amsterdam, 1764); cited hereafter as *NR*.

80. Beaumont-Linguet to Duclos, May 3 [1764], in Brengues, "Duclos dupé par Linguet," 65.

81. *Ibid.*, 64; Beaumont-Linguet to Duclos, Estreuval, Aug. 19, 1764, Sept. 1 [1764]. in *ibid.*, 69, 71.

82. Beaumont-Linguet to Duclos, Abbeville, May 3 [1764], in *ibid.*, 65.

83. *Ibid.*, 64, 65, 65 note c.

84. Linguet-frère to Duclos, n.p. [beginning of May, 1764], in *ibid.*, 67.

85. Beaumont-Linguet to Duclos, Estreuval, Sept. 1, 1764, in *ibid.*, 71. See also police report of Aug. 2, 1764, in the papers of police inspector d'Hémery, BN, MSS, nouvelles acquisitions françaises, no. 1214, fols. 440 bis, 441.

86. Beaumont-Linguet to Duclos, Estreuval, Aug. 19, 1764, in Brengues, "Duclos dupé par Linguet," 69.

87. For the phrase "attorney for the Neros and Caligulas," see Lanjuinais, *Supplément à "l'Espion anglois,"* p. 205.

88. Beaumont-Linguet to Duclos, Estreuval, Sept. 1 [1764], in Brengues, "Duclos dupé par Linguet," 71, 72.

89. Between Oct., 1764, and Jan., 1765, Linguet was inscribed in the Faculty of Law of the University of Reims. Gustave Laurent, "La Faculté de Droit de Reims et les hommes de la Révolution," *Annales historiques de la Révolution française,* VI (1929), 340. It would seem, however, that Linguet bypassed formal course requirements for the *licence ès lois* because the *licence* was the prerequisite for inscription as a probationary lawyer and Linguet was inscribed in October, 1764. During the 1750s and 1760s, the Faculty of Law in Reims had a reputation for venality, but I have found no direct evidence that would indicate what Linguet did to obtain his certification. For discussion, see Laurent, *ibid.,* 329-32; 353-57; Francis Delbeke, *L'Action politique et sociale des avocats au dix-huitième siècle: Leur Part dans la préparation de la Révolution française* (Louvain and Paris, 1927), pp. 47, 63-67.

90. Quoted, with no reference given, in Cruppi, *Avocat journaliste, Linguet,* p. 46.

91. Linguet, *L'Aveu sincère, ou Lettre à une mère sur les dangers que court la jeunesse en se livrant à un goût trop vif pour la littérature* (London and Paris, 1768), pp. iii, v, xv, 22; this work cited hereafter as *Aveu.*

92. In a letter to the King of France published in 1776, Linguet described his double career and reflected upon its advantages—but above all on its liabilities and perils: "It was my misfortune to cultivate letters and jurisprudence at the same time, to bring together the two qualities of author and advocate. The fatality which dogs me willed that in one of these careers, my intimate conviction, the love of what seemed to me to be the truth, would lead me to attack powerful and implacable sects; and that in the other, I would be charged from the beginning with the most delicate affairs, the most interesting perhaps of any that have come up in a long time. Consequently, I had to come into collision with many passions and attract many very violent enemies. So my literary rivals prevailed to decry me everywhere for the devotion with which I followed the impulse of my duty and my conscience in the bar. My rivals in the bar charged my literary essays against me as a crime...." Linguet, *Très-humbles, très-respectueuses représentations adressées à Sa Majesté, par Me Linguet, avocat, sur la défense à lui faite d'imprimer sa "Requête" en cassation, contre les arrêts des 4 février & 29 mars 1775* (Brussels, 1776), p. 10.

93. These verses by Linguet were written at the time the Jesuit order was suppressed in 1762 and were published anonymously under the title *Epître d'un J[ésuite] .....de D ....à un de ses amis* (Lisbon, 1764).

94. Cruppi, *Avocat journaliste,* pp. 73-74. See also Dominique Holleaux, "Le procès du Chevalier de La Barre," in *Quelques Procès criminels des XVIIe et XVIIIe siècle présentés par un groupe d'étudiants,* ed. Jean Imbert, Travaux et recherches de la Faculté de droit et des sciences économiques de Paris, ser. "Sciences historiques," no. 2 (Paris, 1964), p. 165.

95. Cruppi, *Avocat journaliste,* pp. 69-70; Holleaux, "La Barre," in *Procès criminels,* ed. Imbert, p. 171; Jean Imbert, "Principes généraux de la procédure pénale (XVIIe-XVIIIe siècles)," in *ibid.,* p. 4.

96. Holleaux, "La Barre," in Imbert, ed. *Procès criminels,* p. 172. Actually, La Barre was executed first, before these tortures were applied to his body.

97. *Ibid.,* pp. 172, 173, n. 1.

98. Marc Chassaigne, *Le Procès du Chevalier de La Barre* (Paris, 1920), p. 165.

99. Cited without reference in Devérité, *Notice pour servir à l'histoire de la vie et des écrits de S. N. H. Linguet,* p. 43.

100. Holleaux, "La Barre," in Imbert, ed., *Procès criminels,* pp. 172-73.

101. Cruppi, *Avocat journaliste,* p. 127; Chassaigne, *La Barre,* pp. 212-13.

102. Cruppi, *Avocat journaliste,* p. 139.

103. Linguet, *Mémoire pour les Sieurs Moynel, Dumesniel de Saveuse et Douville de Maillefeu* (1766), in Linguet, *Mémoires et plaidoyers de M. Linguet, avocat à Paris,* 11 vols. (Liège and Amsterdam, 1776), I, 7.

104. *Ibid.*, 6ff.

105. *Ibid.*, 123.

106. *Ibid.*, 25.

107. *Ibid.*, 10-11.

108. Duval de Soicourt to Joly de Fleury, July 5, 13, 1766, in BN, MSS fr., Collection Joly de Fleury, vol. 418, doss. 4817, fols. 132-39.

109. Linguet to Joly de Fleury [July, 1766], in *ibid.*, fol. 129. For the official record of Moisnel's disavowal of his lawyers, see *ibid.*, fol. 131.

110. Linguet to Joly de Fleury, Paris, Aug. 27, 1766, *ibid.*, fols. 203-4.

111. Holleaux, "La Barre," in Imbert, ed., *Procès criminels*, p. 174.

112. Grimm et al., *Correspondance littéraire*, VII (July, 1766), 77.

113. *Ibid.*, 77.

114. Chassaigne, *La Barre*, p. 246.

115. Linguet to Jean Dérodé, Sept. 19, 1766, in BM, uncat. MSS, Coll. Gosset, no. 30.

116. Duval de Soicourt *fils* to Joly de Fleury, June 21, 1767, in BN, MSS fr., Collection Joly de Fleury, vol. 418, doss. 4817, fols. 188-91; *Arrest de la Cour du Parlement, Qui supprime le "Discours préliminaire" étant en tête du livre intitulé "Théorie des lois civiles, ou Principes fondamentaux de la société," imprimé à Londres, en M DCC LXVII, sans nom d'auteur, & c. Du quatorze juillet mil sept cent soixante-sept* (Paris, 1767).

117. Linguet to the baron de Tournon, March 27, 1767, in BM, uncat. MSS, Coll. Gosset, no. 17.

The Sociology of Law

A Theory of Paradoxes

The *Théorie des lois civiles, ou Principes fondamentaux de la société* was Simon Linguet's magnum opus. In February, 1767, Linguet submitted the work to Voltaire: "I conform gladly, Sir, to a very sound custom that I see quite generally established, that young authors send a copy of their works to you, and solicit a place for their productions in your library. It is quite natural that a tree's first fruits be gathered by the hand that has contributed most to strengthening its roots. The progress of reason and taste among us is due for the most part to you. Those who profit from it are obliged to express their gratitude to you."[1] There was much that was novel in his work, Linguet ventured, "but there will be many [things] also that surely you have thought before me." Voltaire would need little prodding to recognize that Linguet's weapons against Montesquieu, "a brilliant mind which is subject to frequent eclipses,"[2] had been selected from his own arsenal.[3]

Linguet was speaking of reform, the kind he had campaigned for in his *Nécessité d'une réforme* of 1764. He suggested similarities between his own views on this matter and Voltaire's. Then, without warning, he began lecturing the philosophes: let there be no confusion between remodeling obsolete institutions and frivolously romping about with blazing candles, enlightenment, in the arsenal that was civil society. The final stage in the progressive diffusion of enlightenment necessarily would be the awakening of the masses, *their* enlightenment, and their revolution. Literature and the arts are useful for the rich and lazy, Linguet argued. They are diverting trifles, playthings quite appropriate for the amusement of those perpetual infants of society, the opulent elites:

> But I firmly believe that such is not the case for the other, infinitely more numerous portion of humanity that we call the people. ...The present state of society condemns them to have only arms. Everything is lost from the moment they are placed in the position of perceiving that they have intelligence also.

> If it were possible to enlighten only one of these two divisions of the human race, if it were possible to intercept all the rays which go out from the small to the large [division] and to perpetuate an eternal night for that one of the two which is useful and submissive only so long as it remains like that [in a benighted state], I would gladly applaud the work of the philosophes and their partisans.[4]

Jean-Jacques Rousseau, in his *Discours sur les sciences et les arts,* had lauded ignorance as the best guarantor of a people's moral purity. Linguet was arguing that its perpetuation was the establishment's final defense against social upheaval. He was preaching this sacrilege at the portals of the Temple of Reason:

> But consider, Sir, it is impossible that the sun rise for the first [division] without the matinal rays extending to the second, no matter how far distant it be. The latter, as soon as it is enlightened, tends necessarily to appraise the other, or to confuse itself with it. It follows from this that the day becomes deadly to them both, and that an obscurity where they live tranquilly, each in its respective limits, is infinitely preferable to those lights that show them only how to mutually disdain or detest one another.[5]

Between class division built into societal order itself, and open class warfare, stood only a fragile barrier, the masses' ignorance, against which the philosophes were ramming with suicidal fervor.

Linguet might reasonably have expected that Voltaire would detect in this social analysis an elaboration of his own sober reflections on the social order: "On our unhappy globe," Voltaire had written, "it is impossible for men living in society not to be divided into two classes; one of the rich who command, the other of the poor who serve.... The human race, such as it is, could not subsist unless an infinitely large number of useful men existed who possessed nothing at all...."[6] Linguet had calculated the force of that human mass, stimulated by an inevitable downward diffusion of enlightenment appropriated initially as an awareness of absolute deprivation. He concluded: everything is lost. Voltaire was preoccupied with other calculations.

The philosophe replied. He was pleased with Linguet's summary appraisal of Montesquieu's system. The apostle of enlightenment was flattered, but he also had been challenged. The people, he reported, were not everywhere a homogeneous mass. The artisan class of Switzerland was a case in point. A discriminating extension of enlightenment among the *bas peuple* need not be disastrous. As for the most numerous portion of the people, those engaged in occupations "that require only physical exertion, and a daily exhaustion," Linguet's legions condemned to have only arms, that is, to possess nothing other than their physical strength, the muscle power in their arms, Linguet needn't fear that they would seek their pleasure anywhere but in the village cabaret and at high mass "because there is where the singing goes on, and they themselves can sing."[7] Having pictured a class of benighted, brutish, and superstitious peasants, Voltaire dismissed the masses with characteristic flippancy. Three months later, he would instruct d'Alembert: "As for the *canaille*, I don't concern myself with it; it will always remain *canaille*."[8] But would this characterization stand against Linguet's observation that the philosophes' highly charged propaganda functioned automatically and uncontrollably to awaken desires, spark hatreds, and generate insurrection among these masses whom Voltaire disposed of with pejoratives? "...the day becomes deadly to them both....everything is lost...."

"No *Sir*," Voltaire insisted, "*everything is not lost when you put the people in a state of seeing that it has intelligence.* On the contrary, everything is lost when you treat it like a herd of bulls. For sooner or later they will gore you with their horns." Voltaire reached his point, at last. Enlighten the people; then they will never allow themselves to be led about by religious fanatics.[9] Awaken the people, all of them if necessary, the better to crush the Infamy once and for all.

Linguet and Voltaire had structured the social order with the same divisions of social classes, each permanently fixed in its condition; their perspectives on the activities of these classes could not have differed more. Linguet saw the philosophes, apologists for society's elite of possessors, cavorting about in pursuit of priestly infamy, while the masses, awakened and enlightened by their inflammatory campaigns, were readying themselves for a great subversion. "...everything is lost...." Simon Linguet shouted his warning. And Voltaire replied with an eloquent discourse on tactics for hunting down the black-robed menace.

Linguet's *Théorie des lois civiles* aged at the Lyons customshouse for at least two months, along with a shipment of Voltaire's burgundy: "...I'll forget about the wine," Voltaire wrote to Linguet, "but I can't stand their depriving me of a work I've been told so many good things about, and in which I was hoping to educate myself. I'm a lot more concerned about my soul than I am about my gullet, and I give in to having the soldiers who are encircling me guzzling my wine on the condition that I can read [your book]."[10] Finally, Linguet's offering in two volumes arrived. Voltaire penned a succinct private verdict on the title page: "*La théorie des lois civiles ou principes fondamentaux de la société, ou théorie des paradoxes en déclamations fastidieuses mais qui annoncent de l'esprit.*"[11] Had it been worth even the hypothetical sacrifice of a shipment of burgundy? "I have said what I believe true," Linguet wrote in the dedication to his work. "Some of my opinions will give the appearance of paradoxes at first sight. It is perhaps these which deserve the most consideration. I have ventured them only after long reflection. It will be remarked readily by the tone I discuss them in that I had no pretensions to a *jeu d'esprit*. I might have deceived myself, but it was not my intention to decieve anyone" (*L*, I, 9).

Voltaire confined his faint praise to the title page of his copy of Linguet's magnum opus. The *Correspondance littéraire's* reviewer damned the book in incendiary declamations: "Monsieur Linguet's works are like straw fires; for a moment they make a great blaze, and then it's over. This is because they are filled with paradoxes and daring opinions, and that whets one's curiosity at first; but these paradoxes are presented in such an unappealing manner that straightaway you get disgusted."[12]

Paradox: the critic was exposing the *Théorie des lois civiles* as a product of brilliant stylistic artifice. He spoke as though he were dismissing some facile verbal trickery contrived by an imaginative and ambitious seeker after novelty and attention. Paradox: puzzles for the logician, ingenious sleights of hand that set the terms of logical statements clashing against one another in dead-ended self-contradiction. Paradox, however, was more than sleight of hand. It was potentially the most deadly weapon an adversary could bring into combat against the man of reason's principal instrument, logic. A reasoner who followed the classic logic in his analytic and critical thought would abide by the rules of internal self-consistency, the laws of self-contradiction. He would use his reasoning powers to judge, to compare, to contrast statements, to discover the variety of connections between them, to eliminate from or add to them, to label them true, or false. "Reason," Deslandes proclaimed in 1741, "is the power or the faculty of our soul which, by means of the ideas it has of things, and in comparing them together, discerns the true from the false, and the certain from the uncertain, whatever the subject of our reasoning."[13] Thirty years later, d'Holbach suggested a definition of reason more congenial to the younger generation of philosophes: "Reason is only the knowledge of what is useful to us, or harmful, furnished by experience and reflection."[14] Paradox, taken with methodic seriousness, could prove the downfall of utilitarian reason and classical logic—the enlightened thinker's guides through all dimensions of reality.

The accusation of paradox hounded Linguet throughout his career. But certainly Voltaire and the literary critics were aware that Linguet was not Zeno's student in the school of paradox, nor Epimenides'; he was Rousseau's apprentice. An easy way to damn Rousseau, although his opponents didn't stop there, was to dismiss his social analysis as the clever paradox of an intellectual lightweight. The *First Discourse,* La Harpe wrote "inaugurated the reputation of its author although it proves only the facile talent of putting intelligence into a paradox. This entire discourse is only a continual sophism, founded upon a commonplace and effortless artifice. The *Discourse on Inequality* is only the sequel to the same paradoxes and a sophism that falls before a simple truth...."[15]

But was this "facile" paradox? "All ran to meet their chains thinking they secured their freedom....Such was, or must have been, the origin of society and the laws, which gave new fetters to the weak and new forces to the rich, destroyed natural freedom for all time, established forever the law of property and inequality, changed a clever usurpation into an irrevocable right, and for the profit of a few ambitious men henceforth subjected the whole human race to work, servitude, and misery."[16]

Rousseau was not intimidated; on the contrary, he invited his readers to throw off thought-fettering conventions: "Common readers, pardon my paradoxes: they must be made when one thinks seriously; and whatever you may say, I would rather be a man of paradoxes than a man of prejudices."[17] And how sophistical was Linguet's paradoxical contention that: "To render [the laws] necessary, meekness had to be subjugated by barbarism. And then justice raised itself up on the earth between the arms of rigor....To prevent [the hunter class of society] from using its weapons arbitrarily, [justice] made it see a dagger all ready to pierce it through. By means of this terrible sight, [justice] brought to the world at least an appearance of calm" (*L*, I, 317).

Linguet and Rousseau invoked paradox to depict and analyze contradictions in social institutions and antagonisms between incompatible social forces and to organize the terms of their resolution. Paradox was the language of their logic of dialectics, a powerful new instrument of social analysis, one capable of structuring the dynamics of transformation through conflict in developing societies.[18]

Many contemporaries found these analyses profoundly unsettling, or unbearable. For a century, philosophes had been applying physical models to impose balance, harmony, law, on social phenomena. Paradoxical arrangements of social realities exposed the contradictions, tensions, conflicts, built into these newly conquered spaces of civil society. The philosophes' charge of paradox and absurdity launched against analyses of mutually destructive oppositions inextricably rooted in society seemed somehow futile and pathetic, like distress signals sent up by a lone survivor after the shipwreck of his models and methods on the reef of social reality. But in that shipwreck everything would be lost. The invalidation of categories and formalisms used to conceptualize, reform, control, and make one's peace with the social environment—both the status quo and the processes of societal development—portended the return of chaos into the world or of massive guilt and terror into the mind.

Paradox, as Linguet and Rousseau used it, was not only a language to structure social analysis; it was also a language to structure societal critiques which pointed simultaneously to the dissolution of contradictions with the explosion of society and their perpetuation in more tolerable expressions under reformed, fundamentally preservative regimes.

The contradictions in the eighteenth-century world that Linguet and Rousseau exposed and deplored in paradoxes were not those which philosophes, by and large, were interested in condemning or even in confronting. Instead, they hammered out "tranquilizing doctrines...ideologies consistent with the wish of the dominant classes."[19] It was not merely fashionable to attack the paradoxes of a Linguet and a Rousseau. For men of good sense, with a vested interest in having social analysis yield predictable, nonthreatening, and guilt-assuaging returns, it became obligatory.

There were exits a thinking person might take from conflict-ridden, "paradoxical" realities, reconciliations if not syntheses that provided safe and comforting ways out of turmoil. Linguet consistently refused to opt for them. Abbé Baudeau, editor of the physiocratic journal *Les Ephémérides du citoyen*, was shocked and puzzled by a theorist who balked at dissipating or resolving in the realm of norms and ideals the conflicts and crises he depicted in historical societies.

> The youth of the author is his excuse. We trust that his heart has no part in the deviations of an ardent imagination....[20]
>
> But for the consolation and instruction of this unfortunate humanity, he ought to have ended with the simple, naïve, and touching exposition of a *society* in perfect harmony with the constitutive principles of *order;* shown innocence, justice, peace, and happiness flowing from the same source; *all interests concentrated in the same object; all wishes, all desires conspiring towards public and private prosperity.*
>
> It is the author of the *Théorie des lois* himself whom we unhesitatingly exhort to edify an honest public rightfully afflicted by what he has just published....[21]

Abbé Baudeau sounded a call for a new recruit, while the defending legions of a heavenly city-that-never-was massed about him: Dupont de Nemours, the baron d'Holbach, Helvétius, Morelly, and Rousseau. Simon Linguet, whom Voltaire had dubbed Paris's Jean-Jacques Rousseau, remained on the sidelines, refusing to flee from existing tensions and impending conflicts in society to search after extra-historical harmonies.[22]

Primitives and Moderns: Anthropology in Support of a Critical Sociology

"La nature crie dans tous les coeurs, elle montre à tous les yeux que les hommes naissent libres et parfaitement égaux" (*L*, I, 181). That inflammatory opening sentence calls to mind Rousseau's "L'homme est né libre." Linguet had offered his magnum opus to Voltaire with the flirtatious deference of a suitor, only to betray his infidelity, once again. His first allegiance was to the social analyst whom Voltaire had dubbed "Diogene's ape" and the "bastard of Diogene's dog."[23]

Nature, Linguet continues, provides man with physical strength for self-defense, senses for fending off danger and finding food, hands for grasping it, organs for perpetuating the species. Man in the state of nature is self-sufficient, perfectly capable of providing for his own physical conservation; once he passes his infancy, there is no one more robust, vivacious, "more exactly free than man imagined in his primitive condition. His destiny in this state would be to be born without ties, to live without remorse, and to die without fear" (L, I, 181-82), a being at one with nature, because immediately related to it. He is Rousseau's "homme sauvage" of the Discourse on the Origin of Inequality. "His desires do not surpass his physical needs; the only goods he knows in the universe are nourishment, a female, and repose; the only evils he fears are pain and hunger."[24]

"...and everywhere he is in chains." Linguet only reinforces the shock of those impassioned descriptions of the opposition: natural man—socialized man, where Rousseau bares the terms of a radical dichotomy, a separation of self from nature past the possibility of reintegration:

> He is no longer there [in nature]. He would not know how to return....
> No sooner does he open his eyes than he is tied to this immense chain that we call society. How they rush to enroll him on the pretext that one day he must compose one of the links. They make him contract obligations that he cannot yet know about or practice.... From the depths of his cradle where he is fettered, his first glances fall upon beings like him, all weighted down with chains, who congratulate one another on seeing a companion ready to share their slavery. [L, I, 183.]

Natural man, Linguet believed, overcomes himself, becomes a social self. The genteel, societal life weakens his body; nature becomes alien to him, an obstacle. "His hands, softened by the arts, no longer can bear him to the tops of trees to search for the subsistence nature has prepared for him... Heat burns him, the cold bites him, rain penetrates him...."[25] The habits of society make it impossible for him to support solitude (L, I, 186). Education only conspires to choke the voice of nature in him. "He accustoms himself to following without repugnance movements that are not his own; allows himself to be swept along by a general agitation to which he hasn't contributed." In a desperate attempt to overcome the loss of his first primitive self, man-immediately-in-nature, societal man drives himself to a radical extreme: imitation, total externalization. He acts on his urge to become the world: "He clings to it [society] in proportion as the reasons for fleeing it become more imperative, as in a collapsing building, the unfortunate beings dragged down by its fall, grasp with all the more force as they fall the debris that's going to crush them" (*L*, I, 185, 187). "Sociable men," Rousseau wrote, "always outside of himself, knows no way of living other than in the opinion of others; and it is, so to speak, from their judgment alone that he derives the consciousness of his own existence" (*R*, III, 193).

Natural man becomes social, historical man. The unity of the present is fractured. Man acquires a past and a future. "Instead of enjoying the present, which he possesses, he only despairs of the past which no longer belongs to him, and shows anxiety about the future which is not yet at his disposal. He is torn by regrets, tormented by curiosity" (*L*, I, 186-187). He has killed the beatific savage in himself, Rousseau's man of nature, whose soul, "agitated by nothing, is given over to the unique sentiment of his present existence, without any idea of the future..." (*R*, III, 144).

Natural man becomes economic man. "Avarice and violence have usurped the earth." In an anguished effort to overcome the alienation he experiences in his economic activity, societal man embraces another extreme,striving frantically to restore that primal wholeness in himself, his first selfhood in nature. He begins by accumulating property in material objects. "Who do you think owns these rotten branches scattered about on the ground by the winds? Don't think for a moment that they've been abandoned to need, who covets them from a distance with tear-bathed eyes. Opulence snatches them away with an insult." More hideous still, he tries to buy back his fragmented wholeness piecemeal by purchasing other selves; he tries to restore his sense of well-being and independence by reducing potential competitors to appropriable property. He forges a new social bond, the master-slave relationship. The suspicions of the propertied master, "always directed against the indigent man he is robbing, makes him look upon independence as an offense and upon liberty as a revolt. He proclaims loudly that the right to think belongs only to him. He directs himself to crushing indigence continually, for fear that in raising itself up, it might be tempted to make of its strength a use other than that which he demands" (*L*, I, 187, 188, 189).

Rousseau's understanding of social-class relationships was similar. "I would prove, finally, that if one sees a handful of powerful and rich men at the summit of greatness and fortune while the mass crawls in obscurity and misery, it is because the rich value the things they enjoy only as long as the others are deprived of them..." (*R*, III, 189).

Law introduces peace into a society shot through with class division, tottering on the brink of war. The price of peace is the perpetuation of radical economic and social inequalities: "Justice is the perpetual and constant desire to render to every man what belongs to him. *Justitia est perpetua et constans voluntas jus suum cuique tribuendi,* the jurisconsults tell us. But the indigent man possesses only his own indigence. The laws, then, cannot guarantee him anything else. They tend to shield the possessor of superfluities against the attacks of those who lack the essentials. That is their true spirit, and if it is a drawback, it is inseparable from their existence" (L, I, 190-91, 196). That was precisely the antithesis which Linguet had offered to his thesis on the necessity for legal reform.[26]

Rousseau had argued in the same vein: "If we follow the progress of inequality in these different revolutions, we will find that the establishment of law and the right of property was its first stage, the institution of the magistrature the second...so that the condition of rich and poor was authorized by the first epoch, that of the powerful and the weak by the second..." (R, III, 187). Society sanctions a major redistribution of the parts of a once-whole man. "From this instant his existence ceased, so to speak, to belong to him. His arms, his thoughts, his life, everything was locked up again in a common depository whose use was no longer at his discretion" (L, I, 193).

Linguet echoes Rousseau, perhaps even surpasses him in the violence and daring of his juxtaposition of extremes: man in nature, man in society. The laws authorize that thieves be hanged, but without society would there be thieves? Would safes be cracked if there were neither locks nor silver? Aren't the crimes that justice punishes born of the unequal distribution of goods? Isn't it an unequal distribution of possessions that makes subsistence so difficult for three-quarters of the human race? Aren't wars and famines the works of society, and aren't they responsible for the great ravisher of humanity, plague? Society's edicts herd soldiers into carnage; society's conventions press men upon one another "in cities and houses, the way African pirates squeeze their slaves into the convict prisons of Algiers or Tunis"; the consequences are plague and famine. Society and the laws sanction the habits of abundance that alone make famine insufferable. The law encourages the accumulation of luxury "at the expense, and under the very eyes of all the unfortunate men whose labor [industry in luxuries] devours" (L, I, 211-12, 213-14, 215-16).

Linguet's critique is in the tradition of impassioned social analysis that begins with Rousseau's Second Discourse. Both Linguet and Rousseau discovered the bifurcation of modern man in civilized society. They represented his experience of radical disequilibration, depicting his alienation. They did not use the word; but they described the state of being-in-radical-separation, a severance of the self from the ground of its own being, from the world, and from other selves. Above all, alienation described psycho-physical and psychological separation. Social man, as Linguet depicted him, incessantly experienced the sense of being cut off from some imagined or recollected oneness and wholeness. But beyond that almost instinctive malaise, modern man was afflicted by the torture that accompanies a real loss of self-control and self-direction in the social and economic spheres.

Primitive man might have triggered the process of self division when he invented instruments to mediate between himself and his world; the earliest societies deepened the split and intensified the pain by consecrating private property in law. This act eternalized expropriation and legitimized the separation of masses of men from the means of self-sufficient existence; it institutionalized their dependence. In modern societies, a self-interested calculator, *homo economicus*, completed the process by appropriating and exploiting the labor of nominally free although absolutely dispossessed and dependent persons, as though their labor was equivalent to a machine's work. The possessor classes could dull the psychological agony of alienation either by appropriating property and exploiting human beings, or by imitative externalizations and identifications with artifice. The dispossessed were caught without hope of diversion or compensation. They were society's perfect victims. Civilization and the civil laws sanctioned their expropriation, their exploitation, their reification.

Rousseau expressed the dilemma of alienated man in historical societies with painful clarity. "What then? Must we destroy societies, annihiliate 'yours' and 'mine,' and return to live in forests with the bears?" (*R*, III, 207). Linguet reached the same conclusion. Man "is no longer there [in nature]. He would not know how to return..." (*L*, I, 183). Society eclipsed nature. "We have to speak about the condition the human species is in, and not about the one it might have been in. It is certain that by remaining dispersed, it would have spared itself great evils. It is not any the less certain that in joining together as it has, and as it is obliged to do, it requires rules for its containment. ...we must be chained up, the way you put hobbles on bad-tempered horses when you let them loose in a common pasture" (*L*, I, 227-28).

Historical existence was antithesis, one raging, ceaseless, irresolvable antagonism. Rousseau brought it to an honorable end only in the political society of the social contract, a utopia beyond the lost domain of nature and outside the bloodied mire of history.

Five years after the publication of the *Contract social*, Linguet still was unable to take Rousseau's leap. Unlike Rousseau, he did not overcome historical pessimism with redeeming anthropological, ethical, political, or theological systems,[27] although he did describe the dissolution or attenuation of contradictions in historical society in theoretical forecasts of imminent social revolutions, breakthroughs into nihilistic anarchy or dictatorships for society's propertyless masses.[28] He undergirded historical pessimism with systems of economic and psychological determinism in which autonomously moral dimensions of the human experience found no place. In Linguet's scheme, the existence of *homo economicus* as the new human archetype was a grim testament to the death of natural man beyond the hope of resurrection, and to the irreversible metamorphosis of primitive man's good instincts into an amoral calculating self-interest.

The chains of society would never be legitimized by the measures of so-called absolute standards. On the contrary, all laws governing the constitution and operation of polities dictated that these bonds be tightened as society perfected itself. The fundamental purpose of the law and the political author-ity that enforced it was to perpetuate the regime of properties and privations. Unless authority was successful in modulating the inevitable tensions between antagonistic social classes, they would break the social bond, opening the civil war of civil society. Rousseau did not have to concern himself exclusively with the details of this war, its causes, its progress, its aftermath, if any. All that was merely history, and history was only the first act. Linguet had no choice. For him, that was all there was. In his sociology of the laws, a *théorie des paradoxes,* Linguet imposed structure on this historical reality with a the-ory of social classes, an analysis of class struggle, a projection of social revolu-tion into the historical future, and a strategy for using reform as an instru-ment of political and social containment.

Property, the Spirit of the Laws in One-Dimensional Society

A tragic, irreversible transformation had happened somewhere in the tran-sition from nature into society: "We must see by what means [men] succeed-ed in stripping themselves of this original independence which imposed upon them no yoke other than their will, no laws other than their desires. We must return to the period of this reununciation, and to the manner in which it was consummated the way we consult the jail warden's registers to determine the date and the case for a prisoner's confinement" (*L,* I, 229).

Political theorists among Linguet's contemporaries agreed that human be-ings brought human establishments into being, not the theologians' *deus ab-sconditus.* But that only begged the question: how did they organize civil societies? The theorists were ready with an answer: via the social contract. Their contractual formulations expressed the man of reason's revolt from secular authoritarianism traditionally justified by appeals to revelation. Rous-seau, Locke, Hobbes, the jurisconsults Grotius and Pufendorff, all invoked some version of the contract theory. Somehow, men had made their own so-cial destiny. Here Linguet was at one with his age. But he went on to insist that political systems and social class relationships were not freely contracted for *all* men of nature.

Fear was not the motive that first brought these wild men together, Lin-guet maintained;[29] and it was not the development of agriculture either.[30] Far from bringing society into existence, agriculture only intensified the pri-mitive farmers' isolation and independence (*L,* I, 240-41, 277).

"Liberty was forging their chains and independence was preparing their subjection" (*L*, I, 279). Realizing itself dialectically through time, the impulse to freedom generates an antithetic force which, overcoming and suppressing natural man's liberty, will perfect and fully realize itself, preparing the next and final stage.

The menace came from the forests, from the deep interiors of tree-covered plains, from the summits of the mountains, from a race of hunters, "another species of men." Hunters, roaming freely in hordes, searching for meat, were the human race's equivalent of packs of wild animals. Although they hunted together, they still remained free, equal, and independent in relation to one another. How account, then, for the foundation of civil society which required "absolutely that among those composing it, some consume without worry, while others expend themselves in hard labor; that the first be embarrassed by nothing but their laziness, while the second have not a single moment in their lives free from toils? " (*L*, I, 279, 282, 285).

Society was born of an accidental, violent confrontation. A band of famished hunters chanced upon a flock belonging to an isolated family of shepherd-farmers. "Hunger, excited by the sight of objects capable of satisfying it, caused them to look upon this particular separation as an infraction of the natural law, or, if you will, as an occasion worth exploiting." "Thus, by an example, repeated forever after, wealth found itself at that time too weak against indigence, and those who possessed everything were from the beginning expropriated [*dépouillés*] by those who had nothing" (*L*, I, 228, 288-89).

The irony of history, Linguet seemed to be implying, was this. When this law first had worked itself out in history, indigent men were the belligerent hunters, and opulent men the retiring and pacific farmers. The next time around, the victims again would be the opulent; only this time, the opulent fated to be vanquished would be the descendants of that first class of indigent victors, and the impoverished race destined to victory the swindled and dispossessed descendants of the class of the originally opulent. The balance would have been redressed, the antagonistic relationship overcome, but society would explode, and as Linguet had forecast in his letter to Voltaire, everything would be lost.

At the moment of gory conquest, the men who perpetrated the primal crime of usurpation were only hunters in search of prey, not power-hungry exploiters. They stumbled across the wealth of the agricultural proprietor and pastor. Instinctual appetite impelled them to devour it (*L*, I, 339). Involvement in the act itself was the occasion of an irreversible transformation of hunter into master, a revolution in the human psyche.

> These bloody trophies became for the ravishers the fatal fruit that opened their eyes and made them blush at their ignorance.... [the

bloody prey] excited in their veins a thirst that nothing could extinguish, set their passions in motion, developed them, the way fiery liquors do that inflame the combustible materials they're poured over. From their shock, from the fermentation that followed, a hideous light was created, illuminating the charms of tyranny to these ignorant men who had known nothing of it, and enlightening them to the means of establishing it. [*L*, I, 289-90.]

Booty, drenched in blood, the first property, had generated *homo economicus*, the first real proprietor. "From the moment the spirit of property began to take possession of [people's] souls, it contracted them, materialized them, so to speak. It closed them off to almost every motive except interest" (*L*, II, 389-90).

The victim of the first society, the farmer and pastor, became a hired hand on his lands, then a domestic slave. On those first days following his "accident," he led his herds to pasture, his eyes filled with tears. "But little by little, habit hardened his heart" (*L*, I, 292).

"...as soon as there were masters and slaves, society was formed: it was tending toward its perfection. It could receive it only from the laws, and it was not long before these burst forth" (*L*, I, 343-44). From this point, society's development was clear. The victorious hunters soon realized that it was inconvenient to own their captives collectively; they decided to divide their booty in men and goods, and to devise laws sanctifying the division. "They conceived that the primitive usurpation had to be regarded as a sacred title..." (*L*, I, 298). "The most ancient of all laws confirmed the most humiliating dependence. The first society that took shape on earth displayed despotism and lowness there, imperious masters and a trembling slave" (*L*, I, 292).

Hunters brought society into being by means of conquest and usurpation. Thieves, their hands still bloodied, signed the terms of societal peace by which property was institutionalized and the expropriated unconditionally enslaved. Society's first law consecrated theft, enslavement, exploitation. "La théorie des paradoxes en déclamations fastidieuses" was a theory to explain the establishment, structures, and dialectic progress of ineradicable socioeconomic class division and antagonism.

Seventeenth-century theorists—Locke, Grotius, Hobbes, Pufendorff—set up states of nature as backdrops for man's contractual agreements inaugurating and legitimizing societal relationships, institutions, and statutes which presumably conformed to natural law. Rousseau retained the concept of contract in his *Second Discourse*, although contract there only sanctioned a travesty of justice; contractual consent in historical society was a trickery practiced by a wealthy, constantly threatened class of possessors upon a willing, downtrodden class of potentially dangerous outcasts (*R*, III, 176-77). For Rousseau, right or law did not exist actually in the state of pre-societal nature—it existed only potentially, and it did not exist in history. The realm of right was on the other side of the pit of history, the dark dwelling place of contingency, accident, and fact. Right was called into being, along with the perfect political society, utopia, when rational men exercising enlightened will signed the social contract.[31]

Linguet rejected all concepts of legitimizing contract in his *Théorie des lois civiles*. He dismissed the contention of the jurisconsults that men had come to terms with societal arrangements and had signed compacts binding themselves to embrace them willingly (*L*, I, 71-72). He exploded the juristic notion of a normative *droit naturel*. What the jurisconsults have agreed to name natural law is only civil law. "This is the title that renders possessions exclusive. This is the law that divides the world into an infinity of little domains..." (*L*, I, 352). A description of man in a state of nature as a totally independent being, physically free and free-wheeling, autonomous, consitutes an enumeration of his rights in this state. But society eclipses the state of nature, along with the "natural rights" men enjoy there. Society emancipates men from their natural freedom. It institutionalizes the inequality of slavery. "Whatever the jurisconsults say, their treatises on natural law are all treatises on servitude. They are epitaphs of this [natural] law and the entire earth is its tomb. No place in the world exists where you could not say, in speaking of it: *hîc jacet*" (*L*, I, 349-50, 351).

Linguet also repudiated the Rousseauan moral and rational legalisms, concepts of law, rights, contract, and general will embodying Rosseau's faith in man's potential for self-redemption. He was even more categorical than Rousseau in his denial of that potential as a possibility for historical man.[32] He insisted that conquest and spoliation, the grim events inaugurating society, fixed for all time the gauntlet historical man would run. The spirit of property "contracted [their souls], materialized them, so to speak. It closed them off to almost every motive except interest" (*L*, II, 389-90).

The social world Linguet depicted was a penitentiary of the human race where all access to extra-societal and pre-societal norms had been barred: "If a prison has twenty doors, it is not enough to close off, to padlock exactly nineteen, because all the prisoners are going to escape through the twentieth, the only one still open" (*L*, I, 350). Linguet appeared to be presenting his *Théorie des lois civiles* as a descriptive or historical sociology of the laws, but he did not foreclose the possibility for critical and constructive sociology— even though he left the critic with no meta-historical platforms and no extra-societal standards for judgment (*L*, II, 296-97). He anchored the logic of his dialectic in history; there could be no exit from socio-historical necessity except through the revolutions that exploded society. Social criticism either committed the critic to programs of institutional reform designed to render more tolerable an unalterable social condition of domination and subjection or it engaged him in the social upheavals that dissolved the bonds of social necessity to inaugurate a new dark age of chaos.

Linguet began his sociology with a narrative of the origin of human society; but was that narrative itself really part of a descriptive science of historical society, or was it only science fiction? Linguet charged the contract theorists with a lack of anthropological verisimilitude in their intellectualizations, but he opened himself to the accusation that his sociology was deficient in historical veracity.

Where on earth, and when, could this wild confrontation have happened? Who in history had assumed the roles of these macabre characters, sanguinary, barbarian hunters, and trembling, tearful farmers, who confront one another in a moment of gory pillage and remain bound to one another forever after in the irremediable social and economic relationship of perpetual mastery and exploitation, and perpetual slavery and expropriation? If Linguet had invented a story to enchain the human race, that is, if that story was not history, why shouldn't someone else contrive another story to liberate it?

Where, even in the admittedly rich archives of the race's experience, had Linguet managed to discover a host of savages far more animalistic in their behavior than even the Hobbesian automata clashing in the wilderness? He discovered them, as Montesquieu had, at the moment when the French nation was founded. However, the *Théorie des lois civiles* was a sociology of law whose categories reflected a reading of history diametrically opposed to Montesquieu's in his sociology, *De l'esprit des lois*. Montesquieu scanned the medieval chronicle to discover foundations for a constitution justifying an aristocratic elite's political resurgence in a nominally absolute monarchy. The valiant Germanic nations of northern Europe descended into Gaul, Montesquieu related, "to destroy tyrants and slaves, and to teach men that, nature having made them equal, reason could not make them dependent, except for their happiness."[33] Drawing upon theories of society's origins advanced by other constitutionalists, Montesquieu clinched his argument in favor of the aristocratic party's pretensions to political, social, and economic dominance in France: "When the Franks, Burgundians, and Goths made their invasions, they took all the gold, silver, furniture, clothing, men, women, young boys, that the army could carry; the whole was pooled, and the army divided it. The entire body of history proves that after the first establishment, that is to say, after the first ravages, they came to terms with the inhabitants and allowed them to retain all their political and civil rights. That was the law of nations in those times; you carried off everything in war, you accorded everything in peace."[34]

Linguet shared with Montesquieu the shadowy images of this historical oc-currence—the descent from the forest, the swift, ravenous pillage. French ci-vil society originated in the conquest and subjugation of Gallic farmers and pastors by barbarian Germanic hunting tribes. Victory was consolidated by expropriation and enslavement. "Also," Linguet wrote, spotlighting details that it was in Montesquieu's interest to obscure, the conquerors "did not re-turn to the original proprietors the possessions they had despoiled them of. On the contrary, they consecrated their slavery forever. They placed the seal of justice on it" (L, I, 345).[35] Linguet raised the historical fact to the power of law. That law, unredeemed by subsequent history or by extra-historical im-peratives, became the norm for society.[36]

From these first events in the history of French society, conquest and sub-ordination, "were born...the true obligations of society,...to command and to obey" (L, I, 94).

The possibility of an authentically political dimension in social existence was destroyed, or rather, political activity was reduced to a function of those economic relationships that now comprised all there was of public life. Lin-guet was hardly content to have his historical sociology of law written off as clever critique and facile caricature of Montesquieu's history of medieval French institutions. He wanted his theory to describe structures and relation-ships in all societies—aristocratic, democratic, monarchical. The spirit of the laws was written into all the laws in history. But that spirit was not a function of time, place, climate, political tradition, and morals; it did not work like Montesquieu's complex of principles and ideal types, simultaneously deter-mining and determined by cultural, physical, moral, economic, and religious diversities in human societies. For Linguet, the spirit of the laws, everywhere, in all times, and for all time, is property: "Their spirit is to consecrate proper-ty" (L, I, 236).

Property undergirded all other formative influences upon any particular society. Property was the single natural law of all civil societies. The civil laws "are in my belief, clear, luminous; they all derive, like [the axioms of] geo-metry, from one unique and incontestible axiom" (L, I, 103).

All political laws could be derived from that axiom also: "It's all in vain that differences have been set up between civil law and political law. These fat books that differentiate them, separate them, are only the compilations of illusions and chimeras....All laws, and above all those two, boil down to be-ing just, and giving to each man what belongs to him, in order to conserve one's own possessions" (L, I, 89).

"...it is easy to convince oneself that society is born of violence, and property of usurpation" (L, I, 347). Linguet recalled the price of order when he analyzed its necessary components. The first society, with its propertied masters and conquered slaves, was threatened with dissolution as soon as it was formed. Women were society's first troublemakers. They aroused passions and jealousies, touching off war among the first rude members of society. Peace could be restored only by making women personal and exclusive possessions, properties like a man's holdings in fields and slaves: "Thus, from the beginning, the two supports of the civil union were, on the one hand, the slavery of most of the men, and on the other, that of all the women. On these distressing foundations the edifice of social institutions was constructed" (*L,* II, 365).

In a social system where liberty was apportioned in landed acres and measured by numbers of heads dominated, the freest men would be outright owners of goods and persons. In the empires of the Middle East, in "Asia," among peoples "worth of becoming our masters in Morality, Jurisprudence, and all parts of government," Linguet found his ideal civil society, uncorrupted by time, revolution, or the aristocratic barbarians of the West. This societal perfection, Linguet revealed, had been achieved by the absolute annihilation of nature and a totalitarian extension of the principles of property. Polygamy in the empires of the Middle East was a case study in the application of the principle *not* of climatic determinism, as Montesquieu claimed, but of property (*L,* I, 115, 381-82).

The earliest divorce laws are extensions of property law. "In contracting the deal, or in calling it off, he was using his property; he was conforming to the laws, or rather, the laws were being forced to conform to his caprices". *Homo economicus,* a psychological type "possessed" by the "spirit of property," "the foundation of society," had rarely been portrayed with more ruthless and deliberate consistency (*L,* 420, 431).

The severity of early adultery laws provided Linguet with further evidence that the principle of exclusive rights in property had been realized in civil law. These laws "showed severity against the seducer of a woman, as against the plunderer of a field" (*L,* I, 474-75).

The first civil laws subjugated sons to fathers unconditionally, again illustrating the principle of property in operation: "...the law that places exclusively in the father's hands the despotic reins with which he must govern his entire family is of about the same date as that which allowed the enclosure of a field by a hedge or a ditch" (*L,* II, 88-89). These legal sanctions for parental despotism were grounded in and entirely justifiable in terms of the psychology of *homo economicus.* Newly materialized man was prey to a morbid fear that his sons would threaten his land and cattle; to destroy in children the idea of robbing their father, the legislators "forced them to consider him as the arbiter of their destiny; they forced them to respect the power he had to give them life by conferring upon him the right of depriving them of life" (*L,* II, 54).

Linguet began his chronicle of humanity's progressive reification with a description of the hunters' appropriation of the cultivators' fields and flocks. The subjugation of the cultivators followed. Then women and offspring were submitted to arbitrary power. "...this happens as the inevitable consequence of an institution whose end is to accumulate all kinds of properties exclusively in the hands of a small number.... [this principle] is as necessary for society's conservation as it was for its establishment. It alone can maintain order and harmony" in society (L, II, 82).

The introduction of the concept of the testamentary will into civil law marked the ultimate extension of the spirit of property, that is, of the passion for materializing and reifying. It made the proprietor omnipotent and immortal; to limit the proprietor's power "would be to degrade it. Restrain it and you destroy it. Whether exercised by the dead or by the living, its essence consisted in complete liberty. Either it shouldn't have been extended beyond the grave, or allow it all the power it had on this side" (L, II, 153, 166).

Always, the terms of the analysis recalled the immensity of what had been lost, an indeterminate natural freedom, and the irrevocability of what had been gained, a social order grounded in class division, organized in rigid hierarchies, and governed by the spirit of property institutionalized in civil law. "However you look at the question, you will always see that once the heredity of properties is admitted, that of privations must be also" (L, II, 267).

This, then, was the tableau of the first societies. They were founded on crime, but they guaranteed order. The system had slaves, but it also had formed citizens. Out of the civil despotism enjoyed by these fathers, antique republics developed, guaranteeing the political liberties of citizens to paternal despots. However, the democracies were evanescent moments in the political history of the Western world,[37] and the Roman Empire offered only a historical example of the fate of civil societies that violated the spirit of the civil laws (L, II, 204).[38]

Only in the Middle East, the *locus classicus* of Montesquieu's political despotism, did Linguet discover the unadulterated historical realization of his ideal type of society, the absolutism of paternalistic monarchy: "I delight to find myself back near the cradle of society. How pleasing to make out in this vicinity the traces of the first steps men took toward civilization" (L, II, 219). The so-called despotic "Asiatic" societies functioned for Linguet as historical exits from the cycles of history. Asiatic peoples never knew the political freedom of the polis; but they could not have lost it either. Linguet made this point in the second edition of his *Histoire du siècle d'Alexandre:* Oriental administrations "were equitable,...mild, if it is permissible to use this term for any kind of social confederation. The same thing is still true in these regions where nothing has changed but the name of the nations that inhabit them"

(*A-1769*, 231-32). The only liberty these peoples lost was the liberty of nature: "One would wish to know to what extent this primitive liberty was already lost, which nature made our most glorious apanage, but which is hardly in keeping with perfected society" (*A-1769*, 225-26). The Asiatic nations were perfect civil societies. The anarchic liberty of nature had been extirpated from them. They knew nothing of democracy, a perfect transplantation of natural freedom into the space of society, but one which "in its essence... was repugnant to the nature of society..." (*A-1769*, 233). The civil existence of Asiatic subjects is one-dimensional. They owe their monarchs unquestioning obedience. The monarch's obligation to his subjects is one-dimensional also. He must guarantee them only justice, that is, protection for their properties: "Legislators were agreed that to obtain for men the kind of happiness they are fit for once they have taken on the chains of civilization, all regulations destined to govern them must derive from property and tend exclusively to strengthen it in all orders of the social hierarchy" (*A-1769*, 225-26).

Revolution, Phase One: The Third Estate

When he presented his "Asiatic" empires as ideal types of civil societies, Linguet was begging a crucial question. How could these paradigms serve as working models for administrators in modern states, heritors of institutions haphazardly constructed by Germanic barbarians on Roman imperial debris?

"Laws in their most general signification are the necessary relations arising from the nature of things," Montesquieu wrote. But civil society, Linguet taught, was the denaturing of all things, their transformation into propertied things. Their true relations, described by the laws, would be property relations. "Everything derives from property; there is nothing in the world that is not related to it: this is a truth which princes and their councils perhaps do not ponder sufficiently" (*L*, I, 61-62).

In the third quarter of the eighteenth century, French administrators still had not established civil laws to protect all properties: "We are still all covered with tatters that barely hid our ancestors' nudity in their savage forests: our national laws are nothing but the thick mud that filthied them in their swamps..." (*L*, I, 120). French civil laws did not reflect the real complexity in propertied relations in the realm. They failed to bind the interests of men holding new forms of property, mobile wealth, holdings in capital, stock, and annuities. They failed to protect the poorest subject's real possessions (*L*, I, 56, 61-63). The perfection of the first societies, the Asiatic empires, had been achieved by the forced containment of forces potentially disruptive of the rulers' and the subjects' security as proprietors. Now, however, that primitive state had degenerated everywhere, except in Asia.

Linguet saw eighteenth-century France as "a monarchy where morals are depraved." Women had been liberated; they were no longer anyone's property. Luxury, their peculiar accessory, had corrupted everything it touched. Fathers no longer ruled their families. Most crucial, medieval monarchs had liberated French serfs. A nation of former serfs now composed a technically free Third Estate (*L*, II, 183, 204, 449, 480). An entire complex of property relations had been irreparably fragmented. Ambitious members of the Third Estate claimed properties in lands and other goods and disputed their claims with noble proprietors.[39]

In these dissolute times, given new conditions of real ownership, the chances for approximating the perfect state of civil law and administrative order in the Asiatic empires would be practically nil. Nonetheless, an effort would have to be made—precisely because "everything derives from property," and because "there is nothing in the world that is not related to it." Heads of modern European states must reform a legal system overweighted in favor of the posterity of predatory aristocrats. They must rewrite the laws and restructure the realm's institutions so that they protected proprietors whom the French monarchs themselves had literally created. Glaring imperfections in the civil law reflected a fatal fault in the structure of the French monarchy.

"Whatever you say, sovereigns reign because they reign. The very exercise of their power is the title to it" (*L*, I, 73). Contracts did not legitimate their reigns, establish their sovereignty, or guarantee that their subjects would obey. What *did* were bonds of real interest. These bonds were formed between monarch and subjects and derived from a common concern for property (*L*, I, 67-72, 89-90). The monarch must become the scrupulous administrator of a civil law reformed to reflect radical transformations in property relations, and to protect new, untitled economic interest groups: "The foundation of my dependence on you, who are superior to me, is my power over other objects which are inferior. How are you going to attach me to your Empire? In what way are you going to tie me to the obedience you demand of me? Isn't it by guaranteeing me the enjoyment of properties I possess, or at least by presenting me with the hope of enjoying those I might have one day?" (*L*, I, 80-81).

Repeating the thesis of his *Nécessité d'une réforme*, Linguet called for legal reform comprehensive enough to contain the fact of revolution in economic relationships in the realm. Perhaps it was true of these "vast arsenals known under the name of compilations, of commentaries," that "it is no more permitted to bring light there than into our powder magazines; and perhaps the care taken to protect them from it is very well advised: the least spark which might penetrate there would cause the entire edifice to blow up…. Nonetheless, it would be a service to human nature to bring about this happy accident." The enterprise was not all that difficult, "and it certainly would be more necessary than one might think to undertake it" (*L*, I, 16).

The clear alternative to reform was upheaval, a revolution of newly propertied, inadequately protected members of the Third Estate whose economic interests in maintaining the social order had been engaged only feebly, or not at all. Revolutions were not historical anomalies confined to Crete. Montesquieu was wrong. Revolutions "are a fruit of all climates." They ripen in states whose monarchs allow civil laws, "which establish property of every kind" to lapse (*L*, I, 78-80).

Linguet described a monarch, shepherd-governor over a vast kingdom of subject sheep. If he decided to banish the flock from the pasture assigned to each member, if he disposed of their pasture lands arbitrarily, he undermined the legitimacy of his own titles: "...the entire flock revolts. These sheep, so gentle, become furious lions: they recover their original independence. Power deprived them of it: power restores it to them. It becomes the remedy for the abuses it caused" (*L*, I, 78).

The prophet of revolution in the Third Estate delivered another forecast. This one was unencumbered by parables: "Woe to governments that forget this truth, or neglect it. Nothing can save them if they remain insensitive to the din of multiplied abuses warning them to protect themselves against their progress....If the administrators of empires disdain to profit from these valuable counsels, revolutions soon will occur which will accomplish for them what they did not want to do; but these violent reforms occur only along with the ruin of the state where they are executed" (*L*, I, 38-39).

Encompassing the dynamics of upheaval in the categories of his sociology, Linguet forecast a revolution of the Third Estate, a struggle pitting all categories of inadequately protected proprietors against a political regime that perpetuated in its civil laws the powers that descendants of aristocratic usurpers wielded over dominions they no longer really possessed and over persons they no longer really dominated. He did more. Employing these same determinants describing the progress of socioeconomic class antagonisms, he warned of the revolution of a class of absolutely dispossessed persons.

Revolution, Phase Two: The Fourth Estate

Linguet was convinced that the fundamental relationships of men in society were class relationships, and that they were radically antagonistic: master/slave; proprietor/expropriated. These divisions and relationships originated with society, in acts of usurpation and subjugation, and were maintained by the arm of might supported by the institutions of justice. Slavery could not be justified in terms of theories of contract and consent. What justified it was its social necessity. Linguet measured necessity in terms of utility. The argument from utility was overweighted to reflect the master class's needs—although these would include, in principle at least, its permanent interest in preserving the lives of the exploited and dominated class that produced and gave value to everything.[40] When this condition was met, slavery, along with every other form of subjugation, became precisely as "useful" to its victims as brute life itself.

Linguet disposed of the legalisms with which the jurisconsults had justified slavery or attempted to camouflage its brutality. He depicted the circumstances under which the enserfed masses in France had been liberated. He argued that emancipation brought most free persons no change in their position as the dominated, exploited class in society. What had changed in the modern world, Linguet observed, with the double triumph of economic liberty (which accelerated the processes of their immiserization) and liberal philosophy (which accelerated the processes of their enlightenment) was their perception of the utility, the "necessity" of their position. Linguet engaged both objective analysis and an intense personal sympathy in the warning that these twin processes of immiserization and enlightenment were generating forces capable of sparking revolution and exploding an order of necessities institutionalized in systems of socioeconomic repression and exploitation—if only to plunge the insurrectionaries into a state of chaotic anarchy.

The master/the slave: this relationship had been treated frequently in the political theories and juristic treatises of Linguet's contemporaries. The urge to apply a metaphysical balm of legitimizing consent to social relations had impelled Hobbes, Grotius, and Pufendorff to construct elaborate apologies for laws of slavery.[41] Both Grotius and Pufendorff are correct, Linguet granted, in assuming that domestic slavery and society originally had the same base.[42] But then they advanced "this chimera of a unanimous and voluntary consent" (L, II, 238):

> This word [slavery] signifies the destruction of all rights of humanity for the human being to whom it is applied. This is no longer a man: this is, depending on the circumstances, an insensate tool or an animate beast of burden. He no longer sees with his eyes. He can only follow the movements of an alien will. As long as he remains in this condition, even his existence is alien to him. Except that he still walks around on his two legs; except that he doesn't know how to neigh, or whinny, and that when he dies, they do not rip into his flesh or his hide, there is no longer any kind of difference between him and a cow or a horse.
>
> He is led, as they, to market. He is made to trot, jump, run, as they are, to test the strength or weakness of his limbs. [L, II, 232-33.]

Men do not voluntarily dehumanize themselves or transform themselves into mechanical appendages. Men do not become slaves out of need; for a free man would never willingly sign a contract containing the clause: "You will produce everything, you will enjoy nothing." Such an exchange could be proposed only to men already reduced to captivity. Only ruthless acts of conquest and expropriation created slaves; contracts did not; and yet, the maintenance of the masses' subjugation was the condition of society's perpetuation. "Any society whatever must have robust, docile, and indefatigable animals, who carry its full weight; and it is this function that slavery imposes upon the miserable men whom it brands" (L, II, 242-45, 257).

At the same time that he attacked the jurists for applying salves in the form of contracts to cut the sting of slavery, Linguet issued a warning to outraged humanitarians, reforming philosophes, and moralizing utopians. They branded societal necessities radical social evils; they publicized these revelations; but then they were structuring the logic of a final remedy—one which they themselves would be unable to accept (L, II, 284-85):

> But between them [the philosophes] and me, there's this difference; that they believe this injustice [slavery] is noxious, and I believe it's necessary; they reject it as the enemy of all rights, while I consider it the foundation of them all; they commiserate with the human species for having adopted it, and they consider its destruction as the first step toward the common happiness of society, whereas I, in pitying it also for having committed this imprudence, am resolutely convinced that it would not know how to rectify it without annihilating this very society which owes its existence to it [such an imprudence]. [L, II, 280-81.]

A fully enlightened philosopher must recognize that his reform programs were capable of activating a dynamics that would drive civilized society into annihilation. The one *genuine* expression of moral revulsion against enslavement in civil society would be an echo of the revolution that ended society along with slavery.

Linguet discussed such an upheaval in his treatment of slavery resulting from conquest. He began by demolishing Pufendorff's argument that contracts legitimated the enslaving of captives.[43] The enslaved captive commits himself "to everything when the whip threatens him; to nothing when the whip is removed, or when he manages to snatch it away, and forges for himself a road to liberty with the instrument of his servitude" (L, II, 330-41).

Having penned a justification for rebellion, the theorist of societal necessities was left with the hopeless task of discriminating between the captive slave's legitimate revolt and revolts of enslaved domestics. In fact, he discovered nothing at all to distinguish the two kinds of slave insurrection, only a utilitarian difference measured by the impact on society of each group's revolt (L, II, 350ff.). A single captive slave's escape is unnoticed, and harmless to society; it is like the wind's displacement of a grain of sand from one dune to another. But what if the winds increased to storm intensity? What would happen if a whole nation of domestic slaves rebelled? "There is the natural emblem of society. A hurricane formed it, but which of us would want to run the risks of the vortex that would restore things to their original position?" (L, II, 356-57).

Linguet further undermined his fragile distinction between revolts of domestic and captive slaves when he admitted that the revolt of large numbers of captives "would not be an injustice: but this might be the cause of a great revolution" (L, II, 357).

Only armed force, not legal hairsplitting, could halt the march of slaves into revolution. "It's up to [the police] to make use of a force that exists to prevent the generation of a force that does not exist, and that would become most deadly to it [the state] if ever it succeeded in developing" (L, II, 357).

But hadn't history itself resolved the problem of slavery, at least in the Western world? The slaves were free. Linguet admitted that much; however, he described their emancipation as though it represented the fullest historical expression of a paradox, and not the historical resolution of it. If the resolution was still to come, then that would be the history of the future.

Medieval monarchs, Linguet wrote, had freed the serfs, les vilains, that is, 999/1000 of the total population of the realm; except for the names, however, nothing had changed. Slavery survived intact in the modern world. Enlightened men perpetuated and perfected the institution; only now, they called it freedom. "...dependence, slavery, lowness, are...the fate of three-fourths of mankind. It is from their distressing subjugation that the voluptuous ease of the other quarter that governs them is acquired. Whatever name you give to these two mobiles of society,...whether you call them domesticity or servitude, empire or liberty, it means invariably, for the one group, a total abnegation of itself, a complete sacrifice of the rights attached to the quality of man; and for the others, a doubling or, if you will, an abuse of these same rights" (L, II, 498-510).

The great divide of civil society was a barrier protecting, from the masses who had nothing, all categories of persons who possessed something. It had been marked out at the moment of society's inception. Society could be maintained only on the condition that this barrier was fortified and patrolled continually. Emancipator-kings were the first to relax the guard. "It is this operation which has corrupted our governments: it has delivered them up to terrible maladies which will kill them sooner or later" (L, II, 480).

Below the clusters of entrepreneurs in the Third Estate, possessors enriched through agricultural, commercial, financial, and industrial exploits; and below all categories of peasant proprietors, teemed masses of men condemned to have only arms, only labor power, a Fourth Estate. These were the emancipated descendants of a race of slaves, and potential engines of the most dangerous revolution, the last. Processes that contributed to the economic, social, and intellectual triumph of the propertied masters and profiteers in modern society were simultaneously preparing the awakening, the disaffection, and ultimately, the revolution of the expropriated victims. That, perhaps, was what Linguet was implying in his warning to Voltaire.[44]

Linguet focused his analysis on two groups within that Fourth Estate of propertyless men: impoverished debtors and wage earners among the rural and urban laboring poor. The debtor was a free man who was compelled under law to offer his person as security for the debt he owed; should he default, civil law reduced him to even less than a thing: "Whoever has nothing annihilates himself in her [society's] eyes; and if, far from owning something for himself, he owes to others even the price of the nourishment that has prolonged his life, his annihilation augments in proportion to the sum he has borrowed. His existence becomes, so to speak, negative. He is bound to society only by his debt. She [society] would let him perish without the slightest qualm if the creditor's interest was not opposed to his death." Society was withholding from the debtor even the right to die. Sociological analysis was a testament to an ongoing vivisection of indigent men (L, II, 365-68, 372).

How overcome the bestial horror? Economic man demands his payment; yet he imprisons the debtor, provides for his nourishment, and never gets paid. Vengeance turns absolutely against the perpetrator of it. In invoking his property rights, he fails utterly to calculate the extent to which he is foiling himself. He bungles the job in imperfectly annihilating or reifying the debtor. *Homo economicus* is moved only by material self-interest. It was his interest that Linguet enlisted when he proposed a humanitarian reform of imprisonment laws for debtors. The logic of the creditor's position would drive him either to release the imprisoned debtor—but that would frustrate his desire for vengeance—or to legislate the only sensible alternative, the debtor's enslavement. "I have said only what I believed was true and apt to facilitate what you most improperly call their happiness in this valley of tears which you embellish with the name of society" (L, II, 390, 448).

Linguet had attempted to suppress sympathy and moral revolt in the interest of achieving a dispassionate, descriptive analysis of societal necessities. However, indignation surfaces in his depiction of the contradictions and the bankruptcy in which the liberal philosophies of *homo economicus* deadended. It is brought under control and given focus and targets in his challenge to authority—implicit in his deliberately shocking reform proposals—to legislate alternatives to the debtors' re-enslavement that would alleviate the intolerable inhumanity of their condition as free men. "Don't be inhuman or compassionate half-way, since modified compassion is as cruel for them as it is ruinous for you, because inhumanity can be useful to you only insofar as it is entire and complete" (L, II, 410, 411-16).

Linguet carried his analysis still further. He depicted the material conditions of farmhands, day-laborers, and workers employed by merchant-manufacturers—a second cluster in the class of propertyless persons. He developed the logic of their progress into an unexampled degradation, desperation, and enlightenment—that is, a perception of their own privation and an expectation of ending it—and beyond, toward revolution.

A society whose members are treated as economic units will be most perfectly organized when most consistently regulated by the laws of the market place. "Everything derives from property; there is nothing in the world that is not related to it" (*L*, I, 61). The *Théorie des lois civiles* had described the origin of civil society and the formation of its two great social classes. Now it became the systematic exposition of the "progress" of these two classes in a universe where all relations between things and between persons are treated as functions of the law of material self-interest. Linguet's analysis of the doctrines of capitalist ethics and classical economics added up to a psychosociology of class exploitation in modern civilizations where all men are free.[45]

> [The modern manual laborer] is free, you say! ah! But there lies his misfortune. He is bound to no one; but then no one is bound to him...
>
> [The free manual laborers] have no master, you say. But this is still another pure abuse of the word. What do you mean? They have no master: they do have one, and the most terrible, the most imperious of masters: need.
>
> They become the valets of whoever has money, which gives an infinite scope and rigor to their slavery. [*L*, II, 466, 470, 471.]

Urban and rural wage earners—day laborers, manual laborers, a new breed of "domestics" in Linguet's vocabulary—were at liberty in a universe where all human values had been transformed into functions of property values, where all human relationships could be described by the formula: appropriate or be appropriated. "The miserable wage he [the manual laborer] is promised hardly matches the price of his subsistence for the day's labor he supplies in exchange." The worker is watched over at all times for fear that he might become interested in his work and waste time; every moment of rest is counted as a theft. After every ounce of productivity has been drained from him, he is summarily dismissed (*L*, II, 466). The wage earner is the pariah of society. His work is the source of all abundance; yet he is excluded forever from any share in it. These day laborers [*les journaliers*] "are born and raised for the service of opulence.... In striking the earth with her foot, she calls out of it legions of laborious men who fight among themselves for the honor of taking her orders...." Misery forces them into the market place to await purchase. "The more the day laborer is pressed by need, the more cheaply he sells himself" (*L*, II, 463, 468, 482). The social analyst had drawn inflammatory word-pictures of the condition of a class of disinherited men, graphic descriptions capable of inciting that fatal awakening of class consciousness against which he had been at such pains to warn Voltaire and the philosophes. He etched into the grain of an age of progress a theory of surplus value, the concept of a rural proletarian reserve army, and the iron law of wages.[46]

Slavery, the state of being of instrumental man in the ancient world, and more to the point, serfdom, the condition of almost all Europeans in the medieval Western world, functioned for Linguet as a measure of the progress of modern, free men into a subhuman existence. Rational, calculating, enlightened men had reduced man the two-legged horse to a nullity that could not even be named, except by calling it a free day-laborer, a domestic, an emancipated manual laborer, a worker in rural industries, or in the new factories.

> He is free! But this is precisely what I pity him for....The slave was valuable to his master by virtue of the money he cost. But the manual laborer costs nothing to the voluptuous rich man who employs him. In the time of servitude, men's blood had a price tag. They were worth at least the going market price. Since we have stopped selling them, they no longer have any intrinsic value. [L, II, 467.]

> I say it with as much candor as sorrow: all they [the free domestics] have gained is to be tormented constantly by the fear of dying of hunger....The slave was nourished, even when he didn't work, the way we provide our horses with feed on holidays. [L, II, 464-65.]

> But the free manual laborer, who is often poorly paid when he works, what becomes of him when he does not work? Who is perturbed over his destiny? Who loses something when he ends by perishing of languor and misery? Who, consequently, is interested in preventing his death? [L, II, 465-66.]

Earlier in his sociology of law, Linguet lamented the murder of natural man by civilization. Now he depicted the dominant classes' vivisection of pre-proletarian free men.

"To be a proprietor, according to the *Théorie des lois*," wrote Abbé Baudeau, editor of the physiocrats' *Les Ephémerides du citoyen*, "is to be absolute master of the person and work of one or several other persons. *Once you have taken this first step, it is impossible that any but the most disordered consequences could follow.*" [47]

Whoever described as a naked exploitation the exploits of rational and enlightened entrepreneurs, and pointed out slaves in the marketplace where propagandists of a new liberty were publicly proclaiming their emancipation, was inviting "the most disordered consequences." He was seeing contradiction, class antagonism, where the new humanitarians read cosmic harmony and coinciding economic interests.

The slave had been freed. Whoever would plunge backward in a flight or retreat was beating vainly against an irreversible deed. The slaves were free, but freedom only completed their dehumanization. That was Linguet's point: "...the emancipation on which poverty congratulates itself is only the garland used to decorate the victim they wanted to sacrifice to opulence...." (L, II, 449-50).

Permanent division and latent antagonism between classes of free men constituted the incurable malady of modern societies. Utopians, utilitarians, and other humanitarians who tried to overcome this antithesis in synthesizing reconciliations—expressed either as projects for classless societies, or as dreams for harmonizing conflicting class interests through universal enlightenment and a perfect economic liberty—would kill the polity. They might pose as society's saviors; but they would function as its annihilators. The antiphilosophic sociologist who enlightened his contemporaries to the prospect of the masses' annihilation within the system, while simultaneously previewing their imminent war against it, presumably was not as dangerous as the philosophes.

From the instant of society's formation, the two classes, a propertied elite and the expropriated masses, had remained pitted against one another in a relationship of latent hostility. The dynamics driving society to its perfection did not dissolve or overcome class antagonism. Development on all fronts only acerbated it, and ripened conflict.

The day civil society was founded was a day of dupes. A thick veil of mystification still hung between the victims of this colossal trickery and those who profited from it. The unprecedented happening of modern times, as Linguet saw it, was that the perpetrators of the mystery suddenly had given themselves new names, men of reason, and had invented for themselves a new task, that of changing men's expectations.

"It is one of the most astonishing, and at the same time, one of the happiest effects of providence, that despair has not turned the head of this immense multitude of human creatures who sleep at night not knowing whether the next day they will have the occasion to earn enough to eat bread" (L, II, 483-84). Suddenly, without warning, the philosopher-magician illuminates, as though for some splendid *fête galante,* the house of horrors that is civil society. With "a twist of the magic ring...societies of men emerge from the bowels of the earth, all equal, all rich, all happy." The philosophic word-pictures, "political fairy tales,.. break through the night of the masses to awaken in them a consciousness of total deprivation. Word-pictures become the objects of collective desires; the frustration of desire generates a great shared rage and intensifies the pain of a new knowledge. Philosophic fairy tales unleash the dynamic force that will realize the last term in a dialectic progress. All is lost, all, that is, connected with artifice and property, civil society itself. "Society makes of the entire world one huge prison where only the prisoners' guards are free....Why can't you see that it will outrage the unfortunate captives to post touching descriptions of the happiness they would enjoy if they were free on the very bar that holds them in captivity?" (L, II, 516, 517).

Society had annihilated the rights of the man of nature to a boundless, indeterminate independence. Then why did jurists, utopian theorists, philosophic reformers, and government administrators—the "guards"—invoke these rights incessantly? Society naturally was divided into two classes. Rights and liberties were instruments in the hands of the appropriators and exploiters, who alone were free. All their lamentations on servitude had "not led to pay raises of one *sou* for our day laborers, soldiers, or domestics: it is the cheapness of this kind of men's services that forms the wealth of society, and the base of governments" (*L*, II, 511-12). The expropriated victims, whether technically "emancipated" or literally in chains, had a right to nothing (*L*, II, 454-55)—unless they had a right to everything.

Linguet propped up a spokesman for civil society's pariah class and forced him to inform against himself, to warn his exploiters, the same who were the agents of his enlightenment, that they were driving him to spark the final holocaust. "What then is the aim of your discourses? I suffer, and according to you, I need not, even more, I must not suffer. I perish in chains, and you cry out to me that no one has the right to bind me. What then is your intention? Is it to force me to join in my heart the sentiment of injustice and that of slavery?" (*L*, II, 519). A benighted masses' ignorance and submissiveness stood between societal order and the last revolution. The great myth that society's flock of sacrificial victims enacted, the myth that all its members together were weaker than one watchdog, must be perpetuated, The sheep in the societal flock "are more easily protected against being devoured by wolves. It's true, that's only so they can be eaten by men. But alas, that is their destiny from the moment they entered a fold. *Before speaking of rescuing them, begin by overturning the fold, that is, society*" (*L*, II, 513, emphasis added). This sober warning was sounding too much like a rebel's dare.

If the day of revolution ever dawned, Linguet warned, it would be society's last day. Humanity's mass would rise up, breaking the bonds of class—invisible chains of free men—while societal superstructures crumbled around it. This happening would mark the end of a cycle of history, if not the end of time. The author of this apocalypse was not privileged to open the seals. He spoke in parables. He refused to structure any development out of chaos or chart the renaissance of civil society. Ruination was his only forecast. "If the sheep that compose it [the flock] should ever decide to present their head to the dog who herds them, wouldn't they soon be dispersed and destroyed, and their master ruined? " (*L*, II, 512-13.)[48]

Linguet's historical determinism was ironclad, but also self-annihilating, and world-destroying. For what he had been describing all along in the operation of his determinants was their bondage to social forces fated to conflict and moving dialectically through time to the gory end of societal necessity in anarchy and chaos. At the edge of the abyss, where he had all but guaranteed that the feat would be impossible, Linguet elected to check these forces—not with constructive reform legislation, and not by reinstating the legal condition of slavery—but by inducing hypnotic paralysis among the members of the pariah class. "...suffer and die in chains: that is your destiny" (*L*, II, 519).

This consoling advice proliferated among the masses would be the work not of superstitious priests but of clairvoyant philosophers. The true philosopher was a social analyst who knew too much to be a philosophe. "...the philosophy that exhorts them to patience is much more reasonable than that which encourages them to revolt" (*L, II, 521*).

Whatever that philosophy was, it was not all that was contained in the *Théorie des lois civiles*. For Linguet had preached submission there, but in a language that impelled to revolution; and he had warned against enlightenment while calculating a French proto-proletariat's power to blow up the world. The reality he depicted was dialectic; the dynamics of the dialectic was the conflict of internal war, socioeconomic class struggle. Simon Linguet's new sociology of law was complete, an exhortation to patience embedded in analyses of class exploitation and a theory of social revolution.[49]

Sociology, Prolegomenon to a New Science of Political Economy

The *Théorie des lois civiles* of 1767 was a first statement. A second edition, revised and expanded into three volumes, came out in 1774. In 1777, Linguet eluded the growing circle of his enemies by going into exile in London. He wrote to his literary agent, Pierre Lequesne, to report progress on yet another revision of the *Théorie*. He planned to include it in a complete collection of his works.

> It is true that my task is enormous: you cannot have any idea of it. In tampering with my works, I am tempted to do the whole thing from scratch. I no longer recognize the *Théorie des lois civiles* and the rest. I am forced to stop myself in order not to denature them too much—because it wouldn't be the same thing, or rather, it would be altogether different things. There are two books added to the *Théorie*...I am completing it; I am completing there the development of my system: after that, I can say...: I will never do anything more than clarify, but I give the core of the ideas. One can criticize. I am certain there will be no reply.[50]

The promised edition never appeared; a long series of Linguet's defenses did. They were self-defenses, but also a vindication of his sociology of law. In 1774, Linguet was fighting for his professional life as an advocate, struggling to prevent a cabal of lawyers in Paris from disbarring him. He was convinced that his ideas and works were being minutely dissected by his enemies; that his anti-Montesquieuan system was being charged against him as a crime. His self-justification, then, had to include a vindication of his literary productions. Precisely what Linguet feared in 1769, he now believed had happened to him: "The person [of the writer] is separated from the work....This will never happen to an orator. His glory is linked in its essence to his person....Everything in him is indivisible..." (*A-1769, 455, 457*). He chose to justify himself in 1774 by describing his *Théorie des lois civiles* as follows:

A work so unworthily, so cruelly judged, so little read, luckily for me, perhaps; a work decried as a panegyric of despotism, and where the dispassionate eye perhaps would see the most service-able memorial that exists to the love of liberty...a work, finally, in which I would not be astonished to find people digging one day for evidence to pursue me as a furious republican—with as much injustice as when they pretended to find motivation there for accusing me of being the flatterer of tyranny. It could be that this strange mistake is the secret of my security. They saw, then, in the *Théorie des lois* what was not there at all: and of what was there, they saw nothing.[51]

Again pleading for himself, this time in January, 1775, before the Order of Lawyers in Paris, Linguet reformulated this strange confession. "I had written in favor of liberty perhaps with an overly republican candor; by the most inconceivable of all misunderstandings, they believed they saw in my principles the germ and the panegyric of despotism."[52]

Apparently, Linguet convinced no one. He stated his plea even more forcefully in a *Mémoire* to Louis XVI published in 1786. He admitted that when his *Théorie des lois civiles* first appeared, everyone looked upon it as "the school of despotism": "...if the partisans of despotism had had the same interest in decrying it, it would have been far easier for them to condemn it as being the *school of independence*. In truth, I must admit it, that is the real fault in it. There reigns there, from beginning to end, a republican haughtiness that I would not permit myself today. To venture it took all the imprudence of youth."[53]

"I had written in favor of liberty...." Linguet depicted the state of nature as a condition of absolute independence for pre-societal beings, lords over an unbounded domain, masters of their destinies, men without any obligations to authorities on any level (parents, employers, kings). "It is he [the child] who can be regarded as exercising a veritable empire over them [his parents], and it is they who are condemned to render him arduous services" (L, II, 19, and discussion, Chapter One, pp. 12-14). In this utopian reconstruction as well as in his juxtapositions of the liberty, equality, and integrated identity of men in a state of nature against the multiple subjections and alienations of so-cietal man in modern cultures, Linguet built a "memorial...to the love of li-berty." "He is no longer there [in nature]. He would not know how to return ....From the depths of his cradle where he is fettered, his first glances fall up-on beings like him, all weighted down with chains, who congratulate one an-other on seeing a companion ready to share their slavery" (L, I, 183).

"...I would not be astonished to find people digging one day for evidence to pursue me as a furious republican...." The forceful language of paradox which Linguet used to depict contradictions in the social condition tends to develop its own revolutionary dynamics, and that dynamics breaks the bonds of social necessity, even while the author, apparently obedient to the dictates of his system, cries for their reinforcement: "I suffer, and according to you, I need not, even more, I must not suffer. I perish in chains, and you cry out to me that no one has the right to bind me. What then is your intention? Is it to force me to join in my heart the sentiment of injustice and that of slavery?" (*L*, II, 519).[54] This revolutionary thrust finds expression not only in the structure of Linguet's language but also in his theory of usurpation and in his dialectic development of the concepts of class and class struggle, where he argues that spoliation and subjugation, raw crime and its institutionalization in class divisions and exploitations, are at the root and foundation of social establishments; that class wars, the revolutions of commoners against aristocratic usurpers, and the war of proletarians against all proprietors, are the motor forces of society's development, and that they drive relentlessly toward a fatal recovery of equality and independence in chaos. "Thus, by an example, repeated forever after, wealth found itself at that time too weak against indigence and those who possessed everything were, from the beginning, expropriated by those who had nothing" (*L*, I, 288-89).[55]

The *Théorie des lois civiles* is a "memorial...to the love of liberty." Nonetheless, Linguet constructed this monument in the shadows of oppressive social institutions and forces of containment. The work expressed the author's commitment—colored, but not cancelled, by his radical ambivalence—to a repressive social order where rulers and subjects were bound to a totalitarian regime of properties originating in criminal acts.

> ...the most brilliant governments soon will be overturned if the property of peoples is not left undisturbed. The power of kings is assured only insofar as their subjects's possessions are solidly maintained; and the reason for this is very simple; it is that they all possess by the same title.... Our titles to the enjoyment of property are the same, that is to say, a force, a primitive violence later legitimated by prescription.
>
> I possess a property in Champagne: by what title? My father left it to me. But from whom did my father hold it? He bought it for himself; and as for the seller, what was his right? Another sale or donation doubtless made to him, or to one of his predecessors. But in going back this way from owner to owner, one would have to find the root of all these successively transmitted properties. And one will find none other than the violence of the original possessor who seized it, and the prescription that covered, consecrated this violence.
>
> But each one of those who successively possessed and transmitted the realty did not communicate to his transferee either more of a title than he received, or another kind of title; so that

the most legitimate, the most sacred possession today, is rooted at one end in the most flagrant usurpation. It is clear, however, that it must be respected, and that whoever violates it becomes guilty toward society....

It is exactly the same with kings, their property has a less circumscribed expression...otherwise the principle of it is the same....Whoever would dare undertake to examine thoroughly the rights attached to sovereignty to demonstrate their injustice would unsettle the whole of society. [*L,* I, 63-65.]

In Linguet's system, a common dedication to preserving an order of properties rooted in crimes bound property-owning subjects to support unflinchingly their ruler's estate in his sovereignty, and it dictated to kings the utility, the necessity, of protecting their subjects' holdings. They must employ every means available—including drastic reform of legislative and administrative institutions—but they owed their subjects no more than this—not liberties, or independence, or a share in the power of sovereignty. The basis for such claims, appeals to extra-societal norms, had no place in Linguet's system. This understanding of the interlocking material interests of sovereigns and subjects formed the core of a political doctrine, an ideology for kings and people (by implication, proprietors in the Third Estate).

Linguet's theory of usurpation embodied a rationale for the revolution of a class of propertyless persons, permanent victims of "flagrant usurpation" and "primitive violence," and yet, the repressive function of authority, which Linguet invoked repeatedly, was to prevent that class's revolutionary potential from developing, to maintain class divisions that safeguarded the propertied order and condemned the masses to a condition of dispossession and degradation. "Later governments have been able to maintain without scruple the state which violence introduced into the world. From this origin which I give to society there are no consequences detrimental to the administrations that develop out of it" (*L,* I, 306).

In his *Théorie des lois civiles,* Linguet offered painfully detailed depictions of deprivation, abandonment, exploitation, and massive insecurity among free, propertyless persons under regimes of economic liberty; he projected the impact of enlightenment on the attitudes and behavior of populations with limited material possibilities, predicting that intensified exploitation combined with perceived deprivation and raised expectations would spark the slave revolution that dissolved society. In these analyses, he revealed a remarkably sympathetic and comprehensive understanding of the roots and social expressions of frustration and aggression—knowledge he was prepared to engage in the service of containment and control.

Linguet did not succeed in his *Théorie des lois civiles* in completing his formulation of a political doctrine. He related how, in modern society, impoverished masses could be driven from resignation into revolution; he

was convinced that revolution would destroy them as it dissolved society:
"...wouldn't they soon be dispersed and destroyed and their master ruined?"
He preached fatalistic resignation to the victims: "Suffer and die in chains;
that is your destiny." He offered authority no blueprints for programs to
check the progress of immiserization or forestall revolution, only a somber
warning that in the modern world, the conditions for society's preservation
were no longer being met.

A few years later, in the heat of escalated combat against physiocrats, the
noblesse de robe, and authorities sympathetic to them, and with the development of a real, if fragile, base of support in the administration, Linguet formulated political principles that completed his sociology. He integrated his
split perspectives on the needs, claims, and revolutionary potential of two divisions of subjects and the prerogatives and obligations of governors into a
comprehensive, coherent political philosophy, a theory of political administration and an anti-physiocratic *économie politique.*

NOTES

1. Linguet to Voltaire, Feb. 19, 1767, in *Voltaire's Correspondence,* ed. Theodore
Besterman, 107 vols. (Geneva, 1953-65), 64, no. 13075, 228. Linguet's *Théorie des lois
civiles* was the first work he had sent to Voltaire, although he had been trying to call
himself and the products of his talent to Voltaire's attention for years. He had hoped
that his *Histoire du siècle d'Alexandre* (Amsterdam, 1762), would be accepted as the de-
finitive work on the first of Voltaire's four great centuries, the last of which, of course,
Voltaire himself had depicted in his *Siècle de Louis XIV.* His tragedy in five acts, *Socrate*
(Amsterdam, 1764), was in part a reply and challenge to Voltaire's *Socrate.* He had written a parody on selected chapters from Voltaire's *Candide,* which he entitled *Cacomonade, histoire politique et morale, traduit de l'allemand du docteur Pangloss par le docteur
lui-même depuis son retour de Constantinople* (Cologne, 1766). Two of his manuscript
plays, "Les Effets des tremblements de terre" and "Une étrange folie," were parodies of
Voltaire's *Poème sur le désastre de Lisbonne,* and his manuscript play "Le Mandarin"
was a parody of Voltaire's *Orphelin de la Chine.* For these manuscript plays, see BM, no.
1921, fols. 104-13, 114-30, 95-103. Linguet's defense of La Barre and his friends was to
some extent a calculated bid for attention and support from the defender of Calas.

2. *Ibid.,* 229.

3. For a comparison of Voltaire's ripostes to Montesquieu with Linguet's in the same
genre, see: Montesquieu, *De l'esprit des lois,* bk. xvii, ch. v, as quoted in Elie Carcassonne,
Montesquieu et le problème de la Constitution français au XVIIIᵉ siècle (Paris, 1927),
p. 304; Voltaire, *Essai sur les mœurs et l'esprit des nations,* ch. XVII, in *Oeuvres complètes de Voltaire,* ed. Louis Moland, 52 vols. (Paris, 1877-85), XI, 269; Linguet, *Théorie
des lois civiles, ou Principes fondamentaux de la société,* 2 vols. (London [Paris], 1767),
I, 36-37.

4. Linguet to Voltaire, Feb. 19, 1767, in *Voltaire's Correspondence,* ed. Besterman,
64, no. 13075, pp. 229-30.

5. *Ibid.,* 230.

6. Voltaire, "Egalité," *Dictionnaire philosophique,* ed. Raymond Naves and Julien
Benda (Paris, 1961), pp. 176, 177, quoted by Peter Gay in *Voltaire's Politics: The Poet
as Realist* (New York, 1965), p. 225.

7. See Voltaire to Linguet, March 15, 1767, in *Voltaire's Correspondence,* ed. Besterman, 65, no. 13143, pp. 47-48.

8. Voltaire to d'Alembert, June 4, 1767, in *ibid.*, 66, no. 13317, p. 6.

9. Voltaire to Linguet, March 15, 1767, in *ibid.*, 65, no. 13143, p. 48.

10. Voltaire to Linguet, April 6, 1767, in *ibid.*, no. 13194, p. 110.

11. M. P. Alekseev and T. K. Kopreeva, eds., *Bibliothèque de Voltaire; catalogue des livres* (Moscow, 1961), entry no. 2136, p. 560.

12. Jakob Friedrich Melchior Grimm, Denis Diderot, Guillaume Thomas François Raynal, Heinrich Meister, *Correspondance littéraire, philosophique, et critique,* ed. Maurice Tourneux, 16 vols. (Paris, 1877-82), VII (Dec., 1767), 509.

13. A. F. B. Deslandes, *De la certitude des connaissance humaines, ou Examen philosophique des diverses prérogatives de la raison et de la foi; avec un parallèle entre l'une et l'autre* (London, 1741), quoted in Albert Soboul, *La France à la veille de la Révolution,* 2 vols. (Paris, n.d.), II: *Le Mouvement des idées dans la seconde moitié du XVIIIe siècle,* Cours de l'Université de Clermont-Ferrand, Centre de documentation universitaire (Paris, n.d.), 78.

14. Paul Henry Thiry d'Holbach, *La Politique rationnelle* (1772), Discours I, cited without page reference by Soboul, *La France à la veille de la Révolution,* II, 79.

15. Olivier de Corancez to Jean-François de La Harpe, published in François Métra, J. Imbert, de Boudeau, et al., eds., *Correspondance secrète, politique, et littéraire, ou Mémoires pour servir à l'histoire des cours, des sociétés, et de la littérature en France, depuis la mort de Louis XV,* 18 vols. (London, 1787-90), VII (Nov. 21, 1778), 118-31. In the passage cited (p. 120), Corancez is quoting from La Harpe's article in the *Mercure de France* for Oct. 5, 1778; reproduced in *Jean-Jacques Rousseau raconté par les gazettes de son temps. D'un décret à l'autre (9 juin 1762-21 décembre 1790),* ed. Pierre-Paul Plan, 3d ed. (Paris, 1912), p. 162. Voltaire tried to dispose of Rousseau's paradoxes in a line: "L'orgueilleux Jean-Jacques," he informed Damilaville in a letter dated June 25, 1762, "est à Amsterdam, où l'on fait plus de cas d'une cargaison de poivre que de ses paradoxes." As cited in Marc Viridet, ed., *Documents officiels et contemporains sur quelques-unes des condemnations dont l' "Emile" et le "Contrat social" ont été l'objet en 1762* (Geneva, 1850), p. 68.

16. Rousseau, *The Second Discourse,* in *Jean-Jacques Rousseau: The First and Second Discourses,* ed. Roger D. Masters (New York, 1964), pp. 159-60.

17. Rousseau, *Emile,* book II, in *Oeuvres complètes de Jean-Jacques Rousseau,* 13 vols. (Paris, 1909-12), II, 60, as cited in *Rousseau...Discourses,* ed. Masters, p. 25. See also Rousseau's countering of charges of inconsistency and contradiction in his *Contrat social,* in *Jugement sur la polysynodie,* in *The Political Writings of Jean-Jacques Rousseau,* ed. C. E. Vaughan, 2 vols. (New York, 1962), I, 422, as cited in *Rousseau...Discourses,* ed. Masters, p. 26.

18. For discussion of paradox in eighteenth-century thought, and for analyses of its uses in the writings of Linguet and Rousseau which parallel my own here, see Hans Sckommodau, "Thematik des Paradoxes in der Aufklärung," *Sitzungsberichte der wissenschaftlichen Gesellshaft an der Johann-Wolfgang Goethe-Universität, Frankfurt am Main,* 10, no. 2 (1971), 56-101, and especially 69, 76-77, 85ff., 91-94, 98-101.

19. The quoted terms are Henri Grange's in his *Les Idées de Necker* (Paris, 1974), p. 213. Grange offers a brilliant analysis of the philosophes' "tranquilizing doctrines." He recognizes two. First, he treats the "doctrine of the concordance between individual interest and general interest" under three headings: "the ethic of expenditure" (and here he includes apologies for an elite's luxuries as the necessary condition for the poor man's enjoyment of a livelihood); "exchange in inequality," a rationalization of social divisions as an inevitable, salutary by-product of the division of labor; and "democratic liberalism," the faith that education will "recreate social harmony" while leaving the propertied order intact. Second, Grange discusses physiocracy, the "mystique of agricultural capitalism" and agent of a cosmic harmonization and reconciliation of the iron law of wages with the law of the net product (see Grange, pp. 212-40). Linguet's social analyses and critiques in the *Théorie des lois civiles* can be interpreted as a critical response to these expressions of an exploitative ideology.

20. Nicolas Baudeau, Dupont de Nemours, et al., eds., *Ephémérides du citoyen, ou Chronique de l'esprit national,* 69 vols. (Paris, 1765-72), 1767, III, 191.

21. *Ephémérides du citoyen*, 1767, III, 203-4. Emphasis added.

22. Voltaire to Marin, Oct. 24, 1770, in *Voltaire's Correspondence*, ed. Besterman, 77, no. 15701, p. 44. Voltaire's phrase was "Paris a donc aussi son Jean-Jacques...."

23. Voltaire, *Voltaire, Lettres inédites à son imprimeur Gabriel Cramer*, ed. Bernard Gagnebin (Geneva, 1952), p. 84, as quoted in Gay, *Voltaire's Politics*, p. 201; *Voltaire's Marginalia on the Pages of Rousseau: A Comparative Study of Ideas*, ed. George R. Havens (Columbus, Ohio, 1933), pp. 21-22.

24. See Rousseau, *Discours sur l'origine de l'inégalité*, notes and intro. by Jean Starobinski, in *Jean-Jacques Rousseau, Oeuvres complètes*, ed. Bernard Gagnebin and Marcel Raymond, 4 vols. (Paris, 1959-69), III, 143.

25. See, for comparison, *R*, III, 135-36.

26. See Linguet, *Nécessité d'une réforme dans l'administration de la justice et dans les lois civiles en France, avec la réfutation de quelques passages de "L'Esprit des lois"* (Amsterdam, 1764), pp. 6-7.

27. If Rousseau was able to overcome the historical pessimism that pervades the *Discours sur l'origine de l'inégalité*, it was because historical pessimism in his thought was counterbalanced by a strain of anthropological optimism (Starobinski's term, introd., *R*, III, 1ix): "cependant l'homme est naturellement bon" (*R*, III, 202). Man's corruptible but essentially indestructible moral potential awaited only purification. Following the extremist style that is his, Starobinski writes concerning Rousseau, "he leads history to a catastrophic terminal point. The curtain falls upon a stage overrun by anarchy and chaos, but it is only the end of the first act" (Starobinski, intro. *R*, III, 1ix). Man was naturally good and could become rationally moral. Struggle between possessors and dispossessed was as real to Rousseau as anything in history could be, but only that real. This social theory in which he charted progressively more violent shocks of confrontation between social forces, culminating in civil war, was only Rousseau's sketchy preface to the chronicle of his own feats of transcendence, whether in retreats inward from history to the interior spaces of self, or in flights out beyond history into utopia. See Claude Mazauric, "Le Rousseauisme de Babeuf," in *Jean-Jacques Rousseau, (1712-1778). Pour le 250ᵉ anniversaire de sa naissance*, ed. Société des études Robespierristes (Gap, n.d.), pp. 75-100. "L'individualisme et le rêve unanimiste de Rousseau exclut tout recours à une conception de la lutte des classes" (*ibid.*, p. 97).

28. See this chapter, pp. 73ff.; and Chap. Five, pp. 181-86.

29. Linguet accused Montesquieu, Pufendorff, and Hobbes of ignoring natural man's limitations. "Fear is even less natural than boldness to one who knows nothing, and curiosity is the first and almost the only passion of ignorance." See *L*, I, 240.

30. Here Linguet would seem to be refuting a suggestion of Grotius, as well as Rousseau's more complex and multifaceted anlaysis of societal origins. See Hugo Grotius, *Le Droit de la guerre et de la paix*, ed. Jean Barbeyrac, 2 vols. (Basel, 1768), I, 228-29; *R*, III, 164ff.

31. Starobinski, intro., *R*, III, 1xvi.

32. Rousseau, it is true, did not categorically foreclose the possibility of intra-historical reconciliations of the great socioeconomic class struggle. But he could not afford to count upon the chance of history. See Starobinski, intro., *R*, III, 1xviii.

33. Montesquieu, *De l'esprit des lois*, book XVII, ch. v, t. II, as quoted by Carcassonne, *Montesquieu et...la constitution française*, p. 86.

34. Montesquieu, *De l'esprit des lois*, book XXX, ch. xi, t. III, quoted by Carcassonne, *Montesquieu et...la constitution française*, pp. 89-90.

35. See also *NR*, pp. 24-29.

36. In some respects, Linguet's argument here resembles Voltaire's. See *Essai sur les mœurs et l'esprit des nations*, in *Oeuvres complètes de Voltaire*, ed. Moland, XI, 271-72. However, Voltaire generally refused to concede that historical circumstance was an iron-clad determinant of the subsequent course of society's development.

37. For an extended discussion, see Linguet, *Histoire du siècle d'Alexandre*, 2d ed. (Amsterdam and Paris, 1769), pp. 232-33.

38. See also Linguet, *Histoire des révolutions de l'Empire romain, pour servir de suite à celle des révolutions de la République*, 2 vols. (Paris, 1766).

39. See *NR*, pp. 28-33.

40. See. for example, *NR*, pp. 7-8.

41. Pufendorff advances one version of this argument legitimizing the subservience of poor to rich: "Thus servitude was established by a free consent of [both] Parties, and by a contract to produce in order that it be given to us." Pufendorff, *Droit de la nature et des gens*, book VI, ch. III, nos. 5, 4, cited by Robert Derathé, *Jean-Jacques Rousseau et la science politique de son temps* (Paris, 1950), p. 197.

42. *Le droit de la guerre et de la paix*, book II, ch. XXVII, no. 4, and *Droit de la nature et des gens*, book VI, ch. III, as given in *L*, II, 237-38.

43. Pufendorff, *Le Droit de la nature et des gens*, book VII, ch. VII, no. 3, quoted in Derathé, *Jean-Jacques Rousseau et la science politique de son temps*, p. 207.

44. Linguet to Voltaire, Feb. 19, 1767, in *Voltaire's Correspondence*, ed. Besterman, 64, no. 13075, p. 230.

45. I borrow the term "psychosociology" from J. F. Faure-Soulet, *Economie politique et progrès au 'siècle des lumières,'* Collection techniques économiques, Séries modernes, tome 4, Séries Histoire et pensée économique, no. 1 (Paris, 1964), p. 207.

46. For Karl Marx's comments on Linguet's formulations of these economic laws, see his *Theories of Surplus Value*, trans. Emile Burns, ed. S. Ryazanskaya, 3 vols. (Moscow, 1969), I, 345-50.

47. As cited in Georges Weulersse, *Le Mouvement physiocratique en France (de 1756 à 1770)*, 2 vols. (Paris, 1910), I, 148. Emphasis added.

48. In this context. Linguet is using the term "sheep" metaphorically to describe the dispossessed masses whom he had just depicted as salaried day laborers, artisans, domestics, and farmhands. Earlier, he had used the image of flocks of sheep each assigned to its pasture to refer to subjects each possessing a domain. "Mais s'il s'arroge le pouvoir de les bannir de l'étendu de pâturage qui est assigné à chacun d'eux..." (see *L*, I, 75-78). Linguet appeared to be suggesting here that it would be possible to include in this depiction of propertied men those men who had properties only in a right to biophysical survival, a right to subsistence (see *L*, I, 76). Five pages later, however, he definitively limits the application of his metaphor. He suggests that the only way the king can bind his subjects to obey is by guaranteeing them the enjoyment of properties: "Comment se feroit-on obéir d'un homme qui ne posséderoit rien, et qui renonceroit sincèrement à rien posséder. Il faudroit le tuer, et alors même il n'obéiroit pas" (*L*, I, 81).

49. Recent studies of prerevolutionary structures and conjunctures lend support to Linguet's vision of a culture where permanent divisions were multiplied and deepened by complex and interrelated developments entailing destabilizing transformations in politics, economy, society, and mentality. For my own understanding of developmental crises in eighteenth-century France, I am indebted chiefly to the following studies: Ernest Labrousse, *La Crise de l'économie française à la fin de l'ancien régime et au début de la Révolution* (Paris, 1943); Labrousse, *Esquisse du mouvement des prix et des revenues en France au XVIIIᵉ siècle*, 2 vols. (Paris, 1933); Fernand Braudel and Ernest Labrousse, eds., *Histoire économique et sociale de la France*, 4 vols. (Paris, 1970–), vol. II: *Des derniers temps de l.âge seigneurial aux préludes de l'age industriel (1660-1789)* (Paris, 1970). I have profited from Georges Lefebvre's commentaries on Labrousse's phase theory, "Le Mouvement des prix et les origins de la Révolution française," in Lefebvre, *Etudes sur la Révolution française*, 2d ed. (Paris, 1963), pp. 197-238; from two volumes of Albert Soboul's *cours*, comprehensive studies of the integration into the larger framework of eighteenth-century French social and cultural history of data and trends presented by Labrousse: *La France à la veille de la Révolution* (Paris, n.d.); and from Pierre Goubert's *L'Ancien Regime*, 2 vols., Collection U, Series Histoire moderne (Paris, 1969, 1973). For insights into the connection between the modernization process and the writings of the philosophes, I am indebted to Arthur Wilson's analysis in "The Philosophes in the Light of Present-Day Theories of Modernization," *Studies on Voltaire and the Eighteenth Century*, LVIII (1967), 1893-1913. I acknowledge valuable discussions with Harriet B. Applewhite concerning crisis in one area of eighteenth-century French modernization, the nation's political development, and communication of several

chapters in her dissertation, "Political Culture in the French Revolution (1788-1791)" (Ph.D. dissertation, Stanford University, 1972); see also Harriet Branson Applewhite and Darline G. Levy, "The Concept of Modernization and the French Enlightenment," *Studies on Voltaire and the Eighteenth Century*, LXXXIV (1971), 53-98. I acknowledge also Samuel Huntington's *Political Order and Changing Societies* (New Haven, Conn., 1968), and Cyril Edwin Black, *The Dynamics of Modernization: A Study in Comparative History* (New York, 1966). If Linguet was imperfectly aware of the operation of all the factors we now recognize, and of their full impact upon French institutions and traditions, still he had begun reading the signs and drawing his conclusion: social class conflict was inevitable and imminent.

50. Linguet to Lequesne, London, Oct. 7, 1777, in BM, no. 1916.

51. Linguet, "Réflexions pour Me Linguet, avocat de la Comtesse de Béthune" (1774) in his *Appel à la postérité, ou Recueil des mémoires et plaidoyers de M. Linguet pour lui-même, contre la communauté des avocats du Parlement de Paris* (n.p., 1779), pp. 173-74.

52. Linguet, *Plaidoyer pour M. Linguet, avocat au Parlement, prononcé par lui-même en la Grand'Chambre, les 4 et 11 janvier 1775; avec l'arrêt intervenu en sa faveur* (Paris, 1775), p. 43.

53. Linguet, *Mémoire au Roi par M. Linguet, concernant ses réclamations actuellement pendantes au Parlement de Paris* (London, 1786), p. 111.

54. Hans-Ulrich Thamer, *Revolution und Reaktion in der französischen Sozialkritik des 18 Jahrhunderts. Linguet, Mably, Babeuf* (Frankfurt am Main, 1973), pp. 124, 284, n. 2, citing my observation on the characteristic power of Linguet's language in an earlier and expanded version of this chapter, "Simon Linguet's Sociological System: An Exhortation to Patience and Invitation to Revolution," *Studies on Voltaire and the Eighteenth Century*, LXX (1970), 219-93. The use of the term "revolutionary dynamics" in this context is Thamer's.

55. In his discussion of these same themes, Thamer speaks of the "relativity of the concept of class" and the "revolutionary function of the theory of usurpation" (*ibid.*, pp. 127, 66).

THREE

Travaux Pratiques:
The Politics of Subsistence

The Paradoxes of Economic Modernization

Some of Simon Linguet's earliest reflections on political economy appeared in his *Mémoire sur un objet intéressant pour la province de Picardie*, published in 1764.[1] The work was ostensibly a proposal for government-initiated programs to promote development in the commercial and industrial sectors of the French economy. Linguet was in Abbeville, impoverished and still profession-hunting. He might have been hoping for recognition by intendants, members of provincial estates, and others on the lookout for recruits who had proven their skills in handling the technical and theoretical aspects of administration.

The *Mémoire* brought Linguet some local notoriety,[2] but no job offers. His talents were obvious; but his public display of them was grossly unpolitic. What the *Mémoire* advertised most conspicuously was Linguet's skill at uncovering the paradoxes of economic development, and depicting the crises that would unroll should the government fail to meet the challenge of resolving them.

Linguet began his *Mémoire* with an ambitious proposal for a canal system to make the Somme river navigable from Amiens to the sea, "a great work with great views," the author's modest description ran, "a bold and magnificent project" (*MOI*, 4) to foster industry and commerce and create prosperity. This ex-candidate for admission to Perronet's engineering school, observer in the tradition of Thales, and disciple in Colbert's school of mercantilist economics, was ready to rechannel Abbeville's waters to revive Picardy's economy. The engineer of abundance concluded, however, that Abbeville would have to pay the price of modernization. Its port would be eliminated as the Somme's bed was redirected (*MOI*, 14-16). In any case, Linguet believed, the city was doomed. Paradoxically, what doomed it was the existence there of the very state-encouraged industry that ought to have guaranteed prosperity and a continuing economic growth.

The chief center of economic activity in Abbeville was a broadcloth industry housed in a vast establishment and operated under a royal privilege granted to the VanRobais family.[3] Linguet was convinced that far from contributing to Abbeville's prosperity, the VanRobais manufactory was killing it; far from providing thousands of workers with a livelihood, "...it is forcing them, in the most literal sense, to perish of hunger and misery." The VanRobais family, under the terms of its privilege, had to employ a fixed number of three thousand workers. During slump periods, fewer full-time workers were needed. Forced to employ three thousand hands at all times, the directors simply reduced the number of working days for each worker. This calculus of interest was most practical for an industrial entrepreneur: "But a worker whose only resources are his arms could not conceive of his work diminishing without his subsistence suffering. He eats as much bread one day as another." If he doesn't work, he will be forced into debt to pay for his food, and this "consumes in advance the fruits of his future work. He will struggle for a time against anxiety and misery and drag himself finally to a public hospital to perish at the first illness brought on by these two plagues."[4] How many fathers every year "perish beside their dismantled looms," leaving moribund orphans to the care of charity? (*MOI*, 17, 18).

In a passage heavy with irony, Linguet speaks of the threat of depopulation in the ranks of the laboring poor, a consequence of life dragged out in unbearable conditions. The statistics ought to concern especially the opulent industrial entrepreneurs: "If those who have nothing did not undertake to produce citizens in the state for the service of those who have everything, riches soon would become worthless there. Imperceptibly, they would even be annihilated because arms would no longer be available to reproduce them. And it is this fortunate reproduction that the exclusive manufacture of cloth attacks at its base" (*MOI*, 18-19).

Are these entrepreneurs barbarous men? Are they capable of sacrificing everything to their interests? Do they treat workers as machines? Do they keep them in working order when needed, and destroy them without regret when they are no longer operative? Let such ideas, Linguet protests, not be attributed to him. The tactic is Antony's as he delivers Caesar's funeral oration. They are all brave and honorable men. The entrepreneurs use their wealth well, entertain lavishly, their probity is common knowledge. Who would accuse them of self-interested cruelty? (*MOI*, 19-20).

Linguet repeatedly forecast Abbeville's imminent death. "She will die, there will remain nothing more of her than her name: *Et campos ubi troja fuit*" (*MOI*, 21). But then to what avail was all this fury unleashed against the inevitable? And why hover over the worker breathing his last, hunched over his idle loom? Was it merely to comfort him in his agony with assurances that though the mechanic must perish, the mechanism too would rot, and the factory crumble, and the enterprise fail, and the city vanish—in time? There was something suspicious about the tone in which Plato in Abbeville expressed passive resignation.

Linguet was not the only critic of Abbeville's privileged broadcloth industry. Rival entrepreneurs in Abbeville, struggling to revoke the privileges of the VanRobais family, charged them with causing misery among their workers.[5] But while industrial rivals called for an end to the family's privilege, Linguet counselled the perpetuation of the situation as the only means of maintaining urban order. If the VanRobais family reduced its work force to provide full employment for those remaining, "if out of three thousand, they fired fifteen or eighteen hundred, they would cause a terrible revolution in the city....The damage was done long ago. Perhaps it would be even more dangerous to try to remedy it now than to put up with it" (MOI, 20-21).

In 1768, Linguet published a second and expanded version of his canal projects, as part of a collection of Oeuvres diverses, and in 1769 he printed a still more complete collection, his Canaux navigables.[6] Here he returned to his observations of 1764. What he had begun as an aside to an appeal for the development of French commerce and industry, Linguet now expanded into a full-scale attack against industrial progress, against the luxury that feeds it, and the squalor accompanying it: "The appearance of any manufactory whatever brings with it all the plagues that the masses used to attribute to the influence of comets." Minuscule amounts of that torrential flow of gold from industry reach the worker, glide through his hands, and vanish: "Their indigence augments in the same proportion as the riches of those who employ them." Linguet invites the reader to follow him on a tour of a luxury cloth shop. Remark that the glowing colors were fabricated with putrid urine—and with how many thousand other infectious ingredients? How quickly we forget that these reams of dazzling cloth "were produced on dung heaps, and that the merchant's opulence necessarily is based upon the poverty of the producer-worker [fabriquant]." The merchant willed his workers' exploitation; exploitation was an iron law of burgeoning industrial enterprise, and the necessary condition of the entrepreneur's profit-making operations (CN, 81-83).

Poverty takes root only in the midst of opulence, "alongside manufactories. These are twin branches appearing at the same time from the same root. The one never flourishes without the other...." Take two cities even in the same state, and equally populated: "...you can be certain that the one where the most human beings are at the point of dying of hunger is also the one where the most hands are employed in operating the shuttle. No city in France has more looms than Lyons, and Lyons is consequently the city of France with the largest number of poor who lack bread." Lyons has a new public hospital, but it is not large enough "to receive all the miserable poor who, having toiled for fifty years over gold and silk, come there groaning, to die on straw mats." The situation is even worse where the industry is a monopoly, and all workers owe their lives to a single entrepreneur. Follow these workers, if you dare, into their "dwellings" in these manufacturing cities: "These are regular burrows, like the ones beavers build; dark holes where herds of laborious animals hide out, breathing only a fetid air, poisoning one another with contamination unavoidable in that crowd, and inhaling at every instant the seeds of death, while toiling without respite to earn enough to protract their miserable lives" (CN, 84-85, 100).

Herds of laborious animals, burrows like beavers', multitudes of human beings at the point of death, gold woven on dung-heaps, workers come to expire moaning on piles of straw: in these phrases Linguet depicted horrors that seemed calculated to evoke reflex responses: revulsion, disgust, outrage, and revolt. But revolt backward, or forward, and with respect to what? The Turks have no factories, no weavers, and they have no public hospitals either. Ought France destroy her factories to clear the fetid air? But no! Medea alone possessed the talent of restoring youth—and we moderns have lost the secret: "When once an empire touches upon its old age,...it's useless to search for secrets to restore lost elasticity" to its fibers. Not even reason can overcome the "vampires of interest." Of course, there remained the brute and still unreasoning force of the indigent "herds," but Linguet had not called attention to their subversive potential in this context. What he had done was provoke moral revulsion as an involuntary response to his exposure of the manœuvres of a "vampire of interest" spreading its shadow over the "burrows" that housed these "laborious animals" (CN, 85, 158).

Linguet set out in 1764 to propose a canal for the province of Picardy. He published grandiose plans for reinvigorating the entire province, encouraging industry, and providing new markets for manufactured goods. He prodded the French to imitate the prosperous Dutch, masters of world commerce and fearless innovators in industrial enterprise. He chided his countrymen for their predilection for costly, useless machines (MOI, 69-70). He ridiculed French indulgence in sterile luxuries. The Bordelais enjoy a splendid promenade, but lack a bridge. The Remois have just erected a statue to the king, and their river is unnavigable. The Dutch don't have theatres, statues, or water towers. "But they have deep canals everywhere, which bring them the riches of the universe" (MOI, 26-27). At the same time, however, Linguet obviously was possessed by another concern that intruded upon his subject, distracted him from the pursuit of his thesis. His message to his countrymen read as a paradox, an expression of irreconcilable contradictions inextricably rooted in the laws and processes of economic development.

In the course of analyzing and evaluating the government's pro-physiocratic theories and policies of agricultural modernization, Linguet eventually un-

covered the same unsettling paradox. The administration in France institutionalized its conversion to a new science of political economy, physiocracy,
with the promulgation of liberal economic legislation in 1763 and 1764. Controller General Henri-Léonard-Jean-Baptiste Bertin's declaration of May 25,
1763, removed all barriers to the free internal circulation of grains; Bertin's
successor, Clément-Charles-François de Laverdy, made an even more dramatic
break with tradition. Laverdy's edict of July, 1764, authorized free grain
export as long as prices remained below a fixed ceiling.[7]

The new policies worked a radical and irreversible transformation in relations between governors and governed on the key issue of distribution, the
government's allocation of goods and services. Traditionally, French subjects
had equated government's distributive role with provisioning. The expectation of government intervention to guarantee subsistence was deeply in-
grained in the French popular mentality. The people saw their relation to
their monarch as that of a flock to its pastor, or children to their father; they
owed their king obedience; he owed them an unfailing delivery of life-sustaining grain and bread during periods of shortage.[8]

The administration's traditional means of meeting distribution expectations and demands was an elaborate regulatory system for keeping agricultural markets conspicuously well supplied with grains of good quality, and at
accessible prices. To achieve an appearance of abundance in times of medi-
ocre or bad harvests, authorities could constrain owners to dispose of all their
grain, or stipulated portions of it, at designated marketplaces within a given
period, no matter what the going price, and to specified persons in a fixed order of priority. Markets were priced—strictly in times of dearth, leniently in
easy times—by officials enforcing complicated regulations and collecting numerous fees for their services. Preventive measures designed to guard against
hoarding by speculators in anticipation of scarcity and soaring prices bridled
those who traded in grain. Merchants normally were required to obtain licen-
ses, to supply specific markets, to buy only on the market, to declare all
stores of grain, to restrict or forego trade between provinces, or on the international market.[9]

Physiocratic theorists of agricultural modernization who commented on
the French economy in the prerevolutionary decades shared a certain number
of economic and political concerns with their opponents. They recognized
that in a realm with an expanding population and a growing number of
important urban centers, government could hardly afford to be indifferent to
questions of national provisioning in grain and grain products, principally
bread. The nation's safety, political stability, and continuing economic
growth were at stake in all controversies over national agricultural policy.
However, both physiocratic theorists and converts to the system among
government officials were convinced that in formulating a national agricultur-

al policy, the government should abandon policies of containment and regulation and should be ruled exclusively by principles calculated to promote economic expansion. Liberty, *laissez-faire* and *laissez-passer*, by favoring the producer and encouraging production, would be the government's best policy for insuring an abundance of grain.[10]

The physiocrats called for thoroughgoing agricultural modernization, a revolution that would transform a traditional economy into a market economy, and farm owners, cultivators, and traders into agricultural capitalists. As incentives to a more rational and profitable cultivation, they advocated the suppression of communal and small, fragmented plots, and the formation of large domains exploitable by modern farming techniques. They called upon government to end restrictions on internal circulation and export of grains, and to abolish controls on marketing. Producers and traders then would be free to buy, sell, and store grain wherever and whenever these transactions were most advantageous to them. Following the natural law of self-interest, the new agricultural entrepreneurs would produce more, and would circulate their grains throughout the realm, and if necessary, outside the realm as well, in order to obtain *le bon prix*, one which would give them a good return, or *produit net.* The more certain the owner was of obtaining his *produit net*, the greater his incentive to produce more, and to market his grains where need was greatest, that is, where the price approximated *le bon prix* most closely. As grain production increased and profits on sales rose to *le bon prix* and remained there, owners would raise agricultural workers' wages. Automatically, naturally, wage-earners would be able to afford higher grain and bread prices.[11]

Initial reaction to agricultural policies modeled after physiocratic maxims was generally favorable; in any case, certain reassuring traditional restrictions governing the Paris grain trade remained in force.[12]

Linguet publicized his own enthusiastic approval of the doctrines of liberalization in 1766, in his *Histoire des révolutions de l'Empire romain.* His motives might not have been entirely disinterested. He had been practicing law for two years, but he was still struggling for survival, and probably trying to impress highly placed potential employers with his talents as a propagandist for government-sponsored causes.[13] And so he praised the economic policies of Roman emperors who recognized their obligation to distribute subsistence, and who invoked a *laissez-faire* politics in fulfilling it.[14]

Linguet's flirtation with physiocratic doctrines, whether ideologically or pragmatically motivated, was short-lived. By 1767, he had repudiated the physiocratic economic system and the principles of a protocapitalist ethic.[15] In 1768, in his *Oeuvres diverses,* and in 1769, in his *Canaux navigables,* he offered strong criticism of the liberal administration's agricultural policies. The physiocrats, in the meantime, had published negative reviews of the *Théorie des lois civiles* and were subjecting Linguet's other essays to even harsher treatment. Their progressively sharper critiques spurred Linguet into retaliating with aggressive anti-physiocratic diatribes.[16] His antipathy to the party, however, was a complex affair. The theorist of civil law declared that the propertied order was a social necessity, even a positive good: security in possession was the condition of social stability; and at the same time he depicted and experienced that necessity as intolerably oppressive and insisted that it was unjust and unnatural because grounded in the raw violence of usurpation and enslavement. The physiocratic party's clean classic apologies for a totalitarian reign of properties would confront Linguet with the challenge of making some kind of political sense out of his own apparently contradictory doctrines.

The philosophic agriculturalists, Linguet charged, sensitive above all to the pecuniary interests of agricultural entrepreneurs, expand their systems, and modernize agricultural operations on paper, regretting all the while "that human industry can burst forth only at the expense of men's lives." Their erudite treatises are "vast cemeteries, where sometimes the entire population of a province has been swallowed up" (*CN*, 265). Who is interested in preserving the farmhand's life? No one.

> After all the accounts are in, what is the value of men's lives to those who direct their labors, and even more, to the millionaires who give the orders?
>
> Today we hear the starlings of philosophy emphatically chirping the word *humanity* into the ears of the rich who degrade it: but what is the result of this cackling invented mainly to amuse women or the men who resemble them, or to fill up lacunae in ceremonial discourse?
>
> Do we see happiness and virtue multiplying on earth? Do we notice the rich becoming more sensitive to the misfortunes of the poor? Do we see them reestablishing between them, on the plane of sentiment, this precious equality which the injustice of chance has banished? No: everything contributes to complete the destruction [of equality].
>
> ...in civilized nations, the poor man continues to be, of all beasts of burden that the rich man uses for his pleasures, the most docile, the most active, and the cheapest. [*CN*, 267-68.]

Linguet had written another exposé. The proponents of a systematic modernization in French agriculture were standard-bearers for a party composed of agricultural entrepreneurs. Their categories of universals camouflaged imperfectly the class-specific economic interests they were working to promote. If progress through agricultural reform, the most certain guarantor of the entrepreneur's augmented profit, constituted the necessary order of the universe, Linguet demanded to know where in this system of cosmic harmonies the deprivation of propertyless and near-propertyless agricultural workers, the rural laboring poor, fitted in, and by what sleight of hand the progressive aug-

mentation of profits had been reconciled with the perfect dehumanization of
the workers who produced it.

> ...it turns out that for everything that is called heavy labor it's
> cheaper to employ men than horses.
> The highest daily wage of an agricultural worker [*manouvrier*]
> is from twelve to fifteen *sols*. A horse eats that much, but the
> master pays for its harnesses....while the agricultural worker,
> with his fifteen *sols*, must live, he and his family....
> If the horse succumbs to fatigue, if it comes down with colic,...
> if it breaks a leg, if it dies, it is mourned: the master is inconsol-
> able when he considers the price he paid for it.
> But the peasant who digs in the earth costs the man who
> makes him work neither money nor anxiety. When he is healthy
> he is worn out. When he is sick he is neglected. When he is dead
> he is forgotten: it doesn't cost a cent to replace him. The coun-
> trysides are vast stud farms where, without interfering, opulence
> observes the propagation of a breed of robust and submissive ani-
> mals, whose destiny is to live in pain and to die on a dungheap or
> in a public hospital. [*CN*, 269-70.]

The development of enterprises in all sectors of the economy was a principle
of national vitality and the necessary condition of economic growth. But the
growth of prosperity only intensified the progress of poverty. The progressive
impoverishment of the masses was at once a deadly social evil and a necessary
condition for the perpetuation and perfection of techniques and structures
guaranteeing the prosperity of an opulent elite and the state's continued economic development. Linguet was a strange reformer. He drafted projects to
revive whole provinces, an entire nation. He proposed to redirect the course
of rivers. At the same time, he cursed the luxury that flowed through these
widened channels. He damned the machines that regurgitated luxury products.
He exposed the foundation on which the machinery for grinding out national
prosperity rested—the systematic exploitation of armies of desperate men. He
could trace the dynamics of economic modernization—urbanization, techno-
logical innovation, the transformation of commerce, agriculture, and industry
into profit-making operations—only by juxtaposing and exposing the ever-
intensified progress of poverty among the proto-proletarian victims of the same
dynamics.

Linguet's propagandizing for national policies to stimulate economic growth
was hardly pioneering campaigning. The most elementary reflections on the
economy of great civilizations had provided Voltaire with material for his *Le
Mondain*, Montesquieu with apologies for luxury as a key factor in the development of national prosperity, and an entire generation of philosophic economists with arguments for the practicability of systematic modernization in agricultural enterprises. The most committed among the apologists for luxury
had insisted that although avarice might have been the psychological ground

for an overproduction of luxuries, the public utility of riches cancelled out the passions of lust and the vice of covetousness. Having followed the modernizers' arguments to this extreme, Linguet made an abrupt about-face, rushed headlong into the camp of the militant moralists, and, as though in expiation of a blasphemy against humanity, began broadcasting the social critiques of a Morelly and a Rousseau. He refused to transmute moral outrage into proclamations of social utility; but neither could he comfort himself with flights from intolerable and irreversible economic realities into morally pure utopia. His paradoxical reports on the French economy read as case studies in the crises of economic development.

Anti-physiocratic Political Economy, an Ideology for a Monarchy in Crisis

French administrators were far from insensitive to the crisis conditions Linguet had depicted in his early essays in political economy. However, in confronting the widespread unrest generated by partially disastrous harvests and soaring grain and bread prices in 1767, 1768, and 1769, they were determined to affirm their commitment to the principles and letter of the liberal legislation of 1763 and 1764.[17] Physiocratic publicists continued advertising the king's subservience to the new maxims. Sympathetic officials stepped up their systematic execution of the new laws.

The government's dogmatic intransigence during this critical period operated to shatter a traditional political relationship between king and people on the distribution question; and it also had the effect of strengthening the position of certain French parlements as centers for an anti-physiocratic opposition politics and as spokesmen for popular interests and demands.

In 1763 and 1764, many of the parlements (and most conspicuously, the Paris parlement) had supported the government's liberal policies.[18] As the subsistence crisis of the sixties deepened, attitudes in these parlements changed dramatically. For example, in December, 1767, the Paris parlement appealed to the king to prove to the people, by his deeds and through his policies, that he had not abandoned his role as their shepherd, provider, and distributor of their subsistence. When the king failed to respond positively to this overture, the Paris parlement ordered a general inquiry into the grain trade; on October 20, 1768, it issued an *arrêt* of remonstrance—a frontal challenge to the politics of liberalization. The parlement followed the *arrêt* with a remonstrance against letters patent where the king had defended liberalization and had assigned blame for the subsistence crisis to a refractory police and an ignorant people.[19] In the fall of 1768, in an even bolder gesture, the Paris parlement convoked an Assembly of General Police where delegates from all three orders discussed the causes of the subsistence crisis and recommended measures to alleviate it. The assembly called for a return to the regime of regulation. The Paris parlement acted upon that recommendation with an *arrêt* on December 7, 1768, in which, in demanding an end to liberalization, it invoked " 'the voice of the people,' " which " '...in this matter more than any other is the voice of God, that is, the expression of the truth itself.' " The king and his ministers rejected the advice.[20]

By now, the Paris parlement had established itself as a base for a politics of subsistence—a politics of opposition to the monarchy's liberalization efforts in the economic sector and a politics for the people.[21]

The resignation of pro-physiocratic Controller General Etienne Maynon d'Invau in December, 1769, in the middle of a fiscal crisis, did not end the subsistence debate; and neither did Chancellor Maupeou's *coup d'état* annihilating the Paris parlement. The abbé Joseph-Marie Terray, Maynon d'Invau's successor, promulgated legislation in December designed to return the nation to regulation and protection. Terray also took a part in Maupeou's *coup d'état* against the parlements.[22] The new controller general may have had good political reasons for wanting those institutions liquidated, especially the Paris parlement. The school and party of liberal economists whom Terray replaced were a manageable political opposition. The Paris parlement, whose interventionist operations the Terray administration finally legitimized in December, 1770, was not. When forced into it, the Paris parlement had repeatedly defied administration and king to support precisely the regulatory system to which Terray was returning only now; and it had become identified as a courageous executor of policies Terray reinstated. The Paris parlement had proved itself more monarchist than the king on the issue of the people's subsistence. It was probably less embarrassing to the new controller general to join the new chancellor in abolishing this institution physically than to risk competing with it openly for the nation's political allegiance.

By the middle of 1771, Terray had reinstated the machinery of a regulatory regime; he had perfected or invented devices for enforcing his legislation. He had helped wipe out a dangerous institutionalized political competitor. He had ousted the last of the physiocratic policymakers and had begun censoring or suppressing physiocratic propaganda. He did not end either the subsistence crisis of the sixties or the crisis of national confidence—a legitimacy crisis in the making as well as a distribution crisis—that had been triggered by the government's vacillations between policies of regulation and liberalization during periods of poor harvests and high prices.

The king's new legislation on grains, notwithstanding Terray's traditionalist phrasing, no longer spoke automatically for the king's intentions, for his understanding of his political role and his political obligations toward a mobilized, partially disaffected nation of consumers. Terray sensed the existence of a dangerous breakdown of trust between the king and the nation on this issue of subsistence.[23] And he was certainly sensitive to the need for exploiting the talents and convictions of opinion makers to clarify and justify the administration's policies.

The abbé Galiani's brilliant critique of physiocracy, his *Dialogues sur le commerce des grains,* was a persuasive first statement of the principles of Terray's *économie politique.* Terray did not solicit the work, but he gave it his protection; he suppressed the abbé Morellet's riposte for the physiocrats; he profited from the success of Galiani's work, and he took steps to reinforce the impression it had made.[24] He extended his protection to Simon Linguet.

Linguet was in the right place at a critical moment. He had removed himself from the relative security of a law practice in Paris and stepped onto the political battlefield when he agreed in February, 1770, to accept the case of the duc d'Aiguillon, Louis XV's former *commandant en chef* in Brittany. Linguet wrote three briefs for d'Aiguillon, defending him against the Parlement of Rennes' accusation of grave misconduct in office.[25]

Maupeou's *coup d'état* against the rebellious parlements and d'Aiguillon's appointment as the disgraced duc de Choiseul's successor in the Department of Foreign Affairs assured the ascendancy of a new ministerial triumverate— d'Aiguillon, Maupeou, and Terray—and launched Simon Linguet into political careers as protected anty-physiocratic publicist, pro-government propagandist for the *thèse royale* against the *thèse nobiliaire,* and star advocate and enfant terrible of the Maupeou parlement.[26]

Operating out of a fragile base at the periphery of the administrative power network, Linguet publicly and explicitly identified the principles and policies of monarchy with incompatible claims for justice of two partisan interest groups in French society—the class of property holders, and a dependent propertyless nation, the victim of oppressive and exploitative injustice that government sanctioned when it protected properties. In government service, more accurately, in his role as a government-protected publicist, Linguet succeeded in giving full and coherent ideological expression to complex political insights and commitments.

One of Linguet's first statements of support for the principles and operations of Terray's administration appeared in 1770, in his *Lettres sur la "Théorie des lois civiles".*[27] Several months before the Paris parlement was suppressed, Linguet was deliberately confusing the programs, political philosophies, and economic and political interests of Anglophiles, *encyclopédistes, économistes,* and Montesquieuan *parlementaires,* his adversaries, and, he assumed, the administration's.

"The world," Linguet announced, "is filled today with certain philosophic, economic insects hatched from the *Spirit of the Laws,* and who nourish themselves on it; the fermentation of this work produced them...." They used to keep busy talking *"liberty," "political constitutions," "balance of powers."*

Now they have "fallen back on grain, bread, milling"; they have spread their corruption there also. Montesquieu's disciples, Linguet charged, were not the people's protectors, not the nation's providers. They were "ravenous vultures who prey upon and mangle" the nation (*LL*, 25, 26, 55).[28]

While Terray was reinstalling regulatory machinery to handle a crisis of political confidence that had weakened traditional political ties between king and people, Linguet was using his pen on Terray's and Maupeou's behalf in an attempt to dissolve a fragile trust and fracture a bond of unity between the parlement and the public.

At the same time, Linguet became involved in another kind of propaganda activity. He turned out several lengthy treatises on political administration. The *Lettres sur la "Théorie des lois civiles,"* a defense of his magnum opus, appeared in 1770 and the *Réponse aux docteurs modernes* in 1771; in 1774, Linguet issued a revised and expanded version of the *Réponse,* composed of a *Du plus heureux gouvernement* in two volumes, and *Du pain et du bled* in a single volume. He also published a new three-volume edition of the *Théorie des lois civiles.*[29]

Linguet built a political ideology into these works, a variation on the *thèse royale.* He assumed that the king and his ministers would follow the dictates of *raison d'état* and publicly commit themselves to the political principles he spelled out; and he intimated that his ideology alone was capable of recapturing the political allegiance of subjects enlightened by physiocratic publicists but alienated by the physiocrats' practice of a monarchical politics of liberty and seduced by anti-physiocratic *parlementaires* championing an aristocratic politics of regulation and political power sharing.

Property was the first principle of Linguet's political doctrine and the hub about which his system of political administration revolved. The litmus test of any political system's legitimacy was its ability to guarantee its subjects' properties—not their liberties, but their possessions. Linguet said precisely the same thing in his *Théorie des lois civiles* when he represented the interests of unprotected proprietors in the Third Estate.[30] The liberty the jurisconsults talked about didn't exist in political societies: "Oh you, men of all nations, of every rank, of every age, who listen to me, they are deluding you: you were born free, they are trying to convince you that you might be so still. This idea is a chimera" (*PHG*, II, 7).[31] The liberty of nature consisted in an absolute independence, "that of a lion, or of a wild bull in the forests" (*PHG*, I, xvii; *LL*, 104). It had nothing to do with society. As for civil or political liberty, whoever speaks of civil liberty "supposes beings subordinated to some kind of government," but subordination is the annihilation of liberty. Liberty and government are as different from one another as life and death. "What is the nature of government? It is to command. What is that of liberty? It is not to obey" (*PHG*, xvii-xviii; *LL*, 104-5).

"Liberty," Montesquieu had written, "is a right of doing whatever the laws permit, and if a citizen could do what they forbid, he would no longer possess liberty, because all his fellow citizens would have the same power.[32] "But who does not see," Linguet retorted, "that this makes liberty consist in slavery? A horse, saddled, bridled, shod, is free then also, as long as it executes all the movements that the hand or the heel of the cavalier commands. Nothing is binding its legs: it advances, it retreats with ease; but each of its progressions is prescribed; and when it bounds from view with the greatest speed it is feeling with the greatest shock the pressure of spur and bridle" (*PHG*, I, xix; *LL*, 105-6). Either liberty in society was a chimera, or it was only a function of dominion: "But if you understand by liberty the submission of one man to another and the state in which he who commands guarantees to him who obeys the possession of the fruits of his work and of his industry in order not to be dispossessed of his own dominion, then I conceive that free men might exist, but then there are just as many different liberties as there are beings who enjoy them; just as there are as many horizons as there are different viewpoints (*PHG*, I, xx; *LL*, 106-7).

The best political system guaranteed all possessions, however distributed, and however acquired. The ruler's political power rested on a foundation of economic empires, as many empires or dominions as there were subjects who possessed something—"the fruits of work and of industry." Possession, then, was the touchstone of all political systems; the guarantee of properties was the condition of any political system's legitimacy. "In the state in which politics places men, *liberty* and *empire* are synonymous. Only those can be free to whom society procures advantages: and unquestionably, the latter are the ones who command. The more absolute their dominion, the more society becomes advantageous to them, and consequently, the freer they are" (*RDM*, I, 252). Subjects were free insofar as they owned something that government guaranteed them the liberty and security to enjoy. They were not politically free in any classical sense, but that was Linguet's point. The governor, a first-rate administrator, guaranteed their economic empires; they forfeited their political autonomy.

The exercise of political authority consisted, first, in fixing the coordinates that determined points of dominion throughout the realm, and then in guaranteeing each of these dominions. Linguet substituted a model of the perfectly administered state for Montesquieu's three ideal types of political system, democracy, monarchy, and despotism. Behind the most imposing constitutional superstructures, rulers exercised power in the same way: "Either it is not true that there are three distinct forms of government, or it becomes necessary to admit a hundred, five hundred, a thousand, as many forms as there are nuances in authority and subjection. Everything we call government consists in two parts only—to command and to obey: now there is essentially only one way

of commanding, as of obeying; so there is essentially only one way of governing" (*PHG*, I, 11; *LL*, 39).

Linguet drew a closed circle; on its circumference, all political administrations could be plotted as points equidistant from a fixed center, property.
The instant any government departed from the "circular line traced in all its
points at intervals perfectly equidistant from the essential fundamental center
of political societies, that is to say, *property*, this sacred principle of all governments, this god of politics—at this instant despotism is generated..." (*PHG*,
I, 12: *LL*, 40). Confusion reigned in civil laws regulating properties when aristocrats dictated and administered them in their chaotic, arbitrary, medieval
fashion, and in effect deprived proprietors of "possession of the fruits of labor
and industry." (*LL*, 68ff.).

When the state was plagued by extremes of wealth and poverty, possession
and dispossession, dominion and deprivation, then it had touched upon the
period of despotism, the last fatal epoch in the cyclical course all historical
societies must run (*PHG*, I, 17-23). Montesquieuan mixed monarchy was Linguet's ideal type of despotism, the one unqualifiedly illegitimate system in his
political spectrum.

The other major historical political systems, democracy and absolute monarchy, were equally legitimate. "The freest of democracies, where everybody
seems to be sovereign; the most absolute monarchy, where everybody seems
to be slave, are two extremities of a circle. In appearance, no [two] things are
so far removed from one another, and in fact no [two] things touch so closely:
no [two] things are so easy to confuse" (*PHG*, I, 11-12; *LL*, 39).[33] Democracy
"is truly the masterpiece of a perfected politics, but its very perfection renders
it subject to many inconveniences....Its greatest prerogative is to maintain
the dignity of the name of *man* and to prevent that of *People* from becoming
degraded because [the name *people*] designates the true Sovereign....It is obvious that this form of administration was the most appropriate for maintaining the rights of the human species..." (*LL*, 49-50).[34]

"All the members of a democracy are free only because they are all *sovereigns.*" Linguet noted (*RDM*, I, 253). Although Linguet had insisted that all
political systems were indifferently satisfactory as long as they revolved about
property (the all-determining principle), still, in the one case of democracy, he
admitted the merit of an irreducible political principle, self-determination. He
acknowledged the theoretical superiority of a democratic politics that functioned to maintain "the dignity of the name of man," a man's property in his
humanity, and not merely the dominion of *homo economicus.* The ancients
had realized political perfection when they united command and obedience in
the person of the democrat. But the democracies were historical ephemera.
Of all governments still existing, the one which most resembled the democracies
was the government of "Asiatic despotism." "And there are no two things that

more closely resemble one another than the laws of alleged *Asiatic* despotism and those of alleged liberty in democracies" (*RDM*, I, 253).

In the democracies, every citizen could share his political sovereignty with every other citizen and yet not sacrifice its indivisibility. This miracle occurred daily in the political space of the democratic assembly. In his house, the democrat's sovereignty was whole but unshared, an absolute power. Every citizen was a master over his slaves, a father protecting and possessing the persons and goods of his wife and children (*L*, I, 186-92). The Asiatic rulers deliberately split the wholeness of democratic sovereignty and then artfully repaired the break. In his home, every subject was a paternal despot. On the public plane, however, every household master was the Asiatic monarch's servant, his property. The monarch would be the only democrat in that system, sovereign in both public and private domains (*PHG*, II, 15-16). In the Asiatic monarchies, as in the democracies, the sovereign's absolute, undivided power would be a safeguard against the tyranny of representative institutions, like those Montesquieu championed—which, far from checking executive arbitrariness, only institutionalized legislative arbitrariness (*LL*, 48). These intermediary bodies, like the parlements and the estates-general, dangerously exaggerated the influence of aristocratic elements in the polity and frustrated the one essential operation of government, that of satisfying nonprivileged subjects' demands for protection of properties (*RDM*, I, 257; *PHG*, II, 23; *L*-1774, I, 89-92).

Administration was the science of governing so that each man in his place might be guaranteed his "liberty," *not* political independence, but the liberty of dominion, possession of the "fruits of his work and of his industry." Linguet's Asia, the Middle East, was a cradle of political perfection. It harbored the pure monarchies (*PHG*, I, 34). With the demise of democracies, the unity of political command and political obedience in each citizen's person had been broken. The Asiatic monarch existed to overcome (in the measure that this was humanly possible) the alienation of his subjects' wills from their political power, to restore wholeness to the public space of his realm. Ideally, his legislation would satisfy needs and demands for protection that subjects—especially those situated in the lowest socioeconomic ranks—could not articulate and satisfy for themselves.

Linguet rejected the arguments of the liberals, for whom liberty in society embraced not only the liberty of dominion but also the civil rights of nonmaterial self-expression and political self-determination. Embedded in that rejection were the convictions that what most proprietors wanted from the political system were guarantees for the goods they had acquired and that what they most feared and what they most needed protection against were the despotisms of aggressive, power-hungry, and land-hungry privileged orders.[35]

But what could political adminstration guarantee to propertyless subjects? What could they possess? Linguet raised this explosive issue in his *Nécessité d'une réforme,* then in his *Théorie des lois civiles;* he suggested there that a monarch could bind his subjects to obey only by assuring them the enjoyment of properties they possessed or might possess one day (*L,* I, 81). Whoever was absolutely dispossessed could not be bound to the system. He could not be tied to its rulers; he would not have any interest in remaining covered by their guarantees. Absolutely dispossessed men would be society's natural revolutionaries.

Asiatic monarchs had taken their precautions. Their beneficence covered everyone. It covered the masses with the security of welfare. Linguet described pensions, guaranteed-wages for court workers, old-age benefits, medical treatment for royal domestics, equitable taxation and customs regulations, the humane treatment of soldiers—in short, the policies of a good Christian king wearing a turban (*LL,* 80-86), an image that could not have been better calculated to provoke physiocrats, encyclopedists, and Montesquieuans among the *parlementaires,* writers who were constructing their models of despotism precisely where Linguet was situating his ideal society and polity.[36]

Linguet's model ruler would legislate on behalf of his propertyless subjects what he assumed they would have willed as self-determining political agents— dominion over their humanity and a property in security—functional equivalents for a liberty they abandoned forever.

> Everything in the customs of Asia breathes simplicity, goodness, humanity, this gentle, this beneficent humanity of which we speak only in order to outrage it, which we bury in our books, and which has never dwelt in our hearts. From the Prince to the lowest manual laborers, all feel that they are men; all love to feel it; all value the rights attached to this name, and respect them in others without causing any weakening of distinction in ranks.... [*PHG,* I, 98; *LL,* 75-76]
>
> ...no place exists there where the lowest citizen could not sense that he is something, that he is being looked after; and where is the place in our country where three-quarters of the men who make up the nation would not find themselves compelled to make the humiliating confession that they are nothing? [*LL,* 90]

The absolute monarch in Linguet's model oriental administration operated as a benevolent absolutist, the only one. He alone was guarantor of his lowest subjects' lives, their security, their humanity—the only property they had. His slightest betrayal of their liberty, that is, their dominion, would be apparent immediately. He would have nothing, no one, to hide behind.

The ideal polity Linguet was depicting was a benevolent paternalistic monarchy where the mutual interest of rulers and subjects dictated that all subjects abandon their political pretensions and obey unconditionally, and that, in return, the ruler, the only sovereign, protect threatened proprietors against rapacious privileged elites while limiting all property rights in the interest of the welfare of propertyless masses. Linguet grounded his political model in a social matrix which he had analyzed already, in his *Théorie des lois civiles,* in his theories of how societies originated in acts of usurpation, were structured into social classes, and progressed through class conflict into civil war. The "Asiatic" model, constructed in part following sixteenth- and seventeenth-century theories of monarchical sovereignty and medieval traditions of Christian kingship, provided Linguet with a frame of reference and a point of departure for his radical critiques of blueprints for a free and open society, economy, and culture capped by a political administration subservient to principles of *laissez-faire.* And this conservative political theory, in combination with a social theory that generated its own revolutionary dynamics, supported Linguet's formulations of violent remedies for intolerable contradictions and inequities that triumphant liberal policies were generating in French political society as well as his proposals for the preservative reform of existing institutions.[37]

When Linguet listed welfare benefits that the benevolent Asiatic monarchs provided for their propertyless subjects, he excluded subsistence. The ruler did not guarantee that (although, in principle, he could have—by virtue of his power of eminent domain, and precisely because every subject and every subject's property was *his* property). In Asia, rice was always available for everyone; it was cheap; anyone could grow his own. "They live only on rice there, and one of the most remarkable benefits of nature, as well as one of the wisest features of their politics, was never to have allowed wheat to be known there" (*LL,* 90-91).

Asia, Linguet added immediately, was not France (*LL,* 91-92). Economic and psychosomatic determinants of political culture there dictated that the ground (if not the full content) of any politics of welfare in France must be a politics of subsistence. Linguet's task was to analyze these determinants.

The French, along with other Western Europeans, Linguet announced in 1770, are addicted to wheat and bread; even worse, the staff of life is a poison. "We live by bread, we Occidentals; our existence depends upon this drug, whose principal ingredient is putrefaction, [and] which we are forced to adulterate with a poison [yeast] to make it less unwholesome..." (*LL,* 91).

The French addiction to grain and bread was a local affliction; bread was unknown not only in the Middle East, but in three-quarters of the world (*RDM,* I, 158-63; *LL,* 92). The addiction was not exclusively physical, it was psychosomatic; but was it incurable? Linguet flirted with the hope that it was not, and that a stiff dose of panophobic propaganda might shock France back into physical and political health.[38]

Linguet opened his campaign against bread with a systematic chemical and economic analysis. Bread was an exorbitantly priced poison. The grain used in its preparation could not even be sown before the earth had been worked over. As soon as the grain germinated, it was attacked by worms, devoured by insects. Frosts and floods easily uprooted and destroyed it. Blight and hail damaged it. The grain that survived this assault of the elements had to be turned and stacked in bundles by workers hunched in back-breaking labor. If the grain survived the rains and the dampness of night, it had to be thrashed in barns: "It must be submitted to the flail; by dint of violent effort it is torn from the asylum of where nature has hidden it." Once beaten, sifted, and passed through the sieve, it was inedible. It was carted to the mill, ground on the millstone. The flour that was produced was kneaded. Then "a mixture of soured and stinking paste is introduced, without which, we are told, it would have no taste...." After it was baked, one had a product which must be eaten at once because it soon acquired "the hardness of stone and the insipidity of sand if it is kept from humidity, or if it is not, it is covered with mold in a week.... There is the natural history of this admirable commodity which we have called bread." If the grain spoiled, or was contaminated, and if the police who were ordered to confiscate it were kept at bay, then a hundred thousand men would be poisoned "to spare a loss of a few crowns to a rich imprudent man" (*RDM*, I, 163-68; *PB*, 18-24).[39]

France's "little septentrional production" was a hotbed of corruption. It had contaminated an entire culture: "Of all the substances the stomach of man can digest without being wrecked immediately, perhaps none is more dangerous than bread. It is so physically, it is so morally, it is so even if you want to look at it only from the viewpoint of politics."[40]

Bread was physically lethal. "You will be convinced that the plow opens the tomb of our species in tracing the furrows where wheat grows." Bread thickened the blood. It impeded circulation. Indigestion caused by bread was fatal. Besides, bread afforded only short-term nourishment; it destroyed the body in the long run.[41] Linguet insisted that the most casual comparison of the stamina, physique, comportment, and numbers of inhabitants of regions where grain was cultivated and consumed with the condition of people living in prairies and wooded mountains and drawing their subsistence from plants growing there would clinch his argument (*RDM*, I, 168, 177-78, 185-90; *PB* 28-29, 37-44).

The moral effects of bread were not any less fatal: "As for the moral side,... I see that slavery, despondency of spirit, lowness of every kind in the little fellow; despotism, the unbridled furor of destructive possession, contempt for men among the great, are the inseparable companions of this habit of eating bread, and emerge from the same furrows in which grain grows" (*RDM*, I, 178-79; *PB*, 30). Everyone was fettered to the lethal grains: both the producer and the consumer—but especially the consumer, who feared death in every grain shortage, in every work layoff; who was torn by anguish over the question of his daily physical existence (*PB, 32*). Watch the day laborer as he drags the ploughshare through the wheat fields: "…if he wasn't in the habit of walking on his two feet, you would often have trouble distinguishing him from the animals he directs" (*RDM*, I, 189-90; *PB*, 44).[42]

Not only was bread physically and morally lethal, it was politically lethal as well. Political systems could be evaluated and their stability measured in terms of the subsistence commodities consumed there. Linguet prefaced this original essay in comparative politics with a graphic depiction of his gastronomic difficulties with English roast beef. "Now a journalist-economist who apparently likes his beef roasted, and his pies stuffed with plums, tells me people in England are better lodged, better dressed, better nourished, than in Asia. *The lowest classes of society on this Island eat abundant portions of* roast beef *and* puddings; from which he nobly concludes that the *trade of being a man is worth more in England than in Turkey,* and consequently, that *the government there is better"* (*RDM*, I, 193-94; *PHG*, II, 213).[43] The reasoning was profound, Linguet granted. And it was true that these tempting English dishes could not be commanded in the Middle East: "But there are some people who would be as content with a good pilaf made with well done lamb, and with good chicken well-simmered, as with a roast beef, all bloody and nauseating in its coagulated grease! There are those who would be better pleased with flavored water ices than with an extract of fermented barley and soured hop" (*PHG*, II, 214).

Here was an international gastronomic guide to political administration. Roast beef, rare, was the specialty of constitutional anarchies. Rice was staple nourishment in the most politically perfect administrations in the world, those of Turkey and Persia, while in the heart of Europe, millions of Frenchmen, subjects in an imperfectly absolute monarchy, were dying of luxury on an epicure's diet of bread: "…from the time the wretched grain forming its base lies hidden in the bosom of the earth, to [the instant] a baker displays it in his shop, [bread] demands the greatest toils as well as the cruellest dependency.…We believe it is impossible to do without it: we are crazy enough to consider it the only nourishment worth of man…but it is also the most certain resource of despotism and the cruelest fetter that ever has been clamped upon Adam's descendants…" (*LL*, 90-92).

Linguet had diagnosed France's national disease as bread addiction. His recommended cure was a more varied diet, but better still, a breadless diet. He even opened an advertising campaign for a variety of bread substitutes—cheap, readily prepared, palatable, immediately available, nonperishable nutrients. He had in mind natural products of the earth or sea, or foods so universally abundant and hardy that every human being could obtain them readily, even in time of national disaster, and keep alive by eating them. Linguet was particularly attracted to rice as a substitute for bread; it happened to be the subsistence commodity of governments Linguet had proclaimed the best administered in the world. Let people eat rice, so easily prepared, and at so little cost, so accessible to every hungry mouth (*PB*, 21-27). Let them eat cassava, ribgrass, bananas, maize, vegetables (*PB*, 9-13). Let them eat fish (*RDM*, I, 182-83). Let them prepare millet, gather chestnuts, eat buckwheat, or potatoes (*PB*, 15-16).[44]

Panophobic propaganda notwithstanding, Linguet never really believed the French addiction to bread was curable. Nothing he could tell the French about bread—that it was physically, morally, and politically dangerous, that it was a poison, that people who ate bananas, fish, rice, and chestnuts were healthier, happier, freer human beings—nothing would stop the French, "les plus grands panivors de l'univers,"[45] from craving bread, from degrading, subjecting, and enslaving themselves to get it, from chaining the nation's political machinery to the task of supplying them with it. "However, I know it well," Linguet lamented, "we will never wean ourselves from the habit of eating it" (*PB*, 44). "...as with these poisons that lead the addict to his tomb, the lack of which would cause death anyway, we can neither renounce it [bread] nor enjoy it" (*LL*, 92).

If the nation was gastronomically enslaved, if France's addiction to bread was unbreakable, then the elder Mirabeau, a physiocratic zealot, was right to insist that "everything holds together in politics." He was right to preach that "all politics takes off from a grain of wheat."[46]

In France, politics, or public administration, could be understood as an applied science of political economy. The most vital issue in French politics was the people's subsistence. It always had been. A politically unorganized people was permanently mobilized on the question of minimum daily requirements for keeping alive. The bread consumers of France formed an interest group, an uninstitutionalized national pressure group. When the government formulated its revolutionary agricultural policy in the 1760s, liberalizing the nation's grain trade and dismantling much of its regulatory apparatus, it also upset traditional assumptions about governments' distributive role, aggravated a permanent popular sensitivity on the subsistence issue (a sensitivity deeply rooted in psychosomatic fears), and contributed to provoking a rash of food riots. The administration made a conspicuous show of its determination to enforce its widely broadcast economic policy changes, even as the subsistence crisis deepened. Its tenacity virtually guaranteed that the people's expression of their one unchanging, unnegotiable demand upon government for bread at a just price would take a violent form.[47]

In his *Réponse aux docteurs modernes*, Linguet expressed that national demand in a conspicuously radical language. He publicized the first principles of an anti-physiocratic, pro-monarchical ideology which both limited and completed the doctrine he had spelled out in his *Théorie des lois civiles* on behalf of kings and insufficiently protected proprietors in the Third Estate. He identified the king's highest interest with a national interest in life; he declared that the monarch's principal political responsibility was that of guaranteeing the people their right to bread; and he proclaimed the inalienable right of this people—a right born of necessity—to test in revolution the legitimacy of regimes which defaulted on that obligation.

Linguet stated a key article in his *économie politique* as a corollary to an axiom in physiocratic economics. Liberal economists and policymakers had declared that government had only one distributive obligation to all subjects: to provide absolute guarantees for their property rights, including an unassailable liberty and security in the possession and disposal of these properties and their fruits. "Is authority," Abbé Baudeau asked in 1768, "anything other than the duty of protecting properites and liberties?"[48] Government filled its distributive obligation to partially or wholly dispossessed subjects when it guaranteed them a property in their physical persons and their time, and a liberty to dispose of both. As the new school of economists and liberal politicians defined it, the property of propertyless men would consist in their possession of their bodies, their manpower, their subsistence-earning potential. You poor people, Condorcet exhorts in one of his earlier lectures to the masses, "...if you are hungry, work for the rich man, he will associate you with his wealth."[49] In the context of the system, men's potential for earning their food was realized naturally, necessarily, eventually, in the course of self-interested operations of buyers and sellers in a free economic market.

How did Linguet define property rights for a population of laboring poor?[50] Not as every person's right to work, but as every person's right to life, to bread, whether he earned it by working, or not. In law, Linguet wrote in his *Réponse aux docteurs modernes,*

> every living being has a right to demand food. His teeth and stomach, these are his license. He holds it from nature, and this is the most respectable of all chancelleries. His first duty, and the most sacred, is to take care for his preservation, to look for his subsistence; from this duty follows the right, when need drives him so sharply as to expose his life, to take possession of everything that can satisfy him. Society has been able to curtail this right: it has been able to determine the manner of enforcing it, to insist on equivalents, to modify the way it is exercised, but it has not been able to annihilate it. [*RDM,* II, 53-54; *PB,* 55.]

In his *Théorie des lois civiles,* Linguet insisted that when society was organized, nature was wiped out. He chanted his *requium mortis* over the rights and liberties men of nature had enjoyed. "Whatever the jurisconsults say, their treatises of natural law are all treatises of servitude. They are the epitaphs of this law and the whole earth is its tomb. There is no place in the world where one might not say, in speaking of it, *hic jacet*" (*L*, I, 351). Now Linguet was boldly resurrecting natural law, the only *natural* law, a law which described the state of man's biological needs and dictated their immediate satisfaction. "Society has been able to curtail this right...but it has not been able to annihilate it." Linguet was by no means the first to express this fundamental maxim. St. Thomas Aquinas gave imperative force to practices deeply rooted in medieval Western culture in his *Summa Theologica,* whether it is lawful to steal through stress of need: "...that which he takes for the support of his life becomes his own property by reason of that need."[51] The physiocrats conspicuously broke with tradition when they embraced an ethic suitable to their new science of political economy. Humanitarian social ethics was not part of the new politics; but then, as Linguet saw the situation, modern statesmen would have to recreate one in defiance of the laws of classical economics and the precepts of a capitalist ethic.

Linguet was not overly scrupulous about acknowledging the sources of his fundamental principles of political economy, but his debt to the social utopian thinkers, Morelly[52] and Meslier,[53] and to Rousseau is undeniable. He rejected the utopians' fantastic otherworldly resolutions of socioeconomic tensions and class wars, but not before adopting something of the outspoken moral indignation that motivated their flight from social injustice.

Rousseau taught in his *Second Discourse* that nature was the preserve of perfectly free human beings. Natural necessity there was not a moral, rational imperative; it was organic. This categorical imperative dictated by the biochemistry of the human stomach marked out an absolutely inviolable domain in which the territorial imperative, the property law expressed in civil law, was without force: "...it is manifestly against the law of nature, however you define it...that a fistful of people is choking on superfluities, while the famished multitude lacks necessities."[54]

The utopians, along with Rousseau, retired from the political scene, their moral strictures intact, to forge paths in nonexistent universes. The philosophizing political economists remained to systematically subordinate the demands of the biological imperative to economic laws governing the operations of a free market.[55] That left Linguet composing revolutionary-sounding manifestos on behalf of the government. These powerful representations of the biological imperative as a right to life, where Linguet may have been projecting, making class typical, a reaction to scarring personal experiences,[56] find their place in a hard-headed political campaign to represent the *thèse royale* as a political philosophy and program capable of reattracting the allegiance of a class of dominated, exploited, and politically alienated persons. Christian humanists and moralists had articulated the interest of that class in staying alive, and the obligation of authority to safeguard it. Executors of a thoroughly secular mercantilist politics and economics had consistently supported the "right to demand food"—until converts to economic liberalism, who were re-placing them in the administration, began throwing a protectionist *économie politique* into question with a new ideology and innovative liberal legislation.

In his *Réprésentations aux magistrats* of 1769, the abbé Roubaud, the phy-siocratic publicist, opposed needs to rights. "I have said it, needs are not rights at all, and rights are before everything, and everything that violates rights is violence and tyranny....I have already said that prior to interests were rights: I will add that the right of a single person must prevail over the interests of all without rights, because justice is the supreme, universal, and unique law."[57] Linguet resolved Roubaud's antithesis between interests and needs on the one hand and rights on the other. He stated this resolution as a first principle of his anti-physiocratic ideology for king and people. The act of satisfying bio-logical needs and protecting one's interest in life is the exercise of a natural right, and the only inalienable property right. Whatever else man is, he is alive, a being endowed with an inalienable *amour de soi.* Life is a right.

Linguet carried this statement of first principles still further. Only one pro-perty right, precisely this right to life, was natural. It was natural because it was grounded in biological necessity. And even then, Linguet argued, the *so-cial* condition of possessing one's only property and one's only right in life, narrowly defined, was both unnatural and reversible—reversible through po-pular revolution: "I present to the unfortunate human beings who form the lowest class in society, and who bear the whole weight of it, the consoling idea that their condition is not natural, that it is a usurpation of their rights, that if they or their posterity have the courage one day to repossess them [their rights] nothing can stop them" (*RDM,* I, 116).

In his *Théorie des lois civiles* of 1767, Linguet stated these themes: in acts of usurpation, expropriation, enslavement, a band of predators first dispos-sessed the multitudes. Modern political societies perpetuated this injustice. They protected properties grounded in theft. They reduced the masses to a property in brute life. Under regimes of economic liberty, they failed to gua-rantee them even that; they offered them freedom instead. Their policies le-gitimated a crime against humanity, against human nature. Under conditions of intolerable duress—which Linguet depicted in graphic detail as the condi-tion of free labor on an open market—an outraged humanity, enlightened by the same philosophers who were programming their exploitation, would summon the force to redress a rank injustice in self-defeating revolution.[58] In the conclusion to his *Théorie des lois civiles,* Linguet cast himself in the role of adviser to the people; he urged them not to risk a destruction of self and society through violence: "suffer and die in chains: that is your destiny." In a pointedly critical review of Linguet's *Lettres sur la "Théorie des lois civiles"* in his *Ephémérides du citoyen* of 1770, Dupont de Nemours called attention to Linguet's depiction of societal order as a tyrannical reign of properties originating in violence and maintained through an almost universal subjugation. He specifically cited Linguet's fatalistic last paragraphs: let the slaves die in chains, consoling themselves for the blows they take by the blows they give... to animals placed still lower down then they in the chain of enslaved being. He made a mockery of Linguet's fatalistic humanism.[59]

In his *Réponse aux docteurs modernes*, Linguet took up the challenge implicit in Dupont's critique. He politicized and radicalized his analyses and gave them ideological coloring and a revolutionary direction. He taught dangerous political lessons drawn from his theories of society's origins in acts of usurpation and subjection, its organization into antagonistic classes of dominators and dominated, and its development through class conflicts. By the measure of their natural rights, presumably to the fruits of the earth which they produced with their labor, the people could have no interest in acknowledging the legitimacy of any political regime, only its provisional acceptability. All regimes originated in criminal acts and perpetuated themselves by exploiting the labor of the dispossessed masses: "...their condition...is a usurpation of their rights...." If this people summoned the courage to challenge fundamentally illegitimate regimes in revolution, it could not lose. Victory and repossession, not self-destruction in anarchy and chaos, not pain and death in chains, would be its destiny—"...nothing can stop them."

"While they are waiting I give them reasons to have patience. I make them see the very masters who dominate them enchained by them, not by any metaphysical networks, but by a sensitive and palpable interest, and obliged to treat them well in order to get work from them..." (*RDM*, I, 116-17).

I submit to these wretched individuals a consoling idea. While they are waiting, I give them reasons. I make them see. I demonstrate to them. Linguet had calculated his effects. He wanted to leave the impression with his enemies that *he* knew how to give expropriated, exploited masses lessons in natural rights, natural law, and rebellion; that he really could enlighten a Fourth Estate, although enlightening the people and inciting them to revolution were not his purposes. He believed he was serving the administration; his intention was to provide Terray with an ideological grounding for his policies. He did not believe the administration could re-cement a fractured political relationship between king and nation merely by enforcing anti-physiocratic legislation. Any simple restoration of the *status quo ante* was out of the question. The liberal *économistes* had seen to that, but so had the conservative *parlementaires*.

Linguet accused the physiocrats of redefining the obligations of kings and the rights of subjects. They had translated the maxims of their system into economic policy. They enforced the policy. They preached the maxims everywhere. "Civil society is a vast prison in which only the guards of the prisoners are free," Linguet had written in his *Théorie des lois civiles*. What were the guards doing? They were occupying themselves by posting "touching descriptions" of liberty on the grills of the prisoners' cells (*L*, II, 517). At precisely this moment, jailbreak was most to be feared. The guards had taught the prisoners to calculate and compare. They had only to contrast their condition with the chimera of liberty depicted by the philosophes among their guards. What was making their condition physically intolerable, Linguet insisted, was that now they believed they were dying in their cells, dying of economic freedom, of *laissez-faire* and *laissez-passer*. Physiocrats had joined the front ranks of the guards.

> All of a sudden [Linguet wrote in 1771] the *économistes*, that is to say, the abbés, gentlemen, clockmakers, provincial judges, etc., arrived on the scene to teach the millers that they didn't know anything about milling; and the people that their appetites were too great; and the bourgeois that they were putting too much good wheat flour into their loaves: and everybody applauded.
>
> From their bakery, they have moved on into jurisprudence and the laws. With hands still all whitened from their dough and their milling, they have taken it into their heads to feed upon our legislation; from behind their millstones well or badly maintained, we were wildly surprised to see their flour-dredged Solons emerging with their pretensions to reforming the entire political machinery: and still, we applauded. [*RDM*, I, 9]

The crusading political economists had found the road to Versailles, their new Jerusalem. Physiocracy was not simply a science of economics. It was an ideology. Preaching it, the school's propagandists liberalized the language of politics, and they tried to convince the nation that the king was speaking it (*RDM*, I, 124-25, 129-30), that he had abandoned the principles and programs of administrative intervention and regulation to embrace the politics of liberty.

Now, on the other side, the consistently vituperative language which Linguet used to attack the parlements as the people's enemies betrayed his very real fear that that was not what the people were thinking. "These phantoms [the parlements] ...have become the true enemies of the people, the surety of their slavery."[60] Linguet deliberately and conspicuously expressed the principles of his *économie politique* in a seductive, radical language which represented to authorities at all levels and to a literate public at large the needs, interests, and strength of disaffected subjects: subjects whom the physiocratic economists had alarmed and alienated from authority with their liberal propaganda and their liberalizing legislation; and subjects whose vital interest in life the *parlementaires* were defending in their own persuasive political vocabulary, following an anti-physiocratic politics that was also a politics of opposition to the monarchy.

Linguet believed that the king, through his network of officers (assuming they adhered to the spirit and the letter of the newly reinstated policing operations) could recapture the allegiance of a partially estranged people. But some of the king's men themselves would have to be reconvinced that regulation made political sense. These converts would have to be won from the camp of the *économistes*. In addition, bonds of trust and allegiance would have to be renewed between the king and his ministers, on the one hand, and, on the other, the officers who had defied these authorities throughout the period of liberalization to remain loyal to regulation. When he presented the case for intervention—for this audience in part, but also for a larger public of Terray's adversaries and supporters—Linguet did not employ traditional rhetoric and reasoning exclusively. In a political atmosphere saturated with liberal propaganda, the rhetoric of paternalism would be unconvincing, almost out of place. Instead, Linguet argued in the vocabulary of a new ideology. He declared that it was the duty of kings to offer the realm's subjects ironclad guarantees of security, and protection for their properties in and right to life.

In formulating his anti-physiocratic first principles, Linguet depicted the biological imperative as a right—the right to a property in life. He radicalized the language of a regulationist political economy. He confronted the liberal philosophers on their own ground, the universe of natural law and natural rights, and demonstrated how, even there, especially there, the case for intervention could be made and must be won for the sake of public order, national security, human life.

Linguet expected that his way of looking at the subsistence question would win supporters for Terray's policies—but only among the elites. He also anticipated that when the people demanded the right to life from their side, that is, without the benefit of the ideological underpinnings with which he had equipped the literate public, they would continue to express a very narrow range of political demands, demands for bread exclusively. Physiocratic policies and publicity in a period of economic crisis might have politicized the nation, but only on one issue. Terray's administration still might bribe the people out of organizing their protests and escalating their demands. The people could be bribed rather cheaply. In 1774, in his *Du pain et du bled,* Linguet used the term "compensation" [*dédommagement*]. The people, the "lower classes," could be compensated for expropriation with bread.

The sole end of political speculations, Linguet wrote, "is to assure to the lower classes who bear the whole burden of society the only kind of compensation that can console them for the privations to which they are condemned. And what is it, this compensation? It is subsistence; it is the opportunity to remain alive..." (*PB*, xxvii-xxviii).

A class of laboring poor still translated liberty as the freedom to obtain twenty-four hours' worth of food, a minimal reserve of strength, measured out in loaves of bread, on which to live by illusions. Its members still believed their property was the stuff of life, and still defined security narrowly as a guaranteed delivery of bread. The laboring poor had asserted no other rights, had made no other distributive demands on government, not yet.

Laissez-faire Politics vs. the Politics of Subsistence: A National Debate

Bread was what the administration had to bargain with. The abbé Terray came to the same conclusion. His design in expanding his administrative operations had been to give himself the option of suspending or limiting property rights whenever the proprietor's unrestrained exercise of them conflicted with the consumer's exercise of his right to obtain food. Linguet offered full polemic support for Terray's policies in his *Réponse aux docteurs modernes*.

Terray's politics of subsistence did not survive the death of Louis XV and the political power struggles of 1774. Louis XVI dismissed Maupeou and Terray, resurrected the parlements, and appointed Turgot as controller general. Turgot, a physiocrat, lost little time in translating the principles of economic liberalism into a remarkable piece of new legislation on the grain trade. His *arrêt du Conseil* of September 13, 1774, returned the nation to the political principles and economic policies of the liberal administrations of the sixties. The wording of the preamble to this *arrêt* was particularly significant. The controller general gave Louis XVI an untraditional language to speak—the language of the sixties. It sounded as though the monarch had switched political principles. Once again, or so it appeared, the king was reinterpreting his political role and redefining his obligations to guarantee his subjects' properties, liberties, and lives. He still called himself a father, his subjects' provider, only now he was making perfectly clear exactly what he was and wasn't going to provide. He committed himself to observing "exact justice," and protecting his subjects' property rights and "legitimate" liberty. To owners of properties in land and grains, he guaranteed rights to possess and dispose of both freely; to owners of labor power exclusively, subsistence-earning potential, he guaranteed *not* bread, but the right to work. The king, in the language of the new legislation, was a father who taught his subjects what their true interests were, and how their self-interested, self-regulating economic activities satisfied everybody. Everybody was part of the system, including the king; but who was its master? Not the king; not anyone; only Nature.[61]

Physiocracy's most articulate and agressive critic was still Simon Linguet. With the fall of the ministerial triumverate, Linguet lost his tenuous hold on an affiliation with the government,[62] but he stepped up his anti-physiocratic propaganda.[63] He timed the appearance of his *Du pain et du bled,* a revised and abridged version of the *Réponse aux docteurs modernes,* to coincide with the promulgation of Turgot's legislation on the grain trade. He also turned out his compilation of earlier attacks on the parlements, and he issued a revised edition of his anti-Montesquieuan sociology of laws, adding the Estates-General to his list of representative institutions that crushed the masses whose interests they claimed to articulate (*L-1774*, I, 89-92). He was still claiming to represent the king's highest political interests—against physiocrats, against an administration filled with physiocratic sympathizers, against parlements, and against all *corps intermédiaires.*

At the same time, Linguet acquired a new base from which to launch his anti-physiocratic propaganda. Charles-Joseph Panckoucke, the publishing magnate, hired him in September, 1774, to edit the government-licensed *Journal de politique et de littérature.*[64]

Turgot's administration had Linguet under close surveillance almost from the beginning. The physiocratic party also was on guard. In the summer of 1770, Dupont de Nemours, editor of the party's *Ephémérides,* branded the author of the *Lettres sur la "Théorie des lois civiles"* a calumniator of bread, a saboteur of the maximum net product, a public enemy, and a political menace. He did not bother to add that Linguet had taken the liberty of calling him "only the trumpet of a troop of charletans," a "detractor liable to punishment," and had eulogized his journal as a "rhapsody composed without trouble and without judgment" (*LL,* 150, 156, 162).

> And how could men expect to escape from the overflow of his bile? Bread, the *daily bread* that nourishes him, isn't exempt!
>
> But he is trying to establish principles which, if adopted, seem to us calculated to cause the ruination of society and to spread countless misfortunes among all humanity.... One of our principal duties, therefore, is to combat Monsieur Linguet's paradoxes with [reasons] and [examples].[65]

Turgot was more sensitive to Linguet's harassment in the fall of 1774 than Dupont de Nemours had been in 1770. He was more politically vulnerable also. He was trying to enforce an *arrêt* providing for free trade in grains. An assumption behind the legislation was that in the long run a *laissez-faire* policy would stimulate national grain production and bread consumption. At this critical moment, in his *Du pain et du bled,* Simon Linguet, panophobic maniac, began to sabotage the precious grains. He was trying to contaminate them with venom from his pen, to turn the stomachs of twenty-five million Frenchmen. He dared question the *idée fixe* the physiocrats were exploiting, an almost universally held conviction that bread was the Frenchman's staff of life, that without it he would die. He proposed to educate French palates to a taste for exotic bread substitutes—bananas, cassava, fish. In short, he was undermining physiocratic policy.

What was to be done? The book must be censored, of course—but that was impossible. Liberty of thought and liberty of grains were both cherished tenets in the physiocratic faith. Turgot started out with a clever private revenge, although he must have known it wouldn't shame Linguet into public silence.

The controller general had a shelf in his library filled with "imaginary books." This false libarary with its *trompe l'œil* volumes was a joke of his. There were fifty-six entries in the catalogue of titles contained in the false library, of which ten represented delicate little reprisals against the nefarious Simon-Nicolas-Henri Linguet. Turgot's Linguetiana included: *"Hobb. Leviathon novo Comment. illustratum a S.N.H. Linguet, tom. 1 et 2"*; *"Délices du gouvernement turc, dédiées au Kislar-Aga,* par S.N.H. Linguet, tom. 1 et 2"*; *"Draconis Leges notis perpet.,* illustratae a S.N.H. Linguet"*; *"Morale fondée sur la force,* par S.N.H. Linguet, tom 1 et 2"*; *"Dangers du pain,* par S.N.H. Linguet"*; *"S.N.H. Linguet, de Suppliciorum ingeniosa diversitate Diatribe."*[66] Turgot's residence was well frequented, but still, his was a private, not a public, false library. As it turned out, dainty intellectual teasers were hardly appropriate weapons of assault against Linguet's *Du pain et du bled.*

The administration would have to escalate its campaign and publicly ridicule *Du pain et du bled* into oblivion; that would be a respectable liberal and philosophic alternative to suppressing it outright. Toward the end of 1774, the abbé Morellet undertook this task for Turgot's greater peace of mind and more certain vengeance.[67] Simon Linguet's *Du pain et du bled*—this was the abbé's profound appraisal—was a *théorie du paradoxe.* Everything that Linguet had ever written was precisely that.[68]

Linguet had refuted the accusation too many times before. He was beyond intimidation although not above taking immediate measures of reprisal. Having obtained the tacit consent of the lieutenant-general of the Paris police, Jean-Charles-Pierre LeNoir (who was only too willing to stab physiocratic policymakers in the back, using Linguet as a foil), Linguet rushed into print with his *Théorie de libelle; ou l'art de calomnier avec fruit; dialogue philosophique pour servir de supplément à la "Théorie du Paradoxe."*[69] Four thousand copies of the work were in circulation when Turgot overrode LeNoir to suppress it.[70]

Linguet's *Du pain et du bled* continued to circulate. The physiocrats were upset by the panophobic propaganda contained in it, but Linguet was the first to admit that the people would not be. No epithet he could apply to bread, no substitute he might offer for it, would shock or tempt the nation out of its deadly addiction. "cependant, je le sais bien, nous ne nous corrigerons jamais de l'habitude d'en manger" (*PB,* 44). The physiocrats were capitalizing upon a national lust for bread. They profited from it, though they had not generated it.

For Linguet, the crucial question in this debate between him and the physiocrats, once he resigned himself to the necessity of talking grain and bread with them, was whether in applying their principles they would be in a position to satisfy the national demand for these commodities.

Most of Linguet's three-hundred-page *Du pain et du bled* is a systematic *anti-physiocratie*, a point-by-point refutation of the physiocratic system for creating and distributing an abundant supply of grain for a nation of bread consumers.[71] Linguet challenged physiocratic arguments with the thesis that the laboring poor—"the lowest class," bearing the "whole weight" of society— were programmed to be victimized daily under a physiocratic system, whether it functioned perfectly or imperfectly. The "lowest class" was victim of its own psychosomatic needs, but also of an iron law of wages and a permanent wage-price lag—laws of self-interested economic operations. Should the physiocratic system break down, even momentarily, every option open to impoverished people who equated bread with life—emigration, death, revolt— would be equally fatal to any administration.

Physiocratic policy-makers were ready to give free play on a free market to grain producers and traders operating on the principles of classical economics and a capitalist ethic. Linguet's first point was this: when the grain trader actually followed the dictates of self-interest, he would create artificial scarcity to raise prices and multiply profits. He would withhold grains which, according to the *économistes*, he was supposed to be circulating. Physiocratic systematizers predicted that once owners had their net product and an insured *bon prix*, they and all other employers would raise the salaries of their work force to meet soaring bread prices. In fact, Linguet insisted, the owners would follow their self-interest, but would be fearful, hence shortsighted. In order to grab their net product immediately, they might even lower wages as prices soared.

In a supposedly self-regulating and harmonious physiocratic system, Linguet announced, the grain merchant directs all his efforts to monopolizing the market, engineering variations in price, and artificially prolonging famines (*PB*, 33).[72] Linguet was exploiting a perfect understanding of how the popular French mentality operated in the face of actual or anticipated food crises. When he evoked images of *monopoleurs* to depict the operations of grain merchants and owners, he was deliberately calling into play a predictable popular dread and hatred.[73]

Political administration was only the science of applying principles of political economy, but Linguet was quick to point out that the economy rested upon a commodity subject to manipulation by self-interested entrepreneurs. If physiocratic theorists-turned-policy-makers gave them free reign to test their laws of production, circulation, and profit, they would not stop short of depriving the people of the only liberty politics could guarantee to it: the liberty to "enjoy" the force of life, the liberty to fill its stomach. The reign of physiocracy would be the most perfect political tyranny on the face of the earth, a tyranny exercised over the physics and chemistry of human existence.

The king who decreed that grain must circulate freely in the realm in search of the highest price, recognizing the omnipotence of the net product, sanctioned not only chronic subsistence crises but also national murder.

Again, recalling and justifying traditional popular suspicions, as if to intimidate reckless administrators, Linguet announced that the speculation in grain commodities so inextricably tied up with the grain trade was the most dehumanized of all the exploits of *homo economicus;* but it was also the most natural. The grain trader operates by accumulating stocks in grain; dearth gives these stores their value. Dearth, contrived or natural, was the source of his profit *(PB, 47).* "It is therefore upon someone's misfortune, and that of the portion of society most to be pitied, that he has made his calculations.... [the trader] has said to himself: I will put a tax upon the misery of the people" *(PB, 49).* He doubles his prices; then he tries to justify a colossal fratricide: "It's true that the workers in this manufactory, the artisans who make this city flourish, the day laborers who fill this countryside, will not have their wages doubled; receiving exactly the same sum as before as the equivalent for their work, they will be foreced into debt to get the same quantity of bread, or to diminish the subsistence of their families by half: but what difference does that make to me" *(PB, 49).*[74]

Even if subsistence crises were self-rectifying, as the physiocrats claimed, even if grain scarcity lasted only until freely circulating grain arrived in poorly provisioned markets, still, the process would take time. Meanwhile, bread prices would rise everywhere, "and beware, the blow has fallen only upon the people" *(PB, 62).* The well-to-do bourgeois did not panic. Either he was well-provisioned in grain or he could afford the daily price whatever it happened to be *(PB, 62-64).* For the day laborer and his seven or eight dependents, these events would herald disaster. Not superfluity, but necessity itself would be grabbed from their reach *(PB, 65).*

The physiocrats moved about in a cosmos that was one vast seller's market. The natural law of this universe was profit, the law of the maximum *net product;* and its by-law was dearth, the most certain guarantor of a high price, the physiocrats' *bon prix.* The *bon prix* was achieved naturally through total liberty: *laissez-faire, laissez-passer (PB,* 80ff.).[75]

From the masses' standpoint, the world was a consumer's market; but the nation, *le peuple,* could not pay the price that gave the agricultural capitalist his maximum net product, his incentive to produce more. The price in question happened to be that of bread. The consumer, then, could not afford to pay the price of life, he could not afford to exist: "But just tell me, when Tantalus, in the midst of the fantastic abundance which surrounded him, beheld water flee from his lips, and apples withdraw as he reached to grasp them, would you then have succeeded in clearly persuading him that he was wrong to complain about the dearth of water and apples, and that this condition was a true abundance for him? The people, this unfortunate people, about whom you affect to speak with such concern, and whom you sacrifice with so little scruple—aren't they, for all your pretty systems, suffering precisely the fate of Tantalus?" (*PB*, 87).

Day laborers needn't fear rising grain prices, the physiocrats argued. The benefits of the net product were all-embracing. They would trickle down to the humblest classes in the form of salary increases. All is for the best. Leibniz was Quesnay's master in the science of engineering cosmic harmonies, and Quesnay was the physiocrats'.

Linguet confronted the physiocrats with a barrage of counter-indications, data for reconstructing social reality and dissolving societal harmonies. Experience, Linguet told the abbé Roubaud, editor of the *Gazette d'Agriculture,*

> this fatal reef of false systems, this incorruptible touchstone of erroneous schemes, could have disabused you; but you have shut eyes and ears to the truth that millions of interpreters exhibited to you; famine, misery, despair, the expatriation that has been desolating our provinces in the ten years since you began to influence their administration, have found in you only insensitive witnesses. You have told the unfortunate men whom your *economics* was killing that they were wrong to die, that with a bit more patience everything would be for the best. Far from attributing these cruel symptoms to liberty, you have cried out that they were [symptoms] of a hidden slavery....

> The scalpel of surgery hacks up only cadavers, yours practices on a living body, a body composed of twenty million beings, three-quarters of whom have been suffering, and suffering horribly for ten years while waiting for your speculations to be solemnly consecrated or proscribed.[76]

Linguet had followed the physiocrats' argument that eventually the day laborer's salary would rise to meet increased costs in subsistence commodities. Scarcity and *le bon prix* would benefit the consumer, sooner or later. Assuming the allegations were true, Linguet argued, *le bon prix* still would be intolerably unjust to the consumer. The net product from which avaricious employers deducted a pittance to increase the laborer's salary was accumulated predominantly from sales of wheat at *le bon prix* to these same laborers. "Don't you see that it is his misery that produced [the grain proprietor's wealth]?...it is from his wages of fifteen *sols* a day that he has been obliged to give the proprietor the means of paying him thirty" (*PB*, 96-97). That was enough of an injustice. In addition, Linguet was ready to document his allegation that the laborer's real salary lagged behind the price of grain and bread. What guarantee did he have, after all, that his calculating employers would raise his wage when scarcity caused a sharp rise in the price of subsistence?

> No, it is not true that the indigent man's wages are raised in the same proportion as the price of the black bread he purchases with so much sweat and tears: it is not even true that they are raised at all....

> Always pressed by the need of the moment, reduced to the alternative of being dead tomorrow of inanition, or fagged out today from work undertaken to earn half their subsistence, they [in this context, "hommes laborieux dévoués aux arts grossiers et nécessaires"] have rented out their scraggy arms at whatever price was named. By the most murderous of all machinations, the value of bread has gone up by half, and the valuation of the efforts which drag it from the bosom of the earth has not varied at all.[77]

In a market regulated by the natural laws of physiocracy, even the iron law of wages broke down.

Ernest Labrousse, in his studies of wages and the price of subsistence commodities in the prerevolutionary years, concluded that increases in the price of bread, "l'élément génerateur par excellence de l'énergie humaine," in most cases, and in most years, far exceeded the pay raises offered the working poor.[78] Linguet began taking account of the signs as early as 1764. By the end of 1774, he had reached the conclusion that the data did not verify physiocratic doctrines and policies. It supported the thesis that the realm was caught up in a grave social crisis.

"In a word," Linguet summed it up, "they pay the poor man only after he himself has paid....This is the most deadly mistake that could ever have been committed in politics" (PB, 98). Between 1764 and 1774, Linguet estimated, bread prices doubled; cultivators' revenues increased; wages of day laborers, domestics, and artisans remained stationary (PB, 113-19).

The physiocrats claimed that with their system in full operation, the grain owner who obtained his bon prix would follow the dictates of self-interest and liberal economics and reinvest his profits in expanded production. He would hire more workers. Linguet insisted that this same owner, if he lived in the countryside, would be more likely to contract his operations than to expend them; he would lay off workers, not hire additional help. He would follow a pre-capitalist self-interest which dictated to him that he emulate aristocratic habits, rather than the ethic and economic operations of the agricultural capitalist. If the profiteering producer lived in the city, he would invest his net product in urban luxuries exclusively. He would be contributing to the progress of urban prosperity and the progress of poverty in the rural work force (PB, 101-2).

The employer knew that the day laborer was at his mercy. "If he does not work today, no matter what the going wage is, he and his family will be dead of hunger tomorrow. So, he goes down on his knees to receive the wage that assures him only half his subsistence...." This rural, proto-proletarian reserve army, as Linguet depicted it, was helpless. Its members could not strike—although the strike, Linguet observed, might have been their best weapon. The legions in this army were absolutely destitute. They had no reserves on which to hold out. Anyway, in competing with one another for work, they would succeed only in lowering their wages still further (*PB,* 116, 123-25).

Was the bourgeois in the city, the cultivator in the countryside, a man of flesh and blood? Then his reaction would be outrage at the spectacle of this human misery. Yet this same entrepreneur was a self-interested calculator. His workers were reduced to depending upon him for their lives. His natural compassion for them was checked by a rational calculation. He could not bring himself to raise the going price of labor for fear that he would lose out when bread and grain prices fell (*PB,* 125-26).

Linguet demanded to know what the freedom of this free man—artisan, loom operator, or domestic—really meant. Public hospitals were overflowing with free men who had come there in the prime of life, to die. And even these asylums might be forced to close their doors as the price of bread rose. At that moment, "...what will be the resource of the artisan, I won't say for living, but for dying?" (*PB,* 128).

They are free! Again, Linguet tried to calculate the functional equivalent of liberty for the laboring poor: "You have never seen horses die of hunger because of an increase in the price of oats.... The same reasoning once applied to the slave....But the agricultural worker[*manœvrier*] who belongs to no one, the agricultural worker whose misery remains unknown, the agricultural worker whom you think you are rid of as soon as you pay him, whose loss injures no one, whose preservation interests no one—you allow him to languish and die in his pigsty without so much as deigning to worry yourselves" (*PB,* 129-30).

Dearth and high prices in 1768 and in the spring of 1775 might have recalled to the ever-sensitive masses the nightmare of death and plague associated with the earlier food crises. The great famine of 1709 remained a living and electric memory. Still, legions of people were not dropping dead in the streets and fields; 1768, 1770, 1775 were not 1709. And yet, physical and psychosomatic factors are hard to dissociate. Correlations of mortality rate with hunger and famine are more easily made in times of absolute disaster than in times of scarcity when people do not die outright. What Linguet had perceived was that people can be consumed by the relentless anguish of uncertainty about the source of their next meal. They can be as much the victims of their dread of starvation as of starvation itself. They can suffer greater agonies from dearth that weakens in times of relative prosperity than from famine that kills in times of national disaster. They are more likely to move from rage into open insurrection in an era of prosperity and abundance than in a period of depression and famine. Linguet had depicted the plight of free, impoverished men and women, victims of socioeconomic conditions and economic policies which intensify their anguish but do not deprive them of the force and signs of life, the prods of hatred, and the strength and incentive to revolt.[79]

Linguet's observations were not lost to the physiocrats. As humanitarians they were uneasy; although as engineers of cosmic harmony, the backdrop against which Linguet insisted a crime against humanity was being played out, they were helpless, or even worse, indifferent with calculation. "The rain that inconveniences the traveller," Quesnay wrote, "fertilizes the earth; and if you calculate without prejudice, you will see that these causes produce infinitely more good than ill; that the evil they cause incidentally results necessarily from the very essence of the properties by which they effect good.[80]

The salaried worker, Turgot announced, would never receive more than a subsistence wage, even in the best of times. His employer "pays him as cheaply as possible, and as he can choose among a huge number of workers, he prefers the one who works most cheaply. Workers are therefore obliged to lower their price in competition with one another. In any case, it must happen, and in truth it does turn out, that the worker's wage is limited to what he needs for obtaining his subsistence."[81] Quesnay's philosophic equanimity in making the same point was unmatchable: "...one profits from the competition of those who fight for work...."[82]

In his *Réponse au mémoire de Graslin,* Turgot figured out what it would cost the entrepreneur to raise his workers' salaries. "We must agree that the more this entrepreneur pays his carters, the bigger the daily wage of his harvesters and other day laborers he employs, the greater his expenditure in charges, and this expenditure is always a deduction from the net product. What should we conclude from this? Isn't this true for all systems?...And is there any inhumanity in agreeing upon a truth that need only be stated to appear evident?"[83] In another context, Turgot tranquilly observed: "The increase in prices in years of dearth not only enters for nothing in fixing the salary scale, but it tends rather to diminish it. In truth, the misery of the multitudes banishes their laziness, and makes labor so necessary to them, that the price [of labor] falls."[84] If the worker really was starving, Turgot suggested, let him send his wife and children out to work to supplement the paternal pittance.[85]

Nonetheless, it was Turgot who questioned a key principle in the *économistes'* system when he called attention to Linguet's anti-physiocratic critiques in 1771:

> It is a terrible truth that in all conditions of known things, the limit of the population is always misery. One would hope that were not the case, but the way to get to that point poses a problem which has not yet been resolved.
>
> If what Linguet said about slavery had been looked upon as a notice posted to philosophes and humane politicians that this

problem was still to be resolved, perhaps people wouldn't have treated his *Théorie des lois* with such contempt. He had to be refuted by proving that slavery didn't resolve the problem and by searching out another solution, but he must be given some credit for having directed attention to the inadequacy of known solutions.[86]

The most deadly and inadequate of known solutions, Linguet insisted, was the physiocrats' *économie politique.*

Slavery was not Linguet's answer. It was simply the most devastating weapon in his arsenal. It was not for having enslaved men that the golden age was golden; and it could not be the policy of modern administrators to forge the chains to re-enslave them. The institution of domestic slavery represented Linguet's irony-laden recollection of a time when slavery still depicted the estate of the lowest order of human beings on earth: "In our cities in Europe, in these retreats of liberty, enlightenment, order, men are treated quite a bit worse than horses and dogs" (*PB*, 131).[87]

"I have read recently," wrote Voltaire in his *Questions sur l'Encyclopédie,* article *Esclavage,*

> on Mont Krapack where everyone knows I dwell, a book written in Paris, full of intelligence, of paradoxes, of opinions, and of courage....In this book slavery is openly preferred to domesticity, and above all to the free estate of the day laborer. [The author] there pities the fate of these unfortunate free men who gain their livelihood where they want to by the labor man was born for, and which is the guardian of innocence as well as the consolation of life. No one, the author tells us, is concerned with their nourishment, with helping them; the masters, on the contrary, nourished and cared for their slaves as well as they cared for their horses. This is true, but the human species much prefers to take care of itself rather than to be dependent; and horses born in forests prefer them to stables.[88]

Let's leave it to the people whose destiny we are fighting over, Voltaire suggested, to decide whether they would rather be free or enslaved:

> Question the vilest day laborer, covered with tatters, nourished on black bread, sleeping on straw in a half-opened hut; ask him whether he would rather be a slave, better nourished, better dressed, better boarded; not only would he answer by drawing back in horror, but there are even some to whom you wouldn't dare put the question.
> Now ask a slave whether he would want to be liberated, and you will see what he will answer. And as easily as that, the question is decided.[89]

From Linguet's perspective, the alternatives Voltaire held out would not have been live options. Linguet had depicted the condition of wage-earning laborers, farmhands, workers in manufactories, artisans, impoverished, near-property-less peasants—emancipated persons who did not have the luxury of a choice between freedom and unfreedom. Calculating monarchs and their policymakers had sold liberty to their ancestors; the direction of historical progress was irreversible. And now, self-interested philanthropists and philosophic economists were completing their emancipation. It was not worthwhile to anyone who had a voice, that is, a pecuniary interest in the matter, to re-enslave them. The physiocrats had already reached that conclusion by applying their economic calculus.[90] Linguet's purpose in invoking his notorious paradox, *free men in modern societies are more perfectly enslaved than subjugated men were in slave societies,* was to throw into glaring relief the real choices open to authority, on the one hand, and to the emancipated, impoverished masses, on the other. Without altogether halting or reversing economic development, the government must make progress compatible with the preservation of life in the work force, source of all national productive strength, or prepare itself for economic paralysis, political crisis, and eventually, society's collapse.

Under a physiocratic administration, Linguet believed, the people's only possible spokesmen in the ranks of the governors would be officials who were willing to violate property laws for the duration of food crises, practicing a politics of insubordination on the people's behalf—unless the people themselves intervened, practicing a politics of violence on their own behalf.

When the people's food supply is threatened, the grain trader who yesterday owned his granary is today only a trustee: "...his prerogative, as all others without exception, gives way to a right even more sacred, source or reef of all rights, necessity....The partial property of the master of several sacks of grain is subordinate to the universal property which a whole body of people has over the soil it occupies and over the fruits that grow there" (*PB,* 66, 67, 69).

The practical application of these fundamental principles followed inexorably in Linguet's anti-physiocratic *économie politique.* Government officials charged with policing grains must disregard the decrees of a physiocratic administration; they must enforce laws of nature and necessity. "March, fathers of the people, protectors of the poor. Combat the monster, tear his prey from him. Don't let yourself be affected by his roars at that instant when the hand of justice seizes him....despise their vain efforts [those of the grain hoarders], and do not be any less firm or less tranquil about the legitimacy of an expedition upon which the welfare of your compatriots depends" (*PB,* 76-77).

Another option remained—revolution—the people's way of testing the legitimacy of regimes practicing a politics of economic liberty that threatened their property in life. Linguet explored it openly in his *Journal de politique et de littérature* in one of a series of three letters to the abbé Roubaud (the physiocrat who edited the *Gazette d'agriculture*). This correspondence deals with Turgot's *arrêt* of September 13, 1774.[91]

In his third letter to Roubaud, in the middle of a discussion of suppressed rights to collect market fees on grain, Linguet recalled a passage from the abbé's *Représentations aux magistrats*: "I have said it, needs are not rights at all and rights are before everything...."[92] Abruptly, for the space of a paragraph, Linguet changed the subject. He read Roubaud's maxim as a paraphrase for the new administration's policy of protecting the inviolability of private properties in grain; and he declared that if the government persisted in guaranteeing property rights that violated the biological imperative—the people's right to life—the people's political response would be revolution.

> It would be hideous to decide that an entire nation, or the most essential part of the individuals who compose it, must be sacrificed without pity to the self-interested caprice of one or several misers who would place impossible conditions on the opening of their granaries. The great law, the most sacred of laws, is the *salut du peuple*. The most vital of all properties is that in life. There are no longer any rights, there no longer can be any when it [life] is compromised by hunger; and in this terrible situation, the screams of unfortunate men would call down thunderbolts to break through these pitiless storehouses if the administration, too blinded, persisted in defending them.[93]

Linguet had given a new name to these "unfortunate individuals" forming the "lowest class of society" and bearing the full weight of it. He called them the nation. He had argued earlier that the king must identify his highest political interest with the national interest in life. But Turgot had given the king another identity: the king was an instrument of a self-regulating *économie politique*. In a system where the king was a slave to natural laws, or in Linguet's phrase, where the administration was "blinded," the nation became politically sovereign. It exercised the distributive function of government for itself—suspending property rights and declaring all men economic and political equals in need.

Linguet's third installment of his answer to Roubaud was his last. Turgot suppressed the sequels.[94] He suspended his liberal policies toward the press to protect his administration's liberal economic programs.

Paradoxes and Crises in Political Development: from the Politics of Subsistence to the Politics of Welfare

Early in 1775, Voltaire published a *Petit écrit sur l'arrêt du Conseil du 13 septembre 1774 qui permet le libre commerce des blés dans la royaume*.[95] He publicly declared himself one of Turgot's most vocal supporters.[96] He was shocked that Simon Linguet, "a man of much intelligence, who appears to have pure intentions, but who perhaps allows himself too much of a propensity for paradoxes," had taken so vehement a position against free commerce in grains. Linguet's contention in his letter to Roubaud, that the people were at the point of starvation, left Voltaire incredulous: "Whatever people say, I have never remarked that any death resulted uniquely from inanition. It is a truth only too well recognized that more men die of debauchery than of hunger. In a word, it has never been such a waste of time to complain about all this as it is today." Even in the direst scarcity, the people had infinite resources: chestnuts, barley, rice, and potatoes.[97]

Let them eat chestnuts! There was a philosophic and humanitarian prescription! But they could not eat chestnuts. They refused to eat chestnuts. That had been Linguet's point in his *Du pain et du bled*. Physiocratic propaganda only reinforced a national *idée fixe*, the people's belief that they would die without *bread*. Their ailment was not physical, it was psychosomatic. A prescription of chestnuts was not a cure; it would function exclusively as an incitement to mass hysteria. Only more bread would do, larger doses of leavened poison.

All of politics takes off from a grain of wheat, Mirabeau had proclaimed; and all of physics and morality too, Linguet would have conceded. Bread was the poison men could not do without. In practical terms, men were dying every time they thought they were dying, and whenever they were at the edge of revolt to prevent themselves from dying. This was hardly the moment to persuade them that their stomachs were not quite empty, and the resources for filling them not yet completely exhausted, that the staff of life hung from a chestnut tree.

Voltaire was not convinced. At the height of the *guerre des farines* of April and May, 1775, a spate of food riots in the region around Paris, Voltaire published his *Diatribe à l'auteur des "Ephémérides,"*[98] a piece addressed to the abbé Baudeau, editor of the recently reorganized *Ephémérides,* the *Nouvelles Ephémérides économiques.* He praised Turgot, and emphasized the importance to humanity of reforms in the French agricultural system undertaken at the controller general's direction. He attempted to cut down the anti-physiocrats and struck several blows against *l'infâme.* He refused to take grain warfare very seriously, minimizing the importance of popular violence provoked by scarcity, soaring grain and bread prices, and persistent, frequently confirmed rumors of grain hoarding and speculation. He indicted fanatic priests, charging them with inciting and directing drunken mobs to confiscate and dump grain in order to discredit Turgot's ministry and the philosophes' work of enlightenment. Voltaire had the solution to all food crises in the realm: a more industrious cultivation of the soil and fewer priests. The tone and content of the *Diatribe* suggest that Voltaire ignored or summarily dismissed *taxation populaire,* price controls imposed by the people on grain and bread, and that he made nothing of violent incidents marking the *guerre des farines* as the most serious of all immediately prerevolutionary popular political manifestations.[99] He had little grasp on the operations of popular mentality during this crisis; he felt absolutely no sympathy with the rioters.[100]

All along, Linguet had been lecturing on this question as though it were a matter of life for the masses and survival for the crown. He depicted conditions of misery and degradation among the working poor, especially in the rural population; and he tried to measure both the people's threshold of tolerance for suffering and their potential for rebellion (*PB*, 211-12). He did not encourage a people's revolution. He forecast such a revolution, he legitimated it, but he did so within the framework of an ideology and economic program he believed would ward it off.

In his anti-physiocratic ideology, Linguet identified the monarch's highest political interest with a national interest in and right to biological life, and the king's will with the general will as life force (*PB*, 69, 55, 76-77). He realized, of course, that the king must intervene with more than a political faith. He must use authority and the machinery of government to resolve a national economic crisis. He must cleanly reject the politics of liberty and embrace a politics of intervention. The administration's task would be threefold. First, it would have to draft and enforce legislation guaranteeing all propertyless or near-propertyless wage-earners that whatever their daily wage was, they would be able to purchase their daily bread with it (*PB*, 216). The government could execute this policy by fixing both the price of grains and the price of labor; or it could insist that before the price of subsistence was raised, the price of labor "which alone facilitates its purchase" be raised (*PB*, 239-42). At the same time, administrators would have to encourage agricultural enterprises, making sure the cultivator received a return equal to the amount of his advances plus an "honest profit" (*PB*, 216). And Linguet believed they should go even further, actually protecting and encouraging small-scale agricultural production in preference to large-scale exploitation. These policies would have the double effect of frustrating agricultural capitalists in their quest for economic dominion and political influence and forestalling a dangerous destabilizing trend toward rural proletarization. Linguet denied that such a policy would affect total agricultural yield adversely (*PB*, 245-54), and he did not believe that it was incompatible with development in the industrial and commercial sectors of the economy. On the contrary—and this was his third point—the administration would have to coordinate its policy of intervention in the agricultural sector with long-range planning for national industrial and commercial growth. All wealth did not come from the earth, physiocratic systematizing notwithstanding (*PB*, ch. XIX). The adminsitration that intended to encourage manufactures and the development of new industry would have to guarantee not *le bon prix* but *le bas prix*. Only if the cost of subsistence remained low could the price of urban labor be kept down without wiping out the urban laboring classes. Only on the condition that cheap labor was linked with cheap bread and low grain prices could the cost of manufactured goods be kept down and their price remain competitive on an international market (*PB*, 222, 241-43).

Political economy henceforth would have to be a principal concern of an administration serving the mutually exclusive interests of antagonistic socio-economic classes—the possessor class for whom the ideal political system would function to protect dominions and the fruits of dominion, including profits; and the class of dispossessed persons, whose interest in a system which perpetuated its daily exploitation indefinitely could be won, if at all, only by ironclad guarantees of adequate indemnification.

The upper limit of "adequate" indemnification could never be fixed absolutely. It would always vary with time, and place, and most important, with the level of the masses' political consciousness and political expectations. The lower limit of indemnification was never open to question. It was bread.

The masses believed that without bread, they could not continue to live. The ideologues who promised them liberty and delivered the right to work, who guaranteed their property in labor power, but not subsistence, risked precipitating popular upheavals, revolutions for food. But by 1774, Linguet half-believed that the masses, the people, were not going to live by bread alone, not for very much longer. They were being enlightened daily, by necessity, by philosophes, by économistes. Linguet stated the core of this conviction in his Théorie des lois civiles of 1767: "Why can't you see that it will outrage the unfortunate captives to post touching descriptions of the happiness they would enjoy if they were free on the very bar that holds them in captivity?" (L, II, 517). "What then is the aim of your discourses. I suffer, and according to you, I need not, even more, I must not suffer. I perish in chains and you cry out to me that no one has the right to bind me" (L, II, 519).

Physiocratic economists, encyclopedists, philosophes—all these national educators, bearers of enlightenment and popularizers of liberal ideologies—were about to precipitate a revolution of rising popular expectations. If one had not taken place yet, that was a political miracle. Linguet tried to warn Roubaud in December, 1774: "...will they ["les peuples"] look favorably upon the maintenance of what they have been taught to view as an unbearable disorder? To the pain of their captivity will be joined the sentiment of the injustice that perpetuates it forever. For all your discussions they will have gained only the deadly knowledge of the weight of their chain, and the impossiblility of breaking it. Now I ask you, what will be the outcome of this terrible position?"[101]

Nothing enraged and alarmed Linguet more than the physiocrats' crash programs for teaching the people their interests, converting them to physiocracy with evidence. He did not think they really would win the masses over. On the contrary, he broadcast the political consequences of their inevitable failure to attach those to whom they were preaching the calculus of interest. Once educated, the "lowest class" would know too much to commit itself to physiocracy.[102] The physiocrats' political faith, which promised the people everything—liberty, happiness—and delivered nothing, not even bread, not even the guarantee of a subsistence wage to buy bread with, would be incapable of binding the general will of an enlightened people. The physiocrats were educating the masses, but they never could convert them. But neither could Linguet with his ideology. Obliquely, he had admitted as much to Roubaud in December, 1774: "...will they [les peuples] look favorably upon the maintenance of what they have been taught to view as an unbearable disorder?"[103]

One consequence of the revolution of rising popular expectations that Linguet seemed to be predicting or diagnosing would be the people's repudiation of the party of physiocrats which had played so central a role in engineering a popular political awakening. But another outcome might be an enlightened people's repudiation of the politics of subsistence. Why should the masses embrace an ideology in which their rights to liberty, property, and happiness (goods the liberal publicists promised and protected) were equated with the right to biological life? An indiscriminate enlightenment was relegating the politics of subsistence to the rank of an ideologically bankrupt proclamation of natural necessity.

In his anti-physiocratic *économie politique*, Linguet had worked out a resolution to a national economic crisis—but only to discover and diagnose a crisis in French political development at the core of that resolution. When Linguet publicized what he believed was the government's intention to reestablish its regulatory machinery to handle its distributive functions, his principal objective was to strengthen and widen the base of the administration's support among a population alienated by the government's innovative agricultural policy during the sixties. He sensed a heightened political awareness, sensitivity, and hostility among the people—a consciousness he nonetheless believed was narrowly focused on a single issue, the bread question. The political crisis he seemed to be uncovering was this: the masses' mobilization under the impact of enlightenment, economic policy innovations, and food crises was outrunning the institution-building and expansion of government functions he originally believed would satisfy national distribution demands, and was threatening the programs and ideology of the politics of subsistence with a premature obsolescence.[104]

In December, 1774, Linguet had no resolution for a paradox that expressed his understanding of a crisis in French political development. The best he could come up with was a two-pronged stopgap measure. His first prong was force, "a coercive force, which at least subjugates actions even if wills escape it. It might be helped along by exhortation which persuades, but it demands in addition a palpable and mechanical authority which subjugates" (*PB*, 288).

His second prong was a collusion with philosophes and economic doctors to withhold or even reverse enlightenment. All parties to the national debate on political economy must stop disseminating propaganda to educate the masses and work ideological conversions. "En deux mots, Monsieur," Linguet told Roubaud, "les Legislateurs sont des Dieux pour la Société." [105] The principles behind legislation, even its content, shouldn't be made to matter to the people. The people's political belief—if one's aim was to attach the people to a political system—would have to consist in a worship of the lawgiver, not in an ideological commitment to his laws.

> Believe me, nothing in excess; for three-fourths of mankind, it's enough to know how to obey. I can see that it is in your interest to make philosophers of them, and philosopher-*economists* at that; but again, believe me, one of two things happens: either once they were educated, the disciples would take leave of their spades and their plows to argue with their *masters* over the best way to sow grain or care for it, mill it, and then govern those who sow it, who care for it, who turn it into flour; or the *masters*, returning to the only true maxims of politics, would go into the villages and weed out this poison plant which turns all who breathe its odor into madmen; they would go into huts and tear up the books they filled them [the huts] with; they would preach publicly to these men who have touched the tree of life, and have become ashamed of their nudity, telling them that these more profound researches are useless, and that for them, evidence must be reduced to the exhortations of their pastor. [*PB*, 305-6]

The trouble with that advice, as Linguet knew only too well, was first, that bread addiction was an incurable national malady, and second, that enlightenment was infectious and irreversible. Pastors too had become philosophes, "docteurs modernes," as Linguet himself observed (*PB*, 310-2). And Simon Linguet, adviser to monarchs and crown officials, who condemned the philosophies of *économistes, parlementaires,* and *encyclopédistes* and excluded their liberties from his model political system, nonetheless contributed with his dissertations on the obligations of authorities and the inalienable rights of subjects to a literature that anticipated an enlightenment of the people and legitimated their revolutions for the recovery of security—a freedom from want.[106]

With every attempt he made to resolve the crisis of political development in 1774, Linguet was becoming more deeply ensnared. It was not until three years later, when he established his political journal, the *Annales politiques, civiles, et littéraires du dix-huitième siècle,* that Linguet began to work his way out.

Linguet advertised the *Annales* as an organ independent of all the authorities of the earth. He published it in exile, from London. He said he would use it to establish himself as the people's protector and teacher.[107] That boast was a threat, but it was clearly an empty one. Linguet had no way of making good on it. Anyhow, he wanted to do something else. When the Establishment left him with no other choice, Linguet acted like a rebel, advertising himself as an unpurchasable independent; but by 1777, he had identified himself as an administrative theorist and publicist whose special knowledge made his advisory and propaganda services indispensable to authority. What he had to sell was insight into elite and popular mentality and behavior, knowledge of societal institutions, and mastery of administrative principles and operations. He handled this knowledge as a power. In his *Réponse aux docteurs modernes* and in his *Du pain et du bled,* he had shown how special knowledge could be used to bolster authority, or to subvert it, although what he wanted for himself was the opportunity to serve the king and save the monarchy, on his own terms.[108]

Linguet used the *Annales* over a period of fifteen years (1777 through 1792) to publicize his plans for rescuing monarchical politics from ideological bankruptcy with a politics to attach propertied subjects and with a popular politics, a politics of subsistence. He presented progressively more complete programs for fusing the interests of king and people. In the process, he exploded his original concept of subsistence—the people's minimum daily requirements measured out in loaves of bread. He replaced it with an ideology and politics of welfare.

Briefly, his plan was to transform the monarchy into a welfare state, and to commit it to recognizing and guaranteeing the people's property in and right to life—and he was giving that right to life progressively broader constructions.[109] The adminstration in a social-welfare state could recapture and hold the nation's political allegiance by delivering full compensation for expropriation, compensation in the form of the security of welfare, a commodity whose material and nonmaterial contents would have to be changed with escalations in popular political expectations and demands. Publicizing the doctrine of welfare, Linguet made his final commitment to monarchical politics and a first commitment to revolutionary politics for a Third Estate and a Fourth Estate in France. He placed his political faith in administration. The real powers behind the sovereign, any sovereign, from king to people, would be first-rate administrators. Responding to changes in political expectations triggered by enlightenment as well as by interrelated crises of development in the economic, social, and political sectors, these master political manipulators would direct the machinery of government to the task of distributing bribes and compensations to the people.

Preaching a secular faith, a politics of welfare (the people's right not just to life, but to a good life, and to the goods of life), executive authority would have a fighting chance at least to convert this "lowest class" to the political regime, if only provisionally, and ward off the spectre of a revolution that Simon Linguet forecast, legitimated, and dreaded nonetheless, a people's revolution against all political systems that functioned to safeguard the propertied order of things.

128   The Ideas and Careers of Simon-Nicolas-Henri Linguet

NOTES

1. The full title is: *Mémoire sur un objet intéressant pour la province de Picardie: Ou Projet d'un canal & d'un port sur ses côtes, avec un parallèle du commerce & de l'activité des François, avec celle des Hollandois* (The Hague and Abbeville, 1764); cited hereafter as *MOI*.

2. See Linguet, *Canaux navigables, ou Développement des avantages qui resulteraient de l'exécution de plusieurs projets en ce genre pour la Picardie, l'Artois, la Bourgogne, la Champagne, la Bretagne, et toute la France en général. Avec l'examen de quelques-unes des raisons qui s'y opposent, & c.* (Amsterdam and Paris, 1769), pp. 4-5; 275-88; see also *ibid.*, pp. 219ff.; cited hereafter as *CN*.

3. See George Ruhlman, *Les Corporations, les manufactures et le travail libre à Abbeville au XVIIIe siècle* (Paris, 1948).

4. See Emile Levasseur, *Histoire des classes ouvrières et de l'industrie en France avant 1789*, 2d ed., 2 vols. (Paris, 1901), II, 490-93.

5. Ruhlman, *Les Corporations*, pp. 75-79.

6. Linguet, *Oeuvres diverses de Me Linguet, avocat au Parlement de Paris* (London and Abbeville, 1768); *CN*.

7. George Weulersse, *Le Mouvement physiocratique en France (de 1756 à 1770)*, 2 vols. (Paris, 1910), I, 79ff.

8. I acknowledge extremely valuable discussions on this point with Steven L. Kaplan, Cornell University. I have also profited from Kaplan's *Bread, Politics, and Political Economy in the Reign of Louis XV*, International Archives of the History of Ideas, 86, 2 vols. (The Hague, 1976), I, xvii, 5-8, 90-91; and from Richard Cobb's illuminating chapter, "Popular Attitudes and the Politics of Dearth," in Cobb's *The Police and the People: French Popular Protest, 1789-1820* (Oxford, 1970), pp. 246-324; and Louise A. Tilly's "The Food Riot as a Form of Political Conflict in France," *Journal of Interdisciplinary History*, II (1971), 23-57.

9. Georges Afanassiev, *Le Commerce des céréales in France au dix-huitème siècle* (Paris, 1894), chs. 1-6, 10.

10. For an excellent general discussion see Tilly, "The Food Riot," 27-35, 45-47.

11. Georges Weulersse, *Les Physiocrates* (Paris, 1931), pp. 232-89; see also Ronald L. Meek, *The Economics of Physiocracy: Essays and Translations* (Cambridge, Mass., 1963), pp. 19-22, 25ff., 315.

12. René Girard, *L'Abbé Terray et la liberté du commerce des grains, 1769-1774* (Paris, 1924), pp. 1-7.

13. See Turgot to Dupont de Nemours, Limoges, Dec. 21, 1770, in Anne Robert Jacques Turgot *Oeuvres de Turgot et documents le concernant*, ed. Gustave Schelle, 5 vols. (Paris, 1913-23), III, 399. For Linguet's reflections on his momentary enthusiasm for physiocracy, see Linguet, *Théorie du libelle; ou L'Art de calomnier avec fruit, dialogue philosophique pour servir de supplément à la "Théorie du paradoxe"* (Amsterdam, 1775), p. 152.

14. Linguet, *Histoire des révolutions de l'Empire romain, pour servir de suite à celle des révolutions de la République*, 2 vols. (Paris, 1766), I, 173, 184-86; II, 133-34.

15. Linguet, *Théorie des lois civiles, ou Principes fondamentaux de la société*, 2 vols. (London [Paris], 1767), II, book v; cited hereafter as *L*.

16. For critical reviews of Linguet's works by members of the Physiocratic party, see *Ephémérides du citoyen, ou Chronique de l'esprit nationale*, ed. the abbé Nicolas Baudeau, Dupont de Nemours, the marquis de Mirabeau, et al., 69 vols. (Paris, 1765-72), 1767, vol III, 191-206; 1769, vol III, 79-125; 1770, vol IV, 161-248.

17. Girard, *L'Abbé Terray et la liberté du commerce des grains*, pp. 7, 11ff.

18. Weulersse, *Le Mouvement physiocratique*, I, 114ff.; Girard, *L'Abbé Terray*, pp. 1-3.

19. For insight into the significance of the parlement's politics of subsistence, I am indebted to Steven L. Kaplan, "Police and Political Economy in Paris: The Crisis of the Sixties" (paper presented at the American Historical Association meetings, Boston, Mass., Dec. 28, 1970). See also Kaplan, *Bread, Politics, and Political Economy*, especially, in this context, II, 410-24. See also Girard, *L'Abbé Terray*, pp. 10-11, 15, 24.

20. Kaplan, "Police and Political Economy in Paris"; Kaplan, *Bread, Politics, and Political Economy*, II, 242-42. See also Girard, *L'Abbé Terray*, pp. 24-26; Weulersse, *Le Mouvement physiocratique*, I, 182-86.

21. Kaplan, "Police and Political Economy in Paris."

22. For a very clear discussion of that collaboration, from the pen of a contemporary with inside information, see Linguet, "Mort de M. l'Abbé Terrai, ancien Contrôleur-général, ministre d'état," *Annales politiques, civiles, et littéraires du dix-huitième siécle*, 19 vols. (London, Brussels, Paris, 1777-92), III (1777), 379-86.

23. Terray had drafted a preamble for his *arrêt du Conseil* of Dec., 1770. That preamble was suppressed, but it indicates nonetheless Terray's concern with combating the effects of the parlements' campaigns to win popular support and restoring the nation's confidence in the king. Terray states there that the king recognizes the numerical superiority of consumers over cultivators and proprietors, and recognizes also that their numbers entitle them to "our paternal solicitude," all the more so because previous legislation had favored the other two interest groups explicitly. See analysis and excerpts in Girard, *L'Abbé Terray*, pp. 50-51; Kaplan, *Bread, Politics, and Political Economy*, II, 532-48.

24. Weulersse, *Le Mouvement physiocratique*, I, 209-27.

25. See Chapter Four, pp. 137-43.

26. I have found no evidence that Linguet was paid or pensioned by Terray; however there can be no question that the new ministers were protecting his libelous polemics against physiocrats and *parlementaires*. For a good indication of the kind of inside information Linguet had on the Terray administration, see Linguet, "Mort de M. l'Abbé Terrai," *Annales*, III (1777), 379-86; Linguet, "Supplément à la notice donnée l'année dernière sur l'administration de M. l'Abbé Terray, & co.," *Annales*, VI (1779), 285-308. For information on Linguet and Maupeou, see [Linguet,] *Eloge de Maupeou*, in Jacques-Pierre Brissot de Warville, *Mémoires de Brissot, membre de l'Assemblée législative et de la Convention nationale, sur ses contemporains, et la Révolution française*, ed. François Mongin de Montrol, 4 vols. (Paris, 1830-32), I, 118-19; the text of the *Eloge* appears in this edition of the *Mémoires*, I, 373-74. See also Henri Carré, *Le Barreau de Paris et la radiation de Linguet* (Poitiers, 1892); Jean Cruppi, *Un Avocat journaliste au XVIIIe siècle, Linguet* (Paris, 1895), *passim*.

27. Linguet, *Lettres sur la "Théorie des lois civiles," & c., où l'on examine entr'autres choses s'il est bien vrai que les Anglois soient libres, & que les François doivent, ou imiter leurs opérations, ou porter envie à leur gouvernement* (Amsterdam, 1770); cited hereafter as *LL*. In August, 1770, the lieutenant-general of the Paris Police, Sartine, asked that the distribution and sale of Linguet's *Lettres* be suspended. However, of the 750 copies printed, all but 10 or 12 had been sold. See BN, MSS fr., Collection Anisson-Duperron, 21,100, nos. 132-35. Sartine's partiality toward the parlements could explain this order, which clearly conflicts with Terray's interests.

28. Linguet seems to have been exploiting a temporary sympathy among the parlements for the legislation of 1763 and 1764; and he deliberately ignores the growing opposition of parlements in the North and East, especially at the end of the decade.

29. Linguet, *Réponse aux docteurs modernes, ou Apologie pour l'auteur de la "Théorie des lois" et des "Lettres" sur cette "Théorie," Avec la réfutation du système des philosophes économistes*, 2 vols. (n.p., 1771); cited hereafter as *RDM*. Linguet, *Du plus heureux gouvernement, ou Parallèle des constitutions politiques de l'Asie avec celles de l'Europe, servant d'introduction à la "Théorie des lois civiles,"* 2 vols. in one (London, 1774); cited hereafter as *PHG*. Linguet, *La Théorie des lois civiles*, new ed., 3 vols. (London, 1774); this edition of the *Théorie* is cited hereafter as *L-1774*, Linguet, *Du pain et du bled* (London, 1774); cited hereafter as *PB*.

30. For discussion, see Chapter Two, pp. 64-66.

31. See also *RDM*, I, 245.

32. Montesquieu, *The Spirit of the Laws*, ed. Franz Neumann (New York, 1949), p. 150.

33. In *PHG*, the term "slave" [*esclave*] is replaced by *"dépendant"*.

34. See also *PHG*, II, 16-18.
35. See Hans-Ulrich Thamer, *Revolution and Reaktion in der Französichen Sozial-kritic des 18 Jahrhunderts. Linguet, Mably, Babeuf* (Frankfurt am Main, 1973), p. 108.
36. *Ibid.*, pp. 94-95.
37. For insight into the relationship between Linguet's model of Asiatic monarchy and his radical critique of liberal economic policies and ideologies, I am indebted to Thamer's analysis in *ibid.*, esp. pp. 93-101.
38. In his study of budgets among the laboring poor in seventeenth- and eighteenth-century France, Michel Morineau shows that bread was the single most expensive item in the family budget; depending on region, bread could account for between half and two-thirds of a family's total annual expenditures. Bread supplied most of the caloric intake of adults and children, although again, depending on region, season, and other factors, products like meat, butter, and vegetables might be included in the family's diet. Although Morineau calculates that bread often did not satisfy minimum daily caloric requirements for active working adults (and especially for the laboring poor woman, who consumed only a child's portion of bread—half the two to three loaves which represented her husband's daily portion), he concludes nonetheless that this strata of the population would not have been able to afford any substitute for bread which supplied as substantial a percentage of the necessary nutrients. See Morineau, "Budgets populaires en France au XVIIIe siècle,"*Revue d'histoire économique et sociale*, L (1972), 203-37; 449-81.
39. Under thick cover afforded by his impassioned rhetoric, Linguet was speeding into physiocratic territory with a formidable weapon. One sure way to break the physiocratic party's stranglehold on the administration would be to convince the public that the commodity being exploited by those who made physiocratic policy and those who profited from it was absolutely unnecessary to the sustenance of life, if not immediately or eventually fatal to habitual consumers—that is, the French nation. There existed in the French popular mentality a deeply engrained suspicion of entrepreneurs who speculated in grain and made their fortunes from a commerce in this commodity. What Linguet conceivably could have been exploiting when he began crying "poison" was an undercurrent of dread—the people's fear that it would be victimized by grain traders plotting to do away with all the poor by poisoning them. For an illuminating discussion of a related topic, see René Baehrel, "Haine de classes en temps d'épidémie," *Annales: Economie, Société, Civilisation*, VII (1952), 351-61; Baehrel, "Economie et terreur, histoire et sociologie," *Annales historiques de la Révolution française*, XXIII (1951), 113-46. What would have to be determined is the extent to which a similar dread was a live and exploitable component in the people's attitude toward merchant-capitalists trading in grains. In this context, see Léon Cahen, "Le prétendu pacte de famine: Quelques précisions nouvelles," *Revue historique*, CLXXVII (1935), 205. Linguet's contribution to this construct of the popular mentality—if his panophobic propaganda had been calculated to strike a popular response—would have been to insist that pure, unadulterated bread itself was its own best poison. The people's enemies were slowly poisoning them to death not only with impunity but with the people's cooperation. They fought among themselves daily for the privilege of buying and devouring the lethal loaves.
40. In an article where he treats the climatic determinants of the quality and quantity of grain harvests in Western Europe, Emmanuel Le Roy Ladurie provides interesting corroborations for some of Linguet's hypotheses. He notes that given the very unfavorable climatic conditions prevailing on the continent through the end of the eighteenth century, the Europeans' obdurate reliance upon cereal grains for subsistence was unfortunate, and at times disastrous. "It is not with impunity that the Europeans for so long made their principal subsistence cereals that originated in a milieu very different from theirs...." Grains require a hot and dry climate; unusually severe cold and frequent rains which figure so prominently in the meteorological charts for Western Europe in early modern times acted as climatic determinants for much of the social, medical, institutional, and political history of the period. "Until they established their economy on a broader basis, the people of Europe paid for this inadaptability with a certain number of famines and crises." Le Roy Ladurie, "Climat et récoltes au XVIIe et XVIIIe siècles," *Annales: Eco-*

nomie, Société, Civilisation, XV (1960), 434-65. Citations from 464-65. Le Roy Ladurie adopts a far more cautious tone on the same question in his *Histoire du climat depuis l'an mil* (Paris, 1967), pp. 280ff.

41. Linguet was serious: bread was a poison. In 1779, in his comment on a published letter from Dr. Samuel Auguste André David Tissot to a Monsieur Hirzel, in which Tissot attempted to refute Linguet's panophobic thesis that bread was indigestible, Linguet referred to his own case history: "...whether it's my own particular constitution, or habit, or the greater attention I've given to this matter than one ordinarily does, I have observed from the time I was a child that bread always disagreed with me; only [bread], in however little quantity I ingested it, always gave me acidity, genuine indigestions, and what perhaps will astonish you is that I digest pastry and unleavened bread in general with no upsets, and even with ease." Linguet provided Tissot with a highly unpalatable graphic description of the metamorphoses of bread in the mouth and stomach of opulent gourmandes. Having done his best to provoke gastronomic revulsions, he concluded his epistle with a rich description of staling bread: "The aliment, triturated in the mill, molded in the kneading-trough, scorched in the oven, and composed in its perfection of a dried-out crust, which dampens in no time, and a soggy crumb that soon toughens up...." Letter from Linguet to Dr. Tissot, Brussels, Nov. 2, 1779, cited in *Annales,* VII (1779), 165-66; 177-78. For a copy of Dr. Tissot's letter to Hirzel of Aug. 1, 1779, see [Linguet], *Dissertation sur le bled et le pain, par M. Linguet, avec la réfutation de M. Tissot, D. M.* (Neuchâtel, 1779), pp. 35-84. For another copy of Linguet's letter to Dr. Tissot, see Linguet, *Du commerce des grains. Nouvelle édition. Augmentée d'une lettre à M. Tissot sur le vrai mérite politique & phisique du pain & du bled* (Brussels, 1788), pp. 143-65. Luckily, Linguet, a Remois, was able to compensate for his constitutional debility by ordering (via his sister in Reims) large quantities of a local specialty, a waferlike product called *gauffres remois,* or *biscuits remois.*

42. For recent elaborations on Linguet's observations, see Abel Poitrineau, "L'Alimentation populaire en Auvergne au dix-huitième siècle," *Annales: Economie, Société' Civilisation,* XVIII (1962), 323-31.

43. The journalist-economist Linguet had in mind was Dupont de Nemours. He is referring specifically to Dupont's review of the *Lettres sur la "Théorie des lois civiles"* in the *Ephémérides du citoyen,* 1770, vol. VI, 161-248, and especially 184-85.

44. Linguet's selection of nutritional substitutes for leavened poison was not outlandish. It was not original either. Eighteenth-century French agricultural literature abounds in encyclopedic treatises on exotic foods and even more common products infrequently consumed in France. See for example, Pierre-Joseph Buc'hoz, *Lettres sur la méthode de s'enricher promptement et de conserver sa santé par la culture des vegétaux exotiques,* 5 vols. (Paris, 1768-70); Buc'hoz, *Manuel alimentaire des plantes tant indigènes qu'exotiques, qui peuvent servir de nourriture et de boisson aux différents peuples de la terre* (Paris, 1771); Antoine Augustin Parmentier, *Recherches sur les végétaux nourrissans qui, dans les temps de disette, peuvent remplacer les alimens ordinaires; Avec de nouvelles observations sur la culture des pommes de terre* (Paris, 1781). Linguet did not approve of ersatz bread products, and was particularly vehement in his opposition to potato breads. He had nothing against potatoes as such as alternatives to bread, but everything against Parmentier and his potato panification projects, "...cette boulangerie *chimique* qui depuis vingt ans tourmente les *pommes de terre.*" Linguet, "Lettre à M. Tissot, 2 novembre 1779," in *Du commerce des grains,* pp. 160-61. Linguet feared that the producers of this kitchen magic would encourage precisely what he was insisting must be rooted out—the French masses' urge to rank subsistence commodities, giving preference to those most closely approximating the texture, appearance, and taste of breads made from the best quality grain. These schemes could only encourage enterprising traders' stratagems for cornering a guaranteed seller's market on necessities, whatever they were. What peasant or day laborer would be content with a lowly potato when he had been conditioned to crave potato bread? *Ibid.,* p. 163. And which commercial capitalist would have even a passing scruple about turning multitudes of men who already were slaves to their own palates and psychological needs into his groveling tributaries? What trader would balk at

invoking time-tested subterfuges to get the maximum return from adroit speculation in the new subsistence commodity, potato bread? "...there will be *granaries, storage bins, monopolies, potato famines,* as there are for *grain* and *bread.* The so-called service that your art will have rendered to the men of our regions will be to contrive for them still another chain with this very production that nature provided to retrace for them a few ideas of independence." *Ibid.,* pp. 163-64.

45. Linguet, *Du commerce des grains.* See also letter from Linguet to Dr. Tissot, Brussels, Nov. 2, 1779, as cited in *Annales,* VII (1779), 167-68.

46. Victor Riquetti, marquis de Mirabeau, "Dépravations de l'ordre légal: 2me lettre de M. B. à M., 18 mars 1767," *Ephémérides du citoyen,* 1767, vol. X, 71.

47. For the insights on which this general conclusion is based, I am indebted to Kaplan, "Police and Political Economy in Paris"; see also Cobb, *The Police and the People,* pp. 246-324; Tilly, "The Food Riot," 23-57.

48. *Ephémérides du citoyen,* 1768, vol. I, 144.

49. Jean-Antoine Nicolas de Caritat, Marquis de Condorcet, *Du commerce des bleds pour Servir à la réfutation de l'ouvrage "Sur la législation et le commerce des grains"* [by Jacques Necker] (Paris, 1775), p. 87.

50. I am using the term "laboring poor" in this context to approximate and characterize the class whose members Linguet describes sometimes as *"le peuple," RDM,* I, 113; *"le pauvre," ibid.,* 117-18; *"le journalier," "le mercenaire," PB,* ch. IX, ch. X. Linguet's best discussion and some of his most precise definitions can be found in an article in his *Annales,* IX (1780), 326ff.

51. St. Thomas Aquinas, *The Summa Theologica,* II-II, Question 66: Of Theft and Robbery, seventh article: Whether it is lawful to steal through stress of need, in Dino Bigongiari, ed., *The Political Ideas of St. Thomas Aquinas,* (New York, 1957), pp. 138-39.

52. Morelly reformulated the categorical imperative of the Thomistic social ethic as follows: "The eternal laws of the universe are that nothing belongs to man in particular except what his present needs demand, what suffices him every day for the support or embellishment of its duration; the field is not the property of the man who farms it, nor the tree of him who gathers its fruits; and even for the products of his own industry, only the portion he uses belongs to him; the remainder, as well as his own person, belongs to all humanity." Morelly, *Naufrage des isles flottantes, ou Basiliade du célèbre Pilpai. Poème héroique,* 2 vols. (Messina [Paris], 1753), I, 205, as cited in André Lichtenberger, *Le Socialisme au XVIIIe siècle, Etude sur les idées socialistes dans les écrivains français du XVIIIe siècle avant la Révolution* (Paris, 1895), p. 111.

53. The curé from Champagne, spokesman for a millenarian and agrarian communist utopia, formulated a natural right to existence as follows: "All men are equal by nature, they all have as well the right to live, and to walk upon the earth, also to enjoy natural liberty there, and to have a share in the goods of the earth." Jean Meslier, *Mémoires des pensées et des sentiments de Jean Meslier,* ch. 42, premier abus, as cited by Albert Soboul, "Le Critique social devant son temps," in *Oeuvres complètes de Jean Meslier,* ed. Jean Deprun, Roland Desné, Albert Soboul, 3 vols. (Paris, 1970-72), I, CVIII.

54. Jean-Jacques Rousseau, *Discours sur l'origine de l'inégalité,* in *Jean-Jacques Rousseau, Oeuvres complètes,* ed. Bernard Gagnebin and Marcel Raymond, 4 vols. (Paris, 1959-69), III, 194. The Encyclopedists had formulated a similar categorical imperative: "Act so that all your actions tend toward your self-preservation and toward the preservation of others: that is nature's call." Denis Diderot, ed., *Encyclopédie, ou Dictionnaire raisonné des sciences, des arts, et des métiers,* 35 vols. (Paris, 1751-80), IV, article *"Conservation."*

55. Abbé Baudeau, editor of the *Ephémérides du citoyen,* printed and fully approved an extraordinary pro-physiocratic rebuttal of a *Lettre sur les émeutes populaires que cause la cherté des grains, et sur les précautions du moment* (Paris, 1767). The critic of the *Lettre* objected to certain measures taken by police agents in Normandy—specifically price-fixing—to counteract effects of grain shortage and high prices. "The first duty is to be *just. Afterwards,* one can be charitable, or an astute politician, but the first thing is to leave to every person that which belongs to him, and never to rob one person under

the pretext of doing good to another.... There has been too much reasoning about grain, as if it belonged to everyone indiscriminately, and as if, consequently, it was the place of the king, the government, the magistrates, to dispose of it with what one calls the public utility in mind.... If, on the contrary, the point of departure had been this truth, so clear, and so important, that the grain belongs to someone, and that this latter person has a right to dispose of it, since it is his, one could have been on guard all the time against sophisms, by recalling these words constantly: the owner of the grain, the rights attached to his property...." *Ephémérides du citoyen,* 1767, vol. XII, 103, 105.

56. For a fuller statement of this hypothesis, see Chapter One, pp. 12-13 and *L,* II, book 4.

57. Abbé Pierre-Joseph-André Roubaud, *Représentations aux magistrats, contenant l'exposition raisonnée des faits relatifs à la liberté du commerce des grains, et les résultats respectifs des règlemens & de la liberté* (n.p., 1769), pp. 395, 399-400.

58. For Linguet's paraphrase of this theme from his *Théorie des lois civiles,* see *RDM,* I, 83ff. For discussion, see Chapter Two.

59. *Ephémérides du citoyen,* 1770, vol. VI, 244-48.

60. *RDM,* I, 257. See also *LL,* 130-34.

61. For the text of the *arrêt,* see François-André Isambert, ed., *Recueil général des anciennes lois françaises depuis l'an 420 jusqu'à la Révolution de 1789,* 29 vols. (Paris, 1821-33), XXIII, 30-39.

62. Well before the change in administration, Linguet had lost his influence with Maupeou and d'Aiguillon. For discussion, see Chapter Four.

63. I have uncovered no evidence linking Linguet's anti-physiocratic propaganda activities to rumored conspiracies against Turgot's administration hatched by the ousted ministerial triumverate. For a critical discussion of the plot thesis (in which, however, the question of Linguet's collusion is not treated), see Douglas Dakin, *Turgot and the Ancien Régime in France* (London, 1939), pp. 186ff.

64. See Chapter Five for details.

65. Dupont de Nemour's review of Linguet's *Lettres sur la "Théorie des lois civiles,"* in *Ephémérides du citoyen,* 1770, vol. VI, 175-76, 180.

66. "Catalogue des livres imaginaires dont le dos figuraient dans une fausse bibliothèque du cabinet de Turgot," printed in Turgot, *Oeuvres de Turgot,* ed. Schelle, III, 683-84.

67. In his *Mémoires,* the abbé recalled the details of his assignment: "Turgot, the Minister, and Trudaine de Montigny were very busy establishing liberty of commerce in grains; Linguet, who saw in this operation one of the principles of the economists whom he was hotly pursuing in all his writings, roused himself, and published a book on *bread and wheat.* He proves there, after his fashion, that *wheat is a poison, that free commerce in wheat is a monopoly, that men should live off potatoes and fish,* etc. Turgot and Trudaine were indignant, with reason, over this extravagance, which might have had unfortunate effects on some minds; but neither of them wanted to suppress the book, or have the author punished, an unjust measure, and contrary to their maxims...." Morellet collected all Linguet's works, and set about to destroy the author. "I shut myself up in my house; I read them, while marking with a stroke of the pencil all the extravagances that I found in them, and which I had transcribed at the same time on separate pieces of paper." When the work was completed, Morellet read it to Madame Trudaine and Messiers de Malesherbes, Turgot, and Trudaine, convoked for the occasion *en salon.* "...I can say that my *Théorie du paradoxe* really mortally wounded him." Abbé André Morellet, *Mémoires,* as cited in *Oeuvres de Turgot,* ed. Schelle, V, 143-44.

68. Morellet, in his *Théorie du paradoxe,* singled out dozens of Linguet's "paradoxes"; i.e., slavery is as necessary as it is horrible (22); oriental despotisms incarnate societal perfection (35ff.); bread, the staff of life, is a poison (57ff.); liberty of commerce in grains is, and is not, desirable (104ff.); the salaried laborer's wage has, and has not, risen (114).

69. The full series of attacks and counterattacks ran as follows: the abbé Morellet published his *Théorie du paradoxe* (Amsterdam, 1775). Linguet responded with his *Thé-*

orie du libelle; ou l'Art de calomnier avec fruit, dialogue philosophique pour servir de supplément à la "Théorie du paradoxe" (Amsterdam, 1775); and Morellet responded to the response with *Réponse sérieuse à M. L^{xx}, par l'auteur de la "Théorie du paradoxe"* (Amsterdam, 1775).

70. Turgot, *Oeuvres de Turgot*, ed. Schelle, V, 144, note a; Matthieu-François Pidanzat de Mairobert, *Journal historique de la révolution opérée dans la constitution de la monarchie françoise par M. de Maupeou, Chancelier de France*, 7 vols. (London [Amsterdam], 1774-76), VII (April 14, 1775), 266. See also Louis Petit de Bachaumont, *Mémoires secrets, pour servir à l'histoire de la république des lettres en France, depuis MDCCLXII jusqu'à nos jours; ou Journal d'un observateur*, 36 vols. (London, 1780-89), VII (March 12, 1775), 338-39. For other incidents involving censorship of Linguet's antiphysiocratic writings, see Georges Weulersse, "Les physiocrates sous le ministère de Turgot," *Revue d'histoire économique et sociale*, XIII (1925), 320, 320 n. 59, n. 60; Mairobert, *Journal historique*, VII (March 13, 1775), 176, 177-78.

71. See pp. 88-89 above.

72. Linguet admitted that such machinations characterized the trader's operations even in regulated economies. When vigilant administrators attempted to buy up grains at exhorbitant prices in order to supply the market at a loss, the merchant capitalized on government-engineered price drops, and swept these artificially garnished markets clean. "Wheat which humanity furnishes reverts to the prisons of opulence; and it can exit only with a passport of avarice; and the indigent man, victim of the very compassion he inspires, owes his loss precisely to the measures devised for helping him" (*PB*, 37).

73. For a physiocrat's corroboration of Linguet's estimation of popular sensitivity on the question of subsistence, see Guy Jean Baptiste Target, *Observations sur le commerce des grains écrites en décembre 1769* (Amsterdam, 1775), cited without page reference in Armand Thomas Hue de Miromesnil, *Correspondance politique et administrative de Miromesnil, premier président du Parlement de Normandie*, ed. Pierre LeVerdier, 5 vols. (Rouen, 1899-1903), V, x-xi.

74. Delivered before a crowd assembled in some village square or marketplace, this tirade would have been registered as an open call to collective raids and popularly enforced price controls. Something in the tone of these rabble-rousing declamations marked Linguet as a populist, the prototype of the revolutionary orator of the people. As much of this populist radicalism as he could recognize and control, Linguet was at pains to convert to the service of what he insisted was a hard-headed politics of social containment. He would use his gift for analyzing motives behind popular explosions to discredit the economic doctors and enlighten the monarch, his policy-makers, and his officials.

75. Pierre-Samuel Dupont de Nemours, *De l'origine et des progrès d'une science nouvelle* [1768], ed. A. Dubois (Paris, 1910), p. 14.

76. Linguet, *Journal de politique et de littérature, contenant les principaux évenemens de toutes les cours, les nouvelles de la république des lettres, & c.*, 1-21 (Oct. 25, 1774–July 25, 1776), no. 5 (Dec. 5, 1774), 192, 193.

77. Linguet, *Journal de politique et de littérature*, no. 6 (Dec. 15, 1774), 235.

78. Ernest Labrousse, *Esquisse du mouvement des prix et des revenues en France au XVIIIe siècle*, 2 vols. (Paris, 1933), I, 584, 593. In a survey of popular budgets in eighteenth-century France, Michel Morineau samples urban and rural areas in carefully delimited time periods. His analyses qualify but do not contradict those of Labrousse. Finally, his findings lend credence to Linguet's *reportage* and analysis. See Morineau, "Budgets populaires en France au XVIIIe siècle," *Revue d'histoire économique et sociale*, L (1972), 203-37; 449-81.

79. For an excellent discussion of this question, see Jean Meuvret, "Les Crises de subsistences et la démographie de la France d'ancien régime," *Population*, I (1946), 643-50.

80. François Quesnay, "Droit naturel," in Quesnay, *François Quesnay et la physiocratie*, ed. Institut national d'études démographiques, 2 vols. (Paris, 1958), II, 734.

81. Turgot, "Réflexions sur la formation et la distribution des richesses," in *Oeuvres de Turgot*, ed. Eugène Daire, 2 vols., Collection des principaux économistes, vols. II-IV (Paris, 1844), I, 10, as cited in Léon Cahen, "L'Idée de la lutte des classes au XVIIIe siècle," *Revue de synthèse historique*, XII (1906), 52.

82. Quesnay, *Sur les travaux des artisans: deuxième dialogue,* in Quesnay, *François Quesnay et la physiocratie,* II, 895.

83. Turgot, *Réponse au mémoire de Graslin,* in *Oeuvres de Turgot,* ed. Schelle, II, 633, cited in Henri Grange, "Turgot et Necker devant le problème des salaires," *Annales historiques de la Révolution française,* XXIX (1957), 24.

84. Turgot, *Septième lettre sur le commerce des grains* (1770), as cited in Roger Picard, "Etude sur quelques théories du salaire au XVIIIe siècle," *Revue d'histoire des doctrines économiques et sociales,* III (1910), 161.

85. Turgot, *Mémoires sur les moyens de procurer des ressources au peuple par le travail* (1775), in *Oeuvres de Turgot,* ed. Daire, II, 451ff., cited (as "Guillaumin") in Picard, "Théories du salaires," *Revue d'histoire des doctrines économiques et sociales,* III (1910), 162.

86. Turgot to Dupont de Nemours, Limoges, Aug. 29, 1771, in *Oeuvres de Turgot,* ed. Schelle, III, 494.

87. See also *LL,* p. 5; *L,* book V, ch. 31.

88. Voltaire, "Esclaves," in *Questions sur l'Encyclopédie,* in *Oeuvres complètes de Voltaire,* ed. Louis Moland, 52 vols. (Paris, 1877-85), XVIII, 602. The book Voltaire is referring to is probably Linguet's *Lettres sur la "Théorie des lois civiles"* (1770). See Voltaire to Marin, Oct. 24, 1770, in *Voltaire's Correspondence,* ed. Theodore Besterman, 107 vols. (Geneva, 1953-65), 77, no. 15701, p. 44.

89. Voltaire, "Esclaves," XVIII, 603.

90. Dupont de Nemours manipulated calculations based on physiocratic laws to demonstrate that free labor in the French colonies would cost the employer less than slave labor. "For if you take into account the expense of the Negroes' purchase, the necessity of rapidly amortizing this initial expense due to the short lifespan of slaves, the poor quality of their work, the expense of supervising them, you find that the salary scale is so high that you can almost always be certain of having free workers for the same price without doing violence to anyone." Dupont de Nemours in *Ephémérides du citoyen,* 1771, vol. VI, as cited in Gustave Schelle, *Du Pont de Nemours et l'école physiocratique* (Paris, 1888), p. 106.

91. Linguet's letters appeared in three numbers of his *Journal de politique et de littérature:* "Lettre de M. Linguet à l'auteur de la *Gazette d'agriculture,*" no. 3 (Nov. 15, 1774), 106-15; "Suite de la lettre de M. Linguet à M. L'Abbé Roubaud, auteur de la *Gazette d'agriculture,*" no. 5 (Dec. 5, 1774), 188-93; "Suite de la lettre de M. Linguet à M. l'Abbé Roubaud," no. 6 (Dec. 15, 1774), 227-36. For Roubaud's side of the correspondance, see *Gazette d'agriculture, commerce, arts, et finances,* vol. for 1774, 709-11, 748-51, 828-32.

92. Roubaud, *Représentations aux magistrats,* p. 395.

93. Linguet, "Suite de la lettre de M. Linguet à M. L'Abbé Roubaud," (Dec. 15, 1774), 232.

94. François Métra, J. Imbert, de Boudeaux, et al., eds., *Correspondance secrète, politique, et littéraire, ou Mémoires pour servir à l'histoire des cours, des sociétés, et de la littérature en France depuis la mort de Louis XV,* 18 vols. (London, 1787-90), I, 163, as cited in Turgot, *Oeuvres de Turgot,* ed. Schelle, V, 144, 144 note a. See also Pierre Fonçin, *Essai sur le ministère de Turgot* (Paris, 1877), pp. 174-75.

95. Voltaire, *Petit écrit sur l'arrêt du Conseil du 13 septembre 1774 qui permet le libre commerce des blés dans le royaume* (1775), in *Oeuvres complètes de Voltaire,* ed. Moland, XXIX, 343-47. See also Voltaire to Condorcet and d'Alembert Jan. 16, 1775, in *Voltaire's Correspondence,* ed. Besterman, 90, no. 18173, p. 16; Voltaire to Condorcet and d'Alembert, Jan. 21, 1775, in *ibid.,* 90, no. 18189, p. 27: "What madness ever took hold of this devil Linguet? First he had written against the bad habit of eating bread, and today he writes against the precious liberty of this essential trade!"

96. See Peter Gay, *Voltaire's Politics: The Poet as Realist* (New York, 1965), pp. 331-33.

97. Voltaire, *Petit écrit* (1775), 346-47.

98. Voltaire, *Diatribe à l'auteur des "Ephémérides,"* in *Oeuvres complètes de Voltaire,* ed. Moland, XXIX, 359-70.

99. *Ibid.*, 367, 369.

100. V.-S. Lublinsky, "Voltaire et la guerre des farines," *Annales historiques de la Révolution française*, XXXI (1959), 137, 140.

101. Linguet, "Suite de la lettre de M. Linguet à M. l'Abbé Roubaud," (Dec. 15, 1774), 229. See also, *PB*, 292-296.

102. Linguet warned Roubaud: "If there was ever on earth a country where the idea prevailed of passing off thus a legislator as missionary and the laws as sermons, this aberration could not be kept up." Linguet, "Lettre de M. Linguet à l'auteur de la *Gazette d'agriculture*," 114.

103. Linguet, "Suite de la lettre de M. Linguet à M. l'Abbé Roubaud," (Dec. 15, 1774), 229.

104. For further discussion of some of these themes, see Harriet B. Applewhite and Darline G. Levy, "The Concept of Modernization and the French Enlightenment," *Studies on Voltaire and the Eighteenth Century*, LXXXIV (1971), 58-60.

105. Linguet, "Lettre de M. Linguet à l'auteur de la *Gazette d'agriculture*," 114.

106. He had publicized the news that the people's original dispossesssion was a forced expropriation; their progressively more intolerable impoverishment at the hands of an elite of exploiters was a theft committed daily against their property in the fruits of their industry; their starvation was an unbearable infraction of laws and rights of nature; unless the state undertook to claim these rights for the people, the people would accomplish the deed for themselves.

107. Linguet, *Lettre de M. Linguet à M. le Comte de Vergennes, ministre des affaires étrangères en France* (London, 1777); for details, see Chapter Five, pp. 176-77.

108. Linguet, "Au Roi, Londres, ce 8 octobre 1777," *Annales*, III (1777), 3, 4.

109. For complete discussions, see Chapters Six, Seven, Eight. For examples of Linguet's early thoughts on this question of social welfare, and his early projects, see: *Annales*, II (1778), 339ff.; *Plan d'établissemens tendans à l'extinction de la mendicité* (Paris, 1779); *Annales*, IX (1780), 326ff.; *Annales*, VII (1779), 203ff. For Linguet's more complete welfare programs, which he offered to the National Assembly, see: *Point de banqueroute, plus d'emprunts, et si l'on veut, bientôt plus de dettes, en réduisant les impôts à un seul. Avec un moyen facile de supprimer la mendicité en assurant à toutes les classes du peuple une existence aisée dans la vieillesse. Plan proposé à tous les peuples libres, et notamment à l'Assemblée nationale de France* (n.p. 1789); "Projets de finance, pour le soulagement et même la libération de l'Etat," *Annales*, XVI, no. 134 (1790), 436-64; "Suite de projet pour l'établissement d'une caisse nationale salutaire," *Annales*, XVI, no. 135 (1790), 465-506.

FOUR

Travaux Pratiques:
Forensic Politics

Linguet and the duc d'Aiguillon: A Rebel's
Brief for the *Thèse Royale*

By 1770, the Fourth Estate's unsolicited advocate and the Crown's over-zealous defender was leading more than a double existence. He had a lucrative practice going in Paris; his clients included prosperous entrepreneurs and well-placed aristocrats.

On a fateful morning in February, 1770, business in Simon Linguet's law offices started out normally enough. Linguet was working on his cases in an inner office. In an antechamber, his four secretaries, swamped with briefs he had dashed off in an almost illegible scrawl, were transcribing and preparing them for printing.[1] Suddenly, a Peer of France, Louis XV's former military governor for the province of Brittany, Emmanuel-Armand de Vignerot du Plessis de Richelieu, duc d'Aiguillon, burst into Linguet's office and insisted on speaking with him, "...I never found out what brought me the fatal honor of being chosen by him to defend him. He didn't know me, I had never seen him when he called upon me one morning in February..."[2]

D'Aiguillon was on trial. At stake were his honor and his chances for appointment to the post of secretary of state in the Department of Foreign Affairs—his political future, in short. But the monarchy and the nominally absolute monarch also were on trial in the d'Aiguillon affair. If the monarch were to exercise political sovereignty, he would have to break up a complex of theological, quasi-legislative, judicial, and quasi-executive institutions, all harboring rival claims to a share in political power. An admittedly hesitant king, goaded and supported by the parlements and the Jansenist party, had recently eliminated the Company of the Jesuits. The parlements remained, however. With their rights of remonstrance, the prerogative of protesting before registering royal edicts, the parlements were able to impede or delay the execution of the king's orders.

In the 1760s, the Parlement of Brittany at Rennes, exercising allegedly constitutional rights, challenged the principles of absolute monarchy by defying d'Aguillon, Louis XV's governor in Brittany. While d'Aiguillon was serving as governor, the Estates of Brittany refused to levy the royal *corvée,* claiming that the tax was illegitimate because it infringed upon traditional provincial rights. Louis-René de Caradeuc de la Chalotais, attorney general to the parlement at Rennes, emerged at the head of a company of magistrates determined to back the estates. To demonstrate its solidarity with the estates of Brittany, the parlement at Rennes suspended its own judicial operations. D'Aiguillon was compelled to oppose this maneuver to defend the king's prerogatives.

Louis XV took his own extraconstitutional action to quash the insurrection. He placed La Chalotais and five principal instigators under arrest. When the Paris parlement protested, Louis laid down the law in his famous *séance de flagellation* of 1766. He was monarch, sovereign lawmaker, overseer of all who executed the law, the judge of all its magistrates.[3]

The monarch won. Yet the parlements emerged triumphant, exalted in the eyes of a public which, with little comprehension of the conservative ends that the *parlementaires'* radical political vocabulary was serving, had appropriated the inflammatory verbiage in which they voiced their demands for constitutional and natural rights. D'Aiguillon was recalled to Paris by Louis XV, but placed on trial by the parlement at Rennes for high crimes against the French constitution. Exercising his privileges as peer of the realm, the duke transferred trial proceedings to the Court of Peers meeting at Versailles, and hired a dozen lawyers to provide a legal justification for his performance as governor of Brittany.

It was not enough. They were getting nowhere when Linguet accepted the case. Linguet was aware that more than the duke's guilt or innocence was at stake. This was really a trial to test the monarch's strength against that of the constitutional pluralists in Brittany's estates and parlement, and throughout France. Linguet's defense of d'Aiguillon was anything but a sellout to a reactionary party of monarchical traditionalists. It was a forceful defense of the Crown's program for centralizing and rationalizing French administrative operations, an essential part of the political modernization process.

Linguet insisted that the duke hand over all memoirs, laws, and executive orders connected with his governorship of Brittany, a complete dossier. The duke complied. Years later, Linguet recalled the moment when he received this supporting evidence:

> A portfolio wasn't what was needed for the transfer, not at all: not even an ordinary wheelbarrow, but a cart; it was filled up, and two horses were hardly enough to get it moving.
>
> I repeat: secretly, I accused myself of presumptuousness; my fear doubled upon seeing the congestion produced in my apartment by these overpowering stacks: chairs and desks were not enough to hold them. We had to spread them out all over the floor, which began to buckle.[4]

The duke's new advocate went through everything. Working at a furious pace, he arranged and classified the entire record, and turned out his *Mémoire pour M. le duc d'Aiguillon.*[5] In it, the duke appeared as an obedient administrator. His task, as Linguet represented it, was exceedingly delicate. He could enforce the king's edicts only at the risk of alienating the Estates and Parlement of Brittany, partisans of a provincial traditionalism justified in the pluralistic categories of a constitutional theory. The duke's execution of the monarch's dictates, Linguet concluded, was legal, in perfect agreement with the "constitution" of a monarchy.[6]

The *Mémoire* was Linguet's testament to d'Aiguillon's innocence. In addition, it apparently was his testament to his own belief in it. Linguet later confessed, more to the public than to d'Aiguillon:

> As a result of my unfortunate makeup, I was more profoundly moved by your affair than perhaps even you were. From the moment I took up my pen on your behalf, I was caught up in enthusiasm; my head flared up from the flame that burns habitually in my heart.... In short, I comported myself in all this the way these indiscreet youngsters do who are betrayed by their temperament and who discredit their favors for want of knowing how to make them longed for.

> Although basically you were innocent, you had a terrible handicap, that of appearing universally hated and dreaded: to dare defend you, a man would have to defy the nation—tear away credulity's blindfold... cover you with his body, and risk his life to save yours.[7]

The lawyer might have been playing a role, but not to win plaudits from his famous client. A man of substance and common sense, a man of the duke's quality and ambitions, was bound to be palpably uncomfortable in the company of this possessed persecuted advocate. True, he had hired Simon Linguet, but for the explicit purpose of drawing up convincing briefs. The duke had retained not one lawyer, but an advisory council of twelve legal experts. He expected that any memoir in his defense would be a group enterprise, subject to his revisions. That was not Linguet's understanding. In presenting the duke's case, he told the truth, but he claimed it as *his* truth. He refused to tolerate modifications, revisions, or suppressions.

Linguet completed his *Mémoire pour M. le Duc d'Aiguillon* in May, 1770; he submitted it to his client. Several days later, it was returned—minus the author's exordium, and filled with someone else's corrections. Linguet rushed to d'Aiguillon's residence. As he told the story, he confronted the duke's secretary, and demanded to know who had deleted his exordium and replaced it with an inadequate substitute. "The exordium is Monseigneur's," the secretary blurted out. He had not intended to implicate d'Aiguillon, since the *littérateur* Jean-François Marmontel actually was responsible. "Monseigneur!," Linguet screeched back—for in that moment of rage, he assumed the culprit was the defendant, his client: " 'Monseigneur is better equipped than I to govern provinces, but, damn it, I am better at briefs and exordia than he! Mine will have preference'; '—no, it won't.' 'Then I absolutely refuse to sign.' "[8]

The brief appeared in June, with Linguet's own revisions of his original exordium and conclusion.[9] In March, Linguet had advised d'Aiguillon, "...your judges, without knowing it themselves, will be subjugated or restrained by the public, by the most widely broadcast opinion. It is the public, then, that must be enlightened, convinced, and won over....Make yourself unassailable on the big points, and I guarantee your success. Prove that you comported yourself so as to merit the nation's love, and your enemies will be vanquished.[10]

The duke's case would be decided in the Court of Peers. However, far more than a key point in law was at stake. The man's honor hung in the balance; but Linguet did not appeal to the judges to vindicate it. He appealed beyond them. Outside the courtroom, he was convinced, the only verdict that counted would be handed down in a voice that rose as a murmur of sympathy, a half-articulate expression of national sentiment against particularist regional loyalty. This extrajudicial verdict of public opinion would be evoked through the advocate's word, and echoed in the streets of Paris and Rennes, and throughout the realm.

The king feared uncontrollable political repercussions from a court decision unfavorable to d'Aiguillon. Advised by his newly appointed chancellor, Maupeou, who already was engaged in heavy-handed maneuvers against the pro-parlementaire secretary of state for the Department of Foreign Affairs, the duc de Choiseul, Louis XV decided to remove d'Aiguillon's case from the Paris parlement's jurisdiction. A prudent d'Aiguillon was in agreement with this policy. On June 27, 1770, in a lit de justice, Louis XV, by lettre-patentes annulled all legal proceedings, declaring "the conduct of his cousin d'Aiguillon irreproachable," and ordering "the most absolute silence" concerning the affair.[11] The Parlement of Paris interpreted Louis XV's coup as an attack on its constitutional prerogatives; in an order dated July 2, 1770, it divested d'Aiguillon of the privileges of his peerage.[12]

The parlement's remonstrance on July 9, 1770, was a model for seditious violence. The king's Conseil d'état annulled the parlement's proclamation.[13] At once, parlements throughout the country were up in arms. On August 14, the Parlement of Brittany condemned Linguet's Mémoire for d'Aiguillon and ordered it lacerated and burned by the public hangman.[14] The king responded to the challenge. Later that month, he summoned a representative delegation from the Parlement of Brittany to his residence at Compiègne, arrested two members, and forced another to witness the registering of lettres-patentes annulling the parlement's decrees against Linguet's Mémoire for d'Aiguillon.[15] The king was in possession of all legal weapons. He had dismissed the case against d'Aiguillon. Now he took steps to annihilate every word of it. On September 3, 1770, Louis XV arrived at the Palais de Justice and ordered that all documents in the d'Aiguillon case be laid at his feet.[16]

At the time, Linguet was confined to his bed; he later assured his public that he had been consumed by fever, frustration, and rage. The king was dispensing his justice, but precisely by dispensing with legal forms. "I have been sick and extremely weak for the past seven days," he wrote the duke, "but yesterday, grief and indignation restored my strength."[17] Linguet had just received the text of the order of the king's Council suppressing the Parlement of Bordeaux's remonstrance against the king's termination of the d'Aiguillon case:[18] "What! the King, in speaking of you and of your affair, claims the right to *dispense grace, abolish crimes,* etc....that means that you are declared guilty, a favored criminal, to be sure, whom the all-powerful saves from punishment, but not from infamy."[19] In his letter, Linguet imagined the duke's reaction to all these developments. D'Aiguillon would bow to the king's will, relieved that the messy affair had been quashed. He would reason that it was not in his power to manipulate events, that he was not the master of the situation, that a man must accommodate himself to the course things take:

> Ah! pardon me, *Monsieur le duc*—a man is always master when it is a question of preventing himself from being dishonored.... What will the effect be now of all our printed matter, after so discouraging an avowal [as that of the king's Council]. I see it with despair, *Monsieur le duc,* but you will never win back the public....I will start work on the reply to the Parlement of *Rennes:* I will defend you once again, I will justify you the way you are worthy of being defended and justified....But what use will my pen be to you if you are betrayed by authority?[20]

Meanwhile, the Estates of Brittany, convened during the recess of the Brittany parlement, demanded the release of detained *parlementaires.* In addition, the Estates commissioned a refutation of Linguet's *Mémoire* of June, 1770, a *Mémoire en réponse à celui de M. le Duc d'Aiguillon.* It appeared in November, 1770. Immediately, Louis XV suppressed the work, and imprisoned both author and printer; and early in January, 1771, by *arrêt du Conseil,* the king suppressed the *délibération* of the preceding December 21, where the estates had registered approval of the commissioned *Mémoire en réponse.*[21] In December and January, the Brittany parlement, newly reconvened and supported by other parlements, entered its boldest protests against the king's maneuvers.

In the midst of this parlementary insurrection, Chancellor Maupeou saw his chance, as he put it, "à retirer la couronne de la poussière du greffe." The duc de Choiseul, the king's first minister and one of the parlement's more reliable spokesmen in the administration, had been dismissed in December 1770. In protest against a *lit de justice* where the king had forced registration of an edict against "illegal coalitions" among *parlementaires,* the Paris parlement went on strike. During the night of January 19-20, 1771, Maupeou exiled the corps from Paris. His suppression of the Paris parlement was a *coup d'état.*[22]

Linguet's briefs for the defense had worked better than the fearful d'Aiguillon ever could have imagined. Once the smoke from his lawyer's immolated *Mémoire* cleared, d'Aiguillon was able to make out for himself an unobstructed path to the post of secretary of state for the Department of Foreign Affairs.

Linguet saw nothing, except that along with his legal brief he himself had been sacrificed, although not consumed. The advocate who had proclaimed his words the expression of his being burned, still lived on, but on what? D'Aiguillon was scheduled to receive his appointment in the summer of 1771. Even before then, and with his customary bluntness, Linguet was demanding palpable marks of the duke's gratitude. At first, he confined himself to requesting d'Aiguillon's intervention to obtain Chancellor Maupeou's consent for a reprinting of his complete works. The chancellor's initial reaction to that request, as Linguet reported it, had been anything but reassuring: "...he looked upon them [Linguet's writings] and feared them, he said, as a school of despotism." Keeper of the Seals Miromesnil offered to approve a complete edition on the condition that Linguet dedicate it to d'Aiguillon. Linguet refused, but he kept on petitioning.[23] In a letter written in March, 1771, he asked for a country retreat, perhaps on the duke's estate at Montcornet, in Champagne: "I am not a flunkey, you know that from experience: buried in my study, naïve, sincere, like my writing paper [sic], disdaining or forgetting to fill even what are called social obligations, or proprieties that make up the great art of advancing oneself in the world...."[24] D'Aiguillon met the demand by offering Linguet the use of a little hut on his estate at Veret, near Tours. The gesture infuriated him: "a damp monk's house, with no garden, with nothing pleasant to recommend it; at very best good for some Tourangean canon; with nothing pretty about it except its name—the Rose Chateau!"[25]

In June, after d'Aiguillon's appointment came through, Linguet escalated his demands. He knew Italian and Spanish and could pick up foreign tongues easily. He had a taste for travel. He was offering himself as an itinerant negotiator for the Department of Foreign Affairs at foreign courts; but d'Aiguillon would have none of it. To prove his worth as political analyst, Linguet turned out a brief on the Polish question in which he "predicted" the partition of Poland by the great powers and recommended that the French profit from the deal.[26] Next, he asked for a license over foreign gazettes introduced into France. When he was turned down, he worked up another project with the publisher Panckoucke to establish a political journal that would fall under d'Aiguillon's jurisdiction. His prospectus was turned down.[27] Then he indicated that he would be content with the post of secretary to the Peers of the Realm, but that sinecure had been auctioned off to someone else. Next he solicited a privilege for publishing the *Gazette de France*. Again, he was refused. He would settle for the post of envoy of the Bishop of Spire to the Court of France. The competition was fierce and the job went to another candidate. Finally, the duke offered him the office of secretary to the comte de Provence's Council of Finances. The post cost four thousand *livres*. Linguet refused to pay. The duke, exasperated, desperate to rid himself of a lawyer for whom, it seemed, the d'Aiguillon case would never be closed, intervened in Linguet's favor and the post was his without payment.

The comte de Provence's new secretary sold his title immediately, netted seven thousand *livres*,[28] and launched into what turned out to be a thirteen-year campaign to obtain justice from d'Aiguillon. He demanded his fee, an indemnification for the risks he had run and for the slander he had suffered at the hand of the duke's enemies.

Linguet's case against d'Aiguillon was not decided until 1787. Intermittently, from 1774 on, he aired his casebook of grievances—not in the courts, but before the bar of public opinion. Repeatedly, he threatened to release the unabridged story of d'Aiguillon's betrayal. He was even prepared to use his grasp on the duke's public image to intimidate the king's ministers and to coerce privileges from them that amounted to political rights.[29] He wanted the kind of recognition capable of blasting open paths into the future for an untitled, ambitious, and talented lawyer on the make. Otherwise, in his defeat, he would drag everything down with him.

This lawyer hardly fitted the stereotype of the advocate in that age. He was anything but a smooth and covert calculator. "For as long as I've been alive," he would write in 1774 to Miromesnil, keeper of the seals, "my heart has always been the master of my reason: that is why I have conducted myself in so unpolitic a manner."[30] Passion with the man was fluid. It overflowed the dikes of form, sweeping everything before it into a shipwreck guaranteed to be disastrous, but sublime, and above all, public, visible. He could not stay put. Something in him burst through the narrow, restrictive professionalism of the lawyer's estate. He demanded the right to make careers for himself in law, journalism, literature, diplomacy, and statesmanship at the highest echelons, on his own terms. He was becoming a new kind of factotum, a political independent in an imperfectly absolute monarchy.

Insurrectionary Law in the Maupeou Parlement

In his battle to bring d'Aiguillon's case into the courts and before the bar of public opinion, Linguet was defeated at the hand of his client's royal protector, and with his client's consent. Nonetheless, the case provided an occasion for Chancellor Maupeou's *coup d'état*. Parlement was annihilated in January, 1771. The king's justice, insofar as it was delegated to and exercised through these intermediary institutions, was suspended. After a brief and unsuccessful period of experimentation with a commission recruited from the king's Council, Maupeou decided on a drastic transformation of legal structures. By creating six *conseils supérieurs* to administer the king's justice outside the capital, he reduced the Paris parlement's jurisdiction. He reformed the Parlement of Paris, now referred to as the Maupeou parlement, abolishing venality of offices and creating seventy salaried positions for *conseillers* or judges to preside over the Tournelle, the Enquêtes, and the Grand'Chambre. He immediately began recruiting *présidents, avocats-généraux,* and lawyers. The Maupeou parlement was functioning by the fall of 1771.

The Order of Lawyers practicing before the Paris parlement ante-Maupeou had strong ties of interest and loyalty to magistrates in the suppressed institution. At first, the Order made a great show of its determination to follow these magistrates into inaction in order to frustrate Maupeou's efforts to crush the parlement. However, such firm resolutions quickly proved unprofitable. A prearranged capitulation following a mock last stand brought many of the Order's members back into the Palais de Justice to plead before Maupeou's parlement.

Linguet had never made a secret of his contempt for the establishment and personnel of the parlements. Under the old institutional setup, as under the new one, any advocate practicing before the Parlement of Paris would be compelled to inscribe himself on the membership rolls of the Order of Lawyers. In 1770, Linguet barely succeeded in getting his name included. He was forced to refute charges of embezzlement and theft constructed by his enemies from the meager shreds of rumor a decade old. More serious, he was called down for his works on political administration and legal reform. His colleagues in the bar were suspicious of this author of warm apologies for Neros and Persian despots because these panegyrics read as attacks against the French nobility and as apologia for absolute monarchy.[31] They interepreted his cavalier disdain for the rank, stature, and values of the *noblesse de robe* as threats to the integrity of their professional existence and as a blanket indictment of the justice they claimed to uphold. While students rioted in the streets of Paris to protest Maupeou's coup, and lawyers closely allied with the ousted magistrates shut their law offices and risked their safety to distribute diatribes against the chancellor and his parlement,[32] Linguet circulated his *Eloge de Maupeou,*[33] a less than gentle satire against the protesting magistrates.[34] This impetuosity did not win him any supporters among colleagues who had not taken any stand, who in fact had made a virtue of their timorous hesitation.

Linguet knew what he was after. While apologists for the dissolved parlement exposed the newly appointed magistrates as upstarts and rabble, and branded lawyers who continued to practice before the Paris bar as vile accomplices, avid rowdies and hangers-on, lawless keepers of illegal laws,[35] Linguet was at work plotting the strategy of his march through muddied ground to fortune and liberty, above all.

The regulations governing the trial of cases before the Maupeou parlements restricted use of written judicial briefs. Lawyers now would be compelled to plead a greater number of cases orally.[36] This innovation virtually assured Linguet the setting for which he had been clamoring for almost a decade. During the few years of the Maupeou parlement's existence, the Palais de Justice would be transformed into an arena where legal victory at last would be the reward of any lawyer who, "studying the springs of the human heart,... rendered himself master of the mind in pleasing the ear."[37] Chancellor Maupeou had fashioned the new institutions following dictates of political expediency, and not in faithful imitation of the ancients. Nonetheless, the system called for advocates who were also orators. For Linguet, whose cult of antique perfections, including the oratorical, was patterned after Jean-Jacques Rousseau's models,[38] that orator was a man whose profession would be to express the truth by "bring[ing] the noble passions into play...and employ[ing] the most vehement expressions without fear of appearing ridiculous."[39] "He had to move his judges: he did not think of convincing them by these shreds of arid citations...."[40]

The stage was set. A frail and delicately structured little man of savage audacity, with his flutelike voice, and his frenzied gestures, strode out onto it, a self-proclaimed Gallic inheritor of the tradition of Demosthenes and Cicero. Those were dangerous postures in a nominally absolute monarchy. First of all, Linguet insisted that the lawyer enjoy special privileges amounting to rights of absolutely free expression:

> Nothing more honorable, but at the same time, nothing more delicate and more painful than our functions....The gratitude that it [our zeal] excites, on the one hand, is only too often purchased with the hatred to which it exposes us, on the other; and if we followed only our interests, the moments when we needed fortitude most would be precisely those when we would display the most spinelessness. It is to support our courage in these perilous junctures that, in all nations, alongside the danger in our profession, have been placed the glory that compensates us for it, and the liberty that effaces the thought of it.[41]

> Liberty is inseparable from a profession which, without it, would have no object, or rather, would have one incompatible with its institutions. Without liberty, instead of being the supports of truth, we soon would become only ministers of the lie.[42]

Second, Linguet was determined to speak a language that moved and affected people immediately and persuaded them of the truth by sweeping them into commitment to it. Such a lawyer was not only an advocate; he was a *de facto* legislator. He convinced in spite of established law, even in blatant defiance of it. The judges whom he exhorted to disregard written law would be doing so as executors of his, the orator's legislation, or as legislators themselves, making the advocate's word their law. Even more provocatively, Linguet was summoning the public to judge. The decisions of a vast public carried away by the force of oratorical persuasion would be breaking the bonds of law—or rather, all these decisions handed down by all these judges might command the force of lawmaking acts. The author of the *Mémoires secrets* was able to see at once what the key was to Linguet's commanding position in the bar: "He is able to treat particular issues...on a grand scale, and to bring them forward as objects worthy of the legislator's attention."[43]

The year was 1772. Linguet had accepted the case of Marthe Camp, the former Vicomtesse de Bombelles. At issue was the validity of Camp's marriage to the viscount, who had since deserted her to marry a Catholic. The viscount claimed in his defense that his marriage to Camp was nonexistent in the eyes of the law because the bride was a Protestant, and the couple had not sought the intervention of a Catholic priest to solemnize the marriage and convert the bride to the Catholic religion.

The viscount's argument from statute law seemed unchallengeable. The law absolved him of all obligations of marriage. Linguet would have lost his suit in Marthe Camp's behalf before he ever brought it into the courts to plead it before the magistrates of the Maupeou parlement; but it was not before any court of law that he intended to argue and win it.[44] From the very beginning he had taken the story directly to the bar of public opinion. It was in the journals, the gazettes, among the "crowds" that Linguet created law in this case, generating it as a spontaneous and universally felt moral sentiment of sympathy and commiseration for Camp's plight. Only then did he plead the case before the Maupeou court—with this warning, almost a threat: "And would you want it said one day that the entire nation pleaded for them [the former viscountess and her daughter] and the principal tribunal of the nation condemned them?"[45]

Immediately, the anticipated echo of public opinion followed, the voices of those in the crowd who counted. The Ecole royale et militaire of Paris roundly denounced the vicomte de Bombelles, an alumnus, mouthing sentiments Linguet had contrived to evoke: "We will leave to others the burden of pronouncing upon the ties you have formed with Demoiselle Camp. But there is a tribunal to which you are accountable for the proceedings you have used in your conduct towards her: that of honor. It is before this tribunal, which resides in the hearts of all honest men, that you are everywhere cited and condemned.[46]

Linguet rose to plead for his client in the Grand'Chambre of the Palais de Justice. The courtroom was packed. A segment of the public which had queued up for admission was there, along with prominent members of the nobility, bourgeois with leisure time and curiosity, law students in whose eyes Simon Linguet was the modern Cicero—a mélange of classes and allegiances. Lines had formed early that morning. The corridors were jammed with an overflow that could not be accommodated in the judicial chambers; this tremendous crowd was flanked by an imposing police cordon dispatched to keep it in check.[47] The spectators roared their support of Camp's lawyer. The Grand'Chambre of the Palais de Justice was not an assembly hall for citizens in a republic, yet the former viscountess's lawyer was declaiming as a citizen-lawyer, exhorting as a legislator.

The king's attorney-general, Martin de Vaucresson, summed up his case against Marthe Camp, and at the same time charged Linguet with insurrectionary pleading. He "exhorted the young orators not to take him [Linguet] as their model,....whether it be in his dangerous art of covering everything with his sarcasms, and of misrepresenting as satires pleadings pronounced in defense of innocence...or, finally, in his unbridled audacity in formulating indecent apostrophes to the public, as though to use it as a rampart to force the judges' votes."[48]

The judges retired for a deliberation that lasted three hours, while the spectators remained rooted in their places, overflowing the Grand'Chambre, the Gand'Salle, and "all the avenues of the Palais."[49] The judges decided to dismiss Marthe Camp's demand that her marriage be recognized as legitimate; they also ordered that her child by the viscount be raised as a Roman Catholic, at his expense, and awarded her and her child damage and interest payments of 12,000 *livres* apiece. The viscount paid a high price for legal victory. Before the law, he won his case on a technicality, but before the bar of public opinion, where Linguet had brought him to trial, he lost his honor. Linguet did not triumph in that lost case by force of brilliant arguments from statutory law. He appealed to a law higher than that, to the natural law of human compassion, and to judges whose verdict would be handed down not in the courtroom, but in the corridors of the Palais and on the streets.[50]

The Bombelles case was a *cause célèbre* for the Maupeou parlement that year. Simon Linguet, *enfant terrible* of the new establishment, and the defending lawyer in the case, was no more secure in his triumph before the public than he had been in oblivion. He still did not fit into the legal establishment. He never would. He had entered the Bar publicizing his hatred of parlement and the *noblesse de robe*.[51] His early appeals for thoroughgoing legal reform betrayed his incorrigible disrespect for established legal procedure and judicial institutions; and his apologies for absolute monarchy had not won him any friends either in the *noblesse de robe* or in the *bourgeoisie de robe*. They showed this monarchist publicist to be a theorist of revolutionary remedies.

If the Paris parlement *ante*-Maupeou had remained intact, Linguet could have been controlled. He would have been an isolated rebel against a powerful corps of lawyers supporting and supported by an entrenched magistrature.

That was not his position in the Maupeou parlement. The chancellor had to establish justice on new foundations, at once. Somehow, in spite of demonstrations staged by exiled magistrates backed by advocates sympathetic to the *exilés*, he would have to legitimize a *coup* and win back a public already seduced by liberal-sounding propaganda launched by apologists of aristocratic reaction. Simon Linguet, an outcast among advocates and a friend of absolutists, a man who drew record crowds into the courtrooms and whose eloquence won their allegiance to the new institution, was Maupeou's greatest asset. He was, that is, when he did not pose the greatest threat to unity in Maupeou's court.

By his conduct in the Bombelles case, Linguet already had alienated two attorney generals and a hard core of their supporters. He made enemies easily. Pierre-Jean-Baptiste Gerbier was the most celebrated lawyer in Paris at the time Linguet made his appearance. Gerbier's bearing, his eloquence as an orator, and his Roman profile, called forth all the facile analogies with the noblest ancients. Gerbier's decision to plead before the Maupeou parlement would have guaranteed him an unrivaled series of spectacular triumphs if Simon Linguet, small, thin, pockmarked, with shrill voice and charismatic powers, had not outperformed him. Linguet pleaded against Gerbier on several occasions while defending the marquis de Gouy in a suit brought against the marquis by his wife. Linguet won the case,[52] but the fervor of his defense was sparked, as usual, by an undisciplined passion. He did not spare Gerbier, and Gerbier never forgave him. Gerbier's colleagues had scores of their own to settle with Linguet and were more than willing to contribute to his fund of resentment. "Young and weak, like David," Linguet remarked, "I dared from the beginning to measure myself as an equal with this new Goliath, and the Philistine never forgave me for it."[53]

Then there was the question of Linguet's behavior in the notorious Morangiès affair. Linguet's client, the comte de Morangiès, a free-spending nobleman, had been indicted on a charge of embezzlement by a family of bourgeois moneylenders, the Veron family. The count's protracted and sensational trial, which began in 1772, enlisted the impassioned suffrage of the Parisian public, which split into two belligerent camps. The "plebs," made up of nontitled entrepreneurs, merchants, shopkeepers—all those who had invested important sums of money in dealings with profligate spenders—rallied to the support of the Veron family. Aristocrats and some philosophes, including Voltaire, took their stand with Morangiès and his lawyer, Simon Linguet. Linguet needed all the help he could get, including Voltaire's. In his pleading for Morangiès, he repeatedly called the entire judicial system into question, and above all, the integrity of attorney generals Jacques de Vergès and Martin de Vaucresson. When these threatened functionaries took action against him, postponing one of his cases, refusing to communicate with him, and demanding that Morangiès change lawyers, Linguet broke the bonds of professional decorum altogether, unleashing a barrage of counterthreats in a letter to one of the *présidents à mortier* of the Maupeou parlement, Auguste-Félicité Le-Prestre de Chateaugiron: "However, they appear determined to sacrifice me to the petty, cowardly vengeance of two attorney generals....So far I have not taken a stand, but I shall, and if I must retire, my withdrawal will be that of the lion: I will not turn my back, and I will fight to the last breath."[54]

On July 2, 1773, de Vergès called for Linguet's disbarment—and this, before Linguet was scheduled to plead on appeal before the Tournelle, and after he had printed his *Observations pour le Comte de Morangiès* challenging the attorney general's first conclusions against Morangiès: "He dared to have *Observations* printed against our conclusions, adopted by your Order, an unheard of, scandalous, inexcusable procedure....This is the height of indecency: what can we do about the author of it all? As men we can pity him, as magistrates we can tolerate him no longer."[55] Acting on de Vergè's indictment, the parlement suppressed portions of Linguet's *Observations pour le Comte de Morangiès* and threatened to strike his name from the membership rolls of the Order of Lawyers if he did not stop his disrespectful outbursts against the king's attorneys.[56]

Linguet reacted to the news with predictably flamboyant defiance. He tacked a copy of the parlement's *arrêt* to his office door.[57] Then, according to one account, he rushed to Versailles to demand Maupeou's protection. "What do you want me to do about it," the chancellor is alleged to have told him, "do you think I am going to set up another Parlement, just for you?"[58] We have no record of Linguet's reply.

On September 3, 1773, Morangiès was cleared of all charges against him.[59] Linguet had racked up another sensational triumph and a martyrdom, his own. Linguet had defended the count as though his own integrity were at stake. The Morangiès affair turned upon a point of honor—but whose honor was in question? The count's name had been dragged through the mud by his enemies. When the trial ended, the victorious advocate was charging that he had been calumniated and disgraced. It is true that as the count's lawyer, Linguet had been maligned publicly by the opposition's counsel and by the king's attorney generals. But Linguet also had contributed his share to the mudslinging. A vicious exchange of epithet, both in published briefs and in verbal exchanges in the courtroom, was part of this new game of public pleading. For one lawyer, however, the professional and private dimensions of selfhood were inextricably welded. Linguet acted as though a lawyer could become the voice of his client—his client's truth. Their persons would be inseparable. "After having studied a case well, I set up the lines of an argument, and two days before pleading I became penetrated with the sentiments I must make the tribunal share—to such a point that I fell victim to fever and insomnia."[60] The advocate Linguet was an actor who broke the bonds of his own art to become the client he was defending, on trial for his honor, his profession, his life. "...alone against a whole world of enemies, I presented my head at the feet of Justice to guarantee that of an innocent man [Morangiès] whom her erring arm was about to assassinate. I forced the Public to see, even in our centuries of degeneracy and inertia, how valuable the profession of lawyer still might be when exercised by an upright, strong man whose courage of mind issues from the righteousness in his heart."[61]

Very suddenly, following the end of the Morangiès trial, and this time in the most literal sense, Simon Linguet learned that he was the accused. Kafka's K had a prototype in the person of an eighteenth-century French advocate, a man in search of his trial, summoned to answer for some unnamed crime. Devoured by the anguish of unrelieved uncertainty, he wanders about aimlessly through the corridors of the Palais de Justice, not knowing before whom he must justify himself, or on what counts, and ends by confessing himself publicly, baring his soul in every spoken and written word, professing his innocence with every gesture as though the crime charged against him were that of having lived his life: "What! on your own admission there exist no detractors at all, and there is a denunciation? There are no accusers at all, and there is an accused? You cannot find any evidence, and there is a crime, and not only a crime, but a condemnation, but a punishment, but a civil death; and this death strikes—I will not say the alleged guilty party—but all those who have any professional connections with him?"[62]

Trouble began in December, 1773, when Linguet returned to Paris following a three-month exile in Chartres, a punishment for having defied legal protocol by circulating briefs in defense of a military officer. His absence had provided his enemies with the time to gather from all sides for the assault. Linguet had accepted the comtesse de Béthune's difficult case against some of the most influential persons in the realm, the marquis de Béthune, the duc de Lauzan, and the brother of the countess, the maréchal de Broglie, all of whom were disputing an inheritance from the countess's father. But the marquis's lawyer, Gerbier, had sworn that he would never plead against Linguet, whose mortifying insults he had received with dignified silence in the affair of the marquis de Gouy. He had no intention of submitting himself again to the tongue-lashings administered by this raging advocate who appealed past the judges to the crowds and who, in his insurrectionary pleadings, broke the bonds of statutory law.

Linguet refused to abandon his client. An ad hoc committee composed of members of the Order of Lawyers, chief among them Gerbier and Gaillard, was prepared to take all steps necessary to silence Linguet. On January 23, 1774, this committee concluded that there was reason to engage Linguet to refrain from pleading for one year.[63] The professional côterie met again in

January, and at the Palais de Justice on February 1. By a narrow margin, this faction of the Order confirmed the decision of January 23 to suspend Linguet from the Paris Bar for a year. When Linguet arrived at the Palais de Justice later in February to plead his client's case, the presiding magistrate simply skipped Linguet's case, the first on the docket, and called up the second case.[64]

Simon Linguet would not disappear, or be silenced. Following Gerbier's maneuvers to disbar him, he rushed into print with his *Réflexions pour Me Linguet, Avocat de la Comtesse de Béthune,* his most impassioned defense, a self-defense against the charge, pressed from all quarters, that he had persisted too adamently in being himself: "...isolated in the middle of this terrible flux and reflux of passions which solicit my downfall and would hope to assure my dishonor, I need a general apology that at last will show me such as I am."[65]

Even if the man were only mouthing the role of a bit-part play actor, still he was being pursued for embodying actions and attitudes his role demanded he portray. Then why didn't he leap from the stage, fall to his knees before his judges, and ripping off his mask, beg for mercy? That was the point. This performance was not a play, and that profession was not a mask, but a self-expression. In some real sense Linguet believed that the totality of his existence had been placed on trial, opened to universal scrutiny, and to the judgment of his contemporaries. He had always believed as much. "Paris a donc aussi son Jean-Jacques," Voltaire had observed. His complete confessions were the eleven volumes of his judicial *Mémoires et plaidoyers.*[66]

Linguet claimed he was the medium through whom his client's truth expressed itself. He was fanatically concerned that the integrity of his person and the essential purity of his existence remain unchallenged and untainted. Only on this condition would his verbal testament to his client's truth ring true to the public. Linguet's practice of his profession was necessarily, then, a perpetual public self-confession. This attitude was difficult to sustain in the 1770s before one's colleagues in the Bar, before magistrates in the Maupeou parlement or higher authorities in the administration. And it would not help to bring to the task the passions, the temperament, and the urge to self-laceration of a Jean-Jacques Rousseau.[67] It certainly would not help in bringing the professionals around.

Simon Linguet knew it. His confessions were deliberately phrased as painful studies in professional incompetency, and they read as declarations of permanent revolt against narrow professionalism, the petty rivalries, the cabalistic intrigues in the bar and magistrature. It was not then to enlighten or win votes from his colleagues that Linguet rushed to confess in print that he was the most inept professional practicing before the Paris Bar. "I roamed about through the Palais without a protector, without a backer; an unknown face, and not a very pleasing one; a shy manner that could be taken for rudeness...."[68] These confessional reflections were a strange self-portrait into which, playing soothsayer to himself, Linguet was incessantly reading the profiles of his greatness and the dark lines marking his impending disaster:

> With a delicate constitution, sapped by work and sorrows; with an outward appearance that was not very advantageous; and with a voice in which I suspected neither range nor flexibility, ought I dare take on the fatigues of the bar? Besides, having never appeared in public in my life, having never destined myself to be a bearer of the word, was it prudent to compromise myself by an attempt which, even if successful, could not prove very brilliant, given the apparent nature of my faculties, and which, were it not successful, would expose me to the kind of degradation from which my enemies would profit?[69]

The confessions would have been lacking in sincerity had their author not confessed also his uncontestable success as an orator, and recalled to his enemies the formidable strength of his following: "For a long while, the Palais had been nothing more than a hideous solitude. Now—and this had never happened before—they had to hire guards to turn the crowds away, or to keep them in order."[70] The crowds were Linguet's support, crowds signaling their approval in peals of applause echoing through the Grand'Chambre. "It is the public, then which must be enlightened, convinced, and won over."[71] The public would guarantee his strength as an independent, his professional autonomy, a property right he raised to the power of political freedom. The crowds would function as his court of appeal. The crowds became Linguet's first and final resort against the judicial establishment, all branches of the administration, and if necessary, against the king himself. If the crowds could be won over, everything would be won.

Certain faces in the crowd, those of the young, ambitous, aspiring student population of Paris, became the particular focus of Linguet's attention; the students had not had time and experience enough to be contaminated by the system. It was to them that Linguet's most intimate confessions of professional incompetence were addressed. He never tired of repeating, for their edification, and for the comfort of their protesting response, that he was as unworthy of the legal profession as Cicero had been; that he was as ungifted as Demosthenes in the arts of oratory, and as lacking as he in purity and moral integrity:

> I was a fanatic, I admit it, concerning the nobility of my profession; drunk with this enthusiasm that the candor of youth is susceptible to; full of reading [men like] Cicero and Demosthenes; inflamed by the recollection of their success; filled with a lively emulation engendered by the idea of the glory attached to the career they followed, I didn't think that these great men owed it

perhaps less to their talents than to the fortune of having been born under an administration that facilitated their development. I forgot that our orators are no longer exclusively those of *Rome* and that among us, the *robe* is something quite different from the *toga*....[72]

As you can see, I brought into this profession at least a part of what was necessary to exercise it with brilliance and bring about my downfall.[73]

Linguet conveniently forgot his estimation of Cicero's merits in his *Canaux navigables* of 1769. There he had depicted Cicero as a man of base character. Cicero was eloquent but also venal, and a coward.[74] His own irreverent debunking nonwithstanding, Linguet was perfectly aware of Cicero's hold over the young. Cicero was a model of perfection to those who had not yet reached the age of disillusionment. Cicero's most outspoken critic was prepared to drop his reservations, and proclaim himself Cicero's double. In every respect, he appeared to be living the role to the point of martyrdom, and beyond. The performance was only too realistic. And the example of the Gallic Cicero would be sore temptation to those "young orators" whom de Vaucresson had attempted to dissuade from imitating Linguet—either in his subversive oratory or in his insurrectionary life-style. The *Réflexions pour Mᵉ Linguet, Avocat de la Comtesse de Béthune* was a confession that read in parts like a manifesto, a declaration of independence against the Bar, the Maupeou parlement, and all powers—and a call for supporters.

Following the committee's secret meetings in January, and on February 1, 1774, resulting in the decision to silence and disbar Linguet, the victim charged publicly that an illegal cabal of lawyers had sentenced him to death. He presented himself as a disembodied voice fighting to repossess his professional selfhood, struggling to carry off the miracle of an auto-resurrection. "To judge is to exercise sovereignty. To judge without power is to usurp it; and to condemn to death without power is a crime of *lèse-majesté* of the first degree. Now I have said already that the loss of professional status is a real death for a lawyer, because he cannot live without honor, and because, necessarily, the loss of this professional status covers him with shame."[75]

A subject in an absolute monarchy was defending his honor and claiming his rights, as though Paris were ancient Rome, as though a professional's properties in honor, career, liberty, and life were inextricably linked. This subject happened also to be the son of a father whose properties in profession and honor had been confiscated without due process by the king's minister. In his *Théorie des lois civiles,* where he proclaimed the sacrosanctity of properties, that son spoke for his father, and for all categories of unprotected, threatened proprietors when he argued that revolution was the only effective recourse against institutionalized injustice.

How could a single man make a revolution?

> Moreover, whatever the outcome of this singular dispute must be, I resort here to a privilege consecrated by custom. Outraged, calumniated by unjust and prepossessed colleagues, I appeal from them to my Order: if my Order does not come to my aid, I will appeal from it to Justice: if Justice, and this is not possible, had the weakness to keep silent; if her laws are compromised; if the most cowardly of assassinations committed under her very eyes in circumstances which double the atrocity of it were unable to move her, I would appeal from her to the Public; and if, finally, prejudices suffocated the universal reclamations of contemporaries, there will remain to me at least the last recourse of feeble and slaughtered innocence, the remorse of the assassins, and the judgment of posterity.[76]

"...I would appeal from [Justice] to the Public..." This was no ordinary appeal. Linguet had summoned the public as an extra-institutional tribunal to act in his special case as adjudicator, as agent of his vindication. In an absolute monarchy, justice resided in the person of the king. Whoever appealed from justice to the public appealed from the crown to the nation, placing his provocative pamphleteering in the service of a revolution for a single beneficiary—himself. Linguet was the kind of publicist who could place his life in the hands of his public because he had mastered the art of evoking an immediate and favorable popular response. In another context, Linguet offered his opinion of public opinion: it ought to be venerated by whoever had directed it before consulting it! The public is competent to pronounce final judgment on what concerns it immediately, and where it cannot be blinded or seduced.[77] He could make his professional existence concern the crowd personally; and if that was not seduction, if that could not be called rigging the people, then one might conclude that Linguet was appealing to them. The gesture, however calculated and contrived, was seditious.

Linguet's *Réflexions pour Me Linguet, Avocat de la Comtesse de Béthune* appeared at the beginning of February, 1774. On February 11, acting on a petition submitted against Linguet by thirty lawyers in Gerbier's behalf, the first attorney general of the Maupeou parlement, Jacques de Vergès, denounced the *Réflexions* in a session before the assembled Grand'Chambre and Tournelle. The court then ordered the *Réflexions* suppressed as injurious, calumniating, and debasing to the Order of Lawyers, and Linguet's name deleted from the Order's membership list.[78]

"If my Order does not come to my aid, I will appeal from it to Justice." Following the parlement's *arrêt*, Linguet rushed to Versailles to solicit the intercession of the duc d'Aiguillon and Madame Dubarry. That same day, the king's Conseil d'état, acting on a petition submitted by Linguet, issued an *arrêt de surséance* suspending the parlement's *arrêt* until the king's minister, the duc de Lavrillière, had gathered all relevant data concerning the case and submitted his report. This order was dispatched from Versailles to the parlement in Paris.[79]

The reprieve was short-lived. Pressured by magistrates in the Maupeou parlement who were afraid that Linguet's triumph would bring the entire institution crashing down, Louis XV instructed the duc de Lavrillière to present Linguet with a special letter annulling the *arrêt de surséance*. Linguet was to suspend his pleading before the parlement until the king ordered otherwise.[80]

Declarations of Professional and Political Independence

"I will appeal to Justice," Linguet had insisted. But how was he to recognize the face of justice? The king made his will known in February. In May, 1774, the king was dead; by the fall of that year, the Maupeou parlement was a doomed institution. Magistrates of the old parlement, whom Maupeou had silenced and banished into inactivity, now hoped for a speedy recall from the provinces.

The Conseil d'état remained closed to Linguet's petitions.[81] Behind closed ministerial doors, in the person of a court favorite, at the word of unknown members of a shifting coterie of potentates, legal vindication, professional salvation, and the self's triumph might lie—if only the lines could be cleared, if only the castle could be fixed in time, and space, and reached by a given route, if only the trial date could be set, a plea entered, the defense heard, a judgment rendered, justice administered, and the man vindicated.

On November 12, 1774, in a *lit de justice* at the Palais, Louis XVI ordered the parlement *ante*-Maupeou restored. Magistrates and advocates who had been unrelenting in their refusal to preside or plead in the Maupeou parlement naturally demanded compensation for a voluntary and financially ruinous abstention. Above all, the abstaining lawyers, *"les avocats romains,"* demanded preferential treatment and privileges sufficient to distinguish them from tainted members of the Maupeou parlement, *"les avocats souillés,"* *"les mendiants,"* and *"les vingt-huit."*[82] They called for harsh penalties against *arrivistes* who had profited from an association with the Maupeou establishment.

Meanwhile, Linguet, who did not fall into any of these groups, continued to demand justice for himself, that is, a clean reversal of the Maupeou parlement's *arrêt*. For everything that divided them, key members of the Bar and the parlement were united in their shared hatred of Linguet. Leading advocates in the parlement *ante*-Maupeou and in the Maupeou parlement had tried to strike his name from the Bar's membership rolls, and had warned against his insurrectionary pleading. They had exposed his populist political tactics, his use of the courtroom as a legislative assembly, his indomitable impudence, and the flamboyant irreverence informing his professional activities. Both factions had singled out his literary work, that is to say, his critiques of aristocratic constitutionalism, his apologies for absolute monarchy, and his theories of popular revolution In their eyes, Linguet was guilty of indecencies and indiscretions more heinous than those committed by all the *"avocats souillés."* taken together. If his downfall could be engineered with the active participation of at least some of these disgraced lawyers, the maneuver might serve as an excuse for a fraternal reconciliation, a closing of split ranks.[83]

Antoine-Louis Séguier, an attorney general practicing before the restored parlement, declared himself for Linguet; with this support, Linguet was given permission to defend himself against the Order's accusations during sessions of the Grand'Chambre scheduled for January 4 and 11, 1775. About thirty members of the Order of Lawyers, refusing to be superseded by the parlement in their jurisdiction on the Linguet affair, held a meeting on December 22, 1774, and decided that the Order would not communicate in any way with the ostracized Linguet.[84] In an explanatory letter, the *bâtonnier* of the Order, Nicolas de Lambon, advised Linguet that in spite of his talents, he was engaging in literary activities unbecoming to a lawyer. His editorship of the *Journal de politique et de littérature* was especially repugnant to them.[85] Linguet had assumed this post in the fall of 1774, launching his first issue with an appeal to his public to join him in his crusades to redeem his name, reclaim his property in his profession, beat his enemies into defeat, and reform the Bar to make it a safe place for a political independent practicing law. Ostensibly an advertisement for subscribers, this prospectus read like an appeal for political supporters, for recruits, for avengers: "...you will be convinced that he has never provoked anyone in his life; if sometimes he has wounded his enemies, it was in self-defense, and after having been cruelly outraged....If he then showed an ardour which his assailants occasionally were forced to regret, that is because he believes that in all things, a combat should not be a game, and that either a man must scorn his enemies, or pin them all the way to the ground once the fight is on." Of course, after he had been avenged, but only then, his enemies would have nothing to fear in the way of his reprisals: "Although there is some difference between a journal and the Empire of Rome or the Crown of France, he [the editor] believes that, as Hadrian, as Louis XII, he could say to his literary persecutors: *There, you have been spared."*[86]

Linguet, it seemed, already had outmaneuvered the arbiters of his professional fate. Before they could judge him, he set his journal up as a bar before which he could try his judges and enlighten his reading public. However unprofessional this career in journalism might be for an establishment lawyer, it was manifestly appropriate for a professional rebel who had identified the practice of law with the exercise of liberty and his "political faculties": "Doesn't a lawyer reduced to this deplorable condition [where his colleagues refuse to communicate with him] become suspect to the public, incapable of all social functions in society, alien and even odious to his colleagues? Doesn't he lose his reputation, his occupation, his rank? Isn't he delivered up to an opprobrium ceaselessly renewed, to a daily despite?...[Excommunication] removes from a citizen in an instant all his political faculties, and almost his liberty, which is no longer a possession when it is besmirched with shame."[87]

Lambon's letter to Linguet indicated that the Order of Lawyers would decide his fate during the session where the membership list for the year was drawn up. Linguet guessed the date of that convocation. It was the same day Lambon's letter arrived, December 29, 1774. He arrived at the Palais de Justice and forced an entry into the judicial chambers.

> ...they told me that they had no desire whatever to listen to me, that they would not hear me out.
>   Then, I admit it, I was overcome by indignation: in the kind of fit which so barbarous and cold an injustice brought on, I threw myself across the doorway, and I cried out, sobbing to these pitiless judges: you will not leave until you have heard me; only by crushing me will you open a passage for yourselves without completing this formality.
>   Well!...at this expression of despair, a furious and almost universal clamor arose, as though I had committed the most violent outrage against the assembly....I marked that instant when sober men, mellowed by experience, age, their occupations, violated the immunity of this floor where they used force to pull from their knees a colleague who bathed them in his tears and who demanded in the name of innocence, truth, justice, the one and only favor of being heard.[88]

There were two courts before which Linguet was compelled to plead, the parlement and the Order of Lawyers sitting as a court. The Order had dragged him off as he was clamoring for the right of offering the most complete testament possible to his innocence—a total confession.[89] The parlement remained open to him. On January 4 and 11, 1775, Linguet defended himself before that body: "I ask of you that you restore to me that most precious portion of a citizen's existence, my profession, which I never deserved to lose. I do not ask for the restoration of honor. I do not believe I ever lost it."[90]

On January 11, 1775, the Parlement of Paris overturned the decision of February 11, 1774, by which it had expelled Linguet from the Bar; and it annulled all preceding action as well as all subsequent action that might be taken against him. However, the parlement took no steps to place Linguet's name back on the Paris Bar's membership rolls. He still could not plead or accept clients.[91]

Linguet described his short-lived legal victory before the parlement as though it represented the formalization of the only verdict that counted, his public's. The verdict of the public and the magistrature "is in my favor," he wrote. "You could not doubt it. I received unequivocal proofs of it on this glorious day when all Orders in the state, drawn to my judgment as to a kind of national ceremony, the solemnity of which was augmented by this assemblage, heard the Court of Peers pronounce my absolution....The public seemed to take the obligation of my gratitude upon itself; the power, the universality of the acclamation...drew tears from me; they compensated me for all previous bitterness."[92]

Still, the parlement's justice was not the Bar's, and the parlement almost immediately showed its reluctance to take any steps that would impinge upon the Order's right to discipline its own members. Under renewed pressure, the parlement reversed itself, placing Linguet's professional fate in the hands of the Order.[93]

Again Linguet maneuvered for an audience before the Bar. He was turned away on the nineteenth of January, and again on the twenty-fifth. At last, on the twenty-sixth, he was admitted to the chamber in which a small segment of the Order was assembled. Linguet opened his defense by challenging the Order's procedure in his case. The Bar was offering him justice, and he announced to his public that the Bar's justice was unjust.[94]

First among the Order's grievances, which Linguet recorded in defiance of protocol, was that he did not like the Roman law code. He was accused of lacking respect for French law. He was reproached for his controversy with the duc d'Aiguillon over the payment of his honorarium. The president of the Bar pointed out to him that his writings were filled with reprehensible opinions.[95] The accusations piled up, eight in all, some trivial, some justifiable, and all revealing as much about the kind of establishment the Paris Bar was as about the crimes Simon Linguet had committed against its members. This assembled fraction of the entire Order, about thirty members, voted to keep Linguet's name off the Order's membership rolls, notwithstanding the parlementary *arrêt* of January 11, 1775. Linguet's appeal had failed.[96]

"...If my Order does not come to my aid, I will appeal from it to Justice." In his *Supplément aux "Réflexions pour Me Linguet, Avocat de la Comtesse de Béthune*, which he published on January 30, 1775, Linguet exposed the injustice of the justice that had been meted out to him, conveniently forgetting his earlier appeals to this very authority: "A citizen's profession, above all when it is bound up with his honor, is the most precious portion of his existence. To take away a citizen's profession and his honor requires the same crimes, the same proofs as to take away his life."[97]

In Linguet's new understanding, a professional fraternity would be incompetent to pronounce upon his professional estate as it then would be disposing of his property in his life.[98] On January 27, 1775, the day after the Order had pronounced for disbarment, Linguet addressed still another appeal to the parlement. He was referred to a General Assembly of the Order of Lawyers. A session was scheduled for the Palais de Justice in the Chambre de Saint-Louis on the morning of February 3, 1775.

At the appointed time, Linguet arrived on the scene, surrounded by an impressive gathering of cohorts, including his client, the comtesse de Béthune, the prince de Hénin, a military escort including several chevaliers of the Order of Saint-Louis, Louis-Léon Félicité de Brancas, comte de Lauraguais, the marquis de Morangiès, and Caron de Beaumarchais.[99] He had been authorized once again to address himself to his Order, but he had changed his tactics. An appeal to the Bar's justice would fall on deaf ears. The parlement had referred him back to the Bar. "...if Justice...had the weakness to keep silent ...I would appeal from her to the Public." Linguet summoned his public. He armed it with his passion for his vindication. His public armed itself with other weapons as well.

When the president of the Bar, Nicolas de Lambon, along with the other lawyers, arrived at the Chambre de Saint-Louis, they found the room filled to capacity by Linguet's supporters. A frantic and disconcerted Lambon announced that judicial proceedings could not be carried out in the midst of a mob. Linguet protested; "...the Public was witness to his defense and became his judge because he considered himself justified in invoking the laws and customs of Athens."[100] The histrionics of it all was calculated to arouse "young orators" among Linguet's disciples to intensified expressions of enthusiasm and support. But there was more to it. The Athenian in Linguet in some sense really had welded his profession to a public and political existence. He would triumph or fall *not* by the pronouncements of a coterie of unjust advocates but by a voice vote of the polis. He had taken the precaution of handpicking the polis. It was assembled.

This unexampled spectacle of rebellion left Lambon stupefied. He refused to conduct his proceedings in that arena, but obtained permission to use the Grand'Chambre of the palais.[101] Only one principal was missing—Linguet. Two lawyers were dispatched to invite him to the proceedings. Linguet refused, insisting upon a written agenda of grievances. The Order responded by sending out a deputation of four lawyers. Again, Linguet refused to appear. Finally, after a deputation of six invited him, he arrived at the entrance of the Grand'Chambre accompanied by the comtesse de Béthune. He was admitted while his distinguished client remained glued to the door that had been slammed in her face, straining to catch something of the proceedings. Linguet's crowd of supporters, a symbolic five hundred at his own count, the "Public," in his phrase, pressed from behind.[102]

Meanwhile, inside, Linguet was refusing categorically to satisfy the president of the Order with "yes" or "no" answers to three questions its members had drawn up. He demanded time, then refused to reply to anything until all lawyers notoriously disposed against him—he estimated one hundred—were removed from the room.[103]   He had prepared an oration, a fiery challenge to the Order's justice, an appeal to his public, the polis. "...I can succumb, as *Socrates*," he intended to announce, "but I do not want my *Anituses* to rest unpunished. You allege that you are judging me. I agree to this: but I will place between you and me this supreme Judge to which the most absolute tribunals are subordinated: *public opinion;* it will dispense justice while you will have refused it to me; and if your voices, against all probability, should unite for my proscription, at least I would be able to say upon leaving this place: *everything is lost, except honor."*[104]

Not only was the orator silenced before he could deliver his oration, but the public was barred from the courtroom. The public, a republic of five hundred, was on the other side of closed doors. From there, the eavesdropping comtesse de Béthune suddenly heard what sounded to her like Simon Linguet's cry for help: "...they are cutting my throat, they are assassinating me, Murder...."[105] Linguet's cry "Murder," one report of the scandalous incident read, was "a cry you might look upon as a kind of war cry, or rallying sign— because it was repeated immediately by the crowd of his partisans...." They rushed into the Grand'Chambre; some held "canes high in the air"; others had "hunting knives ready at hand...." The hall was in tumult. Linguet's polis was literally up in arms.[106] At this clear sign that they were dealing with a gang of insurrectionaries, the more prudent advocates beat a retreat. At the same time the comtesse de Béthune summoned up all her energies for a fainting spell, and Linguet, rising to his sense of the melodramatic and the expedient, demanded a postponement of the proceedings, just as a shaken Lambon, gathering the fragments of his shattered instinct for decorum, called for the court bailiff, who managed to clear the invaders, along with the defendent, from the room. In relative safety, the Order took a vote. Of 210 voices counted, 197 were for Linguet's disbarment.[107]

One last step remained. The parlement would be called upon to confirm the Order's action. On February 4, the day following the insurrection at the palais, as Linguet's *Discours destiné à être prononcé par M*e *Linguet, dans l'Assemblée générale des Avocats le 3 février 1775* was being distributed, the assembled parlement heard Nicolas de Lambon's account of Linguet's crimes against the Bar, "his repeated deviations":

> His self-generated principle has been to recognize none; in his writings, he has attacked natural law, that of governments, the public law of the realm, ecclesiastic law, and the civil laws....he has not even respected the Bar as a whole, of which he paints the most horrible picture; he has crowned his excesses, first by seizing —along with people he had assembled in large numbers—the place indicated for our general assembly, and then by violating the sacred refuge of this august sanctuary where *Monsieur le président* gave us shelter so we could pass our resolutions....[108]

The king's attorney, Séguier, who had supported Linguet earlier, now concurred in the Order's decision to strike his name from its membership rolls:

> It is not possible for us to conceal that, in spite of all Sieur Linguet's talents, the character of his mind, the brusqueness of his proceedings, the nature of his principles, the violence of his expressions, and the occurrences yesterday in the heart of the sanctuary of Justice—all these motives together argue against his being kept in the heart of an Order whose union, its most secure and desirable bond, he would not fail to trouble.[109]

Acting on Lambon's remarks and Séguier's conclusions, the parlement drew up an *arrêt* suppressing Linguet's *Supplément aux "Réflexions de M. Linguet, Avocat de la Comtesse de Béthune"* as "injurious to the Order of Lawyers and tending to stir people up," and confirming the decision to strike his name from the Order's membership rolls.[110]

In his exegeses of concepts of law, nature, liberty, and constitution, Linguet undermined the parlement's pretensions to a share of monarchical sovereignty. In politically charged pleading, he broke the bonds of statutory law, reforming the law single-handedly. He made a mockery of the Bar in his subversive and insurrectionary appeals beyond it and beyond the parlement, to a formidable and enthusiastic public following, presenting his case to the public as the titanic struggle of a talented independent against despots, and he explicitly identified the despots. They were the magistrates in the parlement, alleged guardians of the French constitution and defenders of French liberties, and the *parlementaires'* satellites in the Order of Lawyers.

The recently strife-torn corps of magistrates in the parlement and the advocates practicing before it were agreed that Simon Linguet's legal practice was a defiant embrace of lawlessness, as much a threat to the restored parlement as to the newly reintegrated Bar. In the cause of fraternal reconciliation, enemies and allies of the now defunct Maupeou administration joined votes to sacrifice an indomitable rebel.

Linguet appealed from the Bar to the parlement several more times. It is not inconceivable that all these appeals were being supported by enemies of the restored parlement who were prepared to use Linguet's *cause célèbre* as a ramming rod to split ranks in the magistrature and the Bar wide open.[111] If that was the tactic, it failed. Every time Linguet appealed, the parlement ended by concurring in the Order's decision to disbar, and even more, recognizing its right to do so.[112]

By the end of March, 1775, Linguet had exhausted all institutional recourse for his vindication, except for the king, the personification of law and justice. Before making this last appeal, Linguet had reviewed in his *Journal de politique et de littérature* a pamphlet entitled *La Censure*, issued by several members of the Order of Lawyers of Paris. *La Censure* contained a statement of the Order's infrangible prerogative to discipline its members. Linguet protested: "For all men who recognize his power, the Sovereign is the guarantor of properties: *that* is the purpose of the institution; and profession and honor occupy the first rank among properties regarded as belonging to all members of a society: it is therefore these above all that the Sovereign must preserve for them."[113]

A man's professional standing was his property, as was his honor, without which he could not practice his profession. These were properties as inviolable as his stake in land and capital. Liberty of professional self-expression, political in scope and function, apparently was his property also. Without it his profession would have no real value. The sovereign had no choice. He was bound to protect all these holdings.

On October 8, 1775, Linguet appealed to the king to save his life, to restore his profession to him, to guarantee his property rights as he now chose to define them.[114] Linguet recounted all his nightmarish gropings through the corridors of the Palais de Justice in search of his accusers, the place of his trial and the bar of final judgment. The verdicts against him, he charged, reflected a pattern of judicial arbitrariness.[115] Linguet rushed to the king's residence at Choisy to fling himself and his *Mémoire* at the monarch's feet. Louis XVI took no action to save a brilliant, unpolitic lawyer whose defeat by his colleagues in the Bar and their backers in the parlement could be explained in part by his reputation as defender of royal authority.[116]

In Linguet's political system, the monarch was the one person who gave orders to everyone and received them from no one. He was the only perfectly free man. However, monarchical rule rested upon a populist base, upon the conditional submission of millions. Subjects measured the legitimacy of kings by their success in protecting holdings.

With his profession wiped out, Linguet believed he had been robbed of the most valuable property he owned, his livelihood, his life. The monarch's only obligation to him, in return for his submission, was to guarantee him these properties, that is, the fruits of his labor, his profession—including, Linguet insisted, an unfettered self-expression. In his political theory, Linguet deliberately dispensed with the concept of constitutional guarantees for men's civil rights; but then every man who owned something was left to determine for himself at what point a king became a tyrant. This understanding of monarchy might prove fatal to the French crown; it conformed perfectly to the constitutional makeup of Simon Linguet who, in his blueprint for the preservation of an oppressive regime of properties, had engineered an emergency exit for himself into the kind of professional independence which touched upon political self-determination.[117]

Measured by Linguet's standards, the king had defaulted on his fundamental political responsibility. Expressing all the while a most profound veneration for the royal arbiter of his professional existence, Linguet embarked upon a treacherous course of *de facto* insurrection. He appealed his case. He did not appeal from the king to posterity. What he wanted could not wait upon posterity's verdict. He appealed from the king back to the public.

The appeal to his public that Linguet scheduled for February 3, 1775, was never made. The most important witnesses, the members of the Paris Bar, refused to convene in the Chambre de Saint-Louis where Linguet and his polis had gathered. The citizens in this polis finally broke into the Grand'Chambre of the palais, knives drawn and swords unsheathed; but they were forcibly removed by officers of the court. Linguet would have to locate another forum where supporters who identified his lost cause with their interests could demonstrate their allegiance and his real strength. He needed a platform from which, with a loyal following as audience, deterrent force, and political support, he could perform in his complicated triple role as spokesman for the conflicting interests and nascent ideologies of propertied and propertyless subjects and as publicist for the *raison d'état* of the one agency capable of satisfying and reconciling the incompatible demands of these antagonistic classes—monarchical administration.

Linguet justified his insurrection for a single beneficiary by invoking laws governing the propertied order of things. But with that appeal, he repudiated the repressive regime of properties, at least implicitly, and in part. In the face of attacks from the camp of the *économistes,* Linguet already had proclaimed that the political obligations of proto-proletarians to obey and submit, to "suffer and die in chains," was limited by their natural rights to a property in life which they might lay hold of in revolution. The experience of professional expropriation at the hands of a privileged corps of lawyers and magistrates drawing occasional support from potentates in a vacillating administration provoked him into revising his understanding of the obligations and prerogatives of proprietors *vis-à-vis* political authority as he broadened his definition of their properties. He continued to argue that subjects renounced all claims to sovereignty, assuming subpolitical postures, in return for protection that the monarch provided for their holdings—only now, holdings were being reinterpreted to include properties in professional independence and liberty, so that the monarch's coverage would be sufficient to protect not only fathers who were "victim[s] of the despotism of the exilers" but also their sons, "victim[s] of the despotism of the disbarrers," and in fact an entire estate of threatened proprietors.[118] Linguet failed conspicuously to indicate how far he might be willing to go to institutionalize the properties in liberty that he was claiming in this one-man revolution.

Disciples among Linguet's supporters, young collegians and future revolutionaries, were quick to appropriate his deeds as models for their own revolts. As a student of law, Brissot de Warville confessed, he had read Cicero, but it was Simon Linguet's example that inspired him. "His example inflamed me, his success was for me this electric fire that in the batting of an eye, leaps through the most distant things, animating them, enlivening them....I resolved to imitate him." Brissot identified in Linguet's character and comportment the admirable traits a man would have to suppress to avoid his martyrdom: "...this philosophic fever, these fits of independence that turn all thinking heads at age twenty...." He concluded that the disciplinary code of the Bar was expressly designed to exclude genius, corrupt virtues, extinguish the lawyer's liberty. His remedy: open the Bar to merit, following the Roman example, and offer prizes for distinguished professional performance.[119]

Linguet may have taught the generation of future revolutionaries some important political lessons. The *bourgeoisie de robe* and the *noblesse de robe* were not united by unbreakable bonds of ideology and interest. On the contrary, irreconcilable principles and interests might make them natural rivals. In his extraordinary and extralegal practice of law before the Maupeou parlement and in his political writings, Linguet, for one, broke these bonds to declare himself a political independent. He paid a price for his revolt at the hands of his colleagues in the Bar, and his enemies in the parlement and in the king's Conseil d'état. The following generation would not have to. Its members might have learned from *l'affaire Linguet* that a lawyer's professional and political interests might turn out to be equally opposed to those of the aristocratic party and the crown. In a showdown, a threatened professional, even the Third Estate's most brilliant spokesman for a reformed and strengthened monarchy, could not count upon the crown to back him against a powerful corps of *parlementaires,* their satellite advocates, and their influential supporters at Versailles; but then whom could he trust? The public perhaps, provided he could rally its support and use it as independent leverage against a regime of institutionalized and prejudicial privilege.

In a backhanded way, Linguet acknowledged that these appeals to the public were acts of treason. In his review of the Paris advocates' *La Censure,* where he clearly stated the omnipotence of the monarch's will in matters of justice, Linguet also discussed an alternative to the monarchical system: "If in republics other maxims are followed with impunity, that is because there are means of warding off abuses, or because these abuses themselves become a necessary evil for the benefits that liberty promotes there...." In a republic, Linguet explained, legal forms might be less scrupulously respected than in a monarchy, because at any moment any citizen could set the machinery of legislative change in motion. He could do this precisely because he himself would be a portion of that sovereignty in whose name such forms were established. "It is of the essence of a republic that everything change there with the will of the people, which governs itself...." In a republic, the people was its own lawmaker. Every citizen there was a political animal. The nation, the people, everyman, was king there. Linguet was calling the Bar to task precisely for indulging in dangerous flirtation with republican forms and practices: "The subjects of a monarch must never cry anything but *vive le roi*, and not *vivent les Grecs, vivent les Romains, vivent les Anglais...*"; and again: in a democracy a man can call the people to his aid because the people is prince. In a *monarchy*, this would be an outrage, a crime of *lèse-majesté*, because it is not the People who is Sovereign."[120]

Linguet described democrats exercising their liberties, appealing to their fellow citizens; but as a theorist of monarchical absolutism, he categorically condemned such activities: kings were obliged to protect properties, not liberties. Nonetheless, he provoked and met opposition from his enemies in the Bar, the parlement, and the administration by claiming independence, liberty, and influence for himself—as aspects of his endangered property in his career. He set an example for others in how to exercise influence; he mobilized a public following to defend his liberty.

When, in the course of exercising power, magistrates, lawyers, the king's Council, and the king encroached upon and expropriated what Simon Linguet was defining as his dominion, this monarchist whose works Maupeou feared as "the school of despotism" recast his political doctrine so it could be read as the charter for a school of liberty and a handbook of complaints and remedies for despotism's victims. "Injustice in the end gives rise to independence."[121]

NOTES

1. Jean Cruppi, *Un Avocat journaliste au XVIIIe siècle, Linguet* (Paris, 1895), pp. 203-4.

2. Linguet, *Aiguilloniana, ou Anecdotes utiles pour l'histoire de France au dix-huitième siècle, depuis l'année 1770* (London, 1777), p. 15.

3. Jule Flammermont, ed., *Remonstrances du Parlement de Paris au XVIIIe siècle*, 3 vols. (Paris, 1888-98), II, 556-57.

4. Linguet, *Plaidoyer pour S.N.H. Linguet, Ecuier, ancien avocat au Parlement de Paris, prononcé par lui-même, en la Grand'Chambre, dans sa discussion avec M. le Duc d'Aiguillon, pair de France, ancien commandant pour le Roi en Bretagne* (London and Brussels, 1787), p. 15.

5. Linguet, *Mémoire pour M. le Duc d'Aiguillon* (Paris, 1770).

6. *Ibid.*, pp. 1-4.

7. Linguet to d'Aiguillon, Sept. 3, 1774, cited by Linguet in "Requête de M. Linguet, avocat, presentée au Roi à Choisy, le 8 octobre 1775," in BN, MSS, nouvelles acquisitions françaises, 1448, p. 10; printed in Linguet, *Requête au Conseil du Roi, pour Me Linguet, avocat. Contre les arrêts du Parlement de Paris, des 29 mars & 4 février 1775* (n. p., n.d.), pp. 109, 108.

8. Linguet to d'Aiguillon, n.d., cited by Linguet, *Plaidoyer pour S.N.H. Linguet*, p. 45. Marmontel's recollection of the incident in his *Mémoires* deviates from Linguet's in certain details. Marmontel, who faithfully recorded an acquaintance's depiction of Linguet as "an *enfant perdu*, a young man whose talent is not formed but who is trying his luck," and who described Linguet's *mémoire* as "a bombastic declamation, a formless

heap of ridiculously figured sentences...," also acknowledged his own role in revising the work. He described a direct confrontation between Linguet and d'Aiguillon on the subject of revisions in Linguet's text; and he reconstructed Linguet's half of the dialogue: "'No, Monsieur le duc,' he told him, 'no, it is not you, it's a specialist who has put his hands on my work. You have wronged me mortally; you want to dishonor me. But I am not anybody's schoolboy; no one has the right to correct me. I will not sign anything except my work; and this work is no longer mine. Look for a lawyer who is willing to be yours; it will not be I from now on.'" Jean-François Marmontel, *Marmontel, Mémoires,* ed. John Renwick, 2 vols. (Clermont-Ferrand, 1972), I, 266-67.

9. *Ibid.,* I, 267.

10. Linguet to d'Aiguillon, March 7, 1770, cited by Linguet in his *Aiguilloniana,* pp. 20-21, 22.

11. Barthélemy Pocquet, *Le Pouvoir absolu et l'esprit provincial, le Duc d'Aiguillon et La Chalotais,* 3 vols. (Paris, 1901), III, 483.

12. Arthur LeMoy, *Le Parlement de Bretagne et le pouvoir royal au XVIIIe siècle* (Paris, 1909), pp. 410ff. See also Marcel Marion, *La Bretagne et le Duc d'Aiguillon, 1753-1770* (Paris, 1898), pp. 575-76.

13. LeMoy, *Le Parlement de Bretagne,* pp. 411-12.

14. *Arrest du Parlement de Bretagne. Rendu sur les conclusions de Monsieur le procureur général du roi, qui ordonne que les deux imprimés, l'un intitulé "Mémoire pour M. le Duc D'Aiguillon," & l'autre "Mémoire à consulter pour M. le Duc d'Auigillon," seront lacérés & brulés au pied du grand escalier du Palais par l'exécuteur de la haute justice. Du 14 août 1770* (Rennes, 1770). See also Le Moy, *Le Parlement de Bretagne et le pouvoir royal,* p. 412.

15. LeMoy, *Le Parlement de Bretagne,* pp. 412-13.

16. "Séance du Roi en son Parlement de Paris du lundi 3 september 1770, du matin," as chronicled by Pocquet, *Le Duc d'Aiguillon et La Chalotais,* III, 490-91.

17. Linguet to d'Aiguillon, Oct. 11, 1770, as cited by Linguet in his *Aiguilloniana,* p. 28.

18. See Pocquet, *Le Duc d'Aiguillon et La Chalotais,* III, 489.

19. Linguet to d'Aiguillon, Oct. 11, 1770, as cited by Linguet in his *Aiguilloniana,* p. 29.

20. *Ibid.,* pp. 29-31. Linguet completed two long briefs in defense of d'Aiguillon: *Mémoire pour M. le Duc d'Aiguillon* (1770); *Procédures faites en Bretagne et devant la Cour des pairs en 1770, avec des observations* (n.p., 1770). He also drew up a brief defending himself. See his *Observations sur l'imprimé intitulé: "Réponse des Etats de Bretagne au mémoire du Duc d'Aiguillon"* (Paris, 1771).

21. LeMoy, *Le Parlement de Bretagne,* pp. 414-16.

22. *Ibid.,* pp. 415-16.

23. Linguet, *Aguilloniana,* pp. 121-22.

24. Linguet to d'Aiguillon, March 18, 1771, cited by Linguet in his *Aiguilloniana,* p. 38.

25. Linguet to d'Aiguillon, cited without reference, in Cruppi, *Avocat journaliste,* pp. 242-43.

26. Linguet, *Aiguilloniana,* pp. 50-51. Linguet's memoir was published under the title *Considérations politiques et philosophiques sur les affaires présentes du Nord, et particulièrement sur celles de Pologne* (London, 1774). See also Linguet, "Mémoire remis en 1771, par l'auteur de ces *Annales,* à M. le Duc d'Aiguillon, Ministre des affaires étrangères de France, sur un partage de la Pologne," in Linguet, *Annales politiques, civiles, et littéraires du dix-huitième siècle,* 19 vols. (London, Brussels, Paris, 1777-92), I (1777), 104-14.

27. Linguet chronicles these episodes in his *Aiguilloniana,* pp. 54ff.

28. Cruppi, *Avocat journaliste,* pp. 248-51.

29. See, for example, Linguet to Maurepas, London, June 30, 1777, in BN, MSS, nouvelles acquisitions françaises, 5215, fols. 364-65; see also Chapter Five.

30. Linguet to Miromesnil [1774], cited, n.p., in Linguet, *Aiguilloniana,* p. 118.

31. Henri Carré, *Le Barreau de Paris et la radiation de Linguet* (Poitiers, 1892), p. 3; Pierre-Etienne Regnaud, "Histoire des événemens arrivés en France depuis le mois de septembre 1770, concernans les Parlemens et les changemens dans l'administration de la justice et dans les loix du Royaume (1770-1775)," in BN, MSS fr., vol. 13, 733, fols. 257, 300.

32. Paul Dupieux, "L'Agitation parisienne et les prisonniers de la Bastille en 1771-1772," *Bulletin de la Société de l'histoire de Paris et de l'Ile de France*, LVIII (1931), 45-47.

33. For a discussion of Linguet's *Eloge de Maupeou*, see Jacques-Pierre Brissot de Warville, *Mémoires de Brissot, membre de l'Assemblée législative et de la Convention nationale, sur ses contemporains, et la Révolution française*, ed. François Mongin de Montrol, 4 vols. (Paris, 1830-32), I, 118-19. The text of the *Eloge* appears in this edition of the *Mémoires*, I, 373-74.

34. See Henri Martin, "Etude sur Linguet," in *Travaux de l'Académie nationale de Reims*, vols. XXX (1858-59), 341-425, and XXXI (1859-60), 81-149; see also XXX, 392.

35. For contemporary comments on the activities of the Maupeou parlement in Paris by an author sympathetic to the exiled parlement, see Matthieu-François Pidanzat de Mairobert, *Maupeouiana, ou Correspondance secrète et familière du Chancelier Maupeou avec son cœur Sorhouet*, 2 vols. (n.p., 1771); Mairobert, *Les Efforts du patriotisme; ou Recueil complet des écrits publiés pendant le regne du Chancelier Maupeou...Ouvrage qui peut servir à l'histoire du siècle de Louis XV, pendant les années 1770, 1771, 1772, 1773 et 1774* (Paris, 1775); Mairobert, *Journal historique de la révolution opérée dans la constitution de la monarchie françoise, par M. de Maupeou, Chancelier de France*, 7 vols. (London, 1774-76).

36. See P. Guilhiermoz, "De la persistance du caractère orale dans la procédure civile française," *Nouvelle revue historique de droit français et étranger*, XII (1889), 21-65. See also Cruppi, *Avocat journaliste*, p. 259; and Linguet, *Réflexions pour Mr. Linguet, Avocat de la Comtesse de Béthune*, in *Appel à la postérité, ou Recueil des mémoires et plaidoyers de M. Linguet pour lui-même, contre la communauté des avocats du Parlement de Paris* (n.p., 1779), p. 178.

37. Linguet, *Histoire du siècle d'Alexandre, avec quelques réflexions sur ceux qui l'ont précédé* (Amsterdam, 1762), p. 200.

38. See above, Chapters One and Two.

39. Linguet, *Histoire du siècle d'Alexandre*, 2d ed. (Amsterdam and Paris, 1769), pp. 262-63.

40. Linguet, *Nécessité d'une réforme dans l'administration de la justice et dans les lois civiles en France, avec la réfutation de quelques passages de "L'Esprit des lois"* (Amsterdam, 1764), p. 94.

41. Linguet, *Réplique à la consultation signée Dobet, pour le Comte Orourke, Mestre de Camp, contre M. Linguet, avocat, en son nom défenseur de Madame la Duchesse d'Ollonne*, in Linguet, *Mémoires et plaidoyers de M. Linguet, avocat à Paris*, 11 vols. (Liège and Amsterdam, 1776), VII, 105-6.

42. *Ibid.*, VII, 106.

43. Louis Petit de Bachaumont, *Mémoires secrets, pour servir à l'histoire de la république des lettres en France, depuis MDCCLXII jusqu'à nos jours; ou Journal d'un observateur*, 36 vols. (London, 1780-89), VI (Jan. 18, 1771), 79; V (Aug. 30, 1772), 181.

44. See Cruppi, *Avocat journaliste*, p. 283. Before Linguet brought Marthe Camp's case to trial before the Maupeou parlement, the pre-Maupeou parlement had established legal precedents for handling *de facto* violations of the letter and the spirit of the law. Linguet's task was to bring these lessons home to the magistrates sitting on the Maupeou court. In doing so, his principal appeal was not to legal precedent, but to universally acknowledged principles of humanity and common sentiments of compassion. For a discussion of cases involving Protestant-Catholic marriages and legal decisions preceding those of the Maupeou parlement in the Bombelles-Camp affair, see David Bien, "Catholic Magistrates and Protestant Marriage in the French Enlightenment," *French Historical Studies*, II, (1962), 409-29.

45. Linguet, *Réplique pour D^lle Antoinette-Louise-Angélique-Charlotte de Bombelles*, in Linguet, *Mémoires et plaidoyers* (1776), V, 336.

46. Council of the Ecole royale et militaire to M. de Bombelles, Nov. 27, 1771, in Poncet-Delpech, *Mémoire à consulter et consultation sur un mariage contracté en France suivant les usages des Protestants, Pour Dame Marthe Camp, Vicomtesse de Bombelles* (n.p., 1772), pp. 114-15.

47. Bachaumont, *Mémoires secrets*, VI (Aug. 7, 1772), 168.

48. *Ibid.*, 169.

49. *Ibid.*, 173.

50. No one was more aware of his power over the public than Linguet. Mairobert, in his chronicle of the activities of the Maupeou parlement, his *Journal historique*, notes that Linguet, who had been boasting before the parlement of his successes as a lawyer, claimed that of seventeen cases undertaken in 1772, he had won thirteen and "one was lost (Madame de Bombelles's) much to the regret of the public...." *Journal historique*, IV (Apr. 1, 1773), 140.

51. Regnaud, "Histoire des événemens depuis le mois de september 1770," vol. 13,734, fols. 212, 268-69.

52. Linguet, *Mémoire pour le Marquis de Gouy contre la Marquise de Gouy*, in *Mémoires et plaidoyers* (1776), VI, 155-405.

53. Linguet, *Réflexions pour Me Linguet*, in *Appel à la postérité*, p. 207.

54. Linguet to the président de Châteaugiron, May 13, 1773, in BM, no. 1916.

55. *Arrest de la Cour de Parlement extrait des registres du Parlement. Du deux juillet mil sept cent soixante-treize* (Paris, 1773), p. 2.

56. *Ibid.*, p. 3.

57. Regnaud, "Histoire des événemens depuis le mois de september 1770," vol. 13,734, fol. 20.

58. Mairobert, *Journal historique*, IV (July 6, 1773), 239.

59. *Arrêt du Parlement, rendu la Grand'Chambre assemblée: Qui décharge le Comte de Morangiès de toutes les plaintes & accusations contre lui intentées, avec dommages-intérêts & dépense....Du 3 septembre 1773* (Paris, 1773).

60. Marie-Jean Hérault de Séchelles, quoting Linguet, cited without reference in Martin, "Etude sur Linguet," in *Travaux de l'Académie nationale de Reims*, XXX (1858-59), 418; see also Hérault de Séchelles, *Hérault de Séchelles: Oeuvres littéraires*, ed. Emile Dard (Paris, 1907), p. 166.

61. Linguet, *Réflexions pour Me Linguet*, in *Appel à la postérité*, pp. 180-81.

62. Linguet, *Discours destiné à être prononcé le 3 février 1775, dans l'Assemblée générale de l'Ordre des avocats au Parlement de Paris*, in *Appel à la postérité*, p. 373.

63. Mairobert, *Journal historique*, V (Feb. 10, 14, 1774), 167, 172-73.

64. Linguet, *Réflexions pour Me Linguet*, in *Appel à la postérité*, pp. 185-87; Mairobert, *Journal historique*, V (Feb. 14, 1774), 173-74; Regnaud, "Histoire des événemens depuis le mois de spetembre 1770," vol. 13,734, fol. 345.

65. Linguet, *Réflexions pour Me Linguet*, in *Appel à la postérité*, p. 165.

66. Linguet published several collections of his legal briefs. See his *Mémoires et plaidoyers*, 7 vols. (Amsterdam, 1773); *Plaidoyers et Mémoires de M. Linguet, Nouvelle édition revue et corrigée par lui-même*, 2 vols. (London, 1787-88); and *Mémoires et plaidoyers de M. Linguet, avocat à Paris*, 11 vols. (Liège and Amsterdam, 1776).

67. Linguet readily admitted this parallel between his character and Rousseau's on the question of their personal integrity and their shared passion for defending their innocence in the face of slander. Commenting in his *Annales* on a letter to him from the abbé Royou supporting d'Alembert's caustic critique of Rousseau on the question of Rousseau's alleged egomania, Linguet rose to Rousseau's defense, and took the occasion to defend himself against the same charge. See Linguet, *Annales*, VI (1779), 46-47.

68. Linguet, *Réflexions pour Me Linguet*, in *Appel à la postérité*, pp. 172-73.

69. *Ibid.*, p. 178.

70. *Ibid.*, pp. 178-79.

71. Linguet to d'Aiguillon, March 7, 1770, cited by Linguet in his *Aiguilloniana*, p. 21.

72. Linguet, *Réflexions pour Me Linguet*, in *Appel à la postérité*, pp. 168-69.

73. *Ibid.*, p. 170. Linguet played up for everything it was worth—and it was worth at least the suffrage of the student population of Paris—this new study in parallel lives, his and Cicero's. Linguet drew the most explicit parallels in his review of the Order of Lawyers' two pamphlets against him, *Consultation sur la discipline des avocats* and *La Censure*. Linguet's reviews appeared in his *Journal de politique et de littérature*, no. 18 (June 25, 1775), 236-48. He reprinted the review the following year as *Consultation de M. Linguet, avocat, en réponse à la "Consultation sur la discipline des avocats" imprimée chez Knapen, en mai 1775* (Brussels, 1776).

74. Linguet, *Canaux navigables, ou Développement des avantages qui résulteraient de l'exécution de plusieurs projets en ce genre pour la Picardie, L'Artois, la Bourgogne, la Champagne, la Bretagne, et toute la France en général. Avec l'examen de quelques-unes des raisons qui s'y opposent, & c.* (Amsterdam and Paris, 1769), pp. 349-55.

75. Linguet, *Réflexions pour Me Linguet*, in *Appel à la postérité*, p. 195.

76. *Ibid.*, p. 214.

77. Linguet, *Annales*, XV (1788), 307, 313.

78. *Arrest de la Cour du Parlement, qui supprime un libelle, ayant pour titre: "Réflexions pour Me Linguet, Avocat de la Comtesse de Béthune," & ordonne que Me Linguet sera rayé du tableau. Extrait des registres du Parlement. Du onze février mil sept cent soixante quatorze* (Paris, 1774). See also Carré, *Le Barreau de Paris*, pp. 6-7.

79. Mairobert, *Journal historique*, V (Feb. 15, 1774), 176. See also, "Extrait des registres du Conseil d'Etat du Roy. Du 11 féver 1774," in BN, MSS fr., Coll. Anisson-Duperron, vol. 22,101, fols. 294-95.

80. Linguet, *Aiguilloniana*, p. 62; Regnaud, "Histoire des événemens depuis le mois de september 1770," in BN, MSS fr., vol. 13,734, fols. 348-50.

81. Regnaud, "Histoire des événemens depuis le mois de september 1770," vol. 13,735, fol. 55.

82. Carré, *Le Barreau de Paris*, p. 2. See also Regnaud, "Histoire des événemens depuis le mois de septembre 1770" vol. 13,735, fols. 55, 326.

83. Carré, *Le Barreau de Paris*, p. 2; Regnaud, "Histoire des événemens depuis le mois de septembre 1770," vol. 13,735, fol. 326.

84. Cruppi, *Avocat journaliste*, pp. 370-71; Linguet, *Plaidoyer pour Me Linguet, Avocat au Parlement, prononcé par lui-même en la Grand'Chambre, les 4 & 11 janvier 1775, avec l'arrêt intervenu en sa faveur*, in *Appel à la postérité*, pp. 258-59.

85. Nicolas Lambon to Linguet, Dec. 29, 1774, cited by Linguet in his *Supplément aux "Réflexions pour Me Linguet, Avocat de la Comtesse de Béthune,"* in *Appel à la Postérité*, pp. 329-30.

86. Linguet, *Journal de politique et de littérature*, No. 1 (Oct. 25, 1774), 6-7.

87. Linguet, *Plaidoyer pour Me Linguet...les 4 et 11 janvier 1775*, in *Appel à la Postérité*, p. 279.

88. *Ibid.*, pp. 261-62.

89. *Ibid.*, pp. 260-61.

90. *Ibid.*, p. 221; for entire speech see pp. 218-90.

91. See Cruppi, *Avocat journaliste*, p. 373; Carré, *Le Barreau de Paris*, p. 11; Linguet, "Arrêt de la cour de Parlement," in *Appel à la Postérité*, pp. 290-91.

92. Linguet, *Discours destiné à être prononcé le 3 février 1775*, in *Appel à la postérité*, pp. 397-98.

93. Carré, *Le Barreau de Paris*, p. 11.

94. See Linguet, *Supplément aux "Réflexions pour M. Linguet,"* in *Appel à la postérité*, pp. 333, 337-38.

95. *Ibid.*, pp. 343, 344-45.

96. Mairobert, *Journal historique*, VII (Jan. 28, Feb. 1, 1775), 66, 77-78.

97. Linguet, *Supplément aux "Réflexions pour M. Linguet,"* in *Appel à la postérité*, pp. 363-64.

98. *Ibid.*, p. 365.

99. Siméon-Prosper Hardy, "Mes Loisirs, ou Journal d'événemens tels qu'ils parviennent à ma connoissance (1764-1789)," in BN, MSS fr., vol. 6682, fol. 26; Regnaud,

"Histoire des événemens depuis le mois de september 1770," vol. 13,735, fol. 332.

100. Hardy, "Mes Loisirs," paraphrasing Linguet's response to Lambon, vol. 6682, fol. 26. The *Journal historique*, VII (Feb. 4, 1775), 89, contained the following entry on the incident: "When the accused was given to understand that he could not remain in the hall with this formidable cohort, he claimed that it was necessary, that these were so many witnesses whom he had taken to determine what the Order's grievances and responses were, as they refused to give them to him in writing."

101. Hardy, "Mes Loisirs," vol. 6682, fol. 27.

102. Linguet, *Discours destiné à être prononcé le 3 février 1775*, in *Appel à la postérité*, p. 370, n. 1.

103. *Ibid.*, pp. 377-79; Carré, *Le Barreau de Paris*, p. 12.

104. Linguet, *Discours destiné à être prononcé le 3 février 1775*, in *Appel à la postérité*, p. 372.

105. Hardy, "Mes Loisirs," vol. 6682, fol. 27. Linguet referred to the incident in his *Discours destiné à être prononcé la 3 février 1775*, in *Appel à la postérité*, p. 370, n. 1. It is likely that Linguet prearranged the dramatic scene himself; in his prepared *Discours destiné à être prononcé* he underscored his legal plight as a martyrdom—complete with the imagery of swords, bloodshed, and other dangerous props. Did he expect that with the aid of his five hundred supporters, the truth of his words would be dramatically borne home to his persecutors in the form of gory deeds? "And when I moan, when I show my colleagues, my judges, my wounds and those responsible, the dagger that has cut into me and the bloody hand that left it in the wound, they grumble, what is more, they become angry. They even hold my sobs against me as a crime. There is less injustice, less cruelty in slaughter houses where the animals' life is sacrificed to support our own. The butchers who slaughter them at least forgive their pushing away the knife: they are not offended by the doleful groans which accompany the spilling of all their blood." *Discours destiné à être prononcé le 3 février 1775*, in *Appel à la postérité*, p. 390. For other accounts, see Mairobert, *Journal historique*, VII (Feb. 4, 1775), 93-94; Jean-François de La Harpe to André Schowalow, n.p., n.d., in La Harpe, *Correspondance littéraire, adressée à son Altesse impériale, Mgr le grand-duc, aujourd'hui Empereur de Russie, et à M. le Compte Andé Schowalow, chambellan de l'Impératrice Catherine II, depuis 1774 jusqu'à 1789*, 6 vols. (Paris, 1804-7), I, letter XI, 94.

106. Hardy, "Mes Loisirs," vol. 6682, fol. 27.

107. Cruppi, *Avocat journaliste*, p. 386. Mairobert, *Journal historique*, VII (Feb. 4, 1775), 94, gives a count of 187 to 10 in favor of Linguet's disbarment.

108. "Arrêt du 4 février [1775] supprimant l'imprimé intitulé: *Supplément aux 'Réflexions pour M. Linguet, Avocat de la Comtesse de Béthune,'* comme injurieux à l'Ordre des avocats, et tendant à soulever les esprits; ordonnant que M. Simon-Nicolas-Henri Linguet sera et demeura rayé du tableau des avocats étant au greffe de la Cour en date du 9 mai 1770, et que le présent arrêt sera imprimé" printed in Hippolyte Monin, *Etat de Paris en 1789, Etudes et documents sur l'ancien régime à Paris* (Paris, 1889), pp. 177-78.

109. *Ibid.*, p. 178.

110. *Ibid.*, p. 177; see also Carré, *Le Barreau de Paris et la radiation de Linguet*, pp. 12-14.

111. Hardy, "Mes Loisirs," vol. 6682, fols. 41-42.

112. See Cruppi, *Avocat journaliste*, pp. 389-90; Monin, *Etat de Paris*, p. 178. For more details see the following entries: Hardy, "Mes Loisirs," vol. 6682, fols. 41-47; Mairobert, *Journal historique*, VII (March 6, 18, 25, April 11, 1775), pp. 157-58, 190-96, 257. See Linguet's accounts in his *Requête au Conseil du Roi, pour Me Linguet, avocat. Contre les arrêts du Parlement de Paris, des 29 mars & 4 février 1775*.

113. Linguet, "Réflexions d'un citoyen sur le libelle intitulé *La Censure,*" *Journal de politique et de littérature*, no. 20 (July 15, 1775), 328.

114. Linguet, "Requête de M. Linguet, avocat, présentée au Roi à Choisy le 8 octobre 1775," in BN, MSS, Nouvelles acquisitions françaises, 1448, fol. 2.

115. *Ibid.*, fol. 4. For printed versions, see *Requête au Conseil du Roi, pour Me Linguet, avocat. Contre les arrêts du Parlement de Paris, des 29 mars & 4 février 1775; Très-humbles, très- respectueuses représentations adressées à Sa Majesté, Par Me Linguet, avo-*

cat, sur la défense à lui faite d'imprimer sa "Requête" en cassation, contre les arrêts des 4 février & 29 mars 1775 (Brussels, 1776).

116. Bachaumont, *Mémoires secrets*, VIII (Oct. 16, 1775), 207.

117. In his *Très-humbles, très-respectueuses représentations adressées à Sa Majesté*, Linguet presented his case as a study in the violation of properties under a monarchical regime: "At a time when the revivification of the laws is announced, along with a respect for properties, the best consecrated of the laws, will the [law] that prohibits condemning anyone without a hearing be violated with impunity? Will the most sacred of properties, honor and profession, be snatched away without formalities, and irreversibly, from a public personality? At a period when Your Majesty has just announced, by a very striking retraction, his repugnance for acts of arbitrary authority; when power itself takes pleasure in reigning itself in and wills that all its proceedings be preceded, justified, by a solemn and searching examination, is it tolerable that there exist, by consent of the tribunals, and in their sanctuary, a company which counts among its privileges that of issuing death orders, not only without giving any account of its motives, but without having any?" pp. 4-5.

118. Linguet uses these terms to depict his victimization and his father's in his *Annales*, VII (1779), 459.

119. Jacques-Pierre Brissot de Warville, *De la décadence du barreau françois, des inconvéniens de l'ordre des avocats, de la manière de les rendre utiles au public, sur-tout dans les matières criminelles*, in Brissot de Warville, *Bibliothèque philosophique du législateur, du politique, du jurisconsulte...*, 9 vols. (Berlin, 1782), VI, 344-45, 362-69, 406-8. See Brissot's comments on his first encounters with Linguet and his appraisal of Linguet in Brissot de Warville, *J.-P. Brissot: Mémoires (1754-1793)*, ed. Claude Perroud, 2 vols., Mémoires et documents relatifs aux XVIIIe et XIXe siècles, vols. II-III (Paris, 1911), I, 82.

120. Linguet, "Réflexions d'un citoyen sur le libelle intitulé *La Censure*," *Journal de politique et de littérature*, no. 20 (July 15, 1775), 328-29.

121. Linguet quoted this line in his review (in the *Journal de politique et de littérature*) of a performance of *Tancrède* at the Opera. He described *Tancrède* as "a singular play, a play full of grandeur, energy, philosophy; a play where there are an infinite number of verses which ought to have become proverbs, and proud proverbs, such as this one, for example: 'L'injustice à la fin produit l'indépendance.'" *Journal de politique et de littérature*, no. 15 (May 25, 1776), 129.

FIVE

Travaux Pratiques:
Political Journalism

Revolution, the Journalist's First Political Forecast

A year and a half after his disbarment, Linguet left France, crossed the Channel into England, and announced that he was embracing a new profession, political journalism in exile, and that he was prepared to exercise it in permanent revolt against all branches of the French establishment.

Linguet began marking out a career in the field in the fall of 1774, while battling Parisian lawyers on one front and physiocratic adminstrators and polemicists on another. Charles-Joseph Panckoucke, the enterprising publisher, had bought up rights to a journal, *L'Avant Coureur,* and had joined it to his *Gazette de littérature, des sciences et des arts.* In 1774, he obtained a new privilege for a *Journal de politique;* merging it with the *Gazette de littérature,* he formed the *Journal de politique et de littérature.* Panckoucke held his lease on the journal from the Department of Foreign Affairs. He hired Linguet as editor. Linguet's contract with Panckoucke called for his receiving a salary of ten thousand *livres* a year, with a thousand *livres* raise for every thousand subscriptions over the first six thousand.[1]

Linguet began an unconventional exploitation of the *Journal* in his first number.[2] He used it to declare his independence from the legal establishment; he launched manifestos against the *économistes;* he publicized the narrow sectarianism of the Académie française and the self-interested propaganda of the philosophes. He named all his enemies in the *Journal,* and made a boastful display of his autonomy. He proclaimed himself an implacable adversary of the establishment in arts, letters, law, politics—but what, besides himself, was he for? He sometimes wrote as though he supported a vast inarticulate constituency, a nation beyond despair and ready for revolution: "The great law, the most sacred of all laws, is the *salut du peuple.*"[3] His commitments were in fact more complicated. Journalism turned out to be as perilous a profession for Linguet as law had been. In practicing it, he established himself as a spokesman for the prerogatives of kings and the claims of subjects, and as an advocate for the special interests of Simon Linguet.

In the summer of 1776, Linguet met the danger head on; and he succumbed to his second in a continuing series of professional martyrdoms. Jean-François de La Harpe, one of Linguet's favorite enemies,[4] was accepted into the venerable Académie française on May 13, 1776. The honor was a universally acknowledged mark of literary success. In 1770, Linguet bid for the recognition that only the most prestigious literary fraternity in France could confer and he was turned away. He retaliated with an impassioned repudiation of the literary establishment:

> ...if they [men of letters] consider as a dangerous enemy, if they vilify in society, if they try to deliver up to a stigmatizing excommunication the simple and unknown man who flees even the shadow of stratagem, who lives alone, who brings to light what he believes true, without stubbornness, disinterestedly, without partisanship of any kind, and whose only crime was to want nothing to do with their fanatic conventicles, *ma foi, Monsieur,* so much the worse for them; I tell it to you straight....[5]

> It is true that I did not attack revelation. I did not give my novelties the encyclopedic varnish, this passport for all the coated-over scrap iron with which so many peddlers of old philosophic hat shout us deaf.[6]

In reporting La Harpe's reception into the Académie in June, 1776, Linguet exploited the opportunity to expose the institution's members as narrowly self-interested sectarians. " *'Knock and it shall be opened to you,'* says a sacred Oracle. *M. de La Harpe* has practiced the Gospel....It is true that he had been in cahoots with the gatekeepers *for a long time.* 'One learns to bay,' says another [Oracle], 'with wolves.' "[7]

What did unsuccessful candidates lack? asked this former aspirant, to whom the doors had never opened: "It's complacency, it's a novitiate that prepares them for initiation. It's the promise of a blind devotion, the courage to keep oneself firmly attached to the *Masters*...unqualified submission to the Saint *Peters* who have this little paradise at their disposal and who...admit into it only the elect marked with the *sign of the beast.*"[8]

This news report was a transparent camouflage for Linguet's repudiation of the literary fraternity that had denied him its passport to honor and fortune, and rejected his ideas because they were anti-encyclopedic, unphilosophic, antiphysiocratic, in short, anti-establishment.[9] Linguet judged the forty immortals, judges of all would-be men of letters in France. He publicized his verdict: they were only sellers of used goods—liberal cant—bent on curbing the upward mobility of talented iconoclasts and tightening their monopoly over ideas, position, and influence.

Linguet's printed insult to La Harpe had been approved by the government's censor for the *Journal de politique et de littérature*; nonetheless, or possibly for that very reason, the article was received as an intolerable slight to an institution whose members commanded substantial support in the power centers of the administration. The duc de Nivernais, seconded by the maréchal de Duras, contacted Keeper of the Seals Miromesnil to voice the Académie's grievances against the impertinent journalist.[10]

Panckoucke, the *Journal's* publisher, who as late as July 8, 1776, was on good enough terms with his editor to have planned a pilgrimage with him to Ferney to see Voltaire, suddenly took his distance, and probably his precautions as well.[11] He wrote to Linguet informing him of a new order of necessities which he presented as having been dictated from above, by ministerial fiat, Miromesnil's and Vergennes's: Linguet's affiliation with the *Journal* must be severed; if Panckoucke disobeyed, his privilege would be revoked. Panckoucke enclosed letters from the director of the *librairie* and from Vergennes, both dated August 2.[12]

Linguet was furious. He wrote his own letter to Vergennes, and enclosed an annotated copy of Vergennes's order to Panckoucke. He seized upon Vergennes's phrase, " '...you must no longer employ on this work [the *Journal*] the person who made the mistake...' ": "They speak here of the *person employed* as of a lackey whom they fire when they are displeased with him." What Vergennes failed to understand, Linguet told him, was that he had been appointed editor with a contract, and for as long as Panckoucke's privilege lasted. "The man of letters, called here a person," would never have added the trouble of editing the *Journal* "to the humiliation of being only a hireling dependent on the whims of a publisher. Unless it has been decided to steal from him without reservation all the rights of citizen, in the bar, and in literature, and unless publishers are above the laws and courts, the way lawyers are, this person will claim his rights: he offered them as a sacrifice to honor, he will never [sacrifice them] to force."[13]

In August, 1776, notwithstanding his contract with Linguet, Panckoucke named the new editors of the *Journal de politique et de littérature*: his brother-in-law, Jean-Baptiste Suard, and La Harpe.[14] This defeat was more than Linguet could bear. He prepared to leave France.

Linguet's self-imposed exile began in 1776. On January 16, 1777, he rededicated himself to the cause of a revolution for a single beneficiary. From the depths of the burning entrails of the hideous John Bull, as he once had described England,[15] he published an open and openly libelous letter to Vergennes. The *Lettre de M. Linguet à M. le Comte de Vergennes, ministre des affaires étrangères en France* was an unambiguous declaration of independence from professional enslavement and political servitude under a despotic regime.

A public personality who exiled himself, Linguet announced, owed an explanation of his motives, not only to government officials, but to his countrymen and to the people of the nation where he was seeking asylum—the public, his public. "...he must place contemporaries and posterity between himself and his persecutors; he must cite them [his motives] before this tribunal, independent of all powers and which all powers respect; this tribunal that is sovereign judge of all the judges of the earth, this tribunal before which one speaks in print...."[16]

"...*every citizen for whom the laws of his country become impotent, ceases to be bound by them.*"[17] He did not stop being a citizen; it was simply that he could no longer lead a public existence in France, under a regime that had presided over the liquidation of his properties in two professions. "As long as I had something they could steal from me; as long as I saw myself as the *Sibyl* of *Vergil,* cakes in hand to feed the gullet of the *Cerbereses* bent upon my perdition, I feared less for my person. My fortune, my profession, my works, my civil properties—they devoured everything, bit by bit, and I suffered patiently. But at last, when my liberty was the only possession on earth I had left, could I then flatter myself that they would not soon swallow that up also? Isn't it, according to our customs, of all properties, the one most flippantly ravished, the one that is robbed with the least outcry and scandal?[18]

In a libel circulated in England, possibly in France clandestinely, and elsewhere on the continent as well,[19] Linguet was representing the story of his disbarment and his dismissal from the *Journal de politique et de littérature* as a case study in victimization under a despotism. He made concrete and specific in the *Lettre* the general definition of despotism he had offered the public in his *Lettres sur la "Théorie des lois civiles"* and in his *Du plus heureux gouvernement:* when governments deviate from the "circular line traced in all its points at intervals perfectly equidistant from the essential fundamental center of political society, that is to say, property, this sacred principle of all governments, this god of politics—at this instant despotism is generated...."[20] In the case of Simon Linguet, despotism existed where magistrates and a corps of lawyers, along with dukes, peers, marshals, the Académie française, secretaries of state, publishers, and the king's advisory councils combined to remove his professional estates arbitrarily, and where the king himself did not have the knowledge, or the power, to render him justice.[21]

Linguet informed the public that his letter to Vergennes was only the first installment in a serial indictment of despotism's agents and abettors in France. He announced a fifteen-volume collection of his works and promised detailed exposure there of the regime's multiple violations of his civil rights.[22]

Clearly, then, Linguet's message was that a despotic French regime had all but wiped him out; but he now claimed that he was not matter to be crushed, but rather, the most indestructible embodiment of the principle of aggressive energy. Suddenly, before his eyes, the world also ceased to be immovable matter. He saw all the old forms crumbling, dissolving into a sublime chaos. Here was a singular piece of news to be communicating in a public letter to the king's secretary of state in the Department of Foreign Affairs. The whole world, Linguet proclaimed, was cracking up. Statesmen met the crisis by continuing to balance international powers, manipulating mechanical laws governing an abstract world where stability, or at most, patterns of rationally ordered change, prevailed unchallenged. But they were working on the stuff of a world about to explode into something incalculable and unmanageable. All these scrupulously exact exercises, Linguet revealed, were ludicrous, irrelevant in the face of the old order's impending explosion:

> You force me to give myself a new existence; if my heart balks at it, my mind is not at a loss. Given the condition of *Europe* right now, I have a great feeling that with courage and indignation a man can go very far.
>
> The political balance escapes you, and your enfeebled hands will not recapture it. Everywhere, the North recovers an ascendancy all but forgotten for several centuries. On the old continent, *Poland's* losses enrich powers which will not hesitate to dictate their laws to the *South*. Beyond the seas, it's the same story: the northern portion of the modern hemisphere escapes from the yoke of its masters, whom it calls tyrants. The latter claim their rights with the resources that time and force bestow; one way or another, the wealthy and the weak possessions of the first dominators of *America* will become before long the victor's prey or the indemnity exacted from the vanquished.
>
> In this collision of the two worlds, in the universal conflagration which cannot fail to follow shortly, all careers are open to a man with sharp eyes and a fearless soul; the voice of liberty resounds from one pole to the other; it promises glory and fortune to whoever has the boldness and the talents to seize them. That is what I clearly make out. From there, I see before me innumerable means for my establishment and my vengeance.[23]

The collision of two worlds, universal conflagration, and careers open to talent: in exile, the journalist had turned prophet and the prophet had gone mad, wildly forecasting the end of superannuated regimes. A raging, furious witness marked the hour of the old order's downfall and heralded new things under the sun—from one pole to the other, the voice of liberty resounds.

He, Simon Linguet, would be the new man for this new time: you force me to create a new existence for myself. Linguet announced to Vergennes that he had appointed himself the chronicler of these unique future happenings. He would publish an independent journal, an *Annales civiles, politiques et littéraires* "from which nothing will be excluded except satire and flattery": "In this way I will continue to serve men. As I am no longer the protector of individuals, I will become [the protector] of the masses [*des peuples*]; at least their rights under my pen will never be sacrificed, or their interests compromised; and perhaps with time, they will be enlightened."[24]

That was a loaded pledge. Linguet had been arguing for years that the masses' enlightenment would precipitate their revolution. He would not allow the administration in France to forget that his sciences of sociology and political economy embodied a special knowledge of societal structures and the dynamics of social-class relationships, knowledge that could cut two ways. In his anti-physiocratic propaganda, where he was engaging his sciences to save the system, he also warned that what he knew could justify, even provoke a social revolution that would explode the criminal foundations of it.

It is clear, however, that threats notwithstanding, Linguet wanted his journal to reach not *les peuples* but rather the reading public as well as the power constellation, including the administration he was blasting in his letter to Vergennes. What he told Vergennes about his reasons for going into exile and setting up the *Annales* was true, only he had not told Vergennes everything. He had to exact justice or revenge for the crimes committed against him; he was prepared to turn the *Annales* into a forum for arguing his case against the establishment in France, and to turn his public, his subscribers, into an international court of appeal: "...he must place contemporaries and posterity between himself and his persecutors...." He was determined to make a big name for himself and a fortune that would be minimal compensation for his losses in professional properties. "...[liberty] promises glory and fortune to whoever has the boldness and talents to seize them." The *Annales* provided Linguet in a more fundamental respect with the means for his "establishment." It gave him a territory, the continent of Europe, in which to hack out a place for himself. Since the 1760s, he had been trying to set himself up in France in a career as political persuader. His field was adminstrative theory for a monarchy in crisis, and his areas of special competence were the theory and practice of civil law on behalf of threatened proprietors and political economy in the interests of an impoverished, exploited population. Several branches of the French establishment combined to liquidate his professional practices with the acquiescence of an administration that never appreciated the comprehensiveness of his vision or the real value of his proffered services. Linguet was gambling that they had not liquidated his public support; and he was convinced that on a continent shaken up by unprecedented internal and international developments, his knowledge and talents would be accurately assessed and put to use. "Given the condition of Europe right now, I have a great feeling that with courage and indignation a man can go very far."[25]

Mounting a journalistic enterprise on an international scale, Linguet reestablished contact with his public and at the same time broadened the base of his support. He made the *Annales* into a quasi-independent force for molding opinion and policy in the power centers of Europe. Maneuvering among the great powers of Europe wielding the power of his public's opinion, Linguet institutionalized political influence for himself, and liberty as well, "the only possession on earth I had left...."[26]

In the late fall of 1776, Linguet wrote from England: "I fulfill my profession of adoptive Englishman as best I can, and with every possible scruple. I drink my tea twice daily, I eat my toasts well-buttered; I read my gazette faithfully every morning and every evening, and I laugh heartily to see ministers passed in review there, named by name, just like private persons. That, Sir, is what you call true liberty."[27] Linguet acquired a house outside London; he installed his greatest liability, a bizarre mistress named Perine Buttet,[28] along with printing presses and numerous weapons for self-defense. The expatriate believed he was a hunted man. His ministerial persecutors would be relentless; he must be ceaselessly vigilant. "By nature I am not timid, but I am becoming *precautious*" he wrote to France's ambassador in London, the marquis de Noailles; "so I will be on guard. What's more, before long, if suspicions are not dissipated by a spectacular move, I will provide myself with a civic guard which will interest the country in my defense."[29]

From London, Linguet published, in April, 1777, the first number of his political journal, the *Annales politiques, civiles, et littéraires du dix-huitième siècle,* with this motto: *uno avulso, non deficet alter.*

At the very beginning, Linguet broke the bonds of self-imposed restraints to report as naked, unadorned news various occurrences he had been predicting for more than a decade, events he had been presenting all along as intimations of future happenings still shrouded in mystery. Now he was free to call the shape of the new order into existence on every printed page. It all poured forth, unrestrained: the news of impending revolution. That explosion would mark the coming of an age of chaos. Everything would fall, all forms would be dissolved and totally re-formed. Simon Linguet named this news event hovering on the farther edge of the present day's happenings the "singular revolution that menaces Europe."[30] In an age of light, reason, order, and harmony, Linguet broadcast the news that the one law applicable to all relationships among social classes was a law of progress through conflict.

Philosophes and *littérateurs* were not slow to recognize the merits and the menace of Simon Linguet's new political journal. "...how many obstacles this great weekly political work is going to expose him to!," Voltaire wrote to Mallet du Pan. "It is such a delicate thing to want to recall a nation's interests to her when she herself has deprived herself of all means of regeneration. I doubt that Xenophone would have dared attempt it with the young Cyrus," a flattery complete with supplementary encomia which Voltaire followed up later with a stab in the back.[31] "I don't understand why his journal is less in vogue than Linguet's," Voltaire wrote to d'Alembert concerning La Harpe's attempt to replace Linguet in the editorship of the *Journal de politique et de littérature:* "I am persuaded that in the end, they will prefer reason and good taste to a madman's paradoxes."[32]

Voltaire was correct: Linguet was still writing in paradoxes, and his paradoxes still cast a lurid light on intolerable contradictions in French society. The madman would continue confronting readers of his paradoxes with the choice of supporting institutional reform designed to contain these contradictions or witnessing the social revolution that resolved or annihilated them.

How was it possible for Linguet to report what was happening the way he believed it was happening? His *Annales* represent a major pre-revolutionary contribution to French political journalism;[33] yet they were intended for a public that did not always use partisan political terms openly. Words were needed to identify and brand special political interest groups who represented themselves in a language of glowing universals as friends of liberty, humanity, philosophy. A vocabulary was needed to shock contemporaries into understanding how social, political, and economic developments affected them, and who among rival political forces might best represent their interest in impeding or promoting these changes. Singling out events, personalities, and trends, Linguet frequently invented labels for them, words which clarified for his readers the critical relevance of the news.

The *Annales* was a testing ground for a political vocabulary. Linguistic purists among Linguet's contemporaries were appalled. One scandalized reader began preparing a dictionary to aid others attempting to understand the *Annales*.[34] Linguet, meanwhile, publicly claimed the title of neologist while his rivals brandished it as an epithet. The French neologist par excellence was in suspiciously perfect agreement with an anonymous "foreigner" who wrote to the editor of the *Annales* to defend Linguet's neologism *"amatrice."* "The French language," Linguet's propped-up foreigner announced, "is a living language which is capable of being perfected and improved all the time."[35] Linguet noted in answer to the foreigner's letter, and with a palpably false modesty, that "geniuses...have the right to create words"—geniuses like Rousseau; "...as for me, I am not one of them...."[36] He continued creating words anyway.

Linguet found the Académie française's much vaunted *Dictionnaire* intolerable, a ridiculous linguistic straitjacket designed by the literary establishment to immobilize what could not be bound—the electric word: "...it's madness to create, at great cost, a court to enchain this elusive Proteus...."[37] Among Linguet's principal political enemies were the philosophes. How do you brand as a sect, as a narrowly self-interested party, those who advertise themselves as the disinterested benefactors of the human race? And how do you rally partisan support against them? Linguet reduced them to size with epithets— new compound adjectives such as *"fanato-philosophique,"* jolting juxtapositions like *"huaille philosophique."* He tossed in other variations of the same epithet, such as *"philosophaille du jour,"* or *"philosopherie,"* or *"pédants emphilosophaillés,"* practitioners of *"philosophisme."* In large part, Linguet's *Annales* read as an exposure of sectarian interests operating in frenzied quest of power and profit under soft-sounding universals, deliberately deceptive misnomers. Linguet identified the authors of the *Encyclopédie*, for example, as preachers of a doctrine of *"Encyclopédisme"*; the politicians were this *"secte cabalante de l'Encyclopédisme"*; one happy invention of a hybrid word sufficed to describe the conspiracy of a special economic interest group of *"politiqueurs,"* dedicated to making the world ripe for the practice of *"encyclopéconomie"*! He named an *"opposition"* in its political sense; he described the *"fluctuations de la politique"*; he took the *"température politique"* of nations; he devised a *"thermomètre des opinions"*; in his *"coup d'oeil politique,"* he reported the *"oscillations de notre gouvernement."*[38]

The striking metaphors he employed to describe the lowest rank of men in the order of civil society, *"l'indigent plus nul qu'un chien vagabond,"* the degraded species of *"bipède"* located at *"les couches de la pyramide sociale"* functioned as bolts of lightning loosed by the political reporter against scandalous realities.[39] They illuminated conditions of unexampled degradation and exploitation that Linguet was urging his contemporaries to reform—before the victims took matters into their own hands, overturning regimes of properties and intolerable privations.

In issues of the *Annales* published between March, 1777, and September, 1780, Linguet offered political analyses of an impressive variety of issues.[40] No other French journalist then practicing the craft could have boasted a political audacity renewed semimonthly with the same tenacious courage, and under circumstances as perilous. In no other journal of the period is political and social analysis so profoundly, forcefully, and brilliantly sustained. Among Linguet's journalistic rivals, none would prove his professional equal before the eve of the Revolution, and then, almost all of them would have been forced to acknowledge him as their master and his journalism as their model.

Political journalism, Simon Linguet's *travail pratique,* was a periodic exercise in fitting the categories of his sociology and his political economy to the day's events. In his first news analysis, his "Preliminary reflections on the present state of European society," Linguet depicted socioeconomic and political transformations in the European nation-states and cultural progress there as paradoxical, dialectic developments; and he pointedly predicted that the outcome of multiple crises occurring simultaneously in these processes of European development would be social revolution.

The journalist saw signs everywhere. Everything was crumbling. He began by examining the state of European legislation, that is, the status of law pertaining to adminstration and to the respective rights of peoples and sovereigns. In the case of Denmark and England the situation was easily summed up: the Danes had allowed their king all prerogatives, and the English people had determined to wrangle with their king over all that nation's prerogatives. (*RA,* 16). Everywhere else on the continent, however, rulers and subjects, elites and masses had lost all sense of their position and identity, their duties and their rights as members of a social order and a political system: "In *France,* for example, the Monarch claims he is the Nation; the Parlements claim they are the Nation; the Nobility claims it is the Nation; and it's only [the Nation] that is unable to say what it is, or even whether it exists. While everyone waits for enlightenment on this point, everything is in confusion; everything seems to provide ground for claims and disputes. Royal authority, advancing or retreating ceaselessly, knows neither what the boundaries are that it cannot surpass, nor what the limits are past which it cannot be forced to retreat" (*RA, 17*).

Scanning the surface of European civil societies, Linguet abandoned himself momentarily to illusion, seeing around him what his contemporaries were depicting in their commentaries on the state of Europe.

> Never has the taste for the arts been more widespread; never have the pleasures of the mind been more sought after, and letters more universally cultivated than at this moment. Printing has facilitated among men of all countries a communication of thoughts that has increased knowledge....
>
> For whoever is content with appearances, society never has been more flourishing, at least in the large states of Europe: although, in general, everything tends toward despotism in this part of the world; although arbitrary authority is just about at its limit there ...still, it is true that her [Europe's] annals have not yet shown an epoch where she has seemed more peaceful and happier.
>
> From all sides, cities receive embellishments which a sustained emulation promises to multiply. Communications are easy and dependable....The countrysides are filled with *châteaux* where luxury joins to the refinements of art all that nature's fecundity can produce. There are few private homes, even in what is called the *low bourgeoisie*, where cleanliness, elegance either of appointments or of table...do not herald abundance and felicity. [*RA*, 57, 83-84]

Then, shattering these rich glittering surfaces, the appearances of prosperity in a brilliant, flourishing European civilization, he dragged forward another nation, the producers of abundance, beauty, and civilized perfection, but also the dehumanized victims, sunk in privation and degradation almost without example in the annals of civil society: "...never have possessions been more general, easier to come by, and more common. But on the other side also, never have deprivations been more universal, more murderous for the class which is condemned to them; it could be that in the midst of her apparent prosperity, *Europe* has never been closer to total subversion, all the more terrible because despair will be the cause of it; or to a depopulation all the more frightening because we will not have resources for reversing it that our ancestors had in cases almost like [this one] (*RA, 84*).

"...it could be that...*Europe* has never been closer to total subversion...." Patterns perceivable in concrete ongoing occurrences—the growth of prosperity, the perfection of culture—all bent to the shape and flowed in the direction of an ironclad dialectical progress of all change through stages to an inescapable terminus. The condition of development in civilized societies was a progressively more murderous victimization of the masses—instruments of prosperity and progress. Irreversible depopulation or total subversion were the only historical resolutions Linguet conceived for this glaring contradiction at the core of the modernization process.

In his sociological system, his *Théorie des lois civiles,* Linguet had described a self-propelling dynamics driving with relentless force towards civil society's civil war; but there his descriptions had been abstractions, analytic containers for all possible historical realities: "And so, by example always repeated since then, wealth found itself at that time too weak against indigence, and those who possessed everything were from the very beginning expropriated by those who had nothing."[41] Now, in his *Annales,* Linguet was using those same categories to contain and explain social patterns and movements discernable in the immediate present. "We have arrived via a directly opposite route precisely at the point where Italy was when the war of the *slaves* inundated her in blood, and brought carnage with fire to the portals of the mistress of the world (*RA,* 84). The slave rebellions in Italy were quashed, leaving the state intact, its servants submissive, and its subjects affectionate: "Whereas if this too imminent explosion ever takes place in *Europe,* all that will remain will be devastated proprietors, with their vast solitudes where nothing can bring back inhabitants whom misery will have chased away" (*RA,* 84).

Modern Europe was at the point of a great upheaval, a revolution of its slaves, Linguet explained; but Europeans had arrived there by a "route directly opposite" that followed by the ancients in Italy. The fatal turning point into modernity and crisis was the decision of late medieval European monarchs to free their serfs, to emancipate the subservient classes by royal proclamation: "Ordinarily, public peace is disturbed by two kinds of men only—those who have nothing to lose, and those whose wealth is portable enough so that they can hide themselves easily from the avenging inspection of the laws" (*RA,* 90). One class in modern times with nothing to lose was composed of descendants of emancipated serfs; they had become or were fast becoming dispossessed persons. The other class was composed of holders of fluid portable wealth, the newly affluent financiers, commercial, agricultural, and industrial entrepreneurs, merchants, *rentiers,* and all newly propertied men who in an age of prosperity had the option of taking their profits in cash.

These two classes, people who had wealth at hand in cash or who could readily convert wealth into cash, and people who had nothing but their arms, the strength to earn cash for a day's bread—these were modern society's natural insurrectionaries. In ancient slave society, Linguet's analysis ran, no one had been that poor, that desperate, and no one had been that rich. The slave was a piece of property, but he was that much at least: "He stopped being a man, that is true, but a despised and rejected man, gnawed by anxiety, placed precisely below the lowest rank in society..." (*RA*, 93). Masters burdened with the care of so many servants were unable to amass dangerous hordes of capital. What was nonexistent in the social order of the ancient world, Linguet emphasized, was this species of directionless, "free" creature who populated the modern European state, whose free labor brought him no social, political, or economic benefits whatever. In modern and enlightened European civil societies, the freed slave was an unprotected agent. He was a freely exploitable instrument for augmenting national production and increasing national wealth. His employers considered themselves freed of all responsibility for his life from the moment they no longer had to make a cash outlay to acquire his body and his labor. In vagabond hordes of beggars, free men roamed unfettered through the realm, "devoured by the most shameful maladies"; they were "pestilential ambulatory hotbeds, carrying debauchery and plague from one population center to another" (*RA*, 92); in mendicant legions, free day laborers scoured the countryside in search of work. They discovered that they had been "surrendered unconditionally to the very avarice they were enriching." On daily earnings only occasionally sufficient to maintain life for twenty-four hours, they were free to feed their families, and pay medical expenses and taxes. As free men, they could be dragged off to fight the king's wars, "and people have dared to say to men handled that way that they were *free*!" (*RA*, 94, 95, 97).

All the while, the "colossi of silver," capitalist exploiters, are calculating their augmented net profit by subtracting the free laborer's wage payments from the estimated cost of caring for a slave: "It is no longer the person of the active, industrious man that has been considered in the reckoning between the insolent proprietor and the humble owner of a liberty reduced to two arms for all retinue: it is [rather] the real profit that the first has been able to draw from the use of the second, and in this computation, minutes have been painstakingly calculated..."(*RA*, 101). A colossal wealth accumulated by a plutocracy of exploiters obeying a capitalist ethic and the laws of liberal economics, including the iron law of wages, was crushing masses of men who were the helpless instruments of its accumulation:

> ...the very insufficiency of the day laborer's pay is a reason for diminishing it. The more he is pressed by need, the cheaper he sells himself. The more urgent the need, the less fruitful his labor: the temporary despots whom he tearfully begs to accept his services do not blush to tap his pulse, so to speak, to convince themselves that he still has enough strength left: it's on the extent of his weakness that they tally the pay they offer him: and the nearer they sense he is to perishing of inanition, the more they withdraw what can save him from it; and barbarians that they are,

they provide him far less with the means of prolonging his life, than with the resources for retarding his death. [*RA*, 98-99]

Nineteen-twentieths of free Europe hung suspended between life and death (*RA*, 98). The most scrupulous calculation failed to convince Linguet that these legions could survive in societies governed by the laws of a free and open market. Intensify men's daily deprivation and at a given point, inevitably, they pass the threshold of tolerance: that would be the "moment of the great revolution," *not* a recurrence in a self-repeating cycle, certainly not a repetition of the revolts of peasant masses in Bohemia and Italy. The new social revolution would be comparable to nothing that had occurred before. These earlier upheavals had been "blind" frenzied leaps upward in an unrelieved darkness, graspings after a "vague amelioration of a misery whose cause their brutishness did not allow them to disentangle" (*RA*, 102). Modern times would open upon quite another spectacle. In an age of prosperity and continuing national development on all fronts, a nightmarish scene unfolded. The producers of national wealth in European states comprised a nation of free, dispossessed, exploited men who, with every increase in national output, were sinking further into abject poverty. This nation-within-the state already was kindling sparks of hatred from a smoldering rage; and rage itself would only be intensified still further by enlightenment, a knowledge of the fullness of one's deprivation, the arbitrariness of it, and the calculation with which it was being perpetuated. And so, Linguet reported, the two armies confront one another, antagonists brought to the brink of an inevitable conflict by the sweep of a dialectic movement against which piecemeal policy and reform are powerless. Pitted against one another on the eve of civil war, the total war, Linguet saw a colossus of opulence and an unexampled capitalist wealth, contained until now within the frame work of governmental order only because it had enervated itself in the process of dissipating its stupendous riches, and a colossus of proletarian poverty, enchained until now within the order of civil society only by the most rigorous military despotism. But these very measures of repression and containment are themselves agents of irreversible dialectic progress. In Linguet's analogy, they are poisons "which only alter even further the internal organization of the body politic" and "hasten the moment of the great revolution...the elements that imperceptibly bring it on already are fermenting on all sides" (*RA*, 102).

In this time of crisis, by all signs the last, Europe's fate was progress following either of two routes into an ineluctable destruction. If restless insurrectionary masses, pariahs of the civil order, could be held in tow by an ever-expanding military despotism, then they would perish of unchecked exploitation. In earlier analyses, Linguet had predicted the mass emigration of rural laborers unable to earn the price of life.[42] Now he wiped out that picture. It was illusory. They would fall before they dragged themselves away. They would die; they lacked the strength to move. They would leave their bones as markers along a route through a wasteland (*RA,* 103).

The alternative to this quiet macabre doom, in which the expiring class, the source, through its productive labor, of all wealth, would drag an entire civil society into extinction, was the revolution that Linguet had hinted would bring society as it always had existed in the Western world to another kind of destruction: "...or some new *Spartacus,* made bold by despair, enlightened by necessity, calling the comrades of his misfortune to real liberty, breaking the murderous and deceptive laws which misprize it, will obtain for some among them an absolute partition of the possessions of nature, and for others, the restitution of this sweet security which assured to slaves a repose of mind in exchange for the wealth they left to their masters, and a peaceful life as recompense for the domination whose yoke they accepted and cherished" (*RA,* 103).

A journalist rushing to the scene of an apocalypse was reporting on the shape of a future on the other side of doom. He saw Western societies bursting apart, social relationships rooted in glaring extremes of possession and privation dissolving. A class of impoverished persons, in acts of totalitarian appropriation, was about to claim an expropriated earth. This revolution of the pariahs would mark the birth of a new regime out of violence, a paternalistic social welfare state, a kind of dictatorship for a proletarian population reorganized into two divisions: the new proprietors who would reap the spoils of conquest, obtaining an "absolute partition of the possessions of nature"; and the ever-propertyless multitudes, to whom the new governor, "some new *Spartacus,*" would offer "the restitution of this sweet security" in exchange for the wealth they generated in productive labor but abandoned to their comrades. Seizing the power of self-determination at the moment of revolutionary upsurge, the proletarians, led by a class-conscious Spartacus ("made bold by despair, enlightened by necessity"), would institutionalize for themselves *not* the multiple liberties with which the liberal establishment was tempting them, but only "real *liberty,*" a liberty of dominion in properties "for some among them" and in security "for the others."

That was perhaps the best Europeans could hope for; and the alternative? the awesome, terrifying, silent death of the masses. "One or the other of these calamities is inevitable, and I will not fail in this *Journal* to note the circumstances which from day to day bring us nearer to them" (*RA,* 103).

Simon Linguet's "Reflections on the present state of European society," appearing in the first two numbers of his *Annales politiques, civiles, et littéraires du dix-huitième siècle,* made sobering, compelling copy. At whom was this copy directed? When he analyzed the state of Europe as a state of acute crisis, Linguet may have been trying to attract a specific class of subscribers— but obviously not the potentially revolutionary masses, not the people. He wanted to make the *Annales* required reading for Europe's propertied elites, and for authority—heads of state (like Louis XVI, to whom he dedicated his first volume), ministers, notables, and officials at all levels of government in all the regimes of Europe. He could win subscriptions in this rich territory if, with his analyses and forecasts, he could convince these European governors and dominators that they were close to losing everything, and if, with his model reform projects and his politics of welfare, he could show them how they still might be able to salvage something.[43]

The International Business of Running
a Conditionally Free Press

Linguet planned to remain in England, publishing the *Annales* from London and distributing them in France through his literary agent, Pierre Lequesne, the Parisian cloth merchant. From the beginning of this venture in political journalism in exile, Linguet and French authorities had been engaged in a complicated series of negotiations concerning the distribution and censorship of the *Annales* in France. Periodically, these negotiations would be punctured by Linguet's hysterical threats of reprisal and boasts of insuperable willpower.

Normally, a journalist who printed abroad but who wanted his journal to circulate freely and legitimately in France would have to obtain permission from the French secretary of state in the Department of Foreign Affairs, who was authorized to exact a payment from the proprietor for entry rights. Then, in principle, the author would owe a pension to the proprietor of the *Gazette de France,* the only journal openly authorized to treat political matters in France. The secretary of state would also have the right to appoint a censor, as it was his prerogative to review all matters touching upon the affairs of his department.[44]

Linguet's opening communication with Vergennes was his notorious libellous letter of January 16, 1777. He boasted to France's ambassador in England, the marquis de Noailles, that no one could have convinced him not to publish it: "...my honor and my personal satisfaction required that it become public."[45]

Vergennes reacted with outward calm at first. The hissing of "serpents," "vipers," did not panic him. He boasted that he had yet to be stung by their venomous bites.[46] At the end of March, Vergennes requested that Noailles take out a subscription for him to Linguet's *Annales,* but using a false name. Vergennes told Noailles that he knew the *Annales* would not be accorded free entry into France; Noailles was to send the journal with his dispatches. That way Vergennes would be certain to receive it, even if the government suppressed it![47]

Linguet was not ready to accept an arrangement which entailed periodic arbitrary interdictions of his *Annales*. His recovery and return following two professional martyrdoms had functioned as demonstrations to his public that the man had inexhaustible courage, that he would persevere, that he had what it took to enlighten subscribers on issues no other publicist dared broach. The *Annales'* value for French subscribers would depend on the annalist's ability to guarantee that all the news he saw fit to print would reach them regularly—and intact. Yet how could Linguet bargain with French ministers for unexampled preferential treatment, and from an advantageous position? He had just directed a barrage of slander at three of them: Vergennes, "un ministre étranger bien plus qu'un ministre des affaires étrangères"; Maurepas, "minister at fifteen, dismissed at thirty, recalled at eighty," who joined in his high office "the frivolty of infancy to the lifelessness, the nullity of decrepitude"; and Miromesnil, Maurepas's favorite, "schooled, because of that, for the highest rank in the magistrature, although he valued only the revenues."[48] Linguet's solution to this problem in public relations was to threaten to increase the number of his libels against the administration. With this tactic he maneuvered himself almost past the point of bargaining and into a declaration of war.

Linguet laid his cards on the table in a strangely cordial letter to the marquis de Noailles. He sent it off complete with enclosures for persons in high ministerial posts. He had something he wanted Noailles to forward to the king (probably one or more numbers of the *Annales,* or a letter of dedication), "providing the avenues to the throne are open to what comes from me...." He had cutting words for the French ministers. He was certain that in their "obstinacy" and "blindness" they had made up their minds to "proscribe" both the *Annales* and a projected collection of his works. They were forcing him to renew hostilities: "...always war, always vengeance." They had reduced him to "living his life in convulsions of despair and anguishes of hate." That was their tactic, and he was ready to play that game. He enclosed a separate memoir for the ministers at Versailles. "This is not a threat; this is not boasting. It is the simple notice of what I will do if I am reduced to it, and of what I very sincerely desire that they do not force me to do."[49]

In the attached memoir, Linguet announced that he already knew his journal had been proscribed, that it would be denied entry into France, with the severest penalties meted out to those who dared defy the ban. By what right had the ministers branded his *Annales* a crime, even before it had appeared? He conceded that it was hopeless for him to press his claim that his *Annales* was a legal enterprise, the continuation of the *Journal de Bruxelles* (the *Journal de politique et de littérature*) he had edited in Paris until his arbitrary and illegal dismissal. Ministers did not understand the language of justice. "Let us see if I will be better understood when speaking interest."

> It is not in the Minister's [interest], no matter how entrenched he believes he is, to expose himself to being compromised twenty-four times a year, namely in a work designed to be sought after because of its nature, perhaps because of the name of its author, and certainly because of its proscription: well, that's what will happen without fail to Messieurs de Maurepas, de Miromesnil, and de Vergennes if my journal does not get at least a tacit tolerance.

Political power, the power of persuasion and coercion via libelous polemic, was the principal weapon, besides nerve, that Linguet had at his disposal. Wielding it, he was treating with French secretaries of state as equal to equal. They had an impressive but unreliable police and censorship network which they could use to try to make good their threatened proscription of the *Annales*. On his side, Linguet counted on mobilizing the public opinion of Europe and enlightening and directing it in every number of the *Annales*.

The ministers would be mistaken, he warned, to assume that he and his public would give up, or that he already was worn out, or had run out of weapons. "I am still all fresh, and I have what is required to keep the public in suspense for a long time on the matter of my persecutors."

To whet ministerial appetites, Linguet included a prospectus for his stockpile of seven libels. A new dedicatory letter to the king was all ready for insertion in the second number of the *Annales* "if the journal does not get into France: and this will be a terrific piece, I post warning." His *Aiguilloniana*, an account of the duc d'Aiguillon's manhandling of his advocate, was in press. He had a history of the trial of the duc de Guines, and he would not hesitate to chronicle the involvement of d'Aiguillon and his successors in the affair. Then, there were some *exposés* of various ministerial follies that would make excellent political pornography, including a narrative of the affair of the chevalier d'Eon, the notorious French diplomatic officer, secret agent, and transvestite. He had prepared a character portrait of the septagenarian Maurepas, "a Buffoon of an old man," and one of Miromesnil, "a Crispin from Normandy." He was ready to offer his own critical analyses of French foreign policy, and a special indictment of Vergennes' American policy, accompanied by a tableau of the calamities which might be the consequence of it.

Holding these arms, his "sample," which he paraded for the ministers in Versailles, "a little private person," as Linguet dubbed himself, felt he could afford to be generous. All the ministers would have to do is allow the *Annales* an unobstructed passage into France. Then he would keep quiet. He gave Vergennes, Miromesnil, and Maurepas fifteen days to answer. After that, he would start his presses rolling. He was ready to sling libel "in the face of Europe." [50]

Vergennes communicated Linguet's memoir to Maurepas,[51] who, in a later dispatch to the marquis de Noailles, would refer to Linguet as "a mad dog who bites on all sides."[52] Maurepas was to forward Linguet's prospectus for libels to Miromesnil. When he read it, Miromesnil advised against ministerial reprisals, convinced that they would only furnish Linguet with more ammunition and a more enthusiastic public following.[53]

Vergennes wrote to Noailles on April 7 with instructions on how to handle Linguet. Noailles was to inform him—but verbally, not in writing—that "...his journal would neither be forbidden nor permitted, that it is up to those who might be curious to read it to make arrangements for obtaining it." Noailles wrote to Vergennes on the eighteenth. The message had been delivered.[54]

Simon Linguet was not the man to accept this verbal jockeying. He announced to Noailles that his second number had been held up by French authorities. Noailles reported that Linguet declared himself ready "to make war, since they wanted it."[55]

On June 30, 1777, Linguet used the harassed and embarrassed Noailles to dispatch another letter to the ministers at Versailles. His *Aiguilloniana* was finished and ready for circulation, as he had promised. That piece of news was calculated to embarrass or panic d'Aiguillon's uncle, Maurepas. He would give the ministers one more reprieve, enough time to meet the conditions of his ultimatum.[56] He confided the details of this ultimatum to Vergennes, along with a reminder that he was a political force to be reckoned with: "... an honest man, made furious as a consequence of iniquitous treatment, and who has placed the sea between the Bastille and himself, is a formidable enemy for a minister, no matter how powerful he might be." He advised Vergennes to assure Maurepas that he was as defiant and as courageous as ever. "They can be certain that I will not give up: many resources are still open to me...." His *Annales,* he told Vergennes, again, were being held up, starting with the second number, and in spite of a solemn promise he had insisted he had received "from the king's minister" that he would meet with no obstacles. All copies, even those for the provinces, were being directed through Paris, causing intolerable delays, as he had been denied permission to use the state postal service. And meanwhile, the rumor was spreading that the *Annales* had been proscribed. Encouraged by this news, editors of pirated editions were stepping up their activities. Linguet boasted that all these maneuvers made no difference. He dared Vergennes to keep the *Annales* out of France. He mocked the entire apparatus of government censorship which had been mobilized to black out irrepressible words, his news:

> Besides, you will never stop it [the *Annales*] from getting through. From the day it was proscribed, I would take care not to leave anyone uninformed, and that would increase curiosity. It will always enter France, the way the aid you give the Americans reaches *Congress.* Corsairs will steal some; and the rest will go to provision colonies of honest souls in revolt against the despotism that aims to crush me. The alleged *tolérance* you would like to chain me with is, therefore, a *chimera* which isn't worth any sacrifice on my part. I must have justice, *Monseieur le comte,* and

only in obtaining it will I renounce the pain of getting it for my-self.[57]

Linguet wrote to Maurepas the same day. He reminded the ministers that he had weapons he would not hesitate to use, alluding to his libel against d'Aiguillon, Maurepas's nephew, and perhaps hinting at his sketch for a libel-ous profile of the "old *Buffoon.*" He demanded Maurepas's help in winning the king's favor—or else: "Choisissez de me faire connaître du Roi, ou d'en être connu." He gave Maurepas until July 15 to give an answer. "If I don't have it, the sixteenth everything will be published.[58]

The ministers were not alarmed. Vergennes informed Noailles on July 12 that the much heralded *Aiguilloniana* had arrived, "the blocks, or rather, the sample of the blocks with which Sieur Linguet proposes to strike us down." Maurepas, Vergennes noted, had found it all hilarious, and even excellent in its satirical portrait of him and Miromesnil. Vergennes was not amused. He in-structed Noailles that the ministers had no intention of negotiating with Lin-guet. If he inquired concerning their response to his ultimata, Noailles was to tell him there was none.[59]

While Linguet was stockpiling libels and political pornography in London, in Paris his literary agent, Pierre Lequesne, was employing less incendiary tac-tics calculated to succeed. Linguet was not making Lequesne's negotiations any easier. According to Lequesne, Linguet was advertising his paper as a journal "ennobled by THE INFLUENCE OF LIBERTY. What more was needed to get it rejected?"[60]

While Linguet was provoking the ministers, Lequesne managed somehow to win a major concession from them; he obtained a "tolérance tacite" for the *Annales,* not an *"autorisation expresse,"* and "not the right to publish everything that fell beneath his pen,...but the liberty of being true without scandal, the privilege of having as his only censor M. the lieutenant-general of Police; precious liberty, honorable privilege, or, if you will, just, necessary condition which could not be awkward for the author, as long as he held to his obligations, and which could not diminish the public's eagerness, because it was generally unknown." With a *tolérance tacite,* Lequesne observed, the *Annales* would be exempt from fees owing to the Department of Foreign Af-fairs for foreign gazettes.[61] Given the state of the censorship in France at the time, Lequesne was probably correct in asserting that the arrangements he had worked out for Linguet were the best the journalist could have hoped for.

The lieutenant-general of Paris Police, Jean-Charles-Pierre LeNoir, was Lin-guet's censor. Linguet himself testified secretly in 1780 that he had given Le-Noir prior access to everything of his that entered France.[62] The decision of the secretaries of state neither to prohibit nor permit Linguet's *Annales* amounted to a *tolérance,* that is, a negative promise that numbers would not be suppressed automatically. In these circumstances, LeNoir was a good censor, and possibly a sympathetic one. In his extensive correspondence with Lequesne, Linguet mentions no instance where LeNoir ordered public retractions or seizures of entire numbers; the first outright suppression of an issue came in the summer of 1780.[63]

Once he had settled the censorhip question, Lequesne tackled the problem of winning the government's consent for Linguet's use of the postal service to distribute the *Annales* in France. In order to deliver the first numbers of the *Annales,* Lequesne had been using *messageries,* "but the slowness of these carriages kills a work which has only a momentary value." Linguet wanted Lequesne to work out an annual arrangement with the postal service for distributing the *Annales* throughout France. Ordinarily, Lequesne explained, the postal service would be authorized to accept and deliver only those periodicals for which the government openly granted permissions.[64] However, without fast and dependable delivery service, Linguet's news would be obsolete long before it reached his subscribers. Speed imparted a sense of urgency and immediacy to the contents of every number of his political journal. Speed was the key to success in another sense. From the outset, the *Annales* were being printed and circulated in counterfeit editions, cutting into Linguet's markets in France and throughout Europe.[65] If he could guarantee quick delivery, Linguet would stand a fighting chance of wiping out these literary pirates. By the end of August, 1777, Lequesne had the government's permission to use the postal service; he began contracting with directors of provincial post offices.[66] Linguet was elated.[67]

Success notwithstanding, the man was incapable of abandoning his provocative attitudes of belligerence and defiance. He continued parading his *Aiguilloniana.* "It is in a safe and inaccessible place," he assured a nervous Lequesne in September, 1777. As long as the administration gave him a square deal, he would hold back this ultimate weapon. "It is an arm I will not use, except if required." The following month, he renewed these less than comforting assurances. He would release nothing until provoked. If the situation changed, then "the bonds that restrain me today would not be sufficient."[68]

Meanwhile, in Paris, Lequesne kept up his barrage of promises and entreaties, and finally was able to secure the release of early numbers of the *Annales* which the government had ordered held up.[69]

The arrangements Linguet and Lequesne made with French authorities for distributing the *Annales* in France did not guarantee the international circulation Linguet wanted to establish. As part of his effort to work up a market for the *Annales* elsewhere on the continent, Linguet hired the young Swiss publicist, Jacques Mallet Du Pan. Mallet had been trying to bring himself to Linguet's attention since 1775, when he published his *Doutes sur l'éloquence et les systêmes politiques,* a justification of Linguet's doctrines and professional conduct.[70] How Linguet responded to this offering is not known; but he did decide to make use of the talents of this ambitious, restless young man. He met Mallet, probably for the first time, when he stopped to visit with Voltaire at Ferney on his way into self-imposed exile.[71] Sometime before Linguet left for London, Mallet became his salaried associate. His job was to gather news and subscriptions for the *Annales* from Switzerland. Later, he took an active part in arranging an agreement between Linguet and the Société typographique de Lausanne for a *réimpression* of the *Annales.*[72]

In May, 1777, Mallet placed an announcement in the *Journal helvétique* which presented precisely the image of the *Annales* Linguet was trying to sell to his public. The *Annales* was advertised for prospective subscribers in Switzerland and Italy as "a journal that is truly free, solely devoted to the defense of peoples and the truth.... [e]xamining the present and the future situation in affairs of state, legislation, military affairs, finance, commerce, religion, letters, and social behavior...."[73]

Once subscriptions began coming in, Mallet joined Linguet in an energetic war against entrepreneurs who were printing pirated editions of the *Annales* in France and Switzerland. With Mallet's aid and Lequesne's, Linguet managed at the end of a year of operations to turn the *Annales* into an impressive profit-making enterprise. In January, 1778, Linguet wrote to his friend, the baron de Tournon, "I have no cause for complaint about the *Annales,* assuredly. If things keep up this way, my enemies will have done me a real service; and it is certain that they will have forced me to make a fortune which I would have found unthinkable in Paris...."[74]

The job of political journalist required skills in blackmailing ministers, battling printers of pirated editions, cultivating collaborators, and attracting subscribers all over Europe. But if that were all there was to it, Linguet could never have extracted a *tolérance* for the *Annales* in France and the privilege of circulating the work through the French postal service.

The young Brissot de Warville remarked that "[t]he uninterrupted publication of the *Annales* is an inconceivable phenomenon in the empire of literature for whoever knows its laws."[75] If this phenomenon was not a miracle, it was an extraordinary feat. How did Linguet manage to carry it off? The man cultivated enemies; the king of France, however, was not one of them—although if anyone had a watertight case against a monarch, based on his own understanding of the nature and limits of royal legitimacy, it was Linguet. In his published letter to Vergennes, Linguet identified himself as a new man, an independent defender and protector of peoples. He had said that much before, in his political economy. It was precisely there, in his propaganda work during the administration of Terray, Maupeou, and d'Aiguillon, that this *ami du peuple* displayed his talents most conspicuously as a passionate, persuasive apologist for a new *thèse royale,* a populist monarchism, a politics of subsistence. On March 24, 1777, from London, the people's spokesman dedicated his *Annales* to Louis XVI.[76] If one judges from the literary columnists' reports, Louis was more than curious about the new journal; he was addicted to it. He was alleged to have confessed that he learned his catechism from Linguet.[77] When Linguet's enemies in the Académie française attempted to have the *Annales* suppressed, the king's minister for the Department of Paris, Amelot, regretfully informed them that he could not oblige them because the royal family, including the king, read Linguet's journal exclusively, and "with an inexpressible pleasure."[78] Rumors of that sort were a kind of protection.

Linguet had other supporters whose influence may have contributed to securing entry for the *Annales:* the queen, because Linguet had declared war against d'Aiguillon, whom she disliked; the clergy and the *dévots,* because Linguet took the trouble in the first numbers of his *Annales* to attack their enemies (and his own) among the philosophes and the *parlementaires;* LeNoir, Linguet's censor, because he sympathized with Linguet's anti-physiocratic biases.[79] The secretary of state for foreign affairs was ambivalent. That was no small asset. Vergennes called Linguet a "viper," and he let him hiss; he also said he was letting him "bark." He even listened. He ordered his ambassador in London, the marquis de Noailles, to subscribe to the *Annales.*[80] Possibly, he anticipated that an Anglophobe in London might be able to perform important services for France in the future.[81]

With this kind of backing, Linguet was assured a fragile viability for the *Annales* in France. Nonetheless, this power constellation was undependable. Linguet's supporters became indistinguishable from his enemies in a showdown. In all camps, the working assumption was that if this publicist, who announced all over Europe that he was establishing a journal "ennobled by the influence of liberty" ever got out of hand, his presses could be silenced, one way or another.

The probability of an Anglo-French declaration of hostilities prompted Linguet to consider moving his establishment to a neutral location like Belgium or Switzerland, or Maestricht. He was ready to demonstrate to French authorities that even in exile—especially in exile, he remained an obedient and patriotic subject: "I could never contain my attachment for France."[82] He told Lequesne that "one of the principal magistrates of the country" had encouraged him to remain in England, but "I do not want to give the appearance to my country of being opposed, and decidedly, at the first cannon shot, I am leaving."[83] He wrote to Vergennes in March, 1778, to announce that he was leaving England. He was inclined to settle in Switzerland, he told the secretary of state, and he wanted assurances that French authorities would remain neutral. He felt he could not ask for more. "I sense that present circumstances do not allow me to claim reparations; besides, I would content myself without difficulty with that which the public gives me daily if, in transplanting myself, I could count on tranquility, and I would count on it if I had your word for security."[84] Later, Linguet published a letter from Vergennes dated April 23, 1778. The minister promised him "complete safety for your person in the new domicile you propose to take up."[85]

Suspending the publication of his *Annales* for several months in 1778, Linguet crossed the Channel to search for a new location. His negotiations with authorities in Lausanne, Neuchâtel, Geneva, Bern, and Soleure were unsuccessful. The Swiss were prepared to admit this French expatriate and to tolerate his *Annales*, but on the condition that he submit himself to government censorship.[86] He would not accept the condition. For a man without a country, Simon Linguet drove a hard bargain. He would not be gagged on any terms other than his own.[87]

At the same time that he was receiving encouragements from Vergennes for his resettlement in Switzerland, as well as polite feelers coupled with *sine qua non* conditions from Swiss authorities, Linguet turned his attention, for the third time in three years, to the possibility of locating in the Austrian Netherlands.[88]

He first announced in September, 1776, that he wanted to move to Brussels to set up his *Annales* there; that was before he left the continent for England. His overtures evoked only the enthusiastic, fruitless support of Patrice-François, Count Nény, president of the Conseil privé in Brussels, and a strong supporter of enlightenment culture in the Austrian Netherlands.[89] The second time Linguet requested permission to settle in Belgium, early in 1777, Austrian officials were in a better position to calculate the risks of welcoming him. His scandalous open letter to Vergennes had just appeared. Austrian Chancellor Kaunitz warned his minister plenipotentiary in Brussels, Prince Starhemberg, "how much experience has demonstrated that the said Linguet must not be given too big a welcome." Prince Charles of Lorraine, governor-general for the Austrian Netherlands, was ready to take fifteen subscriptions to the *Annales*.[90] That was safer than taking Linguet.

By the summer of 1778, however, Linguet had persuaded Austrian authorities to reopen discussions on conditions for his relocation in Belgium. Linguet wrote to Lequesne in June to explain the advantages and disadvantages of a settlement in Brussels.[91]

Austria's secretary of state and war for Belgium, Crumpipen, informed Count Nény on July 19 that Linguet had presented his ideas on relocating in Brussels to Starhemberg, and that Starhemberg had delegated Nény to pursue talks. With matters still in this state of uncertainty, Linguet sent off a prematurely optimistic dispatch to Lequesne: "I thought I hit at the right time. I conquered everything. I have not dissipated, but rather, eluded obstacles that would keep me from printing here, at least for the beginning."[92]

Meanwhile, as late as September, 1778, Starhemberg freely admitted to Kaunitz that he had been reluctant to sanction Linguet's relocation of his journalistic enterprise in Belgium; but then Linguet himself had taken the initiative of returning to France and personally obtaining Vergennes's consent to the move. Under these conditions, Starhemberg felt easier about giving Linguet a trial period of residence in Belgium, providing he could keep his "haughty and perhaps vexatious temperament" under control, curb his impulse to "involve himself in affairs which are none of his business," and tone down his "burning style that does not seem accessible to rules of circumspection." Starhemberg reported that Linguet had taken a house outside Brussels and was preparing an edition of his legal briefs.[93] Kaunitz also was wary. He cautioned Starhemberg to warn Linguet that whatever he printed would have to go through ordinary government machinery for policing the press.[94]

On his side, Linguet was creating the impression that he would acquiesce, but he did not intend to submit his *Annales* to policing and censorship in Belgium. He already had an arrangement with a bookseller at The Hague for a Dutch reprinting of the journal; and he cemented a new agreement with his associate Mallet Du Pan for an expanded international distribution. Mallet's understanding of the arrangement was that in a territory that embraced Switzerland, Italy, Germany, and the South and East of France, he would have exclusive rights to distribute an edition of the *Annales* printed up by the Société typographique de Lausanne.[95] Censorship from Brussels, added to controls already exercised by LeNoir in Paris, would cause fatal delays in the printing, reprinting, and distribution of all these editions and possibly undermine Linguet's fragile reputation for independent *reportage*. Besides, Linguet was constitutionally incapable of putting up with any more. Austrian censorship didn't fit his character or his plans.

In July, 1778, Linguet began making arrangements with Lequesne, from Brussels, for the clandestine transport of a printing press and accessories into Belgium. He planned to install this equipment, along with an *équipe*—a director for the press and some assistants—in a country house he was purchasing in Waerbeck. In September, he was talking about hiring two typesetters and a printer to assist his director; and by November, when he finally settled in at Waerbeck, he was seriously calculating the advantages and drawbacks of a second press and thirteen more workers to handle the printing of his complete works in addition to the *Annales*.[96] He did not bother to confide to Lequesne his plan for concealing the existence of this installation from Austrian authorities responsible for overseeing his operations.

Meanwhile, Chancellor Kaunitz had convinced himself that all arrangements for controlling the content of the *Annales* had been disposed of. He was ready to broach the subject of buying Linguet's pen. Linguet would be his propagandist, an agent paid to publicize and win sympathy for Austria's pretensions to the Bavarian succession.[97] Starhemberg had major reservations. His considered judgment on Linguet was that the man was an incorrigible and unmanipulable independent. He was far from certain that Linguet could be counted upon to do his propagandizing from the Austrian government's perspective, unless he happened independently to believe in the justice of Austria's policies. He might make too much noise. His price might be too high; or even worse, he might not want money. He might have his eye set on higher sights. In a later dispatch, Starhemberg again urged prudence, and he promised to work to "prevent the inconvenience that might arise from employing so superior a genius, but at the same time so seething, so vain, absolute, and exigent."[98]

Linguet let it be known that he was prepared to lend his support to Austria's claims, even though Prussia and Russia and, above all, France had denounced Austrian maneuvers to claim possession of Bavaria. He apparently had no objection to submitting his work on the subject to Starhemberg before printing it.[99]

Linguet began research in the fall. However, if he was not deliberately procrastinating, he certainly was not turning out manuscript material on the Bavarian question fast enough for his employers. Starhemberg started apologizing for Austria's new propagandist in December, 1778. Then, after he read a sample of Linguet's uncensored and uncoaxed pro-Austrian apologies in the *Annales,* Starhemberg became uneasy himself. Linguet's principal statement of Austrian policy needed to be subject to a superior and enlightened censorship.[100]

By the spring of 1779, the Austro-Prussian crisis was near settlement. At this point, Linguet's *grand'œuvre* still was unpublished, and Austrian officials concluded that the time had passed for the kind of apology they had authorized Linguet to turn out, this "major deduction by which we expected to attach votes and opinions to our cause." Linguet readily agreed.[101]

Kaunitz, however, was still eager to have Linguet continue defending Austria, "as if by accident." He instructed Starhemberg to review the minutes of whatever Linguet intended to publish.[102] Linguet was willing. He set to work on a retrospective apology for Austrian policy in the Bavarian affair. In close collaboration with Crumpipen, he began working on new articles to appear in the *Annales.* He gracefully, even docilely, submitted this propaganda to Crumpipen for correction. "I will be most flattered, Monsieur," Linguet told Crumpipen, "if I can speak in my work for the views and ideas of the minister [and] I thank you profusely for having been willing to make yourself the interpreter [of these views]...."[103]

What kind of enterprise in independent journalism was this? Whatever else Linguet was doing, he did not believe he was compromising himself. He refused to be bought. While Austrian officials haggled among themselves over payments for masterpieces of propaganda promised and fragments completed, Linguet kept an intriguing silence on the matter and manner of his reimbursement. The government was anxious to settle accounts with its publicist.[104]

However, when officials first began prodding him, Linguet protested that he did not want to talk about monetary compensation.[105] He explained that he had defended Austrian policies gladly, voluntarily, and he wanted to remain disinterested.[106] "If it is true that I have had some little merit concerning the issue at hand, I would be upset at losing it in putting a price on it."[107] Count Nény was momentarily puzzled by Linguet's obstinate refusal to receive his reward for telling Austria's truth. He finally concluded that the most appropriate gesture would be to offer Linguet a jewel.[108]

Simon Linguet did not need cash, and jewelry would have offended him. He wanted formal guarantees of freedom from government interference in his publishing business. By the summer of 1779, he was displaying more than his usual sensitivity on the matter. He had begun to encounter serious opposition to his entire undertaking from a formidable figure in Belgian political circles, the Archbishop of Malines. As spokesman for ecclesiastic autonomy in the Austrian Netherlands, the archbishop led a powerful, conservative political opposition to the systematic secularizers and centralizers among Austrian administrators in Belgium. He was a vigilant ecclesiastic watchdog who operated as an independent censor of printed material circulating in Belgium. The archbishop began criticizing Linguet's journalistic operation in June, 1779. At first he confined his complaints to Linguet's irregularities in performing religious obligations. The journalist's workers, he reported, were as lax as their employer. They rarely attended church. Linguet was running his presses in his home on Sundays, setting a bad example not only for his employees, but for the whole neighborhood around Waerbeck.[109]

The archbishop had touched upon some delicate and explosive issues which might prove extremely embarrassing to Austrian authorities in Belgium. Linguet had never received formal permission to install presses in his country house or to publish his political journal without regular supervision.

Crumpipen forwarded the archbishop's complaint to Count Nény for comment.[110] Nény, whose passionate commitment to Austria's systematic secularization program for her Belgian provinces was an open secret, turned in a report obviously biased in Linguet's favor. He did not see why the archbishop considered church attendance so palpable a mark of good Catholic behavior. Certainly the archbishop would concede that a command to attend church was not the ideal tactic for bringing an apostate back into the fold. Besides, Simon Linguet was a foreigner, in temporary residence in the Austrian Netherlands. What made him useful to the government was his pen, not his piety. The archbishop, Nény counselled, should be told as much, and advised to judge Linguet's conduct as he would that of a Protestant![111]

Austrian officials started encouraging Linguet to move from his country headquarters to a city, where his professional acitivites would be less likely to provoke trouble.[112]

Linguet was easily persuaded; he apparently had had the idea himself.[113] He announced to Lequesne on August 1, 1779, that he was determined to move to Brussels, and that he had obtained the government's promise that "nothing will be seen. That's all I ask for."[114] But Linguet was also piqued by the Archbishop of Maline's interference, and he made sure Nény knew.[115] It is not unlikely that Linguet had decided to exploit his brush with ecclesiastic authority to win the most favorable conditions possible for his move to Brussels. He was willing to relocate, but he wanted formal recognition for the *de facto* freedom from censorship he had enjoyed for his presses in Waerbeck, and which he could not hope to maintain in Brussels on the same casual basis.[116]

Count Nény, after spending an evening with Linguet, was able to figure that much out. "He desires nothing more than that we show a willingness to protect him from difficulties, so he can continue to print his *Annales* freely." Nény thought Linguet might be granted extraordinary permission to install presses for printing the *Annales* in his home, that is, that he might be excused from obtaining the required *lettres patentes d'octrois*, and from all other formalities. Nény suggested that the Fiscal Bureau of Brabant be notified that the government had decided to grant these extraordinary dispensations and privileges.[117]

Crumpipen reported back to Nény, giving him Starhemberg's reaction to his notes on his meeting of July 30 with Linguet. Starhemberg was willing to allow Linguet to operate his presses without police surveillance, but exclusively for the purpose of printing the *Annales*. Even then, Crumpipen noted, Starhemberg was uneasy. He wanted to know whether Linguet would be authorized to give Brussels as his place of publication if he received special privileges The government could not hope to keep the details of its extraordinary arrangements a secret in the middle of Brussels. And it would not be able to avoid giving the impression that Linguet's news was government sanctioned and protected. Some measure perhaps would have to be taken "to prevent him from inserting in his writings *things that are shocking* to *Courts* or *Ministers* whom we would have to handle gingerly, so that the government would not be *exposed to embarrassing complaints.*"[118]

Nény answered Starhemberg's observations with a lengthy "*Note ultérieure*" defending Linguet's request for extraordinary liberties. He argued that Linguet was engaged in a special kind of enterprise. His *Annales* would keep one printing press running constantly. The printer could not engage in any other activity at the same time; and the work required very close and exacting proofreading. The author would have to be on the spot to supervise the whole operation. Obviously, the press must be in his house. The same permission, Nény observed, already had been granted by the duc de Bouillon to Pierre

Rousseau, editor of the *Journal encyclopédique.* Besides, no printer in Brussels was capable of offering the quality service Linguet required. Nény conceded that government ordinances of 1729 and 1731 stipulated that all material printed in the Belgian provinces, with the exception of certain legal works like briefs, would be subject to prior approval by government censors. Linguet's intention, however, was to print the *Annales* from Brussels—without indicating the true place of impression, just as he had been doing since his arrival. "That is one more reason for not creating difficulties over the permission he is asking to be able to print this work in his house."

Nény noted that "the object of censorship is to prevent the printing of anything that directly attacks *Religion, the State, or Morals....* M. Linguet has always handled Religion and Morals with the greatest respect; and as for the State, I don't believe we have anything to complain about." Nény recalled to Starhemberg the letter he had written to Linguet in September, 1776. He felt he had made it emphatically clear to the journalist that no resident of Belgium whose conduct antagonized a foreign power could continue to enjoy asylum and protection under the Belgian constitution. Starhemberg need only reinforce the point in his correspondence with Linguet. As for Linguet's battle of epithets with his personal enemies, the philosophes, for example, Nény did not think these little wars of words should concern Austrian authorities. Even Nero, Nény remarked, had allowed Persius to satirize his poetry. Besides, he argued, everyone knew that the French government allowed Linguet's journal to be distributed through its own royal post office in the heart of Paris. "I think, therefore, that our government has no more interest than the French ministry does in interposing itself in the petty literary quarrels which may enter into the *Annales.*"

On the basis of these arguments, Nény recommended that Linguet be granted permission to install his own printing presses in his home; that he be allowed to print the *Annales* unsupervised and uncensored, without indicating place of impression; that he not be allowed to print other material, such as his complete works, without special permission; that he be warned against printing things shocking to foreign courts and ministries; and that, finally, he be advised that in what he wrote, he would be expected to respect religion and morals, "so that the government not be exposed to embarrassing complaints which might place it under the troublesome necessity of putting an end to the asylum he has been given, with pleasure, by the way, in the states of the Empress."[119]

The government formalized its arrangements with Linguet in February, 1780. They were almost precisely the arrangements which the exuberant Nény had recommended and under which Linguet had been operating independently for two years. Crumpipen asked Nény to inform the Fiscal Bureau of Brabant in the name of the duc de Lorraine of the government's agreement with Linguet. The duke's letter was to stipulate that this agreement had been made with Linguet "provisionally, and pending other arrangements."[120]

Escape clauses notwithstanding, Austrian authorities in Belgium now were committed to Simon Linguet's unpoliced and uncensored political journal. Linguet had wrested extraordinary liberties for himself from government functionaries acting with deliberation and calculation. They thought that with these concessions they had purchased the gratitude and occasional propaganda services of a proven master of political persuasion who was also a champion of strong monarchy. High level Austrian officials in Belgium had sensitized themselves to a new order of political necessities in an age of enlightenment, reform, and irrepressible information flow. They acknowledged their need for assistance from talented writers with experience in drafting and publicizing legislation and a record of success in molding and changing public opinion. They thought Linguet had been tamed and could be used, but already Linguet had used them better. He used them to free his pen and his presses. In an admirable maneuver, he traded a commissioned defense of Austria's position on the Bavarian question, a piece which appeared in print only after the crisis was over (and even then, only as a fragment of a masterpiece promised but never delivered) for recognition of his professional independence, a kind of political liberty.

The Bastille, A Political Journalist's Tomb and Cradle

From the first number of his *Annales* printed in London in 1777 to the seventy-first, which came out from Brussels in September, 1780, Simon Linguet was able to cover both domestic and international political scenes without encountering fatal interference from French ministers, from Austrian officials, or from his only official censor in France, LeNoir. Still, for all the relative show of restraint in official circles, Linguet did not lack political enemies. In a sense, enemies were what he wanted. He almost courted antagonists on all sides the way more prudent and cunning men collected patrons and protectors. In the act of defying or provoking them, he would be convincing his reading public of his political independence.

In the batteries of Linguet's enemies, the parlements occupied the front ranks. Since the 1760s, Linguet had been arguing that the Crown's work of administrative and legal reform must include a drastic limitation of parlementary prerogatives. In 1775, after several shifts of position, the Paris parlement failed to deliver Linguet from "civic death," that is, it refused to annul the Order of Lawyers' decision to disbar him. From that date, the theoretical and personal dimensions of his opposition became indistinguishable. He seized every occasion to attack the parlements in the *Annales*. Lequesne was uneasy. He could do nothing. Linguet freely admitted to his agent that he had a grudge against the parlements. "Well, who doubts that I have one? Who thinks it's bad that I have one? It's precisely because I write for the public that I must not lose a chance to undeceive it concerning these tyrants in robes who assassinated me; who assassinate honest men every day....by God, yes, I have a grudge: I will have one my whole life: and if circumstances are ever favorable, I will give them a far better idea of it."[121]

Beginning with the first number of the *Annales*, Jean-Jacques Duval d'Eprémesnil, a counsellor in the Paris parlement, had been building a collection of Linguet's attacks on the parlement and its members, although he also included evidence of Linguet's commitment to the despotism of kings and the revolutions of subjects. D'Eprémesnil presented this dossier before the Chambres des enquêtes in July, 1780. His aim was to win a vote from the parlement suppressing the *Annales*.[122] He need not have taken the trouble.

Early in April, 1780, in the fifty-ninth number of his *Annales*, Linguet turned out heavily editorialized reports in full and incriminating detail on a suit in civil law involving the duc de Duras. Duras was one of the two Academicians who, in July, 1776, had filed the Académie française's complaint against Linguet's article on La Harpe's reception into the Académie. That complaint had led to Linguet's dismissal from the *Journal de politique et de littérature*. Compromised and infuriated by Linguet's *exposé*, Duras persuaded French authorities to seize Linguet's entire fifty-ninth number.[123] On April 7, 1780, in self-acknowledged exasperation, Linguet wrote a mad, raging letter to Duras. The publicist Grimm reported that Linguet had referred to Duras there as "a son of a...fully spelled out, signed Linguet."[124] Linguet took the misplaced precaution of sending a copy to his censor, LeNoir.[125]

Duras did not demand reparation. He did not waste time answering Linguet's letter. Even before Linguet wrote it, the maréchal had obtained his first satisfaction. He had wiped out Linguet's fifty-ninth number. Now he took more direct paths to vengeance. On April 18, 1780, a *lettre de cachet* was issued against Linguet. It was a virtual guarantee to the offended Duras that as soon as he could be lured from Brussels to Paris, the annalist would be suppressed along with his *Annales*.[126]

Linguet arrived in Paris toward the end of September. He seemed to have been aware that he would be courting trouble in leaving Brussels,[127] but he had urgent business with Lequesne, his agent for the *Annales* in France. He had been threatening since August to stop publication unless Lequesne gave him a report on the financial state of his enterprise.[128] The Paris police were ready for Linguet. They arrested him at noon on September 27, 1780, in front of the Bastille.[129]

While most observers in Paris attempted to explain to their public or to their superiors in foreign courts how Linguet had been brought low by the maréchal de Duras,[130] French ministers and police agents were hot on the trail of evidence for a more serious charge than defamation of a maréchal's character. LeNoir wrote to Vergennes the day after Linguet's arrest. He advised the secretary of state that he had been informed there might be some interest in seizing Linguet's papers in Brussels. He had dispatched a police agent to Brussels to collect them.[131] One observer of these mysterious maneuvers, the bookseller Hardy, noted in his journal that Linguet was rumored to have written a libelous anti-ministerial manuscript found during a raid on a secret printing establishment maintained by the king's brother in his château at Brunoy.[132] If Vergennes was looking for evidence of such a manuscript among Linguet's papers in Brussels, he never found it.[133] Writing to his *chargé d'affaires* in Brussels on October 12, Vergennes acknowledged the failure of LeNoir's police mission to locate incriminating documents among Linguet's papers.[134]

Lack of evidence did not provoke Vergennes to work for Linguet's release. He had had enough of a journalist whose comments on international affairs frequently ran interference with his Genevan, American, Austrian, and Prussian policies.[135] Linguet's enterprise did not correspond in the least to Vergennes's idea of a tolerable political journal.[136]

Linguet's reporting of European affairs was probably not the only source of complaint. Some of the most infuriating and effective material in the *Annales* and in brochures issued as bonuses to subscribers concerns Simon Linguet, or rather, the case of Linguet against the French establishment. All over Europe, he broadcast the news of his disbarment, his dismissal from his post as editor of the *Journal de politique et de littérature,* his harrassment by hostile *économistes, littérateurs,* magistrates, lawyers, and ministers as indicative of what was rotten in the system and as typical of what could happen to talented, unprivileged men who took on the authorities.[137] He had arraigned the duc de Duras before a special international court of public opinion composed of his subscribers and was weighing the evidence against him in the fifty-ninth number of the *Annales* when Duras succeeded in having the number confiscated.

Expelled from conventional institutions and careers in which contemporaries were channeling their ambitions and making their influence felt, Linguet made journalism into a one-man political institution. He placed himself and the *Annales* between the authority of all the regimes of Europe and the force of an international public, his newly aggregated political power, the power of public opinion.

Authorities in France interpreted his career in political journalism as a crime. His punishment was supposed to have been an indefinite term in the Bastille. Linguet experienced this third civil and political death as the regime's most colossal crime against him: "And so, *giggling away,* they told me every day that I must not worry about what was going on in the world *because everyone out there thought I was dead;* they carried the joke to the point of recounting in detail the circumstances which mad rage or a hideous levity was tacking on to my alleged end." (*MB, 92*).

Confined in the Bastille, Linguet insisted that he had been buried alive, with the intention that he continue to breathe, but gagged, bound, deprived of his pen, his public, his presses—once again a victim of vivisection, lingering on by some frightful design of his executioners. He was a disembodied voice speaking to walls twelve feet thick; the voice of a defendant pleading before a nonexistent judge; the voice of an orator declaiming his innocence in unrelieved soliloquy. He could reach neither the king nor his public. If only he could be heard, he would vanquish by force of sustained eloquence. He had to know at once who his accusers were. He would plead his case before them. "It's only too obvious that it's not the government. It has no interest in ruining me, in stifling me the way they're doing. It has no reason. I'm not at all a conspirator, or factious, I'm not even suspected. This entire business is only an affair of clerks, of minor considerations, and perhaps, of money handed over...."[138]

His was the unprecedented case of a man under arrest and "accused of nothing," he wrote to Lesquesne. "I can answer very well for what I do, for what I say, but not for what they attribute to me; and closed in here as I am, not even knowing what they are imputing to me, unable to hope either for an investigation or a confrontation, it is easy for them to make me appear suspect, or even guilty."[139] When was his trial, or his execution? He insisted on knowing. "I asked a thousand times, verbally, and in writing, for a *legal proceeding,* or for *death;* and then the bath of Seneca, or the dagger of Trasea, would have seemed a favor to me" (*MB,* 132-33). One might imagine Linguet as a prototypical "K." The Castle existed. From the Bastille where he was, his words, his verbal testament to his innocence, never would reach the ears of the Castellan. But they would—if only he could confront the monarch immediately, if only, somehow, his call for help and his proclamations of his innocence could pass through myriad intermediary channels, each a cul de sac—as if by magic. Impossible. He wrote beseeching letters, concocted plots from his cell, issued painstakingly detailed instructions to his literary agent, Lequesne. In October, 1781, Linguet surmised the birth of a dauphin from the firing of the Bastille's cannon, and dashed off at least two poems celebrating the event.[140] The king, he instructed Lequesne, must find his verses in the dauphin's cradle, and added, "I know how difficult that must be to obtain and I don't ask you even to try for it."[141]

The feat Linguet was obsessively intent on accomplishing was to reach out from behind bars and walls to touch the person of the king, to move the heart of the royal master of his fate, and, barring that, to recall himself, to represent himself to the king in words. "The king is just, he is severe but good. He is deceived. It is not possible that if he were informed, he would abandon a man whose patriotism is above suspicion to such an outrageous captivity as this...."[142]

Linguet wrote several letters to the duc de Duras; and apparently, at one point, he was ready to hand over important sums of money, presumably to Duras, as payment for the crime of defaming a French peer. A handsome cash settlement might have appeased Duras. French authorities with whom the decision to liberate Linguet rested could not be bought off as easily.[143]

There had to be another way to reach the castle from the Bastille. Linguet found it. He would transmit his innocence directly to the king; he would signal it to him with the speed of light. In the early months of 1782, Linguet announced to Lequesne that he had invented a communications system from his prison cell. He took care to envelop the project in mystery, and even when he said he was describing it, he was more concerned to impress Lequesne and the public with what the system could do than with how he planned to do it.[144] Even his written instructions to Lequesne from the Bastille reveal little about the details of the mechanism he had put together, if there were any.

Speculation on the nature of the invention began as soon as Lequesne broadcast the news that Linguet had formulated an experiment in long-distance communication and had asked for provisional liberty to try out his system. One account passed off the invention as a system for launching a bullet-like device with a coded message inside from one relay station to another. Another described a kind of electric telegraph. Other chronicles have interpreted the novelty as a light-signal system,[145] or a phonograph or telephonelike device—a rather unlikely possibility.[146]

The editor of the *Courrier du Bas-Rhin,* who had access to a copy of Linguet's memoir, offered a running *précis* in two installments. According to this report, Linguet's invention was not an ordinary signal system. He did not use flares, or flags, or straw or fire, or wood, or cannon, or pigeons. Linguet's "aerial correspondence" would provide a safe, dependable, and economical means of communication, with sight the only interpreter. But it would be fast also, like a cannon. Orders and detailed information could be communicated whole and without delay. The message, whatever its length, could be transmitted in absolute secrecy. Intermediary agents would know nothing of what they were relaying. The message could be returned immediately to the sender for verification, if necessary. One machine per station would suffice—not a magnifying glass, not a telescope, or any other instrument requiring special skills. Linguet boasted that in the time required to copy a message of any length six times, he could communicate it from Brest, or Toulon, or Bayonne, to Versailles and return the answer. He could extend the system to Constantinople or St. Petersburg. He modestly disclaimed credit for inventing the equipment; the two principal parts were used every day "in two of the best known, commonest crafts." His contribution was to have figured out how to "get correspondence going between distant places without more distance or less making any palpable difference in the speed."[147]

The mechanism of Linguet's mysterious device, if there ever was one, may have been electric. Linguet was intrigued by the properties and nature of light and the potential of electricity. He himself owned an "electric machine."[148] He lamented that since its discovery, electricity had not been put to one good use.[149]

What is certain, although in no sense conclusive, is that during his twenty months in captivity, Linguet had become obsessed with light, its essence, its properties. What fascinated him was not exactly light as a physical phenomenon, but rather light as the bearer of messages—light the conveyor of the self instantaneously through infinitely great intervals of space, the restorer of wholeness in a dichotomized world. Might not light serve then as the instrument of the prisoner's liberation and self-vindication, the agent of his political resurrection? Light, Linguet wrote in a treatise he would publish in 1784, but which he had worked out while he was in the Bastille, was the unifying principle of the universe. Light, "the image of the Deity by its brilliance, diffused as it is, everywhere in nature, couldn't it be [the Diety's] immediate agent?"[150] Was Linguet suggesting that in one of its forms light would be the ideal messenger, capable of bearing the word, the self's expansion through time and space, and bearing it without distortion, without loss of energy or vital force? Linguet himself had described his experiment to the public as a new use for light "imagined in a time when I wasn't seeing it" (MB, 11).

Linguet wrote to Lequesne on March 30, 1782, instructing him on how they would prepare the experiment for testing his communication system. Lequesne was not to insist too strongly on Linguet's being given provisional freedom to test the device. It would not matter whether he was liberated, provided they could obtain permission to see one another to agree upon the materials to be used and the operation of the mechanism. If they were forced into it, Linguet would operate from the Bastille and Lequesne was to station himself at a point somewhere in the vicinity of Paris from which "this Hell would be visible." He cautioned Lequesne that if they went through with the experiment, "it would be necessary to have in hand the assurance that, at least at the moment of success, the chains would fall...." Lequesne was to be certain to get witnesses for the trial-run of the new mechanism. He urged Lequesne to pull some answer out of the authorities. The uncertainty was unbearable, "above all in such a case; that is to say, with a resource as singular as the one we have in hand, although deprived of everything. I have substituted for everything I was lacking: I have performed my experiment, I do it every day!... In truth, it is on a small scale, and very small, but what difference does it make. Here, there are neither false witnesses, nor defects in materials to fear. There never was a more fortunate idea. In the genre of singularities it can be snuffed out only by the coldness or the disdain that would be interested in suppressing it." After all his boasting to Lequesne about the invention, Linguet still was fearful that he had left too much unexplained. He had the feeling that Lequesne had not caught on—and he had good reason to be afraid. He had told Lequesne virtually nothing. "Although you understand the thing very well, you do not seem to me to have caught on to the means of speed yet: it is true that it is singular: but at the same time so simple, so simple.... I do not dare say the word, but perhaps the time to say it will finally come."[151]

In the letter of March 30, Linguet told Lequesne to let the news of the experiment out: "...it is too interesting not to pique curiosity—finally, and at least. It is in this getup that utility often must be presented to be accepted." On April 29, Linguet wrote to Lequesne expressing his astonishment at the amount of publicity stirred up, especially as they had finally decided to keep the project secret. "I admit, however, that I would have preferred by far to owe my resurrection to justice which has always spoken for me, than to an idea due to accident, and which very well might never have come to me." Several days later, he ordered Lequesne to stop pushing for a demonstration of the invention; it looked as though the minister "did not want to create the impression of having given me back my liberty at a price,...if they do want to restore it, it will be without condition, or at least without that one...." He admitted that this might after all be the better move. He would be able to test the idea once he had been freed, and once it had been perfected.[152]

By May 11, Linguet knew he was going to be released. He instructed Lequesne to contact the duc de Castries, the new minister for the Navy, who apparently had written a favorable letter on Linguet's behalf, which now would no longer be needed. Lequesne was to "insist again on the certainty of the discovery, on the reality of my promises; my first care will be to thank them; and the second, to convince them." He then turned his attention to the capital question: "I do not know what conditions they will place on the opening of portals so long closed. If they knew me, the best thing for them would be not to give me any: but in any case, you will let it be known that I am not eager to become the object of public curiosity; there would be as much danger in it as indiscretion." He had the idea of renting a house at Passy under a pseudonym, "absolutely incognito." While he was recuperating there, he and Lequesne could prepare for the trials of "our air service."[153]

Linguet was released from the Bastille on May 19, 1782, but his freedom was hedged with conditions. Bastille rules required that all prisoners sign a promise that they would never speak of the place and of what had happened to them while they were there. Linguet signed. He was forced to promise that he would go directly from Paris to the village of Rethel-Mazarin, in Champagne, and that he would remain there until further notice. Again, he signed.[154] Still, he found the conditions of freedom intolerable (*MB*, 14). Almost immediately and without authorization, he left for Brussels. A few months later, he embarked for England. He might have promised to respect the realm's laws, morals, and religion. But he fled France to safeguard his property in his liberty, and to continue practicing his suspect profession, that of political communicator, a mediator between throne and nation.

Linguet's *Avis aux souscripteurs,* his first public announcement that he would resume publication of the *Annales,* was dated London, January 1, 1783: "In the lion's den of the modern Babylon, inaccessible even to celestial messengers and to the consolations which sometimes got through to the [den] of the ancient [Babylon], they could afflict my heart by all kinds of privations, they could *rend* it by all kinds of attacks; they have not been able to degrade my spirit. My strength is diminished: my courage, my love for the truth, are not."[155]

Linguet's sensational *Mémoires sur la Bastille* appeared in the first pages of the tenth volume of the *Annales,* under a motto descriptive of his miraculous reestablishment: *Surrexit ex mortui.* The work was published separately as a pamphlet, translated into several languages, reprinted in multiple editions, and circulated clandestinely all over France and throughout Europe.[156]

Linguet presented his *Mémoires sur la Bastille* as a rebellious survivor's testimony about his living death under an absolute despotism. "I am in *England,*" the new Job wrote in the first lines of his *Mémoires:* "It must be shown that I could not help returning there. I no longer am in the *Bastille:* it must be shown that I never deserved to be confined there" (*MB*, 1). To prove his innocence, he brought the machinery and personnel of monarchical administration in France to trial in his *Mémoires.* He accused the regime of committing a perfectly arbitrary criminal act. It had murdered him; robbed him of his property in his life. The Bastille was the administration's tomb for political men. When he was released, he stepped out of the sepulchre "a new Lazarus, free of the funereal shroud which for twenty months intercepted all movements of my mouth and my heart..." (*MB*, 48).

The subject of this modern miracle was fully aware that he was releasing dangerous knowledge: "All the subjects I discuss here—can I treat them without qualms? In *all good conscience,* can I let the public in on the secret of the terrible mysteries into which the 27th of September, 1780 initiated me?" (*MB*, 5). Knowledge was the motor of revolution; still, the people, Linguet admitted in his *Avis aux souscripteurs,* have a right to know. And nothing, no one, could keep his knowledge from them: "There is no human means of annihilating them [the *Mémoires*] ....they would transpire through all the pores of the realm."[157]

He had been wrong about England: "The Bastille makes an excellent telescope for evaluating England and its laws." At first, he was prepared to state outright that the English Constitution, guaranteeing personal liberty and rigidly stating both the instances in which it could be denied and the forms following which it might be defended and restored, was "the most perfect."[158] Later, he qualified himself without reverting to the fanatic Anglophobia of his earlier writings. What was beginning to redeem England for Linguet was its political climate, the openness of English public space, that preserve in which Englishmen could be political selves: "...but it seems to me that there is something noble and consoling for the *English* in being able to claim, at least every seven years, a right which all the rest of the human race has lost: [the right] to designate for the sovereign magistrate assistants who must guide him in the name of the *People*; [the right] to give moderators to power, create mouths which will not only carry the vow, the desires of the Nation to the foot of the throne, but if necessary, will force the prince to listen to them, to comply with it."[159]

Corruption, the failure of electors and elected to live up to their principles, and the growth of power, had checked the full realization of English political liberty. Traces remained, however, barriers against every kind of tyranny, "and the rest of the known world provides none. Finally, if it were true that in reality, liberty did not exist here any more than elsewhere,...still, it is a great accomplishment for the *English* to have preserved the image of it, to have made it the object of their cult, and to have kept possession of these rights which, marking the place where [liberty's] altar used to exist, can still be used as the material for reconstructing it."[160]

Liberty in civil society, Linguet had proclaimed countless times, was only the liberty of dominion; but the liberty of dominion might be enough, provided a man could enlarge the domain infinitely. Linguet had hinted already in the first numbers of his *Annales* that for the propertyless, the domain might be enlarged from the size of the human stomach to embrace a human being's security, his welfare. He now suggested that for everyone, that domain was not only biological and psychological, but political also. The liberty of dominion touched upon everything every man might want to possess in the world, including a political existence.

Simon Linguet was the new Lazarus. He had come back from the dead, prepared to tell all. Every revelation to his public was calculated for its inflammatory content. A prisoner in the Bastille is the most helpless of victims; each of his guards is his potential executioner. Every meager meal might be his last; he must fear poison in every morsel of nourishment he can bring himself to swallow. And even if such wild fears were only a sick man's ravings, still the inevitable onset of the disease had been calculated as part of the prisoner's torture (*MB*, 71-75). Lowly subordinates made a sport of opening, reading, and then burning or diverting every attempted communication with the outside world. The prisoner, sequestered in his cell, sees none of his fellow prisoners, but he clearly hears their sighs, their sobs, their pacings, the sounds of their arrivals and departures (*MB*, 62, 51 bis, 62 bis, 63 bis). "Here are combined [the tortures] of *Tantalus, Ixion, Sisyphus*" (*MB*, 63 bis). The Bastille was a "political purgatory, where the slightest faults, often innocence, are submitted arbitrarily to the tortures of Hell" (*MB*, 130, n. 23).

Linguet fashioned these word-pictures to touch his reader's every sense, to inspire outrage, horror; they were words that leapt from atrocity to abomination, sparing no detail, no matter how minuscule or how scandalous, no matter how incendiary. For now he aimed to arouse public rage and the public's passion for action by revealing the facts of a political and civil annihilation, his own; a total eclipse of liberty, his in particular. In England, and this time Linguet himself and not his adversaries among philosophes, *encyclopédistes, parlementaires*, was making the comparison, in England, "an arbitrary detention would be a crime of *lèse-peuple*, almost as rigorously pursued as [a crime] of *lèse-majesté...*" (*MB, 142*, n. 23). The Bastille was the institutional perpetuation of a crime of *lèse-peuple*, a crime against the nation. Linguet pleaded with the king to authorize its destruction. His frontispiece showed the Bastille in ruins with citizens bowing in gratitude before the statue they had erected to honor Louis XVI. The statue speaks: "Be free, live." But Linguet anticipated at the same time that his appeal to the king might fall upon deaf ears. Nature, then, would accomplish the deed: lightning, "the thunderbolts of heaven," an untamable nature's instrument of salutary violence, like the lightning that strikes down the Bastille in the frontispiece—or maybe an enlightened nation in arms, "the anathema of men" (*MB*, frontispiece, 105).

Linguet expressed in the *Mémoires*, and with a disarming boldness, what can best be described as an overpowering urge to blow up a regime that had become for him a prison and tomb of the political self. He quickly recovered, to argue, as he had in the past, that the reinforcement of institutional constraints on liberties must be the highest end of political endeavor. He reverted to his quest for systems and programs of social, economic, and political containment. He continued to insist that subjects owed obedience to kings whose only obligation to them was to provide protection for their properties— although he did not repudiate a line of his *Mémoires sur la Bastille*, where he taught by example, his own, that in France, monarchical authority had degenerated into a despotism where estates in life and profession (including properties in the kind of professional liberty that conferred political influence) were attached and arbitrarily wiped out with impunity; and that under these conditions a subject was justified in exercising rights of self-protection and self-determination.

There was no easy way for Linguet to retreat from this position. A band of unsolicited proselytes and half-courted disciples already was taking lessons in revolutionary attitudes in the school of this monarchist and subversive. Linguet's most observant public enemies had predicted as much. In reporting Linguet's arrest, a writer for the *Correspondance littéraire* remarked that Linguet recruited his supporters among the clergy, the court, the military, "and above all in the cafes of Paris, where the violence of his pen is advantageous to malignity, amuses the idle, and causes him to be admired by blockheads as one of the most sublime models of French eloquence."[161]

While Linguet was still a prisoner, a strangely independent character, although no apostle of revolutions, Louis-Sébastien Mercier, in his *Tableau de Paris*, praised Linguet's iconoclasm and his martyred-rebel stance: "...the hypocrite is cowardly, and he escapes; the passionate man gives himself up to his fire, and he destroys himself. I will regret, along with all just and impartial men, not having heard for longer the voice of the only orator the bar had; and his exclusion, his disbarment, will be an eternal stigma upon the *Order.*" Concerning Linguet's captivity, Mercier wrote: "There groans or groans no more, the famous Linguet. What is his crime? No one knows. 'The consequence of it is abominable, the cause is unknown.' Voltaire."[162]

As soon as Linguet checked out of the Bastille, young Camille Desmoulins, the future revolutionary radical, tried to convince himself that a hero modeled after the ancient republicans had just been restored to life. He prepared a poem celebrating Linguet's freedom, and announcing his discipleship:

> Et toi, rentre, o Linguet! dans le temple des arts.
>
> Vous ses lâches persécuteurs [the Academy, the
>   magistrature],
> Tremblez qu'en traits de feu sur vos fronts im-
>   posteurs
> Sa main n'imprime un sceau d'ignominie
>
>   ...
>
> Toujours la fortune ennemie
> Fut le creuset de la vertu,
> Et donna la trempe au génie.[163]

Brissot de Warville, if only momentarily, was no less completely carried away. "His courage and his intelligence, his fiery nature, as his energetic pen, everything pleased me, everything interested me, attracted me; and when, following his release from the Bastille, I found him again in London, I did not run, I flew into his arms."[164]

Perhaps more than the philosophes whose work as educators he condemned, Simon Linguet was contributing to a national enlightenment when he depicted the Bastille as an instrument of despots in full control of the machinery of monarchical administration, and as the symbol of a despotism which threatened security, liberty, life.[165] He was making it necessary to regard monarchical statecraft as the impossible art of restoring the shattered confidence of a politically educated nation.

NOTES

1. Linguet, *Précis et consultation dans la cause entre Simon-Nicolas-Henri Linguet, Ecuyer, et Charles-Joseph Panckoucke, libraire à Paris* (Paris, 1787), pp. 5-6.

2. Linguet, *Journal de politique et de littérature, contenant les principaux événemens de toutes les cours, les nouvelles de la république des lettres, & c.,* 21 nos. (Oct. 25, 1774–July 25, 1776), no. 1 (Oct. 25, 1774), 6-7.

3. Linguet, "Suite de la lettre de M. Linguet à l'Abbé Roubaud," *Journal de politique et de littérature,* no. 6 (Dec. 15, 1774), 232; and see Chapter Three.

4. For details of Linguet's *guerre de plume* with La Harpe, see Jean Cruppi, *Un Avocat journaliste au XVIIIᵉ siècle, Linguet* (Paris, 1895), pp. 195-99.

5. Linguet to d'Alembert, printed by Linguet in his *Réponse aux docteurs modernes, ou Apologie pour l'auteur de la "Théorie des lois" et des "Lettres" sur cette "Théorie," Avec la réfutation du système des philosophes économistes,* 2 vols. (n.p., 1771), II, 237-38. See also François Métra, J. Imbert, de Boudeaux, et al., eds., *Correspondance secrète, politique, et littéraire, ou Mémoires pour servir à l'histoire des cours, des sociétés, et de la littérature en France depuis la mort de Louis XV,* 18 vols. (London, 1787-90), XIII (Paris, Oct. 9, 1782), 302-4.

6. Linguet, *Réponse aux docteurs modernes,* II, 243.

7. Linguet, "Discours de MM. de la Harpe et Marmontel, à la réception du premier dans l'Académie françoise," *Journal de politique et de littérature,* no. 21 (July 25, 1776), 403-4.

8. *Ibid.,* 405.

9. Linguet feared the worst repercussions from his inflammatory reporting of La Harpe's reception into the Académie française. "They are making an affair of state out of the criticism of the choice of the Academy, which has prostituted itself to Hapula [La Harpe]," he wrote to Brissot. "The minister is getting mixed up in it: but then try to be a man of letters without being base!" Linguet to Brissot de Warville, Paris, sometime after June 20, 1776, in Jacques-Pierre Brissot de Warville, *J.-P. Brissot: Correspondance et papiers,* ed. Claude Perroud, Mémoires et documents relatifs aux XVIIIᵉ et XIXᵉ siècles, vol. IV (Paris, 1912), p. 2.

10. Eugène Hatin, *Histoire politique et littéraire de la presse en France,* 8 vols. (Paris, 1859-61), III, 338. See also Louis Petit de Bachaumont, *Mémoires secrets, pour servir à l'histoire de la république des lettres en France, depuis MDCCLXII jusqu'à nos jours; ou Journal d'un observateur,* 36 vols. (London, 1780-89), IX (Aug. 2, 4, 8, 1776), 178, 180, 183-4; Brissot de Warville, *J.-P. Brissot: Mémoires (1754-1793),* ed. Claude Perroud, 2 vols., Mémoires et documents relatifs au XVIIIᵉ et XIXᵉ siècles, vols. II-III (Paris, 1911), I, 83-85.

11. Linguet to Voltaire, Geneva, July 8, 1776, in BM, uncat. MSS, coll. Gosset, no. 23.

12. See Linguet, *Précis et consultation,* pp. 16-18.

13. See Linguet's annotation on Vergennes to Panckoucke, Aug. 2, 1776, allegedly communicated by Linguet to Vergennes and printed in Linguet, *Lettre de M. Linguet à M. le Comte de Vergennes, ministre des affaires étrangères en France* (London, 1777), pp. 17-19; see also Linguet, *Précis et consultation,* p. 20.

14. For La Harpe's commentary on the incident, see La Harpe to Jean-Baptiste-Joseph-René Dureau de la Malle, Paris, Sept. 13, 1776, in Jean-François de La Harpe, *Correspondance inédite de Jean-François de La Harpe,* ed. Alexandre Jovicevich (Paris, 1965), pp. 29-31. For detailed discussion, see Christopher Todd, *Voltaire's Disciple: Jean-François de La Harpe* (London, 1972), pp. 24-26.

15. Linguet, *Lettres sur la "Théorie des lois civiles" & c., où l'on examine entr'autres choses s'il est bien vrai que les Anglois soient libres, & que les François doivent, ou imiter leurs opérations, ou porter envie à leur gouvernement* (Amsterdam, 1770), pp. 124-25 (Cited hereafter as *LL*). On the eve of his departure for England, Linguet was viewing his new location in quite another light. "Since I saw you, many things have happened," he wrote to a correspondent (probably Samuel-Frédéric Osterwald, director of the Société

typographique de Neuchâtel), "and I have seen many countries: I went to England for the express purpose of feeling out the ground: because in the position I am in, I need a solid one. I hesitated between this island and your mountains. The desire to see you made me lean to the side of the latter; but the proximity, the complete liberty [*la grande liberté*] decided me for Great Britain. I will not tarry in returning there, and we will see what will come of it." Linguet to correspondent unnamed, Brussels, Dec. 25, 1776, in Archives de la Société typographique de Neuchâtel, in Bibliothèque publique de la ville de Neuchâtel, MS 1175, fol. 441.

16. The text I cite in this passage is the manuscript copy of Linguet's *Lettre*, Lettre de M. Linguet à M. le de Vergennes, ministre des affaires étrangères en France, London, 1777, avertissement, fol. 2, in BM, no. 1917. In my edition of the printed *Lettre*, the phrase "...he must place contemporaries and posterity between himself and his persecutors" is omitted. See Linguet, *Lettre de M. Linguet à M. le Comte de Vergennes, ministre des affaires étrangères en France* (London, 1777), p. 4.

17. Linguet, *Lettre de M. Linguet à M. le Comte de Vergennes*, p. 22. Emphasis is Linguet's.

18. *Ibid.*, pp. 33-34.

19. In his *Les Imprimeries d'Yverdun au XVIIe et XVIIIe siècles* (Lausanne, 1945), pp. 303-4, Jean-Pierre Perret provides a brief but suggestive discussion which covers the reprinting of Linguet's *Lettre* by the Société littéraire et typographique d'Yverdon (a Swiss publishing house which specialized in pirated editions of political literature and distributed to French customers); the *Lettre's* proscription by Swiss authorities; and its continuing appearance in catalog listings of available works.

20. LL, p. 40; Linguet, *Du plus heureux gouvernement, ou Parallèle des constitutions politiques de l'Asie avec celles de l'Europe, servant d'introduction à la "Théorie des lois civiles,"* 2 vols. in one (London, 1774), I, 12.

21. Linguet, *Lettre de M. Linguet à M. le Comte de Vergennes*, pp. 9-27, 46-47.

22. *Ibid.*, pp. 9-12, 56, 62.

23. *Ibid.*, pp. 43-44.

24. *Ibid.*, p. 56.

25. *Ibid.*, pp. 4, 43-44.

26. *Ibid.*, pp. 33-34.

27. Cited without reference in Louis-Alexandre Devérité, *Notice pour servir à l'histoire de la vie et des écrits de S.N.H. Linguet*, new ed. (Liège, 1782), p. 130.

28. Perine Buttet, wife of a successful merchant-manufacturer from the town of Nogent-le-Rotrou, and mother of two teen-aged daughters, first latched onto Linguet sometime early in 1771. By August 11 of that year, she was writing to "le sage éclairé" to request that he find her a copy of the *Système de la nature* and keep his eye out for other diverting readings, particularly philosophically oriented works. Buttet to Linguet, Nogent-le-Rotrou, Aug. 11, 1771, in BM, no. 1916, no. 1. On Oct. 6, 1771, she recalled to Linguet her last trip to Paris and "les douceurs de votre société," Nogent-le-Rotrou, Oct. 6, 1771, no. 2. She carefully followed Linguet's pleadings in the Bombelles case, taking care to overload her letters with lavish praises for Linguet's public performances, Nogent-le-Rotrou, Dec. 29, 1771, no. 3. In January, 1972, she invited him to visit Nogent-le-Rotrou, to take on one of her husband's legal suits, Jan. 29, 1771, no. 4; see also nos. 5 and 6. She followed these invitations with a present of a *pâté* in February, Feb. 26, 1772, no. 6. At the end of March, she announced to Linguet that she was prolonging her stay in Paris to hear "le Ciceron de la France" plead a case, and requested that he allow her to call for him in her carriage and accompany him into the courtroom as his secretary. Paris, March 30, 1772, no. 8. Sometime later, she was openly avowing her undying passion, n.p., "ce samedi soir," no. 10. She paraded the news of her separation from her husband for Linguet's sake, and her suffering at Linguet's hand—"homme cruel!" Paris, "vendredi matin," no. 12. By the spring of 1774, Zulaire's Zélie was a full-fledged mistress lost in a torrential love: "...je te voyais sans cesse dans cette chambre: tu t'es reposé près de moi sur cette automane [*sic*] et ce lit....ah Zulaire! [*sic*] tu n'y viendras pas ce soir. Mais je t'ai vu écrire sur cette table, ma plume t'a suivie, ces livres sont de toi aussi. Je m'envi-

ronne de tout ce qui a touché à mon amant,..." n.p., "mardi à sept heures du soir" [end of March, beginning April, 1774], no. 13. For a complete chronicle of major episodes in Linguet's stormy liaison with Madame Buttet, see selected letters from Madame Buttet's correspondence with Linguet, and with M. Buttet; Linguet's correspondence with Le-quesne (Linguet to Lequesne: Brussels, July 30, 1778; Waerbeck, June 27, 1777, July 5, 1779, and *passim*); Mme. Buttet's correspondence with Lequesne; Mme. Buttet's corres-pondence with Linguet in the Bastille, all in BM, no. 1916. See also Mme. Dérodé, Lin-guet's sister, to Linguet, July 13, 1774, and *passim*, in BM, uncat. MSS, Coll. Gosset, nos. 30-76.

29. Linguet to Noailles, London, April 6, 1777, in AM, Angleterre, vol. 522, fol. 358v. Siméon-Prosper Hardy, "Mes Loisirs, ou Journal d'événemens tels qu'ils parviennent à ma connoissance (1764-1789)," March 12, April 17, 1777, in BN, MSS fr., vol. 6682, fols. 335, 347. The ministers in France apparently had no intention of kidnapping Lin-guet or doing away with him. Miromesnil admitted that the administration was respon-sible for Linguet's excesses of insolence. "If, at the time of his first delinquency, he had been thrown into an oubliette for life, the source of this torrent of insults would have been dried up." Nonetheless, Miromesnil was not recommending these "assertive acts of authority" [*coups d'autorité*] in Linguet's case. See Miromesnil to correspondent un-named, April 6, 1777, in AM, Angleterre, vol. 522, fols. 357, 357v. See also Vergennes to Noailles, Versailles, April 19, 1777, in *ibid.*, fols. 452, 452v. Still, Linguet was not mistaken in his suspicion that while he was in England, he was under constant surveil-lance. Several reports by government agents shadowing him were filed with the Depart-ment of Foreign Affairs in France. One report, dated May 13, 1777, records the follow-ing mad incident: "82 [code for Linguet's name] brought a hussy here [Madame Buttet] whom he allowed to pass for his wife. One fine morning (two or three days ago), the goddess took it into her head to change her quarters, which she managed with such se-crecy and dexterity that the poor modern philosopher had no inkling of the matter until the time when, wanting to look for some socks in his wardrobe, he didn't find a single pair; everything was carted away. This adventure makes the poor forlorn creature look frightfully ridiculous; this would be just the right time to finish up portraying him [pro-bably a reference to a biography of Linguet in preparation, commissioned by this agent, or by a superior, for the Department of Foreign Affairs]." AM, Angleterre, vol. 523, fol. 67.

30. Linguet, "Réflexions préliminaires," *Annales politiques, civiles, et littéraires du dix-huitième siècle*, 19 vols. (London, Brussels, Paris, 1777-92), I (1777), 83. Cited here-after as *RA*.

31. Voltaire to Jacques Mallet Du Pan [1777], in *Voltaire's Correspondence*, ed. Theodore Besterman, 107 vols. (Geneva, 1953-65), 96, no. 19545, 209-10. Brissot also had been impressed by Linguet's determination to publish a political journal. Brissot de Warville, *Avertissement* to *Fragments sur les lois criminelles tirés des "Annales poli-tiques, et civiles" de M. Linguet*, in Brissot de Warville, ed., *Bibliothèque philosophique du législateur, du politique, du jurisconsulte...*, 9 vols. (Berlin, 1782), IX, 76. Later, Brissot reversed his first judgment on the merits of the *Annales*. In all its parts, political, civil, literary, legal, Linguet's eighteenth century, Brissot concluded, was an unrelieved distortion: "He presents it through a prism, and because he has been careful to place himself between this prism and us to keep us thinking about his person, the author of the *Annales* turns out to be the most important figure of his time." Brissot de Warville, *Brissot: Mémoires*, ed. Perroud, I, 94.

32. Voltaire to d'Alembert, April 8, 1777, in *Voltaire's Correspondence*, ed. Bester-man, 96, no. 19473, 139.

33. When Linguet published the first number of his *Annales*, in April, 1777, the com-petition in political journalism was almost nil. The *Courrier de l'Europe* (1776-92) is the nearest thing to a comparable enterprise. The young Brissot de Warville was among the contributors. See, for comparative purposes, the first French daily, the *Journal de Paris*, which began publication on Jan. 1, 1777; the *Journal général de l'Europe*; the *Journal de littérature française et étrangère*, an enterprise of J.-G. Dubois-Fontanelle; the *Gazette*

des Deux-Ponts; the *Nouveau spectateur;* the *Nouvelles Ephémérides économiques;* the *Gazette du commerce, de l'agriculture et des finances.*

34. *Dictionnaire à l'usage de ceux qui lisent les "Annales" de M. Linguet,* announced in Bachaumont, *Mémoires secrets,* XV (Sept. 15, 1780), 324.

35. Linguet, "Problème proposé aux personnes jalouses de la pureté de la langue françoise, par un Etranger," *Annales,* IV (1778), 388. See also *Ibid.,* 248.

36. Linguet, "Réponse" to "Problème proposé aux personnes jalouses de la pureté de la langue françoise, par un Etranger," *ibid.,* 392.

37. *Ibid.,* 248. Linguet had referred to the members of the Acadèmie française as "ces prétendus inspecteurs de la pureté des mots." Linguet, "Réponse" to "Problème proposé aux personnes jalouses de la pureté de la langue françoise, par un Etranger," *ibid.,* 396.

38. Ferdinand Gohin, *Les Transformations de la langue française pendant la deuxième moitié du XVIIIe siècle: 1740-1789* (Paris, 1903), pp. 234, 238, 242, 254, 268, 269, 289, 292, 294, 344, 355, 360, citing Linguet's *Annales,* I (1777), 63, 306, 411; II (1777), 274, 459; III (1777), 15, 355, 450, 473; V (1779), 67, IX (1780), 270; XII (1784), 45, 255; XIII (1788), 84, 272, 415. See also for "*économisme,*" *Annales,* III, 250. It would appear that Linguet really invented many words in his political lexicon; but he also borrowed some remarkable expressions from the anti-philosophe Elie Fréron—*philosophism* and *philosophistes,* for example. See Jean Balcou, *Fréron contre les philosophes* (Geneva, 1975), Histoire des idées et critique littéraire, no. 151, pp. 185-87. Linguet proclaimed countless times, as Fréron had, that he was attacking the philosophes the better to defend morals, religion, and the government. However, Linguet went further than Fréron had in politicizing his opposition to *économistes, encyclopédistes, académiciens,* and others in the party of humanity who were making their power and connections felt in royal government. In conjunction with his theoretical work on the principles of monarchical society and administration, Linguet's protests against the authorities' violations of subjects' properties, including his own, read as frontal attacks on the legitimacy of constituted authority. When Fréron had to face *coups d'autorité* against his "estate" in his journalistic career, he shrank from phrasing his protests as general indictments of monarchical administration.

39. *Ibid.,* p. 352. citing Linguet, *Annales,* XIII, 425; *Annales,* II, 133.

40. Indexes are available for volumes I through VII. Linguet analyzes political affairs in major states: England, Africa, the American colonies, Germany, Geneva, Turkey, Bavaria, Austria, Spain, Poland, Russia, and the Scandinavian countries. He evaluates the careers of public officials, including d'Aiguillon, Terray, Necker, Maynon d'Invau, Saint-Germain, among others. He offers running analyses of French institutions: the Estates-General, the parlements, the Acadèmie française, other academies and societies of arts and sciences, French professional corps (like the Order of Lawyers of Paris). He reviews cases in civil and criminal law, and among the most celebrated, those involving the comte de Morangiès, the maréchal de Richelieu, the duc de Guines, the chevalier d'Eon, the chevalier de La Barre, the maréchal de Duras. He offers analyses of European finances; observations on war; evaluations of crown policies toward Jesuits and Protestants; critical appraisals of physiocracy; reflections on poverty, criminal-law reform, tax reform, the national debt, property, liberty, mendicity. A systematic comparative analysis of political content and material conditions governing the publication of the *Annales* and other French language journals circulating during the period 1763-89 forms the subject of a separate monograph which I am preparing.

41. Linguet, *Théorie des lois civiles, ou Principes fondamentaux de la société,* 2 vols. (London [Paris], 1767), I, 288-89.

42. Linguet, *Réponse aux docteurs modernes,* II, 184-85.

43. I have not discovered complete lists of subscribers to the *Annales.* The evidence I do have indicates that subscribers to Linguet's edition of the *Annales* and to other editions, authorized and unauthorized, were drawn from a mixed elite of notables in England, all over France, and in western and eastern Europe. Linguet occasionally mentions subscribers by name in his correspondence with Lequesne, preserved in BM, no. 1916. So does

Mallet Du Pan, in his correspondence with the directors of the Société typographique de Neuchâtel, in Bibliothéque publique de la Ville de Neuchâtel, MSS, no. 1178. E. Berthoud, in his "Un Commerce de librairie entre Neuchâtel et Prague, de 1777 à 1789," *Musée neuchâtelois*, 3me série, VI (1969), p.136, briefly discusses orders for the *Annales* that were placed by a correspondent of the Société typographique de Neuchâtel in Prague. Many of the Société's correspondents were booksellers who would not have included the names of their custormers in their letters requesting copies. The kind of evidence Berthoud offers us is valuable principally for what it tells us about the geographic distribution of the *Annales;* Robert Darnton's forthcoming studies of the role of the Société typographique de Neuchâtel in distributing political literature will shed even more light on the matter. Another untapped source of information about readers of the *Annales* is documentation on printers of unauthorized editions. The Société typographique et littéraire d'Yverdon, for example, distributed a pirated edition of the *Annales* and advertised for subscribers all over Europe. At the time the Société was liquidated in 1778, it had 260 subscribers. See discussion in Perret, *Les Imprimeries d'Yverdun au XVIIe et au XVIIIe siècles*, pp. 293, 306-7. For additional information, more valuable for assessing the number of Linguet's subscribers in France than for compiling lists of names, see Pierre Lequesne, *Mémoire judiciaire pour le Sieur Pierre Lequesne, marchand d'étoffes de soie, Rue des Bourdonnois, à Paris, contre le Sieur Simon Nicolas Henri Linguet, ci-devant avocat à Paris, demeurant actuellement à Bruxelles, sur les demands en suppression de quatre libelles diffamatoires et calomnieux, en réparation d'honneur, et en 100,000 livres de dommage-intérêts, par forme de réparations civiles, formées par le Sieur Lequesne contre le Sieur Linguet, les 6 décembre 1783 et 20 juillet 1784* (n.p., n.d.); Linguet, *Défenses pour M. Linguet, sur la demande en réparation d'honneur et en dommages-intérêts formée contre lui au Châtelet de Paris par le S[ieur] P[ierre] Le Quesne, marchand d'étoffes de soie* (n.p., n.d.).

44. See Eugène Hatin, *Les Gazettes de Hollande et la presse clandestine aux XVIIe et XVIIIe siècles* (Paris, 1865), p. 44; Hatin, *Bibliographie historique et critique de la presse périodique française...*(Paris, 1866), xxx,lxxxix; Aimé Azam, "Le Ministère des affaires étrangères et la presse à la fin de l'ancien régime," *Cahiers de la presse*, no. 3 (July-Sept., 1938), 428-38.

45. Linguet to Noailles, London, June 30, 1777, in AM, Angleterre, vol. 523, fols. 333-333v.

46. Still, he regretted the government's laxity in allowing "vipers" like Linguet the liberty of going to England "to exercise the infamous trade of libelists." Vergennes to Noailles, March 7, 1777, in *ibid.*, vol. 522, fol. 37.

47. Vergennes to Noailles, Versailles, March 21, 1777, in *ibid.*, vo. 522, fol. 115v. Vergennes was certain that Linguet's *Annales* would be filled with invective against him although he conceded that in other respects "...his work might be interesting...." See also Noailles to Vergennes, London, March 28, 1777, in *ibid.*, fol. 146. Vergennes wrote to Noailles on April 5, 1777, acknowledging receipt of the first number of the *Annales:*"I have received, M. le marquis...the copy of S[ieur] Linguet's new journal, a work in which one must be prepared to find few good ideas, but much spitefulness and venom. He is in a place where he can indulge his character with impunity, thanks to the impunity that reigns there and to the neglect of all respect and obligation, which they pride themselves on there. Soon England will be for France what the bilge is in a ship, the receptacle for all the filth." Vergennes to Noailles, Versailles, April 5, 1777, in *idid.*, fol. 352.

48. Linguet, *Lettre de M. Linguet à M. le Compte de Vergennes*, pp. 50-51.

49. Linguet to Noailles, London, April 1, 1777, in AM Angleterre, vol. 522, fols. 294-295v.

50. Mémoire from Linguet enclosed with letter to Noailles of April 1, 1777, in *ibid.*, fols. 296-297v.

51. Vergennes to Maurepas, Saturday, April 5, 1777, in *ibid.*, fol. 346.

52. Maurepas to Noailles, Versailles, April 15, 1777, in *ibid.*, fols. 408-408v.

53. Miromesnil to correspondant unnamed, April 6, 1777, in *ibid.*, fols. 357, 357v.

54. Vergennes to Noailles, April 7, 1777, in *ibid.*, fols. 362, 362v;Noailles to Vergennes, London, April 18, 1777, in *ibid.*, fols. 427-427v. See also Maurepas to Vergennes, April 28, 1777, in *ibid.*, fol. 502.

55. Noailles to Vergennes (paraphrasing Linguet), London, May 23, 1777, in *ibid.*, vol. 523, fol. 124. About this time, a spy in the department's pay reported to Vergennes that notwithstanding police measures, Linguet had recruited at least one agent of his own, "a certain Desbrugnières," to get the *Annales* into France. Agent's report, May 16, 1777, in *ibid.*, fol. 87. Vergennes refused to be intimidated by Linguet's "second declaration of war"; and he assured Noailles that Maurepas wasn't either. He thought the best procedure would be to let Linguet "bark" [*aboier*] . Vergennes to Noailles, Versailles, May 31, 1777, in *ibid.*, fols. 189, 189v.

56. Linguet to Noailles, London, June 30, 1777, in *ibid.*, fols. 333-34. Early in March, 1777, Caron de Beaumarchais, who at the time was in communication with Vergennes, wrote to announce Linguet's *Aiguilloniana* and to offer his services as mediator of the administration's outstanding disputes with Linguet. "I liked him, this Linguet. His eloquence charmed me. He seemed to have a good enough opinion of my character....It is horrible that such honest ministers are vilified by such a sharp pen. It is distressing that France is deprived of such an eloquent man." Beaumarchais to Vergennes, Paris, March 8, 1777, in *ibid.*, vol. 522, fols. 47-48. It is not clear whether Vergennes made use of Beaumarchais's offer. In any case, other agents continued turning out reports on Linguet's plans for distributing the *Aiguilloniana*. One agent reported that Linguet's *"D'Aiguillonade"* was ready for circulation, and that the author had men in Holland who were prepared to transport copies into France; several "notable persons" had offered their homes as warehouses. See agent's report, London, April 25, 1777, in *ibid.*, fols. 473-74. See also agents' reports, London, May 2, 13, 1777, in *ibid.*, vol. 523, fols. 4, 67.

57. Linguet to Vergennes, June 30, 1777, in *ibid.*, vol. 523, fols. 331-332v.

58. Linguet to Maurepas, London, June 30, 1777, in BN, MSS, nouvelles acquisitions françaises, no. 5215, fols. 364-65.

59. Vergennes to Noailles, Versailles, July 12, 1777, in AM, Angleterre, vol. 523, fol. 436.

60. Lequesne, *Mémoire judiciaire*, p. 13.

61. *Ibid.*, pp. 13-14.

62. Charpentier, *La Bastille dévoilée, ou Recueil des pièces authentiques pour servir à son histoire*, 3 vols. (Paris, 1789-90), III, 117-18. Before he shipped copies for public distribution in France, Linguet supplied both Lequesne and LeNoir with advance printed copy on every number of the *Annales*. Only when each number cleared did he send Lequesne the full edition for distribution to French subscribers.

63. For a discussion of the *tolérance*, see J. P. Belin, *Le Commerce des livres prohibés à Paris de 1750 à 1789* (Paris, 1913), p. 28. Linguet and Lequesne both refer to the arrangement as a *"tolérance tacite."* Linguet's correspondence with Lequesne is preserved in BM, no. 1916.

64. Lequesne, *Mémoire judiciaire*, p. 14, n. 1.

65. For brief discussions of counterfeit editions of the *Annales* being printed and distributed from Yverdun and Avignon, see Perret, *Les Imprimeries d'Yverdun au XVIIe et au XVIIIe siècles*, pp. 140, 293, 303-7; René Moulinas, *L.Imprimerie, la librairie et la presse à Avignon au XVIIIe siècle* (Grenoble, 1974), p. 417; Frances Acomb, *Mallet Du Pan (1749-1800); A Career in Political Journalism* (Durham, N.C., 1973), pp. 109-10. In January, 1780, Linguet announced to his subscribers that he had counted five new pirated editions of the *Annales;* they were being advertised from Marseilles, Aix, and Nancy. And he reminded his readers that fourteen pirated editions were already in circulation before January, 1780—for a grand total of nineteen unauthorized editions! Linguet, *Annales*, VII (1780), 453-56.

66. Lequesne, *Mémoire judiciaire*, p. 14, n. 1. For details of the arrangements from Linguet's side see Linguet to Lequesne, July 25, Aug. 26, 1777, March 3, 1778, BM, no. 1916.

67. "Eh oui, mon cher ami, Dieu soit béni, c'est donc chose faite, que cette maudite poste, Cela va, à ce que j'espère, tout déterminer: il étoit tems." Linguet to Lequesne, London, Aug. 29, 1777, in *ibid.*

68. Linguet to Lequesne, London, Sept. 23, Oct. 7, 1777, in *ibid.* In his study of Linguet, Jean Cruppi refers to a dossier of unedited correspondence relating to the *Aiguilloniana,* which he consulted at the Archives du ministère des affaires étrangères. Although Cruppi announced that he was publishing these documents, which would have shed light on Linguet's negotiations with French ministers for the withdrawal of his entire edition of the *Aiguilloniana,* the material never appeared in print. Archivists whom I consulted at the Ministère des affaires étrangères have not been able to locate this dossier. See Cruppi, *Un Avocat journaliste au XVIIIe siècle, Linguet* (Paris, 1895), pp. 206-7, n. 1.

69. Lequesne, *Mémoire judiciaire,* p. 18.

70. The complete title of Mallet Du Pan's work: *Doutes sur l'éloquence et les systémes politiques, adressés à M. le baron de B^{xxxx}; chambellan de S.A.R. le prince H. de P. Par M.N., citoyen de Genève* (London [Neuchâtel], 1775). The Société typographique de Neuchâtel forwarded Mallet's *Doutes* to Linguet in October, 1775, requested his aid in getting it distributed, and seized the occasion to advertise its printing and marketing services. See Archives de la Société typographique de Neuchâtel, in Bibliothéque publique de la Ville de Neuchâtel, MS 1101, fols. 174-75. I am grateful to Robert Darnton, Princeton University, who called my attention to material in these archives concerning Linguet's relations with the Société typographique de Neuchâtel.

71. Voltaire to François-Louis-Claude Marin, Jan. 24, 1777, in *Voltaire's Correspondence,* ed. Besterman, 96, no. 19385, 42; Acomb, *Mallet Du Pan,* p. 46.

72. I am indebted to Acomb's study of Mallet Du Pan for valuable details concerning the Mallet-Linguet collaboration. Acomb was able to make use of unpublished correspondence between Mallet Du Pan and the Société typographique de Neuchatel housed at the Bibliotèque publique de la ville de Neuchâtel, MS 1178. See Acomb, *Mallet Du Pan,* pp. 39-60; 106-33.

73. *Journal helvétique,* 1777, II, 71, as cited in translation in Acomb, *Mallet Du Pan,* p. 107.

74. Linguet to the baron de Tournon, London, Jan. 27, 1778, in BM, uncat. MSS, Coll. Gosset, no. 19. See also Acomb, *Mallet Du Pan,* pp. 109-10. For discussion of Linguet's profits, see for example Métra, *Correspondance secrète,* XIII (Paris, Oct. 19, 1782), 336-37, citing Devérité's *Notice pour servir à l'histoire de la vie et des écrits de S.N.H. Linguet.* The author, speaking of Linguet's "prodigious success," estimated his readers at 6,000 to 7,000, or 20,000 if readers of pirated editions were included; he calculated Linguet's profits at 100,000 crowns. See Devérité, *Notice pour servir à l'histoire de la vie et des écrits de S.N.H. Linguet,* new ed., p. 125. See also Brissot de Warville, *Brissot: Mémoire,* ed. Perroud, I, 99-100. Mallet Du Pan's comments on subscribers to the *Annales* are reported in Acomb, *Mallet Du Pan,* pp. 108-9. The question of the number of Linguet's subscribers and the amount of his profit during the first three years of publication formed the subject of a contest in civil law between Linguet and Lequesne. For details, see Linguet, *Défenses pour M. Linguet;* Lequesne, *Mémoire judiciaire.*

75. Brissot de Warville, *Avertissement* to *Fragments sur les lois criminelles tirés des Annales politiques et civiles" de M. Linguet,* in Brissot de Warville, ed., *Bibliothèque philosophique du législateur, du politique, du jurisconsulte,* IX, 76.

76. *Annales,* I, 3-4.

77. Mathurin-François-Adolphe de Sescure, *Correspondance secrète inédite sur Louis XVI, Marie Antoinette, la cour et la ville de 1777 à 1792,* 2 vols. (Paris, 1866), I, 249.

78. *Ibid.,* I, 133.

79. For excellent detailed discussion of points covered here, see Acomb, *Mallet Du Pan,* pp. 110-14. On LeNoir and Linguet, see earlier in this chapter.

80. For the viper image, see Vergennes to Noailles, March 7, 1777, in AM, Angleterre, vol. 522, fol. 37; for Vergennes on Linguet's bark, see Vergennes to Noailles, Versailles, May 31, 1777, in *ibid.,* vol. 523, fols. 189, 189v. On Vergennes's decision to subscribe to

the *Annales,* see Vergennes to Noailles, April 7, 1777, in *ibid.,* vol. 522, fols. 362, 362v.

81. Acomb, *Mallet Du Pan,* p. 114.

82. Linguet to Lequesne, London, Dec. 26, 1777, in BM, no. 1916. To these effusive declarations of loyalty to France, Linguet was careful in subsequent correspondence to append the qualifier that in leaving England he did not want to give French authorities the idea that he was begging to come back: "Because either I will obtain justice, or I will return only after having made a fortune to indemnify myself, and even then, after the downfall of my enemies, who will not remain in office forever." Linguet to Lequesne, London, Feb. 10, 1778, in *ibid.*

83. Linguet to Lequesne, London, Feb. 10, 1778, in *ibid.*

84. Linguet to Vergennes, London, March 13, 1778, in BM, uncat. MSS, Coll. Gosset, no. 22.

85. Linguet, *Mémoires sur la Bastille, et la détention de l'auteur dans ce château royal, Depuis le 27 septembre 1789 jusqu'au 19 mai 1782* (London, 1783), pp. 8-9. Cited hereafter as *MB.*

86. Acomb, *Mallet Du Pan,* p. 115.

87. Describing his reception in Switzerland, Linguet complained that the Swiss looked upon his pen as an "electric conductor"; they thought his portfolio was a "Pandora's box", and they feared him as a "new Titan." Linguet, *Annales,* IV (1778), 15. He painted the same picture for Vergennes: "I am not a proscribed person with whom the slightest contact could be pestilential. At least, I do not think so...." Linguet suggested that perhaps the best way to correct false impressions was for Vergennes to give him "a mark of esteem and protection on your part which precisely fixed ideas about me. Your earlier letters warrent my believing you worthy and capable of this effort. In every respect, at the least, it would be even more honorable for you than it could prove useful to me"! Linguet to Vergennes, May 24, 1778, in AM, correspondance politique, Geneva, vol. 83, fols. 328, 328v. Vergennes wrote to Linguet in June to assure him that "the ministry's dispositions concerning you are ever the same." Still, he warned Linguet against yielding to the temptation to play diplomatic envoy without letters of appointment, and involve himself in other countries' internal disputes. "They [these domestic disputes] must remain irrelevant to you, and I cannot exhort you too much not to have anything to do with them." Vergennes to Linguet, Versailles, June 5, 1778, in *ibid.,* fol. 333. Lequesne, who apparently had been in contact with Vergennes, communicated the core of the minister's message before Vergennes's letter of June 5, 1778, could have reached Linguet. Responding to Lequesne's comments in a letter to Lequesne from Geneva on June 7, 1778, Linguet commented appreciatively on Vergennes's advice; by July, he was complaining about Lequesne's opposition to his publishing laudatory material on Vergennes in the *Annales* to signal his changed attitudes to his public. Linguet to Lequesne, Geneva, June 7, 1778; Brussels, July 22, 1778, in BM, no. 1916.

88. Linguet to Lequesne, Geneva, June 7, 1778, in BM, no. 1916.

89. Nény to Linguet, Sept. 22, 1776, cited by Nény in his Note ultérieure sur les affaires de Monsieur Linguet in AG, MSS divers, no. 1498, fols. 35, 35v. See also Charles Piot, "Linguet aux Pays-Bas autrichiens," *Bulletin de l'Académie royale de Belgique,* 2d ser. XLVI (1878), 789-90. I have profited immensely from two excellent studies which treat Linguet's relocation of his journalistic enterprise in Belgium: Piot's "Linguet aux Pays-Bas autrichiens, and André Puttemans, *La Censure dans les Pays-Bas autrichiens,* Académie royale de Belgique, classes des lettres et des sciences morales et politiques, mémoires, 2e série, XXXVII (Brussels, 1935). In my own research, I consulted archival sources used by Piot and Puttemans but also integrated material from French, Austrian, and Swiss sources which Piot and Puttemans did not use in their studies.

Having submitted his legal briefs and his complete works to a royal censor, Linguet withdrew them precipitously and apparently abandoned the idea of settling in Belgium. He might have assumed that the censor's delay in turning out a favorable report was typical of the obstacles he could expect to encounter. Linguet's sudden change of mind caught Austrian officials just as they were cautiously weighing the option of authorizing him to issue his works and briefs from Brussels, but on the condition that he print a foreign place of publication on the title page. That way, Linguet would have had his *de facto permission tacite*, and the Austrians would have avoided the embarrassment of giving official approval to his diatribes against French ministers and other prominent personalities. See Starhemberg to Kaunitz, Brussels, Oct. 26, 1776, in OS, Belgium, Ber. 219, fols. 277-78; Kaunitz to Starhemberg, Vienna, Nov. 6, 1776, in *ibid.*, Belgium, Weis. 36, fol. 438.

90. Kaunitz to Starhemberg, April 9, 1777, as cited from "Repertoire de la Chancellerie des Pays-bas à Vienne (1777)," in Piot, "Linguet aux Pays-bas autrichiens," 791.

91. Linguet was concerned principally with the difficulty of printing from Brussels. Under existing censorship regulations no journal could be printed openly and distributed in the Austrian Netherlands which had not been approved by the authorities and submitted to a regular government censor. To circumvent these regulations, Linguet explained, he would have to do his printing either in London or in Maestricht. If he printed in Maestricht, and he himself worked out of Brussels, physically removed from the scene of printing operations, the printer could easily be tempted to pass copies on to editors of counterfeit editions. In these circumstances, Linguet felt London would be the safer location for printing, except for the obstacle of Anglo-French hostilities. Linguet to Lequesne, Geneva, June 7, 1778, in BM, no. 1916.

92. Crumpipen to Nény, Brussels, July 19, 1778, in AG, MSS divers, no. 1498, fol. 1: Linguet to Lequesne, Brussels, July 22, 1778, in BM, no. 1916.

93. Starhemberg to Kaunitz, Sept. 8, 1778, in OS, Belgium, Ber. 233, fols. 37-38. For reactions from the Department of Foreign Affairs in France to Linguet's plans for relocation, see Count d'Adhémar to Vergennes, July 17, 20, 1778, in AM, Angleterre, vol. 530, fols. 93, 110-111; Vergennes to Adhémar, Versailles, July 20, 1778, in *ibid.*, fols. 110-11.

94. Kaunitz to Starhemberg, Vienna, Sept. 19, 1778, in OS, Belgium, Weis. 40, fol. 174. Starhemberg informed Kaunitz that Linguet knew his writings would be subject to ordinary police measures for the press. See Starhemberg to Kaunitz, Sept. 29, 1778, in *ibid.*, Ber. 233, fol. 210.

95. For discussion of Mallet Du Pan's reading of his agreement with Lingeut in 1778, see Acomb, *Mallet Du Pan*, pp. 116-18, 124. The arrangement was altered in 1779. Mallet moved his operation from Lausanne to Geneva. The separate Lausanne edition had been liquidated. Mallet agreed to buy from Linguet exactly the number of copies he needed, at a fixed price. For full discussion of Mallet Du Pan's role in Linguet's journalistic enterprise, as agent, distributor, news source, and occasional writer, based principally on Mallet's correspondence with the Société typographique de Neuchâtel, see Acomb, *Mallet Du Pan*, pp. 116-33. Linguet fills his letters to Lequesne with complaints and questions about Mallet's handling of his end of the enterprise. See, for example, Linguet to Lequesne: "ce vendredi" [received Aug. 9, 1779] ; Aug. 24, Sept. 5, 13, Oct. 18, 19, 24, 1779, in BM, no. 1916. Linguet expresses his doubts and suspicions about Mallet's interpretation and exploitation of the 1779 arrangement in a remarkable letter to the Genevan pastor Jacob Vernes. See Linguet to Jacob Vernes, n.p., n.d. [probably summer or fall, 1779] , in Bibliothèque publique et universitaire de Genève, MS Supp. 1036, fols. 98-99.

96. Linguet to Lequesne, July 23, 1778, in BM, no. 1916; see also Linguet to Lequesne, Brussels, July 30, 1778; Linguet to Lequesne, Waerbeck, Sept. 8, 10, Nov. 14, 1778, in *ibid.*

97. Kaunitz to Starhemberg, Sept. 26, 1778, in OS, Belgium, Weis. 40, fol. 197. Kaunitz indicated that he thought the content of Linguet's defenses of Austrian policy on the Bavarian question could be controlled if he published with approval, and after government censorship. Kaunitz to Starhemberg, Vienna, Oct. 17, 1778, in *ibid.*, fols. 236, 236v.

98. Starhemberg to Kaunitz, Oct. 6, 27, 1778, in *ibid.*, Ber. 233, fols. 262-264v, 430. In the Oct. 27 dispatch, Starhemberg reiterated his conviction that a character such as Linguet would have to believe in what he wrote, otherwise he could not be effective in as Linguet would have to believe in what he wrote, otherwise he could not be effective in sustaining an argument. "I will try to assure myself that he undertakes it [the defense of Austria's position] only on the basis of a very complete personal conviction...."

99. Copy of dispatch from Nény, to Crumpipen, Nov. 5, 1778, enclosed with Starhemberg to Kaunitz, Brussels, Nov. 7, 1778, in *ibid.*, Ber. 234, fols. 27-28.

100. Starhemberg to Kaunitz, Brussels, Dec. 19, 1778, in *ibid.*, Ber. 235, fol. 232. See also Starhemberg to Kaunitz, Brussels, Dec. 29, 1778, Jan. 19, Feb. 23, 1779, in *ibid.*, Ber. 235, fol. 335; Ber. 236, fol. 152, fols. 489-97; Jan. 30, 1779 (n.p.) in *ibid.*, Ber. 236, fol. 450. For the article in the *Annales,* see Linguet, "Russie," *Annales,* IV (1778), 341-67.

101. The quotation is from a letter from Crumpipen to Nény, Aug. 9, 1779, in AG, MSS divers, no. 1498, fol. 31. On this subject see Starhemberg to Kaunitz, Brussels, Feb. 27, 1779, in OS, Belgium, Ber. 236, fol. 526, 526v; Kaunitz to Starhemberg, Vienna, March 6, 1779, in *ibid.*, Weis. 41, fol. 240; Starhemberg to Kaunitz, Brussels, March 16, 30, 1779, in *ibid.*, Ber. 237, fols. 142, 238-39.

102. Kaunitz to Starhemberg, April 10, 1779, in OS, Belgium, Weis. 41, fol. 324. See also Starhemberg to Kaunitz, Brussels, April 20, 1779, in *ibid.*, Ber. 238, fol. 29.

103. Linguet to [Crumpipen], April 5, 9, 13, 22, 1779, in AG, MSS divers, no. 1498, fols. 5, 6, 7, 8. The citation is from Linguet to [Crumpipen], Waerbeck, April 9, 1779, in *ibid.* See also Starhemberg to Kaunitz, Brussels, May 4, 1779, in OS, Belgium, Ber. 238, fol. 254. For Crumpipen's observations on Linguet's pro-Austrian apologies, see AG, MSS divers, no. 1498, fols. 62-65v. For the article in the *Annales,* see Linguet, "Allemagne," *Annales,* V, 279-93.

104. Crumpipen to Nény, July 13, 1779, in AG, MSS divers, no. 1498, fols. 18, 19a.

105. Starhemberg to Kaunitz, Nov. 7, 1778, in OS, Belgium, Ber. 234, fol. 26.

106. Linguet to [Crumpipen?], July 23, 1779, in AG, MSS divers, no. 1498, fol. 24.

107. Linguet to Nény, July 25, 1779, in *ibid.*, fol. 25.

108. Count Nény, "Notes sur les affaires de M. Linguet," Aug. 5, 1779, in *ibid.*, fols. 28, 28a; Starhemberg to Kaunitz, Brussels, Nov. 7, 1778, in OS, Belgium, Ber. 234, fol. 26; Crumpipen to Nény, Aug. 9, 1779, in AG, MSS divers, no. 1498, fol. 31v. The question still was being raised the following year. See Crumpipen to Nény, Feb. 16, 1780, in *ibid.*, fols. 38-39v.

109. Report of the Archbishop of Malines to Starhemberg, June 26, 1779, in AG, MSS divers, 1498, fols. 9-10.

110. Minutes of letter from Crumpipen to Nény, July 2, 1779, in *ibid.*, fol. 12.

111. Nény, "Note sur l'extrait qui m'a été, communiqué d'une lettre du Cardinal Archévêque de Malines, concernant M. Linguet," Brussels, July 6, 1779, in *ibid.*, fols. 14-15. To appease the archbishop, and above all, to avoid a direct confrontation between ecclesiastic and secular authority, Prince Starhemberg wrote to Malines, informing him that the government was fearful of a scandal, and that therefore all protest about Linguet's failure to attend church must be suppressed—Protestants, after all, were tolerated in the Pays-Bas! He added, however, that Linguet's operation of his presses on holidays could be viewed as a matter for public concern, and suggested that he would speak with the journalist about it. Starhemberg to the Archbishop of Malines, Brussels, July 13, 1779, in *ibid.*, fols. 16-17.

112. Crumpipen to Nény, Brussels, July 13, 1779, in *ibid.*, fols. 20v-21.

113. Crumpipen to Nény, July 25, 1779, ibid., fol. 25v. Reporting on his meeting of July 30 with Linguet, Nény noted that Linguet traced his initial run-in with ecclesiastic authority more to a dispute over payment for some straw he had purchased from the *curé* at Waerbeck than to any offense against religion. Linguet told Nény he was disgusted with the kind of country living that came complete with an ecclesiastic spy system; he had decided to move to Brussels. See Nény, "Notes sur les affaires de M. Linguet," Aug. 5, 1779, in *ibid.*, fols. 28v-29v.

114. Linguet to Lequesne, Waerbeck, Aug. 1, 1779, in BM, no. 1916.

115. Linguet to Nény, n.p., n.d. [received Aug. 4, 1779], in AG, MSS divers, no. 1498, fols. 26, 26v.

116. Linguet mentioned two letters during his interview with Nény on July 30, 1779. He had sent one off to the Archbishop of Malines, and had completed the draft of another. He sent copies of both to Nény. These letters produced a generalized consternation (which Linguet doubtless intended). Nény was all the more certain that Austrian authorities should make it worth Linguet's while to put an end to the dispute with the

archbishop and move to Brussels. Nény, "Notes sur les affaires de M. Linguet," Aug. 5, 1779; Crumpipen to Nény, Aug. 9, 1779, in *ibid.*, fols. 30, 30v.

117. Nény, "Notes sur les affaires de M. Linguet," Brussels, Aug. 5, 1779, in *ibid.*, fol. 30v.

118. Crumpipen to Nény, Aug. 9, 1779, in *ibid.*, fol. 32.

119. Nény, "Note ultérieure sur les affaires de M. Linguet, relativement à la lettre de M. le sécretaire d'état de guerre, du 9 août 1779," Brussels, Aug. 26, 1779, in *ibid.*, fols. 33-37.

120. Crumpipen to Nény, Brussels, Feb. 16, 1780, in *ibid.*, fols. 38, 38v. See also Charles duc de Lorraine, to Conseillers fiscaux de Brabant, Feb. 17, 1780, in AG, Office fiscal, no. 1024.

121. Linguet to Lequesne, London, Feb. 10, 1778, in BM, no. 1916.

122. See Chapter One.

123. See Charpentier, *La Bastille dévoilée*, III, 117ff.

124. Jakob Friedrich Melchior Grimm, Denis Diderot, Guillaume-Thomas-François Raynal, Heinrich Meister, *Correspondance littéraire, philosophique, et critique*, ed. Maurice Tourneux, 16 vols. (Paris, 1877-82), XII (Oct. 1780), 441.

125. Linguet explained this strange procedure in the course of a police interrogation. He had sent his copy to LeNoir "following the rule he had imposed upon himself since he was abroad to do absolutely nothing without informing either the king's ministers, or the lieutenant-general of police of Paris, for what concerns France...." Charpentier, *La Bastille dévoilée*, III, 117-18. Three years later, Linguet recalled the incident in quite another light. He cited from his alleged covering letter to LeNoir of April 8, 1780, in which he enclosed the copy of his libelous epistle of April 7 to Duras. He might not have been telling the public the strict truth, but he *was* telling it what he knew it wanted to hear: at least one political journalist was turning out an independent coverage of political events. The proof of his independence was the price he had paid for exercising it: " '...no one had imposed the condition [for the unobstructed circulation of the *Annales*] that I would respect the cowardly villainies of *maréchaux de France*, if any of them committed them, or the prevarications of tribunals. There were never any [conditions] stipulated; I would not have accepted them.... I never agreed to submit myself to any kind of censorship; on the contrary, I protested openly. I printed it several times, that I would never have any censor other than my own delicacy.' " Linguet to LeNoir, Brussels, April 8, 1780, printed by Linguet in *MB*, pp. 33-34.

126. See Chapter One.

127. See Linguet's correspondence with Lequesne, Brussels, year 1780, in BM, no. 1916.

128. Linguet to Lequesne, Brussels, Aug. 14, 1780, in *ibid.*

129. See opening pages of Chapter One.

130. See, for example, Mercy-Argenteau to Starhemberg, Dec. 22, 1780, cited in Eugène E. Hubert, ed., *Correspondance des ministres de France accrédités à Bruxelles de 1780 à 1790, Dépêches inédites*, 2 vols. (Brussels, 1920-24), I, 5.

131. LeNoir to Vergennes, Paris, Sept. 28, 1780, in AM, Pays-Bas autrichiens, vols. 172, fol. 232.

132. Hardy, "Mes Loisirs," in BN, MSS fr., vol. 6683 (Oct. 3, 1780), fol. 351. See also Starhemberg to Kaunitz, Brussels, Oct. 24, 1780, in OS, Belgium, Ber. 237, fol. 404. In an earlier dispatch, Kaunitz had asked Starhemberg to try to find out why Linguet had been arrested. Starhemberg reported that some sources attributed the arrest to Linguet's notorious letter to Duras. Others thought he was suspected of having had something to do with alleged anonymous letters against Necker's administration. See also Starhemberg to Kaunitz, Brussels, Nov. 21, 1780, in *ibid.*, Ber. 248, fol. 140. Apparently, Starhemberg was puzzled by the persistence and urgency with which French authorities were demanding the extradiction of Linguet's papers. Starhemberg reported that the French *chargé d'affaires* in Brussels had presented a new memoir, "attesting that because this was a question of a Prisoner of State, the king was not in a position to unfold the motives of his conduct at greater length." As late as December, 1780, Starhemberg was still trying to figure out what crimes the French hoped to pin on Linguet. He had received

Mercy-Argenteau's report from France, stating that the Duras affair was the only cause of Linguet's arrest. "...in this case, it must be admitted that the French court has not acted candidly in requesting, for reasons of state, an extradition of papers, subject besides to many difficulties, because as for old grievances, they were already pardoned because of the liberty granted to return to France." Starhemberg to Kaunitz, Brussels, Dec. 25, 1780, in *ibid.*, fol. 459.

133. For details of international negotiations between Vergennes and the Belgian government for possession of Linguet's papers, see: AM, Pays-Bas autrichiens, vol. 172, fols. 232-304, *passim*; AG, Repertoire, Chancellerie autrichienne, vol. 304, fols. 81ff.; Documents concernant le Sieur Linguet, prisonnier de la Bastille, ses papiers, et son argent, in OS, Fonds de la Secrétariat d'Etat et de Guerre, Belgium, DD, B 192^b (56).

134. Vergennes to La Grèze, Versailles, Oct. 12, 1780, in AM, Pays-Bas autrichiens, vol. 172, fols. 252, 252v.

135. For examples of articles in the *Annales* which alternately support and contradict the broad lines of Vergennes's policies, compare *Annales*, VII, 43-48 with *Annales*, VII, 63-85 (on Genevan affairs); and *Annales*, IV, 65-103 with *Annales*, IX, 441-48 on American affairs.

136. Bachaumont reported that Vergennes had tried to buy Linguet off, offering him a pension if he would stop reporting on political matters, but that Linguet had turned him down. Bachaumont, *Mémoires secrets*, XVI (Oct. 15, 1780), 24. For discussion of Vergennes's attitudes concerning political journalism in the context of his treatment of Mallet Du Pan's efforts to obtain entry into France for his continuation of Linguet's *Annales*, see Acomb, *Mallet Du Pan*, pp. 127-43.

137. Linguet's indictment of the Paris Bar provides a good example of his mode of operation. In 1779, Linguet issued an *Appel à la postérité, ou Recueil des mémoires et plaidoyers de M. Linguet pour lui-même, contre la communauté des avocats du Parlement de Paris* (n.p., 1779), a collection of materials documenting his case against the Paris Bar. He opened the work with a dialogue between a Frenchman and an Englishman. The Frenchman speaks: "It's up to you to believe me or not; but what I have told you is true, nonetheless. There exists in Europe, I repeat, a society which has the privilege of not recognizing any kind of law, or power, or authority...which tries its members without writing down anything, without verifying anything, without examining anything, without alleging anything; which condemns them to civil death, and executes them without there being any way in the world for someone to elude its *arrêts*." Linguet, *Appel é la postérité*, p. 1. Linguet sent the brochure to Lequesne to distribute in France. When Lequesne made some critical comments about the dialogue, Linguet answered him as follows: "You are right to say that the dialogue is a rough piece; but it is even truer than it is rough: and if the people on top were not the [illegible], the most irresponsible, the most dastardly fellows alive, they would sense how useful it is that there exists a man capable of revealing truths, and at the same time, how ridiculous it is, or how abominable, to let the effects of such a despotism remain. But everybody will feel it, everyone will say it, and nothing will be done." Linguet to Lequesne [Brussels, "ce 28," "reçu 2 janvier 1780"], in BM, no. 1916.

138. Linguet to Lequesne, the Bastille, Feb. 14, 1782, in BM, no. 1916. All letters from Linguet to Lesquesne mentioned hereafter in this chapter were written from the Bastille and are found in BM, no. 1916, unless otherwise noted.

139. Linguet to Lequesne, Feb. 14, 1782, Aug. 30 , 1781.

140. A copy of one of these poems, and the original of another, can be found in BM, no. 1916.

141. Linguet to Lequesne, Oct. 27, 1781; see also Linguet to Lequesne, Oct. 31, 1781.

142. Linguet to Lequesne, Feb. 14, 1782.

143. For Linguet's mention of his negotiations with Duras, see Linguet to Lequesne, Oct. 6, 1780, Oct. 31, 1781. For Linguet's discussion of cash payments to an unnamed person, possibly Duras, see Linguet to Lequesne, Feb. 8, 11, 1782.

144. Linguet informed his public that this sensational device was capable of transmitting "news over the farthest distances, no matter what kind it is, no matter how long the dispatch might be, with a rapidity almost equal to that of the imagination." *MB*, 121, n. 13. Someday, Linguet boasted, his invention in communications would be as valuable for

commerce as electricity in medicine, and the steam engine in all work requiring huge outputs of power. *MB*, 121.

145. Bachaumont, *Mémoires secrets*, XX (May 16, 19, 1782), 293-94, 297; Métra, *Correspondance secrète*, XIII (June 5, 1782), 84; Henri Martin, "Etude sur Linguet," in *Travaux de l'Académie nationale de Reims*, vols. XXX (1858-59), 341-425; and XXXI (1859-60), 81-149; see XXXI (1859-60), 100.

146. *L'Intermédiaire des chercheurs et curieux, correspondance littéraire, historique et artistique, questions et réponses, lettres et documents inédits, communications divers à l'usage de tous*, 103 vols. (Paris, 1864-1940), XI, 606; Métra, *Correspondance secrète*, XIV (Paris, May 7, 1783), 302-3.

147. *Courrier du Bas-Rhin*, 1782, no. 41 (Wednesday, May 22, 1782), 331-33; no. 42 (Saturday, May 25, 1782), 340-41.

148. Martin, "Etude sur Linguet," in *Travaux de l'Académie nationale de Reims*, XXXI, 103n; see also Linguet to Lequesne, Brussels, Nov. 17, 1779, and London, Nov. 25, 1777, in BM, no. 1916.

149. Linguet, "Réflexions," *Annales*, I, 68-69. "...electricity," Linguet laments "has not made any real progress since the time of its inventors," 68. Not even the electric eel, "a living Electricity," "a more sensitive depository than any other of this salutary and formidable fire" has proved sufficient stimulus to scientific investigation and innovation, 69. See also, *Annales*, XIX (1792), 270.

150. Linguet, *Réflexions sur la lumière, ou Conjectures sur la part qu'elle a au mouvement des corps célestes*, new ed. (Brussels and Paris, 1787), pp. 3, 11. See also pp. 30, 53-54.

151. Linguet to Lequesne, March 30, 1782.

152. Linguet to Lequesne, March 30, April 29, May 9, 1782.

153. Linguet to Lequesne, May 11, 1782.

154. Livre des sorties de la Bastille, Nov. 12, 1771–Dec. 26, 1782, in Bibliothèque de l'Arsenal, Paris, MSS, 14,566, entry no. 263.

155. Linguet, *Avis aux souscripteurs des "Annales politiques, civiles, & c.* [London, Jan. 1, 1783] (n.p., n.d.), p. 1. For copy of the *Avis* in the *Annales*, see *Annales*, IX (Jan., 1783), 449-72.

156. For a brief but illuminating and suggestive discussion of French and European markets for the *Mémoires sur la Bastille*, based on sample studies of orders placed with the Société typographique de Neuchâtel, see Elie Berthoud, "Un Commerce de librairie entre Neuchâtel et Prague, de 1777 à 1789," 134-39; Robert Darnton, "Un Commerce de livres 'sous le manteau' en province à la fin de l'ancien régime," *Revue française de l'histoire du livre*. nouvelle série, V (1975), 5-29.

157. Linguet, *Avis aux souscripteurs* (London, Jan. 1, 1783), p. 18. In a letter to the editor of the *Courrier du Bas-Rhin* which appeared in that journal on Jan. 1, Linguet wrote of his *Mémoires* that "...they contain revelations which I owe to the public and a justification—which I owe to myself." *Courrier du Bas-Rhin*, 1783, no. 1 (Wednesday, Jan. 1, 1783), 2. Spies and libelists in the pay of the Department of Foreign Affairs in France did not share Linguet's certainty that nothing could stop him or his *Annales*. For discussions of projects and plots against the author of the *Mémoires sur la Bastille*, see letter of the French ambassador in London, Moustier, to Vergennes, London, March 17, 1783, in AM, Angleterre, vol. 541, fols. 204-204v; Report of Thomas Evans to Moustier, London, April 7, 1783, in *ibid.*, vol. 541, fols. 369-75. Evans, apparently an informer in Moustier's service, suggested that one sure way to get rid of Linguet would be to persuade his mistress's husband to initiate proceedings against the journalist on the charge of adultery. Evans was certain that Linguet would be indicted. "I think he would stand a chance of being brought to a prison in England where his treatment (according to his own account) would not be quite so civil as in the Bastille in France, and from which no prostituted oath or promise of future good behavior should ever release him." Thomas Evans to Moustier, April 7, 1783, in *ibid.*, vol. 541, fols. 377-377v. See also Thomas Evans to Vergennes, Oct. 31, 1783, in *ibid.* vol. 545, fol. 262. Fully supported by the French Ministry of Foreign Affairs, Evans published a brochure in which he attempted to undermine Linguet's credibility as a witness to and victim of despotism. See Thomas Evans, *A Refutation of the "Memoirs of the Bastille," on the General Principles of Law,*

Probability and Truth; in a Series of Letters to Mr. Linguet, Late Advocate in the Parliament of Paris (London, 1783); translated into French as *Réfutation des "Mémoires de la Bastille," sur les principes généraux des loix de la probabilité et de la vérité, dans une suite de lettres à M. Linguet* (London, 1783).

158. Linguet, *Avis aux souscripteurs* [London, Jan. 1, 1783], p. 2.

159. Linguet, "Angleterre, Dissolution du Parlement; Tableau abrégé des révolutions arrivées dans le ministère anglois depuis vingt ans," *Annales*, XI (1784), 186.

160. *Ibid.,* 187.

161. Grimm, *Correspondance littéraire*, XII (Oct. 1780), 441-42.

162. Louis-Sébastien Mercier, *Tableau de Paris*, new ed., 12 vols. (Amsterdam, 1782-88), II, ch. CXVII, article *Avocats*, 44-45, and III, ch. CCLXXXII, article *Bastille*, 290.

163. Camille Desmoulins, *Révolutions de France et de Brabant*, 86 nos. (Paris, 1789-91), no. 14 (1790), 34-36, n. 1.

164. Brissot de Warville, *Brissot: Mémoires*, ed. Perroud, I, 96.

165. In a recent case study, Robert Darnton analyzed the stock in trade and distribution operations of Bruzard de Mauvelain, a correspondent of the Société typographique de Neuchâtel who ran an underground trade in prohibited literature in Troyes in the 1780s. Linguet's *Mémoires sur la Bastille* ranks high on the local best-seller lists of underground literature compiled by Darnton from records of Mauvelain's book orders. When demand is measured by numbers of copies of prohibited books ordered by Mauvelain from the Société typographique de Neuchâtel, the *Mémoires* holds seventh place, on a list of thirteen titles (with orders recorded for thirty copies). And when demand is measured by numbers of separate orders placed, the *Mémoires* ranks fourth on a list of six (with seven orders placed). Robert Darnton, "Trade in Taboo: The Life of a Clandestine Book Dealer in Prerevolutionary France," in Paul J. Korshin, ed., *The Widening Circle: Essays on the Circulation of Literature in Eighteenth-Century Europe* (Philadelphia, 1976), p. 49. Darnton believes Mauvelain's stock may be typical of the bulk and content of underground literature that was being traded in prerevolutionary France, *ibid.,* pp. 63-64, 68. In that case, the *Mémoires sur la Bastille* will have to be recognized and evaluated further as a major title in a library of proscribed political literature which shaped the attitudes of a generation of revolutionaries.

For other discussion suggesting the impact of the *Mémoires sur la Bastille* on the revolutionary generation, see Chassin, *Les Elections et les cahiers de Paris en 1789*. Collections de documents relatifs à l'histoire de Paris pendant la Révolution française, 4 vols. (Paris, 1888-89), III, 233ff. For one interesting piece of evidence which suggests the kind of connection the public may have been making between the *Mémoires sur la Bastille* and the events of July 14, 1789, see ["Mauclerc, de Chalon en Bourgogne,"] *Le Langage des murs, ou Les Cachots de la Bastille dévoilant leur secrets* (n.p., 1789). "Mauclerc" describes how he walked through the ruins of the Bastille and sought out the clock in the courtyard to which Linguet had called attention in the *Mémoires:* "(O LINGUET! all the workers who are laboring on the destruction of the Bastille are Gods for you, you owe them your homages)." "Mauclerc" also describes his visits to the ruins of the prisoners' cells: "But nothing held my attention more than this sentence, which I found in the cell where I was assured M. LINGUET had been detained. I do not claim it as his, but let me say, nonetheless, that the style really does bear his marks....Here it is: 'Ordinarily, the constitution of a state is only the work of accident, which time has shaped by rolling it by slow degrees over the slope of abuses.' " *Ibid.,* pp. 2, 7.

LINGUET.

Il brûle, mais il éclaire.

Portrait of Linguet, engraved by Mariage, with Voltaire's epigraph, "Il brûle, mais il éclaire." *Bibliothèque nationale, Paris.*

Frontispiece for Linguet's *Mémoires sur la Bastille*. *Bibliothèque nationale, Paris.*

NOUVELLE PLACE DE LA BASTILLE

Ami le temp. passé n'est plus rendons a Cesar ce qui appartient a Cesar et a la Nation ce qu. est a la Nation

"*Nouvelle place de la Bastille*," an engraving that suggests a borrowing from the frontispiece and text of Linguet's *Mémoires sur la Bastille*. Even in the aftermath of the conquest of the Bastille by the Paris crowds, the king is portrayed as restoring French liberty. *Musée Carnavalet, Paris.*

"The Taking of the Bastille on the 14 July 1789, Drawn on the Spot by an eminent Artist." Note, in the lower right corner, among the papers strewn on the ground, a volume entitled *"Mémoires de la Bastille"*—possibly a reference to Linguet's *Mémoires. Bibliothèque nationale, Paris.*

The interior of the Palais de Justice in Paris, site of Linguet's confrontations with the Paris Order of Lawyers and the Paris parlement. The mid-eighteenth century engraving is by Janinet, after a painting by Durand. *Musée Carnavalet, Paris.*

Portrait by Saint-Aubin illustrating themes from Linguet's *Appel à la Posterité*. *Bibliothèque nationale, Paris.*

S. N. H. LINGUET.

Né à Reims en 1736.

Engraving by Vangelisty from a portrait of Linguet painted from life by
Pujos, 1774. *Bibliothèque nationale, Paris.*

Propaganda for Contradictory
Ideologies and Interests

International Crises in the Service of Private and Public Interests

The ministers who consented to Linguet's release from the Bastille in May, 1782, were probably less impressed by his aerial communications system than by the names and positions of those who supported the invention and his plea for freedom. No one, however, could pressure them into tolerating his *Annales.*

Linguet had been liberated to a banishment of indeterminate length in the village of Rethel-Mazarin. He would be allowed to move about freely there on the condition that he not speak or write publicly; but that was not his idea of freedom.[1] He left for Brussels almost immediately.

As soon as Austrian authorities learned that Linguet was planning to return to the Belgian capital to recover his possessions, they began formulating conditions for his permanent reestablishment. Chancellor Kaunitz raised the subject with Joseph II in June, 1782. He underlined the importance of paying Linguet off with 200 *louis* for pro-Austrian propaganda he had been commissioned to write in 1778 and 1779. "...occasions could arise when we might need the pen of this able writer again."[2] Joseph thought the price was too high for the particular goods and the man they had purchased. "As I do not at all like to buy the votes of these insignificant writers, it will suffice for Prince Starhemberg to give Linguet 100 *louis* as if he were offering it on his own initiative."[3]

Linguet had no way of knowing what Joseph II thought of him; but he was thinking rather highly of himself in the summer of 1782. In August, while he was still in Brussels, he stated his conditions for remaining there. He wanted the rights and the protection enjoyed by Belgian citizens, or at least advance warning of French designs against him. He asked permission to pursue these matters in a private conversation with the emperor in Vienna.[4]

Starhemberg communicated Linguet's thoughts on this matter to Kaunitz, who commented on them in a dispatch to Joseph. Kaunitz thought the

French would allow Linguet to remain in Brussels, provided he could be kept from exploding into print against the administration there; but Kaunitz thought he knew his man too well. Linguet could not be kept in tow. His hatred of Vergennes was uncontrollable. If he launched his verbal assaults from Brussels, an already fragile Franco-Austrian alliance might be further imperiled. Kaunitz wanted to avoid even hinting to Linguet that he could count on protection against the French. "In addition, the censorship of his writings would have to be confided to a prudent and enlightened man who, without impeding him too much, would not approve anything which a foreign power might justly complain about to the government under which a talented man like Linguet has settled himself."[5] Joseph attached a note to Kaunitz' letter: he saw no difficulty in Linguet's coming to Vienna; he enclosed a personal letter to the journalist.[6]

Early in September, Starhemberg reported to Kaunitz that Linguet was grateful for Joseph's interest, eager to come to Vienna, and ready to abandon the *Annales* and his other publication projects; he had proposed an interlude of European travel. Linguet had also assured him that even if at some future date he had the urge to write, the thought that he would be censored probably would put an end to it.[7]

Toward the middle of November, with Austrian officials prepared for his arrival in Vienna, Linguet wrote to Secretary of State and War Crumpipen, from London! He enclosed a letter for Joseph. He had changed his mind. He told Crumpipen only that "a serious affair for me, deference for friendship [probably Madame Buttet's] brought me here: the cruel experience I have had of the French ministery's fury and perfidy will stop me here."[8] The emperor, who had received Linguet's apologetic letter *via* Kaunitz, returned it to him with the following note: "You will see by this that he is still as mad and as imprudent as before. I do not intend to answer him any more, and this way, I think everything will be settled."[9]

Safe in London, the self-styled Lazarus was free again to publish his *Annales.* He demanded more. He demanded everything. He would advertise for the enlightenment of all Europe that the despots who influenced and ran the government in France had wiped him out totally, repeatedly. A duke and former secretary of state for foreign affairs refused him adequate compensation for professional services rendered. A fraternity of advocates encouraged by this potentate as well as by magistrates in the Maupeou parlement and in the Paris parlements *ante* and *post* Maupeou, robbed him of his profession in law. A publisher in league with another secretary of state for foreign affairs, who in turn was supported by ministerial colleagues and a literary rival waiting in the wings, cheated him out of an editorship, under contract, of the *Journal de politique et de littérature.* A French *maréchal* tapped power from the administration to liquidate him altogether, to take away his political journal, his liberty—his life, he said. It was not in Linguet's character to relinquish his claims to the benefits of estates in two professions, or to full compensation for their loss, indemnities from the French courts, and if necessary, from the French crown.

From England, Linguet once again began negotiating for favorable conditions for a return to the continent—not to France, but to the Austrian Netherlands. He sent out fresh feelers to Count Belgiojoso, Joseph's new minister plenipotentiary in the Austrian Netherlands replacing Prince Starhemberg. Belgiojoso suggested outright that the emperor "make the acquisition of Linguet."[10] Linguet did not confine himself to discreet inquiries. To add weight to his credentials as a publicist for monarchical causes, master of the craft of political persuasion, he plunged headlong into the most explosive issue in European diplomacy. In the eighty-eighth number of the *Annales*, he published a dissertation defending Austrian demands that the Scheldt river, blockaded by the Dutch to stop Belgium's ocean-bound traffic, be reopened.[11]

The man had nerve, but he also had a keen sense of what would flatter and impress Austrian officials. His first defense of Austria's position, in number 88 of the *Annales,* was unsolicited; Linguet would not allow it to remain unacknowledged. He submitted it to Crumpipen. "Better informed, better assisted, I would have done better. But here is what my heart dictated."[12]

Impatient for a reading, Linguet wrote to Crumpipen from London in late November, 1784, noting that he was not fishing for compliments, only for reactions, and enough information to prove his devotion to Joseph, to demonstrate the truth, and to "contribute as much as I can, in revealing it, to preventing the terrible war which menaces if it is ignored." He repeated his avowal that he had completed the work "abandoned to my heart and to my own resources." With government backing, it would have been even better. He announced that his next defense of the Scheldt issue would appear in the eighty-ninth number of the *Annales*; and he warned that his archenemy Vergennes would try to keep the number out of France.[13]

Vergennes's refusal to lend full French support to Joseph's claims against the Dutch had provided Linguet with an ideal opportunity. He would sabotage Vergennes's foreign policy by rallying international public opionion behind the cause of Vergennes's alienated ally—the opinion, that is, of the *Annales* subscribers and readers.[14] He had other compelling reasons also for soliciting imperial favor.

On November 29, Linguet advised Crumpipen of shipment of his eighty-ninth number. He again enclosed copies for Joseph, Marie-Antoinette, and Austria's ambassador in France, Mercy-Argenteau. He assured Crumpipen that he had ways of smuggling this propaganda into France.[15] That same day, November 29, 1784, Joseph had instructed Belgiojoso to try "to make use of this man," to supply him with necessary documentation, and to offer "pecuniary means" as encouragement and as a sign of imperial pleasure. He enclosed a personal letter for Linguet.[16]

Crumpipen wrote to Linguet on December 13, acknowledging receipt of his latest work and enclosing Joseph's letter. Crumpipen informed Linguet that his work already had been reprinted and translated into German, and that by order of the Imperial Council, he was sending Linguet the sum of two hundred guineas, although "...I know your delicacy...." The Austrian government was ready to commission him to write up new apologies of Austria's position in the Scheldt dispute. Austria's ambassador in England would provide Linguet with government documents. "You will easily sense how rushed and impatient we are to put out something good. Your way of handling matters increases this impatience infinitely."[17]

Meanwhile, on December 14, 1784, before Crumpipen's letter of the thirteenth could have reached him in London, Linguet grabbed the initiative and wrote a letter filled with complaints: Austrian authorities had failed to respond to his eighty-ninth number; his shipments were being delayed; counterfeit editions of the work were being circulated everywhere. He had one constructive suggestion: the eighty-eighth and eighty-ninth numbers of the *Annales* should be combined into a larger work: "...we have reason, justice. But this is not enough: it must be shown that in fact, they are on our side. People must be persuaded; the largest possible number of people must be convinced: it would appear that this kind of canon does not count for as much as the ones made of bronze. It doesn't make as much noise at first; but in the long run, it can prove to be a big support for the latter, and sometimes makes its use unnecessary—which would be a very great benefit."[18]

In fact, Austrian authorities *were* impressed by Linguet's arguments, but understandably wary. Writing to Joseph on December 19, 1784, Kaunitz enclosed the eighty-ninth number of the *Annales*. He expressed his admiration, but also his concern. Linguet's "Discours tenu, ou à tenir par un ministre de France...," the content of his number 89, for the most part, was bound to offend Vergennes. In his marginal comments on Kaunitz's dispatch, Joseph agreed that Linguet's work had made a big impresison: "It's not an indifferent matter that a man such as Linguet, read all over Europe, employs his talents in the defense of our cause....But it is impossible to guide the pen of a man like that, who follows only the impulse of his imagination, and his own way of looking at things." Nonetheless, in January, 1785, Joseph ordered Kaunitz to pay Linguet a thousand ducats from the imperial treasury.[19]

On December 19, 1784, Linguet wrote again to Crumpipen. He acknowledged receipt of letters of praise for his pro-Austrian propaganda, including a letter from the emperor. He also expressed his impatience: source materials promised him by the government had not arrived, and he was eager to make use of them to mount what he outlined as a three-part propaganda campaign for the government: an imperial manifesto on the Scheldt crisis; an essay providing historical background on the crisis; and finally, a reprinting of a Dutch manifesto, with his own observations juxtaposed, article by article—a kind of propaganda Linguet believed would be particulary effective: "When what you have to do is win people over, you must not rely entirely on the inclination everybody should have to enlighten himself and to compare documents that contradict one another: this comparison must be made [for them] ; and lazy readers must be spared the trouble they would not take, or which perhaps would prejudice their judgment if they forced it [forced themselves into this kind of effort]."

Linguet accepted, even welcomed, government corrections in his texts. He offered to make the trip from England to Belgium to cut revision time and speed publication.[20]

By December 28, 1784, Linguet had worked himself into an atypically positive frame of mind about his assignment and about progress toward completing it. He assured Crumpipen that he had stopped worrying about counterfeiters who were reprinting articles from the *Annales* treating the Scheldt crisis—in the heart of Brussels, and of course, without authorization. Literary pirates no longer irritated him because in fact they were multiplying avenues for the circulation of works that vindicated the emperor's Scheldt policies: "So, let's not speak about it any more. Let's concentrate exclusively on the big case concerning which you did me the honor of consulting me." He boasted freely about a new justification of imperial international politics, an *oeuvre* on which he was hard at work, the "Observations sur le manifeste des Etats-Généraux, relativement à l'ouverture de l'Escaut." "The work which exists today, and which will reach you for sure, in any case, will establish your rights; I am not afraid to tell you that it will silence the canon of... [Holland], provided that treacherous and unfortunately only too dangerous interventions [those of France] do not come to their aid." In this same letter, Linguet announced that he was shipping eight hundred copies each of reprints of numbers 88 and 89 of the *Annales;* and he announced another shipment of eight hundred copies of the work which combined the two numbers, his *Considérations sur l'ouverture de l'Escaut.* He expected that Austrian authorities would make it their business to filter this propaganda into France; he knew that they could manage the feat if they would agree to use the good offices of Austrian minister plenipotentiary in Paris, the comte de Mercy-Argenteau, with whom, Linguet implied, he already had a working arrangement for clandestine distributions. He told Crumpipen that he had in hand the good news that his separate reprintings of the eighty-eighth and eighty-ninth numbers of the *Annales* probably would be allowed to circulate in France.[21]

What Linguet did not suspect when he expressed himself with such unguarded enthusiasm to Crumpipen was that the secretary of state for war did not share his eagerness to implicate Austrian authorities in the task of distributing pro-Austrian copy. Instead, government officials preferred to have it sold. Linguet objected violently to this plan, insisting that the government must assume its share of responsibility for getting his texts to the public, free of charge. "I know very well that the government should not place its approbation on this brochure [the *Considérations sur l'ouverture de l'Escaut*, in this context]. But I am not any the less persuaded that it may be very useful in the present circumstances that it be known and circulated: and administrations, like private persons, have—and to a far greater degree than private persons do—a thousand ways of getting through to the public, without compromising themselves, things which concern them." He again recommended that part or all of his shipment be dispatched to Mercy-Argenteau, who, in turn, could be instructed to pass it on to Linguet's literary agent for distribution, gratis. If the government was still unwilling to handle the matter his way, Linguet had a final solution: "...there is a very simple way to get out of this difficulty—throw the edition into the fire and look upon it as if it had never been printed up."[22]

On January 13, 1785, Linguet wrote to Crumpipen to announce that he was sending off a first installment of his "Observations": "Here is the beginning of our work...." But what he had done in addition, and without authorization, was print up what he was sending, doubtless confirming the worst fears of the Austrian authorities that he could not be controlled, that he would elude every attempt to shape or censor his writings.[23]

In this same letter of January 13, Linguet harped on the necessity for speed in getting his work to the public (implying that the major obstacle to a speedy delivery of the *Considérations* would be the government's delaying tactics, and above all its insistence on interminable reviews of what he was doing): "Because promptness is essential. Your scoundrel adversaries saw very well how advantageous it would be for them to monopolize opinions: they have done that already; they are continuing to do it. I hope the enclosed will begin to prove embarrassing, at least to their writers, while we wait for you to harrass their warriors."[24]

When he received the first installment of Linguet's "Observations," Crumpipen responded with effusive praise for a "*chef d'oeuvre*"; "Monsieur, it took energy, which you know how to combine so well with eloquence—and this striking manner you seize upon so perfectly—to show the truth and confound trickery...." Crumpipen assured Linguet that once clearance came through from Vienna, the "Observations" could be printed in final form and circulated through the office of the director of the Belgian postal system. Best of all, Crumpipen reported that "...altogether, nothing was found that needed changing."[25]

On February 4, 1785, Linguet sent Crumpipen the bulk of the text for the "Observations": "...here is our completed work"—four numbers for the *Annales,* which he intended to distribute together, unless the government wanted the work published separately, as its own—a procedure Linguet opposed (probably with full knowledge that Austrian authorities would be even more opposed than he).[26]

When he wrote to Linguet on February 14, 1785, having received in the meantime the completed "Observations," Crumpipen made it clear that all previous instructions were being superseded by new orders. Count Belgiojoso had instructed him to ask Linguet to correct the "Observations" following a detailed critique, which he enclosed. Once Linguet had taken care of all corrections—and Austrian authorities were agreeable to his making them following a kind of honor system, that is, without having to resubmit corrected copy—he was to print the final version, but in a single volume rather than as four numbers of the *Annales,* and was to send it to Brussels via special messenger on call at the residence of Austria's ambassador in London. Crumpipen informed Linguet that he (and not Linguet) would handle all shipments of copies to Mercy-Argenteau in Paris and that Linguet's correspondence with the ambassador was to flow through the office of the secretary of state for war.[27]

The trouble with these orders was that Linguet did not receive them, or in any case, he insisted that he had not received them, until February 21. Meanwhile, he was flooding Crumpipen's office with letters in which he confessed that he was confounded and panicked, and with unauthorized shipments of his final, uncorrected printed copy. On February 15, on his own initiative, he sent 250 copies of his "Observations" to Crumpipen and the same number, minus the first part, "the only one where there might be some changes necessary," to Mercy-Argenteau in Paris; and he expressed his fear that the government's sudden eclipse might have something to do with baleful influences emanating "from the bawdy-house of Versailles" [le tripot de Versailles] ."[28]

Finally, on February 22, 1785, Linguet wrote to Crumpipen to acknowledge that he had received—but only the previous day—Crumpipen's letter and instructions of the fourteenth. He confessed that the news blackout from Brussels had made him literally sick. "...for two days, I didn't leave my bed...." Then he came to the heart of the matter; he had not been able to incorporate Crumpipen's list of corrections into the "Observations" because he didn't have the list when he printed and shipped off his final copy. He urged Crumpipen to send fifty copies of an earlier shipment for Brussels to Mercy-Argenteau; he calculated that fifty copies would be left for this purpose after a hundred copies went to Mannheim and another hundred to Belgium. He promised a second shipment of seventy-five copies for Paris, and felt confident that somehow he and Austrian authorities would overcome impediments to their distribution "...and the ill-will of the minister who is the sole author of all obstacles and of the danger Europe is in perhaps even now."[29]

Confronted, even more, deluged by Linguet's *fait acompli*—hundreds of copies of the "Observations"—Crumpipen could do little more than acknowledge that Linguet's instructions for distributing the "Observations" were being carried out "to the letter, and in this way, Europe will be enlightened and our adversaries confounded." He also expressed his regret that Linguet had not had time to attend to the suggested corrections; he hoped Linguet would provide them shortly, in a supplement; and he reiterated the government's wish that its collaboration with Linguet be kept secret.[30]

What was Linguet after this time? He was continually declaring his independence of all the powers of the earth; periodically, he hovered on the edge of compromising it scandalously. Linguet made his objectives perfectly clear in his letter of July 15, 1785, to Belgiojoso. Austrian authorities had invited him to express himself freely concerning his "views and desires for the future." He did exactly that. He included in his letter a copy of a memoir for Louis XVI—the memoir that appeared in print in the *Annales* in the first numbers published after those in which he had defended Austria's interests in the Scheldt crisis. Linguet recommended the memoir to Belgiojoso as an account of "a persecution of a type as new as the details are distressing. Given my misfortunes, given the slander and the arbitrary acts of authority to which I was subjected in my country; given maneuvers and insinuations which I can only suspect, but about which I can have no doubt, it was essential for me that the facts be brought to light definitively, once and for all."

Linguet told Belgiojoso that he was determined to make Belgium his permanent residence, but that he was determined also that "my arrival and my stay there be honorable." Letters of naturalization and some kind of diploma would suffice as unambiguous marks of the emperor's favorable disposition toward him and also as a sign that he had entered into the imperial service. He assured Belgiojoso that he had no vaulting ambitions. He said that the government's cooperation with his efforts to acquire a piece of property, an unused priory in Melle, near Ghent, would make it possible for him to satisfy all his needs.[31]

Linguet enclosed for Belgiojoso's inspection a copy of a letter to Joseph which he was asking the minister to forward to the emperor, along with the memoir for Louis XVI, in which he stated his grievances against government officials and other notable persons in France: "Sire, the Scheldt's defender is known to Your Majesty, even now, only because of his zeal: the memoir which I take the liberty of sending him will explain his conduct, his misfortunes, his rights, and his soul, if I may say so. If he deigns to read it through, he will find there, I am sure of it, more than one cause for astonishment and shock."

He informed the emperor that whatever favors were dealt out would be of great help to him in his pursuit of justice on French soil against all his enemies, but principally against his arch-foe Vergennes, who, just as he had opposed Joseph's determination to open the Dutch-controlled portion of the Scheldt to seagoing traffic from the Austrian Netherlands, now was opposing Linguet's fight to bring his civil law suits into the French courts: "My real adversary at this moment is, in fact, the same person who was [the adversary] of the Scheldt. It would be worthy of Your Majesty to force him to pull back in the one case as in the other"![32]

In a letter to Crumpipen written that same day, July 15, 1785, Linguet spoke even more freely about what he wanted from Austrian authorities: "...that His Majesty be willing to have a request made directly to the king, through the mediation of his ambassador in Paris, for permission for me to enter into his [the emperor's] service." Linguet explained that this mark of favor would make his letters of naturalization even more flattering; and that it would give him still greater protection against the "dangerous secretary," Vergennes. "This would also be a more unambiguous title to His Majesty's protection when I bring civil action [in the courts]." Armed with imperial support, he could be certain that his enemies would not dare block his access to the courts: "...in short, His Majesty would gain little from this acquisition; but in France they perhaps might begin to suspect that they had lost something."[33]

Relying on Crumpipen's and Belgiojoso's promises and encouragements, Linguet made plans to pull up stakes in London; he took a house, a former soap manufactory in the neighborhood of Brussels, and hired a ship to transport his furniture to Ostend and a boat to carry it from there directly to "my humble chateau."[34] Appearances notwithstanding, Linguet did not sell out to Joseph. He engaged his political journalism in Joseph's service, but he was ingenious enough to calculate that he could manipulate an international diplomatic crisis to serve his own highest interest in France: self-vindication, revenge, and his reestablishment—the restoration of properties in profession, honor, capital, liberty, and political influence.

Joseph tempered his admiration for the talented Linguet with a wariness justified by his insight into the man's volatile and indomitable character. Belgiojoso's enthusiasm for this dedicated pro-government publicist and opinion-maker was unbounded. Belgiojoso seemed to be looking upon Linguet as Austria's best buy in philosophers with proven practical skills, a match for Prussia's Voltaire, or Russia's Diderot. In a long dispatch to Kaunitz in September, 1785, the Austrian minister plenipotentiary in Brussels again pushed his discovery. "It has been my honor already to propose to Your Highness the idea of making the acquisition of Monsieur Linguet...." He urged Kaunitz to grant Linguet letters of naturalization, free of charge, and a diploma of nobility, a reasonable procedure for "attaching M. Linguet, and even employing him...." He testified to the zeal and courage with which Linguet first pleaded the emperor's case in the Scheldt affair "on his own initiative, and without having been invited to do it...." He alluded to Linguet's "rare talent," his informed mind, and his style, "a unique style in which the cast of the writing persuades singularly: he is right for all work that might interest a government, and without speaking of the resources one might find in him for drawing up declarations, memoirs, or manifestos that the Court might desire or want to have published, I will not even go outside the interior of government to find the necessity and convenience of employing M. Linguet." He credited Linguet with having singlehandedly turned the tide of public opinion in Austria's favor in the Scheldt affair; he was certain that the government should be attributing to Linguet's first production on the subject "the shock which unsettled people's opinions and caused them to tend to favor us." He noted that Linguet's journalism would enlighten, direct, gently prepare public opinion in the Austrian Netherlands, weaning it from prejudice. Should Linguet be offered a post as "professor of eloquence"? Would he accept? Belgiojoso seemed to think better of that idea. Perhaps a wiser move would be to appoint Linguet as the emperor's historiographical adviser, award him a membership in the Academy of Brussels, and give him a salary of from 3,000 to 3,500 florins. For some reason, Belgiojoso thought that under such an arrangement, Linguet's services to the government could be kept secret.

Belgiojoso added one precautionary note. He was concerned about the "printed minutes" of Linguet's memoir to the King of France—the memoir Linguet had sent him. Linguet had assured Belgiojoso that he would not make any use of it "before having been informed about what His Majesty might have decided to do in his favor...." Nonetheless, Belgiojoso had warned Linguet that he could count on nothing from the emperor if he persisted in offending the French court; and, Belgiojoso told Kaunitz, Linguet in turn had reassured him that he had only a few copies of the memoir on hand, in the form of minutes, and that they would remain "hidden and buried."[35]

In communicating Belgiojoso's proposals to the emperor, Kaunitz agreed that it might be in Austria's interest to "attach Linguet," but he qualified his support. Linguet would have to stop his phobic outbursts against Vergennes and other French authorities—especially the magistrature. What worried Kaunitz particularly was Linguet's printed minutes of his memoir to the King of France: "As a matter of fact, in order for this request to have been susceptible to being favorably received, he ought not to have designed it to be made public in his *Annales,* and even less, filled it with sarcastic outbursts against the minister of France, and specifically, against the comte de Vergennes, whom he reproaches, among other things, with not having paid him for the *Annales,* which he had to have been receiving nonetheless." He noted, possibly without much conviction, Linguet's promise to Belgiojoso to "suppress this memoir." And he concluded that Linguet would have to accept a censor who would preview everything he intended to print; the government would also have to obtain Vergennes's explicit consent. In the meantime, Kaunitz noted, if Linguet's rancor against ministers and magistrates in France continued to boil over, the journalist might exacerbate the near-crisis in Austro-French diplomatic relationships occasioned by the dispute over the Scheldt: "...at the present time, when we have much more important affairs to discuss with this secretary of state [Vergennes], it is hardly appropriate to put this one on the agenda; judgment on this matter must be deferred until the conclusion of the peace." At that time, unless the French court voiced strong objections, the Austrians could safely accord Linguet letters of naturalization, titles of nobility, membership in the Academy of Brussels, and a pension. Kaunitz was against appointing the journalist to the post of historiographer. It would be dangerous to have so unpredictable a character directly attached to the imperial service.[36]

When he received Kaunitz's dispatch, Joseph wrote out a signed note for the chancellor. He apparently wanted to make this his last word concerning *l'affaire Linguet:* "By all means, and insofar as we can, we must avoid attracting this man into the country; his pen is already too well known as venal and fertile in paradoxes for anything he writes to make an impact in the world; so you will instruct M. Belgiojoso to act accordingly, and attempt to dissuade Linguet from setting himself up in the Netherlands by making him see that he would run the risk of being sought out by the French Court at the first occasion, and of being delivered up to it, something he would not risk in England."[37]

On March 19, 1786, in Vienna, Linguet received letters of naturalization; three days later, the emperor presented him with a certificate of nobility "in view of the regard he has acquired as much by his various literary works as in the exercise of his profession as a lawyer."[38]

What accounts for the emperor's sudden reversal of position? It is not improbable that in appraising Austria's position after the peace settlement with the Dutch Republic, Joseph II recognized that in spite of a sizable monetary indemnification from the Dutch, Austria had suffered a real loss not only in commercial advantage but in stature and prestige. A professor of eloquence, of sorts, who had argued Austria's case so convincingly in the past, might be just the man to repair the damage. In addition, Joseph may have sensed the need for an effective propagandist to persuade openly hostile subjects to accept the sweeping institutional reforms he projected for his Belgian provinces. And finally, he may have been moved by an appeal from Linguet, who made the trip from Brussels to Vienna to present it in person.

Almost immediately following his ennoblement, Monsieur de Linguet began applying new pressure on Joseph II to intervene with French authorities on his behalf. He asked for safe-conduct for his return to Paris. He wanted guarantees that once he arrived there, magistrates who in 1775 had forbidden any court functionary to accept his case against the Paris Order of Lawyers would be ordered to consent to hear his suits against everyone who had violated his civil rights. In the memoir he addressed to the King of France, circulated among Austrian authorities, and published, eventually, for his public, and in a cluster of related memoirs issued separately, Linguet enumerated these grievances.[39] Chief among them was his unsettled account with the duc d'Aiguillon. He demanded adequate payment, 120,000 *livres,* for services rendered, dangers incurred, and reputation risked during his defense of the duke sixteen years earlier.[40] In addition, he was suing the publishing magnate Charles-Joseph Panckoucke for breach of contract; Panckoucke, he charged, had consented to, if not intrigued with ministers in Versailles, to force his dismissal in 1776 from the editorship, under contract, of the *Journal de politique et de littérature:* "...in short, within four days, the Academy complains, the publisher plots, the bureaus draw up their documents, the ministers sign, and I am expropriated!" and again: "Is it therefore part of our morals; is it in accordance with our laws; it is in the sovereign's sacred name, that a property can be destroyed, without investigation, without following formalities, merely by virtue of ministerial orders?"[41] He had still another case pending, this one against Pierre Lequesne, his former agent for the distribution of the *Annales* in France, whom he accused of conspiring to defraud him. He was suing Lequesne for 100,000 *livres.*[42]

Finally, through all these suits in civil law, Linguet pressed his least concrete and most compelling claim. He demanded full indemnification from the literary, administrative, and judicial branches of the French establishment. He accused statesmen, magistrates, publishers, *littérateurs,* and his own agent for the *Annales,* of snuffing him out—physically, professionally, politically— and repeatedly. He presented, in the French courts, with the backing and intervention of Austrian imperial authority, an indictment against the regime and *le monde,* in France.

By April, 1786, Linguet had persuaded Joseph II to lend imperial support to his claims. The emperor instructed Mercy-Argenteau to do everything possible for Linguet "with regard to his creditors," while respecting Vergennes' sensitivity.[43] Kaunitz also wrote to Mercy-Argenteau, reiterating that Joseph keenly desired to help Linguet: "...what Linguet demands, seeming to him [the emperor] to be of the kind that cannot be refused to anyone, and consequently in the category of these things to which one can lend one's good offices without difficulty." Kaunitz even added his own plea on Linguet's behalf. Mercy-Argenteau was to arrange things so that "if possible this poor man at least gets something from all his claims...." Kaunitz feared only an explosion of Linguet's hotheadedness the minute he was free of guardians, advisers, and censors: "...because underneath it all I have found him a good fellow, capable of listening to reason, but at the same time a man with a great deal of spirit lodged in an unruly head, and who would always be needing the advice of a man like me." Kaunitz left it to Mercy-Argenteau's discretion to determine whether the queen's support should be solicited in this matter. Mercy-Argenteau reported to Kaunitz from Paris on April 18 that only the chancellor's backing could have moved Vergennes "with respect to the case of the writer in question, against whom he has long held a grudge, and who, by his various works, had often enough provoked him in a way that is not easily overlooked."[44]

Finally, in May, 1786, Mercy-Argenteau was able to report to Kaunitz that he had obtained everything: guarantees for Linguet's personal safety, permission for him to bring his suits into the courts, and a promise that he would encounter no obstacle in finding lawyers to handle his cases. All these guarantees were accorded on the condition that Linguet refrain from libeling his enemies.[45] That, as Kaunitz knew only too well, was the unique condition which Simon Linguet wouldn't respect.[46]

Assured of imperial goodwill, the friendly disposition of Louis XVI, and the neutrality of the king's ministers, Linguet left Brussels for Paris. He claimed for himself what he had been demanding since 1764 on behalf of every French subject: legal protection for properties or adequate compensation for expropriation. Linguet intended his grievances to be those of a propertied, though absolutely unprivileged and justifiably outraged bourgeois, a commoner, a *roturier*. His noble titles had not changed him, he assured his friend Jean-Frédéric Perrégaux (the Swiss banker in Paris who took over some of Lesquesne's work as agent for the *Annales* and who also handled certain of Linguet's financial transactions): "I would use it [his title] only against my enemies. Only for them am I pleased to be *noble* in name and heart; for my friends, I will never be other than *homme* and *bon homme*; therefore please treat me on this footing, and let there be no more question between us of *barony* or even *knighthood,* or all these demonstrations...."[47]

Flanked on all sides by powerful foreign and domestic protectors, Linguet was ready to launch his assault upon highly placed enemies who had almost wiped him out. Three years later, the Third Estate *en masse* would be stating for itself, Linguet's accusations that for decades the French adminstration had been robbing him of properties that were bound up inextricably with his liberty and his life. But already, in October, 1786, Linguet knew that his public, "my old confidant, my only support," "this public" which he had taken care "to take for arbiter between my oppressors and me" was making that vital identification between his interests and rights, and its own.[48] In publicly presenting his case against the regime in France, Linguet was reinforcing earlier lessons to members of the Third Estate on how to identify his grievances with their grievances. In expressing his interests, he was simultaneously articulating an emerging national interest in civil and political rights.

In September, 1780, Linguet had arrived in Paris from Brussels under the sinister auspices of Louis XVI's *lettre de cachet.* In July, 1786, he reappeared under the auspices of Joseph II's *cachet de noblesse,* a far more promising sign. The news of his arrival spread like wildfire. All Paris knew that Linguet was planning to bring suit against his former client, and a former secretary of state for foreign affairs, the duc d'Aiguillon. Linguet had worked up a stunning array of charges. D'Aiguillon had failed to provide adequate compensation for Linguet's legal briefs in his defense; the duke had entered into collusion with the Parlement of Paris and the Paris Bar to disbar him illegally; and had aided and abetted all authorities who illegally forced his dismissal from the editorship of the *Journal de politique et de littérature.* Finally, d'Aiguillon had actively solicited Linguet's arbitrary arrest and confinement in the Bastille.[49]

Once Linguet decided to plead for himself before the Parlement of Paris, the magistrate scheduled to preside in the case, the président, d'Ormesson, anticipating a mob, ordered the guard service quadrupled; all avenues leading to the Palais were to be closed, and barriers set up to contain the crowds. Only spectators in line with tickets for the 7 A.M. session on August 26 would be permitted inside the Grand'Chambre.[50]

During the session of the twenty-sixth, overflow crowds of Linguet's vociferous supporters threatened several times to disrupt the proceedings. Linguet spurred them on to wilder manifestations of allegiance. Informed by a court usher, at d'Ormesson's direction, that for his own safety he must enter the chambers by a side door, Linguet announced, mostly for the crowds waiting inside, and for the young lawyers who insisted on accompanying him into the courtroom: "J'entre point par les détours: je suis fait pour entrer par les grandes portes...." Following an hour-and-a-quarter-long opening statement, Linguet emerged and was escorted to his carriage on the shoulders of his public.

Before dawn on the morning of September 2, crowds began lining up for the second session of the trial; from five o'clock on, they had been packing the courtroom, plastering themselves to every available observation point. Spectators sat astride the mantelpiece, hung in from windows, or fastened themselves onto the ledges; women besieged the magistrates' benches.[51] It was reported that at the end of the session the Grand'Chambre had to be disinfected with burning vinegar to remove the stench; magistrates collapsed from the heat and pestilential odors; spectators swooned; the corridors of the Palais de Justice were transformed into hospital wards.[52] Again, "ex-lawyer Baron Linguet" exited triumphant.[53]

Originally, the final session of the trial had been scheduled for September 6; Linguet managed to extend his testimony through seven sessions, expanding the number of his charges against d'Aiguillon in each one. The court did not reach a decision in the case until March 11, 1787. D'Aiguillon was ordered to pay Linguet a supplement in legal honorariums of 24,000 *livres.*[54] Technically, the court found d'Aiguillon guilty on only one charge. Still, overflow crowds could not be expected to make distinctions among issues which Linguet, in his perorations, had intentionally confused. The mob simply went wild: to the flourish of trumpets and the congratulations of fish-wives, the victorious Linguet, as reported in the *Mémoires secrets*, was carried to his carriage by "riff-raff" [*la canaille*].[55]

Counter-prerevolutionary Polemic

Linguet won a legal victory in the Grand'Chambre of the Palais de Justice, but he engineered this victory in the antechambers and in the Austrian imperial court. The circumstances of his success in the courtroom only added weight to his long-standing contention that the judicial system in France was corrupt, despotic—a scandalous, dangerous failure.[56] For decades, he had been campaigning against the parlements. Earlier in his career, he had exposed the self-interested political maneuverings of the *parlementaires*. Now, in the spring of 1787, just following his legal triumph, Linguet aligned himself with a powerful monarchist party and began contributing to a propaganda campaign aimed at discrediting and depoliticizing the parlement and reorganizing French administration.[57] Thoroughgoing administrative reorganization was Linguet's preferred alternative to his private stratagem of undercutting institutionalized arbitrariness by pull and pressure. Revolution, which cancelled out this despotism by force of arms, was the other option he recognized.

When Linguet began operating as spokesman for a monarchy in crisis, he resumed work interrupted in 1774, when Terray, Maupeou, and d'Aiguillon fell from power. As ad hoc government adviser and publicist, Linguet played a role in formulating and advertising reforms which gave royal administration the power, institutions, and programs to quell a smoldering civil war between propertied and propertyless subjects, adjudicate their conflicting claims for justice, and direct their behavior in the general interest of preserving the oppressive societal order of properties. He was free at last to identify and represent the interests of monarchical authority and the contradictory interests of two classes of subjects simultaneously.

The crown was faced with the threat of bankruptcy when Controller-General Calonne, in a move to by pass the parlement's opposition to fiscal reform, called a handpicked Assembly of Notables into session and presented it with a financial scheme to end the crisis. The keystone in Calonne's program was a tax to be levied on all property owners without discrimination of estate. Provincial assemblies composed of all three estates of property-holders would be convoked periodically to consent to this taxation. In order to stimulate commercial activity, Calonne proposed liberating commerce in grains from all internal tariffs.[58]

Calonne's mistake was to have banked too heavily on the predominantly pro-aristocratic Assembly of Notables. Convened in February, 1787, the Assembly discovered threats to traditional privilege everywhere and declared itself incompetent to pass on financial matters. In April, with the financial crisis still unresolved, Louis dismissed Calonne; he eventually appointed as his successor the Archbishop of Toulouse, Etienne-Charles de Loménie de Brienne. Unable to negotiate with the Notables, Brienne dissolved the Assembly and prepared to face the parlement's opposition.[59]

Linguet lent the support of his publicity to the Calonne property tax, modeled in large part after the project for a *dîme royal* first proposed by the economist Vauban at the end of the seventeenth century.[60] He had only to represent his own version of Vauban's program, his *Dixme royale* of 1764.[61] Linguet revised and reissued the work, with the title *De l'impôt territorial,* just after the Notables turned down Calonne's master plan.[62]

In his preface, Linguet hinted that Calonne's program failed because philosophes had infiltrated the government. The philosophy he had in mind was physiocracy.[63] Linguet was publicizing this property tax, collectible in the form of farm produce, for purposes which neither Calonne nor his successor Brienne had envisaged. They favored the property tax principally as a means for ending a financial crisis and restoring commercial and agricultural prosperity. Linguet viewed it as a means by which the government, provisioned in grains, could compete with entrepreneurs, control the market price of wheat, and in that way guarantee the lives of an impoverished and progressively more restless population of dispossessed persons. Linguet saw the unpopular tax program as a key government stratagem for warding off two spectres—bankruptcy and a people's revolution.[64]

As anticipated, the Paris parlement protested a royal edict decreeing a general property tax. Proclaiming its incompetence to pass on questions of financial reform, the parlement asked for an Estates-General. Louis XVI, resorting to a *lit de justice,* forced the parlement to register the royal edict on August 6, 1787. The following day, the parlement declared *nul* the proceedings of the *lit de justice* and opened an inquest against the deposed Calonne.[65] To quash the Paris parlement's insurrection, Louis exiled its members to Troyes. It proved to be an unhappy move. Supported by the provincial parlements, the Paris parlement-in-exile drew up formal demands for the convocation of an Estates-General while throughout the realm, sympathizers drawn from all orders were rallying to the parlements' revolutionary cant. In the face of this united front, Brienne abandoned the principal tenets of Calonne's financial reform program and recalled the parlement to Paris.[66]

Brienne's only recourse was to fall back on old tax remedies—the *vingtièmes,* and to call for a national loan. In a fitful show of prerogative, Louis ordered the parlement to register these edicts. At the same time, he promised a convocation of the Estates-General for 1792. The parlement responded by declaring the king's forced registration illegal.[67] This was more than a customary intransigence; it was an aristocratic revolution perpetrated by the *noblesse de robe* and supported by vast numbers of subjects mouthing radical slogans.

By now, Brienne had exhausted all ordinary measures of containment. One extraordinary maneuver had yet to be invoked—a *coup d'état* in the tradition of Chancellor Maupeou's *coup* of 1771. In May, 1788, Brienne, seconded by Keeper of the Seals Chrétien-François de Lamoignon, took that step in an effort to quash the parlement's claim to exercise political sovereignty.

This *coup d'état* made a strange counter-revolution. In many ways it was more revolutionary than the aristocratic prerevolution it was engineered to suppress. The *coup* of May, 1788, was Linguet's kind of revolution. He had been urging the monarchy to provoke it for three decades. The way Linguet viewed the matter, the *coup,* if properly executed, would make an aristocratic revolution impossible and a revolution of the Third Estate unnecessary.

In the beginning of May, Brienne and Lamoignon prepared an edict under which the jurisdiction and operations of a Plenary Court in existence since 1774, at least on paper, were radically expanded. In fact, they created a new institution, one Plenary Court to replace the several parlements of France in their function of registering edicts. The ministers carried their reorganization further still, drafting sweeping reform legislation in the area of French civil and criminal law.[68] These reforms were calculated to strike at abuses in the administration of the law which reformers and victims had brought into glaring relief. By assuring a more rapid and more certain justice, and a more direct means of obtaining it, the reforming ministers would be securing a protection for real properties which might win the support of the Third Estate.

Parlementary opposition to the ministerial *coup d'état* was a last-stand insurrection. Simon Linguet reacted with a militant propaganda campaign to win support for the ministers' audacious schemes. He also claimed full credit for originating major provisions in the ministers' program.[69] He had something of a case. In his *Dixme royale* of 1764; his *Nécessité d'une réforme dans l'administration des lois* of 1764; his *Mémoire pour les Sieurs Moynel, Dumesniel de Saveuse et Douville de Maillefeu* of 1766, and his *Théorie des lois civiles* of 1767, Linguet urged these kinds of reform in French civil and criminal law. In several of these works, as well as in his *Du plus heureux gouvernement*, his *Lettres sur "La théorie des lois civiles,"* and his *Annales*, he had warned repeatedly that for the safety of the Crown, aristocratic privilege would have to be drastically curbed, and parlement depoliticized. Linguet was convinced that the inevitable revolution of the Third Estate, should the ministry's *coup* fail, would be far more ruinous to the monarchy than the probable insurrection of the Second Estate in the wake of a successful reform program. Faced with violent opposition from the parlements in the opening days of the crisis,

Brienne is alleged to have remarked: "I have anticipated everything, even civil war."[70] Simon Linguet out-anticipated him, having forecast civil war as the prelude to the revolution of the Third Estate.[71]

In defending the ministerial *coup,* Linguet lashed out against the aristocratic party. "What! some gentlemen from Dauphiné dare to ask what the King of France would be, at the end of the eighteenth century, without the Nobility. What would he be! He would be what he is—the sovereign."[72]

Linguet had just begun to propagandize for the reform program when the king retreated. Faced with another acute financial crisis and chronic insurrection in the parlements, Louis XVI accepted Brienne's resignation, and recalling Jacques Necker to Paris, demanded that Lamoignon step down. In his declaration of September 23, 1788, the king axed the reform program. He recalled the parlements, annulled all judicial reforms, and announced a convocation of the Estates-General for 1789, as the parlements had demanded.[73]

Writing to his friend Perrégaux, Linguet described the Crown's defeat as "a very strange revolution. Where is it going to lead us? I have no idea: but a dreadful absurdity reigns. I am very sincerely sorry for Monsieur, the Keeper of the Seals [Lamoignon], whose views were pure and whose operation was useful. Perhaps he and the principal minister [Brienne] can reproach themselves for having counted too heavily on being justified in their motives. They wanted only to be reasonable: they ought to have been firm. That's the way to succeed."[74]

Still supporting the crown, Linguet carried on his campaign to discredit the insurrectionary *parlementaires* and ward off the Third Estate's revolution. He printed in the 116th number of his *Annales* a proposal for fiscal reform which he had first publicized in his *Annales* in 1778 and 1779, an expedient for terminating once and for all the chronic state of financial crisis that had precipitated Louis's capitulation to the aristocrats.[75]

Financial crisis had been brought on by the crown's unsuccessful appeals for short-term loans from bankers, speculators, and investors to stave off bankruptcy—but why was the Crown bankrupt? Only because from the beginning of the century, French monarchs had been inheriting an increasingly onerous burden of debts which they transmitted to their successors shamefully augmented. These transactions, Linguet announced, were robberies against the properties of subjects not yet born who would be burdened with taxes used to repay loans contracted generations earlier. Parties to an illegal contract could not expect compensation: "If a Prince hasn't the right to sell even the private properties of his family, he has even less [right] to alienate the possessions of all the families in his Realm." The monarch was free to break contracts made with financiers and speculators in government loans and stocks. "That's stealing from their pockets! But no: they gave voluntarily, and they *gave unwisely,* that's all." The king could repudiate all debts incurred before his reign, as well as those accumulated during it.[76] Linguet did not bother to point out—although the conclusion was only too obvious—that in dissolving the financial crisis by royal fiat, Louis XVI at the same time would be freeing national wealth from a clique of court capitalists, breaking Parlement's stranglehold on the throne, and sapping the aristocratic party's political strength.[77]

The king ignored Linguet's lesson in political and economic pragmatism. Financiers and capitalists were up in arms against it,[78] as was the Paris parlement. The aristocratic party could not afford the pose of a dignified and supercilious silence. After all, Linguet was arguing that one firm exertion of royal will would end the financial crisis from which the parlements were profiting in their push to political ascendancy. On September 27, 1788, the Parlement of Paris, all chambers assembled, heard and approved Advocate-General Antoine-Louis Séguier's motion that the 116th number of Linguet's *Annales,* containing the proposal that the king repudiate the national debt, be lacerated and burned at the foot of the grand staircase in the courtyard of the Palais de Justice.[79] While his *Annales* burned, Linguet, for a change, was consumed by rage.[80]

Linguet's next postmortem on the administration's reform effort was his *La France plus qu'angloise,* of October, 1788.[81] He included in it a thinly veiled warning to the king that his next blunder, a fatal one, would be to retreat headlong into the arms of aristocratic reactionaries more English in their pretensions to exercising legislative supremacy than Commons or Lords.[82] This move would signal disaster for the monarchy, as it would alienate the Third Estate from the throne as well as from the aristocratic party, driving it into isolation, and from there into independence and the revolution Linguet had been predicting all along.

Linguet's position was delicate. He explained it to Louis XVI in a dedication: "I have taken upon myself the hard and dangerous occupation of holding a kind of *Office of the Public Prosecutor,* and that of defender of legitimate authority...."[83] While professing perfect submission to the king's authority,[84] and administering blistering rebukes to rebellious parlements, Linguet at the same time was educating the Third Estate—in his *La France plus qu'angloise,* but also in his *Annales,* a work read, he boasted, "simultaneously, the same day, by 20,000 readers" and generating "reflections, discussions, and researches." He was teaching the Third Estate's members how to recognize their rights and act in their own best interest. "Already it [the parlement] also takes measures to master these *Estates* [the Estates-General], in order to turn them into an imposing machine whose movements it will direct, a mighty body whose soul will be the magistrature."[85] *La France plus qu'angloise,* Linguet announced in his *Annales,* was a treatise "in which we give palpable proof of the imminent danger from the Robe's enterprises, [a danger] which threatens the *Nation* as well as its leaders; and [in which we demonstrate] the urgent necessity for the Third Estate to enlighten itself, to concert, to league together to defend its existence, to reestablish its honor."[86]

If Linguet's aim was to disengage the Third Estate from its alliance with the parlements, he could realize it only by persuading notables in that Estate that self-interest dictated their taking an independent stand. He would have to unravel the partisan maneuvering behind the parlements' refusal to register royal edicts on legal reform, reveal the class-interested scheming behind the parlement's demands that approval of these sweeping reforms await a convocation of the Estates-General following the forms of 1614, explain that the parlements' demands for an Estates-General masked a dread that these demands might be realized, and expose a reactionary traditionalism motivating the Aristrocratic party's appeals to the constitution of the realm, the "general will," and the natural rights of citizens.[87] Notwithstanding all these revelations, the journalist still was begging a question. How independent of the aristocracy might the Third Estate become without moving into insurrection against the king? Linguet was only too well aware that at this critical moment Louis XVI was still vacillating before the necessity of throwing his allegiance either to the defiant old guard of the aristocracy or to the still cautious *avant-garde* of the Third Estate. Depending upon the king's final decision, Linguet's advice to the Third Estate could be interpreted either as proof of his determination to save the monarchy or as a sign of his traitorous commitment to the cause of revolutionaries.

Why hadn't the king taken a more forceful stand, Linguet asked in his *La France plus qu'angloise*. The government and the king might have had their reasons for proceeding so cautiously against the insurrectionary aristocratic party, "...but these scruples bear so strong a resemblance to timidity...that an absolute silence on the part of the prince himself perhaps might have been preferable to this feeble and impotent impulse to speak."[88]

What enraged Linguet even more than Louis's timid behavior toward traitors was Louis's ministers' treacherous betrayal of loyal subjects, in particular himself. He was referring to an *arrêt de Conseil* suppressing numbers 109, 110, and 111 of the *Annales* because, as Linguet put it, he had taken a few swipes at dead ministers in the course of defending the reform efforts of living ones. "In every age, in every country, an administration that allows itself to be led around this way can hardly ever be victorious: it compromises itself almost as much by its severity as by its indulgence: not supporting anyone, it makes anyone's support of it equally impossible."[89]

When he dismissed Brienne, Louis XVI turned for the second time to the Swiss financial wizard Jacques Necker in search of a way out of financial crisis. Necker was not ready to attempt two miracles simultaneously—the equilibration of a tottering fiscal system and the resurrection of Brienne's and Lamoignon's defunct scheme for administrative reform. Necker's silence on this second matter discouraged even the faintest hopes. On one issue, however, he spoke out. The fierceness of public debate dictated that the government make some pronouncement concerning the forms under which the Estates-General would be convened. In search of advice, Necker recalled the Assembly of Notables.

Linguet had been following the issue for some sign that the government had emancipated itself from the aristocratic party and was prepared to take the initiative in working out an alliance with the Third Estate: "...it was the *Third Estate* which really should have been assembled; one should have IN-VESTED ONESELF with the *opinion*, the votes of the *Third Estate.* It was necessary to crush between *throne* and *people* these rebellious bodies who favor, who tolerate the enterprises of the one [the throne] only insofar as these help them to tyrannize the other [the people]: from this shrewd and salutary league it might have been possible to realize the *public* regeneration; and the *Third Estate,* as will be seen, is very disposed to it."[90] Necker's reliance on the Notables gave Linguet further proof that the Third Estate's interests were being sold out to a party of aristocrats only too understandably committed to preserving the forms of 1614 intact.[91]

When the Notables failed to allot a double representation to the Third Estate in the Estates-General, Necker was forced to override them. Louis XVI accepted the principle of double representation for the Third Estate in December, 1788. By that time, the Third Estate was already beginning to demand not concessions, favor, or privileges, but rights; not the promise of paternalistic alliances, but marks of autonomy and equality. In demonstrations staged throughout the realm, and in particularly vehement manifestations in Brittany and Dauphiné, the Third Estate was making its weight felt.[92] In his *Annales,* Linguet referred to these numerous nationwide demonstrations for equal representation as insurrections, "domestic uprisings," "revolts."[93] He justified them, exonerating and encouraging the perpetrators. The paradoxical truth, Linguet observed, is that the reign of a weak monarch is the most tyrannical, *"un règne à révolutions."* The people react to repeated violations first by "secret discontent," and then by "open complaint," and finally, when they are utterly scorned, by "revolts." Their unassuaged discontent already had driven them to the second stage. The people, Linguet continued, swarm about the throne, "where they have a *right...*to find asylum and a *rampart....*in a century such as this, at a moment when the *Third Estate's* advances announce that it will combine the enlightenment revealing its true prerogatives with the courage and unity necessary to sustain them, what is inconceivable is that they [the government] seem to prefer making a public show of their determination to defy it [the Third Estate], to embitter it, to degrade it by curbing it." In such circumstances, Linguet concluded, the

Third Estate's projects of confederation "were as praiseworthy, as legitimate as those of the nation's oppressors are odious and criminal...."[94]

Linguet presented his most forceful argument for the Third Estate's declaration of independence in his *Avis aux parisiens,* a masterful piece of polemic, direct, incendiary, persuasive.[95] He began with a provocative announcement. The Third Estate of Paris did not know what it was or who its natural leaders might be. It had no grasp of political reality. It did not know where its political interests lay—if not spread out over all the gambling tables of the capital. For everything they had enlightened themselves to, the Third Estate remained politically pre-conscious, oblivious to the "revolution in preparation." In their appalling political naïveté, Parisians in the Third Estate were about to delegate to their natural enemies in the First and Second Estates the power to represent their political interests. "Rise up against the clergy, the nobility, the magistrature [all of whom have leagued together]. Do not allow something like six hundred thousand men to dictate the law to twenty-four million. Listen as the clergy claims its immunities and its franchises, the nobility its privileges, the magistrature its prerogatives—as if it were not shameful to speak of franchises, of immunities, of privileges, when the state has its needs, when the major part of the nation is in misery" (*Avis,* 3, 4, 5). Linguet's tactic was to persuade the Third Estate that its best strategy would be to unite with the king against the First and Second Estates. But the one question Linguet conspicuously begged was whether the king could be convinced that his interests and political destiny were bound up inextricably with those of the Third Estate.

Not only must this French nation of twenty-four million begin to forge common political interests, and devise means, institutions and operations to satisfy national political demands, it must also identify independent national leaders, representatives emancipated from servile attachments to the magistrature, men who could be entrusted with power proportional to the nation's numbers and to its taxable wealth,[96] and whose duty it would be to express the will of a national constituency. "Let us unite in heart and sentiment; since the clergy, the nobility, and the magistrature want to form a corps apart, let us break all communication with them.... People, think of the burden you carry, look around you—palaces, chateaux constructed with your sweat and your tears. These roads you have opened up still echo from your groans. Compare your situation with that of these prelates, these profiteers, these great men, these senators. What do you get from them for all the services you heap on them, for all the respect you give them? Contempt. They call you CANAILLE. Show them that the CANAILLE is the one who lives at your expense and who fattens himself on your labors" (*Avis,* 9-11, 13).

The Crown's self-styled Public Prosecutor had given important advice to Parisian commoners on the uses of political power; and he identified the

Third Estate's interests with a national interest of "twenty-four million" people well in advance of the Third Estate's political coming of age.

In his *Avis aux Parisiens,* Linguet cemented a working alliance with the Third Estate; but it was a shaky one. He came into the Revolution fresh from prerevolutionary combat against the aristocratic insurgents, but disillusioned with the vacillating, self-defeating politics of the monarchists and disaffected with the self-interested ideology of the liberals. It was in the logic of his position that he would reject the aristocrats' claim to represent the nation, but he never fully supported the claim of notables in the Third Estate to the power of sovereignty. Their leadership might prove suicidal, given the narrow class interests of property-owning dominators, given the incompatibility of their interests with the needs and claims of a dispossessed nation.

By 1789, Linguet already had determined for himself the real political worth of liberal principles first mouthed by philosophes, economic doctors, and propagandists of aristocratic insurrection, and now reappropriated by the Third Estate's leaders. He had disposed of the principle of general will;[97] he was convinced that rights and liberties were only functions of real economic dominion.[98] He mocked notions of constitutions and constitutional guarantees; he already had exposed the constitution of all polities. It was a grim master plan of socioeconomic necessities, the substructure on which all political constructs must rest. Before there could be any question of a National Assembly, Linguet had written off representative institutions as inoperable and representative exclusively of the dominant class's interests (including those of notables in the Third Estate).[99] As for the egalitarian principle, he marked the instant of its demise as precisely that of civil society's origin.[100] He forecast also that the day true liberty was reestablished in the world would be the doomsday of all political societies in which the Third Estate and other dominators and exploiters were struggling to keep public identity and private properties intact. If that doomsday did not herald the return of chaos, then it would mark the inauguration of a political regime dedicated to rewarding victorious proletarians with possessions in domains and dominions in security.[101]

Linguet made a conspicuous show of rejecting the ideological baggage of liberalism which the Third Estate's leaders dragged with them into revolution; he offered instead a disarmingly simple utilitarian argument justifying obedience to sovereigns and revolutions against them. He stated his thesis, a variation on themes from his *Théorie des lois civiles,* in an article in the *Annales* on the nature and use of force in political societies.[102] Revolution, Linguet announced there, is the penalty a monarch always pays for violating the only constitution of his realm—the constitution of civil society, that is, of the propertied order. A realm of expropriated proprietors, robbed by the crown, needn't bother appealing to rights, constitutional guarantees, or institutional checks upon the king's power. This realm had been tied to that king only by "the eternal and unalterable bond of interest." The limits of monarchical power were fixed "in the nature of things, which wills that everything have [limits] , in morals as in physics. Who will set them down? Necessity" ("Force," 229, 207).

But where, toward which tribunal, could subjects turn for a final disposition of their case in civil law against a robber monarch? "Where! I've told you; to [the tribunal] which is the origin, the foundation of all others; to this principle whose influence can neither be contradicted nor limited, and is always discernible where it becomes necessary; to what the *Président de Montesquieu* calls an *Insurrection;* to what the Polish name a *Confederation;* to the result of the nature of things; to the use of a corrective force superior to [that force] whose abuses are to be reformed" (*ibid.,* 219). The instant property is in danger, or laws with respect to properties are enforced capriciously and arbitrarily, "...then, without prior understanding, without conspiracy, all are thrown into revolt; all take up arms: this is not by virtue of a law; this is not in reclaiming a prior pact ceremoniously drawn up: this is following the very constitution of society; following its fundamental nature; following the principle which commands that it [society] cannot be otherwise than it is" (*ibid.,* 220). In this pattern of necessities, Linguet read imminent disaster for the Crown. Let the monarch beware.

> ...lightning strikes the frontispiece of temples as it does the threshold of the humblest shanties....heaven, the sole arbiter between master and rebellious subjects, reveals its intentions only through victories: do not reduce them to the necessity of imploring these formidable oracles.
> ...These maxims fix simultaneously the rights of princes and those of peoples. [*Ibid.,* 227, 228.]

It was in his definition of property that Linguet betrayed—although in a backhanded way—his identification with the Third Estate's interests and a remarkable correspondence between his principles and the liberals' ideologies. Property was the loaded category in Linguet's system; he had imparted to it a wonderful flexibility and an infinite expansibility as a ground for staking out claims to rights and liberties. A man's holdings were his property, as was capital in movable goods. His profession was his property, as well as his unfettered exercise of the liberty necessary to practice it (even where that liberty touched upon the political power to legislate or to articulate a constituency's demands and represent its interests). To remove a man's profession arbitrarily was tantamount to robbing him of property in his civil existence; that was murder.[103] A man's thoughts were his property, even when, in expressing them, he put himself in the position of competing with the government for the public's allegiance. Any arbitrary suppression of these thoughts in print would amount to an attack upon his estate.[104]

Simon Linguet professed obedience to an absolute monarch, but that monarch's legitimacy as he understood it, was conditional nonetheless, and measured by his success in guaranteeing properties. Following every attack upon his professional holdings, this supersensitized son of a professor whose property in his academic career had been confiscated without due process escalated his own demands for protection and compensations—his condition for a continuing recognition of the crown's legitimacy—to the point where the only acceptable compensation for expropriation, both for himself and for the nation, would have been the power of self-determination and self-protection, political autonomy.

Split Perspectives

On the eve of the Revolution, Linguet stretched the Third Estate's property rights to embrace the exercise of political influence needed to protect holdings against destruction by arbitrary power; but he carried his expansionist analyses of property still further, too far perhaps for the comfort of the Third Estate's emerging political leadership.

A subject's most vital property, Linguet announced in his *Réponse aux docteurs modernes* and later in his *Du pain et du bled,* was his property in his stomach. His right to fill it with bread was another inalienable property right, a basic right of nature and necessity before which all other claims for protection of properties would have to be treated as secondary; but by whom?[105] Linguet was wary of all attempts by proprietors, including those in the Third Estate, to arrogate to themselves the exclusive authority to protect properties in life. They wouldn't be able to do it. They were narrowly self-interested: "and as the Third Estate is composed exclusively of deputies chosen from among the wealthiest persons in the order of *roturiers,* their interest in almost all these noisy and useless assemblies is always far more to crush the people than to defend it, and to join [the people's] oppressors rather than to disarm them."[106] Linguet reserved for administration, presumably the party in society with the greatest vision and most general interest in preserving properties, the gargantuan task of reconciling incompatible, class-based demands for justice and claims to property, and of staving off a civil war pitting all categories of possessors against a class of dispossessed persons, a confrontation that must end inevitably in anarchical chaos or in the establishment of a welfare state for victorious proletarians.[107]

In January, 1777, Linguet announced the forthcoming publication of his *Annales* to France's secretary of state for foreign affairs, Vergennes, and to his public. He declared: "As I am no longer the protector of individuals, I will become [the protector] of the masses [*des peuples*]; at least their rights under my pen will never be sacrificed, nor their interests compromised; and perhaps, with time, they will be enlightened."[108] With his annual subscription rate of 48 *livres tournois,* Linguet was not exactly courting readers among *les peuples.* He *was* reaching monarchs, crown officials, and other influential individuals and groups among Europe's notables, barraging them with information concerning socioeconomic conditions and developments on the continent and with political guidelines and programs for preventing the explosion of class antagonisms into civil war.

Ethics and politics, Linguet announced in his *Annales,* are plagued, as all the sciences are, by great insoluble problems. How is it possible to reconcile "liberty and *order,* the rights of *war,* and those of *humanity,* but above all, the *disproportion* in wealth with the public weal. The *great achievement* in the art of government would be to have no *poor,* or at least no *indigent,* and to banish from the surface of this earth the extreme *misery* which until now always has been the inseparable companion of this local augmentation of *riches* that we call the *prosperity of states*" (*Annales,* II [1777], 78-79). This depiction of civil society's paradox—the existence and progressive augmentation of the masses' indigence in an age of unexampled prosperity for the few—expressed Linguet's understanding of the most pressing socioeconomic crisis confronting administrations in modern states.

In the first two numbers of the *Annales*—his bimonthly forum for communicating empirical evidence to support principal theses in his systems of sociology and political economy—Linguet identified several groups composing this dangerous class: soldiers,[109] mendicants, day laborers, and farmhands; and he predicted that a force sufficient to crack society apart could develop within the ranks of this pre-proletarian population (*RA,* 83-102).[110]

In a later article, Linguet formulated a clearer working definition of the class of the poor. He was reviewing a work by a Walloon pastor in Namur, Jean-Baptiste Briatte, entitled *Offrande à l'humanité, ou Traité sur les causes de la misère en générale, et de la mendicité en particulier.*[111] Briatte, Linguet informed his readers, begins by identifying a class of the poor, "'...this class as populous as [it is] unfortunate, for whom poverty is the only appanage.'" He quoted Briatte's definition of this class's members: "'...it contains,' he says, 'all men without properties and without revenues, without pensions or without wages [*gages*]; who live from earnings [*salaires*] when they are sufficient; who suffer when they are too low; who die of hunger when they are cut off.'" Such a population was composed of day laborers [*journaliers*], and also agricultural workers [*manouvriers*], artisans—especially those who are " 'instruments of unskilled trades [*métiers grossiers*],...and, in general, all workers who work on the land, or in the arts, in factories [*fabriques*], in manufactories of staple commodities...[and manufactories] of superfluities...; in a word, all citizens whose subsistence and that of their families depends on the capacity of their arms, or the skill of their hands, and the use one makes of them'" (*Annales,* IX [1780] 326). Briatte delineated precisely the members whose progressive pauperization Linguet had depicted in his political economy.

Linguet was satisfied with Briatte's description of the plagues of poverty and mendicity.[112] He concluded his review by announcing that he planned to offer his own contribution—a remedy for the spreading social plagues of mendicity and poverty—conspicuous and dangerous social expressions of the great paradox of modern societies.[113] Linguet explained that he was in no hurry to publish his work; governments were too busy harming one another "to have time to think of benefiting the people..." (*Annales,* IX [1780], 355-56).

In France, at least, the government's policy concerning the disposition of the most conspicuous group in the population of the desperately poor—the mendicants—varied considerably from 1764 through 1789. Generally, the government favored removing intractable mendicants from circulation. They might be confined in *dépôts de mendicité* (combination prisons and workshops), or in *ateliers de charité* (government workshops), in *hôpitaux* (combination asylums and workhouses), or imprisoned pending an eventual return to their home parishes for employment in local enterprises.[114]

Linguet and other reformers were quick to point out the injustice in treating as criminal deviants those for whom no real possibility existed of finding life-sustaining work (*Annales,* III [1778], 340). As Linguet viewed it, entrepreneurs and statesmen must assume a formal obligation toward this class. They must incorporate it into a pre-capitalist economy, raising it to the position of a working class, bestowing on its victimization a kind of dignity compatible with the laws of liberal economics and a utilitarian ethic.

At the very least, then, the poor must have work. In an article in the *Annales* supporting the decision of the Archbishop of Paris to suppress eleven Catholic holidays, Linguet admitted that administrators could prevent the starvation of the working poor only by multiplying occasions for their exploitation. "...with a crown, you have your choice of slaves; our societies have become immense markets where need, always pressed, every morning sells the largest portion of the human species to the smallest which has appropriated the metal without which living is no longer permitted. Every day this sale does not take place, the unfortunate man who has no other means of subsistence is in danger of dying of hunger (*ibid.,* 181). The humanitarian in this grim environment would be a reformer who, "with as much care as it once required to diminish them" now multiplied the number of days on which "... active indigence is allowed to exchange its sweat against the niggardly distributions of wealth..." (*ibid.,* 181-82).

Lengthening the working year was a necessary beginning; it was hardly the final solution. In a number of the *Annales* appearing in February, 1778, Linguet advertised for one, offering an essay prize of fifty *louis* to the best entry on the causes of and cure for mendicity, "a universal epidemic," a "pestilential leprosy," "one of the most dangerous plagues which torments Europe." Entries were to be judged by the *curés* of Paris (*ibid.*, 339, 341, 342, 343).[115] Linguet was advertising for a way out of a revolution of the laboring poor— victims of faulty financial structures, and of an economic conjuncture characterized by sudden price hikes and permanent wage lags.

> Can the apex of a pyramid be secure when its foundations, already dissolved by a murderous humidity, are further menaced with the shock of a torrent? Such is the position of Europe today.
> ...The sudden increase in the price of staple goods; the disproportion between its [the people's] salary, and the price of its subsistence; the multiplicity of taxes, are sources of a misery which is hardly about to end. These are the Pandora's boxes at the bottom of which you won't find even hope. [*Ibid.*, 348.]

The essays, if they were submitted, were never published. Linguet was compelled to abandon the contest when he encountered difficulties in retaining judges.[116]

When Linguet publicized his essay competition, he announced also that he was holding a project of his own in reserve. He published parts of it in 1779, a *Plan d'établissemens, tendans à l'extinction de la mendicité.*[117] What was more remarkable than the details of Linguet's program was his fixation on voluntary and involuntary unemployment and escalating pauperization among French urban and rural masses as expressions of grave social and economic crises.

In his *Plan*, Linguet projected the establishment of Companies of Commerce and Assistance, with central offices in Paris, and eighty branches in the provinces. Their function would be to locate work in agricultural and industrial enterprises for an unemployed, indigent population (*Plan*, 9-13). "...the withdrawal [of the indigent classes' means of subsistence] is even more dangerous than the perpetuation of their misery" (*ibid.*, 8). *Directions* of these Companies would be empowered to set up job-training centers and employment bureaus. But the *Directions* would also be able to create new manufactories to turn out products previously supplied through foreign markets; and they would provide encouragement and financial backing to entrepreneurs who, for lack of materials, workers, and resources, had hesitated to establish new industries (*ibid.*, 9, 13). Finally, in every city in the realm, Companies of Charity would be opened to accept private donations to be used to purchase food, clothing, and furniture for the destitute. Surplus funds would be diverted into public works projects employing jobless laborers (*ibid.*, 24-26).

Linguet emphasized repeatedly that his proposal was designed to benefit all sectors of the economy, and net profits to financiers, speculators, and entrepreneurs, as well as subsistence wages in all seasons to a population of worker-producers living at the threshold of mendicity (*ibid.*, 14, 17-18, 20-21.)

Destitute and unemployed men refusing to participate in these work programs, that is, mendicants by choice, would be imprisoned until they understood their obligation to respond positively to expressions of paternal beneficence within the government and exuberant entrepreneurship among private persons (*ibid.*, 27). Jean-Jacques Rousseau would have coerced men to enter into the obligations of a self-willed political destiny in forcing them to be free. Linguet, who was much less the theorist than the pragmatist in this context, asked what the cash value of a chimera of political freedom was—what in the world it would get for men who were free to starve and free to be exploited. Their liberty, he concluded, would give them no returns unless they could be forced to be secure first. "…liberty," he remarked later, "is a Circe's brew for them [the day laborers] , or rather, it produces an even more deplorable effect than the magic brew; it persuades them that they have become men when, in fact, they are no longer even animals" (*Annales*, XIV [1788], 72n).

Linguet believed his project was immediately practicable. He was ready to try it out on a small scale; he was waiting only for an overture from the government and an indication that entrepreneurs would be willing to collaborate with him (*Plan*, 30). The go-ahead signal never came.

There were striking similarities between Linguet's program and seventeenth-century projects and policies for stimulating the economy; however, Linguet's focus and sympathies were not identical to those of his predecessors among the *étatistes* and mercantilists. He had convinced himself that government and society owed the poor the dubious service of locking them into the vise of a protocapitalist economy in the throes of a rapid if uneven development. He was convinced that if they were abandoned to allegedly self-regulating economic operations, the unemployed poor would be reduced to intensified misery and driven into revolution. In 1779, Linguet still believed that government, in collaboration with enlightened entrepreneurs, could divert them by finding or creating opportunities to sustain brute life within a system which otherwise would become deadly to them in proportion as it proved momentarily profitable to their exploiters.

He added, in an article in his *Annales* for November, 1779—a re-presentation of themes from his *Du pain et du bled*—that a job and regular wages were not enough; the laboring poor must be able to buy bread with what they earned. Government must guarantee them that. Once admit the worker's infrangible right to subsistence, and you must admit also his right to whatever wage was required to buy bread or else his right to bread at the price his wage dictated he could pay. Linguet seemed to be suggesting that the government had two regulatory options open to it. Either it must establish rigorous price controls on grains, or it must enforce a sliding salary scale.[118] In any case, the administration must reject the liberal economists' argument that as soon as government adopted policies and attitudes of *laissez-faire*, agricultural entre-preneurs would produce more in expectation of higher grain prices on an un-regulated market. From the standpoint of the wage-earner, Linguet argued, high prices were not any more bearable just because large quantites of grains were conspicuously displayed in marketplaces; for him the vital relationship was between the cost of bread and his wage. A realm might be said to be in a state of famine and grave political crisis when the disproportion between wages and bread prices reached the point where the wage-earner could not purchase his subsistence—no matter how much grain and how much bread was available. At this dead-end, "...very shortly, they must revolt, they must die, or they must flee" (*Annales*, VII [1779], 204-5, 209).

Theorists who argued that liberal economics was a self-correcting system had miscalculated everything when they insisted that wages would rise natu-rally, automatically, to meet increases in grain and bread prices. The entre-preneurs themselves would never find it in their interest to raise wages vol-untarily (*ibid.*, 212-24).

The laboring poor, the productive class in society, that is, the class whose productive power was the source of all wealth (Linguet is thinking specifically of agricultural laborers), had a weapon at hand to raise the price of their labor —the strike. The irony was that with every attempt they made to use it, they would only gun themselves down more effectively. "Alarm would spread in houses where the harvest is the foundation of opulence [if] fields, vineyards [were] in danger of remaining uncultivated. They would hire these necessary hands which remained idle, [and] at a higher price, and necessity would dic-tate the law to avarice." However, without substantial savings, agricultural workers could not afford to strike; and without the leverage of the strike, they could never pressure their employers into raising their wages. "The more his stomach goads him, the less he is in a position to bargain over the price he is offered" (*ibid.*, 216-17).

Linguet was not prepared to offer a foolproof solution, nor even a model reform program at this point. He insisted only that commerce in grains was commerce in human life; therefore, that far from guaranteeing liberty and high prices to those who traded in subsistence goods, administrators must per-fect a thoroughgoing regulatory system. However, regulatory powers would have to be exercised with such practiced subterfuge that agricultural and com-mercial entrepreneurs would not sense the slightest restraint on their econo-mic liberty (*ibid.*, 233). This engineered reconciliation of the entrepreneur's economic liberty with the dictates of humanity and the categorical imperative of the life-force would be a major feat of administrative genius. Linguet be-lieved the preservation of political and economic systems based on private properties depended upon the success of such operations. They were the sys-tem's last line of defense against the revolution that would dissolve property relations altogether.

During the decade of the eighties, the administration maintained its attitude of relative passivity in the face of escalating social and economic crises, soaring unemployment in manufacturing and commercial centers, and intensified misery, often approaching famine, in the countrysides. In 1788, Linguet reported a layoff of between five and six thousand master-craftsmen and their apprentice-journeymen in the luxury cloth manufacturing establishments at Lyons. He noted that the merchant-manufacturers had offered these men and their families—twenty-thousand human beings—a total compensation of five *sous* a head, "not a day's subsistence."

> What! Enriched from their work, you would believe your debt to them paid, your sensitivity would be satisfied, once you announced in stentorian voice that you would no sooner give them bread than employment! You lack silk!—but not money. Shouldn't your luxurious ease nourish their painful, distressing inaction?
>
> Your profits are cut off; but their lives are extinguished. The increment in the fortunes you have willed your children is suspended; but the respiration of their own is about to cease; and while you calculate at your leisure just when you will set your machines going, hunger this very day will consume at your door the unfortunate beings you have chased away. [*Annales*, XIII (1788), 222-23.]

"Irrevocable laws of politics and society" dictated that the entrepreneur's philanthropy yield a profit and that his humanitarianism bear interest. "... very well: let your beneficence be a salary and not a charity. I agree." Linguet proposed that the government of Lyons, with financial backing from its silk manufacturers, set up municipal works projects to open roads through the mountains surrounding the city, and hire the idle silk workers. "You grow pale: you are still frightened by the expense. The momentary outlay seems more onerous to you than hope for the future is consoling: you tremble to consecrate 1,200,000 *livres* to save twenty thousand useful men—your providers, the true authors of your fortunes, the benefactors of your families; show me your account books, and let's see what your theatre cost you" (*ibid.*, 224).[119]

Just when he had declared himself solidly for the Third Estate, and was enlightening its leaders to their property rights over against a reactionary aristocracy and an impotent monarch, Linguet suddenly reentered his paradox-riddled plea in defense of the "property" rights of a Fourth Estate. This free and freely exploitable population should never have been emancipated. Linguet was repeating his challenge to philanthropic philosophers, humanitarian entrepreneurs, and administrators. Time was running out. They must devise some alternative to the masses' reenslavement that would neither starve them to death nor propel them into an all-annihilating revolution. They must make a cash commitment to human life—if they were interested in eliciting a political commitment from the masses.

...my system boils down to saying that a *slave* BOUGHT FOR SILVER, guaranteed consequently to have at least one man in the world who in order not to lose his investment is interested in his existence; assured consequently of being boarded and nourished every day; certain of being cared for in illness; occupying in society at least the position of a horse...is less unfortunate even in his degradation than a *day laborer*...for whom the only fruit of liberty is to be literally slave in every respect, and nonetheless deprived of the unique compensation that makes servitude bearable, that of having in the master a protector interested in preserving the serf....[*Annales,* XV (1788), 158.]

In another article, Linguet exposed a new kind of humanitarian—a witness if not a party to the exploitation of free white labor, who launched campaigns to demand that the American slave trade be humanized: "The *Negroes* live, after all: for this will always be my humane and real *cry of Philosophy:* either they must be nourished, or sold, or given up; they fall under the safeguard of the avarice that purchased them. But what about FREE *day laborers?* who will feed them? who does feed them when they are out of work?" (*ibid.,* 22-23). A group of humanitarians in Paris had just completed its prospectus for a center to care for and feed the horses of the capital. "...show me, in any country, a comparable establishment in favor of men, of workers." What enterprise guaranteed rural day laborers and artisans in the city against fluctuations in prices of their daily fodder, their bread? Who would offer to provision the working poor with first-class foodstuffs at below-market prices? Who would save them from being duped daily by retailers of necessities? Why was the horse such a privileged animal, one so worthy of philanthropic solicitude? Why was a free and starving man considered so vile, despicable in the eyes of humanitarian benefactors, lower than an animal? Why? Linguet had the answer. The horse was a slave. Someone had paid a price for it. The modern working man was unattached, free. *"Il est libre."* (*Ibid.,* 24-25.)

What was to be done? At very least, horse-lovers and champions of the rights of black slaves must stop parading through the powder magazine of European societies waving flaming torches for distant causes. No one dared champion the reenslavement of free white men (*ibid.,* 38; see also *Annales,* XIV [1788], 87-88). Then someone must fight publicly to alleviate the conditions of their intolerable freedom.

A year before the Estates-General was convened—and in the middle of his propaganda campaign to teach the propertied Third Estate its political interests, Linguet announced that he was prepared to represent a vast, silent constituency, a class of the poor, a Fourth Estate.[120] He wanted to be its deputy: "The general malaise of the lower classes in *Europe* has produced the almost universal ferment I forecast and announced in the first lines of this work [i.e., in the second number of the *Annales,* vol. I (1777), 83]. It could be that everyone has cause for grievance: but at this moment, when we are concerned with an assembly destined to operate a general reform, there must be at least one interpreter of the cries of the largest, most maltreated class, and [the one] most totally deprived of the means of making itself heard" (*Annales,* XV, 38-39).[121]

Over a period of a decade and a half, Linguet had been demanding bread and work for the class of the poor. At first he believed that food and employment were what its members were most painfully aware of lacking and the most they hoped to get. He did not insist upon a change in their position at the base of the societal pyramid, only on a steady supply of minimal nourishment, enough to sustain life. He applied his ideology and politics of subsistence to a variety of crises afflicting the French realm, expressing traditional demands in a philosophic and juristic language, in terms of rights and laws of nature and necessity.

If ever the class of the poor appropriated this ideology, there would be no reason to expect it to conceive its rights that narrowly—as rights to brute biological existence. In that case, then, the functions of this class's spokesman—who already had elected to identify the interests of Crown and Third Estate—must be to direct and channel the people's evolving political consciousness also, to articulate its escalating demands, and to devise programs and construct institutions capable of satisfying them.[122] The people, too, a Fourth Estate, would have to be reintegrated into the system.

Prescience and Social Sciences, Some Reflections

Linguet's knowledge of the political climate in France on the eve of the Revolution was remarkable. His foreknowledge was more remarkable still. What is it about the man, or his social science, or both, that accounts for the penetrating accuracy in his political reports and forecasts?

Linguet brought his special reading of the historical sociology of law to his understanding of political confrontations shaping up between the propertied Third Estate and the monarchy, but he also offered an ongoing self-analysis as documentation for his depictions and predictions. "There are circumstances where the adventures of an ordinary individual can occupy their place in the general history of his century...and I have paid dearly for the sad satisfaction of thinking that the events of my life constitute one such set [of circumstances]" (*Annales,* II, 194).

Linguet's science of society was supposed to be a complete system. He stated the principles in this science in a set of propositions that accounted for the origins, structures, and transformations of fundamental societal institutions and relationships. These propositions were presented from the perspective of an unprivileged, unprotected member of the Third Estate, a great-grandson and grandson of farmers, and the son of a dispossessed professional.

The totality of societal phenomena, Linguet argued, could be explained as functions of property. Property was generated in acts of brute force, a spoliation and enslavement of farmers and herdsmen by hunters (ancestors of the French nobility) who consecrated theft in civil law and maintained it by the arm of authority. All the institutions of society—class, family, political system, economic structures, culture—derived from and supported this order of properties. From the standpoint of propertied subjects, the legitimacy of the political authority which maintained fundamental societal divisions was conditional, rigorously dependent upon authority's success in safeguarding holdings. In the Western world, the administrative task of protecting properties was complicated. At the end of the middle ages, monarchs practiced a politics of emancipation as part of a more general plan to consolidate their political strength while weakening that of the nobility. They liberated a serf population which formed a Third Estate. Economic transformations generated new opportunities; a sizable minority in this unprivileged Estate acquired properties in land, capital, merchandise, and various forms of portable wealth. Authority became responsible for guaranteeing all possessions that new categories of owners enjoyed.[123]

Early in his career, Linguet argued that French judicial institutions and the personnel of a magistrature subservient to the interests of a resurgent aristocracy posed the greatest threat to holdings of commoners. The triple expropriation of this ambitious member of the Third Estate, who had amassed impressive if contestible properties in capital, profession, honor, liberty, and influence, provoked him into indicting not only *parlementaires* but secretaries of state, potentates in the world of letters, and others in the interlocking branches of the French establishment. In Linguet's understanding, rulers who robbed their subjects or who tolerated theft were despots. And despotism was the one absolutely illegitimate system in Linguet's constellation of political regimes. In exasperation, but also to generate support and prepare his revenge, Linguet compiled notebooks of his grievances; they read as case studies in French tyranny; and they circulated, in the *Annales* and in pamphlet literature, all over Europe. In the end, Linguet claimed for himself and on behalf of all threatened proprietors the direct political influence without which they could neither enjoy nor protect their multiple holdings—everything from shops and parcels of land to careers. He crystallized out of personal, family, and class history a set of political objectives and an ideology which, by 1788, embodied at least some of the emerging political concerns of his contemporaries in the Third Estate. The logic of Linguet's social and political theories dictated the revolution he forecast, and the publication and broad circulation of his intensely personal, universally appropriable experiences of victimization under the French regime invited it.

In his treatises and in his polemic literature, then, Linguet self-consciously grasped the principles and the dynamics of his confrontations with authority. He represented this intimate knowledge so that one man's progress through conflict into a real if unstable professional and political independence recapitulated and anticipated chapters in the political history of the propertied Third Estate. In the "adventures of a simple individual" he read episodes in the history of France's revolutionary future.

Linguet's evaluations of the revolutionary potential in crisis-marked relationships between authority and the Fourth Estate are informed by his theoretical perspectives on the fundamental principles of society and government and by his observations of the impact of innovative political doctrines and legislation and of enlightenment propaganda on the life conditions, attitudes, and behavior of impoverished urban and rural populations composed of day laborers, peasants, workers in rural industry, artisans and urban wage earners, mendicants, and other people living on the margins of society.

All social and political relations revolve around properties originating in crimes of spoliation and subjugation; the principal obligation of political authority is to perpetuate class divisions and fundamentally exploitative class relationships on which the regime of properties rests. Under these conditions, the fate of the disinherited masses, whether they are formally enslaved or technically liberated, would be the same. Their fate would be to have nothing except bread; to derive no benefit other than subsistence from the system. From their standpoint, assuming their expectations remained low, assuming they continued accepting their fate, political utopia would be a regime where the sovereign, a severe but just patriarch-king, placed rigid boundary conditions on the prerogatives their dominators enjoyed and on the privations they suffered as the dominated class—so that the liberty of dominion did not cancel out the liberty to keep oneself alive, a freedom from visceral want. And political despotism would be any regime which identified completely with special interest groups whose priorities and programs, as the masses perceived both, were prejudicial to their continued enjoyment of their property in and right to life.

Linguet's model of regimes of regulation and protection—where property rights were safeguarded and at the same time limited to protect the masses' property in life—provided him with critical leverage for depictions of crises in modern societies in the throes of transition and development—where the sovereign vacillated between a traditional exercise of regulatory powers and an innovation limitation of his political role to one of protecting his subjects' liberty to buy and sell commodities, including grain and labor, on an open market.

In his *Théorie des lois civiles*, in the *Réponse aux docteurs modernes*, in his *Du pain et du bled*, and in the *Annales*, Linguet anatomized—and with a systematic, brutal rigor unequaled by any of his contemporaries—the networks of socioeconomic oppressions in which the dominated were becoming entrapped as the authority of government was engaged unqualifiedly to support a politics of economic modernization through liberalization. Where he focused specifically on the doctrines and policies of the *économistes*, Linguet showed how relationships between buyers and sellers of labor on an open market were governed by mechanisms and laws which dictated the intensification of the wage-earners' deprivations and exploitation. He depicted the operation and impact of an iron law of wages, the law of the proletarian reserve army, and the mechanisms of surplus value. Juxtaposing liberal economic theory against socioeconomic realities, he demolished the liberalizers' contentions that the system would be self-correcting and universally beneficial. He mapped situations where acquisitive instinct and tastes among agricultural entrepreneurs dictated that their profits would be directed into luxury spending instead of being plowed back into augmented productivity as the system dictated; where agricultural products were withheld from the market in anticipation of dearth and rising prices instead of being marketed where need was greatest; where the demand for labor fell with the introduction of labor-saving techniques and machinery, and where the price of labor dropped below the cost of subsistence in violation of the iron law of wages, as desperate armies of unemployed persons competed for work; where employers subordinated any residual humanitarian concerns for their employees to an overriding drive for immediate profits.[124]

If one accepts Linguet's demonstrations of the intractable precariousness of the laboring poor's position under any economic system; and if one admits with him the likelihood of further deterioration where regimes of economic liberty prevail in a still predominantly traditional economy-in-transition, then his conclusion at least becomes tenable: a politics of intervention—incessant regulation and manipulation of economic operations, and limitation of private property rights—must be invoked to protect the masses' property in life. Government, then, can have no higher or more pressing interest than that of covering the poor with guarantees of life. Labor is the source of all wealth, hence of all power in society. If workers perish in droves of an overdose of liberty, the economy collapses, the political power network dissolves, all the superstructures of the culture crumble. Government's complicity in mass murder would be absurdist politics, although, as Linguet understands the matter, the multitudes' alienation from the system in death was not the worst to be feared from a politics of economic toleration. Their alienation might find expression in revolution, not a "blind frenzied uprising," but a self-consciously initiated and directed popular insurrection that would end an economy of possessions and privations, a society of exploiting and exploited classes, and the political regime which safeguarded both.[125]

Linguet's understanding of how economic laws operate as ironclad determinants of the masses' material conditions and real options within the system gave him a basis for projecting the explosive impact of economic policy changes and enlightenment propaganda on popular attitudes and behavior. Economic policy fluctuations, more specifically, physiocratic policy innovations, shattered the people's traditional belief that even in times of food crises, they would be able to provide for their subsistence (the only welfare benefit they had ever claimed from the system)—provided their physical efforts were combined with government vigilance, that is, with the customary policing operations.

The systematic enlightenment the *économistes* championed would do more than dissolve traditional beliefs and expectations; it would spark in the ranks of the dispossessed a revolution of rising expectations. Linguet warned repeatedly that the people's educators were teaching them to demand extravagant material and nonmaterial returns from the economic and political systems when in reality they themselves were calculating prosperity and profit on an assumption of the people's continuing subjugation to ironclad economic laws dictating their permanent degradation and exploitation.

Beginning with an analysis of the people's material capabilities within the system, Linguet was able to forecast rapidly escalating popular expectations under the impact of enlightenment, the brutal, repeated frustration of those expectations under regimes of economic liberty, the buildup of aggressive potential, and finally, its explosion into popular revolution. He did more. During the 1770s, Linguet publicized a popular political ideology, recapitulating, albeit for the education of the propertied elites exclusively, the tenets of a politics of subsistence; anticipating by two decades the demands of radical revolutionaries for subsistence, for welfare, and even for the dissolution of an oppressive social order and the redistribution of the goods of the earth. Linguet's ideology for a people and a monarchy in crisis may have politicized his deeply personal claims upon authority for security, welfare, and nurture, and legitimated his irrepressible nihilistic and anarchistic impulses; his ideology also crystallized and politicized universally experienced, class-appropriable biological imperatives.[126]

Whether Linguet was analyzing and forecasting confrontations between a "despotic" monarchical regime and the propertied elites, or between that regime and the masses, he always built into his depictions and previsions the polarizations that characterized his war-torn relations with authorities. He predicted popular insurrections; he legitimated them as the people's natural, necessary reactions to societal and governmental tyrannies exercised over the physics and chemistry of existence. When revolutions of the people occurred, Linguet arranged on paper for their termination in surrenders of autonomy to administrative authority in exchange for the promise and delivery of security. He forecast that property holders in the Third Estate would be successful in their struggle for independence and the power of self-protection against French despots in power; he educated them to demand both. When they did, and when they triumphed, he began calculating the cost and benefit to an enlightened administration of buying them off with material goods, compensation for a surrender of real political control, if not nominal sovereignty. Applying utilitarian measures, Linguet legitimated expressive revolutionary acts by the Third and Fourth Estates and a repressive administrative politics of total containment.

Linguet's remarkable, if flawed, prescience concerning the shape of France's revolutionary future was informed by his social science; and his "scientific" understanding was deepened and colored by personal experiences of ambivalence and conflict with authority which he projected onto the divided culture he was analyzing and which predetermined in part the patterning of his revolutionary political commitments.

NOTES

1. "Livre des sorties de la Bastille," Nov. 12, 1771–Dec. 26, 1782, in Bibliothèque de l'Arsenal, Paris, MSS, no. 14,566, entry no. 263.

2. Kaunitz to Joseph II, Vienna, June 13, 1782, in AG, Chancellerie autrichienne, vol. 506, D. 107, ad litt. L 1, no. 1. For interpretive studies of Linguet's relations with authorities in the Austrian Netherlands during the 1780s, see Charles Piot, "Linguet aux Pays-Bas autrichiens," *Bulletin de l'Académie royale de Belgique,* 2e série, XLVI (1878), 787-826; André Puttemans, *La Censure dans les Pays-Bas autrichiens,* Académie royale de Belgique, classe des lettres et des sciences morales et politiques, mémoires, 2e série, XXXVII (Brussels, 1935), 298-305; 314-15. Puttemans draws heavily on Piot's study. For my own analysis, I consulted and used archival sources which Piot and Puttemans cite, as well as French and Austrian manuscript and printed material not incorporated into their studies.

3. Joseph II's autograph note in Kaunitz to Joseph II' Vienna, June 13, 1782, in AG, Chancellerie autrichienne, vol. 506, D. 107, ad litt. L 1 no. 1.

4. Starhemberg to Kaunitz, Brussels, Aug. 6, 1782, in *ibid.*, no. 3, P.S., no. 80.

5. Kaunitz to Joseph II, Vienna, Aug. 17, 1782, in *ibid.*, no. 3, P.S. no. 88.

6. Joseph's autograph note in Kaunitz to Joseph II, Vienna, Aug. 17, 1782, in *ibid.*

7. Starhemberg to Kaunitz, Brussels, Sept. 3, 1782, in *ibid.*, no. 3. See also Linguet to Joseph II, Brussels, Sept. 7, 1782, in *ibid.*, ad no. 4: "...from the moment my tranquillity depends only on my exactitude in conforming to what he [the emperor] intends, and to the laws, I will consider myself the most secure among men." For Linguet's later reflections on the conditions Joseph had spelled out for his return to Belgium, see Linguet to Crumpipen, London, March 6, 1783, in AG, MSS divers, no. 1498, fols. 40v-41.

8. Starhemberg to Kaunitz, Brussels, Nov. 16, 1782, citing from a letter from Linguet to Crumpipen in AG, Chancellerie autrichienne, vol. 506, D. 197, ad litt. L 1, no. 5, P.S., no. 110.

9. Joseph's autograph note to Kaunitz in Kaunitz to Joseph II, Vienna, Nov. 27, 1782, in *ibid.*, no. 5.

10. Belgiojoso's report, Sept. 3, 1783, cited in Charles Piot, "Linguet aux Pays-Bas autrichiens," *Bulletin de l'Académie royale de Belgique*, 2d ser. XLVI (1878), 809.

11. Linguet, "Ouverture de la navigation sur l'Escaut, Etat de la question agitée entre Sa Majesté impériale et les Provinces-Unies à ce sujet," *Annales politiques, civiles et littéraires du dix-huitième siècle*, 19 vols. (London, Brussels, Paris, 1777-92), XI (1784), 443-509.

12. Linguet to Crumpipen, London, Nov. 12, 25, 1784, in OS, DD, B192^b (56).

13. Linguet to Crumpipen, London, Nov. 25, 1784, in *ibid*. The second article appeared in no. 89 of the *Annales*, with the title: "Nouvelles considérations sur l'ouverture de l'Escaut." Linguet included here a "Discours tenu, ou à tenir, par un ministre de France au Conseil d'état à Versailles, sur les vrais intérêts de la Nation, relativement à l'ouverture de l'Escaut," *Annales*, XII (1784), 3-58. Meanwhile, Crumpipen *had* written to Linguet to thank him for his first number: "Nothing is better viewed, better thought out, better stated than the writing you were kind enough to send me a copy of. I devoured it, and re-read it with an unbelievable avidity. Every page, every line leads to admiration: that is the effect that this writing has had here on all opinions." See draft of letter from Crumpipen to Linguet, [Brussels], n.d., in OS, DD, B192^b (56).

14. Linguet to Crumpipen, London, Nov. 25, 1784, in OS, DD, B192^b (56). Linguet made no secret of his intense hatred of Vergennes. He was ready to exploit the Scheldt issue to prove his point. He stated his case most strongly in his letter to Crumpipen of Nov. 29: "...it would be really shocking if the false policy of a single man, of a minister who must begin to be known to you, exposed Europe to the disorder that menaces her: in the past, when I wanted to make you understand that personal resentment was not what made me clairvoyant concerning the disposition of the comte de V[ergennes], and that your court should not have put any trust in them, you didn't believe me; you even seemed to be afraid of appearing to understand me! You will see now whether my ideas were exact...." Linguet to Crumpipen, London, Nov. 29, 1784, in *ibid.*

15. Linguet to Crumpipen, London, Nov. 29, 1784, in *ibid.*

16. Joseph II to Belgiojoso, Nov. 29, 1784, in Felice Calvi, *Curiosita storiche e diplomatiche del succulo decimottavo* (Milan, 1878), p. 463, as cited in Adrienne D. Hytier, "Joseph II, le Cour de Vienne, et les philosophes," *Studies on Voltaire and the Eighteenth Century*, CVI, 249-50, n. 46.

17. Minutes of letter from Crumpipen to Linguet, Dec. 13, 1784, in OS, DD, B192^D (56).

18. Linguet to Crumpipen, Dec. 14, 1784, in *ibid.*

19. Kaunitz to Joseph II, Dec. 19, 1784, with Joseph's commentary appended; Kaunitz to Joseph II, Jan. 31, 1785, with Joseph's commentary appended, as cited in Eugène E. Hubert, ed., *Correspondance des ministres de France accrédités à Bruxelles de 1780 à 1790. Dépêches inédites*, 2 vols. (Brussels, 1920-24), I, 116-17, n. 2.

20. Linguet to Crumpipen, London, Dec. 20, 1784, in OS, DD, B192^b (56).

21. Linguet to Crumpipen, London, Dec. 28, 1784, in *ibid.*

22. Linguet to Crumpipen, London, Jan. 11, 1785, in *ibid*. In the end, of course, Austrian authorities rallied; they rescued the "Considérations" from the flames. They tried to do even more. Count Belgiojoso, who was altogether carried away by Linguet's persuasive rhetoric, and altogether prepared to take extraordinary measures to see that the Belgian population would be as well, ordered the suppression of the comte de Mirabeau's retort to arguments in Linguet's 88th and 89th numbers, Mirabeau's *Doutes sur la liberté de l'Escaut. Reclamée par l'empereur; sur les causes & sur les conséquences probables de cette reclamation. Par le Comte de Mirabeau. Avec une carte du cours de l'Escaut, depuis Anvers jusqu'à la mer* (London, n.d.). The emperor, however, was not willing to go that far. He counter-ordered that no measures be taken against Mirabeau's anti-Austrian brochure. See Belgiojoso to Kaunitz, Brussels, Feb. 27, 1785, in OS, Chancellerie autrichienne, Belgium, Ber. 288, fols. 98-103; Kaunitz to Belgiojoso, March 9, 1785, in *ibid.*, Weis. 53, fol. 19. Joseph's comment, dated Vienna, March 29, 1785, appended to a letter

from Kaunitz to Joseph II, March 30, 1785 [*sic*], in *ibid.*, Weis. 53. For Linguet's comments to Crumpipen on Mirabeau's anti-Austrian propaganda, see Linguet to Crumpipen, n.p., n.d.; Linguet to Crumpipen, London, Feb. 22, 1785, in OS, DD, B192[b] (56).

23. Linguet offered several remarkable excuses for having printed up the beginning of his "Observations." He himself could not evaluate his own work, except from printed proof. His secretary was his printer, and the only person in his entourage who understood French. Printed copy could be viewed, criticized, and corrected by more people, and simultaneously, than could manuscript copy. The secrecy the government was so eager to preserve would not be penetrated: Linguet himself would see that his plates were broken. As for his workers, they knew nothing; they thought they were working on nothing more unusual than another number of the *Annales*. Linguet to Crumpipen, London, Jan. 13, 1785, in OS, DD, B192[b] (56).

24. Linguet to Crumpipen, London, Jan. 13, 1785, in *ibid.*

25. Crumpipen to Linguet, Jan. 24, 1785, in *ibid.*

26. Again, Linguet had prepared a barrage of reasons to support his contention that the work should appear as his own. Published to all outward appearances without any aid from Austrian authorities; published, furthermore, in the *Annales*, and from England, "presque Anglais," the work would be more likely to strike the public as containing an objective account of the Scheldt crisis. Again, if so timely a work appeared in the *Annales*, literary pirates would be certain to reprint it! "...in a week, 20,000 copies will be in print; there will be perhaps 100,000 readers. It is this consideration which decided the Dutch to make their gazettes their arsenals: I believe that, at least on this point, we can approximate their politics a little." Furthermore, Linguet argued, any errors that appeared would be attributed to him, and he could correct them, without embarrassment, in later numbers of the *Annales*. Then also, there were issues relating to the Scheldt crisis which he, a journalist, could broach, but which neither the Austrian nor the Dutch governments would be free to handle. Finally, distribution of the "Observations" in the *Annales* would guarantee an automatically wide publicity for the emperor's cause. See Linguet to Crumpipen, Feb. 4, 1785, in *ibid.*

27. Crumpipen to Linguet, Brussels, Feb. 14, 1785, with appended "Note de quelques changemens qui paraissent pouvoir être faits dans l'ouvrage intitulé 'Observations sur le manifeste des Etats-Généraux,'" in *ibid.*

28. Linguet to Crumpipen, London, Feb. 15, 1785, in *ibid.* In a letter to Mercy-Argenteau on Feb. 19, 1785, Linguet gave a fuller development to his fears. He believed the government's silence might be a sign that he had lost the emperor's confidence; and he thought France's "cordoned Tartuffe," Vergennes, might be responsible. He complained and boasted to Mercy-Argenteau that had he received inside government information two months earlier, "...everything would perhaps be over already." Had he been able to publicize Austria's position earlier than that, maybe the crisis would never have developed, because while Vergennes might have been able to close his eyes to the truth, "...he would not have closed them to Europe." Linguet to Mercy-Argenteau, London, Feb. 19, 1785, in BM, 1916.

29. Linguet to Crumpipen, Feb. 22, 1785, in OS, DD, B192[b] (56). On March 23, 1785, Linguet sent off a package with still another 150 copies—this time of an edition he had put together by combining his four numbers of the *Annales* into a single volume. These copies, he instructed, must go to France, "in order to make up, insofar as I can, and for the good of the cause, for the interference which the distribution of the numbers is still encountering, as I expected."

30. Minutes of Crumpipen to Linguet, March 1, 1785, in OS, DD, B192[b] (56).

31. Linguet to Belgiojoso, London, July 15, 1785, in AG, MSS divers, no. 1498, fols. 46-48. For Linguet's earlier reflections on his hopes and plans for a resettlement in Belgium, see Linguet to Crumpipen, London, May 3, 1785, June 3, 1785, in OS, DD, B192[b] (56). For Crumpipen's invitation to Linguet to speak freely about "the marks of approbation, the encouragements, the facilities, or whatever the favors are that you desire," see Crumpipen to Linguet, Brussels, July 2, 1785, in *ibid.*

32. Copy of letter from Linguet to Joseph II, enclosed by Linguet with his letter to Belgiojoso, London, July 15, 1785, in AG, MSS divers, no. 1498, fol. 49.

33. Linguet to Crumpipen, London, July 15, 1785, in *ibid.*, fols. 51-52v. On July 22, 1785, Linguet sent Crumpipen another copy of his memoir to the French king; he asked that it be forwarded to Mercy-Argenteau. Linguet to Crumpipen, London, July 22, 1785, in *ibid.*

34. Linguet to Crumpipen, London, Aug. 30, 1785, in *ibid.*, fols. 54-59.

35. Belgiojoso to Kaunitz, Brussels, Sept. 3, 1785, in AG, Chancellerie autrichienne, vol. 524, D. 109, ad litt. L 4, no. 1, P.S. ad no. 92. For discussion of the motives of Austrian authorities, including Belgiojoso, in encouraging Linguet to return to Belgium, see Piot, "Linguet aux Pays-Bas autrichiens," 812.

36. Kaunitz to Joseph II, Vienna, Sept. 24, 1785, in AG, Chancellerie autrichienne, vol. 524, D. 109, ad litt. L 4, no. 2. Kaunitz's hunch was not misplaced. Vergennes was furious, and had been for months, over Linguet's politicking against him on an international scale. He confided as much to Louis XVI: "When a Linguet is hired by a foreign court to speak ill of me; when he attacks me on the subject of my personal comportment, that is a very unimportant matter, but it ceases to be so when, in criticizing the direction of political affairs, it is no longer I whom he attacks but rather the principles Your Majesty has in view. The same observation holds for all departments, because all with one exception, are the object of the most irreverent criticism...." Copy of Vergennes to Louis XVI, Feb. 6, 1785, in Archives, Ministère des affaires étrangères, Mémoires et documents, France, vol. 1897, fol. 148. I am grateful to Svetlana Kluge Harris for locating the original of this dispatch for me in AN, K164 (no. 3).

37. Joseph's commentary on Kaunitz to Joseph II, Vienna, Sept. 24, 1785, in AG, Chancellerie autrichienne, vol. 524, D. 109, ad litt. L 4, no. 2. Kaunitz communicated Joseph's decision to Belgiojoso in Brussels. See Kaunitz to Belgiojoso, Vienna, Sept. 28, 1785, in OS, Belgium, Weis. 54.

38. See Piot, "Linguet aux Pays-Bas autrichiens," 813. See also Kaunitz to Belgiojoso, Vienna, March 15, 1786, in AG, Rapports du Chancelier de Cour et D'Etat pour demandes de titres de noblesse, vol. 794, G. 10, ad litt. 218, ad A 23. Linguet's coat of arms showed two silver pens [for Linguet's accomplishments in letters] set on a blue background, with a silver chief of shield decorated with three langued gules [standing for Linguet's name, or for his oratorical skills] ; the coat of arms was topped by a silver helmet decorated with a golden crown, and the motto: *Decus et tutamen*. Piot, "Linguet aux Pays-Bas autrichiens," 813, n. 1. See also "Lettres patentes de noblesse avec la couronne d'or en faveur de Simon-Nicolas-Henri de Linguet [Vienna, March 22, 1786], in AG, Chancellerie autrichienne des Pays-Bas, vol. 779, fols. 224-26. Reporting details of Linguet's forthcoming ennoblement to Belgiojoso, Kaunitz noted that the Austrian government was conferring these honors to thank Linguet for his support during the Scheldt dispute, and to protect him against the French magistrature's schemes to foil his attempts to obtain justice in French courts. Kaunitz instructed Belgiojoso to contact Mercy-Argenteau in Paris to try to appease Vergennes. He was to inform the French secretary of state that Linguet would be better watched in Brussels than in London, "where he cannot be supervised in any way." He also remarked that the Austrians had now made themselves responsible for Linguet's conduct: "...doubtless, measures must be taken so that he doesn't fall back into his old errors...." Kaunitz to Belgiojoso, Vienna, March 15, 1786, in AG, Chancellerie autrichienne des Pays-Bas, Rapports du Chancelier de Cour et d'Etat sur demandes de titres de noblesse, vol. 794, G. 10, ad no. 218, P.S. ad no. 23.

39. Linguet, *Mémoire au Roi, par M. Linguet, concernant ses réclamations actuellement pendantes au Parlement de Paris* (London, 1786).

40. See Linguet, *Plaidoyer pour S.-N.-H. Linguet, Ecuier, ancien avocat au Parlement de Paris, prononcé par lui-même en la Grand'Chambre, dans sa discussion avec M. le duc d'Aiguillon, pair de France, ancien commandant pour le Roi en Bretagne* (London and Brussels. 1787).

41. See Linguet, *Précis et consultation dans la cause entre Simon-Nicolas-Henri Linguet, ecuyer, et Charles-Joseph Panckoucke, libraire à Paris* (Paris, 1787), pp. 31, 38.

42. Linguet, *Défenses pour M. Linguet, sur la demande en réparation d'honneur et en dommages-intérêts formée contre lui au Châtelet de Paris, par le S[ieur] P[ierre] Le Quesne, marchand d'étoffes de soie* (n.p., n.d.).

43. Joseph II to Mercy-Argenteau, Vienna, April 1, 1786, as cited in Jules Flammermont and Alfred d'Arneth, eds., *Correspondance secrète du Comte de Mercy-Argenteau avec l'Empereur Joseph II et le Prince de Kaunitz,* 2 vols. (Paris, 1889-91), II, 14-15.

44. Kaunitz to Mercy-Argenteau, Vienna, April 1, and Mercy-Argenteau to Kaunitz, Paris, April 18, 1786, as cited in *ibid.,* 15-16, 18. Mercy-Argenteau added that with wisdom and the pull that Kaunitz had deigned to offer him, Linguet could win out.

45. Mercy-Argenteau to Kaunitz, Paris, May 23, 1786, as cited in *ibid.,* 26.

46. See for example Kaunitz to Mercy-Argenteau, Vienna, "the first of the year" [1787], as cited in *ibid.,* 65.

47. Linguet to Perrégaux, Brussels, May 17, 1787, in BM, Collections d'autographes, première collection de la ville, vol. II, 81. For details of Linguet's business relations with Perrégaux, including Perrégaux's handling of subscriptions for the *Annales,* see Linguet to Perrégaux, Brussels, May 22, 1787, in *ibid.,* 82; Linguet to Perrégaux: Paris, July 29, 1787; Brussels, Jan. 13, Jan. 25, April 17. Sept. 18, 1788, July 26, 1789; Paris, May 10, 1790, in BM, Collections d'autographes, première collection de la ville, vol. II, 83.

48. Linguet, *Mémoire au Roi,* pp. 30-31, 32.

49. Louis Petit de Bachaumont, *Mémoires secrets, pour servir à l'histoire de la république des lettres en France, depuis MDCCLXII jusqu'à nos jours; ou Journal d'un observateur,* 36 vols. (London, 1780-89), XXXII (July 23, 1786), 213-14; XXXII (Aug. 4, 1786), 242. For details of Linguet's other suits in civil law pending at this time see Linguet, *Défenses pour M. Linguet;* Linguet, *Précis et consultation dans la cause entre Simon-Nicolas-Henri Linguet, ecuyer, et Charles-Joseph Panckoucke, libraire à Paris* (Paris, 1787); Linguet, *Mémoire au Roi.*

50. Bachaumont, *Mémoires secrets,* XXXII (Aug. 25, 1786), 296.

51. *Ibid.* (Aug. 26, 29, 1786), 304-5, 315.

52. *Ibid.,* (Sept. 3, 4, 1786), 326-27, 332. For another account of the pandemonium at the Palais de Justice, see: [M.Q.,] *Lettre d'un jeune clerc, adressée à M. Linguet, sur l'audience du 2 septembre 1786* (n.p., n.d.). The writer, in his lightly satirical account, recorded that by 4:30 in the morning, a thousand spectators had gathered (p. 7). The account concludes: "Your return, Sir, into our capital, is that of a Roman general who, having won a battle, received his laurels from the hands of friendship and was led in triumph by the people whose rights he had just upheld" (p. 14). See also Siméon-Prosper Hardy, "Mes Loisirs, ou Journal d'événemens tels qu'ils parviennent à ma connoissance (1764-1789)," entry for Sept. 2, 1786, BN, MSS fr., vol. 6685, fol. 421.

53. The term is Hardy's. See Hardy, "Mes Loisirs," entry for Sept. 2, 1786, in BN, MSS fr., vol. 6685, fol. 421. See also anon., *Au Public. Sentiment sur Linguet* (n.p., n.d.), p. 6. For an excellent account of these sessions, and an appraisal of their import, see Marcel Marion, *La Bretagne et le Duc d'Aiguillon, 1753-1770* (Paris, 1898), pp. 590ff. For Linguet's appraisal, see *Mémoire au Roi,* pp. 30ff.

54. Bachaumont, *Mémoires secrets,* XXXIV (March 11, 1787), 274ff.; in the entry for April 1, 1787, the *Mémoires secrets* records that the King's Council annulled the Paris parlement's decree of March 11, although it was noted that d'Aiguillon already had paid Linguet, and that the whole episode had been engineered as a face-saving device for d'Aiguillon. Bachaumont, *Mémoires secrets,* XXXIV (April 1, 1787), 346. See also Hardy, "Mes Loisirs," entry for April 3, 1787, in BN, MSS fr., vol. 6686, fol. 40. The day this decision was handed down, rumors began to circulate that Simon Linguet was about to clinch a second victory; that the Paris Bar would be forced to reinstate him. See Hardy, "Mes Loisirs," entry for March 10, 1787, in *ibid.,* fol. 15. These triumphs were almost too miraculous. Was some party out to disgrace d'Aiguillon? See Hardy, "Mes Loisirs," entry for Sept. 7, 1786, in *ibid.,* vol. 6685, fol. 425. An even more intriguing possibility was that powerful political figures in high places had joined forces to reinstate Linguet in

order to signal to the Paris parlement and the Paris Bar, which together had sealed his professional fate, that their days were numbered.

55. Bachaumont, *Mémoires secrets*, XXXIV (March 11, 1787), 280-81.

56. Linguet, *Mémoire au Roi*, pp. 4-5, 43.

57. One historian of the prerevolution noted that Linguet was well qualified to come to the ministry's aid; his enmity toward the *parlementaires* was notorious. The aristocratic party went further, and accused the government of buying Linguet's propaganda services. Marcel Marion, *Le Garde des sceaux Lamoignon, et la réforme judiciaire de 1788* (Paris, 1905), pp. 209-10. See also Jean Egret, *La Prérévolution française, 1787-1788* (Paris, 1962), p. 273. I have turned up no evidence to support the allegation that Linguet was being paid by the government during the period of the prerevolutionary crisis. What is clear is that he was in close contact, at least with Keeper of the Seals Lamoignon, during the government's struggle with the *parlementaires*. In May, 1787, Linguet made use of an offer by Madame Perrégaux, the wife of Jean-Frédéric Perrégaux, his friend and banker in Paris, to have a letter hand-delivered to Lamoignon. However, I have not located this letter, and in his references to it, Linguet offers no hint of its contents. Linguet to Perrégaux, Brussels, May 17, 1787; see also same to same, May 22, 1787, in BM, collections d'autographes, première collection de la ville, II, 81, 82. Linguet throws further light on his services to Lamoignon in a letter of Feb. 18, 1789, to Count Trauttmansdorff, Joseph II's minister plenipotentiary in Brussels. In a bid for Trauttmansdorff's support for his attempt to acquire a piece of property in Belgium, Linguet recalled that at the beginning of 1788, he had the possibility of assuming a high position in France as *avocat aux conseils*. The post had been bequeathed to him by his half-brother Antoine. "The circumstance was favorable...for me to get myself received. The French minister at the time had the will and the power to support me. I was, at the time, his counsel, as I was his defender later, I dare to say his savior." He added, by way of explanation for his refusal to take up the position, "But if I believed that without doing any injury to the gratitude, the fidelity, I owe to the emperor, I could give to administrators in my former country pieces of advice which unfortunately they only half-adopted, and an aid which contributed a great deal in France to the present revolution, I did not believe that I could, in the same way, contract engagements which would have taken from his majesty a useless subject, to be sure—because instead of his being used, he was not stopped being insulted...—but a very submissive subject, a very devoted one, who swore never to recognize any other sovereign." Linguet to Trauttmansdorff, Brussels, Feb. 18, 1789, in AG, MSS divers, no. 5117, no. 11.

58. Egret, *La Pré-révolution française*, pp. 20-21.

59. *Ibid.*, pp. 39-54.

60. See J. B. M. Vignes, *Histoire des doctrines sur l'impôt en France: Les Origines et les destinées de la dixme royale de Vauban* (Paris, 1909), *passim*.

61. Linguet, *La Dixme royale, avec de courtes réflexions sur ce qu'on appelle la contrabande et l'usage de regarder comme inaliénable le domaine de nos rois* (The Hague, 1764).

62. Linguet, *L'Impôt territorial, ou la dixme roiale, Avec tous ses avantages* (London, 1787). Linguet first reintroduced this project in 1779, in an article appearing in his *Annales:* "Réflexions sur les finances et sur l'établissement d'une dixme royale," *Annales*, VI (1779), 457-504. He included further reflections on the project in his *Annales* of February, 1780: "Eclaircissemens sur le projet de la dixme royale," *Annales*, VIII (1780), 29-59, 85-116.

63. Linguet, *L'Impôt territorial*, pp. 7-8. See also Egret, *La Pré-révolution française*, p. 29. Linguet was making an oblique reference to physiocratic sentiments professed by Notables who objected strenuously to Calonne's property tax because it taxed a gross, not net agricultural product. Vignes, *Histoire des doctrines sur l'impôt*, p. 61.

64. See Chapter Seven, pp. 291-92. Calonne saw the tax exclusively as an expedient financial measure; in the face of persistent opposition from the Notables he was prepared to abandon the provision for a tax collectable in the form of foodstuffs.

65. Egret, *La Pré-révolution française*, pp. 169-71.

66. *Ibid.*, pp. 173-82.

67. *Ibid.*, pp. 188-203.

68. *Ibid.*, pp. 249, 247, 122-32. Lamoignon was a *président* of the Grand'Chambre of the Paris parlement when Linguet made his debut as a lawyer in the 1760s. It is possible that he read Linguet's *Nécessité d'une réforme*. In his propaganda campaign to win support for his program of radical administrative reform, Lamoignon was clearly exploiting Linguet's talents for publicizing pro-monarchical convictions.

69. "Would it be necessary for me to change systems today, just because I no longer have any grounds for complaint? Would I have to disown my own doctrine just because enlightened, virtuous ministers are reconciled to it, because they finally have the courage, coupled with the power, to do the good which for the past twenty years I could only point out, recommend?" *Annales*, XIV (1788), 371-72. In his *Lettres de M. Linguet au Comte de Trauttmansdorff, ministre plenipotentiaire pour l'Empereur aux Pays-bas en 1788 et 1789* (Brussels, 1790), Linguet modestly indicated the reason for his keen interest in Lamoignon's reform program. It was, after all, his own: "...it was the subject of his debut in literature, of his first work, rare today because he never had it reprinted; unpublicized by the journalists because he never lowered himself to the little strategems which govern these announcements—but well known to impartial, informed men...." He named his *Nécessité d'une réforme dans l'administration de la justice et dans les lois civiles en France, avec la réfutation de quelques passages de "L'Esprit des lois"* (Amsterdam, 1764). He then went on to note that Lamoignon had taken all his ideas from the *Nécissité d'une réforme*, but had completely denatured them, although those very ideas were echoed "in almost all the *cahiers*," p. 18, n. 1.

70. Guy-Marie Sallier, *Annales françaises, depuis le commencement du règne de Louis XVI, jusqu'aux Etats-généraux (1774-1789)*, 2d ed. (Paris, 1813), p. 194, as cited in Egret, *La Pré-révolution française*, p. 263.

71. See Linguet, *Annales*, XV (1788), 180-82. Linguet warned in his *Annales*, XV, 283-86, that civil war might turn out to be only the prelude to a universal upheaval of the "Nation," the "people."

72. *Ibid.*, 98.

73. Egret, *La Pré-révolution française*, pp. 313-17, 320.

74. Linguet to Perrégaux, Brussels, Sept. 18, 1788, in BM, Collections d'autographes, première collection de la ville, vol. II, fol. 83.

75. Linguet, "Réflexions sur la dette nationale en France: la Nation y est-elle obligée comme en Angleterre?" *Annales*, XV, 218-36. Linguet republished the proposal in 1789 as *De la dette nationale et du crédit public en France* (Brussels, 1789). Linguet first presented the issue much earlier. See "Supplément à la notice donnée l'année dernière sur l'Administration de M. l'Abbé Terrai, & c.," *Annales*, VI, 285-314. See also Linguet's "Arrêt du Conseil d'état du 18 octobre 1778, portant établissement d'un nouvel ordre pour toutes les caisses de dépenses," *Annales*, IV, 257-70; V, 10-33.

76. Linguet, "Réflexions sur la dette nationale en France," *Annales*, XV, 223-27. Linguet himself was not averse to risking his fortune in these speculations. He insisted, however, that they were just like any other risky venture. He might lose everything he had put in, without acquiring any special right to claim anything. Linguet stated his position in a letter to the banker Perrégaux. He was discussing the financial crisis that had led to the dismissal of Lamoignon and Brienne. The crisis itself was precipitated by the government's inability to find bankers to supply enough money to pay off short-term loans and contract new ones, and this failure had led to a sharp drop in the worth of the loans. Linguet announced to Perrégaux that he was very lucky to have escaped speculating in government issues. Had he been in Paris at the time, he would have taken his chances. "Right now I would not risk the same speculation, and everything considered, I am not all that proud of having missed out on the other one. Because although basically there isn't anything alarming about limiting oneself absolutely to running the risk of a scheme that could turn out well, or badly, I also am firmly convinced, as you will see in number 115 [116?] of my *Annales* that there wouldn't be anything unwarranted in the revolution which annulled all these alleged obligations of the government: if I had my pocketbook filled with these securities, I would not have struck out a line of what I say about them."

Linguet to Perrégaux, Brussels, Sept. 18, 1788, in BM, Collections d'autographes, première collection de la ville, vol. II, fol. 83.

77. For an illuminating discussion of the politics of prerevolutionary capitalism, consult George V. Taylor, "The Paris Bourse on the Eve of the French Revolution, 1781-1789," *American Historical Review,* 67 (1962), 951-77.

78. See for example [Etienne Clavière], *De la foi publique envers les créanciers de l'état...* (London, 1788).

79. Address of Antoine-Louis Séguier, Advocate-General of the Parlement of Paris, to all chambers of parlement, Sept. 27, 1788, reprinted in *Introduction historique, contenant un abrégé des anciens Etats-généraux, des Assemblées des notables, et des principaux événements qui ont amené la Révolution* (Paris, 1847), pp. 335-37. The *Introduction historique* is the unnumbered first volume of the *Moniteur universel, Réimpression de l'ancien "Moniteur," seule histoire authentique et inaltérée de la Révolution française, depuis la réunion des Etats-généraux jusqu'au Consulat...* 32 vols. (Paris, 1847-50). Séguier acknowledged that Linguet had created for himself a profession in journalism that included statesmanship, international law, and political administration: "He would like ...to make use of peoples and crowns for his own purposes; and in the delirium of his blind presumption, he has set himself up as critic, as reformer of all nations, of all political bodies, of all governments." *Ibid.,* p. 355.

80. Linguet, *Onguent pour la brûlure, ou Observations sur un réquisitoire imprimé en tête de l'arrêt du Parlement de Paris du 27 septembre 1788, rendu contre les "Annales" de M. Linguet, avec des réflexions sur l'usage de faire brûler les livres par la main du bourreau* (London, 1788).

81. Linguet, *La France plus qu'angloise...* (Brussels, 1788).

82. Linguet, *La France plus qu'angloise,* p. 26.

83. *Ibid.,* p. 3.

84. Linguet, "Au Roi de France," *La France plus qu'angloise,* p. 16.

85. *Ibid.,* p. 7, p. 30 n. 2.

86. Linguet, "Protestations de l'auteur des *Annales* tant contre l'Arrêt ci-dessus [the arrêt of the Paris parlement against no. 116 of the *Annales*] que contre les précédens, et subséquens," *Annales,* XV, 388.

87. Refuting the parlement's protests that the edicts of May, 1788, were unconstitutional, Linguet countercharged: "The abuses which this salutary reform attacks are the *Constitution* of the *French* magistrature unfortunately: but they are not the *Constitutions of the monarchy.*" Linguet, *La France plus qu'angloise,* p. 28, n. 1. Linguet insisted that if the Estates-General was convoked according to the forms of 1614, the First and Second Estates would join forces on every issue: "...it is obvious that by the force of things alone, a secret league will be established between these powerful bodies, all the more indissoluble because a mutual interest will be its bond, and all the more preponderant because it will find in the protests of the *Third Estate...* only an easily surmountable obstacle." *Ibid.,* p. 44, and see pp. 43ff. Linguet added that if the forms of 1614 were followed, then the representatives elected from the Third Estate would turn out to be men who owed their position to the aristocratic magistrature and who, therefore, would be only "the slaves of the magistrature." *Ibid.,* pp. 44-45, 50-51. Once convened, he argued, the Estates-General would reform civil and criminal law from the bottom up, and therefore, "As for this assembly [the Estates-General], the parlements therefore would not want it; on the contrary they would fear it...." Linguet disposed of the principle of the general will quickly enough: the general will was only aristocratic self-interest expressed in a vocabulary of universals: "The outcry—not *public,* but self-interested—from *bodies* which for several months have been invoking the *general will* in order to bring about the triumph of their own—this outcry tends to deprive the throne of its own [will]." *Ibid.,* p. 121.

88. Linguet, *La France plus qu'angloise,* p. 77.

89. *Ibid.,* pp. 104-5.

90. Linguet, Commentary on "Discours prononcés à Versailles à l'ouverture de l'Assemblée des Notables du 6 November 1788," *Annales,* XV, 430.

91. Linguet, "France: Nouvelle Assemblée des Notables," *ibid.,* 417.

92. Egret, *La Pré-révolution française*, pp. 364-65, 354.

93. Linguet, "Nouvelle insurrection bretonne, mais raisonnable et fondée. Vœux légitimes que forme le Tiers-Etat à Nantes et dans toute la Bretagne," *Annales*, XV, 431.

94. Linguet, "Efforts de Tiers-état pour parvenir à une libre et égale représentation dans l'Assemblée nationale," *Annales*, XV, 449, 450.

95. Linguet, *Avis aux Parisiens. Par M. Linguet. Appel de toutes convocations d'Etats-généraux où les députés du troisième ordre ne seroient pas supéieurs en nombre aux deux autres* (n.p., 1789). The dating on the first edition of this pamphlet is uncertain. Ambrose Saricks, in *A Bibliography of the Frank E. Melvin Collection of Pamphlets of the French Revolution in the University of Kansas Libararies* (Lawrence, Kans., 1960), no. 160, dates the pamphlet 1788, although the copy he refers to there is undated. The 1789 edition is cited hereafter as *Avis*.

96. "Representatives must be in proportion to represented, therefore twenty-four million must have more deputies than 600,000." *Avis*, p. 12.

97. *L*, I, 65; Linguet, "Développement et conséquences de ce qui a été dit ci-devant sur les lits de justice. Quand, pourquoi, où les enregistremens des loix sont nécessaires. De la nature du pouvoir des Etats-généraux," *Annales*, XV, 172.

98. Linguet, *Réponse aux docteurs modernes, ou Apologies pour l'auteur de la "Théorie des lois" et les "Lettres" sur cette "Théorie," Avec la réfutation du système des philosophes économistes*, 2 vols. (n.p., 1771), I, 245-51; Linguet, *Du plus heureux gouvernement, ou Parallèle des constitutions politiques de l'Asie avec celles de l'Europe, servant d'introduction à la "Théorie des lois civiles,"* 2 vols. in one (London, 1774), I, xx; *L*, I, 181.

99. See for example, Linguet on the Estates-General, in *La Théorie des lois civiles*, new ed., 3 vols. (London, 1774), I, 90-92, cited hereafter as *L-1774*.

100. See Chapter two.

101. Linguet, "Réflexions préliminaires," *Annales*, I (1777), 102-3; Linguet, *La France plus qu'angloise*, pp. 144-46.

102. Linguet, "Explication du principe avancé dans le numéro 26 de ces *Annales*, sur les effets de la force en politique," *Annales*, IV, 199-234; article cited hereafter as "Force."

103. Linguet, *Supplément aux "Réflexions pour Me Linguet, avocat de la Comtesse de Béthune,"* in Linguet, *Appel à la postérité, ou Recueil des mémoires et plaidoyers de M. Linguet pour lui-même, contre la communauté des avocats du Parlement de Paris* (n.p., 1779), pp. 363-64.

104. Linguet protested the parlementary *arrêt* that condemned his 116th number to be suppressed and burned. He charged that the *arrêt* was "une infraction des lois sociales, un violation réfléchie de toutes les espèces de propriétés..." *Annales*, XV, 382.

105. Linguet, *RDM*, II, 53-54.

106. Linguet, *L-1774*, I, 90-91.

107. Linguet discussed the second possibility briefly in his *Annales*, I, 102. He refuses in the *Théorie des lois civiles*, I, 65, to say more than that "all society" would totter.

108. Linguet, *Lettre de M. Linguet à M. le Comte de Vergennes, ministre des affaires étrangères en France* (London, 1777), p. 22.

109. Linguet depicted in detail how armies of recruits were dehumanized with calculation, debased as a matter of policy into platoons of men-machines: "Isn't [the soldier's] first duty and his greatest merit to be deaf, pitiless, as obedient as his gun?" *Annales*, I, 23. He observed that a soldier's wages were equivalent in purchasing power to exactly what had been doled out to him in the middle ages: "...they showed more consideration for horses." *Ibid.*, 27-28. He was not even adequately equipped. The calculus of interest dictated to war ministers that the cost of replacing him was lower than the cost of equipping him. "Now philosophic ministers have made a very simple calculation: finding that it would cost less to buy and nourish a gunner than to accoutre him in bronze, they have embraced the policy of delivering him up under fire entirely naked; in this way, he turns out to be, of all weapons, the one which is obtained and squandered most cheaply." *Ibid.*, 31. He warned that if these automaton defenders, these "ravenous grasshoppers," ever unleashed themselves and turned against the interests they were being prodded to

support, their upheaval would be fatal to the existent socio-political order. *Ibid.*, 20, 24. Linguet followed these preliminary reflections with an article in his *Annales* for February, 1778: "Réflexions sur le droit de la guerre en lui-même." *Annales*, III (1778), 351-64.

110. See discussion in Chapter Five.

111. Linguet first announced Briatte's work in a number of his *Annales* in 1779. To enlighten several confused readers, he pointed out that the author really existed, that he himself had not adopted "Briatte" as a pseudonym to write concerning mendicity. He identified Briatte as the pastor of a Walloon church at Namur. See Linguet, "Réflexions sur les finances et sur l'établissement d'une dixme royale," *Annales*, VI, 503-4, n. 1. The complete title of Jean-Baptiste Briatte's work was: *Offrande à l'humanité, ou Traité sur les causes de la misère en général, et de la mendicité en particulier; sur les moyen de tarir la première, & de détruire la second. Ouvrage imprimé au profit des pauvres par M. Briatte, Pasteur de l'Eglise wallonne de Namur*, Vol. 1 (Amsterdam, 1780).

112. In typical fashion, Linguet noted Briatte's frequent borrowing from his own works. *Annales*, IX (1780), 322, 323.

113. For an excellent recent study of poverty in the *ancien régime* (measured in terms of the incidence of mendicity, vagabondage, criminality, etc. in the region around Lyons) see Jean-Pierre Gutton, *La Société et les pauvres: l'exemple de la généralité de Lyon (1534-1789)* (Paris, 1971). Gutton offers a survey of changing views among administrators, theorists, and reformers concerning society's obligations to various classes of the poor (although he does not single out Linguet's critiques and programs). See also Olwen H. Hufton, *The Poor of Eighteenth Century France, 1750-1789* (Oxford, 1974).

114. Christian Paultre, *De la répression de la mendicité et du vagabondage en France sous l'ancien régime* (Paris, 1906), pp. 410ff., 512ff.

115. Shortly before Linguet publicized his essay contest, the Académie des sciences, belles-lettres et arts de Chalons-sur-Marne issued a similar announcement for entries on the subject: "Sur les moyens de détruire la mendicité en France en rendant les mendiants utiles à l'état sans les rendre malheureux." See Camille Bloch, *L'Assistance et l'état en France à la veille de la Révolution* (Paris, 1909), p. 211.

116. See François Métra, J. Imbert, de Boudeaux, et al., eds., *Correspondance secrète, politique, et littéraire, ou Mémoires pour servir à l'histoire des cours, des sociétés, et de la littérature en France depuis la mort de Louis XV*, 18 vols. (London, 1787-90), XIII (Paris, Oct. 19, 1782), 338. At least one observer, the young Madame Roland, found Linguet's contest revolting. This devotee of republican principles considered Linguet's practice of political journalism insolent; she found his evaluation of the psycho-economic motivations of philanthropic gestures in modern society blatantly vulgar. "What presumption for a private person without titles to offer a sum of money to excite talent! ...Who would allow himself to be aroused by sordid gain, and who would be willing to submit himself to judges chosen by Linguet?...but again, for a man sprung from the mob to set himself up as the arbiter of genius and to make a show of paying from his wallet is a ridiculous insolence...." Madame Roland "aux deux sœurs" [Demoiselles Cannet], May 7, 1778, in Marie-Jeanne Phlipon Roland de la Platière, *Lettres de Madame Roland, nouvelle serie, 1767-1780*, ed. Claude Perroud, 2 vols., Collection de documents inédits sur l'histoire de France, publié par les soins du ministre de l'instruction publique, series IV, vol. 7 (Paris, 1913-15), II, 265. Madame Roland's attitude toward Linguet was somewhat inconsistent, however. See Madame Roland to Sophie Cannet, April 22, 1778, in *ibid.*, 258.

117. Linguet, *Plan d'etablissemens tendans à l'extinction de la mendicité* (Paris, 1779). The work was printed with French Government approval and, Linguet intimated, with government backing. Cited hereafter as *Plan*.

118. For a tentative interpretation of Linguet's proposals as a call for a mandatory sliding salary scale for workers, see J. Conan, "Linguet, précurseur de l'échelle mobile des salaires?" *Annales historiques de la Révolution française*, XXIII (1951), 86-87.

119. Linguet continued the discussion in a later number of his *Annales*. See "Lettre à l'auteur des *Annales* sur ce qu'il a dit dans son no. 99 de la souscription proposée par la Communauté de la fabrique de Lyon," *Annales*, XIII, 355-62; Linguet, "Réponse. Ré-

flexions sur l'état actuel des manufactures françoises, et sur la préférence donnée presque en tout genre par les François même aux productions des manufactures angloises," *ibid.*, 363-86. Here Linguet began by apologizing for his harshness toward the manufacturers of Lyons; he now saw them as pawns within an ironclad economic system and described their position as that of victims and victimizers—at one and the same time. Then he turned around and accused French manufacturers and traders of lacking the cunning, ambition, skill, and entrepreneurial spirit of their successful English rivals; he urged the French on to a more energetic and inventive competitiveness with the English, 371ff. See Chapter Seven, note 40.

120. Linguet himself never uses the term Fourth Estate. For a critical analysis of the term in the context of social and economic group structures and relationships under the *ancien régime*, see Albert Soboul, *La Civilisation et la Révolution française*, 2 vols. (Paris, 1970-), I, Part IV: Le Quatrième état.

121. Linguet was not entirely alone in having distinguished the separate, still unrecognized interests of a class of the poor, over against the interests of the Third Estate. See Jean-Baptist Bremond, *Premières Observations au peuple françois sur la quadruple aristocratie qui existe depuis deux siècles, sous le nom de haut clergé, de possédants fiefs, de magistrats, et du haut tiers; et vues générales sur la constitution et la félicité publique* (Versailles, 1789); Louis Pierre Dufourny de Villiers, *Cahiers du quatrieme ordre, celui des pauvres journaliers, des infirmes, des indigents, & c., l'ordre sacré des infortunés; Ou Correspondance philantropique entre les infortunés, les hommes sensibles, et les Etats-généraux: pour suppléer au droit de députer directement aux Etats, qui appartient à tout François, mais dont cet ordre ne jouit pas encore,* no. 1 (Paris, April 25, 1789). Both cited in René Roux, "La Révolution française et l'idée de la lutte des classes," *Revue d'histoire économique et sociale,* XXIX (1951), 258-59.

122. See Chapter Seven for discussion.

123. For detailed discussion of themes summarized here, see Chapter Two. For Linguet on the origins of property, see *L*, I, 278-353; on property as the central determinant of societal institutions and relationships, *L*, I, 61-62; on measures for the legitimacy of political sovereigns, see *L*, I, 80-81; on the origins of the Third Estate, *L*, II, 449, 480ff.; on new kinds of propertied holdings and the Third Estate's claims for protections, *L*, I, 56, and *NR*, pp. 32-33; on the legitimacy of revolutions by expropriated property owners, *L*, I, 78-80.

124. For detailed analysis of themes recapitulated here, see Chapter three. For Linguet's analyses of the permanent condition of the masses, see *L*, II, 509-10; for his discussion of the impact of economic laws on the lives of the poor, see, for example, *PB*, p. 123; *L*, II, 466, 468, 482; *Annales*, XIII, 500. For Karl Marx's commentary on Linguet's analyses, see his *Theories of Surplus Value*, trans. Emile Burns, ed. S. Ryazanskaya, 3 vols. (Moscow, 1969), I, 345-50; for Linguet's refutations of physiocratic principles, see *PB, passim*, but especially, pp. 33ff.

125. For Linguet's discussion of the highest political priorities of monarchical administration, see *PB*, xxvii-xxviii; for his analyses of the consequences of government's failure to assign priority in its policy-making to government guarantees of provisionment in subsistence commodities, see "Suite de la lettre de M. Linguet à M. l'Abbé Roubaud," in *Journal de politique et de littérature*, no. 6 (Dec. 15, 1774), 232.

126. For Linguet's views on the nature and consequences of the revolution of rising popular expectations in the context of the non-elites' rigidly limited material circumstances, see Linguet, "Suite de la lettre de M. Linguet à M. l'Abbé Roubaud," *Journal de politique et de littérature*, no. 6 (Dec. 15, 1774), 229; and also *ibid.*, no. 5 (Dec. 5, 1774), 192, 193; *PB*, pp. 292ff.; *L*, II, 511-19; *Annales*, I, 102-3.

❖

Master Plan for
Harnessing a Revolution

Revolutionary Forecasts and Correctives

"Right now a very turbulent, very restless spirit hovers over Europe," Linguet wrote in April, 1788.[1] For decades, the French Cassandra had been broadcasting unsettling analyses of societal crises and forecasts of revolutions. He specialized in analyzing the explosive potential in contemporary events and trends: the French public's appropriations and application of American revolutionary ideology, for example; or a runaway enlightenment, "philosophisme"; or economic slumps, intensification of misery and unrest among the masses, chronic financial crises, aristocratic insubordination expressed as insurrection in the judiciary.[2]

He read natural upheavals also as though they portended imminent societal disturbances. It was customary in eighteenth-century political parlance for theorists to invoke nature to justify rebellions against societal injustices, as though nature were order, harmony, equilibrium, and reason, and as though the laws of nature offered rational political models for imitation. Linguet's understanding of the matter was different. He insisted that in civil society, where all laws were artificial contrivances designed to contain classes of men dragged from nature by violence, nature itself intruded only as the grand avenging annihilator—the untamable bolt of lightning that would destroy political society, its laws, its reason, its harmony, and its institutions, starting perhaps with the Bastille. Nature was a power-generating plant for revolutionaries. In Linguet's preromantic vocabulary, nature was the haven of chaos—an unordered energy; natural disruptions were signs of a coming explosion of societal institutions. Unseasonable heat and drought, flash floods, storms—all presaged civil disorder (*Annales,* XV [1788], 55-56). The eruption of a volcano signaled an internal seething of elements in the state (*Annales,* VII [1779], 28-31). Wasn't there some secret connection, Linguet queried, between natural calamities and social and political catastrophes, between the violent storms of nature and the revolutionary upheavals of states? A canton in Spain had been submerged and a city destroyed; the island of Rhé in France had disappeared;

"and right now, hear the deadly signal resounding, and its deadly accompaniments have not failed to manifest themselves"—signs of internal war and international disorder (Annales, XIV [1788], 105-7). Astronomers have predicted the return of the "great comet" for the year 1788. If natural phenomena portended revolutions in the course of human events, then surely the moment would be ripe for the comet's reappearance. "All Empires in general, all societies in particular, even all leaders from one end of Europe to another, harbor and display germs of a fermentation that menaces the most terrible explosions" (Annales, XIII [1788], 450). In violent natural disruptions, Linguet read ominous signs. He augured the triumph of revolutions of nature and necessity against European societies and political regimes. Little in Simon Linguet's reading of events would bear comparison with the ancient augurer's craft. This theorist of societal containment heralded splendid, terrible revolutions. He read signs the way a nineteenth-century romantic would, finding the terrible only the more sublime, and the violent attractive in proportion as it was destructive.[3]

The Bastille was a potent sign. Linguet was understandably sensitive to the contradictory meanings for the present and future that could be read there. He had invented many of them himself. For twenty months he had considered the Bastille his tomb.[4] Vomited up from the great Leviathan, cast onto English shores, the new Jonah branded the Bastille an institutional embodiment of the tyranny, arbitrariness, and injustice which had infected and ravaged the French regime (MB, 22-23). He marked the Bastille for destruction—but how? By whom?

"Speak," he urged the king. At the monarch's word, the walls of this "modern Jericho" would crumble (MB, 105). What if the king kept his silence? It would not change anything. The king's strength was not the only available destructive force. In a breath with his appeal to Louis XVI, Linguet named two other engines of salutary annihilation: the "anathema of men" and the "thunderbolts of heaven" (MB, 105).

Among the minor Bastille horrors Linguet pointed out was a clock in the prison courtyard. It was decorated with two enchained figures (MB, 78, and frontispiece). After reading Linguet's description, one of the king's ministers, the baron de Breteuil, ordered that the two figures with their chains be torn down. He left everything else standing.[5]

Linguet revived his appeal to the king to tear down the Bastille in a Mémoire of 1786. He addressed it to Louis XVI, but as with his Mémoire sur la Bastille, he published it for his public. He recalled the circumstances of his twenty-month long civil death, the murder of an innocent man in the name of the king's justice, a crime which was still unpunished. He announced that in his Mémoire sur la Bastille he had not revealed all the crimes practiced against him. "Future centuries, you would not believe all these abominations if Providence, which had condemned one man only, an irreproachable man, to be the victim of them, had not granted him as well the time to be the historian of them." The monarch had announced the construction of the port of Cherbourg; this was to be "one of the finest monuments to human industry....The destruction of the Bastille would be one of the most splendid victories of humanity...one of the most illustrious triumphs of royal authority over [the authority] of ministers...."[6]

While the king kept a perfect silence concerning the Bastille's fate, Simon Linguet was sealing it by publicly provoking the "anathema of men," bearer of "the thunderbolts of heaven."[7] Linguet repeatedly offered the Bastille to Louis XVI. That was a dangerous gift. Linguet had overcharged it with all the crimes of monarchical administration. When he finished with it, the Bastille was fit for only one fate—immediate destruction. He pleaded with the king to accomplish the deed at once. In this one concrete act, a feat supercharged with symbolic significance, the king would be deploying the crown's physical power to forge new bonds of national unity and purpose.

Louis XVI perhaps did not have the head for recognizing signs; he was not endowed with the qualities of imagination, brilliance, and courage that would inspire him to act upon them. Linguet insisted (after the event, however, calling upon the secretary of state for foreign affairs, the comte de Montmorin, to verify his allegations) that at the end of June, 1789, he was at Versailles, urging the king's ministers, and Montmorin in particular, to adopt his project for demolishing the Bastille and constructing several useful monuments on the razed ground.[8] In a letter allegedly written on July 28, 1789, but which he did not publish until the following year, Linguet exposed his plan. His aim, he declared, was to persuade the monarch and the Third Estate that their interests were identical. The initiative ought to have come from the king. He should have accomplished a deed that would have had universal symbolic value and an immediate political impact. "Exactly one month ago today, day for day, I urged the ministers to demolish the *Bastille* themselves; as the sole indemnity for the sufferings, the horrors I endured there, I asked for the happiness of striking the first blow of the pick, of working together on this ground watered with so many tears, on the execution of a very beautiful project consecrated to the public utility, to the king's glory." The ministers, Linguet reported, had hesitated, stalled for more time.[9]

Time was an essential commodity; time for negotiations and reconciliation, time for the administration to carry out the necessary institutional reforms. Above all, however, the monarchy lacked time. Immediately, then, the king must create a charmed space— a *place de la Bastille*. In a magic gesture meticulously engineered behind the scenes, he must cause the walls to fall. A great illusion of unity would be generated amid the spectacle of a mountain of debris. All obstacles to reunion would vanish. In the aftermath of a perfect demolition job, the king and his advisers would be able to realize the all-saving institutional regeneration. Linguet had learned, perhaps from a reading of Jean-Jacques Rousseau's account of the festival of the *vendages* at Clarens,[10] that magic happenings cast potent and effective spells, instantaneously; that magic forged reunions and dissolved antagonisms, immediately. Louis XVI was not a magician.

When Simon Linguet left Paris on July 13, 1789, to return to a friend's house in the Parisian suburb of Antony, sections of the capital already had been transformed into an armed camp. As rumors flew that the king had summoned foreign mercenaries to march on Paris, a population terrified of pillage, fearful that its food supply would be cut off, began raiding arsenals, monasteries, and storehouses.[11] In the environs of the capital, Linguet learned that day, the population was similarly agitated. Linguet had almost reached the house of a friend at Wissous, near Antony, when, according to his account, the attack began. A menacing peasant crowd surrounded his carriage, "not yet furious, but very disposed to become so," and began shouting accusations at him. He was the emperor's envoy; his mission was to help an enemy party round up support to crush the Third Estate; he had led a contingent of German troops into France, and they were now in the outskirts of Paris; even his coachman was German-speaking—a sure sign of Linguet's complicity in a nefarious plot; besides, the news of his betrayal was circulating at the Palais Royal; the French Guards were determined to come to Wissous, burn down his friend's house, and do away with him; they might be on their way already, and the entire village would be burned and pillaged.[12]

Linguet refused to capitulate to this fear-maddened crowd. Retreating into his friend's house, he held the peasants at bay for two hours, "half the time threatening to oppose force with force, the other half haranguing the assailants from a window." Just as he was about to bring them around, new arrivals on the scene, mostly half-drunk peasants from a local cabaret, renewed the menaces and threats, forcing Linguet to make his escape on horseback, pistols drawn.[13]

He was back in Paris on July 14. The peasant crowd had been right. Rumor had it that Linguet had conspired with the enemies of the Third Estate.[14] The way events turned out that day, Linguet could well have argued that, after all, he had been the greatest of all conspirators on the Third Estate's behalf. He had conquered the Bastille for them, with his pen.

"A prudent man," Linguet did not wait around for the victorious Third Estate's expressions of gratitude to come pouring in. He did not attempt to defend himself publicly against rumors hatched at the Palais Royal. However, he was insulted; privately, he took the trouble to dismiss the charge as groundless calumny.[15] He had seen enough, having witnessed not only the fall of the Bastille, but also the bloody *"portage des têtes"*: "...a great capital was now only an immense theater of assassinations commited in hordes. An entire people having become all at once constable, judge, and hangman, arresting, condemning, executing in the same cry, puts no greater interval between sentencing and punishment than between detention and sentencing"[16] A few days after the fall of the Bastille, Linguet was on his way to Brussels: "Besides, there was almost nothing more I could wish for in Paris, having seen with my own eyes the capture and the beginning of the destruction of the Bastille; and I decided to return here to await the consequences of this conquest, so interesting for honest men...."[17]

Linguet seemed to have decided very quickly what these consequences would be. In a published letter of July 28, 1789, to Austria's minister in Belgium, Count Trauttmansdorff, Linguet offered his interpretation of one of them. While the king's ministers were sitting on his project for tearing down the Bastille, the Third Estate had marched to its historic assault alone: "... the infernal monument has been conquered...."[18] The monarch had survived; the monarchy was doomed. The king had lost his final chance to win the Third Estate's confidence.

> The Crown remains with the shame of having placed its confidence in this horrible expedient for the past two centuries; with the opprobrium of having used it; of having wanted to keep it, and of not having been able to defend it: [the Crown remains] with the ignominy of appearing as an accomplice of this abominable murderer of a Governor, whose entire life was a series of moral assassinations, and whose final crime was an accumulation of physical assassinations; it [the Crown] cannot take the credit even for this reform; *from now on it will not be able to* [take credit] *for any.*[19]

Linguet perceived still another consequence of this happening. "...the Third Estate marched alone; the infernal monument has been conquered: the People has found in this inconceivable exploit the secret of its strength, of its independence."[20]

Linguet dedicated the sixteenth volume of his *Annales,* the first number of which appeared in June, 1790, to Louis XVI. In his letter to the king, Linguet depicts this People and describes "the famous detonation of the fourteenth of July" which "fixed all our destinies":

> What proves that it is not the fruit of a passing effervescence; what must really convince you, SIRE, what must finally familiarize all your courtesans with the idea that this is the outcome of a truly *popular* vow, that consequently it will have lasting effects, is that the first convulsion, the shock that changed the face of everything, went off precisely at the spot where the immobility, the eternity of servitude seemed most perfectly established....it is from the most disdained *class* of its citizens, the least dangerous in appearance, the most bereft of resources, that the forceful cry

went up which called the Nation to the recovery of its rights; it is [this class] which set the first example by repossessing them.

At this terrible cry, as at the sound of *Joshua's* trumphets, the walls of this hell which horrified *Europe* and defiled *France* crumbled; from this miracle of the fourteenth of July, 1789, all the others derive: the happy blows directed at the ramparts of the *Bastille* sparked *universal liberty,* the way an *electric* plate throws off sparks when pressed by an industrious hand. [*Annales,* XVI (1790), 34-35.]

The revolution Linguet witnessed on July 14, 1789, and analyzed in his letters to Trauttmansdorff and Louis XVI, was not the revolution of the people he had been forecasting since the 1760s. On July 14, the people captured the Bastille, "*called the nation to the recovery of its rights,...*put itself back into possession of them [these rights],...sparked *general liberty.*" And still, the people's revolution left the regime of properties and the social class structure intact.

Until the events of July 14 proved to him that his mapping of popular political culture had been inaccurate, Linguet had always maintained that regardless of who did the educating, and no matter how the message was worded, the impact of enlightenment on the political attitudes and behavior of the people would be the same. Inevitably, in the glaring light of knowledge, the people would become aware of the "fundamental principles of society." What would they know? In his *Réponse aux docteurs modernes,* where he interrupted his railing against the *économistes* to take on their task of educating the people, Linguet took the credit for telling them what they were bound to perceive anyway, regardless of how the enlighteners directed their rays. "I present to the unfortunate human beings who form the lowest class in society, and who bear the whole weight of it, the consoling idea that their condition is not natural...." What was unnatural was their condition in society; and what was it?—the condition of being dispossessed and exploited. He told them that their condition was a "usurpation of their rights." What had been usurped were the people's natural rights to a full enjoyment of the earth's riches which they produced by their labor. Presumably, they would conclude for themselves that their exploiters were the usurpers. He announced that "if they or their posterity have the courage one day to repossess them [their rights] nothing can stop them." Enlightened members of the lowest class would know, then, that if they deployed their collective strength, they could dissolve civil society; and that with its end, they would begin to recover the rights and goods that were theirs.[21]

In the second number of his *Annales,* Linguet clarified his understanding of what they might claim and redeem. He predicted that proletarians in arms, enlightened and led by "some new Spartacus," would recover the security of welfare in a postrevolutionary regime—they would, that is, if they did not expire first at the hands of their exploiters, before they summoned the strength and leadership for revolution. He envisioned the regime as a permanent dictatorship for the proletariat, where property confiscated from a vanquished class of ruthless dominators and usurpers would be reapportioned selectively and the exploitation of its riches presumably regulated so that the propertyless masses were guaranteed, in exchange for their productive labor, a "repose of mind" and a "peaceful life"—security as a functional equivalent for autonomy and dominion (*Annales*, I [1777], 102-3).

In July, 1789, the people, the most "disdained...citizens" saved the revolution for the propertied Third Estate. They did not complete the revolution Linguet had scheduled for them. It is clear from what Linguet wrote in the months following the July revolution that he quickly understood why. In his analyses and forecasts, he had been collapsing a multiple-stage process of popular politicization. He rectified his error. He incorporated into his science of society a revised understanding of the dynamics of the radicalization process. The people's revolutionary attitudes and behavior were still being shaped by a powerful myth. Enlightenment, at least temporarily, had blinded them to reality rather than illuminating its fundamental principles. They were still seeing nothing but an illusory identity between their own political interests and those of their exploiters.

Why, then, didn't Linguet inform the people that the rights they repossessed on July 14, 1789, were worthless, and that the liberty they sparked was ephemeral? Why didn't he complete the enlightenment of the people? In the prerevolutionary decades, Linguet had been printing declarations of the Fourth Estate's rights and sending them to his readers in the regime and among threatened elites all over Europe. Now the populace was fully mobilized. It could be reached. It would respond. Already in 1789, in the *cahiers,* and in a pamphlet literature with specifically popular roots, publicists professing to speak for popular interests, needs, and demands were defining their constituency as Linguet defined a proletarian class, limiting property rights by the measure of popular needs, documenting the antagonism between socioeconomic classes, concentrating popular discontent into popular ideology, measuring the power of the poor to dissolve the entire propertied order of things.[22] A Marat, a Sylvain Maréchal, a Théophile Leclerc would make revolutionary careers as spokesmen for the people and as their radicalizers. Not one had Linguet's insight into the fundamental principles of society and his grasp on the mechanisms behind popular political radicalization. Before they published a word of their revolutionary rhetoric for the people, Linguet saw what its final expression must be—a politics of nihilism—the annihilation of an intolerably oppressive regime of properties and privations. He made the politics of nihilism into a theoretically coherent political option, an ideology for the class of society's victims. He saw how political nihilism might be placed in the service of a popularly supported and led revolution for the recovery of rights and possessions in the security of welfare.

As it turned out, when the chips were down, the revolution Simon Linguet was most vitally interested in completing was not the Fourth Estate's, not the Third Estate's, but his own. While all revolutionary parties were struggling to institutionalize the political sovereignty they had conquered in revolution, Linguet enveloped himself in the unstable political identity he had staked out before the revolution. Brandishing his explosive knowledge of the criminality of all political systems and his personal dossier of the French government's crimes against him, this lonely rebel against despotic authority negotiated behind the scenes to arrange an honorable settlement of his war against the *ancien régime* while pursuing an interminable quest for an ideal regime—an administration with which he could identify and collaborate in the work of social containment and control.

On July 1, 1789, two years after he returned to Paris to recover his properties in fees, honors, profession, and political influence, Linguet quietly wrapped up a revolution for a single beneficiary. His revolution was a resounding success; that success heralded the failure of all his attempts to stake out a career for himself in the French Revolution—either as a spokesman for the people, or as the Third Estate's representative, adminstrative adviser, or barely loyal opposition. On July 1, Linguet received an unpublicized payment of ten thousand *livres* from France's secretary of state for foreign affairs, the comte de Montmorin.[23] He had not spent all his time at Versailles advising the ministers to demolish the Bastille; the "happiness of striking the first blow" against the fortress was not the only indemnity he was out after. In the spring of 1792, after the administration failed to deliver three annual installments on what was clearly some kind of pension, Linguet launched a barrage of accusations against the parties who had contracted with him. Minutes of this correspondence reveal that Linguet rationalized what he was getting from the regime as a monetary equivalent for justice. He stated that he was exacting an indemnity for atrocities committed against him by the king's ministers while he was in the Bastille, compensation for arbitrary suppressions and condemnations (probably of the *Annales* and other works), and payment for a sacrifice of claims he had threatened to bring before the Estates-General.[24] In one letter, he promised a public scandal unless he received three years' worth of back payments within twenty-four hours: "...on en va faire trainer l'expédition indéfiniment jusqu'à——la contre-révolution peut-être."[25]

After July 1, 1789, Linguet continued a fitful, inconstant support of the monarchical regime he had been serving in an advisory capacity since 1787. By July 14, 1789, he knew and admitted to Trauttmansdorff that the monarchy's loss of political initiative was irretrievable; he acknowledged the poverty of the Crown's administrative vision: "...it [the Crown] cannot take the credit even for this reform [the destruction of the Bastille]; from now on it will not be able to take credit for any." The ministers might have had enough cash on hand to pay him the first installment on his indemnity; he conceded that the institution over which they presided and in which he now had a not insignificant pecuniary interest was ideologically and fiscally bankrupt.

In 1788, Linguet announced his ambition to serve the people. In July, 1789, he recognized that this people was fully mobilized, and by his own measure, imperfectly politicized. He could not commit himself to a career in popular enlightenment which must end, should his forecasts prove correct, in the completion of their social revolution. He had too much to lose, beginning with the spoils of his own revolution, his fragile conquests within the system of security, justice, political influence, independence.

By 1789, Linguet was publicly identifying his cause with that of the Third Estate; but he did not cement the identification with convincing revolutionary deeds. He never confused the highly partisan interests of propertied commoners with the *raison d'état* which only an all-powerful administration could translate into programs for defusing explosive class antagonisms in the general interest of preserving society.

What Linguet did commit himself to in this revolution was a grand administrative design for generating material satisfactions and reinforcing political illusions in both classes of society, in part with bribes and pensions! He made a commitment to institutionalizing for revolutionary France the material gains of a private revolution of July 1, 1789.

The Politics of Social Welfare: A Program for Completing the French Revolution

Amid triumphant shouts, in a din of crumbling walls, bastions yielding before an irrepressible revolutionary upsurge, Linguet resolved the paradox of modern societies. Revolution had inaugurated a new politcal age, it had not ended the propertied order. Everything was not lost, not yet. The fall of the Bastille, an "inconceivable exploit," had been almost a magic happening, sparking "universal liberty" and enlightenment in one shock. This revolutionary jolt had worked an irreversible universal politicization. That spiritual transformation must be fixed, given objective correlatives, institutional embodiment; it must be made specifically functional in the new regime; otherwise, civil society, as Linguet defined it, would not survive.

In September, 1789, Linguet rushed into print with his most complete reform project, an appeal for a reconciliation of classes at the brink of a final civil war. He called it: *Point de banqueroute, plus d'emprunts, et si l'on veut, bientôt plus de dettes, en réduisant les impôts à un seul. Avec un moyen facile*

de supprimer la mendicité en assurant à toutes les classes du peuple une exist-
ence aisée dans la viellesse. Plan proposé à tous les peuples libres, et notam-
ment à l'Assemblée nationale de France.[26]

He appealed to the National Assembly to take immediate action, prefer-
ably on his project, but in any case on some plan for promoting the same
goal—a negotiated settlement between civil society's radically antagonistic socioeconomic classes, before they marched against one another into civil war.
If no one else came forward with as feasible a plan, "...I would dare to say
to the *National Assembly,* to the *Nation: His uture mecum*" (*P,* 73). Linguet
addressed his plan to members of the National Assembly in a position to as-
sess for themselves the progress of a great popular awakening, as well as the
growth of militant activism, especially among the urban laboring poor and a
marginal population composed of vagabonds and mendicants who were
swarming into Paris looking for work or doles and finding only companions in
misery, the nucleus of a grim fraternity of the impoverished in arms. Necker
remarked their penchant "to observe among themselves a kind of order, to
obey chiefs, a real savage horde at the gate of the most civilized city."[27] The
one institution that provided work for this population, the *ateliers de charité,*
was suppressed, then reestablished from month to month by a desperate administration. Already the *ateliers* had proven inadequate. Perhaps a hundred
thousand persons were demanding work and bread in the summer of 1789 in
Paris alone. The *ateliers de charité* could employ only a fraction of eligible ap-
plicants. By August, the National Assembly was drafting legislation to pay
non-Parisian workers to get out of Paris and return to their local parishes to
look for jobs. That expedient merely displaced the crisis. In September, the
ateliers reopened, proclaiming every worker's right to subsistence. Only a vast
administrative operation could redeem that pledge, and it was not yet in
working order.[28]

Linguet offered his project in the fall of 1789 as a comprehensive substitute for programs that relied on volunteer contributions to solve the nation's
financial crises. "Malheureusement les capitalistes ont encore plus d'argent-
isme que de patriotisme." His offering to the National Assembly would
testify to his good faith and his return to common sense following his scandalous call for a repudiation of the national debt, an alarming departure from
capitalist sanity.[29] "And nonetheless, payment must be made: from all sides
this word resounds, this great word of money, money" (*P,* 8, 7).

"This plan," Linguet announced, "incorporated, amalgamated to the *Constitution,* makes friends of all classes in the State which the present state of
affairs transforms into implacable enemies of one another." He expected to
win the confidence of all proprietors by enlisting their interest. He would
hold out to a class of impoverished persons "a perspective of ease, of well-being
at a certain end-point in its career, by giving it in its first years the motives

for emulation, resignation, and attachment, as well as for docility toward the wealthy classes" (*P,* 71, 18).

Linguet urged the creation of a new financial institution, a *caisse nationale,* a national bank whose administrators would be responsible for achieving national economic stability, a *sine qua non* condition for further expansion of commercial and industrial enterprise.[30] At the same time the bank's administrators would establish a comprehensive state-supported pension system, keystone in a social welfare program designed to attach the French laboring poor and other marginal classes by that same unbreakable bond of self-interest. Linguet announced that if his project were adopted, he would be ready to pledge twelve thousand *livres* from his own capital resources for the purchase of "shares" in this institutional novelty (*P,* 12-13, 74).

Early the following year, Linguet recalled his unsuccessful efforts to interest the National Assembly in his project. He described the plan as an "inestimable relief" for the masses, a sure means of guaranteeing the Assembly a tranquility essential to its success, and an indispensable measure for stabilizing the nation's financial situation.[31] He said he had sent copies of his proposal in brochure form to all ministers, asking them to pass it on to deputies in the National Assembly. He had written to Necker on October 1, 1789, enclosing the brochure—"*La voici, Monsieur.*" He had announced to Necker that he was at work on a supplement, a project "for making the *price of bread* and the wages of *day laborers [journaliers]* invariable, or at least for binding them so closely to one another that the one cannot undergo an increase without the other automatically rising proportionally."[32] Though he had instructed every minister to distribute copies in the National Assembly, they were never received.[33] Of all the ministers, Linguet reported, only Necker answered, two weeks after Linguet had written. He announced that he had received the brochure, but had not read it (*Annales,* XVI, 55).

Linguet did not abandon the idea. In two numbers of his *Annales* for 1790, he presented a revised version of his proposal—expanded and fully accommodated to the revolutionary setting.[34]

The project was not original. Linguet acknowledged an "anonymous" work, *Le Bonheur public,* as the source of some of his pension plans, and the inspiration for his proposals concerning the debt. The author of *Le Bonheur public,* one Vatar Desaubiez, first published the work in 1780-82 in three volumes, allegedly as a proposal for extinguishing the English national debt.[35] He re-presented it in 1789, offering it in abridged form to the French National Assembly as a solution to that body's financial crises.[36] In piecemeal form, most of Linguet's suggestions already were in the air by 1789.[37] What is remarkable in Linguet's master plan is his vision of an all-embracing reunion of the two great classes in the French polity, a reunion planned and executed under the aegis of the national bank's administrative head. Following the dictates of political necessity, the new establishment would commit itself to guaranteeing the worth of all kinds of propertied wealth. In addition, the bank would administer a welfare program designed to bestow on propertyless people—wage-earners, soldiers, domestics—*not* landed property, but real equivalents for it.

In 1790, Linguet was advertising his projected national bank, with headquarters in Paris and branches throughout the nation, as the keystone in the revolutionary architecture ("Projets," 455ff.; *P*, 16). Linguet's scheme is suggestive of Alexander Hamilton's financial program for achieving unity in the new American nation by manipulating a convergence of many moneyed interests. Linguet's project was necessarily more inclusive. He had designed his national bank to serve as the instrument for overcoming open class conflicts in the French nation which were nonexistent or only embryonic in America. Linguet's bank would provide a sure foundation for the economic interests and exploits of all holders of capital. At the same time, it would create a real, a palpable stake in the French economy for a propertyless or near-propertyless nation that had never been anything but the victim of national prosperity and economic development.

The *caisse nationale* was to be the principal political and financial institution in the nation. Its administrators would be responsible directly to the National Assembly. All payments in the name of the nation, payments to the army, the clergy, ministries, payments of pensions, and of interest and principal on the national debt, would be issued in the form of bills. The *caisse* would create them, and mobilize popular confidence to maintain them at par value. It would exchange them against gold or silver on demand. By creating its own currency the bank could save itself and the nation the costs of borrowing at exorbitant interest rates ("Projets," 439-40, 452). The *caisse* would handle the retirement of all *assignats* in circulation, exchanging them for gold and silver. Starting on the day the *caisse* was established, all taxes in the nation would be suspended to give the country a two-year breathing period (*ibid.*, 441, 444; *P*, 16-17).

By enlisting the support of some of the most influential financial magnates, "*de vrais patriotes*," "*tous les capitalistes sensés*," (*P*, 35; *ibid.*, 463) *caisse* officers would be able to inspire the nation with the confidence to keep this bold venture going. Investors would follow the example of those who had most to lose but who still were ready to risk their fortunes to prove the value of *caisse* bills—a fictional value that could only augment the real value of their wealth. The nation and its capitalists would refrain from precipitating a run to exchange bank notes against specie. In addition, the bank could call for totally voluntary patriotic contributions to give real specie backing to its bills; it could sell confiscated church properties to meet the nation's most pressing obligations calling for payment in specie (*ibid.*, 455-64).[38] Capitalists, Linguet insisted, would have everything to gain from this operation. With all taxes suspended during a two-year period, all funds necessary for carrying on government operations would be created *ex-nihilo* by the *caisse*'s administrators. In these extraordinary circumstances, the capitalists of France finally would be free to augment national wealth spectacularly by investing impressive reserves of newly created capital in industry and commerce. The offer of generous tax incentives could only stimulate private enterprise, augmenting private profits, swelling the gross national product, and expanding the base of national prosperity (*ibid.*, Projets, 452-53).

Even if the notables holding resources in capital could be bound to this great state enterprise by ties of interest, was it possible to bind the laboring poor by the same ties? Linguet believed it was. The expedient he proposed would "save *France* and...it is perhaps the only one that could produce this effect" ("Suite," 472n). The methods Linguet had in mind were ingenious, although again, not altogether original.[39] Branches of the *caisse* in Paris and in the provinces would be authorized to accept small sums of money for deposit from propertyless and near-propertyless artists, domestics, manual laborers, and others in similar circumstances. For a period of twenty years, the sum deposited would yield no interest, but at the end of this period the depositor would be entitled to collect annually, and for the remainder of his life, the total amount of his original capital investment (*ibid.*, 471; *P*, 39). Employment by the state in any capacity whatever would be conditional upon the candidate's depositing a minimum of fifty *livres*—the worth of a "share"—with the *caisse nationale*. Eventually, a government employee might cash in up to one half of his shares for the support of his family. The other half would be used exclusively to benefit day laborers, domestic servants, or artisans who had not yet been promoted to the position of master-craftsmen. A 10 percent withholding tax on all salaries paid out by the French government automatically would be deposited in the *caisse nationale;* one half this sum would be used to aid day laborers and other workers in such circumstances. Minimum fifty-*livre* marriage and baptism fees payable to the state, as well as fees for drafting wills and testaments, would be deposited by the wealthy only, and one half of the sum on deposit would be used for the support of day laborers or domestics. Appointment to ranks in the army, beginning with that of colonel, and ranks in the navy, beginning with that of ship captain, would obligate the appointee to deposit one-hundred *livres* annually, or to buy two shares of bank "stock" in favor of a day laborer or a domestic worker, starting at age twenty-five. Deputies to the National Assembly could not claim their seats before fulfilling the same obligation.

Every soldier, in addition to his army pay, was to receive thirty *livres* a year from the bank; at the end of fifteen years of service, he would be retired on a sliding pension of from two hundred to four hundred fifty *livres* annually. Special compensation in the form of pensions would be awarded soldiers disabled before their fifteen years of service had expired ("Suite," 471, 474-76; P, 39-43). In this way, Linguet planned to seduce and tame this "formidable class," composed of "frightening multitudes of armed men, without estate, without country, without ties of any kind, except those that devote them to being the blind instruments of an unbridled despotism" ("Suite," 477, n. 1).

Widows with two children, holding certificates of poverty, but with no deposit in the *caisse nationale,* would be entitled to three hundred *livres* of revenue; widows whose husbands had made desposits would be entitled to draw pensions immediately—and if the initial sum deposited was less than three hundred *livres,* the state would supplement it. Widows of impoverished workers, with one child or childless, would be allowed proportionally reduced compensation. Destitute orphans would be supported by the state through the bank until their twentieth birthday. Public works projects initiated at the parish level and providing jobs for unemployed workers were to be financed out of funds in the *caisse nationale* (*ibid.,* 477-78; P, 44-45).

Linguet expected that at the end of the two-year tax-free breathing period all these payments from the bank to a staggering number of creditors could be made out of revenues from one tax, a national property tax collected in grains in the countryside, and as a tax on city dwellings. Once this single tax was being collected, shares which had been deposited in the bank would be available to pay interest on the national debt and to extinguish the principal gradually. A repudiation would not be necessary ("Suite," 480, 502-3; P, 46-48).

Linguet's aim was perfectly clear. A French nation composed of laboring poor and the destitute now was able to calculate its vital interests. The philosophers of enlightenment had dangled a dangerous utilitarian measuring rod within the grasp of millions. Necessity had impelled them to lay hold of it. They would find it in their interest to remain tied to such a system only if they could be raised out of their nullity and into the ranks of the propertied, hence, the "interested"; only if they could be guaranteed real economic returns from a system which always had operated exclusively in the interest of the propertied elites, only if they could be convinced that the same system that perpetuated their exploitation also augmented their compensation for this state of affairs out of the pockets of their exploiters. Then they would finally be committed to reinforcing and supporting the establishment. Linguet thought his enticements would work like a kind of feudalism in reverse. The wealth of capitalist lords would be channeled through the national bank and directed to reach and enrich the lowest vassals, emancipated descendants of serfs. These free men, too impoverished to be able to deposit funds in the *caisse* on their own behalf, now could expect that their capital, that is, their property, would increase in direct proportion as the taxable wealth of the opulent classes. Masters of national wealth were not capable of a disinterested philanthropy; by imposing fees on marriages and wills, and by bringing other similar devices into play, Linguet would force them "to consign to the *caisse* out of expediency [*politique*], if not out of humanity" ("Suite," 484, 485).

"...once *inaugurated*,...with *Royal sanction*, this establishment would be, I dare say, of all those that have ever been created, the one most favorable TO THE PEOPLE, the most certain source of prosperity that has ever been opened." Linguet anticipated and met all objections with a remarkably modern sense of pragmatic necessities and a typically cavalier impudence. How will the *caisse nationale* be able to pay a vast army of creditors—artisans, widows, orphans, invalids, soldiers, wage-earning laborers? Over a period of two decades, the nation's administrators would take appropriate measures to promote national economic growth—key to national prosperity. They would regularize and simplify the tax system, provide an initial two-year tax-free breathing period, and establish a government-backed and regulated currency: "As it would be only at the end of *twenty years* of exemption, of restoration, that this increase [in government spending] would occur, as it would have been forecast; as the sources of prosperity multiplied by the renewal of industry, commerce, the arts, agriculture, would have given to the body politic a vigor it had not known to this time, it would painlessly bear this burden, which, after all, would be only a real relief for it" (*ibid.*, 482, 495).

Linguet presented several further considerations to allay fears. Then he all but dismissed the practical problem. It did not frighten him, he boasted. These masses would have been promised. They would be clamoring for their payment. A way would be found to pay them. "...what does frighten me is the criminal abandonment in which these beings, so necessary and so unfortunate, whose services are so useful and whose persons are so cruelly forgotten, have languished until now. From the moment I took pen in hand, I have not ceased for an instant to protest on their behalf. I showed that, until now, their alleged *liberty* had been only a trap prepared by opulence to assure itself the fruits of their strength *at a cheaper price*, and to discharge itself altogether of concern for their old age" (*ibid.*, 496).

An unelected deputy claimed to represent a floating constituency, a nation, a Fourth Estate. He presented this Estate's case before the bar of national conscience: "...public interest, public safety, public honor dictate that we hasten to end the unjust, calculated misery that menaces, that overwhelms a million precious families" (*ibid.*, 497).

Whom has the nation always considered as its creditors, Linguet asked. The moneylenders, most of whose aid, he hinted (in an oblique reference to his notorious, now-abandoned plan for repudiating the national debt), could easily have been dispensed with anyway. But the nation's real creditors, "doubtless the most legitimate *creditors* you have," had never even been named (*ibid.*, 499). Legislation on behalf of this dispossessed population to reinstate a portion of its usurped patrimony was not simply a wise police measure. It would mark the beginnings of a repayment—the reimbursement of an infinitesimal fraction of society's unpayable debt to its victims, a debt incurred at the moment of society's foundation. Society's possessors had never before regarded their usurpation as a loan and their exploitation of the dispossessed as a debt with interest compounded daily. Then again, the possessors had never been this close to losing everything, and at the hands of those justified in reclaiming not simply the beginnings of a repayment but the inheritance of the entire earth, starting with the fruits of an expropriated soil. Linguet was not playing with words when he renamed this usurpation a loan solemnly contracted. He was forging rights in the vocabulary of classical economics and drafting contracts that would bind modern civil society's two great parties—before one of them passed the point of being bound.

> ...those in favor of whom I solicit have given you their arms, their youth, their health. Of all the possessions nature bestowed on them, as it has on you, they have known only those which tend to augment yours.
> ...For the past two centuries, above all, there is almost no country in *Europe* where the burdens of the indigent portion of populations have not been augmented annually by *millions,* by HUNDREDS *of millions*: it is delivered·up to an eternal and abominable transfer of *taxes, loans, lotteries,* etc.. Everywhere I see governments fighting about which one will dream up the more vigorous bloodsuckers to drain the last drops of its blood, but not one to give it back [*ibid.*, 499.]

Who speaks for the have-nots? Linguet's answer was that no one spoke for them, because no one was interested; more to the point, every potential legislator on their behalf came from the ranks of the propertied and was incapable of directing his views further than his class-interest. The calculus of interest had always dictated to those in power that it would be in the general interest to perpetuate the nullity of the dispossessed indefinitely. As for the dispossessed, they had never known enough to recognize their interests: "...in all *societies,* this part of the *people* has no plan, no leaders, or if it has them, it is soon betrayed by them, or quickly becomes disgusted with them; it is almost always as dangerous to serve it sincerely as to displease it; today it tears its tyrants to shreds, and tomorrow it will stand by while its defenders are torn to bits; it drinks the blood of the *Foulons* in hatred of what it calls *aristocracy;* and soon after, will stand by without flinching while *aristocrats* become drunk on [the blood] of the *Gracchi*" (*ibid.*, 499, 500).

Here, Linguet was describing his constituency as a pre-conscious multitude, lurching out in blind, frenzied rage against its oppressor, moving with a pitiful inconstancy and total absence of inner direction. But in both versions of his project, he gave his constituency all the credit for having reached the age of reason and self-regarding calculation. When he proposed pensioning off soldiers, and supplementing their salaries with an annual bonus, he pointed out that the soldier no longer could be manhandled like a robot precisely because under pressure of a progressively intensified misery he was transforming himself into an enlightened, indignant human being. "You cannot lead him around any longer as though he were a machine: only by *reason* can you make him like his profession and contain him within boundaries outside which this job is only a brigandage" (*P,* 72; and see also, for a similar statement, "Suite," 477 n. 1).

Linguet had not convinced himself that his constituency was a latter-day Roman plebian mob. He was operating on the principle that the poor were anything but benighted madmen. Maybe they had been. In the first months of the Revolution, they no longer were. They had to be persuaded to give their allegiance to the economic system and political establishment only because they would enlighten themselves eventually to the fact that they had the strength, hence an option, to withdraw that allegiance and annihilate everything. The harsh truth Linguet was publicizing when he printed his project in the *Annales* was that the French Revolution of 1789 was not the last revolution. It was not the people's revolution. Social class structures, a system of economic constraints, and the political regime that guaranteed their perpetuation, were intact. But unless the revolution of the Third Estate could be made a revolution for the people, the people would make one for itself.

Linguet was careful to emphasize that his project for a *caisse nationale* operated entirely within the framework of a now triumphant capitalist ethic and a still imperfectly developed capitalist economics. In Bern, Linguet noted, the government sponsored handouts to destitute workers; but a public dole was not the point of his proposed program: "...here I would want [the worker's pension] to be a *right* exercised by the poor, a right all the more sacred in my plan because he would pay for it by *pecuniary* advances; in that way he would be conforming to a regrettable system, but one inseparable from the very essence of societies, under which the opulent classes, receiving everything from the indigent class, give back to it nothing that it has not *earned back*" ("Suite," 501).

Linguet's project for a *caisse nationale* deliberately introduced a massive, state-administered welfare program into a protocapitalist economy. One way or another, the nation of have-nots within a nation of possessors would have to be annihilated. In 1777, Linguet had calculated the possibility that this nation would perish of starvation. Now that seemed hardly likely. Either the masses would annihilate the nullity in themselves, precipitating not *their* self-destruction but society's, or the government, guardian and caretaker of an exploitative system, would have to transform them, buy them off, converting them into a class with a stake in the existent order, with a cash interest in society's preservation. Now there are only a limited number of ways one can buy off desperate men and women whose power is in proportion to their staggering numbers. One option would be to redistribute properties, or make ownership collective, although that reform, as Linguet understood the matter, could only be the work of the victors in society's final internal war. Linguet programmed something else—guaranteed lifetime revenues, fixed annual income, a prestigious, universally coveted property. Provided the entire nation could be bound by the tie of self-interest to maintain the value of the national currency with an unflinching confidence, capital might be among the most valuable properties a person could hold.

Linguet had hit upon a very likely bribe to win the allegiance of the French masses—the guaranteed lifetime income, "*rentes*" from investments in or outright gifts of government-sponsored "shares." He had assessed the mentality of the laboring poor, had probed their fears and their still unexpressed drives and ambitions. He concluded that those with almost nothing craved after all nothing more than what was always just beyond their reach, what the bourgeois Third Estate and the nobility had been scrambling to acquire and possess for themselves in the immediately prerevolutionary years—maximum security.[40] Linguet observed that security in the bourgeois mentality meant dependable annual returns or lifetime income from capital investments (*rentes viagères,* or *rentes perpétuelles*). Peasants, artisans, and those on the fringe of the bourgeoisie still were making major sacrifices to emulate bourgeois and aristocratic investors in their quest after security.[41] Linguet expected that the have-nots' aspirations would be toward that same assured status and safety enjoyed by those among the *petite bourgeoisie,* the *hautre bourgeoisie,* and the nobility who had guaranteed incomes. The system was designed to satisfy the French laboring poor's deep-rooted lust for security—and in a form, that of *rente* or guaranteed income, which this population might readily recognize as the object of its conscious aspirations.

After all this, however, a guarantee of income some time in the future and a limited amount of relief in the present, would mean nothing to people living from day to day unless, out of the sums they earned, they were able to purchase their daily bread.[42] Natural disaster or monopolistic hoarding and speculation in grains, or a combination of natural catastrophe and artificial manipulation, would inflate prices and send bread soaring out of the worker's reach, sabotaging Linguet's entire project, to say nothing of the regime of properties. Linguet spelled out the difficulty in his *Du pain et du bled* of 1774.[43] He raised it once again in his *Du commerce des grains,* a new edition of *Du pain et du bled* which he published in 1788. Here, Linguet restated a thesis he had been developing for at least fifteen years. The availability of bread to a propertyless nation would be the great determinant of the course revolutionary events took. The inexorable directive forces behind the masses' acts of appropriation and destruction were their stomachs and their psyches—the dictates of nature and necessity. "I have said it already: the principal physical duty of every living being is to live: in this respect the same holds true of political bodies as of private persons. All the prerogatives consecrated and maintained in their midst have and are capable of having as their object only the conservation of their existence..." (*Commerce des grains*, 137-38).

True, government existed to safeguard property rights: "...but you forget that it [this property] could not entail a rigorous and exclusive right, exempt from exceptions" (*ibid.*, 139). The machinations of self-interested speculators in agricultural produce could hardly be called self-regulating when the day laborer and artisan were unable to purchase enough bread to live; and the whole operation was anything but harmonious when the masses had to break down doors of granaries and bakeries to correct a murderous inequity.

That appearance of harmony and that semblance of self-regulation could be achieved only by government, and would have to be evoked at once, provided the government was interested in surviving: "Any kind of increase in the price of bread, when it is not followed without the slightest delay by an increase in the day laborer's salary, is the most abominable of larcenies committed against this unfortunate class: it is a murderous and mad injustice, which, in condemning [that class] to death, prepares and necessitates the decadence of the states where it happens" (*ibid.*, 141).

Somehow, Linguet insisted, the government must regulate this affair so that whatever the worker's salary was, or, no matter how high prices soared, he would be able to purchase his bread every day: "The peoples of Europe, then, will always be unfortunate, and *Governments always uneasy* until, as I have said, they succeed either in giving to grain an unalterable value, or to salaries an irresistible mobility to force them to follow necessarily and without delay all variations [in grain prices] " (*ibid.*, 142).

The government's options were a guaranteed sliding salary scale or rigid government-administered price controls over grains. The leaders of the people, of course, had others. At the end of *Du commerce des grains,* Linguet hinted that this scaling of grain prices to wages could be achieved by subterfuge, so that speculating entrepreneurs in grain products, not knowing what was going on, would believe themselves free when actually they were "giving themselves up to an impulse they could not elude....This harmony between *liberty* and *obedience* exists, the theologians say, in metaphysics: the true benefactor of the human species will be he who points out the means of transferring it into administration. And not only do I believe this operation is possible, but I believe it is easy" (*ibid.*, 142).

In a brief note appended to his project for a *caisse nationale,* Linguet revealed how the government could create this "harmony." The National Assembly would have to legislate a tax on rural properties collectible in the form of food commodities ("Suite," 504n; *P*, 65-66, n. 1). This was the project Linguet had originally proposed in his *Dixme royale* of 1764. He presented the plan again in an article written for his *Annales* of 1779, his "Réflexions sur les finances et sur l'établissement d'une dixme royale" (VI, 457-504), and then in his *Impôt territorial* of 1787. In the light of all his earlier statements, the connection between the national property tax and his project to promote dovetailing of class interests becomes clear. Linguet observed in his "Réflexions sur les finances" that a national property tax, collected in food products, principally grains, and stored locally in government granaries, would act both "as a bridle to muzzle the deadly cunning of speculators in grains, and also as a guaranteed fund for the nourishment of the poor." Which speculator, seeing "40,000 citadels provisioned against him all over the realm," granaries equipped to cater to the needs of destitute consumers out of reserves adroitly administered, would dare to monopolize or hoard grain? The unemployed rural laborer would find the public granary "a kind of workshop always opened, and its contents available *in toto,* to serve in exchange against the labor of the able poor, or for the gratuitous nourishment of the disabled poor" (*ibid.,* 501, 502).

In his project for a *caisse nationale,* Linguet again argued for a national property tax payable in the form of agricultural produce, principally wheat. The government would store its revenue in this vital commodity in granaries located in every city and village in the nation. Whenever the price of bread in any area rose beyond the capacity of the lowest-paid day laborers, artisans, and other wage-earners to purchase it, the administrators of the granary in the affected locality would order the wheat processed and would market it at a price fixed in accordance with the worker's ability to purchase in that area and at that critical moment. To compete with these government enterprises, private entrepreneurs, speculators in grain products, hoarders, and monopolists all would be compelled to temper their acquisitive instinct with self-interested calculations and price-cuts to avoid disasterous competition ("Suite," 504n). It then would be in their best interest, that is, their highest economic interest, to lower prices with all deliberate speed.

Without such a program, Linguet insisted, chronic economic and political calamities would be inevitable: "...society will never be other than it has been, above all for the past three centuries, a brigandage exercised by the rich against the poor, and supported with naked force by *economic constables,* & c., but sometimes suppressed using the same means by *popular* insurrections, more distressing than blameworthy as we have been seeing continuously for several months now." If his project for a *caisse nationale* were adopted at once, Linguet predicted, not one invalid, widow, or orphan would lack an income sufficient to live on by 1812. "Few *day laborers, soldiers* will fail to enjoy easy circumstances, as almost all will have an income of 300 *livres* at least, and the majority, 600 to 800 *livres,* maybe more. Then you will be able to say of *France* that it is a FAIR *realm:* until then it will be only a very astounding one, and right now, it is a *very unfortunate* one" (*ibid.,* 504n, 506).

Linguet never claimed to be the utopian novelist of the French polity, only its most prescient and profound social analyst, the first to understand how explosive antagonisms between the two classes of French revolutionaries might still be controlled; the first to show how laws of human behavior proclaimed by the utilitarians could serve as the foundation for a preservative science of public administration. Linguet acted on the recognition that self-interest, taken in its narrowest definition, was at once a universal psychological and economic motor force. Pecuniary interest and acquisitive instincts were not an exclusive property of the possessor class; they were fundamental psycho-economic drives which could be activated and regulated in both classes of society.

The state would be that great regulator. The state's real governor would be a meta-politician, an administrative genius, the power behind the throne, or behind the people. This master-manipulator would hold out to investors, speculators, and industrial, agricultural, and commercial entrepreneurs a variety of bribes designed to convince them that the national currency was stable, the economy sound, and economic expansion feasible and profitable. He would offer to the propertyless class, in return for its tacit consent to expropriation and exploitation, compensations indistinguishable from valuable mobile properties.

Linguet discarded his long-held conviction, borrowed from mercantilist theory, that the total wealth in the world was strictly limited:[44] he replaced it with the idea that the state could invent wealth, as much as it needed, from above, out of nothing but the materials of confidence and self-interest. The state could proliferate wealth following the dictates of national necessity and national security. The state's administrative head would offer shares and promises of future returns on capital in the form of pensions, annuities, and similar benefits, as well as immediate guarantees of present security in the form of extraordinary pensions, aids, and a virtual price control exercised over the nation's subsistence commodity, bread. The worth of government-backed "shares" or promises of properties would depend absolutely upon national political, social, and economic stability. For the first time in history, it would be in the Fourth Estate's interest to lend full, unflinching support to the administration which validated and maintained the worth of all properties. Furthermore, as the total number of "shares" or properties available would depend absolutely upon the number of wealthy persons who could be fleeced, this again would be the first instance in the annals of social history when a proto-proletariat could almost calculate by how much it would be in its own best interest to be exploited. Finally, because in a sense a propertyless population would enjoy ownership over an estate that consisted of something other than stomachs and manpower, it would also enjoy for the first time a liberty that was not a mirage, the liberty of *dominion,* the only kind of liberty Linguet considered meaningful in civil society.

This last-moment reconciliation of the two great classes at the brink of a yawning abyss could only be the work of a master mind, a great administrative genius capable of operating the *caisse nationale* to make of it the most powerful institution in the realm, the fount of national prosperity and harmony.

The administrator in Linguet's last project emerges in a role similar to that assumed by the Jesuit manipulators whom Linguet had lauded in a work written in the 1760s, when he described the paradise they engineered for Paraguayan natives in their wilderness.[45] Only now, the dupes in question are not ignorant and childlike natives, but a nation of calculating revolutionaries. Crafty administrators, dumping government grain supplies onto a competitive market, deceive agricultural capitalists and speculating profiteers into lowering grain prices to save themselves from financial disaster, and these dupes end up saving the masses from starvation. Other government strategists trick holders of substantial capital resources, bent on following their exclusive self-interests and advancing themselves socially, economically, and politically, into making deposits in the *caisse nationale* as a *sine qua non* condition for promotion; and these deposits operate to the advantage of day laboreres, artisans, and soldiers. Financial "capitalists" calculate the risk of accepting the national bank's bills as repayment for loans over against the risk of a debt repudiation and total loss of their capital investment; and they throw their support to the new bank and its currency. Their backing generates a national confidence in the soundness of the currency and the whole administrative operation. State managers seduce a nation composed of proto-proletarians into believing that with the acquisiton of a promise of future property in annuities and pensions it at last has come into a great inheritance when, in truth, it is only perpetuating its exploitation at the hands of its permanent masters with every compensation it receives from them for its expropriation. All the while, the administrator of the *caisse nationale* would be exploiting both classes of "free" self-interested citizens secretly directing their movements to achieve social harmony, maintain public order, and promote national expansion on all fronts. He would be the real, though hidden master of a nation of imperfectly free, because perfectly and universally materialized one-dimensional men, *homo economicus* raised to the estate and status of a universal type.

Linguet had programmed for French revolutionaries a policy worthy of the most ruthless and realistic practitioner of a politics of social containment through total administrative manipulation. Linguet's project for a *caisse na-*

tionale amounted to a grim evaluation of the real worth of liberal principles proclaimed by the revolutionaries of 1789. Linguet assumed that citizens who called themselves political sovereigns could nonetheless be seduced into surrendering real power to administrators because they confused political control with economic dominion or subordinated it to the lust for material security. He operated on the premise that what they named their drive for self-direction could be checked and diverted as soon as they obtained for themselves certain narrowly defined goods—property, success, security, welfare. The propertyless class, once it had been raised into the ranks of a propertied or share-holding class, could be moved about on the same leading strings.[46]

Had his project been adopted, Simon Linguet, of course, would have placed himself outside the system immediately. He always did that. He would have applied for the post of administrator of the *caisse*, guaranteeing autonomy for himself while a divided nation of revolutionaries was plied with material ial compensations for its surrender.

Linguet offered his project for a *caisse nationale* to a revolutionary establishment he profoundly mistrusted but which he could not afford to abandon. It was his program for exploiting a reprieve from doom which the people's incomplete radicalization made possible. An enlightened absolutist would have appreciated the project. Members of the National Assembly, had they seriously entertained it, would have found it repugnant. The Assembly's vocal majority was not sensitive, in its rhetoric or in its legislation, to the clean class divisions and ideological splits Linguet advertised, and it never abandoned the politically useful illusion of a natural harmony among economic interest groups. It would not have embraced a plan designed to stabilize property values in society and strengthen the economy but which at the same time undercut the Assembly's political authority with all-powerful administrative institutions and made a mockery of liberal ideology—beginning with the faith of the nation's representatives in their capacity to legislate in the national interest.

The government, racked by internal division, suffering from power deflation, lacking in personnel with strength, vision, conviction, and staying power, was in no condition to take Linguet's program under serious consideration.

The people—*sans culottes*, rural laborers, and other categories in Linguet's class of dominated and exploited persons—would have been the first to repudiate the scheme. With his cash bribes, Linguet was offering material benefits that the revolutionary establishments never matched. From the people's perspective, these material returns would have been only poor functional equivalents for the democratic political sovereignty they were claiming in addition to security and welfare and which they were institutionalizing as their only certain means of obtaining both.

In his blueprints for achieving administered order in a revolutionary setting, Linguet orchestrated a reconciliation of the conflicting material interests of revolutionary elites and masses. He did nothing about safeguarding their rights as political participants; or rather, he undermined and in effect dismissed both classes' claims to political self-determination when he concentrated really effective political control in administration. While Linguet was making his commitments on paper, the power of administration was dissolving before his eyes. Where the revolutionary elites legislated on the issues Linguet raised, they did so following liberal principles. Finally, the expectations and demands of the people had changed with the development of democratically based participatory institutions and the penetration of revolutionary ideology. This rapid radicalization of the political revolution within the social revolution left Linguet without any real bases of support—within the administration, among the nation's legislators, or among the people—from which to work toward the realization of his special revolutionary vision of the perfectly administered postrevolutionary society.

The Poverty and Power of Philosophic Irony

A detailed blueprint for celebrating the first anniversary of the storming of the Bastille began to circulate in Paris as preparations for that civic event got underway. It was called *Adresse au peuple français concernant ce qu'il faut faire et ce qu'il ne faut pas faire pour célébrer la fête mémorable et nationale du 14 juillet 1790. Et sur-tout la nécessité de n'y admettre aucun cheval.*[47] Linguet wrote it, although a disciple of Rousseau might have, as a supplement to Rousseau's descriptive analysis of the *fête des vendanges* at Clarens.

The author of the *Adresse au peuple français* was contriving to achieve, against a deceptively natural backdrop, Rousseau's grand illusion: fraternal equality embracing all people, regardless of social or economic position; unity overcoming separateness; harmony diffused everywhere; all-penetrating, dissolving all antagonisms—all by magic, at once—for the duration of the spectacle. The actors would be the spectators, the public, generating the charmed space of the *patrie* in the act of fraternizing. Although all estates would participate, the directors would evoke the grand illusion principally for the Fourth Estate, which at the close of the first revolutionary year, still had little more than illusions to live by. These festivities would "compensate them with an instant of happiness for the long privations to which their position condemns them." The author pointed out that the custom during French civic celebrations was to toss food and money to crowds of celebrators as to packs of ravenous animals, or to open the theaters to the people, allowing them to feast upon scenes of pleasures and leisures which the opulent elite enjoyed: "But isn't this flash of felicity that you allow them more likely to stimulate their desires than to satisfy them?...isn't the regret of privation joined here to the sentiment of ignominy?" (*Adresse au peuple français*, 9-10).

Without any appearance of constraint or artifice, the crowds must be contained, directed, and at the same time impressed. The author suggested that at the Place de la Bastille two elaborate stage settings be constructed, replicas of the catafalque of despotism and the altar of liberty. From the latter, Liberty herself would come forward, "like Minerva, all armed, all Goddess, from the head of the People, helping them to strike down ministerial Titans, to crush the Encelades of Versailles beneath the ruins of this Etna." This spectacle was to be the people's substitute for dangerous, provocative theatrical performances (*Ibid.,* 17, 12-13).

In addition, the author of *L'Adresse au peuple français* would divide the capital into sections; a public feast of the people would be arranged in each one. An orderly repast would replace traditional scenes of near-riot in which food was thrown to celebrators. To lessen the shock of a return from surfeit into a deprivation bordering on famine, prudent officials would provision the poor with wine, meat, and bread the day after the celebration. Finally, dowries for impoverished girls planning marriage would be provided for by contributions made in advance; they would be distributed the day of the celebration in the form of products for the couple's use and a fund for the nourishment and education of their children (*ibid.,* 19, 21, 22-24).

Welfare conceived and distributed in this way was little more than a dole. Bread and wine were opiates for the masses; they lessened the acuteness of suffering among the urban destitute long enough to dull the impulse to revolutionary violence until the next distribution. These kinds of tricks, ephemera of a day and a night, were not reforms but emergency police measures, and this civic celebration, with its feast, singing, dancing, and popular amusements, had been designed as an invisible line of defense. This stratagem was necessary *not* because all programs of reform had proved insufficient, but rather because in this first year of the Revolution, the National Assembly had legislated none at all in the interest of the Fourth Estate, none of the variety Linguet outlined in his *Point de banqueroute* of 1789. In that prospectus for thoroughgoing institutional reform, a blueprint for the beginnings of a broadly constructed state-administered social-welfare program, Linguet took as his point of departure the existence of a nation of angry laboring poor, enlightened enough to be able to calculate its interest in conforming to the existent socioeconomic order, materialized, rational, and frustrated enough to act on the basis of that kind of calculation. The bribery Linguet worked out in his *Point de banqueroute* might have been trickery, but it was higher-order trickery. It bore no comparison to feats of magic by which prestidigitator-administrators propped up Bastilles, sent the Goddess Liberty marching to demolish them, and disguised handouts to beast-men as banquets for citizens.

Linguet might have been trying to engineer trances among the people in his *Adresse,* although untempered irony was not a convincing language for a spell-caster. Why legislate against the presence of horses at a civic celebration? At the beginning of his *Adresse au peuple français*, Linguet recalled an incident at another public celebration where mounted police with sabres drawn had charged into the crowds to keep order: "If new things exist in France, I cried out, they aren't here: there are quite enough reformers, but there is not any reform. All the equipment of despotism is still intact....Every day you tell the People that it is Sovereign: he! *Messieurs, ne bourrez donc pas Sa Majesté.*" That phrase could easily be translated as an admonition not to trample His Majesty the People to death or not to cram His head full of vain promises. Having promised the people everything, the nation's legislators must *do* at least this much: "present an Address to the people, to bring about a Decree, by which it would be ordered IN THE NAME OF THE PEOPLE that in the future NO HORSE will be admitted into any ceremony where the people are invited or have the right to be present" (*ibid.* 5, 8).

Irony was an acceptable mode under the *ancien régime* for expressing moral outrage against the injustice of the inevitable. In a revolutionary setting, nothing was presumed inevitable, least of all the continuing degradation of the people. The reigning belief among all revolutionary parties was that necessity, however defined, would dissolve before the force of ideologues in arms. Linguet could not subscribe to that belief. "There are quite enough reformers, but there is not any reform."

Irony was an ineffective solvent for resistant revolutionary myths, and an inappropriate language for producing trances in the people, although Linguet would have insisted that in wielding it he had exposed the hard truth about the revolutionary situation: the regime of oppressive necessities would yield, if at all, only to the enlightened manipulation of metapoliticians, experts capable of administering on behalf of the new national sovereign an honorable, if necessarily subpolitical settlement of the war between the haves and the have-nots. Irony was the weapon not of a counterrevolutionary but rather of an unaligned rebel whose political vision, in the context of revolutionary developments, turned out to have been prematurely postrevolutionary.

NOTES

1. Linguet to Jean-Frédéric Perrégaux, Brussels, April 17, 1788, in BM, Collections d'autographes, première collection de la ville, vol. II, fol. 83.

2. For samples of Linguet's analyses and forecasts in these areas, see the following articles from the *Annales politiques, civiles, et littéraires du dix-huitième siècle*, 19 vols. (London, Brussels, Paris, 1777-92): on America, XIV (1788), 398-401; on enlightenment, "Considérations générales et préliminaires," XIII (1788), 64-65; on misery among the masses, VII (1779), 215-23; "Mémoires sur les finances, par feu M. l'Abbé Terray," VII, 276ff., n. 1, 280ff., n. 1; on financial crisis, "Réflexions préliminaires," I (1777), 38-46, and "Réflexions sur la dette nationale en France: la Nation y est-elle obligée comme en Angleterre?" XV (1788), 218-36; on insubordination in the nobility of the robe, "Lit de justice mémorable du 8 mars [mai] 1788. Idée de la révolution qui s'y est opérée," XIV, 173-82.

3. Vesuvius erupted Aug. 8, 1779. Linguet, reporting this natural disturbance, remarked that these eruptions, more and more frequent in the eighteenth century, "seem to herald the progress of internal inflammation and presage more terrible disasters in the future." He then went on to describe volcanic eruption, giving full play to his passion for depicting the sublimity of the terrible. *Annales*, VII, 28, 31.

4. Linguet, *Mémoires sur la Bastille, et la détention de l'auteur dans ce château royal, depuis le 27 septembre 1780 jusqu'au 19 mai 1782* (London, 1783), pp. 48-49; cited hereafter as *MB*.

5. Charpentier, *La Bastille dévoilée, ou Recueil des pièces authentiques pour servir à son histoire*, 3 vols. (Paris, 1789-90), I, 18-19.

6. Linguet, *Mémoire au Roi, par M. Linguet, concernant ses réclamations actuellement pendantes au Parlement de Paris* (London, 1786), p. 146n, 148-49. Linguet relived the torture of life in the Bastille during the court trial of his case against d'Aiguillon. See Louis Petit de Bachaumont, *Mémoires secrets, pour servir à l'histoire de la république des lettres en France, depuis MDCCLVII jusqu'à nos jours; ou Journal d'un observateur*, 36 vols. (London, 1780-89), XXXII (Sept. 3, 1786), 327-28.

7. See for example Jacques Godechot, *La Prise de la Bastille, 14 juillet 1789*, Trente journées qui fait la France, vol. 17 (Paris, 1965), pp. 123-24; Jean-François Barrière, "Notice sur la vie de Linguet," in *Mémoires de Linguet sur la Bastille et de Dusaulx sur le 14 juillet*, ed. Saint-Albin Berville and Jean-François Barrière, Collection des Mémoires relatifs à la Révolution française, 2d ed. vol. 14, (Paris, 1822), x-xi. The phrases are from *MB*, 105.

8. Linguet, *Lettres de M. Linguet au Comte de Trauttmansdorff, ministre plénipotentiaire pour l'Empereur au Pays-Bas en 1788 et 1789* (Brussels, 1790), p. 82n. By this time, several other projects had been suggested and discussed publicly. See for example Godechot, *La Prise de la Bastille*, p. 26. Hippolyte Monin, in his preface to an edition of Linguet's *Mémoires sur la Bastille*, (Paris, 1889), suggests that much of the public discussion and the rash of projects for razing the Bastille were sparked by Linguet's *Mémoires*, and above all by the engraving that served as its frontispiece. "L'idée de Linguet avait donc fait fortune," xxxiv.

9. Linguet to Trauttmansdorff, Brussels, July 28, 1789, in Linguet, *Lettres...au Comte de Trauttmansdorff*, pp. 96, 97.

10. Jean-Jacques Rousseau, *Julie, ou la Nouvelle Héloïse*, ed. René Pomeau (Paris, 1960), pp. 596-97.

11. Jules Flammermont, "Introduction," *La Journée du 14 juillet 1789. Fragment des mémoires de L.-G. Pitra*, ed. Flammermont (Paris, 1892), c1xxi-c1xxiv.

12. Linguet, *Lettres...au Comte de Trauttmansdorff*, p. 85n.

13. *Ibid.*, pp. 85-86n.

14. *Ibid.*, pp. 86-87n.

15. Linguet to Perrégaux, Brussels, July 26, 1789, in BM, MSS, collections d'autographes, première collection de la ville, vol. II, fol. 83. Later in the summer, Linguet was still being plagued by these kinds of charges—only now they were coming from the Belgian patriots, not the French revolutionaries. Linguet asked Count Trauttmansdorff for permission to publish his half of their private correspondence. He believed that, among other things, his letters would clarify the purpose of his trip to Vienna the previous March—an expedition which patriots were interpreting as a sure sign of his counterrevolutionary allegiances. "Besides, it [the publication of his letters] will lead quite naturally to revealing the purpose of my trip to Vienna last March, which is still an enigma for you, and even more of one for His Majesty, but which nonetheless provided the occasion for the most odious suspicions, the most dangerous utterances against me, both here and in Paris; however you look at it, it [this publication] is necessary." Apparently, what Linguet was hoping to show was that he went to Vienna to present his claims upon Austrian authorities for their support as he placed his bid for a suppressed Belgian monastery in Awerghem. Linguet to Trauttmansdorff, n.p., n.d., in AG, no. 5117, n. 30. And see Chapter Eight.

16. Linguet, *Lettres...au Comte de Trauttmansdorff*, pp. 91-92n.

17. Linguet to Perrégaux, Brussels, July 26, 1789, in BM, MSS, Collections f'autographes de la ville, vol. II, fol. 83.

18. Linguet to Trauttmansdorff, Brussels, July 28, 1789, in Linguet, Lettres...au Comte de Trauttmansdorff, p. 97.

19. Ibid.

20. Ibid.

21. Linguet, Réponse aux docteurs modernes, ou Apologie pour l'auteur de la "Théorie des lois" et les "Lettres" sur cet "Théorie." Avec la réfutation du système des philosophes économistes, 2 vols. (n.p., 1771), I, 116. In 1767, Linguet warned Voltaire that there was no way to keep enlightening rays, once they were loosed, from striking the minds of the people. Once the people were informed, their attitudes and behavior would be transformed irreversibly, in a way that must prove fatal for them, and for society: "...the day becomes deadly to them both... [possessing elites and dispossessed masses]." Linguet to Voltaire, Feb. 19, 1767, in Voltaire's Correspondence, ed. Theodore Besterman, 107 vols. (Geneva, 1953-65), 64, no. 13075, p. 229. In his Théorie des lois civiles, Linguet warned that the revolution that dissolved the bonds of society would lead the victors into chaos and self-destruction. See Linguet, Théorie des lois civiles, ou Principes fondamentaux de la société, 2 vols. (London [Paris], 1767), II, 512-13. Linguet did not repeat that argument in passages cited from the Réponse aux docteurs modernes and the Annales. He cancelled it out with forecasts of a victory of the people followed by a reorganization of authoritarian society as a dictatorship for a triumphant proto-proletariat.

22. For discussion and examples, see Henri Grange, Les Idées de Necker (Paris, 1974), pp. 244-46 and notes. Grange documents in these pages the striking correspondence between Jacques Necker's prerevolutionary analyses of exploitative institutions and relationships and depictions of exploitation being turned out in 1789 and after by publicists with roots in or ties to popular culture. Grange calls attention repeatedly to the anatomies of exploitation which Linguet had written prior to the publication of Necker's works treating the subject. Grange categorizes both Linguet and Necker as "resolute defenders of order." I would agree, with some qualification. The strains of utopianism and populism which found their way into Linguet's social analyses and forecasts, his position as outsider; his multiple experiences as victim of coups d'autorité—all fed Linguet's ambivalence towards "order," although he defended it nonetheless. I find this ambivalence less apparent in Necker's thought. See Grange, Les Idées de Necker, p. 242.

23. A statement acknowledging receipt of this sum, signed by Linguet, but not countersigned, is preserved in BM, uncat. MSS, Coll. Gosset, no. 26.

24. Copies of letters corrected and annotated in Linguet's hand, addressed to a Monsieur de la P[orte], a functionary in the king's household, and dated end of February [1792], March 8, 12, 20, 1792, are preserved in AN, W 397-921, 4me partie, no. 8.

25. Linguet to Monsieur de la P[orte], March 20, 1792, in ibid.

26. Linguet, Points de banqueroute, plus d'emprunts, et si l'on veut, bientôt plus de dettes, en réduisant les impôts à un seul... (n.p., 1789), cited hereafter as P. The pamphlet bore the motto Dic verbo et sanabitur Patria nostra. Linguet was exploiting, and with an unmistakable irony, a title Brissot had used in 1787 for a brochure against bankruptcy in which he called for a convocation of the Estates-General. Jacques-Pierre Brissot de Warville, Point de banqueroute, ou Lettres à un créancier d'état sur l'impossibilité de la banqueroute nationale et sur les moyens de ramener le crédit et la paix (London, 1787).

27. Cited without reference in Yvonne Forado-Cunéo, "Les Ateliers de charité de Paris pendant la Révolution française, 1789-1791," La Révolution française, LXXXVI (1933), 327.

28. Ibid., 322-35.

29. I am using "capitalist" here the way Linguet meant it in this context, as a description of the activities of finance or court capitalists. For an excellent discussion of this category of eighteenth-century French capitalist activity, consult George V. Taylor's illuminating article, "Types of Capitalism in Eighteenth-Century France," English Historical Review, 79 (1964), 478-97.

30. Linguet deliberately flaunts the word caisse (bank), a term of opprobrium in the French vocabulary ever since the disastrous scandal of 1720 involving John Law.

31. Linguet to Camille Desmoulins, Feb. 18, 1790, printed by Desmoulins in his *Révolutions de France et de Brabant,* 86 nos. (Paris Nov., 1789-July 1791), no. 14 (1790), 39.

32. Linguet to Necker, Oct. 1, 1789, printed by Linguet in *Annales,* XVI (1790), 55-56, 57.

33. Linguet to Camille Desmoulins, Feb. 18, 1790, printed by Desmoulins in *Révolutions de France et de Brabant,* no. 14, 40.

34. See Linguet, "Projets de finance, pour le soulegement a même la libération de L'Etat," *Annales,* XVI, no. 134 (1790), 436-64; cited hereafter as "Projets." Linguet, "Suite de projet pour l'établissement d'une Caisse nationale salutaire," *Annales,* XVI, no. 135 (1790), 465-506; cited hereafter as "Suite."

35. M. D—Z [Vatar Desaubiez], *Le Bonheur public, ou Moyen d'acquitter le dette nationale de l'Angleterre; de trouver une ressource constante pour les besoins du gouvernement, sans taxes ni impositions; de rendre les hommes heureux autant qu'ils peuvent l'être par les richesses. Présenté aux Chambres du Parlement,* 3 parts in one vol. (London, 1780-82).

36. M. D—Z, *Extrait d'un ouvrage intitulé "Le Bonheur public," & c. Imprimé a Londres en 1780, contenant, 1° la liquidation de la dette nationale, et faisant le bonheur de la société; 2° un plan d'adminstration sur les grains, afin d'éviter à jamais la disette; présenté à l'Assemblée nationale en 1789* (n.p., 1789). Here Desaubiez raised the question that concerned Linguet, how government might manipulate the utilitarian principle to generate harmony among disparate interests: "How could it be that no one has thought of binding men to the common interest using the very interest which is the principle of all their actions?" p. 5. He presented a pension system, pp. 5ff., but one which benefited primarily the middle classes; he asked for a year's moratorium on all taxes, p. 37. He outlined a program for government regulation of commerce in grains, which, like Linguet's plan, provided for state competition with private speculators. The government would be sufficiently provisioned in wheat to be able to force prices down, and it also would be authorized to regulate exportation to drive prices up when the private entrepreneur suffered unfair losses, pp. 42ff.

37. Among pamphlets of the day dealing with the establishment of a national bank and a national currency, Boyd C. Shafer, in his "Bourgeois Nationalism in the Pamphlets on the Eve of the French Revolution," *Journal of Modern History,* X (1938), 46, n. 48, singles out the following: *L'Etat libre (1788); Plan d'une banque nationale de France, ou d'une caisse de recette et payement des deniers publics et particuliers* (1788); *Mémoire pour l'établissement d'une caisse publique nationale ou française* (1788).

38. In his *Pointe de banqueroute,* p. 22, Linguet speaks of a kind of magic by which the nation, "simply by applying its all-powerful hand," was able to bestow upon "the most lightweight paper the value of gold." He contrasted the nation's salutary power of creating with its humiliating prerogative of requesting.

39. Linguet noted that he had borrowed the idea of an initial year's deposit eventually yielding an annual pension equivalent to the sum originally deposited from Desaubiez's *Le Bonheur public.* See "Suite," 471. For details of other insurance programs, see Camille Bloch, *L'Assistance et l'état en France à la veille de la Révolution* (Paris, 1909), pp. 155ff., 361ff., 375ff., 385ff. Linguet acknowledged that his entire plan for a *caisse nationale* had been modeled after plans for a similar banking establishment in Venice. See "Suite," 482.

40. Linguet had convinced himself by the end of 1788 that the typical French bourgeois, whatever his psychological makeup, was not the ideal type of the successful industrial capitalist entrepreneur—not yet. England's *homo economicus* had assumed the role more naturally, and more profitably. The French bourgeois's heart and interest, Linguet concluded, were not yet in this form of risky economic adventure. He had not adopted the character, the drives, the kind of ruthless dedication which this new mode of production demanded of its successful practitioners, and he was far from having revolutionized the techniques and financing of French industry. See Linguet, "Réflexions sur l'état actuel des manufactures françoises...," *Annales,* XIII, 369, 371-76. Linguet did not endorse unequivocally the laws of industrial capitalist development, but he recognized what some

of them were, and how an economy even partially dependent for its vitality on a progressively augmented industrial productivity would have to operate in order to satisfy them. See *ibid.*, 366-67, 369-70, 371. What he found intolerable in French "capitalist" enterprise was its sloppiness, its lack of system, its wasteful and damaging disorder. The French entrepreneur, the merchant-manufacturer, for example, was frequently as exploited as his workers were; his business was unprofitable to him as well as dehumanizing and physically lethal for his workers. See *ibid.*, 365. In other words, the French manufacturer had failed to become what we might recognize today as the modern capitalist entrepreneurial type; and he had failed to transform traditionalist French enterprises into smoothly functioning modern concerns capable of holding their own in competition with English capitalist enterprises. See *ibid.*, 363-86. In his forecasts for the year 1811, marking the end of the national bank's first two decades of existence, Linguet seemed to assume that major psychological and economic obstacles to modernization of the economy would have been overcome. But he does not indicate how. See Linguet,"Suite," 495.

41. See Linguet, *P*, pp. 70-71. For a recent historical perspective on Linguet's observations, see George V. Taylor, "Non-capitalist Wealth and the Origins of the French Revolution," *American Historical Review*, 72 (1967), 469-96; Taylor, "Types of Capitalism," 490; Taylor, "The Paris Bourse on the Eve of the Revolution, 1781-1789," *American Historical Review*, 67 (1962), 958-66.

42. Linguet, *Du commerce des grains. Nouvelle édition' Augmentée d'une lettre à M. Tissot sur le vrai mérite politique et phisique du pain et du bled* (Brussels, 1788), pp. 140-41.

43. Linguet, *Du pain et du bled* (London, 1774), cited hereafter as *PB*.

44. For typical expressions of Linguet's earlier commitment to the principles of mercantilism, see Linguet' *Réponse aux docteurs modernes*, II, 222-23, 226-27; *PB*, pp. 268-69.

45. Linguet, *Histoire impartiale des Jésuites. Depuis leur établissement jusqu'à leur première expulsion*, 2 vols. (n.p., 1768), II, 232ff.

46. In his *Point de banqueroute*, Linguet broached this delicate question of the transformation of proto-proletarians into *bons bourgeois* with a remarkable combination of cynical condescension and pragmatic commitment. A mere ten years ago, he estimated, or even a mere three months ago, there are some who would have dismissed *le peuple* as "too insolent." Today, whoever thinks these things, keeps his mouth closed. "...as for me, I will note that the prospect of this affluence will be still another bond between the well-to-do class, which will have the means to make it commonplace, and the lower classes, which will have to merit its choice." A domestic with a guaranteed annuity of 50 *livres* from his master was a relatively submissive fellow, p. 70. "If, at the date of maturity, at the end of *forty, fifty years*, with a *house of their own* and 1000 *livres* in income, they think of themselves as *bourgeois*, where is the harm in that? Won't they have paid their debt to society?" And if, on the contrary, they are still enchained in their penury, "... then it will be hope which moves them, by raising their spirits without making them prideful," p. 71. Of extreme interest in this context would be a study in depth of the French wage-earner's image of the bourgeoisie. For some research in this area see M. Vovelle and D. Roche, "Bourgeois, Rentiers, and Property Owners: Elements for Defining a Social Category at the End of the Eighteenth Century," in Jeffry Kaplow, ed., *New Perspectives on the French Revolution: Readings in Historical Sociology* (New York, 1965), pp. 25-46.

47. Linguet, *Adresse au peuple français, concernant de qu'il faut faire et ce qu'il ne faut pas faire; pour célébrer le fête mémorable et nationale du 14 juillet 1790. Et surtout la nécessité de n'y admettre aucun cheval* (n.p., 1790). See also Linguet, "Cérémonie et serment du 14 juillet: De l'espèce de cirque où elle a eu lieu. Réflexions tant sur ce grand événement que sur les accessoires," *Annales*, XVI, 225-42.

EIGHT

Revolutions

Revolutionary *Engagements,* Brussels and Paris

"You stand on a mine which might blow up just from the heat generated in the environs of *Paris:* and what will happen if live sparks from this blazing Vesuvius fall directly here?"[1] Linguet delivered himself of this alarming portent veiled in transparent metaphor in a letter to Count Trauttmansdorff, Joseph II's minister plenipotentiary in the Austrian Netherlands (replacing Belgiojoso). He wrote from Brussels on July 28, 1789, having just returned from Paris.

Ministers whom Linguet favored with his previews of revolution always failed to respond with appropriate gestures of gratitude or adequate measures of precaution. In European diplomatic circles, Linguet was becoming a splendid suspect. He was wild, that is ungovernable; and he was a seer. It was impossible to know exactly on whose behalf and from which perspective he was foretelling the shape of imminent catastrophes. He did not seem to belong anywhere; he acted as a roving international troubleshooter might, who had been dispatched on his own orders in the interest of preserving society. That made him fair game for all sides. "I'm a little like a turtle dove," he confessed to Trauttmansdorff in August, 1789, "who moans in the middle of a storm: the tree beneath whose foliage it hides is not any less shaken by the winds; these expressions of its woe and fright serve only to indicate its retreat simultaneously to hunters who are undaunted by the bad weather, and to poachers who take full advantage of it."[2]

When Linguet arrived back in Brussels, Joseph's position in his Belgian provinces was precarious. His crash reform program had aroused protests from all quarters. By the summer of 1789, rumor had it that plots to overthrow the government were being engineered under the eyes of the governors.[3] Joseph's plans included a revamping of traditional judicial, administrative, religious, and educational systems, and a substitution of centralized administration for feudal establishments. He planned to set up an executive directly responsible to him. He took steps to impose toleration and to make the clergy dependent upon him for its salaries. He forbade church burials, and in a program of systematic secularization, suppressed convents and episcopal seminaries. The emperor calculated that by imperial fiat, he could wipe out local traditions to which all orders in the population, bourgeoisie, clergy, and nobility, were strongly attached.[4]

Opposition to imperial reform in the Brabant, the area of Belgium with its capital at Brussels, had been sporadic and badly organized before the victories of the French Third Estate. From then on, spurred into political action by Joseph's suppression of the Brabant Estates in June, 1789, and by a revolutionary upheaval in Liège, in August, insurrectionaries had been operating in at least two camps, consolidating public sentiment and plotting revolutionary action. Henry Van der Noot, a wealthy Brussels lawyer with strong ties to the nobility, headed one of these insurrectionary factions. His goals were to bring the British, Prussians, and Dutch to the aid of an insurrectionary Belgium fighting to regain autonomy over traditional political institutions, and to preserve a predominance of conservative forces in them.

The other principal resistance came from the followers of Jean-François Vonck, also a lawyer practicing in Brussels. Vonck drew his support from lawyers, merchants, small proprietors, townspeople, and other middle-class elements. He gathered his following into a clandestine organization, the Society Pro Aris et Focis. The Vonckists hoped for structural revision in the traditional Estates—including the creation of a Fourth Estate representing broadly based middle-class interests.[5]

Linguet's position in the middle of this ferment was highly ambiguous. Following his return to Belgium, Linguet's praise for Joseph was effusive (for example, *Annales*, XIII [1788], 427, 437-39). But his support for the emperor's reform programs and his response to the measures Joseph invoked to execute them was sometimes remarkably tepid; and he was conspicuously piqued by the authorities' failure to consult him on ways of conciliating the Belgian public.[6] Late in 1787, he announced in his *Annales* that grateful as he was to the emperor, he was equally sensitive to the Belgians' traditional rights under the *joyeuse entrée*, a convention of long standing contracted between the inhabitants and their prince, and unilaterally dissolved by Joseph when its provisions began to interfere with his reforms (*ibid.*, 72-80).

Linguet signaled his coming defection even more clearly a few months later, when he reported an incident that had taken place in Brussels on January 22, 1788.[7] The previous day, the Judicial Council of Brabant had refused to publish the Austrian minister's declarations of administrative and judicial reforms for Brabant. Trauttmansdorff ordered the Council locked up until it came around. A crowd gathered on the twenty-second in an open square in front of the Council's meeting place to protest Trauttmansdorff's action. The area was being patrolled by soldiers under the command of General d'Alton, Joseph II's special military emissary. The crowd began pelting the soldiers with stones and potatoes. A soldier opened fire, gunning down several spectators.

Trauttmansdorff reacted to Linguet's article by accusing him of having sold himself to the patriots.[8] "Ah, Monseigneur," Linguet replied, "if I were for sale, the entire country would not suffice as the price I would demand. The late Monsieur le comte de Vergennes wanted to buy me, and at a high price, to use me against the emperor. The comte de Mercy [Argenteau] has the proof of it, as well as my answer. It was to *give* myself to the emperor."[9] He asked for a private interview to explain himself; after that, he would be willing to meet with the offended Austrian Commander-General d'Alton. "At least I will convince him, perhaps, that for the public good, for the common advantage, there must not be a scandal. I will ask him to judge for himself what he might be able to do to avoid one. There have been only too many already."[10]

D'Alton wrote to Trauttmansdorff to accuse Linguet of false and calumniating reporting, of censuring ministerial and military operations, and of "publishing infamies all over Europe." He insisted on a "rigorous censorship" for the *Annales* and called for Linguet's written retraction in the next number of his periodical.[11] In a dispatch to the emperor, Trauttmansdorff described Linguet's stand as an attack against the government and the military. While he admitted that he would have preferred to place himself above "all these scribblers," he recognized that the military commander had become too agitated over Lingeut's presentation of the affair in his *Annales*. In order to put an end to such journalistic slips he had summoned Linguet to his residence, "and after the funniest session, mixed with tears and contortions worthy of a Frenchman," Linguet "committed himself to a retraction of what he said... and to all the reparations I prescribed to him."[12]

Linguet was not that compliant. He wept. In the end, he refused to retract.[13] Even before he could have printed up a retraction, d'Alton commissioned an Austrian officer, Colonel Moitelle, to write and circulate two letters challenging Linguet's report of the incident of January 22. Linguet was now convinced that d'Alton was out to compromise him fatally. At this point, he only aggravated the issue further and at the same time strengthened his public image by publishing Moitelle's second letter in his *Annales*, along with his own observations.[14]

An infuriated population began to recognize Linguet as its defender against Joseph's military despotism.[15] Count Trauttmansdorff began to see the advisability of giving Linguet a censor.[16] Admitting that Linguet "is forever imprudent," Kaunitz gave his full support to the idea of a censor for him, to prevent "other scandals from his camp."[17]

Linguet had also miscalculated Joseph's threshold of tolerance for impartial news reports. Joseph wrote to d'Alton in April, 1788, that Linguet's pen was venal. He echoed d'Alton's assertion that Linguet had found in the bourgeois opposition party a higher bidder than himself, and for that reason had presented the incident of January 22 in a light favorable to it: "...we must scorn that, not answer, and if he becomes too insolent, have him chased out of my States."[18] Notwithstanding all these threats, no action was taken.

Linguet dubbed his retirement from the revolutionary scene in Paris in mid-July, 1789, the retreat of a "prudent man."[19] A retreat to Brussels, however, was a march from one revolution directly into another. Linguet knew it.[20]

He would have to take a position at once. The insurrectionaries in the Belgian Third Estate were almost daring him to commit himself. Distrustful patriots already had aroused suspicions against him by publicizing detailed reports of his handsomely rewarded collaborations with the emperor and his ministers.[21] Remembering Linguet's earlier deviations from the imperial line, Trauttmansdorff and d'Alton were on their guard also. Linguet really might be an agent for the patriots.

Simon Linguet was everything both sides accused him of being. He was working in both camps to achieve an all but impossible reconciliation at the brink between the Belgian Third Estate and Austrian authorities. In issues of the *Annales* and in widely circulated polemic pamphlets, Linguet continued to publicize clashes between government authorities and Belgian citizens. He did not conceal his sympathies for the Third Estate. He had become their apologist and advocate.[22]

Linguet was a government informer also. The government had not solicited advice from him on the execution of Joseph's reform program for Belgium, but he was giving it voluntarily. What Linguet volunteered to tell was hardly what the Austrian administration was prepared to hear. He admitted that he was being kept in the dark; far from being able to support the government's program, he confessed that his tendancy was to "contradict its measures."[23]

The French revolutionaries had ignited an irrepressible political explosive in the world, the force of popularly based national sovereignty. "Live sparks from this blazing Vesuvius" were about to fall on the Austrian Netherlands. Earlier, Linguet explained to the French Third Estate that its natural enemies were aristocratic pretenders and that its power, if only it dared aggregate and consciously wield it, would be insuperable.[24] It is true that Linguet had turned out a pamphlet arguing for a limitation in the scope of the Estate's competency when it was convened.[25] Still, he was able to recognize that after July 14, the triumph of national sovereignty was a foregone conclusion. The French monarch had defaulted. Whether the new sovereign, catapulted out of political nullity and into power, would be capable of executing systematic reforms and organizing the machinery of administration was another question, one which a social analyst and critic might legitimately raise. That, however, would be a question after the fact. That unconjurable fact was the revolutionaries' success.

Almost from the day he returned to Brussels, Linguet began giving Trauttmansdorff authoritative lessons in the art of staving off the inevitable. "Monseigneur, ever since I had the misfortune to dare write on political matters,
I have not stopped maintaining that the *Sovereign* and the *Third Estate,* for
their common interests had to be inseparable."[26] The opening, of course,
begged the question who the Belgian Third Estate was, that is, whether its
membership should be limited to predominantly traditionalist elements represented in the Brabant Estates which Joseph had just suppressed, or broadened
to include the newer wealth of bourgeois lawyers, merchants, and small landowners who were beginning to demand representation; but it did not understate
Linguet's point that the emperor's policy of indiscriminate military repression
was driving all factions of the Third Estate—and even more, the entire population—into an irreconcilable opposition. He outlined in detail the course events
had taken in Paris: "...le Tiers-Etat a marché tout seul...."[27]

> Monseigneur, I am fearful that you are being deceived, that you
> are deceiving yourself about the true state of affairs, about the
> disposition of minds, about the means by which you think you
> can enchain them, about the time you perhaps fancy you have
> left for staving off an irremediable explosion, right up to the
> moment when you could no longer not be fearful of it [this ex-
> plosion]: I fear I see all that only too clearly, and I see nothing
> but the most alarming [things].
>   Again, a terrible light is reflected here from the blazing crack-
> ling hotbed in the middle of France. For several years now,
> peoples have been playing out with their kings a terrible tragedy
> in which we already have had three acts....[28]

Belgium, Linguet forecast, would be the stage where the fourth act in this
"terrible tragedy" of revolutions, Dutch, American, and French, would be
played. "I do not know what will happen in the fourth act; but truthfully,
woe betide the administrators in the countries where it takes place."[29] Linguet's clairvoyance was astounding. He knew almost too much to be only an
innocent seer.

Linguet wrote still another cryptic note to Trauttmansdorff on August 3.
He insisted on seeing the minister that day. He hinted that if Trauttmansdorff
chose not to profit from his advice, he would act on his own preview of revolutionary spectacles: "...having had the honor of writing to him [Trautt-
mansdorff] as a faithful subject and true citizen, I am determined to act the
prudent man, by leaving tomorrow to go look for......distractions, at least:
because as for real safety, I don't know where it exists this side of the Rhine.
It's only too true that everything hangs by a thread, and what if it breaks!"[30]
Whatever the man knew, it obviously was something more than he was willing
to tell Trauttmansdorff.

Again, later in August, Linguet alerted Trauttmansdorff to the danger of a
revolution engineered from the ranks of the Third Estate. He had failed con-

spicuously to take his own advice and clear out to look for "distractions." He
advised the minister that six weeks earlier, he had sounded the same alert, to
the same danger, in his conversations with France's minister in the department of foreign affairs, the comte de Montmorin, "…counseling a condescension which had become indispensable in the state things were in; urging authority to *grant,* so as to sidestep the danger of seeing things *grabbed* from it."
He pointed out that in Paris his efforts had been rewarded by calumniating
charges from the Third Estate that he had conspired with the government
against the people; while in Brussels, he had been accused of conspiring with
the people against the government. Linguet insisted that Trauttmansdorff was
mistaken to suspect him: "…if there was someone from whom the emperor
and you might hope to receive real truths and services, above all right now, it
is from me, independent by my character, by my fortune, or rather by my
moderation; I, who wish no offices; who have neither the taste for nor the
need of money…." Trauttmansdorff could hardly be blamed for not recognizing this self-portrait as Linguet's. "I hope that this expression which I'm
told everyone so ridiculously wants to ask me the meaning of, of *a mine
which the heat from the environs might cause to blow up,* is only a hyperbole
of rhetoric, and unfounded….If I am mistaken in my lugubrious prognostica-
tions I will recant with great joy: but in this case, it is to the goddess *fortune*
and not to the god *Consus* that I will believe my thanks due."[31]

Trauttmansdorff was impatient and irritated with the visions of seers. "I
scorn these children's stories that are broadcast to scare us," he wrote to the
emperor.[32] Meanwhile, Linguet kept up his stream of correspondence with
Trauttmansdorff, begging clemency for suspects whom the emperor had
ordered arrested; suggesting the withdrawal of the Austrian military from Brussels; proposing a reestablishment of the suspended Estates of Brabant and a
restitution of the suspended constitution; and urging a reconciliation with the
Third Estate before its revolution made the feat impossible.[33]

Trauttmansdorff in turn was dutifully communicating the contents of Linguet's letters to Joseph, and without taking any of it very seriously, was drawing piquant character sketches of the writer:

> M. Linguet, turned away from the general assembly in France,
> and dying of envy to play a role, thought he had arrived here at a
> favorable moment. The point was to reconcile himself with the
> nation, which had not been happy with him when he left, and
> this intention had to be combined with the confidence he wanted
> to win with me. He wasn't in Brussels twenty-four hours before
> he set about writing me two or three consecutive letters, all
> charming in style, but all calculated to make me fear the fate of
> those who had been immolated to the fury of the masses in
> France.[34]

The minister had analyzed at least this much correctly: Linguet had engaged
himself in Belgium's political affairs with a foot firmly planted in the camp of

each antagonist, a natural and necessary position for him. His pen had been double-edged in the service of a complex political philosophy decades before Joseph II suspected it of being venal. He could lend his support to the Belgian Third Estate's claim for justice (protection of properties) because at base that had been his own claim against the regime in France. Before 1789, he had passed through all the stages in the Belgian and French Third Estates' politicization and radicalization processes. For all that, Linguet was incapable of cutting his ties with absolute authority and of making a whole ideological commitment to the revolutionaries; his identification with their interests was real, and permanent, but permanently incomplete. He never abandoned his idealizations of an administrative authority embodying the vision, justice, humanity, and force necessary to maximize the propertied class's chances for survival in a society rent by civil war. Linguet's prerevolutionary careers had been studies in split political commitments. Revolutions in France and Belgium only further exposed and exaggerated these polarizations.

Committed to balancing radically contradictory political alignments, Linguet set to work on a petition to be submitted on behalf of the inhabitants of the Austrian Netherlands requesting the restoration of Belgium's ancient constitution, the *Joyeuse entrée*. Naturally, he informed Trauttmansdorff, announcing to the minister that he had discovered in Joseph's act suspending the constitution a technical error that might provide the occasion for an honorable constitutional restoration: "...it's astonishing, but fortunate, that no one has noticed it." It would "not be impossible to conciliate everything without compromising the *restoring* authority, or running the risk of having it appear opposed to the *abolishing* authority."[35] Later, he told Trauttmansdorff that plagued by accusations from both sides, each charging that he was the blind instrument of the other, he had abandoned his work on the petition."... I'm tired of raising Temples to Peace which the combatants use only to throw stones at my head." He also expressed his regrets that his popular pamphlet dealing with the abduction, forced conscription, and eventual release by the Austrian government of several citizens of Brussels had been badly received by the minister. Finally, he issued another warning: "Doubtless, lots of stories are going around, but among these stories there are some which, by force of being repeated, engender the idea and the means needed for transforming them into truths *quod omen deus avertat!*"[36]

Joseph, for one, was genuinely concerned that Linguet was engaged in flinging stones himself—at the Austrian administration. He wrote to Trauttmansdorff on August 25: "If this insolent character of a Linguet takes it into his head to write and have printed, the way he has, things that are hardly proper, and unapproved by the Government—the sole condition on which we gave him asylum in the Netherlands—we could very well send him packing."[37] Linguet's continued defenses of the Third Estate, especially his protests against d'Alton's military despotism, provoked the emperor to command in

September, 1789, that authors of "all insolent brochures" against the military must all be punished, "whether they're named Linguet or Windischgraetz."[38]

During the night of October 17-18, 1789, Austrian authorities in Brussels uncovered what they depicted as a conspiracy to overthrow the Austrian administration in Belgium. Among the suspects seized in a midnight raid was one Daubremez, a wine merchant, a member of the Vonckist association Pro Aris et Focis, and a secretary to Simon Linguet; Claude-Antoine Joseph Fisco, an engineer in Brussels and one of the founders of Pro Aris et Focis; Philippe-Abraham-Louis Secrétan, tutor to the son of the Duke of Ursel; and Simon-Nicolas-Henri Linguet, adviser to emperors and propagandist for revolutionaries.[39]

Trauttmansdorff broke the news to Joseph on the eighteenth, borrowing for the occasion Linguet's explosive metaphor which had been intriguing them all. In the end, it had turned out to be something more than a "hyperbole of rhetoric." "The mine is really laid bare, or is going to be." He reported the seizure of "three in conference," Secrétan, Fisco, and Daubremez, along with notes, papers, a manifesto, and plans for a general insurrection.[40] On the nineteenth, he announced that Linguet had been caught in the dragnet. "Linguet has been indulging himself in violent outbursts, notably in a brochure which he has just published under his name...." Trauttmansdorff admitted that the brochure in question (possibly Linguet's *Point de banqueroute* or the second edition of his *Avis aux Parisiens*) dealt primarily with French, not Belgian affairs, but that it contained "passages designed to be applied to our own, and which it is impossible to tolerate. Besides, his connections are suspect, his principles are still more so, and it is more than probable that the examination of his papers, which is under way already, will shed more light....I admit that this is a severe operation, but circumstances have made it indispensable."[41]

Trauttmansdorff wrote to Joseph again on the twentieth, to fill him in on the details of this expedition to lay bare mines. He emphasized that unless the government obtained a "perfect conviction," there could be trouble in one case, "that of the notorious Linguet, who is going to cry murder all over Europe, and who, suspected of working on the manifesto which it was said was ready to appear, had to be arrested by the police to get him out of a state of causing harm." The minister went on to note that he personally had "as little belief in the existence of such a manifesto, as in an imminent explosion of that with which we have been threatened for so long." Nonetheless, "Linguet's ...conduct, above all, finally, his mania for writing and playing a role and the privilege he has enjoyed up until now of having presses in his house, lent too much support to indications the Government had received for us to have done nothing at all in his case."[42]

The hunches might have been deadly accurate. The evidence was circumstantial, hardly the kind that would win "perfect convictions." The manifesto in question did exist, and had been found on Daubremez's person, but a prosecutor would have been hard put to demonstrate that it reflected Linguet's principles or his style.[43]

Joseph was delighted. He did not see why the government should follow judicial formalities in prosecuting its case against Linguet. He wrote to d'Alton on October 31, expressing his satisfaction at the course events had taken and his eagerness to see the Linguet affair terminated: "You've done very well to arrest Linguet with all his accomplices, but on the condition that a prompt judgment and example follow."[44] Kaunitz was "charmed that this horrible conspiracy had been discovered," although he was somewhat more concerned than Joseph to see that the suspects received a fair trial.[45]

Linguet was beside himself. He refused to admit anything. He wrote to Joseph on November 1 "from the Bastille in Brussels": "Yes, Sire, from the BASTILLE: it is destroyed in Paris....It is restored here, for me—and restored crueller, more ruinous, more scandalous, if that's possible—in all senses—than it ever was on the banks of the Seine." He demanded a hearing at once. Even more, he demanded special treatment. "I perish of pain, of distress, not knowing of what I am accused, or even whether I am accused; informed of nothing other than that for the past fifteen days my physical, civil, political, literary, pecuniary existence is in the hands of people I do not know....I ask finally what I am accused of; I ask for judges; I ask for a rigorously examined legal proceeding, with a precise order that it pass before Your Majesty's eyes; and I beg him to set aside a few moments to evaluate my justification. Ah Sire, how glorious it is . But will I survive until then?"[46]

Linguet was released during the first week of November. The official explanation was consideration for his health. The more likely reason was lack of clinching evidence, for by the time the minister and his aides were beginning to despair of implicating Linguet or anyone else.[47] By December, the Austrians had fled before a victorious Patriot party which reestablished the Estates of Brabant and accepted Van der Noot's leadership.

Linguet first made use of his liberty to address petitions to the Patriots demanding the return of properties pillaged during the Austrians' search of his house.[48] He took time out on December 22 to write a frank and sober letter of farewell to Joseph, a letter which he printed for public distribution. He had been trampled under by imperial ministers who now were vanquished, and swept into celebrity by the victorious Belgian Third Estate. Through all this, *he* had managed to keep in step with the march of an inexorable dialectic. Joseph had not. "For your peace, for ours, for that of all *Europe,* it must be flatly, openly stated: *the veil is torn,* at least on this side of the *Rhine:* it's no longer possible to conceal the nakedness of crowns when the law ceases to be their shield, or their impotence when justice is no longer their support. *Royal* authority, even where this epithet is retained, from now on will be nothing more than an *entrusted* and supervised dispensation of *national* authority."[49]

Linguet followed this sober statement of the new order of political necessities and realities with a barrage of raging republican tirades when he learned from correspondence published by the insurgents what Joseph really thought of him.

> Sultan Joseph does not speak of a *procedure,* a *verification.* It's not with trifles of this sort that the Aga of his *Janizaries* must amuse himself: what he has to have is a prompt *judgment* and *example.* It's Linguet's blood to suck that he demands, *immediately,* and *poste courante;* it's *Linguet's* head and that of *all his accomplices* that he's longing to devour.[50]

> ...if ever peoples were wise enough to decide to suppress it [royalty] in *Europe;* if ever a *crusade* were organized for this beautiful and noble project, then my help could be counted on: I enlist in advance. If I am dead, my dried bones will wake up, regain sensation, to applaud the trumpet which will herald this great, this memorable judgment, this last triumph of reason and liberty.[51]

Once he recovered his equilibrium, Linguet would be able to express his Republican allegiance in terms that excluded all radical political extremes. He had been arrested along with well-known Vonckists in October. In December he was ready to side with the triumphant party of Van der Noot, which controlled the newly reestablished Estates of Brabant. The Estates subscribed to twelve-hundred copies of Linguet's *Annales* when he resumed publication;[52] and Linguet became an outspoken proponent of the Estate's struggle for independence against Joseph's successor, Leopold.[53]

Linguet came closest to clarifying his position concerning the Belgian revolution in his *Lettre à un membre de la Société patriotique de Bruxelles* of March, 1790. The principle behind his propaganda for Van der Noot's party of conservative nationalists was simple. The revolution had given the Belgians their sovereignty; it had not liberated them into a state of nature. Property, "the essential object, one could say the only one, of everything that is called Government, or Constitution," was still intact. What kind of victory would a successful revolution be "if, behind the blasted despotism, there remained for them nothing more than.....nothingness." The Belgian constitution itself, *not* institutional novelties imitative of the French National Assembly, was the nation's best guarantor of sovereignty and properties.[54]

Linguet was not particularly comfortable arguing on the constitutionalists' ground. But he was even less at home with the revolutionaries' vision of an omnipotent legislature executing the dictates of a popular will. He was a maverick revolutionary. He seemed to have thrown himself headlong into two revolutions for the express purpose of bucking the tide, but not as a counterrevolutionary would, by swimming against it. There could be no question of a return: "the veil is torn." His opposition was that of a postrevolutionary. He plunged transversely into revolutionary turmoil, and then forged madly ahead with only the slimmest hope of reaching some farther shore.

In Brussels a victim of Joseph II's enlightened absolutism was abandoning his role as imperial seer and adviser and embracing a career as Belgian patriot and publicist for Van der Noot's conservative nationalists. Meanwhile, in Paris, young Camille Desmoulins, editor of a new political journal, *Révolutions de France et de Brabant,* was trying to invent a republican hero for himself. The hero Desmoulin propped up had engaged himself fearlessly in two great struggles for liberty. In advance of the assault on the Bastille, before the patriots took Brussels, Desmoulins's hero had slipped "beneath the flags of triumphant liberty, and he was in the wooden horse with the most courageous Greeks....Who has bent his head fewer times than he beneath the despotism of ministers, parlements, and his colleagues?"[55] The opposition of Desmoulins's hero to all branches of the French political establishment amounted to a one-man revolution.

However, the rebel Desmoulins had in mind, Simon Linguet, was too complicated a character to be heroic in any classical sense, that is, in the one Desmoulins took as his model for all virtue and achievement. Surely the man's complexity was a sign of his impurity. Linguet's writings, Desmoulins was forced to admit, have not always been those of a free man. The corruption in a world where a man could defy ministers at Versailles only by prostrating himself before emperors in Vienna disgusted Desmoulins. He recovered immediately, to pardon Linguet his errors: "...but he did far more to bring on the revolution by his examples than he did to retard it with his paradoxes...."[56]

Desmoulins printed Linguet's response to this qualified panegyric in the eleventh number of *Révolutions de France et de Brabant.* Linguet confined himself to refuting the familiar charge of paradox. He recommended his recent writings on the Belgian revolution: "You will read that, you will weigh that, and you will judge whether these are paradoxes, whether my paradoxes lead to slavery." Borrowing the rhetorical forms of St. Paul answering his detractors, Linguet suggested that the liberty Desmoulins and his contemporaries had just begun to fight for, now that its triumph was assured, was the same that he, a generation older, had been reclaiming alone, unprotected, for twenty years.[57]

Desmoulins was enchanted. He was impatient for Linguet's return to France, and he burned to see Linguet resume publication of his *Annales*: "... how is it that Monsieur Linguet, the only periodic writer who, in the time of Egypt's servitude, dared to proclaim several bold truths to the Pharoahs, and who joined courage to the talent of a great writer, does not show himself among those who lead the people to the promised land, and has withdrawn his pillar of light?" In full view of the promised land, where the freedom of the press he had always reclaimed is guaranteed, "...will Monsieur Linguet, as Moses, have died having seen it, and before having entered?"[58]

Linguet could not afford to ignore this flattery. He assured Desmoulins that he was ready to return; he had taken his leave of the French revolutionary scene only because he had been under sentence of death from Desmoulins's cohorts at the Palais royal: "It's up to you, Monsieur *le Procureur-général de la Lanterne*, to disabuse them and their agents. Admit that it takes a destiny as undecipherable as mine to have run the risk in 1789 of finding myself suddenly coupled and decapitated with dear *de Launay*, *l'Embastilleur*, after having spent in 1780 and 1781, twenty [months], twenty great centuries between his claws." The new Lazarus admitted that after all his martyrdoms, "I have not seen the shores of the dead twice, but two Bastilles, which is getting pretty close." He apologized for having let French affairs drop, in particular his project for the establishment of a *caisse nationale*: "...before turning my head in any direction, I had to assure myself that it was still on my shoulders"; now, at least he could be certain that his proprietorship "over this effect will no longer be transferred by the arbitrary act [par le bon plaisir] of any Majesty...."[59]

He would return, he promised Desmoulins. "It will not be long before you see appearing over the national horizon not, as you too poetically state it, my column of fire, but my peaceful lantern." He would resume publication of his *Annales*. He was ready to take his civic oath. He wanted to join Desmoulins, Danton, and Fabre d'Eglantine in the District of the Cordeliers.[60]

Desmoulins concluded that Simon Linguet had become a patriarch of the Revolution. Linguet was less the patriarch than the coquette on this occasion. He was playing hard to get. In February, 1790, Desmoulins reported that Linguet had ordered discreet inquiries made for him concerning the Cordeliers. He had even requested that formalities connected with his initiation into the district be suspended. Desmoulins would hear nothing of these precautions and procrastinations. "But I had taken the initiative; the sound of bells had announced the joyous news; I had been complimented on my procuration; and when I gave notice of the counterorder, the protest was universal. We want to keep Monsieur Linguet, he will not back out; we have inscribed him on our roll and he will not be stricken from it. We have already prepared his *cocarde* for him, his musket, his sabre, and his cartridge pouch.

Oh! *parbleu,* you will be one of us, Monsieur Linguet; you will belong to the Cordeliers' District. *Ac veluti te Judaei cogemus in hanc concedere turbam."*[61]

Linguet surrendered at once. "I have no news for you," he wrote to a friend, "if not that last Friday...I swore my civic oath at the District of the Cordeliers. So there I am, a bit the son of St. Francis. Tomorrow I will have my national uniform. When I'm wanted, I'll go on guard, and then, we'll see."[62]

Linguet's alliance with the Cordeliers was a short one.[63] It served to advertise his commitment to the revolution, but the advertisement was misleading. Linguet was pledged to his own permanent rebellion and determined to work toward postrevolutionary social settlements of a French civil war. He never identified completely with the revolutionaries' revolution. The patriarch who resumed publication of his *Annales* in what Desmoulins called the promised land immediately began broadcasting his message. He had not arrived there after all; nobody else had either. He had undertaken to present in his *Annales* "the tableau of the progresss of the human mind in this *fin de siècle."* He now lamented that he could perceive "only palpable indications of its impending retrogradation." The triumph of the Third Estate, Linguet announced, was incontestable, and uncontested. It has "become *Nobility,* become *Clergy,* become *Everything....*but where is it going? where does it want to go?" The real difference between him and the younger generation of revolutionaries, Linguet was suggesting, was that he knew exactly where he wanted this revolution to go. The first step in the right direction would be the immediate adoption of his project for a national bank, the project he had outlined in his *Point de banqueroute,* "the only expedient perhaps that could prevent....., what cannot be named, [the expedient] to which they will want to return, but too late, after having disdained it, repulsed it, when it could have saved everything" (*Annales,* XVI [1790], 269, 274).

Camille Desmoulins was 29 years old when the revolution began. Robespierre was 31, Brissot de Warville was 35, Danton was 30, Saint-Just was 22, Siéyès was 41. Simon Linguet was 53 years old on July 14, 1789. Linguet's younger contemporaries were still serving their apprenticeships in revolutionary journalism, oratory, and politics in the summer of 1789. Linguet had become past master of these disciplines by then.

More than one of these younger men, such as Brissot de Warville, whose admiration for Linguet at one time bordered on fanatic devotion, could recall that Linguet, iconoclast and rebel, had been a prerevolutionary political role model. "But I confess it, the heat, the accent of truth that breathed in some of Linguet's writings, had seduced, enchanted my novice youth....With every line that issued from your pen, I thought I saw your entire soul escaping in streams of fire." Brissot recalled also that Linguet had deceived him, that Linguet was impure and unworthy of taking a place among revolutionaries. "Ah!

Linguet! Linguet! why has a fatal enlightenment dissipated the sweet prestige which drew me toward you?...Linguet tribune of the people! Linguet friend of liberty! no, no, and Camille and Danton will not persuade anyone." He had defended the Chevalier de La Barre, but also d'Aiguillon. He was about as much a friend of the people as Marat, "since he has not hesitated to make himself Nero's apologist." "He saw the Club of the Cordeliers as a piscina where all his sermons in favor of despotism would be washed away."[64]

Brissot wrote to expose an impostor. Desmoulins perhaps thought he was saving a sin-stained republican. Simon Linguet, a model rebel against despotisms and a theorist of revolutions, believed he was applying his schooling in the statecraft of absolutism and his scientific knowledge of societal necessities to the task of saving the revolution from the revolutionaries, if necessary.

Nothing in Linguet's character or theories attracted him into the counter-revolutionaries' camp. "La révolution est faite; je la crois irrévocable...." At the very beginning of this revolution, Linguet set himself up as the theorist of a postrevolutionary order of things. He was certain he understood the driving force behind the great upheaval and knew what demands would have to be satisfied, and how, before the revolution could be successfully concluded. "I repeat, the revolution happened without anyone's *wishing* it, without anyone's *believing* it was happening: one was necessary, that is to say, a change, a reform, was necessary: the upper classes were too well off, the lower ones too badly off: it was *everything* and *nothing*. Another proportion, or rather, less of a disproportion became indispensable" (*Annales*, XVI, 268, 270).

In the aftermath of a major disturbance at Nancy in August, 1790, an insurrection carried out by a garrison against its commander, Linguet volunteered some general reflections on the French Revolution as a social revolution.

> On all sides, everyone sizes up everyone else, everyone threatens everyone else, terrifying plots are revealed. Everywhere, without a great deal of mystery, the great quarrel unfolds, the endless quarrel of those who *have nothing* with those who *have something:* this destitution on the one side, this abundance on the other, is a necessary fruit of the *social* condition. Society cannot exist where the subsistence of the most numerous portion of individuals composing it does not depend upon a daily labor. This principle is true; it is incontestable: in the hearts of all those whose dependence seemingly is eternalized by [the operation of this principle], an inextinguishable fund of resentment arises...the unique end of laws is to contain ceaselessly the explosion [of this resentment]. [*Ibid.*, 529-30.]

The expedients flung into this operation of containment would have to be satisfactory to all parties. Everyone was demanding everything. Enlightened declarations proclaimed all men's equality in rights: "From the equality of rights [the people] conclude for the equality of possessions" (*ibid.*, 530).

After the initial explosion in 1789, Linguet saw what revolutionary necessity dictated. He convinced no one. The National Assembly ignored his *Point de banqueroute*, his master plan for achieving societal containment in a revolutionary setting. The Assembly took no official cognizance of the project for a *caisse nationale* which he printed in his *Annales* (*ibid.*, 126-28).

"I would rather keep my silence than risk either being accused of a criminal disobedience or of contributing to weakening the respect due from every good citizen to an assembly which right now is *France's* only resource" (*ibid.*, 318). He could not keep his silence. The trouble with the French Revolution was that it had not yet been *révolue*, "that is to say, finished, that is to say, reformed, and consolidated so as to fix all authorities within limits which alone can assure them an efficacious and salutary preponderance..." (*Annales*, XVIII [1791], 431). Linguet confessed that he was uneasy, even confused. He insisted that he was not a counterrevolutionary, that he was militantly opposed to counterrevolution, the "violent shake-up which in a sudden movement backward would destroy even what has been badly done in the past two years" (*ibid.*, 431); but he could not align himself with leaders who were unable to satisfy the masses and unwilling to depoliticize them, and who, in their failure to "contain ceaselessly the explosion [of their resentment]" were inviting the completion of a people's social revolution and the dissolution of the "social condition": "From the equality of rights [the people] conclude for the equality of *possessions.*"

Linguet suspended publication of his *Annales* in October, 1791. His first declaration to his subscribers when he resumed publication in February, 1792, was that he wanted out. He modestly announced that he had entered into a career in political journalism "committed to *telling nothing but the truth....*" In the midst of revolutionary confusion he no longer could lay hold of it. He had lost whatever perspective he had once possessed on it. "The kind of uncertainty I'm speaking about is that which today extends to principles, to the very foundations of society....nothing is more certain: the Constitution is a cracked-brained notion, or today's representatives are brazen perjurers....Then where is the truth?" he wrote. "...either there is no truth at all now for the impartial historian who searches for it; or if it exists for a philosopher detached from all interests, it is the kind that proves troublesome for all sects, for all factions; and must this philosopher expose himself to the danger of revealing such [truths] or to the annoyance of reiterating that he knows no others?" (*Annales*, XIX, [1792], 1-2, 4, 34).

The truth Linguet knew was that unless France's governing elites institutionalized security for her revolutionary masses, the myths of liberty and equality would only feed their resentment and prepare its explosion and the dissolution of the existing regime of properties. The most pressing need in revolutionary France was the need for a social settlement: "...the upper classes were too well off, the lower ones too badly off: it was *everything* and *nothing*.

Another proportion, or rather, less of a disproportion became indispensable." Linguet envisioned this work of reapportionment, of dispensing material satisfactions universally but in new combinations, as an administrative operation on a vast scale, a task for a *caisse nationale*. Clearly, however, the nation's political sovereigns were not ready to accept salvation through administration. They were not prepared to delegate broad-ranging powers to an executive body which, although responsible in principle to the national legislature, seemed designed to undercut its authority, leaving it in the subordinate position of a control body. Even in 1792, Linguet was correct to insist that his truth was troublesome.

The Mayor of Marnes-les-Saint-Cloud

As part of his opening confession to *Annales* subscribers in February, 1792, Linguet revealed that his demanding reading public had called him from his "rural speculations, rustic labors, where I found repose at least, and health, to immerse myself again in the chaos of historical narratives, in the whirlpool of all our civil and political movements, or others. May I have [narratives] to follow which will be stained neither with tears nor the blood *of the people*" (*Annales*, XIX [1792], 34).

For all his protests against being called out of retirement, Simon Linguet had not entered into it all that willingly in the first place. In the early months of 1791, he was behaving singularly like an active candidate for political office. In January, he was anticipating future elections for delegates to the new assembly that would be convened under the first French constitution. He had been asked, he wrote his sister in Rheims,

> ...whether I would accept some part in the next, or at any rate future legislature. Truthfully, I don't think that it would be by Rheims that I would be called. Besides, there have already been insinuations, but I refused. I have suffered storms enough, and I don't want any more of it. Anyway, as I say, it wouldn't be at Rheims that you would find anyone working to overcome my repugnance. You have not justified the coldness, the forgetfulness of these good *Champennois*. They haven't [forgotten] me, granted; but Bordeaux, Marseilles haven't [forgotten] me, or more, and I have not only readers there, but enthusiastic friends; and in Rheims?[65]

He would not run for elected office except at the slightest provocation or barest hint of encouragement. He even supplied his sister with campaign literature, an issue of the *Annales*, and his *Mémoires* on behalf of the Santo-Dominguan Assembly, works which he instructed his sister "you will have circulated in your fool city in order to try to make me known there. Admit that that's ludicrous: By God, how well represented your fellow citizens are in the National Assembly by M. La Beste. How well chosen that deputy is."[66]

Linguet came closest to a real retirement from European revolutions not in 1791 but in 1789, several months before the conquest of the Bastille. He told Trauttmansdorff in February that "If His Majesty ever founds a convent, I want to be the first monk in it. I told it to him, and wrote when I took leave of him that I had made myself a *Josephien* for the rest of my life. While awaiting the Pope's approval for this Order, which should be that of all honest men..., and [while waiting] for His Majesty to set up an Institute in correct form, I become the inhabitant of one of these he has torn down."[67] That was the kind of anticlerical witticism Joseph might have appreciated and rewarded had he not been ready to boot Linguet out of Belgium at the time.

The retreat into a monastic ruin would open splendid prospects for Linguet. Here at last he would have the freedom and authority to reform and administer the world on a microcosmic scale. He would direct the physical reconstruction of the monastery in question, create manufactures, hire and pay workers, and in short, achieve nothing less than the dead calm thought to exist in the eye of a tornado. "Nature," he wrote to Trauttmansdorff in January, 1789, "has endowed me with an activity for which I don't know whether I should congratulate myself or pity myself, but it exists, and it must have nourishment or distraction. Monseigneur, I must keep busy."[68] He later admitted to Trauttmansdorff: "The occupation of my youth has been to point out this good by my writings: the consolation of my old age, wherever I establish myself, will be to execute it myself, as my abilities allow."[69]

Linguet had placed a bid with Austrian authorities for the abandoned monastery of Awerghem, in Belgium. He had plans for setting up several manufacturing establishments there, a wax bleaching factory, a candle manufactory, and a foundry which would make use of a new process for manufacturing characters for printing.[70] He planned to appoint his brother, Jean-Baptiste-François-Augustin Linguet, as curé of this community, "the Aaron whom I'll make pontiff of my tribe," and he wanted to bring in a surgeon at his own expense.[71] The plan was grandiose—a little world dedicated to industrial progress and societal harmony, under the administrative direction of Simon Linguet.

The deal fell through.[72] Nonetheless, Linguet was determined to retire, in his strange sense of the term. He informed his sister in Rheims in December, 1790, that he had considered, then rejected, the idea of purchasing a farm with extensive vineyards in Champagne. He feared the interference of members of his family in his private affairs, probably in his twenty-year-old love affair with Madame Buttet. "I do not want any master. I want the right to say what I think when I'm right, and when I'm not: and I suspected that as for that latter right, I would no longer have it once I was...where a man is never prophet." Linguet wrote again in January, 1791, to announce that he had passed up several opportunities to acquire choice properties because "...it's stolen goods. I strongly blame the priests' present resistance to the civil constitution they want to give them: but I don't approve the invasion of their property any the more. I don't want to be an accomplice in it. If I make an acquisition I want to sleep without anxiety and without remorse." Several weeks later, he had changed his mind; he no longer was convinced that purchasing former church lands was immoral; even the clergy was buying them up as private property. Still, he hesitated.[73]

May 8, 1791, found Simon Linguet complaining of a ruinous frost on the night of the sixth. He had become a farmer. "...in my new quality of rustic, I am very grieved....I already had the apricots trimmed and the apples & c. I would be consoled if I didn't fear for the vineyards, which are another matter."[74]

Linguet had just purchased a splendid estate, a château and gardens in the park of Marnes, located in the tiny municipality of Marnes-les-Saint-Cloud, between Versailles and the town of Sèvres. Marnes was a choice property situated in the forest of Saint-Cloud. Its well-tended paths, mazes, and gardens were known to and frequented by Marie Antoinette—until Simon Linguet put an end to this royal trespassing.[75]

Linguet's château commanded a view onto terraces embellished with statues and offering magnificent perspectives onto a long tree-lined avenue. To the right of the principal terraces was a large *orangerie* planted in the middle of a terrace covered with orchards and gardens; to the left of the château were ponds and woods camouflaging the water works for the house. Behind the château, to the right of an avenue in the form of a long narrow carpet of grass planted on either side with a double row of trees, there was a large wooded area broken up by long walks; to the left, a garden planted with fruit trees, and finally, in the far western corner of the property, a thicket arranged in the form of a multi-wheeled labyrinth. Beyond the main courtyard of the château were the stables and barnyard, the carriage houses and other farm buildings.[76] Linguet had installed in this setting a large library of handsomely bound volumes, his sumptuous interior appointments, and his mistress, Madame Perine Buttet, alias Poulet, alias Madame de St. Germaine, newly divorced, at last, from Monsieur Buttet.[77]

Linguet described the park as a property "in fields and in woods, not too good but very pleasing, because they are planted and pruned in the style of the *ancien régime*, which gave more thought to display than to utility. I will try to reform that a little, as I did for the rest, and more successfully than it turned out for the rest."[78]

He was settled at the château in Marnes in June, 1791. He suspended publication of his *Annales* in October, but also renounced his plans to retire. He threw himself back into revolutionary turmoil.

Linguet had given ample publicity to his key political programs for achieving societal harmonization through institutional innovation and administrative manipulation of civil society's two great classes. Still, the project for a *caisse nationale,* published in two formats, was unrealized in any form. He had dutifully announced his "repugnance" to stand for election to the Legislative Assembly—only to discover that no one in any quarter had the slightest interest in overcoming it. All his revolutionary political activity would have to be scaled down to the proportions of Marnes-les-Saint-Cloud, a minuscule township containing barely thirty families, fewer than two hundred persons—some tradesmen, a few large landholders, and many impoverished laborers subsisting on day-to-day wages.

Linguet's name first appeared on the register of Marnes-les-Saint-Cloud in May or June, 1791, at most a matter of weeks after he settled there; he had been designated a notable of the commune.[79] He was called upon in July, 1791, to prepare the petition of the township of Marnes to the director of the District of Versailles for the return of twenty-two acres of formerly communal property, originally "usurped" by the ecclesiastic Chapter of Saint-Cloud, then passed on to the *curé* of the parish of Marnes, and finally appropriated as national property and put up for sale. Three months later, the mayor of Marnes called an extraordinary general assembly of the commune's inhabitants and formally addressed them on the matter. The minutes of his address bear all the marks of Linguet's forensic style and patterns of thought. The land in question, the inhabitants were informed, had been usurped "at a time when there seemed to be included in the number of rights accorded to the great the principle that the little man could be stripped with impunity." The authorities must be made to see "that what is in question is the welfare of an entire commune, perhaps one of the most indigent communes in the realm, although it is surrounded by places of the opulent; that the parish of Marnes, squeezed in on all sides by parks of the greatest sumptuousness, hasn't an inch of land that its inhabitants can develop, and by the cultivation of which the poor heads of households composing it can supplement the inadequacy of their daily work, when they can obtain it."[80] Linguet was appointed *commissaire délegué* for this case in November, 1791. At the same time, he was elected municipal officer and town notable. He wrote to his nephew, Antoine Dérodé:

> I have just had honors conferred upon me; first I was elected notable, and then municipal officer: you can sense how much my pride must have been satisfied. Nonetheless I did what I could to excuse myself from these glorious favors. There was no way out. They inscribed my name, in spite of me, in the minutes; and for the title of former lawyer, I will be able to substitute that of municipal officer of——of Marnes-les-Saint-Cloud, so it's known that it's not in the Department of Marne that this mark of confidence and esteem has been bestowed upon me.[81]

Every recrimination Linguet heaped upon the *bons Remois* and the *bons Champennois* who had scorned his talents and ignored his availability for national office only betrayed his ambition to have made his mark as a reforming legislator and administrator on the national political scene. Still, he was elated at the turn political affairs had taken in his commune. A newly elected municipal officer in Marnes-les-Saint-Cloud, especially one who edited a political journal with a national circulation, still could draw attention to the merits of his master plans for national regeneration. For one thing, if he could win the assent of a majority of the township's voting members, he might be able to turn Marnes into a testing ground for at least part of his project.

He had failed to evoke the slightest positive response from Necker, and from the National Assembly, to his plea for a *caisse nationale*. Nonetheless, he undertook to revive another portion of the plan, his program to bind the laboring poor to the Revolution before they detached themselves irrevocably.

The fate of the Revolution, as the fate of society itself, hung on the relationship that existed, or that could be made to exist, between the price of bread and the price of labor. Linguet had been hammering this thesis home for two decades. He would have claimed that what looked like uncanny prescience was only a predictability built into a social science that conformed more perfectly to human nature and social reality than the fairy tales systematically spun out by his contemporaries. His foresight was only analytic insight into the great motor forces of society's grim progress into higher stages of development.

"This calm [in political administration], it is not *bayonnets* that will bring it: It's BREAD," he wrote in his *Annales* in February, 1792. He pointed out to his readers that in 1789 the possessor classes were just beginning to complain of oppression under the *ancien régime*. "...they would have put up with the bit that bloodied their mouths for still longer; the SCARCITY OF BREAD gave them for support the poor, whose rage brought on the explosion" (*Annales*, XIX, 42). These poor, as Linguet depicted them, resembled the new Spartacus he had described in the first number of his *Annales*. They were "made bold by despair," "enlightened out of necessity" (*Annales*, I, [1777], 103).

> The true causes of the revolution are sought; there are two, one long-range, the other short-term, and decisive: in general, the opulent classes were *too well off;* the destitute classes were *too badly off.*
> Both this good and also this evil had, and always will have their source in the instability of bread prices... [*Annales,* XIX [1792], 42.]

Doubling the price of bread yields a handsome gain to the speculating grain merchant, to the grain-growing farmer. But who gets hit? The poor, the agricultural workers, the bourgeois in some cases—all who depend absolutely upon a daily wage, a small profit, or fixed pensions. Once reduce the people to this condition, and "...they must perish, or they must revolt. For some time now, they have submitted to perishing...." Until 1789, "...as the only response to the cries of suffering which hunger tore from them, they received a TROUNCING: the time came when they TROUNCED BACK: you are well aware that since this testing of their strength, it is impossible to reduce them to their former diet. You multiply efforts to bring bread down to their reach, now that they have the means of getting it for themselves with *Bayonets*" (*ibid.*, 42-43).

Linguet wrote on the eve of the food riots of February and March, 1792. The region surrounding Versailles lay in the area hardest hit by grain scarcity.[82] Existing police measures would never forestall revolutions of nature and necessity: "But I dare predict it, efforts will be useless in this respect: as soon as they [the people] are hungry, the *patriotic* militia will not restrain them any more than *aristocratic* regiments did. There are only two expedients for living in peace with them. *Put your finances in order;* and arrange things in such a way that the price of bread is *no longer disturbed*" (*ibid.*, 43).

It was precisely the remedy Linguet had asked for in 1779, 1789, and 1790. Now he only recalled his grand project, he did not present it again. Until the national legislature approved a national property tax collectible in grains, Linguet's permanent solution to the food crisis could not be tried out. He had an alternative plan, however. "...and as for *bread*, I intend not to *propose* one [a project] but to *execute* one which will be as effective. As I'm putting this to press, arrangements are being made, by my requisition, in a municipality of the realm, by which it will be certain that the price of bread henceforth will be only *two sous* a pound" (*ibid.*, 44).

Linguet's idea was that any rise in bread prices above two *sous* a pound be borne in common, in the form of a tax on the citizens in any given municipality. The tax would be levied proportionally, with the poorest citizen paying little or nothing (*ibid.*). This was communal price control, but price control with a difference. Linguet's plan was an attempt to conform to revolutionary legislation decreeing free trade in grains, but also to reconcile the agricultural producer's and enterprising middleman's demands for free trade and maximum profits with the people's right to life. Linguet had as little sympathy for the principle of free trade in grains as he had for the unchecked reign of capitalist ethics and a classical economics. He resigned himself to executing reform within the framework of the new economics, ethics, and politics as a last resort.

In March, 1792, Linguet presented a more comprehensive version of his proposal. He observed that a commitment to free trade was forcing the legislature to authorize massive grain purchases to keep the markets supplied, "and to issue civic sermons to the people to enlighten them, to convince them to become enlightened while waiting for bread."[83] What Linguet found inconceivable was the *naïveté* of those who formulated and practiced a *laissez-faire* politics:

> ...but to claim that this iniquitous maneuver is tolerated without opposition by all the classes whose basic right, whose most precious interest it compromises; to imagine that the justifiable unrest it causes them will yield without the least repugnance at the first philosophic word, at the first so-called *civic* grimace of a municipal officer—that's to lull oneself with extravagant hopes; that's blinding oneself voluntarily with an absurd confidence, above all—I can't repeat it too often—since the People is *King*, and since they have put back into its hand the pointed scepter which does not designate sovereignty, but which exercises it. [*Annales*, XIX, 358.]

Impoverished masses would have to be guaranteed their bread, regardless of their daily wages, notwithstanding the entrepreneur's demands for his profits, and especially in the midst of grave economic crises. The best regulatory agent of grain prices on the open market, Linguet insisted, would have been a stockpile of grains, collected under a national program of commodity taxation, stored locally, and placed on the market by the administration at below-market prices whenever grain and bread prices rose above a fixed ceiling (*ibid.*, 359-62). While waiting for "*re-dimification*," Linguet developed an alternative solution. In every municipality in the nation, one merchant would be selected to guarantee delivery of a given amount of grain. It would make no difference what the going market price was that he had to pay. The grain would be distributed to every citizen "according to his needs," and at a fixed price which everyone could afford; the entire commune would be responsible for indemnifying the merchant should the going market price rise above the price fixed by the municipality. Just as each citizen would be guaranteed cheap bread according to his needs, each citizen also would be taxed for the supplement due the grain merchant at a rate proportional to his means (*ibid.*, 364-66).

Linguet proposed his latest plan without any illusions. He could not have been more perfectly aware that reform along these lines only furthered the development of an economic system which netted profits to enterprising agricultural capitalists while perpetuating the laboring poor's exploitation and dehumanization, even as they were compensated with bread, at best. Linguet had spelled out a more ambitious program for attenuating social class conflict: massive, state-sponsored welfare; the legislature ignored it. And he had envisioned a radical alternative to all reforms, another route into the resolution of class antagonism: proletarian revolution and the people's redistribution of wealth. Now, in the spring of 1792, with the nation mobilizing for war and with local officials struggling to quash civil war, the time had passed, if ever it had been ripe, for realizing comprehensive reform. As for the option of popular revolution, Linguet did not want to see it materialize any further. As much as he might have been for the French revolutionary masses, he was not of them. They had only their chains to lose should they decide to escalate their politics of violence. He had at stake the chateau and park of Marnes-les-Saint-Cloud. No expedient that promised to stave off the great and last civil war of civil society seemed too radical to him.

The people of Marnes-les-Saint-Cloud had debated the merits of his project, and had authorized him to consider it accepted; then they voted it down. Linguet analyzed the cause of his defeat. The large landowners held firm in their support. The small farmers and non-proprietors, however, had defected. Several had stocked a grain supply, and were unwilling to risk being taxed for the commune's purchase of a commodity that would prevent someone else's starvation. The attitudes of the day laborers in his municipality left Linguet particularly exasperated: "...not very assiduous in assemblies, [they] allowed opposition to prevail against an agreement which could have been useful only to them." The propertyless population of Marnes-les-Saint-Cloud still had a lot to learn. It might have known it was free. Simon Linguet concluded that it knew very little else. "To my great surprise, here I am, convinced that it's not any easier for reason to prevail in a village commune than in a *national assembly*" (*ibid.*, 368).

Linguet offered his final critical analyses of French revolutionary events and crises in numbers of the *Annales* appearing in the winter and spring of 1792. In the first article, Linguet discussed food riots instigated by the people of Paris in January and February.[84] A galloping inflation, combined with shortages caused by hoarding in anticipation of a suspension of commodity shipments from the French West Indies, sent prices of sugar and coffee soaring out of the reach of laboring poor men and women, for whom these items had become essential sources of nourishment and energy. The rioters, mostly women, seized sugar and other supplies from warehouses, fixed the prices themselves, and conducted the sales.[85] Linguet pronounced a scathing indictment of the hoarders; he exposed the legalistic facades behind which they perpetrated their crimes against the working poor: "Isn't it he [the hoarder] who provides the example of making a game of the original contract, the truly fundamental pact of all society, this tacit agreement between the rich and lazy man and the poor and industrious man, by which the latter consents to exchange his time, the use of his strength, the totality of his life, against a crude nourishment, and even less elaborate clothing?" He insisted that sugar and coffee must be regulated as necessities (*Annales*, XIX, 227-28, 221-22). He charged that the Revolution had failed to yield the least return for the people; yet it was the people whose commitment to society's preservation the government would have to win before the revolutionary regime could be stabilized.

> Notwithstanding all our philosophy, all our constitutional, and
> anti-constitutional, royalist or republican declamations, how far
> away we still are from even the first elements of a secure society,
> of a general corporation where public tranquillity would be the
> common interest of all members! I have been saying it unavailing-
> ly for thirty years; but in another thirty years, perhaps, people
> will begin to be convinced. There will never be a solidly estab-
> lished civil *society,* save the one where they will have found and
> put into practice the solution to the political problem here stated.
> [*Ibid.,* 228.]

The problem was subsistence. Somehow, the people's wages and the price
of their subsistence commodities would have to be made directly proportional to one another. As though deliberately to place the nullity of revolutionary
social achievements in glaring relief, Linguet risked a final presentation of his
most misunderstood instrument of critical social analysis, the model of imperial Rome as an ideal type of the well-administered state. In calling attention
to the Roman emperors' daily dole, he was not suggesting that heads of modern states resort to handouts to appease the masses. You did not throw bread
to an enlightened proletariat. Besides, that would only ruin industrious entrepreneurs and cripple critical sectors of the national economy. Nonetheless,
the administration must make some arrangement for "interesting" this nation
of dispossessed men in society's preservation, and the state's. Something must
be done that would be as effective for the new political order as Roman solutions had been under the Empire. French revolutionary leaders must make liberty as worthwhile to the people as slavery had been beneficial (*ibid.,* 228,
230-31):

> Its inept fabricators [the constitution makers] wanted the people
> to hold all power. They forgot the *necessary* relationship that
> exists between their *arms* and their *stomachs.* They forgot that
> when they were proclaimed sovereign, they ought to have been
> guaranteed, as all other Kings, at least the certainty of not dying
> of hunger; and in diminishing for them, because of the number of
> *assemblies,* the opportunities, the means for earning enough to
> live on, they ought not to have exposed them either to tax in-
> creases or to [increases] in the price of goods of prime necessity.
> They forgot.....it would be less time-consuming to ask what they
> remembered. [*Ibid.,* 232.]

Linguet distributed the final numbers of his *Annales* in the summer of
1792. One of his last articles was an analysis of the state of affairs in Paris in
the late spring of that year and an evaluation of the French Revolution. After
thirteen centuries, the people, a nation in blood-stained rags, "symbol and
proof" of its "misery, lowness and servitude," had taken up arms. "Only the
explosion of 1789 is what can be called a revolution." The people, Linguet

observed, have demonstrated unprecedented sangfroid, character, energy, and moderation. "Je ne suis pas Jacobin: J'ai une culotte." Other allegiances and interests dictated Linguet's qualified support of the Parisian democrats' tactics and demands (*ibid.*, 333, 334, 335).

Nonetheless, the Revolution had gone wrong. If the people merited praise, the nation's political leaders did not. They had missed opportunities for stabilizing a revolutionary situation and institutionalizing revolutionary gains; now these occasions were irrecoverable. "...by a fatal haste, the nation was made to lose the advantages of a moment she had been expecting for a thousand years, which in the next thousand years perhaps will not recur" (*ibid.*, 333). The "general liberty" sparked on July 14, 1789, had been, after all, only a single flare. The advantages of liberty, a dominion payable in the form of general welfare and security and a public tranquillity, already were beyond the revolutionaries' reach three stormy years later.

With these despairing reflections, Linguet abandoned revolutionary political journalism. He did not forsake the Revolution. The voting inhabitants of Marnes-les-Saint-Cloud, meeting on October 10, 1792, elected him mayor by a vote of sixteen to three. Linguet was already filling the post of officer for *l'état civil.*[86]

The new mayor was not a visionary; within the bounds of the possible, he seemed determined to make of Marnes-les-Saint-Cloud a model commune for revolutionary France. He discounted the failure of his efforts to begin cooperative grain purchases in his commune; or rather he drew a lesson from failure. Now, in legislating the common welfare, he bypassed the democratic voting process, creating welfare funds from his own capital and administering them at his discretion. He and two other citizens of means put up three hundred *livres* apiece to indemnify citizens volunteering to defend the local borders, and he offered to outfit volunteers for the national army. He planted potatoes on his properties and distributed the harvests to citizens unable to obtain food, although the opposition to this handout was vehement.[87]

The mayor was not building sandcastles, feeble barriers against onrushing events. He had staked out a place for himself in the Revolution. He intended to stand his ground: that ground was property in land, profession, and political liberty, and dominion over a unique revolutionary ideology, style, and behavior.

Threatened with foreign invasion and civil war, the Republic moved toward a government of terror in the summer and fall of 1793. The Convention passed a law of suspects on September 17, 1793. The law stated that "those who, by their conduct, relations, or language spoken or written, have shown themselves partisans of tyranny or federalism and enemies of liberty," were suspect.[88] Armed with general directives, zealous exegetes and local troubleshooters, members of municipal committees of surveillance and volunteer informers, began making their roundups.

The mayor of Marnes-les-Saint-Cloud, with every cause for apprehension, refused to retreat. His patriotism was hardly open to question in his commune. He had come under suspicion in August, 1792, when rumors circulated that he had entertained suspicious-looking guests in his home, but he had been cleared.[89] Since then, Linguet had made certain that his patriotic activities would be a matter of public record. He kept the record himself, scrupulously noting all the details of his administration of municipal affairs. He spelled out his efforts to recruit volunteers for the national army and remarked, explaining his conspicuous zeal: "...the danger of present circumstances oblig[ed] him to prove his civic-mindedness by all means that are and will be in his power."[90]

Even if he had been perfectly safe in Marnes, elsewhere in the vicinity—and particularly in the neighboring town of Sèvres—Linguet had made himself highly suspect. He was known to be a stickler for legal forms, combative, quick to contest administrative irregularities.[91]

On September 26, 1793, the Committee of General Security signed an order for the arrest—"whether at Marnes where he lives, or anywhere he might be"—of Citizen Linguet, "former lawyer" and "very suspect man."[92] This order reached the Revolutionary Committee of Sèvres and was made public at a meeting of the committee on September 27, 1793. Immediately, a deputation of seven citizens from Sèvres was dispatched to Marnes to arrest "Linguet, Mayor and former lawyer."[93]

The register of the Hotel de la Force, one of the prisons operated by the Committee of General Security in Paris, records the entry on September 28, 1793, of Linguet, mayor of the commune of Marnes, measuring five feet two inches, with fair hair and eyebrows, a long, thin face, "hidden" eyes, and a long chin; he had been arrested by order of the Committee of General Security for "reasons unexplained."[94]

Two weeks after he was committed, Linguet wrote to the president of the Committee of General Security. He demanded justice and a statement of the reasons for his arrest. "I find in my conduct, in my writings, and in my heart only what ought to have preserved me from such a fate." He reminded the president that his municipality "reclaimed" him, that the abundant testimony of its citizens in his behalf was sufficient to acquit him. "By what fatality, then, am I treated as suspect?" He sought speedy acquittal in order to return to "my people who call me their Father, and on whose behalf, in truth, I have worked to deserve this title."[95]

The citizens of Marnes recorded their activities on Linguet's behalf in their communal register. They were "penetrated with the most profound sadness."

The mayor's "zeal and beneficent attentions are for this commune of the most important utility." They requested Linguet's immediate release and return to Marnes.[96]

The Committee of General Security apparently was still trying to build up a case against Linguet at the end of October, 1793. A member of the committee, Etienne-Jean Panis, writing to his colleagues on October 27, urged them to release the mayor of Marnes. "There is no report to make on Linguet. It's on his name that he was arrested, and that he perishes in prison." He warned the Committee against judging the prisoner on the basis of snatches of phrases he had written years earlier. "The law against suspect persons does not stipulate returning to the deluge."[97]

Linguet exposed his situation again on December 1, 1793, this time in a letter to Minister of Interior Jules Paré: "In the name of reason, of justice, of liberty, today the sole objects of the cult of true Republicans, I ask of you your attention and protection." He was still a prisoner in La Force; he was being detained "without having been able to obtain either communication of grievances, interrogation, or any kind of enlightenment." He had learned that the most meticulous examination of his papers at Marnes did not furnish any evidence against him. He informed Paré of his precarious state of health, his need for immediate medical attention. "Not only am I not *suspect,* but I cannot be....My principles are known to you personally: I never departed from them, either in my conduct or in my writings. My life until 1789 was spent in defying, in unmasking every kind of despotism. Ought I to have anticipated that I would be [unmasking] as well the caprices, the prejudices and indifference, and if I must say it, the cruelty of [despotism's] annihilators?" He demanded his freedom, or at least his release from prison and permission to return to Marnes, under guard, if necessary.[98]

That same day, two doctors visited La Force, examined Linguet, and confirmed his own fears that his maladies were serious.[99] On the strength of their report, Linguet was transferred to the Maison Belhomme in Paris, a convalescent home converted into a prison hospital. A prudent man might have managed to survive here. For all his boasting, Linguet was not a prudent man. He was prepared to risk and lose his property in his life to provoke a showdown with revolutionary authorities over the question of his property in his liberty.

The People's ministers, Linguet informed the members of the Committee of General Security in January, 1794, were more despotic than Louis XVI had been. If they had bothered to read just one of his works, if they had obtained the least information about the kind of life he had led, "...you would be quite convinced by now that the third Bastille, where by your order I am detained, is more unjust, more tyrannical, than the first two. For the despotism that plunged me into the latter was motivated: it was consistent. I had unmasked it and defied it. Whereas today I am deprived of my liberty in the name of the reason, the *liberty,* whose *provocateur anticipé,* whose intrepid defender I was when it did not yet exist." He then went on to argue for his immediate liberation in the interest of maintaining order and administrative regularity in his commune.[100]

The Committee of General Security was hardly likely to acknowledge that its members' republican zeal was a thin mask camouflaging the operations of a new ministerial despotism. Still, the Committee had some compunction about executing suspects for *"cause non expliqué,"* although it apparently had none about keeping Linguet imprisoned indefinitely while the Committee and its researchers combed all available sources for convincing evidence on which to base an indictment.

The Committee was ready with its indictment on 29 Prairial Year II (June 17, 1794). An incriminating document had been turned up, at last, although it had been available for months for conversion into evidence of treason: "In view of M. Linguet's letter, annotated by the hand of the late Tyrant, to whom it was addressed on the fourth of April, 1792...the Committee, considering that M. Linguet, in light of the perfidious advice contained therein, can only be regarded as one of the most intimate advisers of the traitor Louis Capet, orders that the named Linguet be brought before the Revolutionary Tribunal...."[101]

The letter in question, signed by Linguet, was discovered in the *armoire de fer* in the Tuileries, where Louis hid his conspiratorial counterrevolutionary correspondence with the Austrian court; the Committee concluded that Linguet was a conspirator "against the liberty, the independence of the French People."[102] The letter contained the writer's sober appraisal of the Revolution. Each party "desired the humiliation, the annihilation of its adversaries, and it was necessary to work for their reunion. It was necessary, to speak in *Constitutional* terms, to have a *justice of the peace——,* respected enough to be able to propose the conciliation of disputes dividing the great family, powerful enough to make it prevail." The writer suggested that the king show himself firmer, more determined, that he present himself to the people, win their confidence, and attempt to merit the title of justice of the peace.[103]

The Committee concluded that for having proffered this counsel, Linguet "cannot be looked upon except as one of the most intimate advisers of the traitor Louis Capet."[104] The Committee did not consider itself responsible for figuring out what Linguet was attempting to say concerning the course revolutionary events had taken, although the tone in which he chided the impotent monarch for his timidity and his impolitic behavior might have indicated to the sensitive reader the extent and seriousness of Linguet's belief in Louis's capacity to win popular favor and play justice of the peace to a hopelessly divided nation. His crime was to have analyzed a fatal flaw in the republican regime—its lack of executive leadership and administrative vision—and to have offered a tepid phrase of flattery to the king.

The Committee sent its report to the Revolutionary Tribunal. The Tribunal, applying the law of 22 Prairial (June 10), drew up its act of accusation against Linguet without the benefit of a preliminary hearing at which the accused would have been questioned and witnesses called. The Tribunal followed the text of the Committee's report almost exactly. The accusation, penned on 8 Messidor by the Tribunal's chief prosecutor, Fouquier-Tinville, and approved by a committee of the Tribunal, stated that "S. N. H. Linguet, formerly a lawyer, age 56 years,… "known by his writings and his sojourn with despots in the Courts of London and Vienna…" had been an adviser to the traitor Capet, and a member of the king's "Austrian Committee." He had betrayed himself in his letter of April 4, 1792, in which he thanked the king for "the justice, which, he said, He had just rendered him…." He had given the king advice on how to win the people's favor. Therefore, although "…Linguet seemed to cover himself with a mask of patriotism, and produce ninety-nine writings in favor of liberty, only vengeance, hypocrisy, conducted his pen…he was always the partisan and apostle of despotism…"—witness the letter of April 4, "where he takes off the mask to declare himself against the people and its representatives."[105]

That same day, Fouquier-Tinville ordered Linguet released from the Maison Belhomme and brought to the Tribunal's prison to await trial.[106] The records of Linguet's trial before the Revolutionary Tribunal on 9 Messidor contain his handwritten sketch for his defense; he must have written it out as the act of accusation was being read to the prisoners. "You cite against me the extract of one single letter, which is not shown to me, and which I do not recognize. Can a judgment be made on such a piece?" He did not deny having written the letter. In fact, he produced minutes of several letters he had addressed to an officer in the king's service. He submitted this correspondence to the court to aid the judges in their exegesis of his letter of April 4, 1792, thanking Louis XVI for having rendered him justice: "These letters written in 1792 had as object an indemnity which was owing to me because of ravages committed against my properties, on the king's orders, in 1780, and later. It will be seen that they are written with the tone and the courage of a Republican, although the Republic was not yet in existence."[107] The judges would not have time to inspect nuances in style and tone, or to evaluate Linguet's claim that he was thanking the king for renewing payments on his pension, an "indemnity" exacted by a victim of political crimes committed under the *ancien régime*.[108]

He attempted to explain how populism and monarchism could interpenetrate in a citizen's political allegiances. "When Kings did good, I praised them, when they became tyrants, I said it. I became the people's defender with the same candor. That's what won me the Bastille in 1780, and what has followed."[109] He could hardly have expected his judges to approve his political theory or subscribe to the principles which undergirded his split ideological commitments.

He warned the judges against reaching unwarranted conclusions after having examined only phrases from his works: "...but can you judge a writer with sixty volumes published in a lifetime on a portion of his writings examined in excerpt and in his absence?"[110] When the life of the Republic rested upon the exposure of suspects and the elimination of traitors, was it reasonable for Linguet to demand that his judges make allowances for the rich, intriguing, and justifiable complexities that might exist in the patterns of a man's life and thought?

In his penciled defense, Linguet summed up his lost cause: "My justification boils down to a word—it is that I experienced all the cycles of despotism before the Revolution, that perhaps I was incapable of becoming either the friend or the accomplice of despots. I accomplished for the Revolution everything my age and my means permitted."[111]

Linguet defended himself by offering his accusers the story of his political life. His judges solemnly rejected his defense of the integrity of his political existence. They condemned him as a traitor to the Republic. His avowed republicanism was hypocrisy, a pose behind which he pursued vengeance against personal enemies. This professed true believer, "with ninety-nine writings in favor of liberty," was "always the partisan and apostle of despotism."

What is true is that Linguet was both liberty's "intrepid defender" and an apostle of authoritarianism, if not despotism. It is true that he experienced "all the cycles of despotism before the revolution" and that he lived his life as liberty's "*provocateur anticipé*" when liberty "did not exist." It is also true, however, that Linguet had devoted his prerevolutionary and revolutionary careers not to the cult of liberty as philosophes, physiocrates, and their disciples in the revolutionary establishments defined it, and not to the institutionalization of rights of self-determinism, but to the search for systems of social security that would guarantee universally some common denominator of the only liberty he considered meaningful in society, the liberty of dominion.

The mayor of Marnes-les-Saint-Cloud justified himself to the president of the Committee of General Security by confessing that he had worked in his commune to merit the title of father. He meant it; he had. His Jacobin judges, who had recently killed a political father to safeguard the myth of their autonomy, could have used his declarations of paternalistic republicanism as further evidence of a crime against the nation. What Linguet respected in "justices of the peace," political "fathers," and bank directors were the virtues and power of great administrators (all of whom, necessarily, whatever the rhetoric they used to legitimate their exercise of power, would be functioning as chief executives for revolutionary France's exploiting elites). In the middle of a civil war, where every party was out after the "annihilation of its adversaries," a justice of the peace (backed presumably by the metapolitician director of a national bank) might have at least a fighting chance to realize the liberty of dominion for society's two fully politicized warring classes, institutionalizing as much of the general will as any human agency could hope to without exploding the order of private properties and dissolving the foundation of an exploitative society. Linguet's *caisse nationale*, the principal arm of a revolutionary executive in his master plan, would not have denied the sovereignty of "His majesty the people,"[112] or contested the legitimacy of the ruling elites' legislative authority in "an assembly which, right now, is France's only resource" (*Annales*, XVI, 318). However, the bank's application of an all-embracing economic power would have left the national sovereign's representatives with control powers exclusively and the sovereign itself with only the clean, extreme options of revolutionary insurrection or wholesale acceptance of the regime of security and welfare.

Linguet's real crime against the Revolution was to have used his political influence to program only the material dimensions of the liberty of dominion for twenty-five million Frenchmen, a liberty which, in the context of reigning revolutionary myths, allegiances, priorities, and achievements was only a poor functional equivalent for political self-direction—a possession of political autonomy and the full exercise of political sovereignty in a democratic setting.

Simon Linguet was condemned to death on the ninth of Messidor, in the second year of the French Republic (June 27, 1794), and was guillotined that day.[113]

He had appealed to his judges, spokesmen for the people of the French Republic, the nation; his judges gave the order to guillotine him. He did not have time to appeal their verdict to posterity; in any case, he probably no longer believed there would be one for him.

NOTES

1. Linguet to Trauttmansdorff, Brussels, July 28, 1789, in Linguet, *Lettres de M. Linguet au Comte de Trauttmansdorff, ministre plénipotentiaire pour l'Empereur au Pays-Bas en 1788 et 1789* (Brussels, 1789), p. 100.

2. Linguet to Trauttmansdorff, Brussels, Aug. 1, 1789, in AG, MSS divers, 5117, no. 19; printed in Linguet, *Lettres...au Comte de Trauttmansdorff*, p. 103.

3. Eugène E. Hubert, *Les Préliminaires de la Révolution brabançonne. Un Complot politique à Bruxelles, octobre 1789*, Académie royale de Belgique, classe des lettres et des sciences morales et politiques, Mémoires, ser. 2, vol. VII (Brussels, 1920), p. 8n.

4. Robert R. Palmer, *The Age of the Democratic Revolution: A Political History of Europe and America: 1760-1800*, 2 vols. (Princeton, 1959-64), I, 341ff.; Henri Pirenne, *Histoire de Belgique*, 7 vols. (Brussels, 1902-32), V, 381-418.

5. Palmer, *The Age of the Democratic Revolution*, I, 348.

6. For example, Linguet to Trauttmansdorff, Brussels, May 20, 1787, April 21, 1789, in AG, MSS divers, 5117, nos. 2, 16. Linguet freely offered his services to Joseph and his agents; he was willing to act as conciliator and intimate adviser, but his advice, he added, was not being asked: "I see by the statute of the fourteenth of this month *that there has been a postponement.......while waiting for people to become more fully informed concerning this important subject*: but I do not see anyone working to procure this knowledge." Linguet to Trauttmansdorff, Brussels, May 20, 1787, in *ibid.*, no. 2.

7. Linguet, "Réponse de l'auteur des *Annales* à un souscripteur concernant l'accident arrivé le 22 janvier 1788 à Bruxelles, et sur ce qui semble encore rester de sujets d'inquiétude dans les Pays-Bas autrichiens," *Annales politiques, civiles, et littéraires du dix-huitième siècle*, 19 vols. (London, Brussels, Paris, 1777-92), XII (1788), 291-314. A diplomatic agent of the prince bishop of Liège, Barthélemy-Joseph Dotrenge, reported in a dispatch dated March 7, 1788, that Linguet sent this article to Joseph a week before he printed it; that the military now had it in for Linguet; that the article was exact on the affair of Jan. 22. See Eugène E. Hubert, ed., *Correspondance de Barthélemy-Joseph Dotrenge, agent diplomatique du Prince-évêque de Liège auprès de la cour de Bruxelles (1781-1794)* (Brussels, 1926), pp. 229-30.

8. Pirenne, *Histoire de Belgique*, V, 446.

9. Linguet to Trauttmansdorff, Brussels, Feb. 1, 1788, in AG, MSS divers, 5117, no. 3.

10. *Ibid.*

11. Copy of d'Alton's note for Trauttmansdorff, Brussels, March 4, 1788, in AG, D. 109, ad litt. L 4, no. 5.

12. Trauttmansdorff to Joseph II, Brussels, March 4, 1788, cited Hanns Schlitter, ed., *Geheime Correspondenz Josefs II mit seinem minister in den österreichischen Niederlanden Ferdinand Grafen Trauttmansdorff, 1787-1789* (Vienna, 1902), p. 81. Trauttmansdorff communicated with Kaunitz three days later. He said he had accused Linguet of incendiary, biased reporting incompatible with the gratitude Linguet ought to be displaying. Trauttmansdorff promised Kaunitz he would review agreements already made with Linguet for the publication and censoring of his *Annales*. What he found unpardonable was Linguet's political independence, that is, the journalist's failure to obtain ministerial clearance "before publishing anything on our affairs, and above all [his failure] to enlighten himself before contradicting approved gazettes and before setting himself up as the only organ of truth." Trauttmansdorff to Kaunitz, Brussels, March 7, 1788, in AG, D. 109, ad litt. L 4, no. 5.

13. Linguet went through all the gestures of preparing a retraction. He even printed one up for insertion in no. 102 of the *Annales*. It was to have appeared as a letter to the editor correcting Linguet's account of the incident of Jan. 22. At the end of the letter, Linguet had inserted an editor's note: "The foregoing proves that it is excessively difficult to write history. The proximity of objects sometimes prejudices one's view. Even pure intentions don't suffice, as can be seen, to keep one from making mistakes or acting imprudently." See Linguet to unnamed correspondent [Trauttmansdorff?], n.p., n.d., with dummied article enclosed, in AG, MSS divers, 5117, no. 4. Linguet explained to Trauttmansdorff that he was reluctant to publish this material only because he feared antagonizing his reading public still further. "It will be impossible to prevent the public from viewing it as having been demanded, coerced." In the meantime, Linguet reported, General d'Alton already had published one violent attack against him: "...the greater the scandal, the less effect the retraction will have." See copy in another hand of Linguet's report to Trauttmansdorff on article to be inserted in no. 102 of the *Annales*, in *ibid.*, no. 4 bis. Apparently, d'Alton was not satisfied with Linguet's opening conciliatory gestures. He wanted Linguet to confess to his reading public that he had fabricated his report on the incident of Jan. 22; and he called for Linguet's retraction of everything he had written. Minute of unsigned note [by d'Alton] analyzing Linguet's proposed letter to the editor scheduled for publication in no. 102 of the *Annales*, in *ibid.*, no. 5. Linguet was appalled. "I? declare that my entire account is fabricated, and that it is inaccurate? but that would be to declare myself a slanderer with premeditation...." He had offered to publish the government's account of the events in his *Annales* and to let the

public decide whether his account or the government's was the more accurate. That was as far as he would go. "I would be slandering myself if I went further than that." Communication from Linguet to d'Alton concerning d'Alton's note on retraction scheduled for publication in no. 102 of the *Annales*, in *ibid.*, 6 bis.

14. "Copie d'une lettre écrite à M. Linguet par M. de Moitelle, Colonel commandant le régiment de ligne, au sujet du récit inséré dans le no. 101 des *Annales*, de l'événement du 22 janvier dernier. Avec des observations," *Annales*, XIII (1788), 415-45. See also d'Alton to Joseph II, March 7, 1788, in *Copies des lettres du Général d'Alton à l'Empereur Joseph II, relativement aux affaires des Pays-Bas, en 1788 & 1789* (Brussels, n.d.), pp. 13-14. D'Alton enclosed copies of two letters from Moitelle to Linguet. He noted that he had urged the government to censor Linguet's *Annales* "to prevent such literary excesses in the future...." *Ibid.*, p. 14. For Trauttmansdorf's comments see Trauttmansdorff to Kaunitz, Brussels, March 21, 1788, in AG, Chancellerie autrichienne des Pays-Bas, Dépêches d'office, vol. 524, D. 109 ad litt. L 4, no. 8.

15. See d'Alton to Joseph II, March 21, 1788 in *Copies des lettres...d'Alton*, p. 17. D'Alton was particularly concerned about the popularity of Linguet's journal. The patriots, he confided to Joseph, look upon Linguet as "their oracle, and now avidly read his productions which they formerly despised. His last two numbers of the *Annales*, calculated in this vein, won him more than 100 new subscribers." D'Alton wanted Linguet banished from Brussels, "a city where he has become one of the most dangerous firebrands." See also Trauttmansdorff to Kaunitz, March 14, 1788, in AG, D. 110 ad litt. S 1, no. 6; Trauttmansdorff to Kaunitz, April 2, Aug. 20, 1788, as cited in Eugène Hubert, ed., *Correspondance des ministres de France accrédités à Bruxelles de 1780 à 1790. Dépêches inédites*, 2 vols. (Brussels, 1920-24), I, 311n, 312n.

16. Trauttmansdorff to Kaunitz, April 2, 22, 1788, in AG, D. 109 ad litt. L 4, nos. 9, 10.

17. Kaunitz to Trauttmansdorff, May 19, 1788, as cited in Huber, ed., *Correspondance des ministres*, I, 312n; see also Kaunitz to Joseph II, March 30, 1788, as cited in Schlitter, ed., *Geheime Correspondenz Josefs II*, p. 600.

18. Joseph II to d'Alton, April 9, 1788, printed in Comité patriotique de Bruxelles, ed., *Receuil de lettres originales de l'Empereur Joseph II au Général d'Alton, commandant des troupes aux Pays-Bas, depuis décembre 1787 jusqu'en novembre 1789* (Brussels, 1790), p. 8; cited in Hubert, ed., *Les Préliminaires de la Révolution brabançonne*, p. 14n.

19. Linguet to Jean-Frédéric Perrégaux, July 26, 1789, in BM, collections d'autographes, première collection de la ville, vol. II, fol. 83.

20. Linguet, *Lettres...au Comte de Trauttmansdorff*, p. 92.

21. A principal source of these accusations was P.H.M. Lebrun's *Journal général de l'Europe*.

22. See for example, Linguet, *Observations d'un citoyen sur les enlèvemens qui ont eu lieu à Bruxelles, le 27 juillet 1789* (n.d.).

23. Linguet to Trauttmansdorff, Brussels, Aug. 1, 1789, in AG, MSS divers, 5117, no. 19.

24. Linguet, *Avis aux Parisiens. Par M. Linguet. Appel de toutes convocations d'Etats-Généraux où les députés du troisième ordre ne seroient pas supérieurs en nombre aux deux autres* (n.p., [1788, and 2d ed., 1789]).

25. Linguet, *Quelle est l'origine des Etats-Généraux* (n.p., 1788).

26. Linguet to Trauttmansdorff, Brussels, July 28, 1789, in Linguet, *Lettres...au Comte de Trauttmansdorff*, p. 96.

27. *Ibid.*, p. 97.

28. Linguet to Trauttmansdorff, Brussels, Aug. 1, 1789, in AG, MSS divers, 5117, no. 19; see also printed version in Linguet, *Lettres...au Comte de Trauttmansdorff*, pp. 104-5.

29. Linguet to Trauttmansdorff, Brussels, Aug. 1, 1789, in Linguet, *Lettres...au Comte de Trauttmansdorff*, pp. 104-5. In consecutive dispatches and memoirs to Trauttmansdorff, Linguet escalated his demands on behalf of the Belgian people. He admitted to Trauttmansdorff that he found the government's repressive police measures despotic and provocative, especially a government-engineered abduction of citizens from Brussels. See Linguet to Trauttmansdorff, Brussels, Aug. 1, 1789, in AG, MSS divers,

5117, no. 19. Here Linguet presented his own observations and a project for the return of citizens abducted by the military from Brussels on July 27, 1789, and summarily condemned to forced military conscription and service in Hungary. *Ibid.*, 19 bis. See also Linguet's *Observations d'un citoyen.*

30. Linguet to Trauttmansdorff, Brussels, Aug. 3, [1789], in AG, MSS divers, 5117, no. 20.

31. Linguet to Trauttmansdorff, Brussels [August, 1789], in *ibid.*, no. 21. For Linguet's initial use of the imagery of the exploding mine, see Linguet to Trauttmansdorff, July 28, 1789, in Linguet, *Lettres...au Comte de Trauttmansdorff,* p. 100.

32. Trauttmansdorff to Joseph II, Brussels, Sept. 10, 1789, cited without date, from Schlitter, ed., *Geheime Correspondenz Josefs II,* p. 375, in Hubert, ed., *Les Préliminaires de la révolution brabonçonne,* p. 3.

33. Linguet to Trauttmansdorff, 2 letters, Brussels [Aug., 1789] ; Linguet to Trauttmansdorff, Aug. 13, 1789; Linguet's draft of a letter of thanks to Trauttmansdorff on behalf of the people of Belgium [Aug., 1789], all in AG, MSS divers, 5117, nos. 21, 23, 24 bis.

34. Trauttmansdorff to Joseph II, Brussels, Aug. 11, 1789, cited from Schlitter, ed., *Geheime Correspondenz Josefs II,* p. 347, in Hubert, ed., *Correspondance de...Dotrenge,* p. 247, n. 2.

35. Linguet to Trauttmansdorff, Brussels, n.d. ["ce mercredi matin," August, 1789], in AG, MSS divers, 5117, no. 27.

36. Linguet to Trauttmansdorff, Brussels [late Aug. or early Sept., 1789], in *ibid.*, no. 29. The pamphlet in question was Linguet's *Observations d'un citoyen sur les enlèvemens qui ont eu lieu à Bruxelles le 17 juillet 1789.*

37. Joseph II to Trauttmansdorff, Laxenbourg, Aug. 25, 1789, in Schlitter, ed., *Geheime Correspondenz Josephs II,* pp. 363-64.

38. Joseph II to Trauttmansdorff, Hetzendorf, Sept. 13, 1789, in *ibid.*, p. 383. The Comte de Windischgraetz, whom Joseph denounced along with Linguet, was one of Linguet's principal public enemies. See Trauttmansdorff to Joseph II, Aug. 11, 1789, in *ibid.*, p. 347, as cited in Hubert, ed., *Correspondance de...Dotrenge,* p. 247, n.2.

39. Hubert, *Les Préliminaires de la Révolution brabonçonne,* pp. 11-13.

40. Trauttmansdorff to Joseph II, Brussels, Oct. 18, 1789, in Schlitter, ed., *Geheime Correspondenz Josefs II,* pp. 430-431.

41. Trauttmansdorff to Kaunitz, Oct. 19, 1789, as cited in Hubert, ed., *Correspondance des ministres de France à Bruxelles,* II, 104, n. 1.

42. Trauttmansdorff to Joseph II, Brussels, Oct. 20, 1789, as cited in Schlitten, ed., *Geheime Correspondenz Josefs II,* pp. 433-34. See also Le Chevalier de la Gravière to Montmorin, Brussels, Oct. 20, 1789, in AM, Pays-bas autrichiens, vol. 178, fol. 39. Gravière explained that Trauttmansdorff had said Linguet was arrested not so much for what he had done as for what he might do.

43. See Hubert, *Les Préliminaires de la Révolution brabonçonne,* pp. 15-24.

44. Joseph II to d'Alton, Oct. 31, 1789, as cited from Comité patriotique de Bruxelles, ed., *Recueil des lettres originales de l'Empereur Joseph II au Général d'Alton,* p. 59, in Hubert, ed., *Correspondance des ministres de France à Bruxelles,* II, 104, n. 2.

45. Kaunitz to Trauttmansdorff, Oct. 31, 1789, as cited in Hubert, ed., *Correspondance des ministres de France à Bruxelles,* II, 103, n. 2.

46. Linguet, *Lettre de M^r. Linguet à l'empereur Joseph II* [Brussels, from the Bastille, Nov. 1, 1789] (n.p., n.d.), pp. 13, 17, 18.

47. See Trauttmansdorff to Joseph II, Nov. 30, 1789, as cited in Hubert, *Les Préliminaires de la Révolution brabonçonne,* p. 45, n. 1. See also Trauttmansdorff to Joseph II, Oct. 30, Nov. 3, 1789, as cited in *ibid.*, p. 36, n. 2.

48. Linguet, *Lettre de M. Linguet au Comité patriotique de Bruxelles, 13 décembre 1789* (Brussels, 1789), p. 10.

49. Linguet, *Lettre de M. Linguet à l'Empereur Joseph Second sur la révolution du Brabant, et du reste des Pays-bas [Dec. 22, 1788]* (Brussels, 1790), pp. 28-29. Emphasis added.

50. Linguet, ed., *Choix des lettres paternelles de Joseph Néron, second du nom, empereur des Romains, à Richard d'Alton, son assassin en chef, aux Pays-bas, en 1788 et*

1789. Avec quelques observations instructives. Par... un intéressé (n.p., 1790), p. 18.

51. Linguet, *Lettre de M. Linguet à un membre de la Société patriotique de Bruxelles sur la requête par cette Société aux Etats de Brabant en mars 1790; et sur la question: Faut-il à la Belgique une Assemblée nationale, ou non [March 19, 1790]* (Brussels, 1790), p. 5. See also Linguet, *Code criminel de Joseph Second, ou Instructions expéditives données aux tribunaux des Pays-Bas en octobre 1789, publiées et commentées par M. Linguet* (Brussels, 1790).

52. See "Extrait des registres des comptes des Etats de Brabant," *Moniteur*, Feb. 26, 1792, as cited in Hubert, ed., *Correspondance des ministres de France à Bruxelles*, II, 271, n. 2.

53. See for example Linguet, "Lettre de l'auteur des *Annales politiques, civilles* [*sic*] *et littéraires* à celui ou ceux des *Annales patriotiques et littéraires* dirigées par M. Mercier, au sujet du Brabant," *Annales*, XVI (1790), 201-23.

54. Linguet, *Lettre de M. Linguet à un membre de la Société patriotique de Bruxelles*, pp. 18-20, 46-48.

55. Camille Desmoulins, *Révolutions de France et de Brabant*, 86 nos. (Paris, November, 1789–July, 1791), no. 6 (1789), 272-73.

56. *Ibid.*, 273.

57. *Ibid.*, no. 11 (1790), 510, 511.

58. *Ibid.*, 513.

59. Linguet to Desmoulins, Feb. 18, 1790, in *ibid.*, no. 14 (1790), 38, 40, 41.

60. *Ibid.*, 39; Linguet to Desmoulins, continuing his letter of Feb. 18, 1790, in *ibid.* See also *ibid.*, no. 15 (1790), 74-76.

61. *Ibid.*, no. 15, 82n.

62. Linguet to Monsieur Gomel [Procurator-general at the Châtelet], ce 19 matin [May?, 1790], in BM, uncat. MSS, Coll. Gosset, no. 9.

63. Henri Martin, "Etude sur Linguet," in *Travaux de l'Académie nationale de Reims*, XXX (1858-59), 341-425, and XXXI (1859-60), 81-149: see XXXI, 130-31. Desmoulins described Linguet's farewell to the district on July 1, 1790, just as new legislation went into effect which broke up the district organization and divided the city into sections. *Révolutions de France et de Brabant*, no. 32 (1790), 386-87. Desmoulins also chronicled a curious incident involving Linguet. Linguet was leading a deputation from the District of the Cordeliers to section headquarters, presumably to register there in accordance with new decrees. However, the *"robins"* [magistrates] refused to acknowledge that Linguet was an active citizen, "as if," Desmoulins exclaimed, "the author of the *Annales*, a citizen who has paid 12 thousand *livres* in taxes, M. Linguet in a word, could be cast back into the class of the proletarians." *Ibid.*, 388-39, n. 1. Desmoulins was perhaps referring to Linguet's offer to contribute 12,000 *livres* worth of shares to the *caisse nationale*, if it were established. See Linguet, *Point de banqueroute, plus d'emprunts, et si l'on veut, bientôt plus de dettes, en réduisant les impôts à un seul...* (n.p., 1789), p.76

64. Jacques-Pierre Brissot de Warville, *J.-P. Brissot: Mémoires (1754-1793)*, ed. Claude Perroud, vols. II and III of *Mémoires et documents relatifs au XVIIIe et XIXe siècles* (Paris, 1911), I, 96, 97, 98, 327.

65. Linguet to Madame Dérodé, Jan. 7, 1791, in BM, uncat. MSS, Coll. Gosset, no. 64. Writing in Dec., 1790, Linguet revealed his sensitivity to the Remois' neglect: "...your cherished city doesn't seem to me to have a very high opinion of me: it's almost ludicrous that I have absolutely no more than two subscribers,... [totaling] in my supposed homeland the number of four readers." To Madame Dérodé, Dec. 17, 1790, in *ibid.*, no. 63.

66. Linguet to Madame Dérodé, n.d. [1791], in *ibid.*, no. 65.

67. Linguet to Trauttmansdorff, Brussels, Feb. 21, 1789, in AG, MSS divers, (5117, no. 12; also Linguet to Trauttmansdorff, Brussels, Feb. 18, 1789, in *ibid.*, no. 11. Linguet indicated his interest in such a retirement as early as May, 1785. See Linguet to Crumpipen, May 3, 1785, in OS, DD, B, 192[b] (56).

68. Linguet to Trauttmansdorff, Brussels, Jan. 18, 1789, in Linguet, *Lettres... au Comte de Trauttmansdorff*, p. 46.

69. Linguet to Trauttmansdorff, Brussels, Feb. 18, 1789, in AG, MSS divers, 5117, no. 11; and Linguet to Trauttmansdorff, Feb. 19, 1789 [sic], in Linguet, *Lettres...au Comte de Trauttmansdorff*, pp. 55-56.

70. Linguet to Trauttmansdorff, Brussels, Feb. 1, 1789, in *Lettres...au Comte de Trauttmansdorff*, pp. 30-48, and notes, p. 48; Linguet to Trauttmansdorff, Brussels, Feb. 18, 1789, in AG, MSS divers, 5117, no. 11.

71. Linguet to Trauttmansdorff, Brussels, Feb. 21, 1789, in *ibid.*, no. 12; see also Linguet to Trauttmansdorff, Brussels, Feb. 5, 1789, in *Lettres...au Comte de Trauttmansdorff*, pp. 49-50.

72. See "Observations sur le Mémoire et les pièces jointes, présentées à son excellence le ministre plénipotentiaire par le Sire Linguet..." [with reference to Linguet's bid for Awerghem], in AG, Chancellerie autrichienne des Pays-Bas, Dépêches d'office, vol. 524, D109, ad litt. L 4, ad no. 12/a; and Linguet to Trauttmansdorff, Brussels, Feb. 28, April 14, 1789; "Observations de Monsieur Linguet, sur le rapport fait au Conseil"; Linguet to Trauttmansdorff, April 21, 1789: all printed by Linguet with explanatory notes in his *Lettres...au Comte de Trauttmansdorff*, pp. 67-80. At first Linguet was content to have Trauttmansdorff present his special case to Joseph; later he prepared to go to Vienna to present his claim on Awerghem, at a reduced price, directly to the emperor. See Linguet to Trauttmansdorff, n.p., n.d. ["ce mercredi matin"] ; and from Brussels, March 3, 1789, April 21, 1789, in AG, 5117, nos. 14, 16.

73. Linguet to Madame Dérodé, Paris, Dec. 17, 1790, June 7, April 7, 1791, in BM, uncat. MSS, Coll. Gosset, nos. 63, 64, 66.

74. Linguet to Monsieur Jacob [his cousin], Paris, June 18, 1791, in BM, uncat. MSS, Coll. Gosset.

75. C[harles] V[ellay], "Marie-Antoinette et Linguet," *Revue historique de la Révolution française*, II (1911), 444-45.

76. "Analyse du plan et du procès-verbal d'estimation et de division d'une maison de campagne sise en la commune de Marnes, Canton de Sèvres, provenant du condamné Linguet," in Archives départementales d'Yvelines, Versailles, IV. Q 169.

77. The *inventory* giving a partial listing of Linguet's possessions as auctioned off from 2 Thermidor Year II to 14 Thermidor Year II, including furniture and clothing contained in some forty-two rooms, is preserved in Archives départementales d'Yvelines, Versailles, IV Q 169.

78. Linguet to Madame Dérodé, Paris, May 11, 1791, in BM, uncat. MSS, Coll. Gosset, no. 67.

79. The first volume, and for the purposes of this study, the crucial volume of the Registre de la municipalité de la paroisse de Marnes-les-Saint-Cloud, contenant cent cinqante deux feuilles, le dit registre commencé en l'an mil sept cent quatre-vingt dix, le 21 février, et finissant quand il plaira à Dieu, has been missing from the municipal archives of Marnes-la-Coquette for several decades. Extensive excerpts from it were made by Arsène Defresne, "L'Avocat Linguet à Marnes-la-Coquette (de 1791 à 1793)," Commission d'histoire économique et sociale de la Révolution française, Comité départementale d'Yvelines, Recherche et publication des documents relatifs à la vie économique de la Révolution, *Bulletin* (1909-10), 52-78. This publication cited hereafter as *Bulletin*, Seine-et-Oise.

80. Defresne, "Partage des biens communaux à Marnes-la-Coquette," *Bulletin*, Seine-et-Oise (1908-9), 66-67, 68.

81. Linguet to Antoine Dérodé [Marnes, fall, 1791], in BM, uncat. MSS, Coll. Gosset.

82. George F. Rudé, *The Crowd in History: A Study of Popular Disturbances in France and England, 1730-1848* (New York, 1964), pp. 110-11.

83. Linguet, "Expédient simple, infaillible, prompt, peu dispendieux, pour concilier le droit juste et sacré qu'a le peuple de veiller à la certitude de sa subsistance, avec la loi qui autorise la libre circulation des grains," *Annales*, XIX (1792), 356.

84. Linguet, "Murmures et mouvemens du peuple à Paris, à l'occasion du renchérissement du sucre, du café, & c. attribué à des accapareurs. Des accaparemens en générale. Y a-t-il un remède à ce fléau?" *Ibid.*, 220-32.

85. Rudé, *The Crowd in History*, pp. 114-15.

86. Defresne, "L'Avocat Linguet à Marnes-la-Coquette," 58-59.

87. *Ibid.*, 54, 56, 57. Linguet wrote to "the citizens and municipal officers" of Marnes on March 4, 1794, instructing them on the disposal of a harvest of potatoes and the planting of new beds. He noted that he had been planning to plant the maximum number of potatoes on his property, but had been informed that a regulation restricting that amount was in force: "This interdiction cannot exist: it would be contrary to the law: consequently, very criminal, and clearly we will not have to pay any attention to it." He instructed his agent, Perchet, to sell his most recent potato harvest at a price fixed by law, reserving the white potatoes for his own consumption: "It is with regret that I am forced to put a price on them, and to accept it, but, fellow citizens and colleagues, *one* of the pretexts that has been used to my greatest disadvantage is that I distributed my harvests of the preceding two years *free of charge.* That is as strange as it is true, and in fact, no harm came to those who gave nothing away, who, on the contrary, have taken advantage of circumstances to sell at the highest price they could get." Linguet to the Municipality of Marnes, Paris [Maison Belhomme], March 4, 1794, in AN, F^{7}477467, dossier I (PERCHET).

88. Robert R. Palmer, *Twelve Who Ruled: The Committee of Public Safety during the Terror* (Princeton, 1941), p. 67.

89. Defresne, "L'Avocat Linguet à Marnes-la-Coquette," 55. In an unsigned and undated autograph preserved in the records of the Comité de surveillance de Sèvres, Linguet justifies himself against this charge. See Archives, Comité de surveillance de Sèvres, in Archives départementales, d'Yvelines, Versailles, no. 1631, fol. 41v.

90. Defresne, "L'Avocat Linguet à Marnes-la-Coquette," 60.

91. *Ibid.*, 55.

92. Police générale, Comité de Sûreté générale, arrestations, détentions, et mises en liberté, Seine-et-Oise, in AN, F^{7}4573.

93. Journal du Comité révolutionnaire de la Commune de Sèvres, session de la séance ordinaire du 27 septembre 1793; séance extraordinaire du 28 septembre 1793, in Archives départementales d'Yvelines, Versailles, Série Q, non classé; see also Etat des arrestations fait par le Comité de surveillance révolutionnaire de Sèvres, in *ibid.,* Série Q, non classé, no. 19; and report of Linguet's incarceration in La Force "pour fait de Police," signed Bauet, in *ibid.,* Série Q, non classé.

94. Entry concerning Linguet, Sept. 28, 1793, in Registre de la Département de Police pour servir au Concièrge de l'Hotel de La Force, in Archives, Préfecture de la Police, Paris; Police report for Sept. 28, 1793, in AN, F^{9}36883, no. 174. For observations and anecdotes on Linguet by those imprisoned with him see Jacques Claude Beugnot, *Mémoires du Comte Beugnot, ancien ministre* (1783-1815), ed. Albert Beugnot, 3d ed. (Paris, 1889), pp. 198-200; *Supplément au "Notices historiques* [Madame Roland's] *sur la Révolution,"* in Marie-Jeanne Phlipon Roland de la Platière, *Mémoires de Madame Roland,* ed. Saint-Albin Berville and Jean-François Barrière, 2d ed., 2 vols. (Paris, 1821), II, 314-15.

95. Linguet to Président, Comité de Sûreté générale, La Force, Oct. 9, 1793, in AN, F^{7}477424, dossier 2.

96. Procès verbal [Marnes, between minutes of Oct. 4 and 13, 1793] in Registre de la Commune de Marnes, vol. 1, as cited in Pierre-Henri Machard, *Essai historique sur Marnes-la-Coquette (Marnes-les-Saint-Cloud, Seine-et-Oise)* (Paris, 1932), pp. 142-43.

97. Etienne-Jean Panis [member of Committee of General Security] to his colleagues in the Committee, Oct. 27, 1793, copy in BM, uncat. MSS, Coll. Gosset; another copy can be found in the Archives départementales de la Marne, Chalons-sur-Marne, J 664. Linguet's mistress addressed a letter to the president of the convention on Nov. 13, 1793. She reported that Panis had assured her that he had written in Linguet's favor, but that he had no report to make in his case. Perine Poulet to President of the Convention, 23 Brumaire Year II (Nov. 13, 1793), in BM, uncat. MSS, Coll. Gosset, no. 28.

98. Linguet to "citoyen ministre" [Minister of Interior Jules Paré], Paris, 11 Frimaire Year II, in AN F^{7}477424, dossier 2. The minister of interior sent a précis of the contents of Linguet's letter of 11 Frimaire to the Committee of General Security, along with the original: "I leave, citizens, to your justice, the care of deciding what you will judge appropriate concerning Citizen Linguet."

99. Copie du Rapport de la maladie de Linguet, détenu à La Force, in AN, F^{7}477424,

dossier 2. Linguet was suffering from dysentery and a severe infection of the urinary tract.

100. Linguet to the Committee of General Security, Paris [Jan. 1794], in BM, uncat. MSS, Coll. Gosset, no. 29.

101. Report of the Committee of General Security, 29 Prairial Year II, in AN, W 397-921, 4me partie, no. 9.

102. Linguet to Louis XVI, April 4, 1792, in AN, C 184, no. 284; Report of the Committee of General Security, 29 Prairial Year II, in AN, W 397-921, 4me partie, no. 9.

103. Linguet to Louis XVI, April 4, 1792, in AN, C 184, no. 284.

104. Report of the Committee of General Security, 29 Prairial Year II, in AN, W 397-921, 4me partie, no. 9.

105. Act of accusation, drawn up by the Revolutionary Tribunal's Procurator-general, Fouquier-Tinville, 8 Messidor Year II, in AN, W 397-921, 4me partie, no. 5.

106. Order of the Revolutionary Tribunal summoning Linguet to appear, signed A. G. Fouquier, in Archives, Préfecture de la Police, Paris, Registers of Maison Belhomme, Messidor Year II, no. 157.

107. Penciled minute in Linguet's hand of his defense prepared for the Revolutionary Tribunal, A.N., W 397-921, 4me partie, no. 7. Copies of the letters corrected and annotated in Linguet's hand, addressed to a Monsieur de la P[orte], a functionary in the king's household, and dated end of February [1792], March 8, 12, and 20, 1792, are preserved in AN, W 397-921, 4me partie, no. 8.

108. See receipt signed by Linguet, reading as follows: "Je reconnois avoir reçu de Monsieur le Comte de Montmorin la somme de dix mille livres tournois, Versailles, ce 1r juillet 1789." BM, uncat. MSS, Coll. Gosset, no. 26. There is no countersignature. Apparently, it is this pension which was suspended, but then renewed in the spring of 1792. For detailed discussion, see Chapter Seven, above, pp. 280-81.

109. Penciled minute, in Linguet's hand, for his defense before the Revolutionary Tribunal, in AN, W 397-921, 4e partie, no. 7.

110. *Ibid.*

111. *Ibid.*

112. Linguet, *Adresse au peuple français, concernant ce qu'il faut faire et ce qu'il ne faut pas faire; pour célébrer la fête mémorable et nationale du 14 juillet 1790. Et surtout la nécessité de n'y admettre aucun cheval* (n.p. 1790), p. 5.

113. Judgment of the Revolutionary Tribunal, 9 Messidor Year II, in AN, W 397-921, 4me partie, no. 1; procès-verbal of execution of the Revolutionary Tribunal's judgment of 9 Messidor Year II, in *ibid.*, no. 6.

Bibliography

1. Archival and manuscript collections

AUSTRIA

Vienna

Osterreichisches Haus–, Hof–, und Staatsarchivs.

Holdings of the Secretariat of State and War. Belgium, DD, B192[b] (56), 1780-88 (correspondence concerning Linguet, prisoner in the Bastille; correspondence between Linguet and Austrian authorities in Belgium relating to Linguet's defense of Austrian interests during the Scheldt crisis (1784-85).

Holdings of the Austrian Chancellery, Belgium, Weisunge, Berichte, 1776-85 (exchange of reports between the emperor and the Austrian chancellor in Vienna and Austria's ministers plenipotentiary in Brussels).

BELGIUM

Brussels

Archives générales du royaume de Belgique

Chancellerie autrichienne des Pays-Bas. Dépêches d'office (original correspondence between Prince Kaunitz and Austrian Emperor Joseph II, and between Austrian ministers plenipotentiary in Brussels and Chancellor Kaunitz, 1782-89).

Chancellerie autrichienne des Pays-Bas. Répertoires, 1776-89 (précis of exchanges between the emperor and the Austrian chancellor in Vienna and Austria's ministers plenipotentiary in Brussels).

MSS divers, no. 1498 (a collection of correspondence between Linguet and Secretary of State and War Crumpipen; President of the Belgian Conseil Privé, Nény; the emperor's minister plenipotentiary in Brussels, Count Belgiojoso. Correspondence between Nény and Crumpipen. Correspondence between the Archbishop of Malines and the emperor's minister plenipotentiary in Brussels, Prince Starhemberg. Crumpipen's [?] notes on corrections to be made in article written by Linguet in cooperation with Austrian authorities: 1778-85).

MSS divers, no. 4111 (Brabant revolution).

MSS divers, no. 5117 (letters from Linguet to the emperor's minister plenipotentiary in Brussels, Count Trauttmansdorff, 1787-89).

Archival and manuscript collections *(continued)*

Pays-Bas, Office fiscal, 1024 (correspondence relating to the publication of the *Journal de politique et de littérature,* 1776; the duc de Lorraine to the Conseillers fiscaux de Brabant authorizing Linguet's uncensored printing of the *Annales,* 1780).

Bibliothèque royale, Albert 1er

MSS, B II 4742, letter 26, Linguet autograph.

MSS, fonds générales, 15,709-725 (a large collection of printed and manuscript materials belonging to Linguet, including annotated documentation concerning the book trade and reform legislation relating to this subject. Autograph signatures of Linguet and commissaire of Paris police Chesnon, dated March 31, 1781, and appearing on fols. 422, 424, 425 of this collection, indicate that this material was probably removed from Linguet's house in Brussels and itemized as part of a *procès-verbal,* in Linguet's presence, at the Bastille.

ENGLAND

Oxford

Voltaire Foundation, Taylor Institution

MS copy of an anonymous, spurious Linguet "autobiography."

FRANCE

Châlons-sur Marne

Archives départmentales de la Marne

Dossiers, Série J: 539, 557, 561, 564, 664 (documents concerning Linguet, the Linguet family, and the Dérodé family).

Paris

Archives nationales de France

AF II, 292, fol. 90 (documents concerning the arrest of Madame Buttet [Poulet], Spring, 1794).

C 184, no. 284 (Linguet to Louis XVI, April 4, 1792, the letter found in the *armoire de fer*).

F^{7}36883, no. 174 (police reports, Sept. 28, 1793).

F^7 4573. Police générale (lists of arrests, detentions, etc., authorized by the Committee of General Security).

F^7 477424. Dossier II (letter from Linguet to French minister of interior from La Force; medical reports on Linguet's physical condition; Linguet to president of the Committee of General Security; police interrogations of Madame Buttet concerning hoarding of potatoes, and arrest of Madame Buttet [Poulet].

F^7 477467. Dossier I, Perchet (contains material of interest on Linguet's relations with the municipality of Marnes-les-Saint-Cloud at the time of his arrest).

T 1641, Sequestre Linguet.

W 397, dossier 921, 4e partie (documents, several written, annotated, or corrected in Linguet's hand, including material on his trial before the Revolutionary Tribunal, and evidence that Linguet produced in his own defense, and a penciled self-defense; also documents on sentencing, execution of sentence, etc.).

Série X^{1}A, 3582, Conseil secret, Parlement of Paris, fols. 81-128v (précis of Du Val d'Eprémesnil's indictment of Linguet before the parlement, July, 1780).

Bibliothèque de l'Arsenal

Mss, 10,169, 10,305, 11,107, 11,197, 12,452 (several manuscripts concerning Jean Linguet, and some of minor importance from the Archives de la Bastille concerning Linguet in the Bastille, confiscations of Linguet's printed works, *gazetins de la police,* etc.).

MSS, 14,566 Livre des sorties de la Bastille (Nov. 12, 1771–Dec. 26, 1782).

Bibliothèque nationale de France

MSS, fonds français, Archives de la Chambre syndicale de la librairie et imprimerie de Paris au XVIIe et XVIIIe siècles, 21,813-22,060 (especially volumes treating suspensions, seizures, suppressions of printed literature, *permissions tacites, permissions simples, privilèges,* for years 1760-89).

MSS, fonds français, Collection Joly de Fleury, vol. 418, dossier 4817 (the case of the chevalier de La Barre).

MSS, fonds français, 13,733-735, Pierre-Etienne Régnaud, Histoire des événemens depuis le mois de septembre 1770, concernans les parlemens et les changemens dans l'administration de la justice et dans les loix du royaume (1770-1775)."

MSS, fonds français,, 6682-86, Siméon-Prosper Hardy, "Mes Loisirs, ou Journal d'événemens tel qu'ils parviennent à ma connoissance (1764-1789)."

MSS, fonds français, Collection Anisson-Duperron, 22,061-193, *passim* (lists of libels and other prohibited books, censors' reports, book seizures, counterfeit editions, especially for years 1760-89).

MSS, nouvelles acquisitions françaises, 1448 ("Requête de M. Linguet, avocat, présentée au Roi à Choisy, le 8 octobre 1775".).

MSS, nouvelles acquisitions françaises, 5215, fol. 364, LINGUET (Linguet's letter to Maurepas, London, June 30, 1777).

Archives, ministère des affairse étrangères

Correspondance politique, Angleterre, vols. 517-49 (1776-84).
Correspondance politique, Autriche, vols. 351-57 (1786-89).
Correspondance politique, Genève, vols. 83-84 (1778-79).
Correspondance politique, Pays-Bas autrichiens, vols. 170-78 (1776-89).
Mémoires et documents, France, vol. 1897.

Bibliothèque et Archives de la Préfecture de Police

AA, 25, Dossiers, Maison Belhomme.
A, B/316, Registre d'entrées, Maison Belhomme.
A, B/327, Registre, La Force.

Reims

Archives municipales

MSS, Collection Tarbé, carton XXI (1793-1842), fols. 43-44 (Pons de Verdun, "Linguet à la Bastille").

Bibliothèque municipale

Uncatalogued collection of manuscripts bequeathed by Dr. Gosset (letters from Linguet to: Brissot de Warville; Monsieur Gomel, procurator at the Châtelet in Paris; Linguet's cousin, Monsieur Jacob; Charles-Joseph Panckoucke, the publisher; Jean-Frédéric Perrégaux, the Swiss banker in Paris; Monsieur Raymond, director of the postal service,

Archival and manuscript collections *(continued)*

Besançon; the baron de Tournon; Tronson de Coudray; the comte de Vergennes, French secretary of state for foreign affairs; Voltaire; the Committee of General Security, Marie-Louise Dérodé, Linguet's sister; Jean-Nicolas Dérodé, Linguet's brother-in-law; unnamed correspondent. Linguet's signed receipt for 10,000 *livres,* from the comte de Montmorin, France's secretary of state for foreign affairs. Correspondence of: Marie-Louise Dérodé; Nicolas-Antoine Linguet; Jean-Baptiste-Marie Linguet; Jean-Baptiste-François-Augustin Linguet; Augustin Dérode; Perine Buttet; the abbé André Morellet. Portraits of Linguet. Genealogy of the Linguet and Dérodé families. Documents relating to Linguet's estate and correspondence among members of the Linguet-Dérodé family on this subject. Material concerning Robert-Hubert Linguet (the brother of Linguet's father, Jean Linguet), a member of the Faculty of Medicine in Paris.

MSS, collections d'autographes. Première collection de la ville, vol. II, fols. 80-86 (Linguet's letters to: unnamed correspondents; Jean-Frédéric Perrégaux [1787-90]. Notes relating to Charles-Joseph Panckoucke.

MSS, collections d'autographes, collection Augustin Duchesne, fols. 198-99 (Linguet's undated letter to Malesherbes; Linguet's signed receipt for subscription to the *Annales*).

MSS, no. 1160, "Poésies diverses, pièces fugitives," fol. 57 (manuscript copy of Linguet's poem, "Le Convoie de la pie, fable"; manuscript copy of Linguet's "A l'occasion de la mort de Made Géoffrin").

MSS, no. 1299, "Muses rémoises," vol. I (copies of Linguet's unpublished poetry).

MSS, no. 1916 (letters from Linguet to: Pierre Lequesne; the comte de Mercy-Argenteau, Austria's minister plenipotentiary in Paris; LePrestre de Chateaugiron, *président à mortier* in the Paris parlement; Monsieur de Tournon; Monsieur Macquer of the Académie des sciences; Monsieur de Bachois, lieutenant-criminel, Paris. Letters to various correspondents from: Pierre Lequesne; Jacques Mallet Du Pan; Madame Buttet. Linguet's verses, written from the Bastille. Fragments of a memoir by Linguet relating to his disbarment. Miscellaneous material concerning Linguet).

MSS, no. 1917, "Lettre de M. Linguet à M. le C. de Vergennes, ministre des affaires étrangères en France," London, Jan. 16, 1777 (manuscript copy of Linguet's published letter to Vergennes of this date).

MSS, no. 1918, famille Linguet (materials of family genealogy, correspondence, family records and papers. Extracts from parish registers of Reims and Senuc, covering the period 1640-1787. Lettre de cachet addressed to Jean Linguet. *Livre-journal* of Jean Linguet. Letters from Jean-Baptiste-Augustin-François Linguet to the Dérodé family [1767-72]. Letters to and from members of the Linguet-Dérodé family and Marie-Louise Dérodé, Linguet's sister).

MSS, no. 1919, Linguet and Dérodé family papers.

MSS, no. 1920, "Journal pour servir à Jean-Nicolas Dérodé, notaire roial à Reims...."

MSS, no. 1921, manuscript literary works of Simon-Nicolas-Henri Linguet (a collection of Linguet's early literary efforts, including poetry and unpublished plays, some of which are parodies of Voltaire's works or adaptations from Spanish and Italian theater).

MSS, no. 1922, Pierre-Augustin Dérodé-Géruzez, "Vie de S.-N.-H. Linguet, écrite par P.-A. Dérodé-Géruzez, son neveu," July 2, 1817.

MSS, no. 1923 (miscellaneous materials concerning Linguet, gathered by P.-A. Dérodé-Géruzez for his biography; includes a bibliography of Linguet's works).

MSS, no. 1924, papers of P.-A. Dérodé-Géruzez (includes reprints of Dérodé's articles on Linguet).

Société des amis du vieux Reims

Nouvelle collection d'autographes, LINGUET.

Versailles

Archives départementales d'Yvelines (Seine-et-Oise)

Série IV Q 169 (plans of Linguet's estate at Marnes-les-Saint-Cloud; inventory of possessions in all buildings on the estate [books are not itemized separately but simply counted and totaled]).

Série L, non classé, Dossier Linguet.

Série, Q, non classé, Journal du Comité révolutionnaire de la Commune de Sèvres.

SWITZERLAND

Geneva

Bibliothèque publique et universitaire de Genève

MSS, MS Supp. 1036, fols. 94-99 (letters from Linguet to Jacob Vernes).

MSS, Collection Coindet, MS Supp. 357, fols. 18-21 (letters from Linguet to Jacob Vernes).

Institut et musée Voltaire, Les Délices

MS copy of an anonymous, spurious Linguet "autobiography."

Neuchâtel

Bibliothèque publique de la ville de Neuchâtel

Archives de la Société typographique de Neuchâtel, MS 1101, fols. 174-75; MS. 1175, fols. 440-41 (correspondence between Linguet and the Société typographique de Neuchâtel).

Archives de la Société typographique de Neuchâtel, MS. 1178, fols. 22-121 (correspondence between Jacques Mallet Du Pan and the Société typographique de Neuchâtel).

2. Works by Simon-Nicolas-Henri Linguet

Adresse au peuple français, concernant ce qu'il faut faire et ce qu'il ne faut pas faire; pour célébrer la fête mémorable et nationale du 14 juillet 1790. Et surtout la nécessité de n'y admettre aucun cheval, N.p., 1790.

Aiguilloniana, ou Anecdotes utiles pour l'histoire de France au dix-huitième siècle, depuis l'année 1770. London, 1777.

A Messieurs du magistrat de Bruxelles. N.p., n.d.

Annales politiques, civiles, et littéraires du dix-huitième siècle. 19 vols. London, Brussels, Paris, 1777-92. Authorized reprintings of Linguet's edition of the Annales: by Pierre-Féderic Gosse, 9 vols., The Hague, 1777-80, and by the Société typographique de Lausanne.

Appel à la nation belgique. Par l'auteur des "Observations d'un citoyen sur les enlèvemens qui ont eu lieu à Bruxelles le 27 juillet 1789." Contre la déclaration publiée au sujet de ces "Observations," sous le nom du Comte de Windisch-Graetz. N.p., 1789. Another printing with the title: Appel à la nation belgique, par l'auteur des "Observations d'un citoyen sur les enlèvemens qui ont eu lieu à Bruxelles," & c. Réimprimé aux fraix & précédé d'une petite préface du Comte de Windisch-Graetz. N.p., 1789.

Appel à la postérité, ou Recueil des mémoires et plaidoyers de M. Linguet pour lui-même, contre la communauté des avocats du Parlement de Paris. N.p., 1779. This work is volume I of Linguet's Collection complette des œuvres de M. Linguet. London, 1777-79. Another edition, The Hague, 1780.

Works by Simon-Nicolas-Henri Linguet *(continued)*

L'Aveu sincère, ou Lettre à une mère sur les dangers que court la jeunesse en se livrant à un goût trop vif pour la littérature. London and Paris, 1768.

Avis aux Parisiens. Par M. Linguet. Appel de toutes convocations d'Etats-Généraux où les députés du troisième ordre ne seroient pas supérieurs en nombre aux deux autres. N.p. [1788]. 2d ed., n.p., 1789.

Avis aux souscripteurs des "Annales politiques, civiles," & c. [London, Jan. 1, 1783.] N.P., n.d.

La Cacomonade, histoire politique et morale, traduit de l'allemand du docteur Pangloss, par le docteur lui-même depuis son retour de Constantinople. Cologne, 1766. Other editions: Cologne, 1767; London and Paris, 1767; Paris, 1797. German trans.: Berlin, 1782.

Canaux navigables, ou Développement des avantages qui résulteraient de l'exécution de plusieurs projets en ce genre pour la Picardie, l'Artois, la Bourgogne, la Champagne, la Bretagne, et toute la France en général. Avec l'examen de quelques-unes des raisons qui s'y opposent, & c. Amsterdam and Paris, 1769.

Catéchisme des Parlements. N.p., 1789.

Ce qu'il faut penser de la permission demandée et accordée pour le passage des troupes autrichiennes sur les terres de France, pour entrer dans la Belgique. Par M. Linguet. Tournai, 1790.

Code criminel de Joseph Second, ou Instructions expéditives données aux tribunaux des Pays-Bas, en octobre 1789, publiées et commentées par M. Linguet. Brussels, 1790.

Collection complette des œuvres de M. Linguet. 3 vols. published. London, 1777-79.

Collection complette des œuvres de M. Linguet, dont les quatre premiers volumes, contenant la "Théorie du libelle," la "Théorie des lois," et l'"Histoire des révolutions de l'Empire romain, depuis Auguste jusqu'à Constantin," paroitront dans le courant de novembre 1777. N.p., n.d.

Collection des ouvrages relatifs à la révolution du Brabant. Paris, 1791.

Du commerce des grains. Nouvelle édition. Augmentée d'une lettre à M. Tissot sur le vrai merite politique & phisique du pain & du bled. Brussels, 1788. Another printing, Brussels, 1789.

Considérations politiques et philosophiques, sur les affaires présentes du Nord, et particulièrement sur celles de Pologne. London, 1774.

Considérations sur l'ouverture de l'Escaut. London, 1784. A separate printing of numbers 88 and 89 of the *Annales.* Trans. into German with the title: *Die Erofnung der Schiffahrt auf der Schelde. Stand des darüber aufgeworfenen Streitpunts zwischen Sr. Kaiserl. Majestät, und den vereinigten provinzen. Aus dem Franzosischen, nach den "Annalen" des hrn. von Linguet.* N.p., 1784. Trans. into Dutch with the title: *Redevœring over het openen en Bevaeren des Schelde, Door den berusten Heer Linguet, Vertaelt uyt het Fransch.* Brussels, 1785.

Considérations sur l'utilité de réformer les loix civiles de France, de supprimer les justices seigneuriales, et de rendre aux présidiaux du royaume plus de pouvoir, & d'étendu: Avec la réfutation de quelques passages de "L'Esprit des loix" à ce sujet. Amsterdam and Paris, 1768. This is a second edition of Linguet's *Nécessité d'une réforme dans l'administration de la justice et dans les lois civiles en France....* Amsterdam, 1764.

Consultation de M. Linguet, avocat, en réponse à la "Consultation sur la discipline des avocats," imprimée chez Knapen, en mai 1775. Brussels, 1776.

Consultation de M. Linguet pour la portion des religieux capucins, designés dans leur ordre sous le nom de frères lais ou laics; au sujet des décrets de l'Assemblée nationale du 19 et du 20 février 1790; sur le traitement des religieux qui sortiront de leurs mai-

sons; suivie d'une opinion concernant les pensions des religieuses. [Paris, May 28, 1790.] N.p., n.d.

Copie d'une lettre écrite à son excellence le ministre par Mr. Linguet le 28 juillet 1789. N.p., n.d.

Défenses pour M. Linguet, sur la demande en réparation d'honneur et en dommages-intérêts formée contre lui au Châtelet de Paris, par le S[ieur] P[ierre] Le Quesne, marchand d'étoffes de soie. N.p., n.d.

De la dette nationale et du crédit public en France. Brussels, 1789.

Discours destiné à être prononcé par Me Linguet dans l'Assemblée des avocats le 3 février 1775. Paris, 1775.

Discours par M. Linguet à l'Assemblée-générale de l'ordre des avocats du Parlement de Paris. Paris, 1775.

Dissertation sur le bled et le pain, par M. Linguet, avec la réfutation de M. Tissot, D.M. Neuchâtel, 1779.

Dissertation sur l'ouverture et la navigation de l'Escaut. Par M. Linguet. Brussels, 1784. This is a separate printing of Linguet's no. 88 of the *Annales.*

La Dixme royale, avec de courtes réflexions sur ce qu'on appelle la contrebande et l'usage de regarder comme inaliénable le domaine de nos rois. The Hague, 1764.

Eloge de Maupeou, printed in Jacques-Pierre Brissot de Warville, *Mémoires de Brissot, membre de l'Assemblée législative et de la Convention nationale, sur ses contemporains, et la Révolution française.* Ed. François Mongin de Montrol. 4 vols. Paris, 1830-32, I, 373.

Epître d'un J[ésuite] .....de D....à un de ses amis. N.p., n.d. Another edition: Lisbon, 1764.

Esprit et génie de M. Linguet, avocat au Parlement de Paris [excerpts from Linguet's writings, edited anonymously]. London, 1780.

Essai philosophique sur le monachisme. Paris, 1775. Another edition, Neuchâtel, 1776.

Examen abrégé d'un nouvel écrit publié contre le Comte de Morangiès, intitulé: Preuves résultantes du procès pour la Dame Romain et le Sieur Dujonquai. N.p., 1773.

Examen impartial des œuvres de Monsieur de Voltaire. Par M. Linguet, auteur des "Annales politiques, civiles & littéraires du dix-huitième siècle." Hamburg, 1784. Another edition with the title: *Examen des ouvrages de M. de Voltaire, considéré comme poète, comme prosateur, comme philosophe.* Brussels, 1788. Trans. into English as: *A critical Analysis and Review of All M. Voltaire's Works; with Occasional Disquisitions on Epic Poetry, the Drama, Romance & c.* Trans. J. Boardman, London, 1790. Another French edition: Paris, 1817.

Le Fanatisme des philosophes. London and Abbeville, 1764.

Les Femmes filles, ou Les Maris battus, Parodie d' "Hipermnestre" [by A.-M. Lemierre]. Paris, 1759.

La France plus qu'angloise, ou Comparaison entre la procédure entamée à Paris le 25 septembre 1788 contre les ministres du roi de France, et le procès intenté à Londres en 1640 au comte de Strafford, principal ministre de Charles 1er, roi d'Angleterre. Avec des réflexions sur le danger imminent dont les entreprises de la robe menacent la nation et les particuliers. Brussels, 1788. 2d ed., Brussels, 1788. 3d ed., Brussels, 1789.

Histoire des révolutions de l'Empire romain, pour servir de suite à celle des révolutions de la République. 2 vols. Paris, 1766. Vol. I of a second edition was published as vol. III in Linguet's *Collection complette des œuvres de M. Linguet* (London, 1777-79). 3d ed., vol. I, London, 1787.

Histoire du siècle d'Alexandre, avec quelques réflexions sur ceux qui l'ont précédé. Amsterdam, 1762.

Works by Simon-Nicolas-Henri Linguet *(continued)*

Histoire du siècle d'Alexandre. 2d ed., Amsterdam and Paris, 1769.

Histoire impartiale des Jésuites. Depuis leur établissement jusqu'à leur première expulsion. 2 vols. N.p., 1768.

Histoire universelle du seizième siècle, pour servir de suite à "L'Histoire universelle sacrée et profane" [by J. Hardion]. 2 vols. Paris, 1769.

L'Impôt territorial, ou la dixme roiale, Avec tous ses avantages. London, 1787.

Journal de politique et de littérature, contenant les principaux événemens de toutes les cours, les nouvelles de la république des lettres, & c. 21 nos. Brussels [Paris], Oct. 25, 1774-July 25, 1776.

Légitimité du divorce, justifiée par les Saintes Ecritures, par les Pères, par les Conciles, & c. Aux Etats-Généraux. Brussels, 1789.

Lettre à celui ou ceux des "Annales patriotiques et littéraires," dirigées par M. Mercier; au sujet du Brabant. Brussels, 1790.

Lettre à Monsieur le Marquis de Beccaria, auteur du "Traité des délits et des peines." Par M. Linguet. London, 1777.

Lettre à Sa Majesté l'Empereur et Roi [Brussels, Sept. 15, 1789]. N.p., n.d.

Lettre de J. Ph. Cobenzl [Luxembourg, Feb. 28, 1790]. *Avec la réponse d'un citoyen vertueux.* N.p., n.d.

Lettre de M. Linguet à l'Empereur Joseph II [Brussels, from the Bastille, Nov. 1, 1789]. N.p., n.d.

Lettre de M. Linguet à l'Empereur Joseph Second sur la révolution du Brabant, et du reste des Pays-Bas [Dec. 22, 1789]. Brussels, 1790. 2d ed., Brussels, 1790.

Lettre de M. Linguet à M. Camille Des Moulins, auteur du journal intitulé "Révolutions de France, et de Brabant" [Brussels, Feb. 18, 1790]. N.p., n.d.

Lettre de M. Linguet à M. le Comte de Vergennes, ministre des affaires étrangères en France. London, 1777. 2d ed., London, 1778.

Lettre de M. Linguet à un membre de la Société patriotique de Bruxelles sur la requête présentée par cette Société aux Etats de Brabant en mars 1790; et sur la question: Faut-il à la Belgique une Assemblée nationale, ou non? [March 19, 1790]. Brussels, 1790.

Lettre de M. Linguet au Comité patriotique de Bruxelles [Dec. 13, 1789]. N.p., n.d. This publication includes a second letter with separate pagination, *A sa Majesté l'Empereur et Roi* [Brussels, the Bastille, Nov. 1, 1789]. N.p., 1789.

Lettre de M. Linguet au ministre, le comte de Trauttmansdorff [July 31, 1789]. Paris, n.d. This is another edition of Linguet's *Copie d'une lettre écrite à son excellence le ministre par M. Linguet le 28 juillet 1789.* N.p., n.d.

Lettre de M. Linguet, au rédacteur de la feuille périodique intitulée, "L'Abeille patriote". N.p., n.d.

Lettre de M. Linguet au Roi [Brussels, Aug. 20, 1776] N.p., n.d.

Lettre du mandarin Oei-Tching à son ami Hoei-Tchang sur les affaires des RR.PP. Jésuites. N.p., 1762.

Lettre missive écrite aux notables, en leur adressant cette dénonciation [Paris, Nov. 12, 1788.] N.p., n.d.

Lettres de M. Linguet au Comte de Trauttmansdorff, ministre plénipotentiaire pour l'Empereur au Pays-Bas en 1788 et 1789. Brussels, 1790. 2d ed., Brussels, 1790.

Lettres sur la nouvelle traduction de Tacite par M. L. D. L. B [Monsieur l'abbé de la Bletterie], avec un petit recueil de phrases élégantes, tirées de la même traduction pour l'usage de ses écoliers. Amsterdam, 1768.

Lettres sur la "Théorie des loix civiles" & c., où l'on examine entr'autres choses s'il est bien vrai que les Anglois soient libres & que les François doivent, ou imiter leurs opérations, ou porter envie à leur gouvernement. Amsterdam, 1770.

Lettres sur les avantages et les inconvéniens de la navigation des ports d'Abbeville, Amiens, Saint-Valery et Le Crotoy. Ed. H. Devérité. Abbeville, 1818.

Mélanges de politique et de littérature, extraits des "Annales" de M. Linguet pour servir à l'histoire du XVIIIᵉ siècle. Ed. Société typographique de Bouillon. 3 vols. Bouillon, 1778-80.

Mémoire à consulter et consultation pour un mari dont la femme s'est remariée en pays protestant, et qui demande s'il peut se remarier de même en France. Paris, 1771.

Mémoire au Roi, par M. Linguet, concernant ses réclamations actuellement pendantes au Parlement de Paris. London, 1786. Another edition, London, 1787.

Mémoire pour M. le Duc D'Aiguillon. Paris, 1770.

Mémoire signifié pour le Sieur Luneau de Boisgermain, défendeur, contre les syndic et adjoints des libraires et imprimeurs de Paris, demandeurs. Paris, 1769.

Mémoire sur les propriétés et privilèges exclusifs de la librairie. Présenté en 1774. N.p., n.d.

Mémoire sur un objet intéressant pour la province de Picardie: Ou Projet d'un canal & d'un port sur ses côtes, avec un parallèle du commerce & de l'activité des François, avec celle des Hollandois. The Hague and Abbeville, 1764.

Mémoires et plaidoyers. 7 vols. Amsterdam, 1773.

Mémoires et plaidoyers de M. Linguet, avocat à Paris. 11 vols. Liège and Amsterdam, 1776.

Mémoires sur la Bastille, et la détention de l'auteur dans ce château royal, depuis le 27 septembre 1780 jusqu'au 19 mai 1782. London, 1783. English trans.: London, 1783; Dublin, 1783; Edinburgh, 1884-87, ed. E. Goldsmid, 4 vols.; London, 1927, J. and S. F. Mills Witham; Swedish trans.: Stockholm, 1783. German trans.: Berlin, 1783. Other French editions (all from Paris): ed. Berville and Barrière, 1821; ed. N. David, 1864; ed. Barrière, 1866; ed. H. Monin, 1889.

Mémoires sur la navigation de l'Escaut, suivis de "Nouvelles Considérations" sur son ouverture. Extraits des "Annales politiques" de Linguet, & terminés par le "Discours d'un ministre de France au Conseil d'état à Versailles, sur les vrais intérêts de sa nation, relativement à l'ouverture de l'Escaut." N.p., 1785. This is a reprinting from nos. 88 and 89 of the *Annales*.

Mémoires sur l'ouverture de la navigation sur l'Escaut: Etat de la question agitée entre sa majesté impériale et les Provinces-Unies, à ce sujet. Par M. Linguet. N.p., 1784. A reprinting from no. 88 of the *Annales*.

Nécessité d'une réforme dans l'administration de la justice et dans les lois civiles en France, avec la réfutation de quelques passages de "L'Esprit des lois". Amsterdam, 1764.

Nouveau mémoire sur l'ouverture de l'Escaut. Edition généralement refondue & augmentée par M. Linguet. Brussels, 1785, with inside title page: *Nouvelle "Dissertation" et "Considérations" sur l'ouverture de l'Escaut, par M. Linguet. Edition généralement refondue & augmentée par l'auteur même.* Brussels, 1785. A separate printing from nos. 88 and 89 of the *Annales*.

Nouvelles considérations sur l'ouverture de l'Escaut. Par M. Linguet. Pour servir de suite à la "Dissertation" du même auteur. Brussels, 1784. A reprinting from no. 89 of the *Annales*.

Observations d'un citoyen sur les enlèvemens qui ont eu lieu à Bruxelles, le 27 juillet 1789. N.p., n.d.

Works by Simon-Nicolas-Henri Linguet *(continued)*

Observations d'un républicain sur un mémoire publié sous le nom de S.A.R. [Son Altesse Royale] le grand-duc de Toscane, comme rédigé du vivant de feu Joseph Second, pour n'être remis qu'après sa mort aux Etats des Pays-Bas, ci-devant autrichiens. Brussels, 1790.

Observations sur l'imprimé intitulé "Réponse des Etats de Bretagne au 'Mémoire' du duc d'Aiguillon." Paris, 1771.

Observations sur le nouvel arrêté du Parlement de Paris, en date du 5 décembre 1788. Brussels, 1789.

Observations sur un imprimé ayant pour titre: "Mémoire pour Me Gerbier, ancien avocat," avec cette épigraphe: Quod genus hoc hominum? Paris, 1775.

Oeuvres de M. Linguet. 6 vols. London, 1774.

Oeuvres diverses de Mr. Linguet, avocat au Parlement de Paris. London and Abbeville, 1768.

Onguent pour la brûlure, ou Observations sur un réquisitoire imprimé en tête de l'arrêt du Parlement de Paris du 27 septembre 1788, rendu contre les "Annales" de M. Linguet, avec des réflexions sur l'usage de faire brûler des livres par la main du bourreau. N.p., n.d. Another printing, London, 1788.

Du pain et du bled. London, 1774. This work is vol. VI of Linguet's *Oeuvres de M. Linguet,* 6 vols. London, 1774.

Le Peuple belgique à la lettre du Comte J. Ph. Cobenzl, datée de Luxembourg, du 28 février 1790. N.p., 1790.

La Pierre philosophale, discours économique, prononcé dans l'académie impériale de Fong-yang-fou, par le lettré Kong-Kia. The Hague, 1768.

Plaidoyer pour le Comte de Morangiès. Paris, 1772.

Plaidoyer pour M. Linguet, avocat au Parlement, prononcé par lui-même en la Grand' Chambre, les 4 & 11 janvier 1775; avec l'arrêt intervenu en sa faveur. Paris, 1775.

Plaidoyer pour S.N.H. Linguet, Ecuier, ancien avocat au Parlement de Paris, prononcé par lui-même en la Grand'Chambre, dans sa discussion avec M. le duc d'Aiguillon, pair de France, ancien commandant pour le Roi en Bretagne. London and Brussels, 1787.

Plaidoyer sur la question, si la maladie vénérienne communiquée par le mari, est une cause de séparation de corps. Paris, 1771.

Plaidoyers et mémoires de M. Linguet. Nouvelle édition revue et corrigée par lui-même. 2 vols. published. London, 1787-88.

Plan d'établissemens tendans à l'extinction de la mendicité. Paris, 1779.

Du plus heureux gouvernement, ou Parallèle des constitutions politiques de l'Asie avec celles de l'Europe, servant d'introduction à la "Théorie des lois civiles." 2 vols. in one. London, 1774. This work comprises vols. I-II of Linguet's *Oeuvres de M. Linguet.* London, 1774.

Point de banqueroute, plus d'emprunts, et si l'on veut, bientôt plus de dettes, en réduisant les impôts à un seul. Avec un moyen facile de supprimer la mendicité, en assurant à toutes les classes du peuple une existence aisée dans la vieillesse. Plan proposé à tous les peuples libres, et notamment à l'Assemblée nationale de France. N.p., 1789.

Précis et consultation dans la cause entre Simon-Nicolas-Henri Linguet, écuyer, et Charles-Joseph Panckoucke, libraire à Paris. Paris, 1787.

Précis politique sur les differends qui se sont élévés entre l'Empereur et les Etats Généraux des Provinces-Unies, relativement à l'Escaut. Paris and Brussels, 1785.

Procédures faites en Bretagne et devant la Cour des pairs en 1770, Avec des observations. N.p., 1770.

La Prophétie vérifiée; ou Lettres de M. Linguet à M. le Cte de Trauttmansdorff, Weynsberg, & c. Ghent, n.d.

Prospectus pour le projet d'une nouvelle académie de musique. Auquel on a joint par occasion quelques problèmes tendans à favoriser l'agriculture. Par Messieurs^{xxx}, entrepreneurs de ce spectacle. Amsterdam, 1762.

Protestations de M. Linguet contre les arrêts du Parlement de Paris des 25 & 27 septembre 1788. [Brussels, Nov. 7, 1788].

Quelle est l'origine des Etats-Généraux? N.p., 1788.

Réclamations de la commune de Marseille, contre les ministres, suivies d'un arrêté du District des Cordeliers, rédigé par M. Linguet. N.p., 1790.

Réflexions des six corps de la ville de Paris sur la suppression des jurandes. N.p., 1776.

Réflexions pour Me Linguet, avocat de la Comtesse de Béthune. Paris, 1774.

Réflexions sur la lumière, ou Conjectures sur la part qu'elle a au mouvement des corps célestes. London, 1784. New ed., Brussels and Paris, 1787.

Réflexions sur la résistance opposée à l'exécution des ordonnances promulguées le 8 mai 1788, suivies de la différence entre la révolution passagère de 1771 et la réforme de 1788, dans l'ordre judiciaire en France. Brussels, 1788.

Réplique pour le Comte de Morangiès. N.p., 1772.

Réponse aux docteurs modernes, ou Apologie pour l'auteur de la "Théorie des lois" et des "Lettres" sur cette "Théorie," Avec la réfutation du système des philosophes économistes. 2 vols. N.p., 1771.

Réponse signifiée pour le Sieur Luneau de Boisgermain, ou Précis signifié par les syndic & adjoints des libraires de Paris. Paris, 1769.

Requête au Conseil du Roi, pour Me Linguet, avocat. Contre les arrêts du Parlement de Paris, des 29 mars & 4 février 1775. N.p., n.d. Another edition, Amsterdam, 1776.

Seroit-il trop tard? Aux trois ordres. N.p., 1789.

Socrate, tragédie en cinq actes. Amsterdam, 1764.

Suite des "Considérations sur l'ouverture de l'Escaut." London, 1785.

Supplément aux "Réflexions pour Me Linguet, avocat de la comtesse de Béthune." Paris, 1775.

Testament de Joseph II, empereur et roi des Romains. Traduit de l'allemand par M. Linguet. Brussels, 1790.

La Théorie des lois civiles. New edition. 3 vols. London, 1774. This work comprises vols. III-V of Linguet's *Oeuvres de M. Linguet.* 6 vols. London, 1774.

Théorie des loix civiles, ou Principes fondamentaux de la société. 2 vols. London [Paris], 1767.

Théorie du libelle; ou L'Art de calomnier avec fruit, dialogue philosophique pour servir de supplément à la "Théorie du paradoxe." Amsterdam, 1775.

Très-humbles, très-respectueuses représentations adressées à Sa Majesté, par Me Linguet, avocat, sur la défense à lui faite d'imprimer sa "Requête" en cassation, contre les arrêts des 4 février & 29 mars 1775. Brussels, 1776.

Véto d'un citoyen, ou Dénonciation à la nation du rapport fait à l'Assemblée nationale, au nom du Comité de l'imposition sur la contribution personnelle, le——Octobre 1790. Extrait des "Annales politiques, civiles, et littéraires du dix-huitième siècle." Par M. Linguet. Paris, n.d.

Linguet, Simon-Nicolas-Henri, ed. *Choix des lettres paternelles de Joseph Néron second du nom, empereur des Romains à Richard d'Alton son assassin en chef aux Pays-Bas, en 1788 & 1789. Avec quelques observations instructives. Par...un intéressé.* N.p., 1790.

——, trans. *Discours sur la prééminence et l'utilité de la chirurgie, prononcé par M.*

Works by Simon-Nicolas-Henri Linguet *(continued)*

Brambilla, Che. de St E. R., premier chirurgien de S.M., à l'ouverture de l'Académie impériale de chirurgie-médecine, fondée à Vienne en 1785 par S. M. Joseph II, et traduit du latin par M. Linguet. Brussels, 1786. Another printing, Brussels, 1787.

——, trans. *Le Sage dans sa retraite, Comédie en cinq actes et en prose melée d'ariettes, traduit de l'espagnol, par M. Linguet.* The Hague, 1782.

——, trans. *Théâtre espagnol.* 4 vols. Paris, 1770.

[Linguet, Simon-Nicolas-Henri, with Claude Joseph Dorat.] *Voyage au labyrinthe du jardin du Roi.* The Hague, 1755.

3. Writings by Linguet's contemporaries

ANONYMOUS WORKS

Analectes critiques pour servir de supplément aux "Annales" de M. Linguet. Vol. I. Brussels, 1777.

["M. de M^{xxx} (ci-devant prisonnier)"]. *Apologie de la Bastille. Pour servir de réponse aux "Mémoires," de M. Linguet, "sur la Bastille." Avec des notes politiques, philosophiques et littéraires, lesquelles n'auront avec le texte que le moindre rapport possible. Par un homme en pleine campagne.* Philadelphia, 1784.

[Lorinet.] *Apostrophe à M. Linguet, sur ses nos. 25 & 26 des "Annales" du 18me siècle.* Paris, 1779.

Le Bon-homme anglois. N.p., 1783.

Conversations entre Messieurs Raynal et Linguet, sur la nature et les avantages des divers governements. Tenue à l'occasion des Etats-Généraux de la France. Brussels, 1789.

Copie de la lettre écrite à M. Linguet, par Mr. de Moitelle, colonel-commandant [sic] du régiment de Ligne, au sujet du récit controuvé de la journée du 22 janvier, publié dans le N. CI de ses "Annales" [Brussels, March 4, 1788]. N.p., n.d.

Copie d'une lettre d'un habitant de Bruxelles, qui analyse celle de M. de Moitelle, colonel-commandant du régiment de Ligne écrite à Mr. Linguet [Brussels, March 11, 1788]. N.p., n.d.

Dictionnaire à l'usage de ceux qui lisent les "Annales" de M. Linguet. N.p., n.d.

Entretien de Me Linguet et de Me Bergasse. Brussels, 1788.

[Delaunay.] *Histoire d'un pou françois, ou l'Espion d'une nouvelle espèce, tant en France qu'en Angleterre, contenant les portraits de personnages intéressans dans ces deux royaumes, & c. & c.* Paris, 1781.

Histoire secrette des plus célèbres prisonniers de la Bastille, et particulièrement du Comte de Paradès, chargé par le gouvernement d'un expédition secrette sur Plimouth, & c. de Monsieur Linguet, & c. & c....... Paris, 1790.

L'Imposteur démasqué, ou Réponse au mémoire intitulé "Quelle est l'origine des Etats-Généraux?" Par M. Linguet. Paris, 1788.

Justification de l'Assemblée nationale, et Confession sincère & générale de l'avocat Linguet, auteur de l'"Ami du peuple," attribué au Sieur Marat. N.p., n.d.

["Mauclerc, de Chalon en Bourgogne".] *Le Language des murs, ou Les Cachots de la Bastille dévoilant leurs secrets.* N.p., 1789.

Lettre à M. Le Quesne, marchand d'étoffe de soye, Rue des Bourdonnois, à Paris. V...... [October, 28, 1780]. N.p., n.d.

[R. L. M. S.]. *Lettre à M. Linguet.* [Ghent, November 23, 1790]. N.p., n.d.

Lettre à M. Linguet sur son projet de banqueroute royale, inséré dans ses "Annales politiques," no. 1. N.p., n.d.

["M^{xxx}. Américain."] *Lettre à M. Linguet, ou Réponse au No. LIV de ses "Annales."*

[M. Q.] *Lettre d'un jeune clerc, adressée à M. Linguet, sur l'audience du 2 septembre 1786.* N.p., n.d.

[Joseph II (pseud.).] *Lettre de l'Empereur Joseph II. A M. Linguet, en réponse à celle du 22 décembre 1789* [Vienna, January 20, 1790]. N.p., n.d.

[Jousse.] *Lettre de M. Jousse à M. Linguet, sur les numéros 65 & 66 de ses "Annales."* N.p., n.d.

Lettre familière à M. Linguet, en réponse au no. 109, du tome 14 de ses "Annales" [July 12, 1788]. N.p., n.d.

Lettres de Mme. de B...et du Comte de L,...mélées d'éloges et de critiques des "Annales politiques" de M. Linguet. London, 1780.

Mémoires d'un prisonnier d'état sur l'administration intérieure du château royal de Vincennes, pour servir de suite aux "Mémoires sur la Bastille," publiés par M. Linguet. London, 1783.

[Dussaulx, Jean.] *Observations sur l'Histoire de la Bastille publiée par Moniseur [sic] Linguet, avec des remarques sur le caractère de l'auteur, suivies de quelques notes sur sa manière d'écrire l'histoire politique, civile, et littéraire.* London, 1783.

["Par l'auteur du Club Infernal," and signed PILPAY]. *Les Paradoxes, ou Cinquième dialogue des morts de la Révolution: entre Linguet et Charlotte Corday. Sur la démocratie, les beaux-arts et la paix.* Paris, Year III.

Preuves que l'on peut réformer pour 150 millions d'abus par an; ou Réponse aux réflexions de M. Linguet sur la dette nationale en France, inserées dans le no. 116 de ses "Annales." Paris, 1789.

Réflexions ultérieures sur la lettre de M. Moitelle, colonel du régiment de Ligne, & Consors. Articles sur lequelles Mr. de Linguet a passé, ou cru devoir passer silence. N.p., n.d.

Remarques historiques sur la Bastille. Nouvelle édition, augmentée d'un grand nombre d'anecdotes intéressantes et peu connues. London, 1783.

[Un Citoyen.] *Réponse à la "Lettre de M. Linguet à Monsieur le comte de Vergennes, ministre des affaires étrangères en France."* Milan, 1777.

Réponse du membre de la Société patriotique de Bruxelles à la lettre écrite à ce membre par M. Linguet le 19 mars 1790. [March 25, 1790.] N.p., n.d.

OTHER WORKS

Alembert, Jean Le Rond d'. *Oeuvres et correspondance inédites d'Alembert.* Ed. Charles Henry. Paris, 1887.

Arrest de la Cour du Parlement extrait des registres du Parlement. Du deux juillet mil sept cent soixante-treize. Paris, 1773.

Arrest de la Cour du Parlement, Qui supprime le "Discours préliminaire" étant en tête du livre intitulé "Théorie des lois civiles, ou Principes fondamentaux de la société," imprimé à Londres, en M DCC LXVII, sans nom d'auteur, & c. Du quatorze juillet mil sept cent soixante-sept (Paris, 1767).

Arrest de la cour du Parlement, qui supprime un libelle, ayant pour titre: "Réflexions pour Me Linguet, avocat de la Comtesse de Béthune, & ordonne que Me Linguet sera rayé du tableau. Extrait des registres du Parlement. Du onze février mil sept cent soixante quatorze. Paris, 1774.

Arrest du Parlement de Bretagne. Rendu sur les conclusion de Monsieur le procureur général du roi, qui ordonne que les deux imprimés, l'un intitulé "Mémoire pour M. le Duc d'Aiguillon" & l'autre "Mémoire à consulter pour M. le Duc d'Aiguillon," seront lacérés & brulés au pied du grand escalier du Palais par l'exécuteur de la haute justice. Du 14 août 1770. Rennes, 1770.

Arrêt du Parlement, rendu la Grand'Chambre assemblée: Qui décharge le Comte de Morangiès de toutes les plaintes & accusations contre lui intentées, avec dommages-intérêts & dépens...du 3 september 1773, Paris, 1773.

Bachaumont, Louis Petit de. *Mémoires secrets, pour servir à l'histoire de la république des lettres en France, depuis MDCCLXII jusqu'à nos jours; ou Journal d'un observateur.* 36 vols. London, 1780-89.

Writings by Linguet's contemporaries *(continued)*

Baret, J.–F. *Lettres à l'auteur des "Considérations sur l'ouverture de l'Escaut," par le Quaker de Lillo.* Bergen-op-Zoom, 1785.

Barnave, Antoine-Pierre-Joseph-Marie. *Introduction à la Révolution française.* Ed. Fernand Rude. Cahiers des *Annales*, no. 15. Paris, 1960.

Baston, Abbé Guillaume A.–R. *Réponse au "Mémoire" et à la "Consultation" de M. Linguet touchant l'indissolubilité du mariage.* Paris, 1772.

Baudeau, Abbé Nicolas. *Avis au peuple sur son premier besoin, ou Petits traités économiques.* 2 vols. Amsterdam, 1768.

——, *Avis aux honnêtes gens qui veulent bien faire. Sur le commerce du bled.* Amsterdam, 1769.

—— ed. *Nouvelles Ephémérides économiques, ou Bibliothèque raisonée de l'histoire de la morale et de la politique.* 19 nos. Dec., 1774–June, 1776.

——, Dupont de Nemours, Marquis de Mirabeau, et al., eds. *Ephémérides du citoyen, ou Chronique de l'esprit national.* 69 vols. Paris, 1765-72.

Berryer, Pierre-Nicolas. *Souvenirs de M. Berryer, doyen des avocats de Paris de 1774 à 1838.* 2 vols. Paris, 1839.

Bertrand de Molleville, Antoine-François. *Mémoires secrets pour servir à l'histoire de la dernière année du regne de Louis XVI.* 3 vols. London, 1798.

Beugnot, Jacques Claude. *Mémoires du Comte Beugnot, ancien ministre (1783-1815).* Ed. Albert Beugnot. 3d ed. Paris, 1889.

Bourdon des Planches, Louis Joseph. *Lettre à l'auteur des "Observations sur le commerce des grains"* [by Target]. Amsterdam, 1775.

Bremond, Jean Baptiste. *Premières Observations au peuple françois sur le quadruple aristocratie qui existe depuis deux siècles, sous le nom de haut clergé, de possédants fiefs, de magistrats, et du haut tiers; et vues générales sur la constitution et la félicité publique.* Versailles, 1789.

Briatte, Jean-Baptiste. *Offrande à l'humanité, ou Traité sur les causes de la misère en général, et de la mendicité en particulier; & sur les moyens de tarir la première & de détruire la seconde. Ouvrage imprimé au profit des pauvres par M. Briatte, Pasteur de l'église wallonne de Namur.* vol. I. Amsterdam, 1780.

Brissot de Warville, Jacques-Pierre. *J.–P. Brissot: Correspondance et papiers.* Ed. Claude Perroud. Mémoires et documents relatifs aux XVIIIe et XIXe siècles, vol. IV. Paris, 1912.

——. *J.–P. Brissot: Mémoires (1754-1793).* Ed. Claude Perroud. Vols. II and III of Mémoires et documents relatifs aux XVIIIe et XIXe siècles. Paris, 1911.

——. *Mémoires de Brissot, membre de l'Assemblée législative et de la Convention nationale, sur ses contemporains, et la Révolution française.* Ed. François Mongin de Montrol. 4 vols. Paris, 1830-32.

——. *Point de banqueroute, ou Lettre à un créancier d'état sur l'impossibilité de la banqueroute nationale et sur les moyens de ramener le crédit et la paix.* London, 1787.

——. *Recherches philosophiques sur le droit de propriété et sur le vol, considérés dans la nature et dans la société.* In *Bibliothèque philosophique du législateur, du politique, du jurisconsulte...*, vol. VI, 261-339.

——, ed. *Bibliothèque philosophique du législateur, du politique, du jurisconsulte; ou Choix des meilleurs discours, dissertations, essais, fragmens, composés sur la législation criminelle par les plus célèbres écrivains, en françois, anglois, italien, allemand, espagnol, & c. pour parvenir à la réforme des loix pénales dans tous les pays; traduits et accompagnés des notes & d'observations historiques.* 9 vols. Berlin, 1782.

Buc'hoz, Pierre-Joseph. *Lettres sur la méthode de s'enrichir promptement et de conserver sa santé, par la culture des végétaux exotiques.* 5 vols. Paris, 1768-70.

——. *Manuel alimentaire des plantes tant indigènes qu'exotiques, qui peuvent servir de nourriture et de boisson aux différents peuples de la terre.* Paris, 1771.

Charpentier. *La Bastille dévoilée, ou Recueil des pièces authentiques pour servir à son histoire.* 3 vols. Paris, 1789-90.

[Clavière, Etienne.] *De la foi publique envers les créanciers de l'état. Lettres à M. Linguet, sur le no. 116 de ses "Annales," par M.ˣˣˣ. Ouvrage dans lequel, après avoir indiqué l'état le plus modique du revenu général de la France, on prouve que la banqueroute n'est ni nécessaire, ni utile, ni politique, et que la confiance doit ranimer l'esprit public.* London, 1788.

Condorcet, Jean Antoine Nicolas de Caritat, Marquis de. *Du commerce des bleds, pour servir à la réfutation de l'ouvrage "Sur la législation et le commerce des grains"* [by Jacques Necker]. Paris, 1775.

——. *Correspondance inédite de Condorcet et de Turgot, 1770-1779.* Ed. Charles Henry. Paris, 1883.

——. *Condorcet: Oeuvres.* Ed. M. R. Argo and A. C. O. Conner. 12 vols. Paris, 1847-49.

——. *Lettres sur le commerce des grains.* Paris, 1774.

Courrier du Bas-Rhin, ou Gazette de Clèves. Clèves, 1778-92.

D——z [Desaubiez, Vatar]. *Le Bonheur public, ou Moyen d'acquitter la dette nationale de l'Angleterre; de trouver une ressource constante pour les besoins du gouvernement, sans taxes, ni impositions; de rendre les hommes heureux autant qu'ils peuvent l'être par les richesses. Présenté aux Chambres du Parlement.* 3 parts in one vol. London, 1780-82.

——. *Extrait d'un ouvrage intitulé "Le Bonheur public," & c. Imprimé à Londres en 1780, contenant, 1° la liquidation de la dette nationale, et faisant le bonheur de la société; 2° un plan d'administration sur les grains, afin d'éviter à jamais la disette; présenté à l'Assemblée nationale en 1789.* N.p., 1789.

Desmoulins, Camille. *Correspondance inédite de Camille Desmoulins, député à la Convention nationale.* Ed. M. Matton. Paris, 1836.

——. *Révolutions de France et de Brabant.* 86 nos. Paris, Nov. 1789–July, 1791.

Dévérité, Louis-Alexandre. *Recueil intéressant sur l'affaire de la mutilation de crucifix d'Abbeville, arrivée le 9 août 1765, et sur la mort du chevalier de La Barre, pour servir de supplément aux causes célèbres.* London, 1776.

Diderot, Denis, ed. *Encyclopédie, ou Dictionnaire raisonné des sciences, des arts, et des métiers.* 35 vols. Paris, 1751-80.

Dotrenge, Barthélemy-Joseph. *Correspondance de Barthélemy-Joseph Dotrenge, Agent diplomatique du Prince-évêque de Liège, auprès de la cour de Bruxelles (1781-1794).* Ed. Eugène Ernest Hubert. Brussels, 1926.

Duclos, Charles. *Correspondance de Charles Duclos (1704-1772).* Ed. Jacques Brengues. Saint-Brieuc, 1970.

Dufourny de Villiers, Louis Pierre. *Cahiers du quatrième ordre, celui des pauvres journaliers, des infirmes, des indigents, & c., l'ordre sacré des infortunés; ou Correspondance philantropqiue entre les infortunés, les homme sensibles, et les Etats-généraux: pour suppléer au droit de députer directement aux Etats, qui appartient à tous François, mais dont cet ordre ne jouit pas encore.* No. 1. Paris, April 25, 1789.

Dupont de Nemours, Pierre Samuel. *De l'origine et des progrès d'une science nouvelle* [1768]. Ed. A. Dubois. Paris, 1910.

[Eprémesnil, Jean-Jacques Duval d'.] *Dénonciation des feuilles du Sʳ Linguet, faite en Parlement, les chambres assemblées, les mardi 11, vendredi 14, et mardi 18 juillet 1780.* N.p. [1781].

Evans, Thomas. *A Refutation of the "Memoires of the Bastille," on the General Principles of Law, Probability and Truth; in a Series of Letters to Mr. Linguet, Late Advocate in the Parliament of Paris.* London, 1783. Translated into French as: *Réfutation*

Writings by Linguet's contemporaries *(continued)*

    des *"Mémoires de la Bastille," sur les principes généraux des loix de la probabilité et de la vérité, dans une suite de lettres à Monsieur Linguet.* London, 1783.

Falconnet, Ambroise. *Preuves démonstratives en fait de justice dans l'affaire des héritiers de la Dame Veron, contre le Comte de Morangiès, avec les pièces justificatives, au nom du Sieur Liegard Dujonquay, petit-fils de la Dame Veron, docteur ès loix. Pour servir de réponse au "Nouvelles probabilités," de M. de Voltaire.* N.p., 1773.

——. *Réponse aux "Observations" du Comte de Morangiès, avec la défense des "Preuves démonstratives."* N.p., 1773.

Feraud, Jean François. *Dictionnaire critique de la langue française.* 3 vols. Marseille, 1787-1788.

Fréron, Elie. *L'Année littéraire.* 292 vols. Paris and Amsterdam, 1754-90.

Galiani, Ferdinando. *L'Abbé Galiani: Correspondance avec Madame d'Epinay, Madame Necker, Madame Geoffrin, etc. Diderot, Grimm, d'Alembert, de Sartine, d'Holbach, etc.* New edition. Ed. Lucien Perey and Gaston Maugras. 2 vols. Paris, 1889-90.

——. *Dialogues sur le commerce des bleds* [1770]. Ed. Fausto Nicolini. Milan, 1959.

——. *Lettres de l'Abbé Galiani à Madame d'Epinay, Voltaire, Diderot, Grimm, le Baron d'Holbach, Morellet, Suard, d'Alembert, Marmontel, la Vicomtesse de Belsunce, etc.* Ed. Eugène Asse. 2 vols. Lettres du XVIIe et XVIIIe siècle, vols. VI-VII. Paris, 1903.

Gazette du commerce, de l'agriculture, et des finances. 21 vols. Paris, April, 1763-Dec., 1783.

Grimm, Jakob-Friedrich-Melchior, and Denis Diderot, Guillaume-Thomas-François Raynal, Heinrich Meister. *Correspondance littéraire, philosophique, et critique.* Ed. Maurice Tourneux. 16 vols. Paris, 1877-82.

Grotius, Hugo. *Le Droit de la guerre et de la paix.* Ed. Jean Barbeyrac. 2 vols. Basel, 1768.

Hérault de Séchelles, Marie-Jean. *Hérault de Séchelles: Oeuvres littéraires.* Ed. Emile Dard. Paris, 1907.

——. *Voyage à Montbar.* Ed. F.-A. Aulard. Paris, 1890.

La Harpe, Jean-François de. *Correspondance inédite de Jean-François de la Harpe.* Ed. Alexandre Jovicevich. Paris, 1965.

——. *Correspondance littéraire, adressée à son Altesse impériale, Mgr le grand-duc, aujourd'hui Empereur de Russie, et à M. le Comte André Schowalow, chambellan de l'impératrice Catherine II, depuis 1774 jusqu'à 1789.* 6 vols. Paris, 1804-7.

——. *Oeuvres de La Harpe,* Ed. Saint Surin. 16 vols. Paris, 1821.

——, trans. *Les Douze Césars, traduits du latin de Suétone, avec des notes et des réflexions, dans lequelles on trouve une réfutation des paradoxes de M. Linguet sur Titus et Néron.* 2 vols. Paris, 1770.

Lanjuinais, Joseph de. *Supplément à l'"Espion anglois," ou Lettres intéressantes sur la retraite de M. Necker; sur le sort de la France et de l'Angleterre; et sur la détention de M. Linguet à la Bastille. Adressées à Mylord All' Eye. Par l'auteur de "l'Espion anglois."* London, 1781.

Le Mercier de la Rivière, Pierre-Paul-François-Joachim-Henri. *L'Ordre naturel et essentiel des sociétés politiques* [1767]. Ed. Edgard Depitre. Collection des économistes et des réformateurs sociaux de la France, no. 3. Paris, 1910.

Lequesne, Pierre. *Mémoire judiciaire pour le Sieur Pierre Lequesne, marchand d'étoffes de soie, Rue des Bourdonnois, à Paris, contre le Sieur Simon Nicolas Henri Linguet, ci-devant avocat à Paris, demeurant actuellement à Bruxelles, sur les demandes en suppression de quatre libelles diffamatoires et calomnieux, en réparation d'honeur, et en 100,000 livres de dommages-intérêts, par forme de réparations civiles, formées*

par le Sieur Lequesne contre le Sieur Linguet, les 6 décembre 1783 et 20 juillet 1784.
N.p., n.d.

Linguet, Jean. *Catalogue des livres du cabinet de M.L.D.G.* [Monsieur Linguet, docteur gradué]. Paris, 1733.

Mably, Gabriel Bonnot, Abbé de. *Doutes proposées aux philosophes économistes sur l'ordre naturel et essentiel des sociétés politiques.* The Hague, 1768.

Mairobert, Matthieu-François Pidanzat de. *Les Efforts du patriotisme; ou Recueil complet des écrits publiés pendant le regne du Chancelier Maupeou...Ourvrage qui peut servir à l'histoire du siècle de Louis XV, pendant les années 1770, 1771, 1772, 1773 et 1774.* Paris, 1775.

——. *L'Espion anglois, ou Correspondance secrète entre Milord All'Eye et Milord All'Ear.* 10 vols. London, 1784.

——. *Journal historique de la révolution opérée dans la constitution de la monarchie françoise par M. de Maupeou, Chancelier de France.* 7 vols. London, 1774-76.

——. *Maupeouiana, ou Correspondance secrète et familière du Chancelier Maupeou avec son cœur Sorhouet.* 2 vols. N.p., 1775.

Mallet Du Pan, Jacques. *Doutes sur l'éloquence et les systèmes politiques, adressés à M. le baron de B*xxxx*; chambellan de S.A.R. le prince H. de P. Par M.M., citoyen de Genève.* London [Neuchâtel], 1775.

——. *Mémoires et correspondance de Mallet Du Pan pour servir à l'histoire de la Révolution française.* Ed. A. Sayous. 2 vols. Paris, 1851.

Mandeville, Bernard. *The Fable of the Bees: or, Private Vices, Publick Benefits.* Ed. F. B. Kaye. 2 vols. Oxford, 1924.

Manuel, Louis-Pierre. *La Police de Paris dévoilée.* 2 vols. Paris, Year II [1791?].

Marmontel, Jean-François. *Marmontel, Mémoires.* Ed. John Renwick. 2 vols. Clermont-Ferrand, 1972.

Mauclerc [signed MAUCLERC de Chalon]. *Le Langage des murs, ou Les Cachots de la Bastille dévoilant leur secrets.* [Paris?] 1789.

Mercier, Louis-Sébastien. *Tableau de Paris.* New ed. 12 vols. Amsterdam, 1782-88.

——. *De Jean-Jacques Rousseau considéré comme un des principaux auteurs de la Révolution.* 2 vols. Paris, 1791.

Meslier, Jean. *Oeuvres complètes de Jean Meslier.* Ed. Jean Deprun, Roland Desné, and Albert Soboul. 3 vols. Paris, 1970-72.

Métra, François; J. Imbert; de Boudeaux, et al., eds. *Correspondance secrète, politique, et littéraire, ou Mémoires pour servir à l'histoire des cours, des sociétés, et de la littérature en France depuis la mort de Louis XV.* 18 vols. London, 1787-90.

Mirabeau, Honoré-Gabriel-Riquetti, Comte de. *Doutes sur la liberté de l'Escaut. Réclamée par l'empereur; sur les causes & sur les conséquences probables de cette réclamation. Par le Comte de Mirabeau. Avec une carte du cours de l'Escaut, depuis Anvers jusqu'à la mer.* London, n.d.

——. *Lettres historiques, politiques et critiques de M. le Comte de Mirabeau, contenant les "Doute sur la liberté de l'Escaut réclamée; sur les causes & sur les conséquences probables," tant de cette réclamation que des principes que l'empereur & l'impératrice de Russie semblent adopter.* New ed. London, n.d.

——. *Lettres originales de Mirabeau, écrites du donjon de Vincennes, pendant les années 1777, 78, 79, et 80; contenant tous les détails sur sa vie privée, ses malheurs, et ses amours avec Sophie Ruffei, marquise de Monnier.* Ed. Louis-Pierre Manuel. 4 vols. Paris, 1792.

Miromesnil, Armand-Thomas Hue de. *Correspondance politique et administrative de Miromesnil, premier président du Parlement de Normandie.* Ed. P. LeVerdier. 5 vols. Rouen, 1899-1903.

Writings by Linguet's contemporaries *(continued)*

Moitelle, Colonel de. *Copie de la seconde lettre écrite à M. Linguet, au sujet du récit inséré dans le no. 101 des "Annales."* N.p. [1788].

——. *Copie exacte de la lettre de M. de M[oitelle], Colonel commandant le régiment de ligne, et signée au nom du corps d'officiers.* N.p., 1788.

Moniteur universel, Réimpression de l'ancien "Moniteur," seule histoire authentique et inaltérée de la Révolution française, depuis la réunion des Etats-généraux jusqu'au Consulat (mai 1789-novembre 1799), avec des notes explicatives...32 vols. Paris, 1847-50.

Montesquieu, Charles Louis de Secondat, Baron de Brède et de. *The Spirit of the Laws.* Ed. Franz Neumann. New York, 1949.

Morellet, Abbé André. *Analyse de l'ouvrage intitulé "De la législation et du commerce des grains"* [by Necker]. Amsterdam, 1775.

——. *Lettres de l'Abbé Morellet à Lord Shelburne, depuis Marquis de Lansdowne, 1772-1803.* Ed. Edmond Fitzmaurice. Paris, 1898.

——. *Mémoires (inédits) de l'Abbé Morellet, suivis de sa correspondance avec M. le Comte R^{xxx}, Ministre des finances à Naples.* Ed. Saint-Albin Berville and Jean-François Barrière. 2 vols. Collection des mémores relatifs à la Révolution française, vols. VI-VII. Paris, 1823.

——. *Réponse sérieuse A.M. L^{xx}, par l'auteur de la "Théorie du paradoxe."* Amsterdam, 1775.

——. *Théorie du paradoxe.* Amsterdam, 1775.

Morelly. *Code de la nature.* Ed. Gilbert Chinard. Paris, 1950.

Necker, Jacques. *Sur la législation et le commerce des grains.* Paris, 1775.

Palissot de Montenoy, Charles. *Oeuvres complètes de M. Palissot.* New ed. 6 vols. Paris, 1809.

Parmentier, Antoine-Augustin. *Recherches sur les végétaux nourrissans, qui dans les temps de disette, peuvent remplacer les alimens ordinaires. Avec de nouvelles observations sur la culture des pommes de terres.* Paris, 1781.

Poncet-Delpech. *Mémoire à consulter et consultation sur un mariage contracté en France suivant les usages des Protestants, Pour Dame Marthe Camp, Vicomtesse de Bombelles.* N.p., 1772.

Prunget des Boissières. *Réponse de M. Prunget des Boissières, avocat au Parlement, à M.^{xxx}, Au sujet du No. 38 des "Annales" de M. Linguet, sur l'affaire du soi-disant Comte de Solar, sourd & muet; suivie d'un mémoire à consulter et consultation.* Paris, 1780.

Quesnay, François. *François Quesnay et la physiocratie.* Ed. Institut national d'études démographiques. 2 vols. Paris, 1958.

——. *Oeuvres économiques et philosophiques de F. Quesnay, fondateur du système physiocratique.* Ed. Auguste Oncken. Frankfort, 1888.

Restif de la Bretonne, Nicolas Edme. *Mes Inscripcions. Journal intime de Restif de la Bretonne (1780-1789).* Ed. Paul Cottin. Paris, 1889.

Robineau, *dit* de Beaunoir, Alexandre-Louis-Bertrand [pseud. Jacques Le Sueur]. *Les Masques arrachés, histoire secrète des révolutions et contre-révolutions du Brabant et de Liège, contenant les vies privées de Van der Noot, Van Eupen, le Cardinal de Malines...*New ed. Anvers, 1791.

Roland de la Platière, Marie-Jeanne Phlipon. *Lettres de Madame Roland, nouvelle série, 1767-1780.* Ed. Claude Perroud. 2 vols. Collection de documents inédits sur l'histoire de France, publiée par les soins du ministre de l'instruction publique. Paris, 1913-15.

——. *Mémoires de Madame Roland*. Ed. Saint-Albin Berville and Jean-François Barrière. 2d ed. 2 vols. Collection des mémoires relatifs à la Révolution française, vols. 29-30. Paris, 1821.

——. *Mémoires de Madame Roland*. Ed. C. A. Dauban. Paris, 1864.

Roubaud, Abbé Pierre-Joseph-André. *Représentations aux magistrats, contenant l'exposition raisonnée des faits relatifs à la liberté du commerce des grains, et les résultats respectifs de règlemens & de la liberté*. N.p., 1769.

——. *Gazette d'agriculture, commerce, arts, et finances*. Paris, 1769-83.

——, Pierre Samuel Dupont de Nemours, Abbé Nicolas Baudeau, etc. *Journal de l'agriculture, du commerce et des finances*. 48 vols. Paris, 1765-74.

Roubaud, Abbé Pierre-Joseph-André, and Louis-Florent Le Camus, eds. *Journal de commerce*. 24 vols. Brussels, 1759-62.

Rousseau, Jean-Jacques. *Correspondance générale de Jean-Jacques Rousseau*. Ed. Théophile Dufour. 2 vols. Paris, 1924-34.

——. *Discours sur les sciences et les arts*. Ed. George Havens. London, 1946.

——. *Jean-Jacques Rousseau: The First and Second Discourses*. Ed. Roger D. Masters. New York, 1964.

——. *Jean-Jacques Rousseau, Oeuvres complètes*. Ed. Bernard Gagnebin and Marcel Raymond. 4 vols. Paris, 1959-69.

——. *Julie, ou la Nouvelle Héloïse*. Ed. René Pomeau. Paris, 1960.

——. *The Political Writings of Jean-Jacques Rousseau*. Ed. C. E. Vaughan. 2 vols. New York, 1962.

Suard, Jean Baptiste Antoine. *Correspondance littéraire de Suard avec le Margrave de Bayreuth*. Ed. Gabriel Bonno. University of California Publications in Modern Philology. Vol. 18, no. 2. Berkeley, Calif. 1934.

——. *Mélanges de littérature*. 2d ed. 3 vols. Paris, 1806.

——. *Mémoires et correspondances historiques et littéraires inédits—1726 à 1816*. Ed. Charles Nisard. Paris, 1858.

Tissot, Dr. Samuel August André David. *A Letter of Monsieur Hirzel from Dr. Tissot, in Answer to Mons. Linguet's Treatise on Bread-Corn and Bread*. Letters and Papers on Agriculture, Planting, & c. Selected from the Correspondence-Book of the Society Instituted at Bath, for the Encouragement of Agriculture, Arts, Manufactures, and Commerce, within the Counties of Somerset, Wilts, Gloucester, and Dorset, and the City and County of Bristol. N.p., 1780.

Toustain-Richebourg, Charles-Gaspard de. *Mes Rêves: 1° sur M. Linguet et d'autres écrivains; 2° sur la Bretagne et d'autres provinces; 3° sur la littérature et les arts; 4° sur la gloire; 5° sur l'étude de la haute antiquité; 6° sur quelques points militaires, politiques et moraux; 7° sur quelques romans et contes allégoriques ou philosophiques*. Amsterdam, 1772.

Turgot, Anne Robert Jacques. *Oeuvres de Turgot*. Ed. Eugène Daire. 2 vols. Collection des principaux économistes, vols. III-IV. Paris, 1844.

——. *Oeuvres de Turgot et documents le concernant*. Ed. Gustave Schelle. 5 vols. Paris, 1913-23.

Vauban, Sébastien Le Prestre de: *Projet d'une dixme royale, suivis de deux écrits financiers par Vauban*. Ed. E. Coornaert. Collection des principaux économistes. New ed. Paris, 1933.

[Vermandois, Auguste de.] *Jugement d'un citoyen sur "L'Apel [sic] à la postérité" de Simon-Nicolas-Henri Linguet, publié en janvier 1780, avec cette épigraphe, Erudimini, qui judicatis...ou L'Apel à la postérité au néant*. Noyon, 1780.

Voltaire, François-Marie Arouet de. *Oeuvres complètes de Voltaire*. Ed. Louis Moland.

Writings by Linguet's contemporaries *(continued)*

52 vols. Paris, 1877-85.

———. *Voltaire, Lettres inédites à son imprimeur Gabriel Cramer.* Ed. Bernard Gagnebin. Geneva, 1952.

———. *Voltaire, Notebooks.* Ed. Theodore Bestermann. 2 vols. Publications de l'Institut et Musée, Voltaire. Series Voltaire, vols. I-II. Geneva, 1952.

———. *Voltaire: Oeuvres historiques.* Ed. René Pomeau. Paris, 1957.

———. *Voltaire: Philosophical Dictionary.* Trans. and ed. Peter Gay. 2 vols. New York, 1962.

———. *Voltaire's Correspondance.* Ed. Theodore Besterman. 107 vols. Geneva, 1953-65.

4. Published collections of eighteenth-century documents

Comité patriotique de Bruxelles, ed. *Recueil de lettres originales de l'Empereur Joseph II au Général d'Alton, commandant des troupes aux Pays-bas, depuis décembre 1787 jusqu'en novembre 1789.* Brussels, 1790.

Copies des lettres du Général d'Alton à l'Empereur Joseph II, relativement aux affaires des Pays-bas, en 1788 & 1789. Brussels, n.d.

Daire, Eugène, ed. *Economistes financiers du XVIIIe siècle: Vauban, Boisguillebert, Jean Law, Melon, Dutot.* Collection des principaux économistes, vol. I. 2d ed. Paris, 1851.

———, ed. *Les Physiocrates. Quesnay, Dupont de Nemours, Le Mercier de la Rivière, l'Abbé Baudeau, LeTrosne.* 2 vols. Collection des principaux économistes, vol. II. Paris, 1846.

Daire, Eugène, and G. de Molinari, eds. *Mélanges d'économie politique.* 2 vols. Collection des principaux économistes, vols. XIV-XV. Paris, 1847-1848.

Flammermont, Jules, ed. *Les Correspondances des agents diplomatiques étrangers en France avant la Révolution.* Paris, 1896.

———, ed. *Remontrances du Parlement de Paris au XVIIIe siècle.* 3 vols. Collection de documents inédits sur l'histoire de France, vol. XXXIII. Paris, 1888-98.

Flammermont, Jules, and Alfred d'Arneth, eds. *Correspondance secrète du Comte de Mercy-Argenteau avec l'Empereur Joseph II et le Prince de Kaunitz.* 2 vols. Collection de documents inédits sur l'histoire de France, vol. II. Paris, 1889-91.

Hubert, Eugène E., ed. *Correspondance de Barthélemy-Joseph Dotrenge, agent diplomatique du Prince-évêque de Liège auprès de la cour de Bruxelles (1781-1794).* Brussels, 1926.

———, ed. *Correspondance des ministres de France accrédités à Bruxelles de 1780 à 1790. Dépêches inédites.* 2 vols. Brussels, 1920-24.

Schlitter, Hanns, ed. *Geheime Correspondenz Josefs II mit seinem minister in den österreichischen Niederlanden Ferdinand Grafen Trauttmansdorff, 1787-1789.* Vienna, 1902.

5. Secondary sources

STUDIES ON LINGUET

Applewhite, Harriet Branson, and Darline Gay Levy. "The Concept of Modernization and the French Enlightenment." *Studies on Voltaire and the Eighteenth Century,* LXXXIV (1971), 53-98.

Au public: Sentiment sur Linguet. N.p., n.d.

Barrière, Jean-François. "Notice sur la vie de Linguet." *Mémoires de Linguet sur la Bastille et de Dusaulx sur le 14 juillet.* Ed. Saint-Albin Berville and Jean-François Barrière. Collection des mémoires relatifs à la Révolution française. 2d ed., vol. 14. Paris, 1822.

Becot, J. "Gerbier et Linguet." Discours, séance publique de l'Académie d'Amiens, 16 août 1863. Published in *Mémoires de l'Académie d'Amiens,* IV (1865), 27-52.

Bonhomme, Honoré. "Etudes d'histoire et de mœurs au XVIIIe siècle: Linguet." *Revue Britannique,* IV (1881), 431-59.

Boss, Ronald. "Linguet: The Reformer as Anti-philosophe." *Studies on Voltaire and the Eighteenth Century,* CLI (1976), 333-51.

Brengues, Jacques. "Duclos dupé par Linguet, ou Quatre lettres inédites de Simon-Nicolas Henri Linguet à Charles Duclos." *Revue des sciences humaines,* XXXV, no. 137 (January-March, 1970), 61-74.

Burmeister, Brigitte. "Les paradoxes de Linguet." *Dix-huitième siècle,* no. 7 (1975), 147-155.

Cardenal, L. de. "Les idées de Linguet sur le crédit public." *La Révolution française,* LXXXVII (1934), 195-209.

Carré, Henri. *Le Barreau de Paris et la radiation de Linguet.* Poitiers, 1892.

Claretie, Jules, Review of Cruppi's *Un Avocat journaliste au XVIIIe siècle, Linguet* (Paris, 1895). *Revue de Champagne,* VII (1895), 933-41.

Cocatre-Zilgien, André. *Un Génie méconnu du XVIIIe siècle: L'Avocat Linguet (1736-1794). Incendiaire, réactionnaire et visionnaire.* Paris, 1960.

Conan, J. "Linguet, précurseur de l'échelle mobile des salaires?" *Annales historiques de la Révolution française,* XXIII (1951), 86-87.

Conti Odorisio, A. M. "La Formazione del pensiero politico di S.N.H. Linguet." *Il Pensiero politico, Revista di Storia delle idee politiche e sociale,* anno V, no. 1 (1972), 62-101.

Conti Odorisio, Ginevra. *S.N.H. Linguet, Dall'Ancien régime alla Rivoluzione.* Instituto di Studi Storici della Facolta di scienze politiche, dell'Università di Roma, 21. [Milan,] 1976.

C...d'Aval [Cousin d'Avallon, C.-Y.]. *Linguetiana, ou Recueil des principes, maximes, pensées diverses, paradoxes, et aventures de Linguet, suivi de l'éloge du [sic] l'art d'un coëffeur de femmes, par le même auteur.* Paris, 1801.

Cruppi, Jean. *Un Avocat journaliste au XVIIIe siècle, Linguet.* Paris, 1895.

———. "Linguet et le procès du chevalier de La Barre." *Revue des deux mondes,* CXXVIII (1895), 123-57.

David, N. "Notice sur Linguet." In N. David, ed., *Mémoires sur la Bastille.* Collection des meilleurs auteurs anciens et modernes. Paris, 1872.

Defresne, Arsène. "L'Avocat Linguet à Marnes-la-Coquette (de 1791 à 1793)." Commission d'histoire économique et sociale de la Révolution française. Comité départementale de Seine-et-Oise. Recherche et publication des documents relatifs à la vie économique de la Révolution. *Bulletin,* (1909-10), 52-78.

———. "Les Biens de Linguet à Marnes." Commission d'histoire économique et sociale de la Révolution française. Comité départementale de Seine-et-Oise. Recherche et publication des documents relatifs à la vie économique de la Révolution. *Bulletin* (1910-11), 64-98.

Denis, Auguste. "Linguet, avocat, inventeur d'un télégraphe éléctrique." *Almanach Matot.* Braine, 1877.

Dérodé-Géruzez, P. A. "Linguet, notes échappés aux biographes." *Chroniques de Champagne,* IV (1838), 39-43.

Secondary sources *(continued)*

———. "Notice sur Linguet." *Annales de l'Académie de Reims,* I (1843), 401-18.

Devérité, Louis-Alexandre. *Notice pour servir à l'histoire de la vie et des écrits de S.N.H. Linguet.* Liège, 1781. New ed., Liège, 1782.

———. *Qu'est-ce donc que tout ce train-là? Pour servir de suite à "Qu'est-ce que Linguet?"* Paris, 1791.

———. *Qu'est-ce que Linguet?* N.p., [1790].

Doré, Francis. "Simon-Nicolas-Henri Linguet (1736-1794)." Thesis presented for the Diplôme d'Etudes Supérieures de Droit Romain et d'Histoire du Droit, Faculté de Droit et des Sciences économiques de Paris, 1961.

Druart, Henri. *Les Aventures de Linguet, avocat et pamphlétaire rémois (1736-1794).* Paper presented before the Société des Amis du Vieux Reims [March 6, 1934]. Reims, 1934.

Dupin. "Notice sur la vie et les principaux ouvrages de Linguet." *Annales du barreau français, ou Choix des plaidoyers et mémoires les plus remarquables, tant en matière civile qu'en matière criminelle,* VI (1823).

Essai sur la vie et les gestes d'Ariste. N.p., 1789.

G......, F. M. [Gardaz, François-Marie]. *Essai sur la vie et sur les ouvrages de Linguet, où ses démêlés avec l'ordre des avocats sont éclaircis, et où l'on trouve des notes et des réflexions dont la plupart sont relatives à cet ordre et à l'éloquence du barreau.* Paris, 1809.

Greaves, H. R. G. "The Political Ideas of Linguet." *Economica,* X (1930), 40-55.

Hatin, Louis Eugène. *Histoire politique et littéraire de la presse en France.* 8 vols. Paris, 1859-61. III, 324-400.

Janne, Raymond. *Linguet, Avocat du diable. Discours prononcé à l'occasion de la séance solennelle de rentrée de la Conférence libre du jeune barreau de Liège, le 10 décembre 1938.* Brussels, 1939.

Levy, Darline Gay. "Simon Linguet's Sociological System: An Exhortation to Patience and Invitation to Revolution." *Studies on Voltaire and the Eighteenth Century,* LXX (1970), 219-93.

Lichtenberger, André. "Linguet, Socialiste." *La Révolution française,* XXV (1893), 97-125.

———. *Le Socialisme utopique: Etudes sur quelques précurseurs inconnus du socialisme.* Paris, 1898.

Martin, Henri. "Etude sur Linguet." *Travaux de l'Académie nationale de Reims,* XXX (1858-59), 341-425; XXXI (1859-60), 81-149.

Martin, Kingsley. *French Liberal Thought in the Eighteenth Century.* 3d ed. New York, 1963.

Marx, Karl. *Theories of Surplus Value.* Trans. Emile Barns. Ed. S. Ryazanskaya. 3 vols. Moscow, 1969.

Meurisse, Marc. "Quelques Vues de Linguet, d'après les *Annales* (1777-1784)." *Revue du Nord,* LIV (1972), 5-13.

Meyer, E. "L'Amerique d'aujourd'hui prédite en 1777." *Grande revue,* CXXX (1929), 604-9.

Minerbi, Marco. "Furtado et Linguet en 1790." *Archives juives, Cahiers de la Commission française des archives juives,* X (1973-74), 67-69.

Monin, Hippolyte. "Préface." *Mémoires sur la Bastille: Linguet, Dusaulx.* Paris, 1889.

Monselet, Charles. *Les Oubliés et les dédaignés.* Paris, 1885.

Phillip, Adolf. *Linguet, ein nationalökonom des XVIII Jahrhunderts, in seinen rechtlichen, socialen und volkswirtschaftlichen Anschauungen. Ein Beitrag zur Geschichte der Nationalökonomie.* Zurich, 1896.

Piot, Charles. "Linguet aux Pays-bas autrichiens." *Bulletin de l'Académie royale de Belgique*. 2d ser. XLVI (1878), 787-826.

Pitou, Spire. "Voltaire, Linguet, and China." *Studies on Voltaire and the Eighteenth Century*, XCVIII (1972), 61-68.

Puttemans, André. *La Censure dans les Pays-Bas autrichiens*. Académie royale de Belgique, classe des lettres et des sciences morales et politiques. Mémoires, 2ᵉ sér. XXXVII. Brussels, 1935.

Soignies, Jules de. "Une Note sur Linguet." In Paul Saintenoy, "Notes sur l'architecture médiévale française à propos d'une excursion à Reims et à Laon," appearing originally in *Annales de la Société d'archéologie de Bruxelles*, XV (1901), and published separately, Brussels, 1902.

Thamer, Hans-Ulrich. *Revolution and Reaktion in der Französischen Sozialkritic des 18 Jahrhunderts. Linguet, Mably, Babeuf*. Frankfurt am Main, 1973.

C. V. [Vellay, Charles]. "Marie Antoinette et Linguet." *Revue historique de la Révolution française*, II (1911), 444-45.

Vyverberg, Henry. *Historical Pessimism in the French Enlightenment*. Cambridge, Mass., 1958.

——. "Limits of Nonconformity in the Enlightenment. The Case of Simon-Nicolas-Henri Linguet." *French Historical Studies*, VI (1970), 474-91.

Whitham, J., and S. F. Mills Whitham. "Introduction." *Mémoirs of the Bastille by Latude and Linguet*. London, 1927.

OTHER WORKS

Acomb, Frances Dorothy. *Anglophobia in France (1763-1789). An Essay in the History of Constitutionalism and Nationalism*. Durham, N.C., 1950.

——. *Mallet Du Pan (1749-1800): A Career in Political Journalism*. Durham, N.C., 1973.

Afanassiev, Georges. *Le Commerce des céréales en France au dix-huitième siècle*. Paris, 1894.

Airiau, Jean. *L'Opposition aux physiocrates à la fin de l'ancien régime*. Bibliothèque constitutionelle et de science politique, vol. 19. Paris, 1965.

Alekseev, M. P., and T. K. Kopreeva. *Bibliothèque de Voltaire; catalogue des livres*. Moscow, 1961.

Althusser, Louis. *Montesquieu: La Politique et l'histoire*. Paris, 1959.

Anchel, Robert. *Crimes et châtiments au XVIIIᵉ siècle*. Paris, 1933.

Applewhite, Harriet B. "Political Culture in the French Revolution (1788-1791)." Ph.D. dissertation, Stanford University, 1972.

——, and Darline G. Levy. "The Concept of Modernization and the French Enlightenment." *Studies on Voltaire and the Eighteenth Century*, LXXXIV (1971), 53-98.

Arendt, Hannah. *On Revolution*. New York, 1965.

Ariès, Philippe. "Attitudes devant la vie et devant la mort du XVIIᵉ au XIXᵉ siècle. Quelques aspects de leurs variations." *Population*, IV (1949), 463-470.

——. *L'Enfant et la vie familiale sous l'ancien régime*. Paris, 1960.

——. *Histoire des populations françaises et de leurs attitudes devant la vie depuis le XVIIIᵉ siècle*. Paris, 1948.

Aron, Jean-Paul. "Biologie et alimentation au XVIIIᵉ siècle et au début du XIXᵉ siècle." *Annales: Economies, Société, Civilisation*, XVI (1961), 971-77.

Azam, Aimé. "Le Ministère des affaires étrangères et la presse à la fin de l'ancien régime." *Cahiers de la presse*, no. 3 (1938), 428-38.

Baehrel, René. "Economie et terreur, histoire et sociologie." *Annales historiques de la Révolution française*, XXIII (1951), 113-46.

——. "Haine de classes en temps d'épidémie." *Annales: Economie, Société, Civilisation*, VII (1952), 351-61.

Secondary sources *(continued)*

Balcou, Jean. *Fréron contre les philosophes.* Histoire des idées et critique littéraire, no. 151. Geneva, 1975.

Barber, William Henry, J. H. Brumfitt, R. A. Leigh, R. Shackleton, and S. S. B. Taylor, eds. *The Age of the Enlightenment. Studies Presented to Theodore Besterman.* University of St. Andrews Publications, no. 57. Edinburgh and London, 1967.

Béclard, Léon. *Sébastien Mercier. Sa Vie, son œuvre, son temps, d'après des documents inédits.* Paris, 1903.

Beik, Paul H. *The French Revolution Seen from the Right; Social Theories in Motion: 1789-1799.* Transactions of the American Philosophic Society, new ser., vol. 46, pt. 1, pp. 1-122, Philadelphia, 1956.

Belaval, Yvon. "La Crise de la géométrization de l'univers dans la philosophie des lumières." *Revue internationale de philosophies,* VI (1952), 337-55.

Belin, J. P. *Le Commerce des livres prohibés à Paris de 1750 à 1789.* Paris, 1913. Reprinted in the Burt Franklin research and source-work series, no. 28. New York [1962].

———. *Le Mouvement philosophique de 1748 à 1789. Etude sur la diffusion des idées des philosophes à Paris d'après les documents concernant l'histoire de la librairie.* Paris, 1913. Reprinted in the Burt Franklin research and source-work series, no. 27. New York [1962].

Bellanger, Claude, Jacques Godechot, Pierre Guiral, and Fernand Terrou. *Histoire générale de la presse française.* 2 vols. Paris, 1969.

Bénazé (de). "Révolutionnaires et classiques." *La Révolution française,* IV (1883), 900-914; 1073-90.

Bénétruy, Jean, *L'Atelier de Mirabeau: Quatre proscrits genevois dans la tourmente révolutionnaire.* Mémoires et documents publiés par la Société d'histoire et d'archéologie de Genève, vol. XLI. Geneva, 1962.

Berthoud, Elie. "Un Commerce de librairie entre Neuchâtel et Prague, de 1777 à 1789." *Musée neuchâtelois,* 3me série, VI (1969), 134-39.

Bickart, Roger. *Les Parlements et la notion de souveraineté nationale au XVIIIe siècle.* Paris, 1932.

Bien, David. *The Calas Affair: Persecution, Toleration, and Heresy in Eighteenth Century Toulouse.* Princeton, 1960.

———. "Catholic Magistrates and Protestant Marriage in the French Enlightenment." *French Historical Studies,* II (1962), 409-29.

Bigongiari, Dino, ed. *The Political Ideas of St. Thomas Aquinas.* New York, 1957.

Birn, Raymond F. "Pierre Rousseau and the Philosophes of Bouillon." *Studies on Voltaire and the Eighteenth Century,* XXIX (1964).

———. "The French-Language Press and the *Encyclopédie,* 1750-1759." *Studies on Voltaire and the Eighteenth Century,* LV (1967), 263-86.

Black, Cyril Edwin. *The Dynamics of Modernization: A Study in the Comparative History.* New York, 1966.

Bloch, Camille. *L'Assistance et l'état en France à la veille de la Révolution.* Paris, 1909.

Bluche, François. *Les Magistrats du Parlement de Paris au XVIIIe siècle (1715-1771).* Annales littéraires de l'Université de Besançon. 2d ser., vol. 35. Paris, 1960.

———. "L'Origine sociale du personnel ministériel français au XVIIIe siècle." *Bulletin de la société d'histoire moderne et contemporaine,* I (1957), 9-13.

Bollème, Geneviève, J. Ehrard, F. Furet, D. Roche, and J. Roger. *Livre et société dans la France du XVIIIe siècle,* vol. I. Paris, 1965.

Bondois, P.M.. "L'Organisation industrielle et commercialle sous l'ancien régime: le privilège exclusif au XVIIIe siècle." *Revue d'histoire économique et sociale,* XXI (1933), 140-89.

Bonno, Gabriel. *La Constitution britannique devant l'opinion française, de Montesquieu à Bonaparte.* Paris, 1932.

Bord, Gustave. *Le Pacte de famine: histoire, légende.* Paris, 1887.

Bouchary, Jean. "Les Compagnies financières à Paris à la fin du XVIIIe siècle: les compagnies d'assurances." *Annales historiques de la Révolution française,* XVI (1939), 492-505.

———. *Le Marché de changes de Paris à la fin du XVIIIe siècle (1778-1800) avec des graphiques et le relevé des cours.* Commission de recherche et de publication des documents relatifs à la vie économique de la Révolution. Mémoires et documents, vol. VIII. Paris, 1937.

———. *Les Manieurs d'argent à Paris à la fin du XVIIIe siècle.* 3 vols. Paris, 1939-43.

Bougeart, Alfred. *Les Cordeliers.* Caen, 1891.

Bouloiseau, Marc. *Le Comité du salut public, 1793-1795.* Series "Que sais-je?" no. 1014. Paris, 1962.

Bourde, André J. *Agronomie et agronomes en France au XVIIIe siècle.* 3 vols. Paris, 1967.

———. *The Influence of England on the French Agronomes, 1750-1789.* New York, 1933.

Bourrinet, Jacques. "Turgot, théoricien de l'individualisme libéral." *Revue d'histoire économique et sociale,* XLIII (1965), 465-89.

Bouyssy, M. T., J. Brancolini, J.-L. Flandrin, M. Flandrin, A. Fontana, F. Furet, and D. Roche. *Livre et société dans la France du XVIIIe siècle,* vol. II. Paris, 1970.

Braudel, Fernand, and Ernest Labrousse, eds. *Histoire économique et sociale de la France.* 4 vols. Paris, 1970–. Vol. II: *Des derniers temps de l'âge seigneurial aux préludes de l'âge industriel (1660-1789).* Paris, 1970.

Brengues, Jacques. *Charles Duclos (1704-1772), ou l'obsession de la vertu.* Saint-Brieuc, 1971.

Brumfitt, J. H. *Voltaire, Historian.* London, 1958.

Brunel, Lucien. *Les Philosophes et l'Académie française au XVIIIe siècle,* Paris, 1884.

Brunot, Ferdinand. *Histoire de la langue française des origines à 1900.* 13 vols. Paris, 1905-53.

Bruun, Geoffrey. *The Enlightened Despots.* New York, 1929.

Burgelin, Pierre. *La Philosophie de l'existence de J.-J. Rousseau.* Paris, 1952.

Burguière, André. "Société et culture à Reims à la fin du XVIIIe siècle: la diffusion des 'lumières' analysée à travers les cahiers de doléances." *Annales: Economie, Société, Civilisation,* XXII (1967), 303-33.

Cahen, Léon. "L'Approvisionnement en pain de Paris au XVIIIe siècle et la question de la boulangerie." *Revue d'histoire économique et sociale,* XIV (1926), 458-72.

———. "L'Idée de la lutte des classes au XVIIIe siècle." *Revue de synthèse historique,* XII (1906), 44-56.

———. "Le Pacte de famine et les speculations sur les blés." *Revue historique,* CLII (1926), 32-43.

———. "La Population parisienne au milieu du XVIIIe siècle." *Revue de Paris,* XVI (1919), 146-70.

———. "Le Prétendu pacte de famine. Quelques précisions nouvelles." *Revue historique,* CLXXVII (1935), 173-214.

———. "Quelques caractères de l'économie française à la veille de la Révolution." *Annales d'histoire sociale,* I (1939), 238-50.

Secondary sources *(continued)*

——. "La Question du pain à Paris à la fin du XVIIIe siècle." *Cahiers de la Révolution française,* I, 50-76.

Camus, Albert. *L'Homme révolté.* Paris, 1951.

Carcassonne, Elie. "La Chine dans 'L'Esprit des lois.'" *Revue d'histoire littéraire de la France,* XXXI (1924), 193-205.

——. *Montesquieu et le problème de la constitution française au XVIIIe siècle.* Paris, 1927.

Caron, Pierre. "La Tentative de contre-révolution de juin-juillet 1789." *Revue d'histoire moderne,* VIII (1906-7), 649-78.

Carré, Henri. "Les Fêtes d'un réaction parlementaire (1774-1775). Etudes sur les préliminaires de la Révolution." *La Révolution française,* XXIII (1892), 5-35.

——. *La Fin des Parlements (1788-1790).* Paris, 1912.

——. *La Noblesse de France et l'opinion publique au XVIIIe siècle.* Paris, 1920.

——. "Un Précurseur inconscient de la Révolution: le Conseiller Duval d'Eprémesnil, 1787-1788." *La Révolution française,* XXXIII (1897), 349-73. 404-37.

——. *Quelques Mots sur la presse clandestine à la fin de l'ancien régime.* Poitiers, 1893.

——. "La Tactique et les idées de l'opposition parlementaire (1788-1789)." *La Révolution française,* XXIX (1895), 97-121.

Cassirer, Ernst. *The Philosophy of the Enlightenment.* Trans. Fritz C. A. Koelln and James P. Pettegrove. Princeton, 1951.

Cauly, Eugène Ernest. *Histoire du Collège des Bons-Enfants de l'Université de Reims depuis son origine jusqu'à ses récentes transformations.* Reims, 1885.

Cerf, Madeleine. "La Censure royale à la fin du XVIIIe siècle." *Communications,* IX (1967), 2-27.

Chabert, Alexandre. "Rousseau, économiste." *Revue d'histoire économique et sociale,* XLII (1964), 344-56.

Chappe, Ignace-Urbain-Jean. *Histoire de la télégraphie.* Paris, 1824.

Chassaigne, André. *Des Lettres de cachet sous l'ancien régime.* Paris, 1903.

——. *Le Procès du Chevalier de La Barre.* Paris, 1920.

——. *La Lieutenance générale de police à Paris.* Paris, 1906.

Chassin, Charles-Louis. *Les Elections et les cahiers de Paris en 1789.* Collections de documents relatifs à l'histoire de Paris pendant la Révolution française, 4 vols. Paris, 1888-89.

Chaunu, Pierre. *La Civilisation de l'Europe des lumières.* Collection Les Grandes Civilisations. Paris, 1971.

Cheinisse, Léon. *Les Idées politiques des physiocrates.* Paris, 1914.

Chevalier, Louis. *Classes laborieuses et classes dangereuses à Paris pendant la première moitié du XIXe siècle.* Paris, 1958.

Choulguine, A. "L'Organisation capitaliste de l'industrie existait-elle en France à la veille de la Révolution?" *Revue d'histoire économique et sociale,* X (1922), 184-218.

Chuquet, Arthur. "La Jeunesse de Camille Desmoulins." *Annales révolutionnaires,* I (1908), 1-26.

Cobb, Richard C. *The Police and the People: French Popular Protest, 1789-1820.* Oxford, 1970.

——. "Quelques aspects de la mentalité révolutionnaire (avril 1793-thermidor An II)." *Revue d'histoire moderne et contemporaine,* VI (1959), 81-120.

——. *A Second Identity, Essays on France and French History.* London and New York, 1969.

Cobban, Alfred. *The Social Interpretation of the French Revolution.* Cambridge, England, 1965.

Cocatre-Zilgien, André. "Les Doctrines politiques des milieux parlementaires dan la seconde moitié du XVIIIe siècle, ou Les Avocats dan la bataille idéologique pre-
révolutionnaire."*Annales de la Faculté de droit et des sciences économiques de Lille*
(1963), 29-154.

Conan, J. "Les Débuts de l'école physiocratique. Un Faux départ: l'échec de la réforme
fiscale." *Revue d'histoire économique et sociale*, XXXVI (1958), 45-63.

Coquelin, Charles, and Gilbert Urbain Guillaumin. *Dictionnaire de l'économie politique.*
Contenant l'exposition des principes de la science, l'opinion des écrivains qui ont le
plus contribué à sa fondation et à ses progrès, la bibliographie générale de l'économie
politique,...et une appréciation raisonnée des principaux ouvrages. 2 vols. Paris,
1852-53.

Cornou, François. *Trente Années de luttes contre Voltaire et les philosophes du XVIIIe*
siècle. Elie Fréron (1718-1776). Paris, 1922.

Corvisier, André. *L'Armée française de la fin du XVIIe siècle au ministère de Choiseul.*
Le Soldat. 2 vols. Paris, 1964.

Cotta, Alain. "Le Développement économique dans la pensée de Montesquieu." *Revue*
d'histoire économique et sociale, XXXV (1957), 370-415.

Courtois, Alphonse. *Histoire des banques en France.* 2d ed. Paris, 1881.

Crocker, Lester G. *An Age of Crisis: Man and World in Eighteenth Century French*
Thought. Baltimore, 1959.

———. *Nature and Culture: Ethical Thought in the French Enlightenment.* Baltimore,
1963.

Dahrendorf, Ralf. *Class and Class Conflict in Industrial Society.* Stanford, Calif., 1959.

Dakin, Douglas. *Turgot and the Ancien Régime in France.* London, 1939.

Daline, M. V. "Babeuf et Marat en 1789-1790." *Annales historiques de la Révolution*
française, XXX (1958), 16-37.

Danière, A. "Feudal Income and Demand Elasticity for Bread in Late Eighteenth Century France." *Journal of Economic History*, XVIII (1958), 317-31.

Darnton, Robert, "Un Commerce de livres 'sous le manteau' en province à la fin de l'ancien régime." *Revue française de l'histoire du livre*, nouvelle série, V (1975), 5-29.

———. "The Grub Street Style of Revolution: J.–P. Brissot, Police Spy." *Journal of*
Modern History, XL (1968), 301-27.

———. "The High Enlightenment and the Low-Life of Literature in Pre-Revolutionary
France." *Past and Present*, no. 51 (May, 1971), 81-115.

———. "In Search of the Enlightenment: Recent Attempts to Create a Social History
of Ideas." *Journal of Modern History*, XLIII (1971), 113-32.

———. "Reading, Writing, and Publishing in Eighteenth Century France: A Case Study in
the Sociology of Literature." *Daedalus*, C (1970), 214-56.

———. "Trade in Taboo: The Life of a Clandestine Book Dealer in Prerevolutionary
France," in Paul J. Korshin, ed., *The Widening Circle: Essays on the Circulation of*
Literature in Eighteenth Century Europe. Philadelphia, 1976.

Daumard, A., and F. Furet. *Structures et relations sociales à Paris au XVIIIe siècle.* Paris,
1961.

Dautry, Jean. "Le pessimisme économique de Babeuf, et l'histoire des utopies." *Annales*
historiques de la Révolution française, XXXIII (1961), 215-33.

Dawson, Philip. "The 'Bourgeoisie de Robe' in 1789." *French Historical Studies*, IV
(1965), 1-21.

Defresne, Arsène. *Extraits des archives communales de la région de Versailles: documents*
historiques se rattachant à la vie des villages avant 1789 et sous la Révolution. Versailles, 1908.

———. "Partage des biens communaux à Marnes-la-Coquette." Commission d'histoire économique et sociale de la Révolution française' Comité départemental de Seine-et-

Secondary sources *(continued)*

Oise. Recherche et publication des documents relatifs à la vie économique de la Révolution. *Bulletin* (1908-9), 66-77.

——. "Les premières transformations économiques dans le Département de Seine-et-Oise (1790-1792)." Commission d'histoire économique et sociale de la Révolution française. Comité départemental de Seine-et-Oise. Recherche et publication des documents relatifs à la vie économique de la Révolution. *Bulletin* (1908), 36-59.

Delafarge, Daniel. *La Vie et l'œuvre de Palissot, 1730-1814.* Paris, 1912.

Delbeke, Francis. *L'Action politique et sociale des avocats au dix-huitième siècle: Leur Part dans la préparation de la Révolution française.* Louvain and Paris, 1927.

Delbez, L. "Les Sources philosophiques de l'individualisme révolutionnaire." *Revue internationale d'histoire politique et constitutionelle,* VI (1956), 241-58.

Delisle de Sales [Jean Claude Izouard]. *Essai sur le journalisme.* Paris, 1811.

Derathé, Robert. *Jean-Jacques Rousseau et la science politique de son temps.* Paris, 1950.

Desnoiresterres, Gustave. *Voltaire et la société française au XVIIIᵉ siècle.* 8 vols. Paris, 1876.

Dibner, Bern. *Early Electrical Machines: The Experiments and Apparatus of Two Enquiring Centuries (1600 to 1800) that Led to the Triumphs of the Electrical Age.* Norwalk, Conn., 1957.

Dommanget, Maurice. "L'Idée de grève générale en France au XVIIIᵉ siècle et pendant la Révolution." *Revue d'histoire économique et sociale,* XLI (1963), 34-55.

——. *Sylvain Maréchal: L'Egalitaire: L'Homme sans Dieu, 1750-1803.* Paris, 1950.

Dramard, M. *Episodes de la Révolution dans le Département de Seine-et-Oise. La Disette de 1789-1792.* Versailles, 1892.

Du Bled, Victor. *Les Causeurs de la Révolution.* Paris, 1889.

——. *La Société française du XVIᵉ siècle au XXᵉ siècle. IXᵉ série. XVIIIᵉ et XIXᵉ siècles. Le Premier salon de France: L'Académie française. L'Argot.* Paris, 1913.

Dupieux, Paul. "L'Agitation parisienne et les prisonniers de la Bastille en 1771-1772." *Bulletin de la Société de l'histoire de Paris et de l'Ile de France,* LVIII (1931), 45-57.

Egret, Jean. "L'Aristocratie parlementaire française à la fin de l'ancien régime." *Revue Historique,* CCVIII (1952), 1-14.

——. *Louis XV et l'opposition parlementaire.* Paris, 1970.

——. *La Pré-révolution française: 1787-1788.* Paris, 1962.

Ehrard, Jean. "Opinions médicales en France au XVIIIᵉ siècle: la peste et l'idée de contagion." *Annales: Economie, Société, Civilisation,* XII (1957), 46-59.

Entrèves, Alexandre Passarine d'. "Mallet du Pan: A Swiss Critic of Democracy." *Cambridge Journal,* I (1947), 99-108.

Etudes sur le "Contrat social" de Jean-Jacques Rousseau. Actes des journées d'études tenues à Dijon les 3, 4, 5, and 6 mai 1962. Paris, 1964.

Faguet, Emile, ed. *L'Oeuvre sociale de la Révolution française.* Paris, 1901.

Faure, Edgar. *La Disgrace de Turgot, 12 mai 1776.* Trente journées qui ont fait la France, vol. 16. Paris, 1961.

——. "Turgot et la Théorie du produit net." *Revue d'histoire économique et sociale,* XXXIX (1961), 273-86, 417 41.

Faure-Soulet, J. F. *Economie politique et progrès au 'siècle des lumières.'* Collection techniques économiques modernes, tome 4. Series Histoire et pensée économiques, no. 1. Paris, 1964.

Febvre, Lucien. "Pour l'histoire d'un sentiment: le besoin de sécurité." *Annales: Economie, Société, Civilisation,* XI (1956), 244-47.

Flammermont, Jules. *Le Chancelier Maupeou et les Parlements.* Paris, 1883.

——, ed. *La Journée du 14 juillet 1789. Fragment des mémoires inédits de L.-G. Pitra, électeur de Paris en 1789.* Paris, 1892.

——. "Le Second Ministère de Necker." *Revue historique,* XLVI (1891), 1-67.

Foncin, Pierre. *Essai sur le ministère de Turgot.* Paris, 1877.

Forado-Cunéo, Yvonne. "Les Ateliers de charité de Paris pendant la Révolution française, 1789-1791." *La Révolution française,* LXXXVI (1933), 317-42; LXXXVII (1934), 29-61, 103-23.

Ford, Franklin L. *Robe and Sword: The Regrouping of the French Aristocracy after Louis XIV.* Cambridge, Mass., 1953.

Fournel, J.-F. *Histoire des avocats au Parlement et du barreau de Paris, depuis St. Louis jusqu'au 15 octobre 1790.* 2 vols. Paris, 1813.

Francastel, Pierre, ed. *Utopie et institutions au XVIIIe siècle. Le Pragmatisme des lumières.* Paris and The Hague, 1963.

Fromageot, P. "Les Fantaisies littéraires, galantes, politiques et autres d'un grand seigneur' Le Comte de Lauraguais (1733-1824)." *Revue des études historiques,* LXXX (1914), 14-56'

Funck-Brentano, Frantz. "La Bastille d'après ses archives." *Revue historique,* XLII (1890), 38-73, 278-316.

——. *Légendes et archives de la Bastille.* Paris, 1898.

——, ed. *Catalogue des manuscrits de la Bibliothèque de l'Arsenal,* vol. IX. *Archives de la Bastille.* Paris, 1892-95.

Furet, François. "Pour une définition des classes inférieures à l'époque moderne." *Annales: Economie, Société, Civilisation,* XVIII (1963), 459-74.

Gachard, Louis-Prosper. *Analectes historiques.* Series 1-17. 5 vols. Brussels, 1856-71.

Gaudemet, Eugène. *L'Abbé Galiani et la question du commerce des blés à la fin du règne de Louis XV.* Paris, 1899.

Gay, Peter. *The Bridge of Criticism. Dialogues among Lucian, Erasmus, and Voltaire on the Enlightenment—on History and Hope, Imagination and Reason, Constraint and Freedom—and on its Meaning for Our Time.* New York, 1970.

——. *The Enlightenment: An Interpretation.* 2 vols. New York, 1966-69.

——. "Enlightenment in the History of Political Theory." *Political Science Quarterly,* LXIX (1954), 371-89.

——. *The Party of Humanity. Essays in the French Enlightenment.* New York, 1964.

——. *Voltaire's Politics: The Poet as Realist.* New York, 1965.

Girard, René. *L'Abbé Terray et la liberté du commerce des grains, 1769-1774.* Paris, 1924.

Glasson, E. *Le Parlement de Paris: son rôle politique depuis le règne de Charles VII jusqu'à la Révolution.* 2 vols. Paris, 1901.

Godechot, Jacques. *La Prise de la Bastille, 14 juillet 1789.* Trente journées qui ont fait la France, vol. 17. Paris, 1965.

Godfrey, James Logan. *Revolutionary Justice: A Study of the Organization, Personnel, and Procedure of the Paris Tribunal.* Chapel Hill, N.C., 1951.

Gohin, Ferdinand. *Les Transformations de la langue française pendant la deuxième moitié du XVIIIe siècle: 1740-1789.* Paris, 1903.

Goldmann, Lucien. "La Pensée des lumières." *Annales: Economie, Société, Civilisation,* XXII (1967), 752-79.

Goubert, Pierre. *L'Ancien régime.* 2 vols. Collection U. Series Histoire moderne. Paris, 1969-73.

——. "Les Techniques agricoles dans les pays picards aux XVIIe et XVIIIe siècles." *Revue d'histoire économique et sociale,* XXXV (1957), 24-40.

Secondary sources *(continued)*

Gonhier, H. "Nature et histoire dans la pensée de J.-J. Rousseau." *Annales de la Société Jean-Jacques Rousseau,* XXXII, 7-48.

Grange, Henri. *Les Idées de Necker.* Paris, 1974.

——. "Rousseau et la division du travail." *Revue des sciences humaines,* no. 86 (1957), 143-55.

——. "Turgot et Necker devant le problème des salaires." *Annales historiques de la Révolution française,* XXIX (1957), 19-37.

Greenlaw, R. "Pamphlet Literature in France during the Period of Aristocratic Revolt," 1787-1788. *Journal of Modern History,* XXIX (1957), 349-54.

Grosclaude, Pierre. *Malsherbes, témoin et interprète de son temps.* Paris, 1961.

Guilhiermoz, P. "De la persistance du caractère orale dans la procédure civile française." *Nouvelle revue historique de droit français et étranger,* XII (1889), 21-65.

Gutton, Jean-Pierre. *La Société et les pauvres; l'exemple de la généralité de Lyon (1534-1789).* Paris, 1971.

Halpérin, Jean. "La Notion de sécurité dans l'histoire économique et sociale." *Revue d'histoire économique et sociàle,* XXX (1952), 7-25.

Hampson, Norman. *A Social History of the French Revolution.* London, 1963.

Harsin, Paul. *Crédit public et banque d'état en France du XVIe au XVIIIe siècle.* Paris, 1933.

——. *Les Doctrines monétaires et financières en France du XVIe au XVIIIe siècles.* Paris, 1928.

Hatin, Eugène. *Bibliographie historique et critique de la presse périodique française, ou Catalogue systématique et raisonné de tous les écrits périodiques de quelque valeur publiés ou ayant circulé en France depuis l'origine du journal jusqu'à nos jours.* Paris, 1866.

——. *Les Gazettes de Hollande et la presse clandestine aux XVIIe et XVIIIe siècles.* Paris, 1865.

——. *Histoire politique et littéraire de la presse en France.* 8 vols. Paris, 1859-61.

Havens, George R., ed. *Voltaire's Marginalia on the Pages of Rousseau: A Comparative Study of Ideas.* Columbus, Ohio, 1933.

Hayem, Julien. *La Répression des grèves au XVIIIe siècle.* Mémoires et documents pour servir à l'histoire du commerce et de l'industrie en France. First ser. Paris, 1911.

Hazard, Paul. *La Crise de la conscience européene, 1680-1715.* 3 vols. Paris, 1934.

——. *La Pensée européenne au XVIIIe siècle, de Montesquieu à Lessing.* 3 vols. Paris, 1946.

——. "Le Problème du mal dans la conscience européenne du XVIIIe siècle." *Romantic Review* (1941), 147-70.

Hecht, Jacqueline. "Trois précurseurs de la sécurité sociale au XVIIIe siècle: Faiguet de Villeneuve, Henry de Boulainvilliers, Du Beissier de Pizany d'Eden." *Population,* XIV (1959), 73-88.

Hermann-Mascard, Nicole. *La Censure des livres à Paris à la fin de l'ancien régime (1750-1789).* Paris, 1968.

Herr, Richard, and Harold T. Parker, eds. *Ideas in History. Essays Presented to Louis Gottschalk by his Former Students.* Durham, N.C., 1965.

Higgs, Henry. *The Physiocrats. Six Lectures on the French Economistes of the 18th Century.* Hamden, Conn., 1963. Reprinted from the London and New York edition of 1897.

Hillairet, Jacques. *Dictionnaire historique des rues de Paris.* 2 vols. Paris, 1963.

Hubert, Eugène Ernest. *Gouverneurs-généraux et ministres plénipotentiaries aux Pays-bas pendant les dernières années du régime autrichien.* Liège, 1920.

——. *Les Préliminaires de la Révolution brabançonne. Un Complot politique à Bruxelles, octobre 1789.* Académie royale de Belgique, classe des lettres et des sciences morales et politiques, Mémoires, Ser. 2, vol. VII. Brussels, 1920.

Hubert, René. *Les Sciences sociales dans l'Encyclopédie. La Philosophie de l'histoire et le problème des origines sociales.* Paris, 1923.

Hufton, Olwen H. *The Poor of Eighteenth Century France: 1750-1789.* Oxford, 1974.

Huguet, Adrien. *Histoire d'une ville picarde, Saint Valery: 1589-1789.* 2 vols. Paris, 1909.

Huntington, Samuel. *Political Order in Changing Societies.* New Haven, Conn., 1968.

Hytier, Adrienne D. "Joseph II, la Cour de Vienne, et les philosophes." *Studies on Voltaire and the Eighteenth Century,* CVI, 225-51.

Imbert, Jean, ed. *Quelques Procès criminels des XVIIe et XVIIIe siècles présentés par un groupe d'étudiants.* Travaux et recherches de la Faculté de droit et des sciences économiques de Paris. Ser. "Sciences historiques," no. 2. Paris, 1964.

L'Intermédiaire des chercheurs et curieux, correspondance littéraire, historique et artistique, questions et réponses, lettres et documents inédits, communications divers à l'usage de tous. 103 vols. Paris, 1864-1940.

Isambert, François-André, ed. *Recueil général des anciennes lois françaises depuis l'an 420 jusqu'à la Révolution de 1789.* 29 vols. Paris, 1821-33.

Jacob, Louis. *Les Suspects pendant les Révolutions 1789-1794.* Paris, 1952.

Jameson, Russell Parsons. *Montesquieu et l'esclavage. Etude sur les origines de l'opinion anti-esclavagiste en France au XVIIIe siècle.* Paris, 1911.

Jolly, Pierre. *Necker.* Paris, 1947.

Jourdain, Charles. *Histoire de l'Université de Paris au XVIIe et au XVIIIe siècle.* Paris, 1862-66. 2d ed., 2 vols. Paris, 1888.

Kaplan, Steven Lawrence. *Bread, Politics, and Political Economy in the Reign of Louis XV.* International Archives of the History of Ideas, 86. 2 vols. The Hague, 1976.

——. "Police and Political Economy in Paris: The Crisis of the Sixties." Paper presented at the American Historical Association meetings, Boston, Mass., Dec. 28, 1970.

Kaplow, Jeffry. *The Names of Kings: The Parisian Laboring Poor in the Eighteenth Century.* New York, 1972.

——. "Sur la population flottante de Paris à la fin de l'ancien régime." *Annales historiques de la Révolution française,* XXXIX (1967), 1-14.

——, ed. *New Perspectives on the French Revolution: Readings in Historical Sociology.* New York, 1965.

Koebner, R. "Despot and Despotism: Vicissitudes of a Political Term." *Journal of the Warburg and Courtauld Institutes,* XIV (1951), 275, 302.

Krauss, Werner. *Studien zur deutschen und französischen Aufklärung.* Berlin, 1963.

——, ed. *Die französische Aufklärung im Spiegel der deutschen literatur des 18 Jahrhunderts.* Berlin, 1963.

——, ed. *Neue Beiträge zur Literatur der Aufklärung.* Berlin, 1964.

Krauss, Werner, and H. Mayer, eds. *Grundpositionen der französischen Aufklärung.* Berlin, 1955.

Kulstein, David I. "The Ideas of Charles-Joseph Panckoucke, Publisher of the *Moniteur Universel,* on the French Revolution." *French Historical Studies,* IV (1966), 304-19.

Labrousse, Ernest. *La Crise de l'économie française à la fin de l'ancien régime et au début de la Révolution.* Paris, 1943.

——. *Esquisse du mouvement des prix et des revenus en France au XVIIIe siècle.* 2 vols. Paris, 1933.

Lacour-Gayet, Robert. *Calonne, financier, réformateur, contre-révolutionnaire, 1734-1802.* Paris, 1963.

Lacroix, Paul [Jacob, P. L., pseud.]. *Bibliographie et iconographie de tous les ouvrages*

Secondary sources *(continued)*

de Restif de la Bretonne... Paris, 1875.

Ladd, Everett C., Jr. "Helvétieus and D'Holbach: 'La moralisation de la politique.'" *Journal of the History of Ideas,* XXIII (1962), 221-38.

Landes, David S."The Statistical Study of French Crises." *Journal of Economic History,* X (1950), 195-211.

Laurain, E. "Essai sur les présidiaux." *Nouvelle revue historique du droit français et étranger,* XIX (1895), 355-407, 522-76, 738-79; XX (1896), 47-104, 273-329.

Laurent, Gustave. "La Faculté de droit de Reims et les hommes de la Révolution,"*Annales historiques de la Révolution française,* VI (1929), 329-58.

Lavergne, Léonce de. *Les Economistes français du XVIIIᵉ siècle.* Paris, 1870.

Lefebvre, Georges. *The Coming of the French Revolution.* Trans. Robert R. Palmer. New York, 1947.

——. *Etudes sur la Révolution française.* 2d ed. Paris, 1963.

——. *Foules historiques et foules révolutionnaires.* Paris, 1934.

——. *La Grande Peur de 1789.* 2d ed. Paris, 1956.

——. *La Révolution française.* 3d ed. Peuples et civilisations. Histoire générale. Vol. XIII. Paris, 1963.

Le Flamanc, Auguste. *Les Utopies prérévolutionnaires et la philosophie du 18ᵉ siècle.* Brest, 1933.

LeMoy, Arthur. *Le Parlement de Bretagne et le pouvoir royal au XVIIIᵉ siècle.* Paris, 1909.

Léon, Pierre. "Tradition et machinisme dans la France du XVIIIᵉ siècle." *Information historique,* XVII (1955), 1-15.

LeParquier, E. "Un enquête sur le paupérisme et la crise industrielle dans la région Rouennaise en 1789." *Bulletin de la Société libre d'émulation du commerce et de l'industrie de la Seine-inférieure* (1935), 127-197.

Leroy, Maxime. *Histoire des idées sociales en France.* 3 vols. Paris, 1947-1954.

LeRoy Ladurie, Emmanuel. "Climat et récoltes au XVIIᵉ et XVIIIᵉ siècles." *Annales: Economie, Société, Civilisation,* XV (1960), 434-65.

——. *Histoire du climat depuis l'an mil.* Paris, 1967.

Lescure, Mathurin-François-Adolphe de. *Correspondance secrète inédite sur Louis XVI, Marie-Antoinette, la cour, et la ville de 1777 à 1792.* 2 vols. Paris, 1866.

Letaconnoux, J. "La Question des subsistances et du commerce des grains en France au XVIIIᵉ siècle. Travaux, sources, et questions à traiter." *Revue d'histoire moderne et contemporaine,* VIII (1906-7), 409-45.

Leuillot, Paul. "Réflexions sur l'histoire économique et sociale à propos de la bourgeoisie en 1789." *Revue d'histoire moderne et contemporaine,* I (1954), 131-44.

Levasseur, Emile. *Histoire des classes ouvrières et de l'industrie en France avant 1789.* 2d ed. 2 vols. Paris, 1900-1901.

Lévy-Bruhl, H. "La Noblesse de France et le commerce à la fin de l'ancien régime." *Revue d'histoire moderne,* VIII (1938), 209-35.

Lewis, Oscar. "The Culture of Poverty." *Scientific American,* CCXV (Oct., 1966), 19-25.

Lhomet, Jean. *Le Banquier Perrégaux et sa fille la Duchesse de Raguse.* Paris, 1926.

Lichtenberger, André. *Le Socialisme au XVIIIᵉ siècle. Etude sur les idées socialistes dans les écrivains français du XVIIIᵉ siècle avant la Révolution.* Paris, 1895.

——. *Le Socialisme et la Révolution française. Etude sur les idées socialistes en France de 1789 à 1796.* Paris, 1899.

——. *Le Socialisme utopique. Etudes sur quelques précurseurs inconnus du socialisme.* Paris, 1898.

Livois, René de. *Histoire de la presse française.* 2 vols. Paris, 1965.

Lodian, Walter. "A Century of the Telegraph in France." *Popular Science Monthly*, XLIV (1893-94), 791-801.

Loubère, Leo A. "The Intellectual Origins of French Jacobin Socialism." *International Review of Social History*, IV (1959), 415-31.

Lublinsky, V.-S. "Voltaire et la guerre des farines." *Annales historiques de la Révolution française*, XXXI (1959), 127-45.

Lutfalla, Michel. "L'Evidence, fondement nécessaire et suffisant de l'ordre naturel chez Quesnay et Morelly." *Revue d'histoire économique et sociale*, XLI (1963), 213-49.

McCloy, Shelby R.. *Government Assistance in Eighteenth Century France*. Durham, N.C., 1946.

Machard, Pierre-Henri. *Essai historique sur Marnes-la-Coquette (Marnes-les-Saint-Cloud, Seine-et-Oise)*. Paris, 1932.

McNeil, Gordon H. "The Anti-Revolutionary Rousseau." *American Historical Review*, LVIII (1953), 808-23.

Maillou, Rioux de. "La Littérature et la Révolution." *Revue de la Révolution*, XIV (1889), 201-22; XV (1889), 117-37, 377-408.

Mallet, B. *Mallet du Pan and the French Revolution*. London, 1902.

Mandrou, Robert. *La France au XVIIe et XVIIIe siècles*. 2d ed. Nouvelle Clio. L'Histoire et ses problèmes, no. 33. Paris, 1970.

———. "Pour une histoire de la sensibilité." *Annales: Economie, Société, Civilisation*, XIV (1959), 581-88.

Manévy, Raymond. *La Presse française de Renaudot à Rochefort*. Paris, 1958.

Manuel, Frank Edward. *The Eighteenth Century Confronts the Gods*. Cambridge, Mass., 1959.

———. *The Prophets of Paris*. Cambridge, Mass., 1962.

———. and Fritzie Prigolizy Manuel, eds. *French Utopias*. New York, 1966.

Mareille, Vital. *La Plaidoirie sentimentale en France*. Paris, 1907.

Marion, Marcel. *La Bretagne et le Duc d'Aiguillon, 1753-1770*. Paris, 1898.

———. *Dictionnaire des institutions de la France au XVIIe et XVIIIe siècles*. Paris, 1923.

———. *Le Garde des sceaux Lamoignon, et la réforme judiciaire de 1788*. Paris, 1905.

Martin, Kingsley. *French Liberal Thought in the Eighteenth Century: A Study of Political Ideas from Bayle to Condorcet*. Ed. J. P. Mayer. New York, 1962.

Masson, Frédéric. *L'Académie française: 1629-1793* Paris, 1912.

———. *Le Département des affaires étrangères pendant la Révolution, 1787-1804*. Paris, 1877.

Mathiez, Albert. "Marat, Linguet, Camille Desmoulins, Danton jugés en juillet 1790 par un pamphlétaire anti-orléaniste." *Annales révolutionnaires*, III (1910), 249-51.

———. "Notes sur l'importance du prolétariat en France à la veille de la Révolution." *Annales historiques de la Révolution française*, VII (1930), 497-524.

Mauzi, Robert. *L'Idée du bonheur dans la littérature et la pensée françaises au XVIIIe siècle*. Paris, 1960.

Meek, Ronald L. *The Economics of Physiocracy: Essays and Translations*. Cambridge, Mass., 1963.

Méthivier, Hubert. *L'Ancien régime*. Series "Que sais-je?" no. 925. Paris, 1961.

Meuvret, Jean. "Les Crises de subsistances et la démographie de la France d'ancien régime." *Population*, I (1946), 643-50.

Mistler, Jean. *Le 14 juillet*. L'Histoire par image, vol. 1. Paris, 1963.

Monin, Hippolyte. *Etat de Paris en 1789, Etudes et documents sur l'ancien régime à Paris*. Paris, 1889.

Morazé, Charles. *Les Bourgeois conquérants*. Paris, 1957. Trans. into English as *The Triumph of the Middle Classes: A Study of European Values in the Nineteenth Century*. London, 1966.

Secondary sources *(continued)*

Morel, Jean. "Recherches sur les sources du *Discours* de Jean-Jacques Rousseau sur l'*origine et les fondements de l'inégalité parmi les hommes.*" *Annales de la Société Jean-Jacques Rousseau*, V (1909), 119-98.

Morineau, Michel. "Budgets populaires en France au XVIIIᵉ siècle." *Revue d'histoire économique et sociale*, L (1972), 203-37, 449-81.

———. *Les Faux-semblants d'un démarrage économique: agriculture et démographie en France au XVIIIᵉ siècle.* Cahiers des *Annales*, no. 30. Paris, 1970.

———. "Y-a-t-il eu une révolution agricole en France au dix-huitième siècle?" *Revue historique*, 239 (1968), 299-326.

Morize, André. *L'Apologie du luxe au XVIIIᵉ siècle et "Le Mondain" de Voltaire: étude critique sur "Le Mondain" et ses sources.* Paris, 1909.

Mornet, Daniel. "Les Enseignements des bibliothèque privées: 1750-1780." *Revue d'histoire littéraire de la France*, XVII (1910), 449-96.

———. *Les Origines intellectuels de la Révolution française 1715-1789.* Paris, 1933.

Moulinas, René. *L'Imprimerie, la librairie et la presse à Avignon au XVIIIᵉ siècle.* Grenoble, 1974.

Mousnier, Roland. "La Participation des gouvernés à l'activité des gouvernants dans la France du XVIIᵉ et du XVIIIᵉ siècles." *Recueils de la Société Jean Bodin*, XXIV (1966), 235-97.

Muller, Maurice. *Essai sur la philosophie de Jean d'Alembert.* Paris, 1926.

Munier Jolain, Julien, ed. *Le Plaidoirie dans la langue française.* 3 vols. Paris, 1897.

Neill, Thomas P. "Quesnay and Physiocracy." *Journal of the History of Ideas*, IX (1948), 153-73.

Nisard, Charles. *Les Ennemis de Voltaire.* Paris, 1853.

Palmade, Guy P. *Capitalisme et capitalistes français au XIXᵉ siècle.* Paris, 1961.

Palmer, Robert R. *The Age of the Democratic Revolution: A Political History of Europe and America: 1760-1800.* 2 vols. Princeton, 1959-64.

———. *Twelve Who Ruled: The Committee of Public Safety during the Terror.* Princeton, 1941.

Palou, Jean. *La Peur dans l'histoire.* Paris, 1958.

Parker, Harold Talbot. *The Cult of Antiquity and the French Revolutionaries: A Study in the Development of the Revolutionary Spirit.* Chicago, 1937.

Paultre, Christian. *De la répression de la mendicité et du vagabondage en France sous l'ancien régime.* Paris, 1906.

Peignot, G. *Dictionnaire critique, littéraire et bibliographique des principaux livres condamnés au feu, supprimés, ou censurés. Précédé d'un discours sur ces sortes d'ouvrages.* 2 vols. Paris, 1806.

Perret, Jean-Pierre. *Les Imprimeries d'Yverdun au XVIIᵉ et au XVIIIᵉ siècles.* Lausanne, 1945.

Petot, Jean. *Histoire de l'administration des ponts et chaussées: 1599-1815.* Paris, 1958.

Picard, Roger. *Les Cahiers de 1789 et les classes ouvrières.* Paris, 1910.

———. "Etude sur quelques théories du salaire au XVIIIᵉ siècle." *Revue d'histoire des doctrines économiques et sociales*, III (1910), 153-68.

———. "La Théorie de la lutte des classes à la veille de la Révolution française." *Revue d'économie politique*, XXV (1911), 624-33.

Pinset, Jacques. "Les Origines instinctives de la Révolution française." *Revue d'histoire économique et sociale*, XXXIX (1961), 198-228.

Pirenne, Henri. *Histoire de Belgique.* 7 vols. Brussels, 1908-32.

Plan, Pierre-Paul, ed. *Jean-Jacques Rousseau raconté par les gazettes de son temps. D'un décret à l'autre (9 juin 1762–21 décembre 1790).* 3d ed. Paris, 1912.

Pocquet, Barthélemy. *Le Pouvoir absolu et l'esprit provincial, le Duc d'Aiguillon et La Chalotais.* 3 vols. Paris, 1901.

Poitrineau, Abel. "L'Alimentation populaire en Auvergne au dix-huitième siècle." *Annales: Economie, Société, Civilisation,* XVIII (1962), 323-31.

Prat, Jean H. *Histoire du Faubourg Saint-Antoine.* Paris, 1962.

Proteau, Pierre. *Etude sur Morellet considéré comme auxiliaire de l'école physiocratique, et examen de ses principaux ouvrages économiques.* Laval, France, 1910.

Puttemans, André. "L'Histoire de la Belgique de 1715 à 1789." *Revue d'histoire moderne,* XV (1940), 105-56.

Reinhard, Marcel. "Elite et noblesse dans la seconde moitié du XVIIIᵉ siècle." *Revue d'histoire moderne et contemporaine,* III (1956), 5-37.

———. "Les Répercussions démographiques des crises de subsistances en France au XVIIIᵉ siècle." *Actes du quatre-vingt-unième Congrès nationale des sociétés savantes* (1956), 68-86.

Rémond, André. "Trois bilans de l'économie française au temps des théories physiocratiques." *Revue d'histoire économique et sociale,* XXXV (1957), 416-56.

Richard, Guy. "La Noblesse de France et les sociétés par actions à la fin du XVIIIᵉ siècle: un essai d'adaptation sociale à une nouvelle structure économique." *Revue d'histoire économique et sociale,* XL (1962), 484-523.

Richet, Denis. "Autour des origines idéologiques lointaines de la Révolution française: Elites et despotism." *Annales: Economie, Société, Civilisation,* XXIV (1969), 1-23.

Robiquet, Paul. *Thévenau de Morande: Etude sur le XVIIIᵉ siècle.* Paris, 1882.

Rocquain, Félix. *L'Esprit révolutionnaire avant la Révolution, 1715-1789.* Paris, 1878.

Rogers, Cornwell B. *The Spirit of Revolution in 1789. A Study of Public Opinion as Revealed in Political Songs and other Popular Literature at the Beginning of the French Revolution.* Princeton, 1949.

Roover, Raymond de. "The Concept of the Just Price: Theory and Economic Policy." *Journal of Economic History,* XVIII (1958), 418-34.

Rose, R. B. "18th Century Price Riots, The French Revolution and the Jacobin Maximum." *International Review of Social History,* IV (1959), 432-45.

Rothkrug, Lionel. *Opposition to Louis XIV: The Political and Social Origins of the French Enlightenment.* Princeton, 1965.

Rouff, M. "Le Personnel des premières émeutes de 1789 à Paris." *La Révolution française,* LVII (1909), 212-38.

Roux, René. "La Révolution française et l'idée de la lutte des classes." *Revue d'histoire économique et sociale,* XXIX (1951), 252-79.

Rudé, George. F. *The Crowd in the French Revolution.* Oxford, 1959.

———. *The Crowd in History: A Study of Popular Disturbances in France and England, 1730-1848.* New York, 1964.

———. *Paris and London in the Eighteenth Century: Studies in Popular Protest.* New York, 1971.

———. "La Taxation populaire de mai 1775 en Picardie, en Normandie et dans le Beauvaisis." *Annales historiques de la Révolution française,* XXXIII (1961), 305-26.

Ruhlmann, Georges. *Les Corporations, les manufactures et le travail libre à Abbeville au XVIIIᵉ siècle.* Paris, 1948.

Sagnac, Philippe. *La Fin de l'ancien régime et la Révolution américaine, 1763-1789.* 3d ed. Peuples et civilisations. Histoire générale publiée sous la direction de Louis Halphen et Philippe Sagnac. Vol. XII. Paris, 1952.

Sicard, Augustin. *L'Education morale et civique avant et pendant la Révolution, 1700-1808.* New ed. Paris, 1913.

———. "Les grands courants d'idées et de sentiments en France vers 1789." *Revue d'histoire politique et constitutionelle,* II (1938), 317-41.

Secondary sources *(continued)*

——. "Pensée sociale et l'œuvre de la Révolution française: 1789-1792." *Revue d'histoire politique et constitutionelle,* III (1939), 402-28.

St.–Jacob, P. de. "La Question des prix en France à la fin de l'ancien régime, d'après les contemporains." *Revue d'histoire économique et sociale,* XXX (1952), 133-46.

Schelle, Gustave. *Du Pont de Nemours et l'école physiocratique.* Paris, 1888.

Schmidt, Charles. "La Crise industrielle de 1788 en France." *Revue historique,* XCVII (1907), 78-94.

Schumpeter, Joseph A. *The History of Economic Analysis.* New York, 1954.

Sckommodau, Hans. "Thematik des Paradoxes in der Aufklärung." *Sitzungsberichte der wissenschaftlichen Gesellschaft an der Johann-Wolfgang Gœthe-Universität, Frankfurt am Main,* 10, no. 2 (1971), 55-101.

Sée, Henri. "Les Economistes et la question coloniale au XVIIIe siècle." *Revue de l'histoire des colonies françaises,* XXII (1929), 381-92.

——. *L'Evolution commercialle et industrielle de la France sous l'ancien régime.* Paris, 1925.

——. *Les Idées politiques en France au XVIIIe siècle: L'Evolution de la pensée politique en France au XVIIIe siècle.* Paris, 1925.

——. "Les origines de l'industrie capitaliste en France à la fin de l'ancien régime." *Revue historique,* CXLIV (1923), 187-200.

——. *La Vie économique et les classes sociales en France au XVIIIe siècle.* Paris, 1924.

Seeber, Edward D.. *Anti-Slavery Opinion in France during the Second Half of the Eighteenth Century.* Baltimore, 1937.

Shafer, Boyd C. "Bourgeois Nationalism in the Pamphlets on the Eve of the French Revolution." *Journal of Modern History,* X (1938), 31-50.

Sicard, Augustin. *L'Education morale et civique avant et pendant la Révolution, 1700-1808.* New ed. Paris, 1913.

——. *Les Etudes classiques avant la Révolution.* Paris, 1887.

Sirich, John Black. *The Revolutionary Committees in the Departments of France, 1793-1794.* Cambridge, Mass., 1943.

Soboul, Albert. *La Civilisation et la Révolution française.* 2 vols. Collection Les Grandes Civilisations. Paris, 1970–. Vol. I: *La Crise de l'ancien régime.* Paris, 1970.

——. "Classes et luttes de classe sous la Révolution française." *La Pensée,* LIII (1954), 39-62.

——. *La France à la veille de la Révolution.* Vol. I. *Aspects économiques et sociaux.* Les Cours de la Sorbonne. Centre de documentation universitaire. Paris, n.d.

——. *La France à la veille de la Révolution.* Vol. 2. *Le Mouvement des idées dans la seconde moitié du XVIIIe siècle.* Cours de l'Université de Clermont-Ferrand. Centre de documentation universitaire. Paris, n.d.

Société des études robespierristes. *Jean-Jacques Rousseau, 1712-1778. Pour le 250e anniversaire de sa naissance.* Gap, n.d.

Spengler, Joseph J. *French Predecessors of Malthus: A Study in Eighteenth Century Wage and Population Theory.* Durham, N.C., 1942.

Spooner, Franck. "Régimes alimentaires d'autrefois, proportions et calculs en calories." *Annales: Economie, Société, Civilisation,* XVI (1961), 568-74.

Starobinski, Jean. *L'Invention de la liberté: 1700-1789.* Geneva, 1964.

——. *Jean-Jacques Rousseau, la transparence et l'obstacle.* Paris, 1957.

Targe, Maxime. *Professeurs et régents de collège dans l'ancienne Université de Paris (XVIIe et XVIIIe siècles)*. Paris, 1902.

Tarlé, Evgenii Viktorovich. *L'Industrie dans les campagnes en France à la fin de l'ancien régime*. Paris, 1910.

Tassier, Suzanne. "Les Belges et la Révolution française, 1789-1793." *Revue de l'Université de Bruxelles*, XXXIX (1934), 452-70.

——. *Les Démocrates belges de 1789: étude sur le Vonckisme et la Révolution brabançonne*. Mémoires de l'Académie royale de Belgique, Classe des lettres. 2d ser. Vol. XXVIII. Brussels, 1930.

Taylor, George V. "Non-capitalist Wealth and the Origins of the French Revolution." *American Historical Review*, 72 (1967), 469-96.

——. "The Paris Bourse on the Eve of the French Revolution, 1781-1789." *American Historical Review*, 67 (1962), 951-77.

——. "Types of Capitalism in Eighteenth-Century France." *English Historical Review*, 79 (1964), 478-97.

Thompson, E. P. "The Moral Economy of the English Crowd in the 18th Century." *Past and Present*, L (1971), 71-136.

Tilly, Louise A. "The Food Riot as a Form of Political Conflict in France." *Journal of Interdisciplinary History*, II (1971), 23-57.

Todd, Christopher. *Voltaire's Disciple: Jean-François de La Harpe*. London, 1972.

Trénard, Louis. "La Crise sociale lyonnaise à la veille de la Révolution." *Revue d'histoire moderne et contemporaine*, II (1955), 5-45.

——. *Lyon de l'Encyclopédie au préromantisme. Histoire sociale des idées*. 2 vols. Collection Cahiers d'histoire, no. 3. Paris, 1958.

Varin D'Ainvelle, Madeleine. *La Presse en France. Genèse et évolution de ses fonctions psycho-sociales*. Paris, 1965.

Vaughn, Charles Edwyn. *Studies in the History of Political Philosophy before and after Rousseau*. Ed. A. G. Little. 2 vols. London, 1925.

Vexliard, Alexandre. *Introduction à la sociologie du vagabondage*. Paris, 1956.

Vignes, J. B. M. *Histoire des doctrines sur l'impôt en France: Les Origines et les destinées de la dixme royale de Vauban*. Paris, 1909.

Villers, Robert. *L'Organisation du Parlement de Paris et des Conseils supérieurs d'après la réforme de Maupeou, 1771-1774*. Paris, 1937.

Viridet, Marc, ed. *Documents officiels et contemporains sur quelques-unes des condemnations dont l'"Emile" et le "Contrat social" on été l'objet en 1762*. Geneva, 1850.

Volguine, V.P. "L'Idéologie révolutionnaire en France au XVIIIe siècle. Ses contradictions et son évolution." *La Pensée*, LXXXVI (July-Aug., 1959), 83-96.

Vyverberg, Henry. *Historical Pessimism in the French Enlightenment*. Cambridge, Mass., 1958.

Waldinger, Renée. *Voltaire and Reform in the Light of the French Revolution*. Geneva, 1959.

Wallon, Henri Alexandre. *Histoire du Tribunal révolutionnaire de Paris avec le journal de ses actes*. 6 vols. Paris, 1880-82.

Weulersse, Georges. *Le Mouvement physiocratique en France (de 1756 à 1770)*. 2 vols. Paris, 1910.

——. *La Physiocratie à la fin du règne de Louis XV (1770-1774)*. Paris, 1959.

——. "Les Physiocrates sous le ministère de Turgot." *Revue d'histoire économique et sociale*, XIII (1925), 314-37.

Secondary sources *(continued)*

——. *La Physiocratie sous les ministères de Turgot et de Necker, 1774-1781.* Paris, 1950.
——. *Les Physiocrates.* Paris, 1931.
Williams, David. "French Opinion Concerning the English Constitution in the Eighteenth Century." *Economica,* X (1930), 295-308.
——. "The Influence of Rousseau on Political Opinion, 1760-95." *English Historical Review,* XLVIII (1933), 414-30.
Wilson, Arthur. "The Philosophes in the Light of Present-day Theories of Modernization." *Studies on Voltaire and the Eighteenth Century,* LVIII (1967), 1893-1913.
——. "Why Did the Political Theory of the Encyclopedists Not Prevail? A Suggestion." *French Historical Studies,* I (1960), 283-94.

Index